DOLLY PARTON
ALL THE SONGS
THE STORY BEHIND EVERY TRACK

DOLLY PARTON
ALL THE SONGS
THE STORY BEHIND EVERY TRACK

SIMON BENOÎT, DAMIEN SOMVILLE, AND LALIE WALKER

BLACK DOG
& LEVENTHAL
PUBLISHERS
NEW YORK

Contents

6_ Foreword

8_ Angels Are Born in Tennessee

Hello, I'm Dolly	Just Because I'm A Woman	In The Good Old Days (When Times Were Bad)	My Blue Ridge Mountain Boy	Always, Always	The Fairest Of Them All
24	**36**	**52**	**64**	**78**	**88**
As Long As I Love	The Golden Streets Of Glory	Joshua	Coat Of Many Colors	Touch Your Woman	Dolly Parton sings "My Favorite Songwriter, Porter Wagoner"
96	**108**	**116**	**126**	**138**	**146**
My Tennessee Mountain Home	Bubbling Over	Jolene	Love Is Like A Butterfly	The Bargain Store	Dolly: The Seeker / We Used To
154	**162**	**176**	**186**	**198**	**204**
All I Can Do	New Harvest... First Gathering	Here You Come Again	Heartbreaker	Great Balls Of Fire	Dolly, Dolly, Dolly
210	**216**	**230**	**240**	**256**	**268**

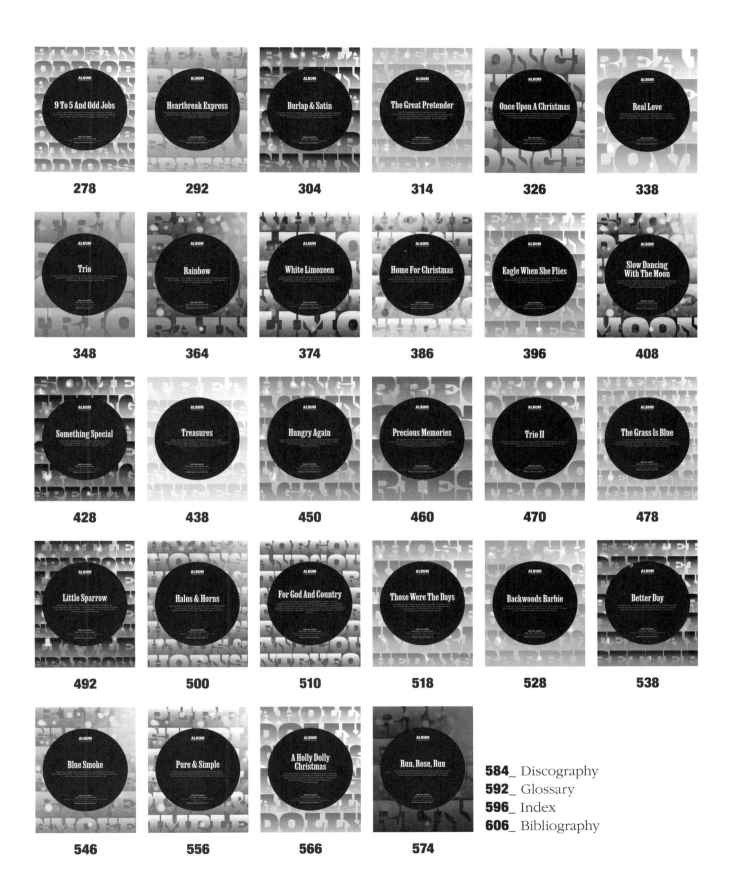

278 9 To 5 And Odd Jobs

292 Heartbreak Express

304 Burlap & Satin

314 The Great Pretender

326 Once Upon A Christmas

338 Real Love

348 Trio

364 Rainbow

374 White Limozeen

386 Home For Christmas

396 Eagle When She Flies

408 Slow Dancing With The Moon

428 Something Special

438 Treasures

450 Hungry Again

460 Precious Memories

470 Trio II

478 The Grass Is Blue

492 Little Sparrow

500 Halos & Horns

510 For God And Country

518 Those Were The Days

528 Backwoods Barbie

538 Better Day

546 Blue Smoke

556 Pure & Simple

566 A Holly Dolly Christmas

574 Run, Rose, Run

584_ Discography
592_ Glossary
596_ Index
606_ Bibliography

In 1999 Dolly Parton was inducted into the Country Music Hall of Fame. In 2022 Dolly was nominated for the Rock and Roll Hall of Fame and eventually inducted, though she initially declined the honor because she felt her music was more country than rock and roll.

Dolly Parton, superstar, in the late 1980s.

Foreword

Dolly Parton All the Songs has been a major undertaking given the longevity of Dolly's career and her prolific output. With more than 3,000 songs written, including nearly 750 recorded, more than 200 compilations, and as many singles, 45 solo albums, duos and trios, Christmas albums, and dozens of collaborations, she is also one of the most award-winning artists. The queen of country music who became a star, then a legend and an icon, is gifted with many talents: singer-songwriter, multi-instrumentalist and writer, actress and producer, entrepreneur, and philanthropist. Exploring the world of Dolly Parton is an exciting adventure that follows the life and career of a star who has shone in the skies over America and the world for more than sixty years. *Dolly Parton: All the Songs* is an opportunity for readers to discover, or rediscover, the life and career of an exceptional artist.

A Note to the Reader

To be consistent with the artist's discography, only albums, compilations, and singles released by the artist's record companies in the US are listed. Where a track has been released in Canada to great acclaim, its chart status has been noted. Some songs that were not released as singles in the US, but which were released elsewhere in the world, are listed if they became hits (this was sometimes the case in the United Kingdom, Australia, etc.).

The references and rankings provided here take into account only a song or an album's first release, unless otherwise indicated. Only the most significant rankings are listed.

The reference rankings for *Dolly Parton: All the Songs* are:
– For the United States: the Billboard Hot Country Songs, Billboard Hot 100 (singles), and the Billboard 200 (albums).
– For Canada: RPM Country Singles and RPM Top Albums.

If we were unable to find certain references, we indicated this with a question mark. When credits were undifferentiated or very long, we opted to include a list of musicians, recording studios, and technical team details at the beginning of the album so as not to clutter the reading process. We have also opted for sources released by the star or her biographers (Alanna Nash, Stephen Miller), and during her major interviews.

Finally, in view of Dolly's immense output, it seemed obvious to us that the focus should be on her solo albums and related singles. The range of singles, compilations, collaborations, bests, remixes, and live albums in her repertoire is so vast that a second volume would have been needed to detail them all. For this reason, we have chosen to list some of her work briefly at the end of the book.

Angels Are Born in Tennessee

A Birth Blessed by the Gods

Dolly Parton's family story begins like a fairy tale...Once upon a time, on a freezing night, in a wooden cabin battered by the wind and snow seeping through the gaps in the floor, a worried couple awaited the birth of their child. Twenty-five-year-old Robert Lee Parton, already a father of three, tries to warm the room by stoking the fire. Avie, his wife, her body tense and aching, prays that the doctor will arrive in time for the birth to go well. Outside, under the gusts of wind, a horse moves carefully along a mountain ridge. One false step and both man and animal will not survive. On the night of January 19, 1946, near the banks of Little Pigeon River in the heart of the Great Smoky Mountains in eastern Tennessee, the Parton family celebrates the birth of their daughter and pays the doctor with a bag of corn. So it was that the life of Dolly Rebecca Parton began, the fourth of twelve siblings.

Dolly spent her childhood and adolescence with the forests and mountains of Appalachia as her only horizon, the wooden shacks with their porches, the scattered neighbors who met at the church where her maternal grandfather, the Reverend Jake Owens, officiated. Her haven, her refuge, and her strengths were her family and her land. Dolly knew nothing of the cities, the suburbs, or the ghettos, nor anything of the countries on the other side of the world from which her ancestors came, and whose songs she hummed from an early age. Despite their immense poverty, she grew up like all little girls, between laughter and sorrow, fears and daring undertakings, hopes and despairs. She knew she was loved, even though, like many children from large families, she did not always get the attention she wanted.

At a very early age, the love she received was sometimes disproportionately important, which made her hypersensitive, a sort of Achilles' heel that accompanied her all her life, but which she nevertheless turned into a strength. When you have nothing, materially speaking, you dream of everything, you invent lives and possibilities, you use a piece of coal for make-up. Everything counts: every glance, every gift, however small and modest, like the piece of gingerbread offered to her by her neighbor, known as "Aunt Marth," who owns the land where her father is a tenant farmer. One day, Aunt Marth improvised a song: "*Tiptoe tiptoe, little Dolly Parton…She got a red dress just like mine…*" In her 1994 autobiography,[1] Dolly said she still remembered her astonishment at imagining that a song was about her. That day she felt really special. Some children are told stories, others have songs sung to them—all of which can

stimulate the imagination and dreams. Dolly was a great dreamer, which enabled her to endure poverty and then to realize what it meant to wear patched clothes or to see her parents toil to feed so many mouths each day. These memories and experiences became material for songs throughout her career, as evidenced by the 1969 album, *In the Good Old Days (When Times Were Bad)*.

A Head Full of Dreams

As a child, Dolly roamed through a natural environment that was as sumptuous as it was rugged, filled with landscapes and sensations that are to be found throughout her work. With poetry, the songwriter created her own symbolism by associating human feelings with this profusion of colors and perfumes, plants, and animals, particularly birds and butterflies—which she made her emblem. As Dolly grew into her teens, the desire to see the country became more and more entwined with her dreams.

In the preface to her autobiography, the star describes herself as follows: "I always loved books. I don't remember learning to read, it was just something I always did. I was hungry for knowledge, I guess, and information; I was a curious kid. I still am." The Parton family's only reading material was a Bible, sometimes a catalogue, and the newspapers that covered the walls of their cabin, which Dolly devoured. Her childhood was spent listening to her mother's stories, working in the fields—which she did not like—playing music together, and attending her grandfather's Pentecostal church, where she was introduced to gospel music and the expression of faith.

At a young age, Dolly heard melodies in her head and had the ability to put them into words and sounds. If she was cut off from the world, the songs of her European and Appalachian ancestors—murder ballads, folk and country songs about murdered women, tragic love affairs, poverty and alcohol that ruin families and couples—made a connection with her, and she soaked them up. She acquired her musical and historical knowledge through this cultural heritage. It was also during this period that she learned to play the guitar, before performing for the first time at the age of eight on local radio stations.

Formative Experiences

As a young teenager, Dolly had a spiritual experience that marked her for life, and she took on certain family values that began to structure her personality and her art. Around the age of eight or nine, hearing her mother and

Dolly Parton gives the camera her most beautiful smile, the one that would build her legend step-by-step.

aunts discussing the young men killed in the war, Dolly wrote a song that showed her talent for storytelling: "Life Doesn't Mean Much to Me" (still unrecorded). In her essay, Professor Lydia Hamessley points out how this text already reveals a profound maturity in the use of rhyme and in the way Dolly immerses her listener in history from the outset: "He's gone from my world / Left this country girl / To fight in a war 'cross the sea / The telegram said / He's been pronounced dead / Life doesn't mean much to me." The Partons were poor, but rich in their love and solidarity, which Dolly expressed in her cult hit song, "Coat of Many Colors," a tribute to her mother enriched with strong lyrics about childhood wounds. In many of her songs, Dolly simultaneously explores a personal detail or emotion in conjunction with an event or a behavior from everyday life.

Her uncle, the songwriter Bill Owens, recognized early on that his niece was not only talented but also serious about music. He gave Dolly her first guitar, encouraged her to write and compose, and took her to her first live session at the *Cas Walker Farm and Home Hour* in Knoxville, a journey that was almost an initiation for Dolly. Even before the age of fifteen, Dolly had already written and composed a lot, and she had performed in front of audiences in several radio and TV shows, which laid the groundwork for her stage and showbiz experience. In 1957,

at the age of eleven, the future star recorded her first single, "Puppy Love," which was released in 1959 by Goldband, a Louisiana-based label. To get there, she traveled more than 120 miles by bus with her grandmother, a journey full of emotions and adventures. Dolly was not a child star. On the contrary—she was a child who decided at an early age to become a country star on her own terms.

Decisive Encounters

When she was about seventeen and on her way to a performance at the Cas Walker show, Dolly was riding in a car with her boyfriend when the assassination of John F. Kennedy was announced on the radio. In shock, as the car sped along, Dolly heard the boy exclaim that it served him right. Horrified, she asked him to turn back; her performance was canceled, and the boy was forgotten. A year later, having just arrived in Music City, Dolly met Carl Dean, the man of her life. For reasons related to her early career, they were married in secret in Ringgold, Georgia, on May 30, 1966. "I never doubted for a minute that we [my husband and I] would be married 50 years as long as we were both alive. Carl is my husband and my best friend so we have had a solid foundation to deal with all of the craziness that comes with a performing career," she said to the British newspaper the *Guardian* fifty years later. Carl Dean was and is her anchor, her other refuge. Little is known about him because, from the start, Dolly has kept her private life private. Their relationship was the subject of a dizzying number of rumors, some of them hurtful. In the same *Guardian* interview, the star told Anita Sethi that she owed a lot to her Uncle Bill. "He's a great musician and songwriter in his own right so I know he sacrificed his own ambitions so I could have mine." Under the guidance of her mentor uncle, Dolly began to make a name for herself as a songwriter. At first it did not earn her a good enough living, but it was enough to give her the desire to go further, higher. This state of mind would always be present in the star, like a spur that drove great determination. Dolly worked tirelessly, wrote tirelessly. In 1966, with "Dumb Blonde," a song written by Curly Putman, she was noticed by the critics and by Porter Wagoner, an extremely popular country singer-songwriter who had his own TV show.

A Collaborative Spirit

The years during which Dolly worked with Porter Wagoner were intense and stimulating. But in 1967 things became tense; the star had finished her five-year commitment to Wagoner, but he refused to let her go. There followed a relational, legal, and media battle. With him, Dolly had learned the tricks of the trade: duets, tours, and shows, which were all new for her. The country world discovered an extravagant blonde who was sometimes outrageous and who embraced the extravagance, ultra-wigged and with ultra makeup, beautiful, and equipped with breasts that in themselves caused too much ink to flow. She was smiling, humorous and self-deprecating, she embodied joie de vivre, and above all, she was talented, even though some people found her voice a little odd.

In the mid-1960s, the country music scene in Nashville was traditional, male-dominated, patriarchal, and sexist, but Dolly navigated it with ease. She knew what she wanted and who she was, and while she sometimes made compromises and even sacrifices, especially in her personal life, she never lost sight of her goals. This did not prevent her from suffering and exhaustion, and even from a depression that made her capsize in the 1980s, from which she emerged stronger. After the adventure of *The Porter Wagoner Show*, which she left with a memorable song, "I Will Always Love You," Dolly invested in pop, became an actress, then a producer, and released a series of albums. Dolly is a generous artist who is not afraid that others might overshadow her; on the contrary, this encouraged her to alternate solo albums with duos or trios. Among her great friends and associates, Kenny Rogers, Willie Nelson, Mac Davis, Emmylou Harris, and Linda Ronstadt, to name but a few, hold a special place throughout her career.

Staying True to Herself

On the one hand, there is Dolly Parton, country star, philanthropist, entrepreneur, talented songwriter. On the other hand, there is Dolly Rebecca Parton, married name Dean, the one with the private life, family, friendship, and spirituality. Managing to have these two facets coexist, without one invading or overrunning the other, is almost a tour de force. To achieve this, very early on, the songwriter set limits between her public and private lives, between the stage and the backstage, between her inner self and her appearance—so much commented upon and criticized that she made a song about it called "Shattered Image." Dolly skillfully presented this artificial image to the media, the record industry, and her fans, while maintaining intact her authentic and honest nature. Perhaps this is one of the reasons why everyone loves Dolly today. She has an unwavering presence—not a year goes by without an event, an album, or a show, without a Dollywood season launch, TV show or book, not a year without giving of herself, like her Imagination Library program. But she consolidates the "other" Dolly, the one of family life, marriage, and friendship, by constantly returning to her origins, her roots. It is a kind of ballet between her present and her past, in order to build the best future she can imagine for herself and her loved ones. In her songs, Dolly also manages to balance this public-private relationship with finesse, intelligence, and talent. Even though Dolly gives voice to personal experiences, she expresses them in a universal form, which is surely the mark of great artists.

A Chronicle of Memories

In 2023, to celebrate her seventy-seventh birthday, Dolly released a new single: "Don't Make Me Have to Come Down There." This was an opportunity for her, through the expression of her faith, to pass on a message to her public: It is time to take action to prevent catastrophes. She refuses to take a political stand, but never hesitates to act whenever she can, as a philanthropist in the face of COVID-19, or (more simply) as a songwriter. And she is a songwriter to the ends of her fingernails, which are as legendary as her outfits, her songs, her laughter, and her presence on the musical and media scene. Because it is indeed as a songwriter that Dolly Parton wishes to be

recognized, which is now an established fact and validated by her fans as well as by the numerous awards and honors she receives and has received, including her induction into the Nashville Songwriters Hall of Fame in 1986 and then into the Songwriters Hall of Fame in 2001.

From the hundreds of interviews and songs published, we will remember in particular her very specific way of navigating between a chronicle of American society and a work of personal memory. To immerse oneself in Dolly's work is to traverse several decades made up of love stories, happy or unhappy, stories of men and women in the grip of passion, the darker sides of their personalities, social constraints, the impact of wealth or poverty. She tirelessly evokes these stories in the numerous TV shows on which she appears. During an appearance on *The Kelly Clarkson Show* in 2022, the star confirmed that she had buried a song in a time capsule under the Dollywood amusement park in 1986, a song that would not be made public until after her ninety-ninth birthday. Dolly Parton's career longevity also lies in her mastery of the media over the long term.

Author and Composer

When Dolly develops a theme—love, for example—she explores all possible variations. Each one improves on the previous one or sheds a different light. One of the strengths

of the songwriter's poetry is the narrative that enables identification in her listeners, hence the success of "Jolene." The star tirelessly examines our emotions, our feelings, our weaknesses, and our strengths, with music that communicates melancholy or joy, the desire to dance or to love, energy, or regret. The year 2023 was the occasion for Dolly Parton to announce on her website the release of her latest book, *Behind the Seams: My Life in Rhinestones*, as well as her partnership with Vinyl Me, Please for a time-limited subscription of twelve records per month.

Taking Risks and Creating a Supportive Entourage

All the big changes Dolly Parton made in her career, all the risks she took, were not so much calculated as due to a sense of necessity, and a vital need to move on. Her survival instinct, her almost innate talent as a businesswoman, and her ability to feel the zeitgeist were certainly a big part of it. Dolly has rarely put a foot wrong in her activities and in her profession, at least never completely. But it has been above all a need for emancipation as a woman and as an artist, and a fierce determination never to be bored, that have pushed her to make sometimes quite radical choices. Leaving Porter Wagoner, first of all, opening up her world beyond the borders of traditional country music, putting

Kenny Rogers and Dolly Parton in 1988, in New York, for a charity dinner for the Foundation to Fight Blindness.

After the film *9 to 5* opened in 1980, the gates to Broadway later opened in 2009 with the creation of the *9 to 5* musical, which toured the country for more than a decade.

herself very much ahead of her time, as well as controlling her image, constantly creating and reinventing her character—a persona, as David Bowie used to call it. Dolly has always known exactly how to respond to her detractors and mockers, in a tone that is sometimes rebellious but always wise, funny, and elegant.

From the beginning of her career, in 1966, she set up her own music publishing company, Owe-Par, with her uncle Bill Owens. In 1986, she took over the "Rebel Railroad" attraction (created in 1961 in Pigeon Forge, Tennessee, on the occasion of the one hundredth anniversary of the American Civil War) and transformed it into Dollywood, her amusement park. Dolly also set up her own label, Dolly Records, in 2007, and masterfully managed the artistic direction of her long career, which has often been held up as a model. Shania Twain, Brandi Carlile, Orville Peck, Miley Cyrus (her goddaughter), and Taylor Swift, to name a few, have all studied Dolly Parton's career closely.

Dolly is a loyal person by nature. She likes to form a "tribe," to surround herself with those close to her and to form friendships with her musicians and professionals whose way of being and talent she admires. We can see this first with her husband, Carl Thomas Dean, whom she married in 1966, but also with her collaborators, producers, and musicians. Sandy Gallin, for example, was her manager for twenty-five years. Before handing the reins to Tom Pick, Al Pachucki was her main sound engineer from 1968 to 1973,

which represents a significant tally of twenty-one albums. We can see that Dolly is above all seeking to surround herself with friends, to constitute a veritable artistic family.

Even after a change of direction, she wants to maintain the special bond that can be formed in the meeting between two people, in collaboration, and in creation. The lyrics of the worldwide hit "I Will Always Love You," dedicated to Porter Wagoner, are certainly the best example. Moreover, she refused to sell her rights to Elvis Presley, who, under the pressure of his manager "Colonel" Tom Parker, would perform a song only if he obtained half the publishing rights. Dolly did not give in, and Elvis never performed the song. This difficult decision shows all her determination, and her acute business sense, which contributed to placing her at the head of a real financial empire.

This sense of loyalty also applies to some of her producers. Besides the first album *Hello, I'm Dolly*, superbly produced by Fred Foster for Monument Records, there was the Bob Ferguson era. When Dolly joined RCA Victor in 1968, Ferguson produced twenty-five of her albums, including her duets with Porter Wagoner. Porter went on to produce five albums for Dolly himself before their musical partnership finally ended. In the case of Bob Ferguson, it is important to note that Dolly was regularly at odds with Wagoner over her artistic choices and career management. Of course, Porter tended to have the last word. "The world and times are changing," as Bob Dylan sang in "The

Blond Dolly Parton and brunette Cher reunited on ABC's *Cher...Special*, broadcast in April 1978.

Times They Are a-Changin'," but they change slowly and not without a struggle. In 1976, Dolly managed to contractually extricate herself from Wagoner and hired producer Gregg Perry for the album *New Harvest...First Gathering*, which was released in 1977. A success and a big step toward the mainstream. To confirm her pop orientation, Dolly decided to call on Gary Klein, a gifted and intuitive producer, known for his way of sculpting sound and creating bridges between genres. In late 1977, they recorded the hit single "Here You Come Again" (written by Barry Mann and Cynthia Weil), and the album of the same name, which would inspire generations of artists and do much to break down the barriers of country music. Never before had the boundaries between pop and country music—the two dominant genres in the United States at the time—been so slim. She made three albums with him.

From 1978, after the collaboration of Dean Parks on the album *Great Balls of Fire*, then that of Mike Post on *9 to 5 and Odd Jobs*, it was the turn of Gregg Perry to take over and to continue to drive toward pop, the work on the synthesizers, and other production techniques, in keeping with the then-current trend. We should not forget that this was the dawn of the 1980s: Traditional country music was not in fashion and the Nashville sound had to undergo, not without a certain amount of pain, an unprecedented mutation. Dolly Parton then tried some experiments with the producers Val Garay, David Foster, and David Malloy, most of them very convincing. George Massenburg was in charge of the two sumptuous *Trio* albums with Emmylou Harris and Linda Ronstadt, then Dolly called upon the talents of Steve "Gold-E" Goldstein, Ricky Skaggs (for the album *White Limozeen* in 1989), and Gary Smith. This is when she met Steve Buckingham, an artistic and friendly meeting of souls. In 1991, they began their collaboration on the album *Eagle When She Flies*, the first to reach number one on the Billboard Top Country Albums since *9 to 5 and Odd Jobs* in 1980. Dolly would work with him on seven albums, including her famous bluegrass trilogy, *The Grass Is Blue* in 1999, *Little Sparrow* in 2001, and *Halo & Horns* in 2002. After two albums produced by Richie Owens, Kent Wells brought a new breath of pop sound to her career from 2003 to 2014, then Richard Dennison and Tom Rutledge together produced *I Believe in You* and *Run, Rose, Run*.

Over the course of these sixty-six albums, the same musicians—sometimes more than thirty years apart—were often involved, such as Lloyd Green (pedal steel guitar), Roy Huskey Jr. (bass), Dave Kirby (acoustic guitar), Hargus "Pig" Robbins (piano), Anita Carter (vocals), Bobby Dyson (bass), Mac Magaha (fiddle and mandolin), or Buck Trent (banjo). They are as much a part of her musical family as they are of her heart. It was certainly just as necessary to create an oeuvre that was of such density and, on the whole, surprisingly qualitative. Because, as we will see in the course of this work, the queen of country always knew how to be surrounded by good people.

The Beginnings of a Vocation

A tin can stuck on a stick, which she wedged between the boards of the veranda, was Dolly Rebecca Parton's first microphone. From then on, she would sing for her family or alone on the porch, imagining herself in front of crowds. Sometimes, in need of an audience, she turned to farm animals as her spectators. From an early age, Dolly transformed both the outside world and her inner world into song. So, when she heard a song in her head but was not yet able to write it down, it was her mother who held the pen. "Little Tiny Tasseltop" was her first composition, revealing a real narrative structure that was amazing for a songwriter who was only five years old. This song expresses her love as a little girl for her doll, made from a corn cob.

The First Show

Bill Owens, an attentive uncle who understood that his niece had a genuine passion for music, gave Dolly her first guitar. He then decided that she should perform on the radio. He knew that sometimes you have to break down doors to get your way, and Dolly was not afraid to do that. When she met Cas Walker, of *Cas Walker Farm and Home Hour* fame, the young girl did not beg for a job as such, but simply said she wanted to work for him. A nuance that made all the difference, and the businessman gave her her chance. So Dolly took her first steps as a professional singer on the radio and soon afterward on television, even though her family did not yet own one. The experience was as decisive as it was fantastic. Dolly stood in front of the microphone and faced the audience. Her dream had come true, but fear had taken her breath away. She was ten years old, terribly intimidated, and even tempted to run away. Instead, she launched herself into her performance, her voice a little impaired by stage fright but quickly asserting itself. In the end, it was a success. People loved Dolly, who in turn loved her first audience with all her heart. This was how she gained an early taste for the stage, just before the taste for staging—clothes, hair, makeup—and everything else she would soon love. Dolly Rebecca Parton definitely knew she was determined to become a star. The other nice surprise was that the show paid $5, which was a fortune when her father barely earned that much for a long day's work in the sawmill.

Taking advantage of the summer school holidays and every opportunity that presented itself, Dolly regularly took part in Cas Walker's shows. The trips back and forth with Uncle Bill become more frequent, and each show brought Dolly Rebecca Parton a little closer to Nashville.

Eddie Shuler and the Goldband Label

Edward Wayne Shuler (1913–2005), known as Eddie, was born in Texas. He moved to Lake Charles, Louisiana, where he and his wife, Elsie, established the Goldband complex in 1945, which included a recording studio and a record and television shop. Initially, Eddie Shuler created his label to promote his own group, the All-Star Reveliers. He then opened the doors of Goldband Records to other artists, including Boozoo Chavis, who recorded his 1954 hit "Paper in My Shoe," and Phil Phillips, who released "Sea of Love" in 1959, the same year as Dolly's first single, "Puppy Love." With Freddy Fender, Rockin' Sidney, and Jo-El Sonnier also in its fold, Goldband became known as the label specializing in swamp pop. Its biggest competitor was the Texan producer Huey Meaux, who released hybrid tracks that combined the sounds of R&B and Mexican music. Cajun and rock remained Goldband's favorite genres. Phil Phillips's "Sea of Love" was a hit—and in 1989 was featured on the soundtrack of the film also called *Sea of Love*, which starred Al Pacino. During the seventies, changes in musical fashion led to the decline of Goldband, which, on the death of Eddie Shuler, was the oldest of the independent labels.[13]

First Guitar

Dolly's first guitar was an old Parton family mandolin, with broken strings—only the two bottom strings remained. Dolly was seven years old when she first used the guitar, and she could not get a decent sound out of it. Her uncle Bill Owens, himself a professional musician, had been following her progress since he heard her singing in the kitchen when she was only three. Certain that she was serious about learning the guitar, he gave Dolly a Martin 5-18 Terz Short Scale and taught her the main chords. Always composing on this guitar at home, Dolly used the Martin from 1954 to 1964 and again from 1991 to 2010.

SIDE A

The singer Kitty Wells, known for her 1952 hit "It Wasn't God Who Made Honky Tonk Angels," in 1954, in Nashville.

Puppy Love

Bill Owens, Dolly Parton / 1:37

Single: Vocals: Dolly Parton **Musicians:** (?) **Recorded:** Goldband Records, Lake Charles, Louisiana, April 1959 **Technical Team:** (?) **Single:** Side A: Puppy Love / Side B: Girl Left Alone **Release:** Goldband Records, 1959 (45 rpm ref.: G-1086) **Best US Chart Ranking:** Did Not Chart Side A: Puppy Love Bill Owens, Dolly Parton / 1:37

Genesis and Lyrics

Co-written with her uncle Bill when Dolly was only eleven, "Puppy Love" evokes the ups and downs of a childish love, of the persistent crush of a girl now old enough to kiss and embrace a boy who does not always treat her well.

A budding star at the time, Dolly would never forget the bus trip from her home to the studio in Lake Charles, Louisiana: thirty hours on the road, the scenery flying by, and the combination of the smells of leatherette, the sweat of the other passengers, and the fuel oil. Her uncle Bill was not available, so Dolly, who was only thirteen, was accompanied by her grandmother, Rena Owens. At one stop, they got off to take a break, but when they returned, the bus had gone, leaving them stranded with nothing to eat or drink! Finally, after many hours, they arrived in Lake Charles on another bus.

"Puppy Love" was recorded and produced by Eddie Shuler of Goldband Records. Eddie had a son named Johnny, who was handsome and kind, with a dark look and a Cajun accent. First single, first crush...definitely a day to remember!

Production

Dolly was hardly a beginner and had the experience of singing on Cas Walker's TV show, but the adventure of making this single was new in many ways. First, the journey to Lake Charles, then the anxiety of recording for the first time on Eddie Shuler's Goldband label. Uncle Bill was not on the trip, and Dolly had to adapt to musicians she didn't know. The arrangement of "Puppy Love" was decidedly rockabilly, the music that teenagers liked at the time. More specifically, the inspiration for this single was the sound of the very popular Collins Kids, Larry—well known for his stage performances, which consisted of playing the

guitar while jumping around—and his sister Lorrie. In just 1:37, Dolly was able to impress with her particularly powerful voice, so strong for a girl her age.

Covers

This first Dolly Parton single was rereleased by Yep Roc Records as a 45 rpm single and MP3 in 2017 under the title "Puppy Love." The digital version contains both sides of the 45 and covers.

"(It Wasn't God Who Made) Honky Tonk Angels" is a 1952 song performed by Kitty Wells, written in response to Hank Thompson's hit "Wild Side of Life," whose chorus stated: "I didn't know God made honky tonk angels." Dolly Parton liked the feminist version sung by Kitty, so she covered it faithfully. "Release Me" by Jimmy Heap and the Melody Masters, itself released in 1953, was a megahit for Engelbert Humperdinck in 1967. "Making Believe" by Kitty Wells dates from 1955. "Two Little Orphans," written in 1925 and recorded by George Reneau in 1926, shows the breadth of Dolly Parton's repertoire. "Little Blossom" is a traditional number, originally recorded by Clyde Moody in December 1947, which her other performers—Hank Thompson, Hylo Brown, and Dolly Parton—all co-wrote. "Letter to Heaven" is the only song written entirely by Dolly, though much later, in 1973.

ON YOUR HEADPHONES
The Collins Kids' delirious, exciting, and joyful rockabilly style seems to have infected Dolly in the Goldband studio in Lake Charles: she moves around so much that at 1:09 you can distinctly hear that she has moved away from the microphone, probably fired up by a short guitar solo completed at 0:56.

The Collins Kids, a rockabilly duo consisting of guitar virtuoso Larry (with his double-necked Mosrite) and his sister, Lorrie, ca. 1970.

Appalachian music, also known as mountain music, is based on vocals, banjo, fiddle, guitar, and mandolin, and is played with a swift, light, virtuosic touch that gave birth to bluegrass. It is totally different from the music of Louisiana, whether it be Cajun style (a corruption of "Acadien," or "Cadien," terms designating a descendant of the first French-speaking settlers who emigrated from Canada) or Zydeco (a linguistic deformation from "Les z'aricots sont pas salés" [the beans are un-salted], a traditional song played by the Black Creole populace of Louisiana)—and also different from the blues.

Girl Left Alone

Bill Owens, Dorothy Jo Owens, Dolly Parton / 2:06

Genesis and Lyrics

Co-written by Dolly Parton, her aunt Dorothy Jo Owens, and her uncle Bill Owens, the B-side of this first single tells a story of loneliness, of an abandoned girl lost in the middle of vast fields, rejected, hopeless, and convinced that she has no place in this world…and maybe not even in heaven, either. Touching lyrics that evoke feelings that anyone might experience in the course of their lives.

Production

For the B-side, there was no question of following the trend of the moment: Dolly Parton sings in the pure style of the Tennessee hills where she was born. This mountain music left the musicians at Goldband feeling hesitant. A touch of bluegrass would have been welcome, but they seem to be wearing concrete boots, especially on the guitar tag at 0:38. It must be said that Cajun rock and East Tennessee music are diametrically opposed, both rhythmically and melodically. However, Dolly's exceptionally clear, high, and true voice is catchy and inspires the Cajun musicians to excel.

Although this single never charted, Dolly Parton has always considered it to be the true beginning of her career.

Album Cover

A smiling girl's face with wavy hair in black and white: Dolly Parton was thirteen years old when she posed for the cover of her first single.

Dolly Parton's career was launched in part by Cas Walker's variety show.

Cas Walker

Born in 1902 in the same area of the country as Dolly Parton: Sevier County, Tennessee, Orton Caswell Walker, known as "Cas," had the makings of a character from a novel.

He left school at fourteen and worked in a variety of jobs, including at the Champion Fiber Company, a well-known paper mill in North Carolina, and in the coal mines of Kentucky. In 1924, he returned to Tennessee and started a business selling goods from a wheelbarrow by going house to house. He then opened a shop with a simple, rural atmosphere, where white Americans and African Americans mingled. From shop to supermarket, his business grew and, eventually, Cas Walker became a multimillionaire: In the mid-1950s, he was the head of a chain of twenty-seven shops that brought in $60 million a year. How did he seduce consumers? By exploiting all the advertising techniques at his disposal. He had coupons distributed by air to inform his customers of the week's promotions. And, above all, he knew how to use radio and television to broadcast his advertisements, which charmed and amused listeners and viewers.

Created in 1929, the *Cas Walker Farm and Home Hour* was first broadcast on the radio and then on television from 1953 onward—it lasted until 1983. It was a huge success. The hall where the show was recorded could not accommodate everyone, so the inhabitants of Knoxville stopped in the street and stood in front of the open door to listen to the artists invited to the show: these included country stars such as Chet Atkins, Roy Acuff, and Bill Monroe, the "father" of bluegrass, but also novices whose careers he helped to launch, such as Dolly.

At the same time, Cas Walker defended the working class throughout his political career. He defined himself as the champion of farmers and workers. He served on the Knoxville City Council, where he became known for his outspoken stances—he threatened to punch another councilman in a heated debate over land assessments—and for his opposition to what he saw as elitist and corrupt practices in the city's governing body. Elected mayor in 1946, acting mayor in 1959, then mayor again in the same year—for the last time—he held municipal office until 1971 and remained involved in political life, even in retirement.

Cas Walker died in 1998 at the age of ninety-six and is buried in Woodlawn Cemetery in Knoxville.

A SENSE OF SHOWMANSHIP, A TASTE FOR CHALLENGES

Cas Walker challenged his audience to climb a very slippery fifty-foot pole: whoever could do it would win $50. Dolly got herself completely wet, then rolled in sand, which enabled her to stick to the greasy surface of the pole and win the prize. Some people were probably put out by the fact that a kid had done better than them, but Cas Walker decided in her favor and the money went to her. Thanks to this challenge, Dolly was able to give her family a television set, as she recounts in her memoir *My Life and Other Unfinished Business*.[1]

A Short History of Country Music

Country music originated in the eighteenth century in the Appalachian region of the American Southeast. It is the music of deepest America, with its share of clichés that are more or less hackneyed today: wide-open spaces full of cowboys and herds of cattle, clicking heels and flashy outfits, and never forgetting the indispensable Stetson. Country music is above all a story that is written, sung, and played out on the other side of the grand narrative of history, from the Old Continent in the southern United States, between migrations and economic depressions.

Mixed Race, the American Creative Force

Whether from Ireland, Scotland, Germany, Switzerland, Hawaii, or Louisiana, both free and enslaved people living on plantations—musicians, singers, and songwriters—shared, through the mutations of country music, its rhythms, emotions, dancing, and yodeling, their hopes and despairs via a diversity of instruments and ways of playing them. Country music has its origins in European folk music and in the Christian musical tradition, which blends with gospel, Appalachian mountain music, Italian mandolin, Hawaiian lap steel, and African banjo. Its followers adopt the polka one day and the blues another; they may divorce themselves from the Nashville sound to get closer to rock. There are also Cherokee traditions, Spanish guitar, Cajun music, Mexican rhythms, the German dulcimer, and swing intermixed. The foundations of the country "house" are the social, familial, and religious values of simple folk, the forgotten, who toil in the fields and the mines, those who starve and receive only the education they can give themselves. The world of country is home to those who, while they work and sing about their despair, dream of a better life, even of transforming their hopes into a fulfilled American dream, as Dolly Parton did. While some become country through the back door or by chance, the many and the more numerous *are* country born.

A Genre That Crosses the Ages

Country music is a mixture of traditions and a constantly evolving mix at that. This is what makes the music so rich and explains why it exists in so many genres and subgenres. This justifies the growing and everlasting interest of the public, and of the record industry, which produces stars and unearths exceptional talents whose hits flourish in the charts. The Bristol Sessions of 1927 and artists such as Jimmie Rodgers, a rock 'n' roll pioneer and one of the first country stars of the early twentieth century, are responsible for the modern form of country music. There are as many genres as there are famous and celebrated musicians and singer-songwriters, because America does not sing with one voice but with a plurality that represents its incredible diversity. A brief overview is given in this book, which is dedicated to Dolly Parton, and this insight enables a better approach to understanding the work of the queen of country music.

Old-Time Music

A music that is learned by ear, such as classic Anglo-Celtic ballads—which are songs coming from Scotland and Ireland that tell a story in a slow rhythm—took root in the American soil. The bagpipes, the fiddle, and the religious hymns intermingled to create the beginning of country music. This was music that sang and gave rhythm to the stories that marked the lives of everyday folks, and it was music that also made you dance. *Old-time music* can be translated as "the music of the good old days," a time that was, as Dolly Parton sings, often downright harsh, in "In the Good Old Days (When Times Were Bad)." Old-time music rhymes with stringed instruments: the fiddle, banjo, and as time went on, the guitar, mandolin, double bass, piano, dulcimer, and cello were all added. The harmonica, the so-called Cajun washboard, and even the musical spoons and the bones complete this rich instrumental palette. It

Country music originated in the Appalachian Mountains of the southeastern United States in the eighteenth century (shown here in the 2000s).

was thanks to the early country musicians, and the travels that they undertook in the territory, that old-time music evolved. The current scene is very much alive, as many are keeping the old traditions and techniques alive. The Library of Congress, along with the Henry Reed collection, and the Digital Library of Appalachia preserve and maintain a historical collection. According to Gérard Herzhaft and Jacques Brémond,[12] what characterizes Appalachian music is the interaction between Celtic tonality in singing and clawhammer banjo playing—a technique that consists of striking the strings with a finger—this creates a "high lonesome sound" that is still present in today's country music. Country music was born in the remote countryside and in inaccessible mountains, as if forgotten by the rest of the world. In the hearts of these communities, past and present, people gathered around their religious convictions and shared music. In its cradle, country music was nurtured by gospel songs and hymns imported from the Scottish Highlands: words, stories, music, and rhythms that crossed time, borders, and cultures and that fed (and feed) all country music.

Hillbilly Music

This variation of country music comes from the American Southeast. Literally, it is the music of the so-called hillbillies of the Deep South. *The Grapes of Wrath*, John Steinbeck's novel, which was adapted to the screen by John Ford, is a wonderful illustration of this. The music of rural life often tells terrible stories and, in this way, bears witness to a certain swath of American life: that of Appalachia, whose isolation after the Civil War worsened with the Great Depression. Country music was expressed in ballads, dances, and songs, and in the early twentieth century, artists performed through vaudeville, the circus, and traveling

"medicine shows" that peddled supposedly miraculous remedies. The hillbilly genre includes the more rocking hillbilly boogie, one of whose most famous representatives is none other than Bill Haley. In 2020, the beautiful documentary *The Last Hillbilly*[9] was released, telling the story of the industrial decline of Appalachia and the desperate situation of many families in the region. A moving film about a world that was about to disappear.

Honky-Tonk

While hillbilly country music belongs to rural America, honky-tonk is urban. Born in the bars where small country bands perform, honky-tonk adopts a binary rhythm, a hoarse, plaintive, or nasal tonality, and it tells of the torments and joys of city life. Intended for entertainment, honky-tonk was considered immoral under the tenets of American puritanism. Tonk music appeared in the 1930s, and its rise occurred during the Second World War. Many of the clichés that still characterize it today in the collective imagination—the alcoholism of its performers, in particular—come from the tonks of the era, a kind of drinking shack where white men gathered. Among African Americans, the equivalent of the tonk is the juke joint. Because of racial segregation, Americans sang, drank, and played music in different places. With the appearance of the Nashville sound, rockabilly, and rock 'n' roll, the honky-tonk sound gradually declined from the end of the 1950s. Hank Williams and Jimmie Rodgers gave it its credentials of nobility and, in 1969, it was the Rolling Stones who paid tribute to it with "Honky Tonk Women." As for Patsy Montana, Patsy Cline, and Kitty Wells, these feminist pioneers of country music, each in their own way, challenged the machismo at work in the world of country music, paving the way for Dolly Parton

Nashville hatter, in the tradition of cowboys and farmers of the Wild West.

and other female artists. The piano provides a bridge between polyrhythmic ragtime and country music; a precursor to jazz, ragtime oscillates between the waltz and the march. When a honky-tonk pianist plays low notes with their left hand, their right hand plays a syncopated melody, causing a shift between the two musical phrases, which are superimposed on the listener's ear. Sometimes, in honky-tonk, the melody occupies a lesser position: in tonk bars, the pianos were often out of tune, and they were often missing keys. Continuing the evolutionary tradition of country music, ragtime and honky-tonk kicked off boogie-woogie.

Hillbilly Boogie

In 1939, country musicians recorded hillbilly songs with a boogie-woogie tempo, a piano style specific to jazz. This gave birth to hillbilly boogie, of which the song "Freight Train Boogie," by the Delmore Brothers, is representative. Born in Alabama, these two brothers mixed country music with blues and boogie-woogie. The Delmore Brothers would in turn influence the Everly Brothers in the early 1960s. This is just one example of the incredible plasticity of the country music scene and its immense capacity to absorb, exchange, and transform different musical trends. In this case, by combining country and blues, we get rockabilly.

Rockabilly

Rockabilly was born in 1954, in Memphis, where Elvis Presley recorded "That's All Right" in Sam Phillips's Sun Records studios. This music was made for dancing while retaining the characteristics of honky-tonk. It found popularity with the public and entered the charts with "Heartbreak Hotel" by Elvis Presley, "I Walk the Line" by Johnny Cash, and "Blue Suede Shoes" by Carl Perkins, to name but a few.

Bluegrass

Bill Monroe founded his band, the Blue Grass Boys, as a tribute to the state of Kentucky, whose nickname is "the Bluegrass State." Led by Lester Flatt and Earl Scruggs—known for having introduced a new kind of banjo playing to bluegrass—the Blue Grass Boys joined the Grand Ole Opry show. More acoustic, though rhythmic, this strand of country music favors three- or four-part vocal harmonies. The sung parts alternate with breaks and instrumental solos. While it remains close to the ballad in sound, because of its specific tempo, bluegrass requires the musicians to demonstrate technical virtuosity. The bluegrass genre has a predilection for strings (banjo, fiddle, guitar, double bass, and mandolin). "Orange Blossom Special," a song by Ervin T. Rouse released in 1938, was successively covered by Bill Monroe in 1941, by the Swedish group the Spotnicks in 1961, and then by the great Johnny Cash in 1965. It was "Foggy Mountain Breakdown," by Earl Scruggs, that Arthur Penn chose to include in the soundtrack to *Bonnie and Clyde*. "Dueling Banjos," a standard from the 1950s, owes its fame to John Boorman's film *Deliverance*. Today, Alison Krauss and Rhonda Vincent carry the torch of women in bluegrass.

Country Western

The Hollywood films of the 1930s and 1940s made cowboy songs very popular. The singing cowboys in turn became the standard bearers of country music. Ken Maynard was the first actor-performer of the genre. In the western category, we find the swing western from 1935 to 1950. This mixture of country and jazz was very popular in Oklahoma and Texas, and as far away as California and Los Angeles, with stars such as Bob Wills and His Texas Playboys, Milton Brown, Speedy West, or Tex Williams and his number "Smoke! Smoke! Smoke! (That Cigarette)." Today, western swing is still successful, with groups such as Asleep at the Wheel, its singer Ray Benson, and the pedal steel player Cindy Cashdollar.

Yodel

Originating in the alpine regions of central Europe, the first American yodels were sung by Jimmie Rodgers in his Blue Yodel series, thirteen "yodeled" songs recorded between 1927 and 1933. In 1935, through yodeling, singer Patsy Montana became the first female performer in the country to sell a million country records. Bill Haley was also a great yodeler. Legend has it that Little Swiss Miss (real name Christine Endeback), a pioneer in the use of yodeling, was known for her yodels that climbed almost as high as the Swiss Alps.

Nashville Sound, Countrypolitan Sound

The Nashville sound marks the economic transition of country music. Famous producers like Chet Atkins decided to make the rural sound "cleaner" in order to win over urban listeners, and thus the Nashville sound was born. The line between country and pop music became porous: The voice was smooth and prominent, supported by a string section and a choir, as heard with the audacious Patsy Cline. Since country music is constantly evolving, the Nashville sound morphed into the countrypolitan sound, embodied by Tammy Wynette, singer and actress, who also questioned the condition of women in country music and in society in general. This was how country music, the daughter of rural life and poverty, was transformed once again and made into an industry juggernaut.

Outlaw, the Austin Scene

America has always distilled a romantic vision of outlaws, such as the enfants terribles Billy the Kid and Bonnie and Clyde. In reaction to the hegemonic Nashville sound, at the beginning of the 1970s some bands decided to distance themselves from Nashville, both geographically and artistically; for them, everything had to change. This begat another revolution in country music: outlaw country.

Distancing themselves from Nashville, the Austin, Texas, scene became the headquarters for these new rebels. The outlaws produced more of a raw sound while still retaining the traditional values of the genre. Among them are Kris Kristofferson and Willie Nelson. After Nashville, Austin became the second capital of country music.

Alternative Country

Other bands rejected Nashville and threw away their Stetsons in the process. They were inspired by roots (white and Black roots of country music), and preserved certain sounds (pedal steel, fiddle, guitars, and vocal harmonies). They are indeed the worthy representatives of country music, bringing together genres and subgenres: country and punk or urban rock, which gives us psychobilly, psychograss, or punkgrass.[12] They are distributed by small, independent labels and have attracted a public in search of a more traditional rock sound. In the hybridizations of country music, we also find red dirt, country pop or rock, new country, Americana, and the Bakersfield sound (a nonexhaustive list!)—some of the many, many constituent branches of the immense genealogical tree of the country music.

Is the World *Country*?

Much of the world listens to country music and dances to it. America is in the lead, of course, followed by the Canadians and Australians, who are also big fans, and also fans of Dolly Parton. In Europe, the United Kingdom, Ireland, Holland, and Germany are especially known to produce artists that stand out. In France, too, singers such as Eddy Mitchell, Dick Rivers, Johnny Hallyday, and Sylvie Vartan have brought back country sounds from Nashville and worked them into their songs, whether rockabilly or ballads.

Country music is mostly listened and danced to in the countryside—those who claim the contrary are often inhabitants of big cities who know nothing about country music! While the Germans, the Dutch, and the British all seem to be fans, this is probably because country music, although born in America, has its origins in old Europe and among the Scottish Highlanders. This is why, when an English or Irish punk hears Dolly Parton sing, they cry—because they find themselves represented in her lyrics.[1]

ALBUM

Hello, I'm Dolly

Dumb Blonde . Your Ole Handy Man . I Don't Want to Throw Rice . Put It Off Until Tomorrow .
I Wasted My Tears . Something Fishy . Fuel to the Flame . The Giving and the Taking .
I'm in No Condition . The Company You Keep . I've Lived My Life . The Little Things

RELEASE DATE
United States: February 13, 1967
References: Monument Records—SLP 18085 (stereo),
MLP 8085 (mono)
Best US Chart Ranking: 11

HELLO, I'M DOLLY
DOLLY PARTON

HIGH FIDELITY MLP8085

For her first solo album, Dolly wrote three of the songs herself; she wrote seven others in collaboration with her uncle, Bill Owens.

The Decisive Meeting with Porter Wagoner

Dolly Parton's first solo album, *Hello, I'm Dolly*, was released on Fred Foster's Monument Records on February 13, 1967. Dolly wrote three of the twelve songs, and seven were co-written with her uncle Bill Owens. While *Billboard* and *Cashbox* magazines gave the album positive reviews, more recently, AllMusic reviewer Eugene Chadbourne gave it five stars.

Iconic Blondes
The year 1967 was marked by the war raging in Vietnam, riots in Detroit, Michigan, and a changing world. It was also an important year for the women's liberation movement in the United States, and for the art scene. In Hollywood, Elvis Presley made a string of films and married Priscilla in Las Vegas, while the Beatles conquered the world with "All You Need Is Love," a song that became the standard for the so-called Flower Power movement. Among the iconic blondes of the era, Marilyn Monroe was depicted in nine paintings by Andy Warhol, who dedicated them all to the late star, and Brigitte Bardot, who had become world famous for her role in the film *And God Created Woman*, proclaimed that she was not afraid of anything on her Harley-Davidson, in a song written

and composed by Serge Gainsbourg. The world of country music now included Dolly Parton, who was celebrating her twenty-first birthday.

And the Dream Became a Reality
With *Hello, I'm Dolly*, Dolly Parton began a turning point in her career, which had already started almost ten years before. The critics were, as always, enthusiastic and...critical. Some found her songs moralistic, while others praised the subtle tracks, but all agreed that the album was very country. Very Dolly Parton. This opus attracted the attention of the very popular Porter Wagoner. The artist contacted her, not, as the young woman had assumed, because she had sent him songs, but to offer her the opportunity to replace Norma Jean Beasler, his show partner, who had left him for family reasons. After this decisive meeting, a fruitful—and stormy—collaboration began, which enabled Dolly Parton to realize her dream: to become a huge star. Thanks to this first solo album and her involvement in the *The Porter Wagoner Show*, the recognition of her talent by both the music world and the public was indisputable: Country to the core, Dolly loved country music, and country music lovers adored Dolly.

In June 1967, in response to a question for *Music City News* magazine, Dolly said she had already written between 400 and 500 songs. She was only twenty-one!

A Chronicle of Lovesickness

In a video that is available on the artist's website, Dolly appears in a very sixties-inspired apple-green dress, her incredible blond mane framing her smiling face while she plays the guitar. The songwriter draws her strength and charm from her roots in her native Tennessee. The album *Hello, I'm Dolly* focuses on love, sometimes unhappy, betrayed, dirty, neglected, and even burning, as in "Fuel to the Flame." The twelve tracks evoke the gap between the lives we dream of living and the lives we actually live. One finds in these songs a sense of gentleness mixed with sadness or anger, specifically on the ballads. A way of testifying to human hopes and despairs: Those of women facing men who do not look at them, or, worse, who forget them, betray them, and abandon them. "Your Ole Handy Man" takes a sharp, uncompromising look at the place of the man within a couple. In 1967, Dolly echoed the demands of women, whether intentionally or not, lending them her voice and carving a new path to industry glory.

Monument Records

The Monument Records label, with which Dolly collaborated for this first album, was created in 1958 in Nashville by Fred Foster. The first artist recorded, Billy Grammer, reached number four on the Billboard charts with "Gotta Travel On," a legendary song that was covered onstage by Buddy Holly shortly before his death in a plane crash in 1959. Bob Dylan would cover this song two years later, before recording it in Nashville, in 1970, for his album *Self Portrait*. With this first hit, Monument became a label dedicated to local artists on their way to success, including Roy Orbison ("Only the Lonely" and "Oh, Pretty Woman"), Kris Kristofferson, Tony Joe White, Willie Nelson, Henson Cargill, revered for his classic "Skip a Rope," Tommy Cash (Johnny's brother), Hank Cochran, Ronnie Hawkins, Sonny James, and Ray Price, as well as musicians Bob Moore, Grady Martin, David Briggs, and Charlie McCoy. The latter were members of the Nashville A-Team, the studio musicians whom the producers would contact first. For this reason, another feature of Monument Records was the creative atmosphere of the sessions in the studios located in Hendersonville, a Nashville suburb where most of the musicians, including Johnny Cash, lived. In 2017, Monument Records was acquired by the Sony label.

A Star in the Making

Three of the songs on this first LP are Dolly Parton's solo compositions, and seven were written in collaboration with her uncle, Bill Owens. The other two songs are by Claude "Curly" Putman, a close friend of Porter Wagoner, and Lola Jean Dillon, a friend of Dolly's, respectively. "I Don't Want to Throw Rice" is an up-tempo country tune with honky-tonk-style vocals that were commonly adopted at Monument Records. Dolly knew that she would soon be signed to RCA, with the help of Porter Wagoner. Furthermore, three of her compositions on this record were triumphs that would be covered by others, such as Skeeter Davis, Bill Phillips, and Hank Williams Jr.

Album Cover

A blond Dolly (not yet platinum) was photographed through foliage, in a bucolic atmosphere bathed in a soft light, (almost) softening the harsh rurality evoked.

Curly Putman hit the jackpot when he wrote "Green, Green Grass of Home" in 1965, a megahit for Elvis Presley, Jerry Lee Lewis, Johnny Cash, George Jones, Merle Haggard, and many others.

Side A

Early on, Dolly learned to play with her image, especially when it came to the stereotypical image of the dumb blonde. "Dumb Pluck," Mutoscope card, ca. 1940s.

Dumb Blonde

Curly Putman / 2:27

Vocals: Dolly Parton **Musicians:** (?) **Backing Vocals:** (?) **Recorded:** Monument Records, Hendersonville, Tennessee, 1964–1966 **Technical Team:** Producer: Fred Foster / Assistant: Tommy Strong / Sound Engineer: Mort Thomasson **Single:** Side A: Dumb Blonde / Side B: The Giving and the Taking **Release Date:** Monument Records, November 7, 1966 (45 rpm ref.: MN45-982) **Best US Chart Ranking:** 24 (ranked for 14 weeks)

Genesis and Lyrics

Dolly Parton mischievously dots the *i*'s and crosses the *t*'s: Blondes are not dumb—far from it, and they are nobody's fools either. In the documentary *Dolly Parton: Here I Am*,[7] Dolly Parton admits that she could have—and even should have—written "Dumb Blonde," which was actually written by Claude Putman Jr. Indeed, this song seems tailor-made for her. It was probably producer Fred Foster of Monument Records who asked Putman, known as "Curly," to write for Dolly. Until then, with the exception of a few singles, Dolly had been writing primarily for Tree Publishing, a music publishing company founded by Jack Stapp in the 1950s in Nashville. Foster mistakenly thought that her energetic soprano voice was that of a bubble-gum pop singer, and Dolly released five such singles for Monument between 1964 and 1966. After the success of Bill Phillips singing "Put It Off Until Tomorrow," which was composed by Dolly, it seemed obvious that her Lolita-esque country persona stoked her evolution toward a style that is specifically both more country and more popular in its sound. In the meantime, it was Curly Putman who, for "Dumb Blonde," lent his pen to the character of the false ingenue who was hiding the fact that she was a lucid and enlightened country girl.

Production

In this song, we find the essential instruments of the Nashville sound of the time: pedal steel and up-tempo

Dolly in 1965, wearing one of her famous wigs, one year after her arrival in Nashville.

drums are at one with an unstoppable strumming (rhythmically strummed folk guitar chords), the tambourine emphasizes beats two and four of each measure on the snare drum, and the electric bass alternates between tonic, third, fifth, and octave on beats one and three. We also notice a less traditional instrument in the world of country music: the Clavinet, a kind of electric harpsichord.

To top it all off, the close harmony backing vocals, worthy of the great doo-wop and bubblegum pop hits of the late 1950s and 1960s, echo Dolly Parton's rebellious voice. A parallel can be drawn with the sublime "You Don't Own Me," a precursor standard sung by Lesley Gore in 1963 and produced by Quincy Jones for Island Records: Indeed, whereas Lesley Gore, then seventeen years old, expressed a feminist rebellion in a confrontational way, very much in advance of her time, Dolly Parton opted, with Curly Putman, for the tone of irony and played with the perspective usually given to the archetype she embodied.

In stereo, the sound is distributed as follows: alone in the center, Dolly's lead voice; on the left, the snare drum, a tambourine, the acoustic guitar, and bass; on the right, the pedal steel, the Clavinet, the backing vocals, and the bass drum. It should be remembered that at this time, mixing desks allowed only for hard left/right for stereo mixing—that is, a track was either completely in the center, completely on the left, or completely on the right; there was no gradation of the stereo field, which required an excellent distribution of the timbres of each instrument and a prior vision of the mix for the recording, which was then still mostly done live in the studio.

The whole album *Hello, I'm Dolly* generally follows this approach, with a few nuances, as we will observe during the analysis of the following titles. It must be said that the formula found here by Fred Foster, Mort Thomasson, and Tommy Strong is devilishly effective.

Your Ole Handy Man

Dolly Parton / 2:09

Vocals: Dolly Parton **Musicians:** (?) **Recorded:** Monument Records, Hendersonville, Tennessee **Technical Team:** Producer: Fred Foster / Assistant: Tommy Strong / Sound Engineer: Mort Thomasson

"Your Ole Handy Man," in some ways, questions the role of each person in a relationship. This focus is on a woman who manages everything. She is fed up. Enough of being a maid for her man, enough of scrubbing, patching up, repairing. A limit has been reached, and this woman may well give up her "handyman" apron and leave. Dolly's composition is very up-tempo country, and sound engineer Mort Thomasson, a true legend of the sound booth, gives the song a depth of relief based on the medium and low frequencies. This second track of the album sets out with the same flying start of the "live in the studio" formula as "Dumb Blonde," with one difference: The Clavinet is supported by an electric guitar backbeat played on beats two and four, which imparts an effective dynamic reminiscent of the first Beatles albums (between 1963 and 1966), which in turn were directly inspired by the Motown sound.

> **MOTOWN**
> Motown is a soul and rhythm 'n' blues music label created in 1959 by Berry Gordy in Detroit. It has notably been home to Michael Jackson and the Jackson Five, Diana Ross and the Supremes, the Four Tops, Martha and the Vandellas, Marvin Gaye, Stevie Wonder...

I Don't Want To Throw Rice

Bill Owens, Dolly Parton / 2:22

Vocals: Dolly Parton **Musicians:** (?) **Recorded:** Monument Records, Hendersonville, Tennessee **Technical Team:** Producer: Fred Foster / Assistant: Tommy Strong / Sound Engineer: Mort Thomasson

An eye for an eye...this time, Dolly plays a woman who is angry at another woman, a man stealer. On the day of a wedding, she seriously wants to throw rocks in the other woman's face instead of the traditional rice. Or better still, why not put dynamite in the traitor's car? Despite her anger and grief, the narrator wonders if she is going too far. In "I Don't Want to Throw Rice," the pain of a broken heart and the feeling of helplessness are mixed with a strong desire to eliminate a rival, and it has the feeling of a murder ballad.

The three-time midtempo (a subdivision of the quarter note into three beats, often performed as a shuffle or swing in American music) that we hear is archetypal of the Nashville sound. Here, the honky-tonk piano replaces the Clavinet, the acoustic guitar moves to the right in the stereo field so as not to be drowned by the snare drum (played mostly with brushes), and the electric guitar backbeat, already present on "Your Ole Handy Man," is on the left, complementing the pedal steel. These subtleties of mixing show the talent of Mort Thomasson, who has no hesitation in creating variations on his magic formula for the needs of the song.

Put It Off Until Tomorrow

Bill Owens, Dolly Parton / 2:25

Vocals: Dolly Parton **Musicians:** (?) **Recorded:** Monument Records, Hendersonville, Tennessee, date? **Technical Team:** Producer: Fred Foster / Assistant: Tommy Strong / Sound Engineer: Mort Thomasson **Single:** Side A: The Little Things / Side B: I'll Put It Off Until Tomorrow **Release:** Monument Records, June 1, 1966 (45 rpm ref.: 45-948) **Best US Chart Ranking:** Did Not Chart

In "Put It Off Until Tomorrow," Dolly Parton and Bill Owens talk about a love that ends with the man's departure, while the woman remains, as though stunned by this painful ending. Wounded, she asks only for a day's reprieve, that this abandonment be put off until tomorrow. This song was the biggest success of the album.

Still in 3/4 time, this is a country ballad in all its splendor: the slow, throbbing shuffle of a rocking chair sways on the front porch of a Southern Appalachian cabin. The counterpoint work of the upright piano dialogues beautifully with the fine embroidery of the electric guitar, a role previously reserved for the pedal steel. Passing through a tape echo circuit, the guitar sound is enhanced by a perfectly timed delay (note the repetition effect). This subtle detail, which brings an additional dimension to the song, suggests the great American plains, the "great wide open." We must think big, since the conquest of America was not limited to the banks of the Tennessee River. Fred Foster, Mort Thomasson, and Dolly Parton understand this very well.

Roy Orbison, pioneering rock 'n' roll singer-songwriter, one of the big stars of the Monument label, in 1967.

In 1966, Bill Phillips covered "Put It Off Until Tomorrow," which he sang with Dolly Parton, though she was not credited on the record. The song reached number six in the country charts. For Phillips, who had sung duets with Kitty Wells and Johnnie Wright, this song was his first real hit. He would never have another comparable success. He died in 2010.

I Wasted My Tears

Bill Owens, Dolly Parton / 2:18

Vocals: Dolly Parton **Musicians:** (?) **Backing Vocals:** (?) **Recorded:** Monument Records, Hendersonville, Tennessee **Technical Team:** Producer: Fred Foster / Assistant: Tommy Strong / Sound Engineer: Mort Thomasson **Single:** Side A: I Wasted My Tears / Side B: What Do You Think About Lovin' **Release:** Monument Records, November 1964 (45-rpm: 45-869) **Best US Chart Ranking:** Did Not Chart

Blinded by love, which leaves only disappointment and sorrow when it disappears, a woman regrets wasting her tears on a man. Released in 1964 on Monument Records, this single has a B-side: "What Do You Think About Lovin'." A good question…

The result of another collaboration between Dolly and her uncle Bill, this country ballad is marked by the influence of Roy Orbison, the rock 'n' roll pioneer nicknamed "Big O," one of the big stars of the Monument label. The sound engineer Mort Thomasson adapts wonderfully to its crying sound, in particular with the contribution of a luxuriant brass band. Here we return to the binary beat, in a march with a fast tempo and a pronounced stomp. In the left stereo channel, the sub-bassophone and tuba double the bass, which contributes greatly to creating a climate that is both danceable and solemn. The spirit of the marching band effectively underlines the central theme: Let it be known that the narrator will no longer cry in vain for this lost love.

Something Fishy

Dolly Parton / 2:06

Vocals: Dolly Parton **Musicians:** (?) **Recorded:** Monument Records, Hendersonville, Tennessee **Technical Team:** Producer: Fred Foster / Assistant: Tommy Strong / Sound Engineer: Mort Thomasson **Single:** Side A: Something Fishy / Side B: I've Lived My Life **Release:** Monument Records, May 1, 1967 (45 rpm ref: MN 45-1007) **Best US Chart Ranking:** 17

"Something Fishy," which went to number seventeen on the Billboard Hot Country Songs chart, juggles emotion and irony. There's something fishy about this song, according to this neglected woman who guesses what is going on: Her man often goes fishing with "an old friend" but only comes back in the night, without fish and with lipstick on his shirt. Written by Dolly Parton alone, this song is in the same vein as "Your Ole Handy Man": Dolly finds her personality as a country Lolita to whom life has nothing more to teach. The pun in the title of this fishing story refers to the hillbilly folk wisdom saying, "Men smell of goats, and women smell of fish."

Instrumentally, we return to the basic formula, with one difference: A dobro is used. This instrument answers to the volutes of the pedal steel with the help of a slide, but with a raw and acoustic tone dear to the Delta blues, represented by Robert Johnson and Bukka White. This bluegrass reminiscence is perfectly suited to the use of bitter and funny metaphors, which are commonly found in hillbilly singing.

Fuel To The Flame

Bill Owens, Dolly Parton / 2:39

Vocals: Dolly Parton **Musicians:** (?) **Backing Vocals:** (?)
Recorded: Monument Records, Hendersonville, Tennessee
Technical Team: Producer: Fred Foster / Assistant: Tommy Strong /
Sound Engineer: Mort Thomasson

"Fuel to the Flame" evokes a love that is all fire and flame, filled with passionate kisses that make you weak but happy. Dolly covers this song; it had already brought good fortune to Skeeter Davis, who had in fact reached eleventh place with it on the Billboard Hot Country Songs chart in January 1967. Unquestionably, this is the most melancholic song on the album. On the right, piano arpeggios, high pedal steel, and electric guitar chords with a sumptuous tremolo effect (altering the volume, not the pitch, probably through the vibrato circuit of a Fender amp, possibly the classic Deluxe Reverb) intertwine to weave a soft carpet of sound. From 0:56, still on the stereo channel, a French horn makes its entrance, an unexpected but sober and timely intervention: Thus, the flame is consumed, the melody settles, we sink and abandon ourselves a little more in the meanderings of this ode to consuming love. The harmonic density of the right stereo channel is remarkable: backing vocals, tremolo guitar, pedal steel, piano, French horn. All the rhythmic parts are on the left: snare drum with brushes and cross sticks, the strumming of a folk guitar, the bass discreetly doubled by an electric guitar played in tic-tac mode—in other words, an exact octave apart from the bass—in order to enhance its percussive character and to make the harmony more readable. A great classic of the Nashville sound.

For Dolly Addicts

In Nashville, Randall Hank Williams, professionally known as Hank Williams Jr. and nicknamed "Bocephus," was very selective in the artists he quoted or recorded. So, it is not surprising that he appreciated "I'm in No Condition" and covered it. Even though the cover was not a huge success, the friendship between the two artists would last.

The Giving And The Taking

Bill Owens, Dolly Parton / 2:25

Vocals: Dolly Parton **Musicians:** (?) **Recorded:** Monument Records, Hendersonville, Tennessee **Technical Team:** Producer: Fred Foster / Assistant: Tommy Strong / Sound Engineer: Mort Thomasson **Single:** Side A: Dumb Blonde / Side B: The Giving and the Taking / **Release:** Monument Records, November 7, 1966 (45 rpm ref: MN45- 982) **Best US Chart Ranking:** 24

Here, on the B-side of the "Dumb Blonde" single, the duo of Dolly Parton and Bill Owens once again explores the theme of troubled love, that of a woman who gave everything but received nothing happy in return: "They say that love is give and take"…A principle not always respected.

On this midtempo country shuffle, the arrangements are sober and tightly controlled. The piano is on the left and all the rhythm parts on the right, in order to leave the floor to a very twangy guitar, that is to say, played in a particular way, by the use of a felt pad fixed on the bridge, or the muffled play of the palm of the hand holding the pick, often accompanied by an intensive use of the vibrato bar. This specifically American sound, very common in surf music, notably with Dick Dale in his famous "Misirlou" (1962), has some of its roots on the other side of the Atlantic, thanks to Hank Marvin, famous guitarist of the instrumental group the Shadows. The addition of the twang guitar seems to have been conceived as a slightly plaintive male response to the singer's tender yet desperate pleas: "You knew I would forgive […] / Now I'm alone and left forsaken." It is very likely that Dolly Parton has overdubbed her own voice here, as the timbre of the second voice seems similar and synchronous.

A son's tribute to his father: Hank Williams Jr. playing and singing Hank Williams Sr. (June 1967, Hollywood).

I'm In No Condition

Dolly Parton / 2:08

Vocals: Dolly Parton **Musicians:** (?) **Backing Vocals:** (?)
Recorded: Monument Records, Hendersonville, Tennessee
Technical Team: Producer: Fred Foster / Assistant: Tommy Strong / Sound Engineer: Mort Thomasson

This is the story of a woman who refuses to let herself be loved, because she is still heartbroken from her last relationship: "Don't smile at me because it's no use / 'Cause I don't have a smile that I can give to you." What stands out right away is the vocal melody floating between the third and major second over a sequence of chords (*F* and *E* flat major on the verses); it is thus strongly reminiscent of the chiseled songwriting of the Byrds, the band that spearheaded the California folk / country rock movement (active from 1964 to 1973) and was carried in its early days by Roger McGuinn, David Crosby, and Gene Clark. The instrumentation also seems to be directly inspired by the Byrds' sound, as all the ingredients are present: on the left, a 4/4 rhythm (as opposed to the 2/4 country rhythm used in the other songs on the album) played with a hi-hat, an arpeggiated twelve-string electric guitar, and an electric bass; on the right, a nylon guitar played with a fingerpicking technique, sounding at times like a harp, a pedal steel, a piano, and a backing vocal. At that time and until the mid-1970s, the boundary between folk music and country music was still extremely porous. Dolly Parton, on the other hand, would not cease, during her career, to make incursions into folk—her global hit "Jolene" is probably the best example—and then into pop. As for the Byrds, their sound became more and more country over the years and with the various line-ups, in particular with the arrival of the legendary Gram Parsons at the keyboard and later the esteemed stringbender guitarist Clarence White.

Dolly prepares for her promotion, smiling and confident. Her career was further helped by *The Porter Wagoner Show*, ca. 1970.

Lola Jean Dillon also composed for Norma Jean Beasler (the singer whom Porter Wagoner replaced with Dolly in 1967), and wrote for Loretta Lynn, Conway Twitty, Billie Jo Spears, and Bonnie Owens (the wife of Buck Owens, then Merle Haggard).

The Company You Keep

Bill Owens, Dolly Parton / 2:33

Vocals: Dolly Parton **Musicians:** (?) **Recorded:** Monument Records, Hendersonville, Tennessee **Technical Team:** Producer: Fred Foster / Assistant: Tommy Strong / Sound Engineer: Mort Thomasson

In this song written by Bill Owens and Dolly—who contributes the lyrics—Dolly seems to have explored with her uncle all aspects of the country mentality, such as advice to give to the younger generation. An older sister, worried about her younger sister, advises her to beware of her friends, who are leading her astray. Without judging her, she explains things simply out of her love and desire to help her.

As for the music, we return to the basics. This country shuffle ballad has a slightly higher tempo than "Put It Off Until Tomorrow," with Mort Thomasson's magic formula at work again. We notice the return of the famous electric guitar, ticking away on the right stereo channel, in addition to the pedal steel. The guitar also provides some exquisite turnarounds, echoing Dolly Parton's benevolent sisterhood: "I'm only trying to help you sis […] / 'Cause I think you're an angel / But folks think that you're cheap / 'Cause you're known by the company you keep." The absence of backing vocals—apart from a few phrases dubbed in thirds, probably by Dolly herself—further emphasizes the intimacy of this song, in the voice of the protective older sister.

I've Lived My Life

Lola Jean Dillon / 2:35

Vocals: Dolly Parton **Musicians:** (?) **Recorded:** Monument Records, Hendersonville, Tennessee **Technical Team:** Producer: Fred Foster / Assistant: Tommy Strong / Sound Engineer: Mort Thomasson

This composition is the work of Lola Jean Dillon, a friend of Porter Wagoner. Through him, she presented the song to Dolly, who liked it and recorded it. In this song, an eighteen-year-old girl, heartbroken by a failed love, thinks her life is over. This ballad is dark, almost fatalistic, even though Dolly Parton's voice counterbalances this perception with its clarity and vitality. The country shuffle strikes again, but this time, the unexpected comes from the presence of a glockenspiel, doubling the melody of the chorus: "I've lived my life and I'm only eighteen." This new piece of exquisite craftmanship brings a welcome delicacy and childlike lightness to this painful theme of early resignation. It is a fine example of what country- and folk-loving Americans—and Dolly Parton herself (listen to the first episode of the excellent *Dolly Parton's America* podcast)—commonly call, not without a sweet irony, a "sad ass song."

An old Appalachian couple sitting on their porch, an image of time passing and echoes of the song "I've Lived My Life."

SINGLE

The Little Things

Bill Owens, Dolly Parton / 2:25

Vocals: Dolly Parton **Musicians:** (?) **Recorded:** Monument Records, Hendersonville, Tennessee **Technical Team:** Producer: Fred Foster / Assistant: Tommy Strong / Sound Engineer: Mort Thomasson **Single:** Side A: The Little Things / Side B: I'll Put It Off Until Tomorrow **Release:** Monument Records, June 1 1966, (45 rpm ref.: 45-948) **Best US Chart Ranking:** Did Not Chart

Through "The Little Things," Dolly Parton and Bill Owens address another aspect of married life: the invisible relationship wounds, the forgotten birthdays, the lack of attention, the flowers or candy never given…These are "little things," but their absence hurts.

"The Little Things" was most likely recorded as a prelude to the *Hello, I'm Dolly* album. The single, which never charted, was released in June 1966, while the LP did not arrive in stores until February 13, 1967.

Surprisingly, this song is available only in mono (instead of stereo), and judging by its clarity, one could argue that it was intentionally mixed that way, which was still common practice at the time. Despite the mono mix, we find the winning Mort Thomasson and Tommy Strong formula, this time in a midtempo, 4/4 pace. One can emphasize the marked presence of the tremolo guitar, as if coating all these small, missing attentions with a comforting, acidulous perfume. Dolly Parton doubles her voice in unison on the verses and switches to thirds on the choruses, which are also embellished with a third voice in fifths. This was certainly how the young Dolly and her family used to harmonize their voices during the long summer evenings spent singing on the front porch of their small Tennessee home. From 1976 on, Dolly often reproduced these three-part harmonies with her singing sisters, Emmylou Harris and Linda Ronstadt. Their collaboration was in fact inaugurated during the *Dolly Parton Show*, at Dolly's invitation, on the song "Apple Jack"; this foreshadowed the long-awaited album *Trio*, which was released in 1987.

ALBUM

Just Because I'm a Woman

You're Gonna Be Sorry . I Wish I Felt This Way at Home . False Eyelashes .
I'll Oilwells Love You . The Only Way Out (Is to Walk over Me) . Little Bit Slow
to Catch On . The Bridge . Love and Learn . I'm Running Out of Love .
Just Because I'm a Woman . Baby Sister . Try Being Lonely

RELEASE DATE
United States: April 15, 1968
Reference: RCA Victor, Nashville—LPM-3949 (mono),
LSP-3949 (stereo)
Best US Chart Ranking: 22 (ranked for 9 weeks)

Women's Liberation Movement demonstration, New York City, ca. 1968, while Dolly lends her voice and pen to the women in "Just Because I'm a Woman."

Also in 1968, at RCA, Dolly Parton recorded several duets with Porter Wagoner, which marked the beginning of a long collaboration: two singles ("Holding On to Nothin'" / "Just Between You and Me" and "We'll Get Ahead Someday" / "Jeannie's Afraid of the Dark") and an album (*Just the Two of Us*).

Emancipation "Dolly Parton" Style

A year had passed since the release of *Hello, I'm Dolly* when, in April 1968, fans flocked to *Just Because I'm a Woman*. A second solo album is perhaps more difficult to produce than the first one, because you know what you are expected to do. However, this is a flawless album from the songwriter, who confirms her talent as a singer-songwriter. Dolly Parton transmits emotion both through the lyrics she writes and through the way she sings them: simply, deeply, and touching the listener in the heart.

Separation and Confirmation

After a rather trying period spent settling in Nashville in 1968, Dolly Parton was now part of the country music landscape. But there was still a long way to go before she achieved the superstar status she had dreamed of since childhood. This second solo album confirms what was already perceptible in *Hello, I'm Dolly*. From week to week, from single to album, Dolly was becoming indispensable. She was there on television, on *The Porter Wagoner Show*; in the studios of Music City (Nashville's nickname), alone, or recording with Porter Wagoner. Quickly, because he was aware of Dolly's potential and because he wanted her on his show, Porter negotiated her move from Monument Records to RCA Victor, his record company. He was even willing to pay out of his own pocket, in case Dolly Parton didn't make enough money for RCA. He would keep his dollars. Dolly transformed the test with *Just Because I'm a Woman*. In *My Life and Other Unfinished Business*,[1] the artist relays how difficult it was for her to tell her friend and producer, Fred Foster, that she was leaving Monument. A first label is (almost) as important as a first love. But Dolly wanted to be a superstar, and that meant making difficult choices.

Evolution and Emancipation

With her move to RCA, Dolly Parton might have been lost, according to Mark Deming of AllMusic, caught between the Chet Atkins style that reigned there—the syrupy violins, the grandiloquent backing vocals—and the influence of Porter Wagoner. Fortunately, as Deming notes, the opposite happened, and *Just Because I'm a Woman* counts among

1968

Chet Atkins, an influential country music figure on the RCA Victor label, with his semi-acoustic Gretsch guitar, ca. 1960.

Chet Atkins (left) and recording engineer Bill Porter, in the control booth of RCA Studio B, Nashville, ca. 1962.

For Dolly Addicts

In 1968, Monument released the single "I'm Not Worth the Tears," written by Dolly with "Ping Pong" on the B-side. In the same year, RCA Victor released the single "In the Good Old Days (When Times Were Bad)," also written by Dolly, with "Try Being Lonely" on the B-side.

the best of her early albums. The album has a honky-tonk sound, refined and organic—to quote Mark Deming—and, from a musical point of view, an ambitious approach, as in "The Bridge." Dolly takes a risk at the end of the song: She cuts it off; we hear no murmur or sigh, nothing, not even a sound of water, just silence.

Dolly Parton wrote four tracks out of the twelve that appear here. In a subtle mixture of fragility and strength, her soprano voice asserts itself, as well as her very specific way of conveying the emotional range contained in her songs, which would be one of her trademarks throughout her career. As for her talent as a songwriter, although it had not yet acquired its full amplitude or its full maturity—Dolly was only twenty-two years old—it was already very sharp. From the first to the last track of the album, it is about love, through the attitude of men especially, but also of women, especially in the couple, what they accept or refuse in the name of love—to suffer, to be unloved, in silence, alone, as if this was their inevitable destiny. "Just Because I'm a Woman," the title track, like the album as a whole, shakes up

a puritanical America, which, at the end of the 1960s, was experiencing the impacts of the women's liberation movement. Since the beginning of the decade, the women's lib movement protested against all forms of sexism and discrimination against women and demanded equal rights for all women. Alanna Nash, in her biography of the artist, thinks it likely that Dolly's progressive attitude was not to the taste of some in Nashville.[3] This second album, however, remained on the charts for a long time, reaching number twenty-two on the Billboard Top Country Albums chart, and the only single, "Just Because I'm a Woman," reached number seventeen on the Billboard Hot Country Singles chart.

Album Cover

Against a blue background, Dolly poses standing, in a classic white dress, as if framed by a canopy, her arms outstretched, palms facing the sky. Was this presentation choice by the decision-makers imposed on her? While waiting for her inimitable style to assert itself—flashy outfits, heavy makeup, and platinum mane—her generous smile radiates.

You're Gonna Be Sorry

Dolly Parton / 2:16

Vocals: Dolly Parton **Musicians:** Wayne Moss: solo electric guitar / Chip Young, George McCormick: rhythm guitars / Lloyd Green: pedal steel / Roy "Junior" Huskey: bass / Jerry Kirby Carrigan: drums / David Briggs, Hargus "Pig" Robbins: piano / Charles Trent: electric banjo / Mack Magaha: fiddle **Backing Vocals:** Anita Carter, Dolores Edgin
Recorded: RCA Victor, Nashville, November 20, 1967
Technical Team: Producer: Bob Ferguson / Sound Engineer: Al Pachucki

Written by the singer, the song that opens the album is rhythmic and soft at the same time, and serious, too. She describes the condition of a woman in a relationship, the ups and downs of love, the wear and the tear. Dolly Parton, who, since childhood, had developed a healthy curiosity and a great sense of observation, noted that in the late 1960s, women were tired of waiting for men and would not hesitate to leave them.

For the recording, Dolly found herself in the legendary RCA Studio B in Nashville, where Willie Nelson, Elvis Presley, and Jerry Lee Lewis had recorded. Chet Atkins usually conducted the sessions, but for this track, he seems to have left it to producer Bob Ferguson. The so-called country-politan formula of Chet Atkins, with syrupy violins and grandiloquent choruses, is not applied. The musicians are all members of the A-Team of Nashville's finest session men. At 0:40, for example, we notice the entrance of Hargus "Pig" Robbins on the piano, with a recognizable style, similar to the vocal technique of melisma; his notes flow into each other naturally, with ease. This style of playing, also practiced by Floyd Cramer, is the opposite of the virtuoso but percussive piano of Jerry Lee Lewis.

Lloyd Green was, at the end of the 1960s, the best pedal steel specialist in the business, and as such he entered the Country Music Hall of Fame. He also played for Johnny Cash and Elvis Presley as well as for Joan Baez. In Europe, he took part in the festivals of Wembley (London) in 1976 and Porte de Pantin (Paris) in 1981 with Wanda Jackson and Jerry Lee Lewis. Endowed with an almost supernatural musical perception, he enhanced the songs of the artists for whom he recorded between 1957 and 1985.

Dolly Parton covers a song written by the prolific songwriter Harlan Howard, with the theme of love, always and forever, and its heartbreak. In this version, the modulation of Dolly's voice as she sings "I've never been loved / The way you love me / I wish I felt this way at home" hooks the listener deeply. Because it is illegitimate, the narrator must give up a stronger love than she is shown at home. "I Wish I Felt This Way at Home" is one of her songs that holds a mirror up to society, as the songwriter accurately and convincingly conveys what she feels.

Dolly sings in the pure honky-tonk style of Loretta Lynn or Patsy Cline. Lloyd Green's pedal steel intro takes the listener to the stage of the Grand Ole Opry and, at 0:50, Mack Magaha's fiddle adds a welcome touch of mountain music. To complete the package, Anita Carter (sister of Johnny Cash's wife, June Carter), provides backing vocals.

I Wish I Felt This Way At Home

Harlan Howard / 2:29

Vocals: Dolly Parton **Musicians:** Wayne Moss: solo electric guitar / Chip Young, George McCormick: rhythm guitars / Lloyd Green: pedal steel / Roy "Junior" Huskey: bass / Jerry Kirby Carrigan: drums / David Briggs, Hargus "Pig" Robbins: piano / Charles Trent: electric banjo / Mack Magaha: fiddle
Backing Vocals: Anita Carter, Dolores Edgin **Recorded:** RCA Victor, Nashville, November 20, 1967 **Technical Team:** Producer: Bob Ferguson / Sound Engineer: Al Pachucki **Single:** Side A: Just Because I'm a Woman / Side B: I Wish I Felt This Way at Home **Recorded:** RCA Victor, June 1968 (45 rpm ref.: 47-9548) **Best US Chart Ranking:** 17

False Eyelashes

Demetris Tapp, Bob Tubert / 2:30

Vocals: Dolly Parton **Musicians:** Wayne Moss: solo electric guitar / Chip Young, George McCormick: rhythm guitars / Lloyd Green: pedal steel / Roy "Junior" Huskey: bass / Jerry Kirby Carrigan: drums / David Briggs, Hargus "Pig" Robbins: piano / Charles Trent: electric banjo / Mack Magaha: fiddle **Backing Vocals:** Anita Carter, Dolores Edgin **Recorded:** RCA Victor, Nashville, November 20, 1967 **Technical Team:** Producer: Bob Ferguson / Sound Engineer: Al Pachucki

This country song, with its strong narrative content, was not written by Dolly Parton, but she could easily have written it. The lyrics recall the young singer's early years, when surviving in Nashville proved difficult—she persisted in wearing

1968

In an improvised studio, Harlan Howard (composer of "I Wish I Felt This Way at Home") records his wife, singer Jan Howard.

heels filled with water and tiny fish, and a dress that did not suit her.[10] The difficulties did not stop her from writing reassuring letters to her family. Dolly Parton has crossed paths with many women who have suffered from not being able to achieve their dreams. "False Eyelashes" is a concentrate of emotions where illusions and disillusions are intermingled.

The musical style is still honky-tonk, with an intro by the virtuoso Lloyd Green, here on the right in the stereo field, the no less voluble fiddle of Mack Magaha making an incursion from the left between 0:41 and 1:13, as if to momentarily let the pedal steel breathe, and a bass part with a relentless but never cumbersome swing by Roy "Junior" Huskey.

I'll Oilwells Love You

Bill Owens, Dolly Parton / 2:16

Vocals: Dolly Parton **Musicians:** Wayne Moss: solo electric guitar / Chip Young, George McCormick: rhythm guitars / Lloyd Green: pedal steel / Roy "Junior" Huskey: bass / Jerry Kirby Carrigan: drums / David Briggs, Hargus "Pig" Robbins: piano / Charles Trent: electric banjo / Mack Magaha: fiddle

Backing Vocals: Anita Carter, Dolores Edgin **Recorded:** RCA Victor, Nashville, November 20, 1967 **Technical Team:** Producer: Bob Fergurson / Sound Engineer: Al Pachucki

Dolly's ironic sense of humor is evident in this song, co-written with her uncle, Bill Owens, the key to the song being a caustic play on the words "always" and "oilwells." This rhythmic song tells of a woman's love for her husband…or, more precisely, for his oil wells. The scene takes place in Texas, a state known for producing this hydrocarbon.

Here again, Lloyd Green's pedal steel playing is fabulous, justifying his nickname of "Master of the Steel Strings." The tempo is much higher, but the recipe is exactly the same as on "False Eyelashes"—one can bet that the two tracks were recorded in the same time. Mack Magaha's three interventions on the fiddle were clearly designed to give the ear a break from the brilliant sound of the pedal steel, while maintaining the upbeat feel necessary for the almost slapstick fun of the track. One can imagine Buster Keaton in the midst of a love affair, with the comical tone that Dolly likes to play with so much and that she would use with panache during her future career as an actress (notably in *9 to 5* (1980) and in *The Best Little Whorehouse in Texas* (1982).

Lloyd Green plays pedal steel at a concert at the Grand Ole Opry, Nashville, ca. 1975.

The Only Way Out (Is To Walk Over Me)

Neal Merritt / 2:55

Vocals: Dolly Parton **Musicians:** Wayne Moss: solo electric guitar / Chip Young, George McCormick: rhythm guitars / Lloyd Green: pedal steel / Roy "Junior" Huskey: bass / Jerry Kirby Carrigan: drums / David Briggs, Hargus "Pig" Robbins: piano / Charles Trent: electric banjo / Mack Magaha: fiddle **Backing Vocals:** Anita Carter, Dolores Edgin **Recorded:** RCA Victor, Nashville, November 20, 1967 **Technical Team:** Producer: Bob Ferguson / Sound Engineer: Al Pachucki

Written by Neal Merritt, this ballad evokes the desperate love of a woman who is willing to give up what little pride she has left to hold on to her man, even if it means getting down on her knees, crawling at his feet, or being stepped on. We find here the darkness of certain country themes. And also, paradoxically, their beauty.

Dolly Parton begins singing in duet with Anita Carter. The two friends are specialists in mountain music and have fun harmonizing in the bluegrass style. Lloyd Green adds a tag at 1:58 and 2:17, and Chip Young responds with sumptuously articulated acoustic guitar phrasing. A surprising detail, revealing the care given to the arrangements: The pedal steel is sometimes doubled in thirds by Lloyd Green himself, in overdub; it is a mirror game of the most beautiful effect, competing with the delicacy of Anita Carter's vocal harmonies.

This stunning ornamentation sounds like a perfect negative counterpart to Lee Hazlewood's song "These Boots Are Made for Walkin'," sung by Nancy Sinatra in 1966; here, Dolly announces "The only way out is to walk over me," when Nancy warned "One of these days these boots are gonna walk all over you." This indicates an evolution of mores, which Dolly Parton will naturally take up later. It is interesting to note that both songs were written by men, one born in 1929 in Oklahoma (Lee Hazlewood) and the other in 1930 in Texas (Neal Merritt).

Little Bit Slow To Catch On

Curly Putman / 2:19

Vocals: Dolly Parton **Musicians:** Wayne Moss: solo electric guitar / Chip Young, George McCormick: rhythm guitars / Lloyd Green: pedal steel / Roy "Junior" Huskey: bass / Jerry Kirby Carrigan: drums / David Briggs, Hargus "Pig" Robbins: piano / Charles Trent: electric banjo / Mack Magaha: fiddle **Backing Vocals:** Anita Carter, Dolores Edgin **Recorded:** RCA Victor, Nashville, November 20, 1967 **Technical Team:** Producer: Bob Ferguson / Sound Engineer: Al Pachucki

After taking over "Dumb Blonde," which fit her like a glove, Dolly Parton covered another song by songwriter Curly Putman, "Little Bit Slow to Catch On," sung with a deceptively candid voice. This marks the end of the image of the dumb blonde, and Dolly never goes back to it. The guitar intro by George McCormick and Wayne Moss evokes a country-pop aspect, a country-rock mix—for the record, Wayne Moss is the rhythm guitarist on Roy Orbison's "Oh Pretty Woman," the main riff being the work of Jerry Kennedy. Note the slight distortion applied to the pedal steel, making the sound extraordinarily mellow and shimmering, as a way of underlining the deliberately rebellious tone of the song: "I'm a little bit slow to catch on [...] / But finally I'm a catchin' on." Curly Putman and Dolly Parton thus settle the score with the dumb blonde on a playful country shuffle, and society moves on. Nancy Sinatra's boots are not so very far off now.

1968

Anita Carter, a friend of Dolly's and a mountain music specialist too, is featured among the backing vocalists on "Just Because I'm a Woman" (ca. 1975).

This aerial view of the Cumberland River, with its string of bridges and downtown Nashville in 1961, is missing only one thing: Dolly's poetry in "The Bridge."

Dolly Parton always followed the musical currents of the country scene very closely. Touched by "Ode to Billie Joe"—Bobbie Gentry's July 1967 single about a pregnant girl who throws her aborted baby off the Tallahatchie River Bridge (Mississippi)—the song became a massive hit. In "The Bridge," Dolly creates her own version of these events.

The Bridge

Dolly Parton / 2:34

Vocals: Dolly Parton **Musicians:** Wayne Moss: solo electric guitar / Chip Young, George McCormick: rhythm guitars / Lloyd Green: pedal steel / Roy "Junior" Huskey: bass / Jerry Kirby Carrigan: drums / David Briggs, Hargus "Pig" Robbins: piano / Charles Trent: electric banjo / Mack Magaha: fiddle **Backing Vocals:** Anita Carter, Dolores Edgin **Recorded:** RCA Victor, Nashville, November 20, 1967 **Technical Team:** Producer: Bob Ferguson / Sound Engineer: Al Pachucki **Single:** Side A: In the Ghetto / Side B: The Bridge **Recorded:** RCA Victor, June 1969 (45 rpm ref.: 74-0192) **Best US Chart Ranking:** 50

Genesis and Lyrics

If there is a dark song on this album, it is "The Bridge." If there is a moving song, it is the story of this lonely and pregnant girl, who, abandoned by her man, returns to the bridge where they met, ready to do anything, even die, to escape her pain. The astonishing thing about Dolly's story is its conclusion: Everything began on this bridge, everything should end there—but the song stops abruptly; we expect a plunge, but there's no sound of splashing water. The finale is poignant.

Production

The paradox of some sad songs is that they sometimes contain no minor chords. "The Bridge" is a perfect example of this. Here, before the late semitone modulation, the song is almost entirely in C sharp and B major. The tension, so palpable in this composition, is generated by the presence of the B flat on the B major chord, giving it that sweet yet disturbing major seventh color. Indeed, this major seventh note is located one semitone below the tonic (the main note of the chord), thus producing a depression. We then feel a continuous effect of tension and release according to the back-and-forth of the major seventh present in the arpeggio of acoustic guitar and in the melody of the song, on words that never really tell the drama that is being played out. For the rest, the dark and theatrical side is essentially due to the haunting atmosphere of a hypnotic bass-drums couple, almost velveteen in texture, evoking the imperturbable current of the river, unaffected by human dramas. However, at 1:35, a bridge as brief as it is subtle and expressive brings about a first change: The usual second chord of the cycle changes from B major to an A major chord supported by its third in the bass (i.e., a $C\#$). This event shifts the piece to an unequivocal major key this time. The tension dissipates subtly, before the final bouquet: At 1:53, the key suddenly rises by a semitone, from C sharp to D major. Majestically reinforced by the pedal steel and its waves of successive chords in swell effect, this rise of a semitone contributes to intensify the dramatic climate through to the fatal moment: the abrupt end of this tragic melody, which leaves the listener in suspense. "Here is where it started / And here is where I'll end it."

Dolly Parton alongside Porter Wagoner, honored as a Wagonmaster, ca. 1968.

Love And Learn

Bill Owens / 2:33

Vocals: Dolly Parton **Musicians:** Wayne Moss: solo electric guitar / Chip Young, George McCormick: rhythm guitars / Lloyd Green: pedal steel / Roy "Junior" Huskey: bass / Jerry Kirby Carrigan: drums / David Briggs, Hargus "Pig" Robbins: piano / Charles Trent: electric banjo / Mack Magaha: fiddle **Backing Vocals:** Anita Carter, Dolores Edgin **Recorded:** RCA Victor, Nashville, November 20, 1967 **Technical Team:** Producer: Bob Fergurson / Sound Engineer: Al Pachucki

Bill Owens, with the lyrics, forms a duet with Dolly Parton, who contributes a very expressive voice to this lesson on life. How to avoid being hurt in love? There's no other solution but to go back, to try again, and to learn from past mistakes.

In this 4/4 ballad, while Dolly's voice bursts forth with all its purity on the musical resolution of each verse ("love and learn"), the words *hurt* and *yearn* are sung in a mezzo register, lower and warmer, unusual for the Queen of Country Music, but which wonderfully underlines the resignation of the subject. On the left stereo channel, the extreme brilliance of the strumming of the acoustic guitar is reminiscent of the sound of a harpsichord, due, probably, to new strings changed that same day, and on the right, the pedal steel, kept in the background until then, gratifies the listener with a melodious take to announce the last verse. The piano answering Dolly's voice has the distinctive David Briggs style, with well-articulated notes and the melody coming in, in counterpoint with the vocals. David Briggs has played with Elvis Presley, Kris Kristofferson, Shania Twain, Tony Joe White, J. J. Cale, and Nancy Sinatra.

I'm Running Out Of Love

Bill Owens / 2:06

Vocals: Dolly Parton **Musicians:** Wayne Moss: solo electric guitar / Chip Young, George McCormick: rhythm guitars / Lloyd Green: pedal steel / Roy "Junior" Huskey: bass / Jerry Kirby Carrigan: drums / David Briggs, Hargus "Pig" Robbins: piano / Charles Trent: electric banjo / Mack Magaha: fiddle **Backing Vocals:** Anita Carter, Dolores Edgin **Recorded:** RCA Victor, Nashville, November 20, 1967 **Technical Team:** Producer: Bob Ferguson / Sound Engineer: Al Pachucki

This country song, written by Uncle Bill in the Nashville tradition, reflects, like other songs on the album, on what many women experience and feel, mostly in silence. Once again, the songwriter's lyrics correspond to Dolly in the sense that it evokes a reality to which Dolly can lend her voice. One has to face facts: By being neglected and deceived, the love a woman has to give eventually dries up, and her patience runs out.

Wayne Moss and George McCormick's intro sounds like a nod to Bill Justis's 1957 instrumental track "Raunchy," a simple and effective riff that has become part of the vocabulary of country guitarists. Its use in this up-tempo track is a great testament to Moss and McCormick's musical relevance. Dolly's voice soars over the whole piece without ever forcing in her high register.

A CD reissue (released in 2003) features two songs recorded live at Sevier County High School in Dolly Parton's hometown of Sevierville in 1970: "Just Because I'm a Woman" and "Coat of Many Colors."

SIDE A

A tribute album entitled *Just Because I'm A Woman: The Songs of Dolly Parton* was later released in 2003 by Alison Krauss, Melissa Etheridge, Norah Jones, Joan Osborne, Shelby Lynne, Mindy Smith, Emmylou Harris, Shania Twain, Kasey Chambers, Sinéad O'Connor, Allison Moorer, and Meshell Ndegeocello.

Just Because I'm A Woman

Dolly Parton / 3:04

Vocals: Dolly Parton **Musicians:** Wayne Moss: solo electric guitar / Chip Young, George McCormick: rhythm guitars / Lloyd Green: pedal steel / Roy "Junior" Huskey: bass / Jerry Kirby Carrigan: drums / David Briggs, Hargus "Pig" Robbins: piano / Charles Trent: electric banjo / Mack Magaha: fiddle **Backing Vocals:** Anita Carter, Dolores Edgin **Recorded:** RCA Studio B, Nashville, November 20, 1967 **Technical Team:** Producer: Bob Fergurson / Sound Engineer: Al Pachucki **Single:** Side A: Just Because I'm a Woman / Side B: I Wish I Felt This Way at Home **Release Date:** RCA Victor, June 1968 (45 rpm ref.: 47-9548) **Best US Chart Ranking:** 17

Genesis and Lyrics

Sometimes, Dolly Parton draws her inspiration from the lives of others. Sometimes from her own life. As she recounts in her autobiography,[1] the idea for this song came from a conversation with her husband, Carl Dean. He wanted to know if the woman in his life had known other men before him. In the interest of honesty, Dolly said yes, and Carl was deeply affected. When she was writing her memoirs, the star wondered whether lying would have saved her from hurting her husband, whom she adores and to whom she is still married. The lyrics of the song, which call for a fair and equitable clemency for the mistakes of the past, both the woman and the man, are simply beautiful, touching, and slightly transgressive for the time. This proximity that the singer knows so well how to create, between her writing and the emotion she transmits to her public, is perfectly rendered here.

Production and Remakes

This midtempo country ballad is clearly one of Dolly's favorites, and she seems to have sung it live a long time before recording it. Her impeccable diction is supported successively by Lloyd Green's pedal steel and Mack Magaha's fiddle arrangements, as well as Chip Young's particularly sophisticated acoustic guitar riffs from 0:48 on. Chip Young (1938–2014) was known and appreciated for his picking style, the thumb on the low strings, the other fingers playing the melody on the high strings. He has played with Willie Nelson, Eddy Arnold, Bobby Bare, Tanya Tucker, Reba McEntire, Billy Swan, and Mickey Newbury.

In 2003, on the covers album *Just Because I'm a Woman*, Dolly Parton herself covers this song as an epilogue to the twelve tribute tracks. This new version, with its pronounced gospel accents, opens with a few sumptuous Rhodes chords (a model of electric piano manufactured by Fender), quickly overtaken by the rhythm section and the electric guitar. The Hammond organ completes the gospel setting, and Dolly can give free rein to the naturally soulful character of her voice. The typically praise sound (the "prayer" song of gospel music), the vibes, and the power are there, impressively so. Norah Jones, Alison Krauss, Sinéad O'Connor, Emmylou Harris, and Shania Twain, among other artists, participate in this splendid album.

In 2016, Stella, the youngest sister of the Parton siblings, and also a singer, took her turn to cover "Just Because I'm a Woman."

Baby Sister

Shirl Milete / 2:39

Vocals: Dolly Parton **Musicians:** Wayne Moss: solo electric guitar / Chip Young, George McCormick: rhythm guitars / Lloyd Green: pedal steel / Roy "Junior" Huskey: bass / Jerry Kirby Carrigan: drums / David Briggs, Hargus "Pig" Robbins: piano / Charles Trent: electric banjo / Mack Magaha: fiddle **Backing Vocals:** Anita Carter, Dolores Edgin **Recorded:** RCA Victor, Nashville, November 20, 1967 **Technical Team:** Producer: Bob Ferguson / Sound Engineer: Al Pachucki

In its subject, this cover of Shirl Milete echoes "The Company You Keep," off the album *Hello, I'm Dolly*: A little sister keeps bad company, trapped by a man who is most certainly a pimp. Dolly Parton seems to say it all, even though she uses her words sparingly. She sings on this midtempo piece with a disconcerting ease, in a range with which most of the country singers of the moment struggle to compete. In the soprano register, of which she is already the queen, Dolly is the new "Honky Tonk Angel" in all her splendor. This song is also introduced by Lloyd Green's steel guitar, in perfect symbiosis with the emotion that Dolly expresses beyond her impeccable vocal technique.

Try Being Lonely

Charles Trent, George McCormick / 2:42

Vocals: Dolly Parton **Musicians:** Wayne Moss: solo electric guitar / Chip Young, George McCormick: rhythm guitars / Lloyd Green: pedal steel / Roy "Junior" Huskey: bass / Jerry Kirby Carrigan: drums / David Briggs, Hargus "Pig" Robbins: piano / Charles Trent: electric banjo / Mack Magaha: fiddle **Backing Vocals:** Anita Carter, Dolores Edgin **Recorded:** RCA Victor, Nashville, November 20, 1967 **Technical Team:** Producer: Bob Ferguson / Sound Engineer: Al Pachucki

"Try Being Lonely," previously performed by the Porter Wagoner–Norma Jean Beasler duo, tells a story in the pure tradition of country love—that is, one of heartbreak, owing to a struggle with loneliness, deep feelings, and passion.

It is hard not to think of Roy Orbison's "Only the Lonely" when listening to this song, which Porter Wagoner recorded before hiring Dolly Parton. The vocals are of a technical level usually reserved for opera, clear and powerful, on the recurrent theme of the inexorable isolation of the artist, always on the road, having, day after day, to find the strength to give the best of himself onstage while love is often so far away. The original idea comes from the album *Frank Sinatra Sings for Only the Lonely*, recorded by Sinatra during his second comeback, in 1958, the concept being that talent breeds loneliness. One notices that, as if to underline this idea, Dolly's voice is exceptionally loud in the mix, the echo chamber taking up a large part of the remaining space. One imagines her, alone in the light, in the middle of the stage, or in one of those artist's dressing rooms that are all alike. Only the low notes of the piano, hammered out by David Briggs, manage to stand out on the left, like a fateful counterpoint to Dolly's tears, whose sobs one might swear are actually heard.

Dolly Parton, probably during the *Porter Wagoner Show* period.

1968

The entire Parton family, ca. 1960. Dolly is in the upper right.

Country, a Family Affair

Dolly Parton has affirmed and reaffirmed her deep attachment to her roots, which originate in eastern Tennessee in the shadow of the Appalachian Mountains. Music and song seem to have always been a part of everyday life for both her mother's family, the Owenses, and her father's family, the Partons, whether telling an old story that has been passed down from generation to generation, playing an instrument, singing, or tapping her heel to the rhythm of the music.

Genealogy and Country

The word *country* refers to both "country" and "countryside." Country music is therefore the music of rural life and the music of a country, for example, the state of Tennessee. The Appalachian Mountains of eastern Tennessee were long home to Cherokee tribes, then migrants from Europe settled and mingled with the Native Americans, with whom they often traded.

On his very informative website, T. Duane Gordon, a great fan of Dolly Parton, has written an article on the artist's genealogy. He explains that, according to various documents, Dolly's mother, Avie Lee Owens (married name Parton), might have Cherokee blood in her veins. In *Dolly*,[3] the authorized biography published in 1978, Alanna Nash writes that Dolly's mother is one-quarter Cherokee; therefore, logically, the songwriter would be one-eighth Cherokee; and on her father's side, she would be Scottish and Irish. However, in the 1970s, Doris Parton, the wife of Bobby, the star's young brother, contested this statement. After tracing the Parton genealogy back several generations, she found no link with the Cherokee people. However, she admits that, as is the case for many people in East Tennessee, there is a family legend about ancestors from the First Nations. Based on her research, Doris has pieced together part of the Parton family tree[24] with roots that turn out to be English, Welsh, and German. In her

Dolly with her first mentor, Uncle Bill Owens, in 2013. The songwriter has written more than eight hundred songs for various artists.

autobiography,[1] Dolly does not mention any Cherokee heritage, nor does her sister Willadeene in her book on their family history.[21]

God, the Land, Family

First, there were the first migrants, those who left the Old Continent to come and settle in America. If they chose Tennessee, it was not for the beauty of the landscape but because land was very cheap. They were poor when they arrived, and many families remained so for generations. Each family was subordinate to geography, climate, and meeting basic needs—food, clothing, shelter. Near Sevierville, the area where the Parton family lives, poverty was perhaps the most common feature of the 1940s and 1950s. The landscape is certainly beautiful and wild, but the environment is harsh, between mountains, forests, and hills, and above all an isolating factor. Scattered around Sevierville, the families gathered in communities, all believers. The church was the place for socializing, the place of hope, but also, in the case of the Owenses and Partons, the first place of initiation to singing, gospel, and African American spirituals—songs born among the Black slaves in the eighteenth century. These inhabitants of deep Tennessee are often called hillbillies, from "hill boys," and sometimes derogatorily referred to as rednecks. Though stereotypical views of this population often depict them as violent, alcoholic, illiterate, inbred, racist, and desperate, people like the Partons are loving and determined to transcend their history. They produced artists and celebrities, and managed to escape a life of poverty.

In his book *Smart Blonde*,[2] Stephen Miller explains the origin of Dolly's surname: Parton is said to come from a medieval English word meaning "pear orchard" and is the name of a town in Scotland or northern England. The Partons are deeply connected to the land, the land of old Europe and the land of Tennessee.

Singing as You Breathe

In this post–World War II Tennessee, leisure time, as we define it today, was what each family invented for itself: Singing and music were the order of the day, including stories that were told either to liven up the meager soup that was available for dinner, or for prayer, or simply for fun. Almost everyone sang and played at least one musical instrument.

Food was obviously a vital part of daily life, and while the Partons did not go to bed hungry, they were rarely full. For many families the table, even the ricketiest, upon which sit the poorest of dishes, is the lifeblood of the home. It is not surprising, then, to find cookbooks written by Dolly's siblings, Willadeene and Stella Parton, and by the songwriter herself. No surprise either that the members of the Owens-Parton family were, for the most part, involved in music, as musicians, composers, or performers. It is also not surprising that writing and books played a major role in the lives of many of the Parton children, given that their father suffered because of his illiteracy. As everywhere else in the world, each generation tries to overcome the conditions of the previous generation. This is what the Parton children have done, and successfully so.

From left to right, Stella, Frieda, and Dolly Parton, in 1981, during the recording of Frieda's album *Two Faced*, in Hollywood.

Dolly's Family

This is a glimpse of Dolly Parton's family tree. This list is not exhaustive, as the Owens-Parton family includes many members, including by marriage, who are not all represented here.

The Uncle

Bill Owens (1935–2021) was the mentor, the man who believed from Dolly's earliest years that she should sing, compose, write, and perform; the man who accompanied her early career and co-wrote many songs with her—in total, he wrote more than eight hundred songs for various artists. At her maternal uncle's funeral, Dolly gave a moving eulogy to the man to whom she says she owes so much. In the eulogy (which can be read on her website at https://dollyparton.com/life-and-career/dollys-touching-goodbye-to-her-beloved-uncle-bill-owens/19249), Dolly states that she would not be here, and certainly would not be what she has become, without her uncle, who gave her her first guitar, taught her how to play it, and instilled in the young girl a strong belief in her talent and her ability to achieve as an artist.

Bill Owens was also a passionate conservationist at Dollywood Park and worked with the American Chestnut Foundation, the University of Tennessee at Chattanooga, and the American Eagle Foundation, contributing toward reestablishing the endangered chestnut tree in the Great Smoky Mountains. This man, fervently convinced that Dolly would follow through on her dreams, lived life to the fullest as the words *country music* imply: in serving the land and the music.

The Grandparents

On her mother's side, the Reverend Jacob Robert Owens, known as "Jake" (1899–1992), was known as much for his fiery sermons as for his prolific songwriting. Jake Owens was married to Rena Kansas Valentine, with whom he had eight children, including Dolly's mother and uncle Bill. While Dolly always thought that her taste for music and storytelling came from her mother's side of the family, she says that she got her entrepreneurial, trailblazing character from her father's side. Her grandfather, William Walter Parton (1888–1982), and her grandmother, Bessie Elizabeth Rayfield (1898–1975), to whom Dolly was very attached as a child, and who was bedridden due to ill health, both witnessed their granddaughter's early life in Nashville.

The Parents

Robert Lee Parton (1921–2000) devoted his entire adult life to his family; he was a sharecropper, then a farmer, and worked in construction—he also produced his own moonshine, a common practice in those days. Avie Lee Owens (1923–2003), Dolly's mother, was the daughter of Rev. Jake Owens. She was a stay-at-home mom and raised eleven children. Avie and Robert were married for sixty-one years.

The Siblings

Willadeene, the eldest (born in 1940), assumed the role of a second mother to Dolly from an early age. She was a creative person who followed her own path and was one of the few siblings who did not pursue a career in music. She published a collection of family memoirs, *Smoky Mountain Memories: Stories from the Hearts of the Parton Family* (1996), with a foreword by Dolly, a family recipe book, and poetry.[21] In 1957 she married Arthur Blalock, and from their union Mitchell was born. She is now divorced.

After Willadeene, her parents had two boys: David (born 1942) and Denver (1943). Little is known about them, nor about Dolly's younger brother Bobby (born 1948). They do not work in music, and they avoid the limelight. In 2017, as

Stella Parton, the other successful Parton sibling, here backstage with singer Mark Hardwick for the musical *Pump Boys and Dinettes*, in 1982.

part of "National Siblings Day," Dolly posted one of the few photos on social media that feature the entire Parton family.

Dolly, the iconic artist, was born on January 19, 1946, under the sign of Capricorn. She has been married since 1966 to Carl Thomas Dean, an entrepreneur, who never appears in public, and about whom we know very little, except what the star has said. Carl Dean is a family man and funny—humor is very present in their relationship— he loves dogs and long walks. They had no children, but the many nieces and nephews of Dolly, who often shared the house of the couple, are also, in a way, a part of them.

Stella (born in 1949), the other successful singer of the siblings, used to sing backing vocals for her sister Dolly as a child. She has had a career as a country singer, with more than forty albums to her credit, and is also an actress, both in the theater and on television, and hosts shows in which she cooks. Stella created her own label and released her first album, *I Want to Hold You in My Dreams Tonight*, in 1975. She has collaborated with Dolly as a consultant or an actress on many projects, such as *Dolly Parton's Coat of Many Colors* and *Dolly Parton's Christmas of Many Colors: Circle of Love*. Stella has also published several cookbooks and her memoirs.[25] She has also developed the YouTube channel Funhouse Church, a virtual church where she regularly ministers.

Cassie (born 1951) is also a singer, but she has never released an album. She works and sings mainly in various Dollywood theme park shows and has often accompanied Dolly on stage.

Randy (1953–2021), singer-songwriter, actor, and businessman, has collaborated on many projects with Dolly throughout his career. He was often seen on stage with his sister, playing bass and guitar, and is credited with vocals on the album *A Holly Dolly Christmas* (2020). He also released a few singles, two of which enjoyed real success:

"Hold Me Like You Never Had Me" (1981) and "Waltz Across Texas" (1983).

Larry, born in 1956, died a few hours after his birth.[1] This was traumatic for Dolly, who was then nine years old. The memory of this brother, whom she would have liked to cherish as Willadeene had cherished her, is often honored by the songwriter.

Freida (born in 1957), was once a punk rock singer and now works as an ordained minister. She opened a wedding chapel in Sevierville that also houses an antique store— Parton Family Wedding Chapel & Antiques. Floyd, her twin, was a singer-songwriter; he passed away aged sixty-one, in 2018. He and Freida were part of Dolly's first band adventure: the Traveling Family Band. Floyd wrote "Nickels and Dimes" for the album *Heartbreaker* (1978) and "Rockin' Years" for *Eagle When She Flies* (1991).

Rachel, the youngest (born in 1959), married Richard Dennison. A retired singer and actress, she and her brother Randy were the stars of the band Honey Creek. She starred in the ABC series *9 to 5,* based on the film of the same name, which gave Dolly her first acting success in 1980. During that decade, Rachel also appeared in several of her sister's TV shows, including *Dolly Parton's Precious Memories* (1999). She also wrote for the TV special *Sunset Music Festival* (1993).

The superstar's family (parents, aunts and uncles, siblings) and friends, including the loyal Judy Ogle, helped make Dolly's dreams come true: by singing alongside her (notably, in one of the episodes of her show, *Dolly*, which ran in the 1976–1977 season), by working on the site at the Dollywood theme park, and even by helping to build her house, along with her husband, Carl Dean. Roots, land, love, and friendship: a beautiful, solid alliance of talents and personalities that have influenced—and still influence—the construction of Dolly Parton's world.

ALBUM

In the Good Old Days (When Times Were Bad)

Don't Let It Trouble Your Mind . He's a Go-Getter . In the Good Old Days
(When Times Were Bad) . It's My Time . Harper Valley PTA . Little Bird .
Mine . The Carroll County Accident . Fresh Out of Forgiveness .
Mama, Say a Prayer . Always the First Time . D-I-V-O-R-C-E

RELEASE DATE
United States: February 3, 1969
Reference: RCA Victor LSP-4099
Best US Chart Ranking: 15

While Dolly loves her native East Tennessee, she also loves to leave it, crossing over the mountains to explore the other side.

Dolly Parton and Porter Wagoner:

Always, Always—RCA Victor LSP-4186

"Always, Always" / "No Reason to Hurry Home"—RCA Victor 74-0172

"Yours Love" / "Malena"—RCA Victor 74-0104

"Tomorrow Is Forever" / "Mendy Never Sleeps"—RCA Victor 47-9799

"Just Someone I Used to Know" / "My Hands Are Tied"—RCA Victor 74-0247

A Growing Popularity

Released on February 3, 1969, *In the Good Old Days (When Times Were Bad)*, produced by Bob Ferguson, is Dolly Parton's third solo album. It reached number fifteen on the Billboard Top Country Albums chart and stayed there for eleven weeks. Since arriving in Nashville five years earlier, Dolly Parton had grown in strength and reputation, and had become one of the most popular country artists.

Back to the Roots

The world was undergoing major changes. Demonstrations against the war in Vietnam were intensifying in the United States, and women and other social minorities continued their struggles for more freedom and equality. Before year's end, a legendary rock festival would be held in Woodstock, New York, and Neil Armstrong would be the first human to walk on the moon.

With this new album, Dolly Parton consolidated her position in the country sphere. She worked hard, and recorded, besides her solo records, singles and albums with Porter Wagoner. She was twenty-three years old, had a dream that was about to come true, and a husband who supported her—even though he preferred to remain discreet. Dolly

was still looking for herself, both personally and in the construction of her public life, and no doubt she sometimes felt a touch of nostalgia when she thought of her native Tennessee, that of her family. *In the Good Old Days (When Times Were Bad)* speaks of her roots, of the landscapes—exterior and interior—of the beauty of nature, but also of the harshness of life there. These are recurring themes in Dolly's world, as well as in country music in general.

Feminine and Feminist

She has often been asked "Are you a feminist?" but Dolly Parton does not claim any party or bias; she acts. Her actions speak for themselves, like her songs. She is a woman, before being an artist, a girl, and a sister who grew up among men and boys in the countryside; she knows the harshness of life. She lacked everything, materially, so she invested in her image: makeup, wigs, clothes. Dolly polished her look. She completely asserts this paradoxical position, which consists in conjugating an artificial appearance and a strong authenticity. And she even plays with it, exuding a mysterious aura that fascinates. And even if she is sometimes mocked, Dolly answers with humor and

1969

Dolly Parton is a woman first, and then an artist, a daughter, and a sister who grew up in a man's environment.

relevance. During an interview she was asked about her support for the women's demonstrations, and she replied that it required an entire fire station to put out the fire that was started when she added her bra to the flames...She is often disconcerting, but her interlocutors are under her spell. She sings "Dumb Blonde," even though she is precisely the opposite of dumb. Some are dazzled by her artifice as much as by her natural beauty, others are confused. Dolly traverses the television, media, and music scenes by assuming her own identity. As she says, her greatest talent is to be herself. In Nashville, men rule and misogyny is still widespread, as it is in all of society. Dolly writes and composes all the time, aware that being a woman in this business means having to do ten times as much as a man to win and keep her place. Perhaps this inspired her to write "He's a Go-Getter." If you listen to her, you will understand that she defends the values of freedom and equality, mutual respect in love—even when it runs out—and the independence of women. To listen to Dolly Parton is to hear the thoughts of her characters, as in "Don't Let It Trouble Your Mind," and to be at the heart of human vicissitudes. In her own way, and with undeniable talent, Dolly Parton, through her songs, chronicles her era both socially and emotionally.

From Yesterday and Today

Dolly gained freedom, and popularity with her audience, through her music, her interviews, and her performances on the *The Porter Wagoner Show*. She won over the show's audience, even though her relationship with Porter was sometimes difficult to manage. The old days were hard, terribly hard, for children and adults alike, but they were also good. The simple things—the beauty of a landscape, friendship, brotherly and parental love—seemed to fill a life. As much as Dolly loved her native eastern Tennessee, she also loved to leave it, to move to the other side of the mountains, to explore the wide world and to be enriched by new experiences. Then she returns, in song or physically, when visiting her family, with all the vitality and joy she carries within her.

The singer knows how to construct irresistible hooks that transform the texture of the story, because she has a keen sense of drama, of conveying every feeling, nuance upon nuance. When *In the Good Old Days (When Times Were Bad)* was released, recognition came not only from the public, but also from critics, such as *Billboard*, who declared it a major album. The key to Dolly's success lies in her empathy, in her way of playing on the heartstrings and making emotions resonate, as in "The Carroll

Musician Jerry Reed was the guitarist for Dolly's album *In the Good Days (When Times Were Bad)*, ca. 1969.

County Accident," or in her humorous touches, as in "He's a Go-Getter." As journalist Alanna Nash notes in her biography[3] of Dolly, in the album's lead track, the songwriter depicts the harshness of an era, without ever exaggerating, and the state of poverty in which she grew up, which she willingly leaves behind. She recounts the love of her family, and the lessons and experiences she learned from as a child, and from which she has made unforgettable songs.

A Folk Album

For her third solo album, Dolly Parton is back in the legendary RCA Studio B in Nashville. The session team assembled by producer Bob Ferguson is much the same as the one assembled for *The Porter Wagoner Show*, but with two more big names: drummer Kenny Buttrey, who the previous year had played with Bob Dylan during the recording of his album *John Wesley Harding*, and guitarist Jerry Reed, who had written "Guitar Man" and recorded it as a solo single and then was guitarist for Elvis Presley's cover version.

In The Good Old Days sounds more folk than the previous two albums, with lots of acoustic guitars in the rhythm and on occasional themes. Advances in sound recording make it cleaner, too. Dolly's voice, still youthful, is much less saturated, and the ensemble covers a wider spectrum.

At that time, sound engineers had to adapt to rapid technical developments. The tambourine, already present in the album *Hello, I'm Dolly*, becomes more important here. By contributing to the folk character of this sound, it marks the strong beats and brings back the sharpness in the percussions. Moreover, we can distinguish two categories of songs in this album: those that describe feelings, family, and Dolly's life, in a rather slow tempo and often in three beats to a bar ("Little Bird," "It's My Time," and "Fresh Out of Forgiveness," for example), and those that tell a story, with a beginning and an end, in a fast tempo, in four beats to a bar, with a number of changes in the structure and instrumentation (like "Harper Valley PTA," "He's a Go-Getter," and "The Carroll County Accident").

Album Cover

At the top left, the album title appears in orange Western font above the artist's name in yellow. In the background, a gradient goes from a dark border to green (signifying hope?), then moves to the halo that illuminates Dolly's face like an Italian Madonna—unless it is she who is glowing—with her eyes raised toward a promising future and a delicate smile on her lips. Dolly is in an orange outfit, also typical of the 1960s fashion, appearing wise and classic.

Don't Let It Trouble Your Mind

Dolly Parton / 2:12

Vocals: Dolly Parton **Musicians:** Wayne Moss, Jerry Reed, Jerry Stembridge: guitars / George McCormick: rhythm guitar / Kenny Buttrey, Jerry Carrigan: drums / Roy "Junior" Huskey: bass / Lloyd Green: pedal steel / Hargus "Pig" Robbins: piano / Buck Trent: electric banjo **Backing Vocals:** Dolores Edgin, June Page, Joe Babcock **Recorded:** RCA Studio B, Nashville, October 9, 1968 **Technical Team:** Producer: Bob Ferguson / Sound Engineer: Al Pachucki

When love is no longer there, we may as well admit it and leave each other. Even though Dolly Parton has already written about the wear and tear of our loves, she has this capacity of renewal from one title to the next, either in the writing and her vocal phrasing, or in the position of the narrator, who is more modern than traditional and who, in "Don't Let It Trouble Your Mind," asserts her independence: She prefers to live alone than be unloved. Here, the singer's delivery is very steady. There is no room for an instrumental part, no breathing. The chord grid is classic, with a change for the bridge. The banjo in the intro and the melodic lines under the lead voice blend well with the rhythm guitar. Dolly's voice becomes more and more powerful as the emotion builds, and the musicians follow the progression. The drop in intensity at the end, back to the original formation, reflects the present serenity of the narrator. If we push the analysis a little, we could see in this song the female counterpart of Bob Dylan's "Don't Think Twice, It's All Right."

He's A Go-Getter

Dolly Parton / 2:03

Vocals: Dolly Parton **Musicians:** Wayne Moss, Jerry Reed, Jerry Stembridge: guitars / George McCormick: rhythm guitar / Kenny Buttrey, Jerry Carrigan: drums / Roy "Junior" Huskey: bass / Lloyd Green: pedal steel / Hargus "Pig" Robbins: piano / Buck Trent: electric banjo / Mack Magaha: fiddle **Backing Vocals:** Dolores Edgin, June Page, Joe Babcock **Recorded:** RCA Studio B, Nashville, October 9, 1968 **Technical Team:** Producer: Bob Ferguson / Sound engineer: Al Pachucki

In this number, the man is a go-getter who goes to get his wife at work ("go get her"…) He does not work, while she is exhausted by her job. This is a song in which humor is mixed with irony, confronting everyone with their responsibilities and flaws.

Dolly sings up-tempo, very close to country rock. A short fiddle solo gives her a break from the vocals. The other melodic instruments settle for themes played during the verses/chorus.

The musicians seem to have more freedom than on the first track of the album. The fiddle intro contributes nicely to the country sound. The guitars improvise during the song. It starts with an electric guitar (on the right). We hear at 0:33 that the guitarist gets lost before finding his feet again very quickly. Then it is the pedal steel's turn (left) after the violin chorus, which performs a nice rise with its bottleneck at 1:15. The drums are very present, with an open or closed hi-hat. This effect always works to slightly fluidify the rhythmic line. The harmonies between guitar, piano, and banjo are very complementary. This is a fairly harmonically rich piece between the guitar-piano rhythm playing, the melodic lines, and the choruses. The subject is light, and the music can go further, to tell its own story.

In The Good Old Days
(When Times Were Bad)

Dolly Parton / 2:45

Vocals: Dolly Parton **Musicians:** Wayne Moss, Jerry Reed, Jerry Stembridge: guitars / George McCormick: rhythm guitar / Kenny Buttrey, Jerry Carrigan: drums / Roy "Junior" Huskey: bass / Lloyd Green: pedal steel / Buck Trent: electric banjo **Backing Vocals:** Dolores Edgin, June Page, Joe Babcock **Recorded:** RCA Studio B, Nashville, September 9, 1968 **Single:** Side A: In the Good Old Days (When Times Were Bad) / Side B: Try Being Lonely **Release:** RCA Victor, October 1968 (45 rpm ref.: 47-9657) **Best US Chart Ranking:** 25

Released in October 1968, the single reached number twenty-five on the charts on December 21; it was on the charts for eleven weeks. Dolly Parton wrote this song while thinking about her younger years. While these were some of her best times, and while life was not all about fame and fortune, she would not want to relive those old times when life was so hard. Dolly's composition is in the fast country style, with a very recognizable beat. She knows how to evoke the poverty in which her family lived in Sevier County, Tennessee, with a voice that expresses emotion intensely—she rerecorded this song for her 1973 opus, *My Tennessee Mountain Home*.

As with nearly every song on this LP, "In the Good Old Days" begins with a single instrument, in this case the folk guitar, playing a cycle (a round of the chords grid). On other songs, it is just one bar, or an anacrusis opening. There is a game of questions and answers with the song, which is reflected by the pedal steel. There is also a progression in the structure of the song. The second verse starts like the first one, with the same intro. The electric guitar plays some kind of discreet rhythmic single note which enriches the

1969

Dolly Parton put away her Martin 5-18 Terz guitar, on which she wrote many of her early songs. She would take it up again around 1991, but for the time being, in 1969, she composed and played on a Grammer Model S, which she used until 1973.

Dolly's Model S Grammer guitar, ca. 1970.

rhythm (in which we note the piano's absence). The choirs, rather discreet, arrive on the beginning of the chorus. On the bridges after the first and third chorus, the tambourine enters in an almost brutal way, to support the power of the subject. The third verse starts without an intro, and the chorus completes the song. Contrary to appearances, there is a lot going on musically, as well as in the lyrics.

It's My Time
John D. Loudermilk / 2:37

Vocals: Dolly Parton **Musicians:** Wayne Moss, Jerry Reed, Jerry Stembridge: guitars / George McCormick: rhythm guitar / Kenny Buttrey, Jerry Carrigan: drums / Roy "Junior" Huskey: bass / Lloyd Green: pedal steel / Hargus "Pig" Robbins: piano / Buck Trent: electric banjo
Backing Vocals: Dolores Edgin, June Page, Joe Babcock **Recorded:**

RCA Studio B, Nashville, September 10, 1968 **Technical Team:** Producer: Bob Ferguson / Sound Engineer: Al Pachucki

This song is a plea of sorts, a vindication of being able to cry, as if it were time to let go. This song was written by John D. Loudermilk, author and performer of monumental country standards such as "Tobacco Road," "Indian Reservation," and "Abilene." Dolly Parton honors him by keeping midtempo and harmonizing with the trio of backup singers. She thus maintains the musical orientation of this album, which is dedicated to her country childhood. Guitar and pedal steel answer each other in the intro, after the chorus, and during the verses. The spatialization of the mix (guitars on the left and chorus on the right) creates an imbalance, especially during the verses. The rhythm section (drums, bass, piano, banjo, rhythm guitar) is constant throughout the song, in an almost heady play. Melodically, at the beginning of the verses, we recognize the first measures of "You Are My Sunshine" (1940) by Jimmie Davis and Charles Mitchell.

Harper Valley PTA

Tom T. Hall / 3:10

Musicians

Wayne Moss, Jerry Reed, Jerry Stembridge: guitars
George McCormick: rhythm guitar
Kenny Buttrey, Jerry Carrigan: drums
Roy "Junior" Huskey: bass
Lloyd Green: pedal steel
Hargus "Pig" Robbins: piano
Buck Trent: electric banjo
Dolly Parton: vocals
Dolores Edgin, June Page, Joe Babcock: backing vocals

Recorded

RCA Studio B, Nashville, September 9, 1968

Technical Team

Producer: Bob Ferguson
Sound Engineer: Al Pachucki

PORTRAIT

Born in Texas, Jeannie C. Riley was a secretary in Nashville when producer Shelby Singleton was looking for a performer to sing a song written by the great Tom T. Hall. "Harper Valley PTA," became a phenomenal success that propelled Jeannie C. Riley to the heights of popularity, including an appearance on the legendary *Ed Sullivan Show*. She knew how to choose good writers and recorded two more songs in quick succession: "The Girl Most Likely" (1968) and "There Never Was a Time" (1969). She signed with MGM Records in 1971 but never found the success she had with Singleton.[24]

1969

Genesis and Lyrics

The song tells the story of a Harper Valley widow who is reproached by the local PTA (Parent-Teacher Association) for her too-short dresses—very trendy during the sixties—her taste for alcohol, and her relationships with men, all of which offend the prevailing puritanism. In response to the indignant reproach, of which her daughter is the designated messenger, the widow, in her defense, draws up in turn the list of the questionable behaviors of her detractors.

Production

The cover of this megahit by Jeannie C. Riley—which sold 6 million copies—enables Dolly to take her revenge on the self-righteous people who have not hesitated to make fun of her and her aspiration to a different life.

The sound and playing of the drums is radically different from the first tracks on the album. The snare drum is more resonant, the hi-hat is very present, and there are even breaks on the toms. The bass drum also gives this impression: it stands out more, because it is not always in sync with the bass. The piano is more prominent in the mix, especially when the pedal steel answers (for example, in the second verse). The pedal steel and banjo play question-and-answer themes throughout the song.

The musical progression is in phase with the text. In the third verse, the first pivotal moment of the story, we hear a modulation of the grid: Everything is raised by a semitone (the smallest distance between two notes). This is a common technique, especially at the end of a song, to revive the listener's attention in a repetition of the chorus. Michael Jackson used it perfectly (listen to "You Are Not Alone" or "Heal the World," for example). It is said, in the business, that it is a very useful writing process when you are running short of ideas! No such failure here; this process is supportive of the text. The backing vocals are discreet, because there is not really a chorus. However, we hear some strings (sustained notes) at the beginning of the first modulation. They stop, then resume at the second modulation and continue until the end. The change of vowel (from "ouh" to "ah") adds a little more power, again in keeping with the lyrics.

Little Bird

Dolly Parton / 1:43

Vocals: Dolly Parton **Musicians:** Wayne Moss, Jerry Reed, Jerry Stembridge: guitars / George McCormick: rhythm guitar / Kenny Buttrey, Jerry Carrigan: drums / Roy "Junior" Huskey: bass / Lloyd Green: pedal steel / Hargus "Pig" Robbins: piano / Buck Trent: electric banjo **Backing Vocals:** Dolores Edgin, June Page, Joe Babcock **Recorded:** RCA Studio B, Nashville, September 10, 1968 **Technical Team:** Producer: Bob Ferguson / Sound Engineer: Al Pachucki

A perfume of nostalgia permeates this song which evokes, in halftone, Dolly's younger years. Time takes its toll on beauty and youth, and memory is like a little bird to whom one might ask: "Fly me away back to yesterday / And drop me off there awhile."

Through this composition, Dolly continues to revisit her childhood, in an up-tempo country ballad and with a moving vocal performance. The guitar intro is reminiscent of the Beatles' "Blackbird" (also about a bird). The song is in three time (like a waltz), the strongest beat being the first. The bass notes mark it well, with a few pivotal bars during which it rises and falls to get the song going again. In the refrains, the pedal steel rises in the highs, probably to suggest the bird's song. The snare drum marks all the beats in the same way, and the piano and choir come in, enriching the instrumentation during Dolly's call to the memory bird.

Mine

Dolly Parton / 2:03

Vocals: Dolly Parton **Musicians:** Wayne Moss, Jerry Reed, Jerry Stembridge: guitars / George McCormick: rhythm guitar / Kenny Buttrey, Jerry Carrigan: drums / Roy "Junior" Huskey: bass / Lloyd Green: pedal steel / Hargus "Pig" Robbins: piano / Buck Trent: electric banjo **Backing Vocals:** Dolores Edgin, June Page, Joe Babcock **Recorded:** RCA Studio B, Nashville, October 9, 1968 **Technical Team:** Producer: Bob Ferguson / Sound Engineer: Al Pachucki

This personal composition by Dolly is a somewhat like the photographic negative of the previous one. The singer slows the tempo considerably to describe her psyche in "Mine," which is a very melancholic piece. Of particular note is that all the instruments play rhythm in the verses, including those that play themes apart from the vocals. Only the pedal steel delivers very long notes, with gentle gaps so as

not to distract the attention from the lyrics. The entrance of the singers is also atypical: they all sing the same note (or with an octave difference, according to the tessitura), and it is the lowest voice that is emphasized. The harmonies arrive with the second verse and the modulation. The emotion rises with the music before the last chorus, then falls, as if to illustrate the sadness of this woman who has been robbed of her love.

The Carroll County Accident

Bob Ferguson / 2:56

Vocals: Dolly Parton **Musicians:** Wayne Moss, Jerry Reed, Jerry Stembridge: guitars / George McCormick: rhythm guitar / Kenny Buttrey, Jerry Carrigan: drums / Roy "Junior" Huskey: bass / Lloyd Green: pedal steel / Hargus "Pig" Robbins: piano / Buck Trent: electric banjo / Mack Magaha: fiddle **Backing Vocals:** Dolores Edgin, June Page, Joe Babcock **Recorded:** RCA Studio B, Nashville, October 9, 1968 **Technical Team:** Producer: Bob Ferguson / Sound Engineer: Al Pachucki

In 1969, Porter Wagoner recorded "The Carroll County Accident" and turned it into a hit, voted song of the year by the Country Music Association. Many times covered, it tells the story of a strange car accident and suspected adultery. Walter Browning, an apparently happily married man, was killed in the accident. At the wheel, a woman, who was said to be respectable but not his wife, survived and explained that, at his request, because he was ill, she was driving him to town. Everyone believed her. When the intrigued narrator searches the wreckage and discovers the deceased's wedding ring in a matchbox stuck behind the dashboard, he understands, throws the ring into a well, and decides to keep quiet…because the county has commissioned a marble monument to his father.

Dolly Parton rerecorded this song as a duet with Buck Trent for the 2018 album *Spartanburg Blues*. For this song with its honky-tonk rhythm, we start quietly with a guitar intro, with a few notes that do not completely make it through. The rhythm is provided by drums, bass (as usual), piano, and guitar with very high notes. The little themes of the electric guitar are quite rhythmic, unlike those of the fiddle and the pedal steel. The violin accompanies the evocation of Walter's wedding, the choirs come in like angels (right), counterbalanced by the return of the themes, this time on the folk guitar (left).

1969

Flanked by two DJs, Dolly poses backstage at the Grand Ole Opry in the 1970s.

Fresh Out Of Forgiveness

Bill Owens, Gene Gill / 2:01

Vocals: Dolly Parton **Musicians:** Wayne Moss, Jerry Reed, Jerry Stembridge: guitars / George McCormick: rhythm guitar / Kenny Buttrey, Jerry Carrigan: drums / Roy "Junior" Huskey: bass / Lloyd Green: pedal steel / Hargus "Pig" Robbins: piano **Backing Vocals:** Dolores Edgin, June Page, Joe Babcock **Recorded:** RCA Studio B, Nashville, October 9, 1968 **Technical Team:** Producer: Bob Ferguson / Sound Engineer: Al Pachucki

How often do we have to forgive the wounds inflicted on us by others? There comes a time when you just cannot keep doing it, when you run out of forgiveness.

In this Bill Owens–penned song, a slow country ballad with a slowed-down tempo, Dolly delivers a vocal performance playing on the interaction of the melody over an original chord line. The piano comes to the fore at last, and a folk guitar provides the answering notes. The rhythm section is pared down to enable the polyphonic instruments to express themselves. The pedal steel, usually the solo instrument, is still present in the first verse and at the end. In fact, the sound is more like an acoustic rhythm 'n' blues, especially on the last guitar phrase. Is that an improvisation to conclude the song on the "blue note" (seventh of the tonic chord), giving this a typical blues sound?

Kenny Buttrey, one of the drummers on *In the Good Old Days*, was Bob Dylan's drummer the year before, in 1968.

Joyce McCord was the sister of Sharon Higgins, who wrote for Loretta Lynn and later for Wynonna Judd. Their brother, Damon Black, was a close friend of Porter Wagoner.

Mama, Say A Prayer

Dolly Parton / 2:45

Vocals: Dolly Parton **Musicians:** Wayne Moss, Jerry Reed, Jerry Stembridge: guitars / George McCormick: rhythm guitar / Kenny Buttrey, Jerry Carrigan: drums / Roy "Junior" Huskey: bass / Lloyd Green: pedal steel / Hargus "Pig" Robbins: piano **Backing Vocals:** Dolores Edgin, June Page, Joe Babcock **Recorded:** RCA Studio B, Nashville, October 9, 1968 **Technical Team:** Producer: Bob Ferguson / Sound Engineer: Al Pachucki

When a girl lives alone in the city, lonely and subject to temptation, she hopes in her heart that her mother, far away, will pray for her at night. "Mama, Say a Prayer" is undoubtedly inspired by personal experience, as faith and prayer were important in Dolly's mother's life as well as her own.

Dolly's Pentecostal upbringing was the strength of the family, and this song contains some of the mysticism of the descendants of the Shakers. Members of this sect, the origin of the Pentecostal Church, evoke the presence of God by swaying. This is probably the reason why this song is not a slow ballad but an up-tempo country song, well supported by the piano and the pedal steel. We notice the layers of the pedal steel on the first verse, the theme of the electric guitar on the second, and the resumption of the pedal steel before a welcome break at 1:29. The drums have not done anything until that point. The melancholy train starts again with the fiddle, then with the choirs during the third verse, before ending gently, for the evening prayer. The chorus is provided by a choir. As a notable change in the spatialization, the rhythm guitar has been moved to the right, and can thus play some phrases in harmony with the folk guitar on the left.

Always The First Time

Joyce McCord / 2:01

Vocals: Dolly Parton **Musicians:** Wayne Moss, Jerry Reed, Jerry Stembridge: guitars / George McCormick: rhythm guitar / Kenny Buttrey, Jerry Carrigan: drums / Roy "Junior" Huskey: bass / Lloyd Green: pedal steel / Hargus "Pig" Robbins: piano / Buck Trent: electric banjo / Mack Magaha: fiddle **Backing Vocals:** Dolores Edgin, June Page, Joe Babcock **Recorded:** RCA Studio B, Nashville, September 9, 1968 **Technical Team:** Producer: Bob Ferguson / Sound Engineer: Al Pachucki

There is always a first time, a first temptation, a first meeting. This is a song that seems meant to remind men that women, too, can turn away from love when it is not what it used to be, when their man does not change. Dolly seems to have chosen the ambiguity of Joyce McCord's composition to explain the parallel lives that a woman can lead.

The electric guitar and the pedal steel were switched in the mix: the latter is placed on the right and the former on the left. The folk guitar plays rising scales twice, to announce the verse to come (at 1:00 and 1:04), like the pedal steel in "He's a Go-Getter." This is an easy but effective device: the musician is confident that all his notes will come through. The resolution will be on the tonic, and away it goes. Like most of the sentimental songs on the album, this is a three-time ballad. The first beat of the bar is very marked with a bass note that holds. This is supported by the piano and drums, especially during the chorus. The instruments that produce notes with little attack, violin and pedal steel, are on the right in the mix, while the two guitars are on the left. We note finally that the violin often accompanies Dolly when she evokes the relations between a man and woman, while the guitar intervenes when she speaks about herself or her family.

D-I-V-O-R-C-E

Bobby Braddock, Curly Putman / 2:43

Musicians
Wayne Moss, Jerry Reed, Jerry Stembridge: guitars
George McCormick: rhythm guitar
Kenny Buttrey, Jerry Carrigan: drums
Roy "Junior" Huskey: bass
Lloyd Green: pedal steel
Hargus "Pig" Robbins: piano
Buck Trent: electric banjo
Dolly Parton: vocals:
Dolores Edgin, June Page, Joe Babcock: backing vocals

Recorded
RCA Studio B, Nashville, September 10, 1968

Technical Team
Producer: Bob Ferguson / Sound Engineer: Al Pachucki

"D-I-V-O-R-C-E" was recorded by Tammy Wynette in 1968, and it earned her a Grammy Award.

Genesis and Lyrics

Recorded by Tammy Wynette in 1968, "D-I-V-O-R-C-E" earned her a Grammy nomination for Best Country Vocal Performance, Female.

The lyrics begin with that trick some parents use, which is to spell out words so that children do not understand what is being said between adults. In this song, words like *divorce*, *hell*, and *custody*, are spelled out to protect a little boy from the harsh realities of the world and parental breakdown.

Curly Putman had already written for Dolly before he and Bobby Braddock co-wrote "D-I-V-O-R-C-E" for Tammy Wynette. It was one of the first times that a story about divorce was narrated by a woman, and it was a huge success, eliciting responses from the likes of Loretta Lynn and Conway Twitty. Earlier, however, Merle Travis had recorded "Divorce Me C.O.D." in 1946. Bobby Braddock and Curly Putman were probably inspired by this first version. Dolly Parton seems to have appreciated the feminine point of view of the song, and you can hear it in her spoken passage at 1:40, where she seems happy to get rid of a troublesome husband. But Dolly is Dolly, and she did not get a divorce, as Tammy Wynette did…four times.

Production

The intro features the piano, bass, and guitar playing in unison. This type of phrase is often heard in Motown productions (such as "My Guy" by Mary Wells, for example). As was often the case, the snare drum is played with cross sticks. As in the previous song, the bass strongly marks the first beats and plays sparingly, except on the chorus, where it rises and falls to resolve on the tonic of the chord each time. During the spoken part, after a modulation of a tone above (again), the musicians play more gently. We also notice a slight decrease in the volume of the music in order to leave room for Dolly's sensitive interpretation. The volume of the orchestra remains unchanged until the second chorus. After the spoken part, the group resumes very strongly, with the very present bass drum. The song could have been ended on the repetition of the intro, but it had to be concluded gently, having dealt with such a painful subject.

My Blue Ridge Mountain Boy

In the Ghetto . Games People Play . 'Til Death Do Us Part . Big Wind . Evening Shade .
I'm Fed Up with You . My Blue Ridge Mountain Boy . Daddy . We Had All the Good Things
Going . The Monkey's Tale . Gypsy, Joe and Me . Home for Pete's Sake

RELEASE DATE
United States: September 8, 1969
Reference: RCA Victor—LSP-4188
Best US Chart Ranking: 6

In this album, Dolly gives an account of the violence and loneliness of the cities. She dreams of her "Blue Ridge Mountain Boy."

The Big City Blues

My Blue Ridge Mountain Boy is Dolly Parton's fourth solo album. It was released on September 8, 1969, by RCA Victor, seven months after *In the Good Old Days (When Times Were Bad)*. This was a busy year for the singer, as she also released a duo album with Porter Wagoner. As with the society of the time, what is striking about this album is the seriousness of the themes addressed by the songwriter, both in her own lyrics and in the covers she has chosen to interpret. Similar to *In the Good Old Days*, this album highlights the quality of the lyrics and the power and clarity of the voice.

The Great Human Torments

The twelve songs, five of which were written by Dolly, express the violence of the world and human tragedies. Looking at the album sleeve, or even at the title, one might expect a very country, even romantic album. *My Blue Ridge Mountain Boy* is about urban violence, the loneliness of cities, and hatred, as in "Evening Shade," as well as the inevitability of poverty and its consequences, as in "In the Ghetto." With a voice that has grown in power, the artist exposes very serious social situations. We are near the end of 1969. In August, the counterculture had been invigorated by the most incredible of festivals: Woodstock. The dream conquering space became real when, on July 20, the images of the first human walking on the moon were broadcast around the world. In the midst of this time of transition, with one foot in

the past and the other in the future, American society revealed its fault lines.

From One War to Another

During the Second World War, women in the United States left the countryside to enter the workforce en masse and replaced the men who had left to fight. Many of them migrated to the cities, where they became independent and participated in economic, political, and cultural life. When the men returned from war, many women did not want to go back home, either to their farms or their stoves. The dynamics of many couples and families, as well as women's social ambitions, were thus considerably altered. Women had developed a taste for independence, and they felt strong enough to divorce when needed, and to demand their freedoms and rights, and they thereby changed the road map that had been handed to them at birth. Such radical and rapid transformations were not without their effects on the minds and feelings of individuals. Dolly Parton is concerned with the outside world, and she is inspired by it. In her songs, we find slices of the lives of these women and men caught up in the great upheavals of modern society. They are like photographic snapshots of what is often intimate and not necessarily seen: including emotions, feelings, and buried dreams. For its part, every day the entertainment industry creates dreams and idols. In 1969, Gene Kelly's musical film *Hello, Dolly!* was released with singer and actress Barbra Streisand as the star and musician Louis

Program poster for *The Grand Ole Opry*, a famous show broadcast live on Nashville's WSM station. The luckiest fans are ones who can attend the live performances.

1969

Armstrong in his own role. Pure coincidence or a nod to the artistic world? In any case, since *Hello, I'm Dolly*, the songwriter had managed to pull herself up by the bootstraps.

Writing: Better Than Therapy

Dolly Parton has often said that there is something therapeutic about writing. So, each song she writes fulfills a double function: It comforts us and heals us from the torments of the world. Listening to these songs extracts us from reality, and yet reality is very present in the lyrics. Her style of singing, which sometimes touches us so deeply, humanizes what could be just another grim event, as in "My Blue Ridge Mountain Boy" or "Daddy." In 1969, Dolly Parton continues her ascent, highlighting with her sharp pen the dramas lived by her fellow human beings. Dolly talks a lot about women, about their feelings, but also about concrete situations: a storm that deprives a family of one of its members, the father, as a metaphor of the war; a couple adrift, a mother who leaves; a young woman who becomes a prostitute in New Orleans, while she was dreaming of

a better life…Poverty is a vicious circle that harshly condemns those who are born into it. An emotional and a social chronicle of a changing world.

What Does a Songwriter Dream Of?

The realities of the world, situations and feelings, are Dolly Parton's raw material. Whether it is faith, jealousy, unrequited love, quarrels between spouses, parents who abandon their children, or extreme poverty, Dolly communicates to us her perception, her feelings, and her poetry. This fourth album portrays a brutalized, even brutal America. In her biography, Alanna Nash[3] notes Dolly Parton's impressive ability to evoke and provoke emotions, both through her lyrics and her melodies, because she has this talent to make fiction almost more real than the reality from which she draws her inspiration. Dolly takes what humanity offers, makes it intimate, and gives it back to us in a striking way on this album. These twelve tracks resonate with the clashes of the modern world, but also with a bittersweet reality, as in "Home for Pete's Sake." "My songs tell how I feel. I get more out of writing than singing. My writing is personal to me. It's my self-expression. It's me," says the artist, adding that she would like to be remembered as a songwriter who contributed something to the world. Dolly Parton's dream of being enshrined as a songwriter, adding her touch to the human edifice, is coming true. *My Blue Ridge Mountain Boy* convinced enthusiastic critics and an ever-growing number of fans.

Album Cover

In the foreground, Dolly is lying on a couch, devilishly feminine, eyes lost in the middle distance, sensual, biting a finger, a shadow of gravity on her face. The background reveals who she is dreaming of: her Blue Ridge Mountain Boy. A contrast differentiates these two shots, like two distinct worlds: that of the woman, dressed as if for a night on the town, and that of the man, sitting on a tree trunk, in front of a cabin, similar to the one in Dolly's childhood. The man is none other than her husband, Carl Dean.

President Nixon meets with community leaders in the wake of the assassination of Martin Luther King Jr.

In The Ghetto

Mac Davis / 2:50

Vocals: Dolly Parton **Musicians:** Fred Carter Jr., Jerry Stembridge, Wayne Moss, George McCormick: guitars / Lloyd Green, Pete Drake: pedal steel / Hargus "Pig" Robbins: piano / Roy "Junior" Huskey: bass / Jerry Carrigan, James Isbell: drums / Mack Magaha: fiddle / Buck Trent: electric banjo **Backing Vocals:** Dolores Edgin, June Page, Joe Babcock **Recorded:** RCA Studio B, Nashville, June 2, 1969 **Technical Team:** Producer: Bob Ferguson / Sound Engineer: Al Pachucki / Assistant Sound Engineers: Milton Henderson, Roy Shockey **Single:** Side A: In the Ghetto / Side B: The Bridge **Release:** RCA Victor(45 rpm ref.: 74-0192) **Best US Chart Ranking:** 50

Genesis and Lyrics

"In the Ghetto" tells the story of a boy born in the Chicago ghetto. One more mouth to feed for a mother who already can't feed the older children, and no one is reaching out to help them. The hungry child grows up, and becomes a thief and a brawler. He finds a gun, steals a car, and tries to run away, but is shot. At almost the same time, in the ghetto, another boy is born, to another desperate mother who cannot feed him. The sense of a vicious circle ("The Vicious Circle" was the original title of the song), inescapable, infernal, is rendered by the very structure of the writing: short, effective phrasing, and the repeated use of the phrase "in the ghetto," like a throbbing pain.

Production

Dolly Parton recorded this Elvis Presley hit on June 2, 1969, shortly after the King's single was released in April. Recording engineer Al Pachucki—along with guitarist Chip Young—had already participated in Elvis's January 20, 1969, recording session at the American Sound Studio in Memphis, which produced this song advocating for individual freedoms. As such, he was one of the few people capable of re-creating the musical setting of this composition, which Mac Davis had written especially for the King. For her part, Dolly was eager to sing this antiracist, controversial song. Producer Bob Ferguson brought in the great pedal steel player Pete Drake. Guitar player Fred Carter Jr. had played with Simon and Garfunkel ("The Boxer," 1969), Bob Dylan, and Waylon Jennings. With Dolly's heartfelt vocal performance, this version of "In the Ghetto" ranks among the best.

Composer Joe South, who wrote for Elvis Presley among others, is the author of "Games People Play."

'Til Death Do Us Part

Dolly Parton / 3:09

Vocals: Dolly Parton **Musicians:** Fred Carter Jr., Jerry Stembridge, Wayne Moss, George McCormick: guitars / Lloyd Green, Pete Drake: pedal steel / Hargus "Pig" Robbins: piano / Roy "Junior" Huskey: bass / Jerry Carrigan, James Isbell: drums / Mack Magaha: fiddle / Buck Trent: electric banjo **Backing Vocals:** Dolores Edgin, June Page, Joe Babcock **Recorded:** RCA Studio B, Nashville, May 14, 1969 **Technical Team:** Producer: Bob Ferguson / Sound Engineer: Al Pachucki / Assistant Sound Engineers: Milton Henderson, Roy Shockey **Single:** Side A: My Blue Ridge Mountain Boy / Side B: 'Til Death Do Us Part **Release:** RCA Victor(45 rpm ref.: 74-0243) **Best US Chart Ranking:** 45

Vows should not, in theory, be broken, especially "till death do us part," when it is spoken with love, hope, and conviction during the wedding ceremony. But what is left of it when the loved one leaves?

This song by Dolly, written early one morning, as always, after her prayer, and composed on her Grammer Model S, is one of the first recorded for this fourth solo album, on May 14, 1969. To set the scene, the song opens and closes with the sound of a pump organ, immersing the listener in the pious and solemn atmosphere of a wedding in a small chapel in the southern United States. The narrator then calls out to the man who is leaving her: "Will you bring your new love to the chapel / To look upon the one that you betrayed?" On the right stereo channel, the warm, lush sound of the tremolo guitar, backed by Mack Magaha's fiddle from the last verse on, responds in turn to the pedal steel and piano on the left. This A-Team of musicians includes Pete Drake on pedal steel, which illuminates the accompaniment of Dolly, who sings in a high register in this song.

Games People Play

Joe South / 2:26

Vocals: Dolly Parton **Musicians:** Fred Carter Jr., Jerry Stembridge, Wayne Moss, George McCormick: guitars / Lloyd Green, Pete Drake: pedal steel / Hargus "Pig" Robbins: piano / Roy "Junior" Huskey: bass / Jerry Carrigan, James Isbell: drums / Mack Magaha: fiddle / Buck Trent: electric banjo **Backing Vocals:** Dolores Edgin, June Page, Joe Babcock **Recorded:** RCA Studio B, Nashville, June 2, 1969 **Technical Team:** Producer: Bob Ferguson / Sound Engineer: Al Pachucki / Assistant Sound Engineers: Milton Henderson, Roy Shockey

This protest song evokes hypocrisy, the small and big daily hatreds that degrade human relationships—"and it's a dirty rotten shame." No one is safe, as the narrator says. Dolly sings this diatribe with the youthful voice of her early days, comparable to that of Brenda Lee or Skeeter Davis. The clarity of the mix is striking; you feel like you are entering the wider, punchy sound of the 1970s. The bass frequencies drop below 150 Hz, the bass drum pulse is felt at 60 Hz. The drums are recorded and mixed in stereo. The piano and fiddle benefit from the new generation of transformers incorporated in the state-of-the-art circuits of the time (probably those of a Neve console) going above 12,000 Hz. On the snare drum, you can clearly hear the compressor attacking in a very musical style to create an exciting and particularly energetic sound.

Big Wind

Wayne P. Walker, Alex Zanetis, George McCormick / 2:18

1969

Musicians

Fred Carter Jr., Jerry Stembridge, Wayne Moss, George McCormick: guitars
Lloyd Green, Pete Drake: pedal steel
Hargus "Pig" Robbins: piano
Roy "Junior" Huskey: bass
Jerry Carrigan, James Isbell: drums
Mack Magaha: fiddle
Buck Trent: electric banjo
Dolly Parton: vocals
Dolores Edgin, June Page, Joe Babcock: backing vocals

Recorded

RCA Studio B, Nashville, June 2, 1969

Technical Team

Producer: Bob Ferguson
Sound Engineer: Al Pachucki
Assistant Sound Engineers: Milton Henderson, Roy Shockey

Genesis and Lyrics

The song focuses on the damage caused by a great wind that ravages the fields and carries away everything in its path, trees and humans alike. The violence of a storm causes the same devastation as a war: It deprives families of their loved ones, and it changes the life trajectory of the survivors. Tornadoes and hurricanes are common in the American South.

This song was co-written by the man known as "Colonel" Alex Zanetis, with George McCormick and Wayne Walker, the composer of "Cut Across Shorty" for Eddie Cochran in 1960. Although Porter Wagoner had already recorded it, it was probably session guitarist McCormick who drew Dolly Parton's attention to the song. In East Tennessee—where even the humblest of homes had a cyclone-proof cellar—the singer had no doubt experienced many severe storms.

Production

We are straight into this up-tempo honky-tonk number. Porter Wagoner closely supervised the playing of his musicians, especially to line up his guitarist, the legendary Fred Carter Jr. Carter plays in a distinctly honky-tonk style, using the famous twang sound developed in parallel in West Coast surf music. Here it's used to emulate the devastating power of a tornado under the impetuous vocals of Dolly Parton and her team of seasoned backup singers. Carter and Dolly know each other well, having shared the Grand Ole Opry stage and the *Porter Wagoner Show* tours. Between Dolly and Wagoner, there was frequent friction: She wanted to stay in the traditional style of her native Great Smoky Mountains; he wanted her to record novelty songs with sound gimmicks. He was sometimes right, as when he made her sing "Mule Skinner Blues" by Jimmie Rodgers and George Vaughn, a rollicking song with whip snaps. "Big Wind" would be a success, but Dolly then devoted her solo albums to mountain music.

Albert Lee, a British guitarist, at a recording session in 1973.

Evening Shade

Dolly Parton / 3:22

Vocals: Dolly Parton **Musicians:** Fred Carter Jr., Jerry Stembridge, Wayne Moss, George McCormick: guitars / Lloyd Green, Pete Drake: pedal steel / Hargus "Pig" Robbins: piano / Roy "Junior" Huskey: bass / Jerry Carrigan, James Isbell: drums / Mack Magaha: fiddle / Buck Trent: electric banjo **Backing Vocals:** Dolores Edgin, June Page, Joe Babcock **Recorded:** RCA Studio B, Nashville, May 21, 1969 **Technical Team:** Producer: Bob Ferguson / Sound Engineer: Al Pachucki / Assistant Sound Engineers: Milton Henderson, Roy Shockey

This song tells a terrible story, painted in few words…an institution for juvenile delinquents, a sadistic director who punishes with an iron or a razor strap, for a wet bed—"The reason we were there is 'cause we had no one who cared / But they cared even less at evening shade"…To get rid of their tormentor, these neglected young people become arsonists, murderers. The subject of the reform school is dear to Dolly Parton, who knows that juvenile delinquency and prostitution can be part of the missteps of young songwriters, and the honky-tonk style in which she sings here marvelously suits the harshness of the theme. As if to bring a little hope and lightness, Mack Mahaga's fiddle makes its entrance in the second verse, then the fabulous guitar arpeggio of the intro, almost swept away, comes tumbling back at 1:32 and starts the machine again. At 1:43, it is the turn of the choirs and the pedal steel to lighten the atmosphere a little, behind the aerial vocals of Dolly dispassionately playing her role of concerned narrator.

I'm Fed Up With You

Bill Owens / 2:00

Vocals: Dolly Parton **Musicians:** Fred Carter Jr., Jerry Stembridge, Wayne Moss, George McCormick: guitars / Lloyd Green, Pete Drake: pedal steel / Hargus "Pig" Robbins: piano / Roy "Junior" Huskey: bass / Jerry Carrigan, James Isbell: drums / Mack Magaha: fiddle / Buck Trent: electric banjo **Backing Vocals:** Dolores Edgin, June Page, Joe Babcock **Recorded:** RCA Studio B, Nashville, June 2, 1969 **Technical Team:** Producer: Bob Ferguson / Sound Engineer: Al Pachucki / Assistant Sound Engineers: Milton Henderson, Roy Shockey

While her songwriting career was growing and she now lived in her own home, Dolly recorded fewer songs by Bill Owens, her uncle, who wrote a lot for Loretta Lynn, Kris Kristofferson, and Ricky Skaggs, among others. In "I'm Fed Up with You," their duet revolves around a story of relationship burnout. This is a one-way trip to traditional 4/4 country. At 0:52, we can hear Mack Magaha's superb intervention with his high-flying fiddle, a concise and melodious solo, of the kind that only the best session men are capable of pulling off at every turn. Then comes the electric guitar to knit its country licks, with chicken-picking inflections, before the pedal steel performs its own tightrope act. Welcome to the pure country hoedown tradition of Bill Owens, far from the more commercial Nashville sound of the other covers on the record.

Roy Huskey's bass imitates the virtuoso playing of James Jamerson (foreground, center), bassist with the Funk Brothers.

Hillbilly, bluegrass, and country music originated from the Blue Ridge Mountains in the eastern part of the Appalachians. The musical capital is Asheville, North Carolina.

My Blue Ridge Mountain Boy
Dolly Parton / 3:32

Vocals: Dolly Parton **Musicians:** Fred Carter Jr., Jerry Stembridge, Wayne Moss, George McCormick: guitars / Lloyd Green, Pete Drake: pedal steel / Hargus "Pig" Robbins: piano / Roy "Junior" Huskey: bass / Jerry Carrigan, James Isbell: drums / Mack Magaha: fiddle / Buck Trent: electric banjo **Backing Vocals:** Dolores Edgin, June Page, Joe Babcock **Recorded:** RCA Studio B, Nashville (TN), May 20, 1969 **Re-Recorded:** 1982 (for "Heartbreak Express") **Technical Team:** Producer: Bob Ferguson / Sound Engineer: Al Pachucki / Assistant Sound Engineers: Milton Henderson, Roy Shockey **Single:** Side A: My Blue Ridge Mountain Boy / Side B: 'Til Death Do Us Part **Release:** RCA Victor(45 rpm. ref.: 74-0243) **Best US Chart Ranking:** 45

In this number, Dolly tells the moving story of a young woman from the country who left to see if life in the city (New Orleans) was more entertaining. When she comes around from her illusions, she feels lonely and becomes a prostitute, thinking with regret of the nice boy back home that she left when he loved her dearly, but who is probably married by now.

A reference to Vernon Dalhart and Carson Robison's 1927 classic "My Blue Ridge Mountain Home," Dolly's composition begins as a classic country shuffle ballad, with Buck Trent's banjo and Pete Drake's pedal steel. But after the first verse, the A-Team switches to a much more modern chord progression. The rhythm goes into 4/4 (never to return to three time, even when it calms down again, from 1:39 to 2:40), the reverb-drenched chorus opens the spectrum, and Roy "Junior" Huskey's bass starts to imitate the virtuoso and bouncy playing of James Jamerson (former bassist with the Funk Brothers, Motown's hit-making session men). As if echoing "In the Ghetto," which opens the album, this larger-than-life sound recalls that of Elvis Presley's big band, which was in residence at the International Hotel in Las Vegas from 1969 to 1976.

Daddy
Dolly Parton / 2:50

Vocals: Dolly Parton **Musicians:** Fred Carter Jr., Jerry Stembridge, Wayne Moss, George McCormick: guitars / Lloyd Green, Pete Drake: pedal steel / Hargus "Pig" Robbins: piano / Roy "Junior" Huskey: bass / Jerry Carrigan, James Isbell: drums / Mack Magaha: fiddle / Buck Trent: electric banjo **Backing Vocals:** Dolores Edgin, June Page, Joe Babcock **Recorded:** RCA Studio B, Nashville, September 9, 1968 **Technical Team:** Producer: Bob Ferguson / Sound Engineer: Al Pachucki / Assistant Sound Engineers: Milton Henderson, Roy Shockey **Single:** Side A: Daddy / Side B: He's a Go-Getter **Release:** RCA Victor, (?) (45 rpm. ref.: 74-0132) **Best US Chart Ranking:** 40

This song's theme has already been treated by the songwriter: neglected love, this time of a woman, mother, and wife who does not ask for anything, does not say anything, does not even seem to notice that her husband does not kiss her or hug her anymore. But one morning, tired of not being loved, she leaves a note on the table and leaves. Dolly Parton dedicates this song to her father, but also evokes her own marriage, which is at the heart of the inspiration for this album, perhaps to express the feeling of abandonment she feels when she has to leave her home to go on tour. This waltz-like ballad features Dolly's vocals. However, the superb melodic counterpoint work of the acoustic guitar on the first half of the first verse is noteworthy. Mack Magaha's fiddle joins her afterward, then come the pedal steel and the backing vocals to complete this country waltz tune with a sound palette already well anchored in the Nashvillian tradition.

We Had All The Good Things Going

Mervin Shiner, Jerry Monday / 2:45

Vocals: Dolly Parton **Musicians:** Fred Carter Jr., Jerry Stembridge, Wayne Moss, George McCormick: guitars / Lloyd Green, Pete Drake: pedal steel / Hargus "Pig" Robbins: piano / Roy "Junior" Huskey: bass / Jerry Carrigan, James Isbell: drums / Mack Magaha: fiddle / Buck Trent: electric banjo **Backing Vocals:** Dolores Edgin, June Page, Joe Babcock **Recorded:** RCA Studio B, Nashville, May 14, 1969
Technical Team: Producer: Bob Ferguson / Sound Engineer: Al Pachucki / Assistant Sound Engineers: Milton Henderson, Roy Shockey

Another of Dolly Parton's favorite themes is that of a sincere love that wears out over time.

This cover of a single by singer Jan Howard (released in 1969) was composed by Mervin Shiner and Jerry Monday. Merv Shiner had started out as a cowboy singer with "Here Comes Peter Cottontail" and "Sonny the Bunny" before writing for Loretta Lynn, Charley Pride, Jan Howard, and Dolly Parton, no doubt sympathetic to her nostalgic style. The up-tempo country shuffle option seems to have been adopted to emphasize Dolly Parton's need not to dwell too much on the nostalgia expressed here. Largely supported by the lively playing of her musicians, who embroider this line of flight with relentless precision, Dolly can return for a moment to the past, at a hundred miles an hour on the tour bus, on the highway to success. It is worth noting the twirling finger-picking of the two acoustic guitars (George McCormick and probably Wayne Moss), in opposition—left/right—and the Hammond organ mixed very low but admirably completing the musical spectrum of this piece made for the road.

The Monkey's Tale

Leona Reese / 1:51

Vocals: Dolly Parton **Musicians:** Fred Carter Jr., Jerry Stembridge, Wayne Moss, George McCormick: guitars / Lloyd Green, Pete Drake: pedal steel / Hargus "Pig" Robbins: piano / Roy "Junior" Huskey: bass / Jerry Carrigan, James Isbell: drums / Mack Magaha: fiddle / Buck Trent: electric banjo **Backing Vocals:** Dolores Edgin, June Page, Joe Babcock **Recorded:** RCA Studio B, Nashville, May 14, 1969
Technical Team: Producer: Bob Ferguson / Sound Engineer: Al Pachucki / Assistant Sound Engineers: Milton Henderson, Roy Shockey

When monkeys behave better than humans and tell better stories than the worst liars…Leona Reese builds here on a long tradition of hillbilly and blues songs, among which one could mention Stick McGhee's "One Monkey Don't Stop the Show," or Chuck Berry's "Too Much Monkey Business." What is immediately striking in this up-tempo with 4/4 time are the high chords played as a backbeat on the Hammond organ. The resulting sound is so unusual and incongruous in country music that it produces a comical effect, inevitably evoking the laughter of the mocking monkey: "the monkey's had a better tale than you."

Gypsy, Joe And Me

Dolly Parton / 3:13

Vocals: Dolly Parton **Musicians:** Fred Carter Jr., Jerry Stembridge, Wayne Moss, George McCormick: guitars / Lloyd Green, Pete Drake: pedal steel / Hargus "Pig" Robbins: piano / Roy "Junior" Huskey: bass / Jerry Carrigan, James Isbell: drums / Mack Magaha: fiddle / Buck Trent: electric banjo **Backing Vocals:** Dolores Edgin, June Page, Joe Babcock **Recorded:** RCA Studio B, Nashville, May 21, 1969
Technical Team: Producer: Bob Ferguson / Sound Engineer: Al Pachucki / Assistant Sound Engineers: Milton Henderson, Roy Shockey

This is the story of a woman and a man and their dog, Gypsy. They have little to live on, they walk on the roads, wear rags, and sometimes find an old shack for shelter. But they love each other and they are free. Death takes the dog, then Joe, as if echoing "The Bridge"—the woman, on a bridge, hears her man and her dog calling her, and she yearns to join them. Dolly Parton's composition evokes, once again, the marginal life of itinerant people and its dangers. A country tragedy.

Dolly sings it with feeling. Not so long ago, she was a budding songwriter, but her vocal technique has progressed to the level of the greatest. With Porter Wagoner, she has learned to magnify the first word of a phrase and then return to a normal volume. Modulations and nuances are now part of her style, especially on the high parts, which she handles with consummate art, without ever making an empty display of them.

On this midtempo number written in 4/4 time, no instrument really comes to the fore from the sound mixture concocted by the A-Team, Bob Ferguson, and Al Pachucki. Only Magaha's fiddle and Trent's banjo stand out in places, as if to evoke the freedom of the hobo.

From the end of the nineteenth century through the Great Depression, the banjo was the emblematic instrument of the American hobo. The violin has been associated with Eastern European musical traditions since the end of the sixteenth century.

1969

"The Monkey's Tale" is in the blues tradition of Chuck Berry ("Too Much Monkey Business").

In the tradition of other songs on this album, the musical concept of "Home for Pete's Sake" is a mix of traditional mountain music and current Nashville sound, enveloping—and even concealing—dark and tragic lyrics.

Home For Pete's Sake

Rudy Preston / 1:59

Vocals: Dolly Parton **Musicians:** Fred Carter Jr., Jerry Stembridge, Wayne Moss, George McCormick: guitars / Lloyd Green, Pete Drake: pedal steel / Hargus "Pig" Robbins: piano / Roy "Junior" Huskey: bass / Jerry Carrigan, James Isbell: drums / Mack Magaha: fiddle / Buck Trent: electric banjo **Backing Vocals:** Dolores Edgin, June Page, Joe Babcock **Recorded:** RCA Studio B, Nashville, May 14, 1969 **Technical Team:** Producer: Bob Ferguson / Sound Engineer: Al Pachucki / Assistant Sound Engineers: Milton Henderson, Roy Shockey

This cover of a composition by Rudy Preston (who was a rockabilly singer working under the name Tex Harper before turning to country music) enables Dolly Parton to evoke themes that are close to her heart. A girl left her country home for the city, broke her lover's heart, and lived another life somewhere else. Now the colors of the city have faded, and she is pregnant, so she thinks of returning to her parents, to find her lost love again—the Blue Ridge Mountain Boy, who will agree

to adopt the child she is expecting. An elegy to the heroine's homeland, this happy conclusion, although surprising, is welcome in this dark album, which mixes tragic destinies, love, and nostalgia for Dolly's Tennessee.

For this track, she opts for a change of pace in the third verse, slowing the tempo considerably. This is beautifully supported by Pete Drake's pedal steel, Buck Trent's virtuoso banjo, and the precision of the Jerry Carrigan–James Isbell tandem on drums, one on brushes, the other on sticks. This production trick consists of doubling the drums played with sticks with a snare drum played with brushes—one of the classic tricks of the Nashville sound. It proves particularly effective here and gracefully supports the abrupt tempo change at the end of the song, perfectly illustrating the point: "So I'm going home for Pete's sake…"

Dolly, Porter, and the Wagonmasters, ca. 1968.

Porter Wagoner with his stylist and costume tailor, the famous Nudie Cohn, Los Angeles, 1973.

The Porter Wagoner Show

Porter Wagoner was born in Missouri, near West Plains, on August 12, 1927. Like Dolly Parton, he had a very impoverished childhood. His first band, the Blue Ridge Boys, played for the local radio station KWPM, which broadcast from a butcher's shop where Porter cut meat. In 1951, he was hired by Si Siman, his first manager, as a performer on KWTO in Springfield, Missouri. The following year, he signed with RCA Victor, which began a long and fruitful collaboration with this label.

Behind All the Glitter, a Determined Man

In 1960, he was offered his own television show: *The Porter Wagoner Show*. He worked tirelessly on this venture, which required all his energy. Not only did Porter work the show, but for much of the year he was on the road touring the country.

The show was primarily Porter Wagoner: a radiant smile, pomaded blond hair, and brightly colored stage costumes with rhinestones and embroidery by talented tailors Nudie Cohn and Manuel Cuevas. There were also guests: a band, including, among other musicians, Mack Magaha on fiddle and Buck Trent on pedal steel, comic interludes by Gilbert Ray "Speck" Rhodes, and the indispensable blond singer, Norma Jean Beasler.

According to Alanna Nash,[3] about 3 million American viewers watched Porter's show on various channels. In 1966, the Country Sound Roundup People's Poll Award named *The Porter Wagoner Show* best country music television program. In 1967, the kings of country music in Nashville were Roy Acuff on radio and Porter Wagoner on television.

In addition to this success, Porter had many hits, such as "A Satisfied Mind" and "George Leroy Chickashea."

Lead-Singer Musical Chairs

Following the 1967 departure of his show partner, Norma Jean, Porter had to replace her quickly. His choice was Dolly Parton. She sang, wrote, and composed, and she was beautiful, funny, and intelligent—and like him, she worked hard. For Dolly, this was a golden opportunity both professionally (throughout this collaboration, her experience was enriched and her fame increased) and financially (she earned nearly sixty thousand dollars per year, a considerable sum at the time). *The Porter Wagoner Show* was sponsored, and Dolly has an amusing memory[1] of the advertisements she sang during her time there, which were not always glamorous (the virtues of a laxative, for example…). But the show was a great springboard for her career, and after a reluctant reception from a public still attached to Norma Jean, Dolly's talent and personality succeeded in winning over the hearts of the audience.

The Porter Wagoner Show was all about co-stars Dolly and Porter from 1967 to 1974. Dolly's success also came from the duets she recorded with Porter for RCA Victor. She had taken advantage of the termination of her contract with Monument to create the Owe-Par label, intended to protect the songs she had written with her uncle Bill Owens.

From 1961 to 1966, 104 thirty-minute episodes of *The Porter Wagoner Show* were broadcast in black-and-white, followed by an additional 582 episodes in color, before the show ended in 1981.

Always, Always

Milwaukee, Here I Come . Yours Love . I Don't Believe You've Met My Baby .
Malena . The House Where Love Lives . Why Don't You Haul Off & Love Me .
Always, Always . There Never Was a Time . Good as Gold . My Hands Are Tied .
No Reason to Hurry Home . Anything's Better Than Nothing

RELEASE DATE
United States: June 30, 1969
Reference: RCA Victor—LSP-4186
Best US Chart Ranking: 5

YOURS LOVE • MILWAUKEE, HERE I COME • NO REASON TO HURRY HOME • THE HOUSE WHERE LOVE LIVES
I DON'T BELIEVE YOU'VE MET MY BABY • ALWAYS, ALWAYS • ANYTHING'S BETTER THAN NOTHING • MY HANDS ARE TIED
WHY DON'T YOU HAUL OFF & LOVE ME • THERE NEVER WAS A TIME • GOOD AS GOLD • MALENA

ALWAYS, ALWAYS
PORTER WAGONER AND DOLLY PARTON

"Always, Always," a title unfortunately contradicted a few years later by Dolly and Porter's separation.

When Everett Corbin asked Dolly what her hobbies were, she answered: fishing and writing, not only songs but also poetry. She would publish in 1979 the poetry collection *Just the Way I Am*, based on her lyrics.

Solo and Duo: The Right Balance

Always, Always was Porter and Dolly's third duet album (due to the large output from the Porter and Dolly partnership, only *Always, Always* and *The Best of Porter Wagoner & Dolly Parton* will be discussed in detail in this book).

Produced by Bob Ferguson, this opus was released by RCA Victor on June 30, 1969. The title *Always, Always* suggests that the two stars hoped their artistic relationship would last forever. The theme of the album is love—always, and above everything else. The critics praised the quality of the duo's work on both the covers and on the three songs composed by Dolly Parton.

The Wagoner House

For the previous two years, Porter and Dolly had been touring as well as performing on *The Porter Wagoner Show*. The relationship between the two artists was at its best. Dolly's confidence was growing, and she was writing new songs in the same way that others would take breath, never stopping. The early days of her stint on *The Porter Wagoner Show* had not been easy for the young woman. In addition to the many things she had to learn in order to be successful, first of all she had to cope with the rather uncharitable attitude of the show's audience—Norma Jean's fans

were not kind to her. For a personality as emotional as the songwriter's, whose need for attention and recognition was powerful, this was torture. In an interview[5] with Jack Hurst, Dolly said that she felt like she was being murdered every time. But she stood her ground, and was eventually not only accepted but also acclaimed.

Evening Dress Required

The Porter Wagoner Show was a live country music show with a band, the Wagonmasters, an entertainer, Speck Rhodes, and the Porter-and-Dolly duo. The show also featured a number of stars, all with the good humor distilled by Porter Wagoner. This was during the late 1960s, when fashion had seized on the psychedelic colors of Flower Power, and dresses and skirts were either very short or very long, floral or graphic. High fashion was inspired by this trend to imagine garments with geometric tendencies. When, on the set of *The Porter Wagoner Show*, the duo sang "Milwaukee, Here I Come," the title that opens the album, Dolly wore a tricolored dress—half blue, half red, with white triangles in between. Other videos from this period show her in blue, yellow, or pink outfits, loose and frilly or straight and tight, sixties style. Porter Wagoner, the long-legged man, had a

A nod to Porter Wagoner quoted in the song "Milwaukee, Here I Come" (downtown pictured in 1970).

Porter Wagoner is as famous for his songs as his Nudie suits.

rockabilly look, with his blond hair slicked back, but above all he wore gleaming suits. The Wagoner house, as a whole, did not do grayness: The Wagonmasters' suits were in pink, red, or green, while Porter liked purple in all its nuances, jackets and trousers coordinated, decorated with rhinestones and sequins in wagon-wheel motifs, sparkling under the glare of the spots. *The Porter Wagoner Show* set had a joyful atmosphere to which the audience was very receptive.

A Happy Time of Partnership

Dolly revealed to journalist Gene Guerrero[5] that when she sings, she does not look at the camera but at the audience. She is naturally gifted at interacting with audiences, she is endowed with a real empathy, and she knows how to intersperse her singing with laughter or comments, as if she were inviting the audience into an intimate conversation. As for the complicity between the two artists, this was undeniable. In 1968, with *Just Between You and Me* the Porter-and-Dolly duo won the Country Music Association and Music City News awards for the best duo of the year. Watching the very first videos of Porter's 1967 show, and then those from 1969 and 1970, one cannot help but notice the giant strides the singer had made. The duo performed, and recorded singles and albums. Porter had found his singing and performing partner, but he did not yet know that Dolly wanted something else. For Dolly, dreaming was not only about letting herself go on an imaginary journey; it was also about constructing projects in the real world, such as when she decided to become an entrepreneur.

The Owe-Par Publishing Company

After the successes of "The Company You Keep" and "Put It Off Until Tomorrow," songs written with her uncle, Dolly realized that she needed to protect their creations and their copyright. In November 1966, she created the Owe-Par Publishing Company with Bill Owens. Dolly, who was only twenty years old at the time, held the majority of the company's shares. It was another step on the staircase of their independence. "As writers we were on the same wavelength. [...] We had the same kind of energy when it came to our careers," Dolly says on her website.

When Uncle Bill left Owe-Par, Dolly offered or sold (there are different versions of this story) 49 percent of her company to Porter Wagoner. They were now 100 percent partners, both artistically and financially.

Album Cover

To the right of the microphone in the photo, Porter, guitar slung over his shoulder, wears a garnet-red suit decorated with cactus and wagon-wheel motifs, highlighted with rhinestones; to the left, Dolly wears a green 1960s dress with a small white collar and a short blond wig. In the background, pale azure blinds and garnet curtains, striped with black and rhinestones, set the scene for *The Porter Wagoner Show*—The Wagoner House. Porter and Dolly have a somewhat rigid posture, she with her hands neatly folded over her dress, and he ready to pluck the guitar strings.

Milwaukee, Here I Come

Lee Fikes / 2:12

Vocals: Porter Wagoner, Dolly Parton **Musicians:** Jean Altshuler: harp / Glenn Baxter, Bill McElhiney: trumpet / David Briggs, Hargus "Pig" Robbins: piano / Jerry Carrigan: drums / Bobby Dyson, Roy "Junior" Huskey: bass / Lloyd Green: pedal steel / Mack Magaha: fiddle / Wayne Moss: guitar / George McCormick: rhythm guitar / Jerry Stembridge: electric guitar **Backing Vocals:** Hurshel Wiginton, June Page, Dolores Edgin, Anita Carter **Recorded:** RCA Studio B, Nashville, April 21, 1969 **Technical Team:** Producer: Bob Ferguson / Sound Engineer: Al Pachucki / Assistant Sound Engineer: Roy M. Shockley

"Milwaukee, Here I Come" was originally written by Lee Fikes and recorded in 1968 as a duo by George Jones and Brenda Carter; it reached number twelve on the Billboard Hot Country Songs chart.

The narrators of the story are about to return to Milwaukee, which they had left for Nashville, and the Grand Ole Opry. On television, Ernest Tubb was singing loudly, and the young woman, convinced that he was the man of her life, wanted to meet him. The *Porter Wagoner Show*'s audience enjoyed this duet, which Porter and Dolly staged with humor and camaraderie.

Listening to the intro, one does not expect such a fast tempo. The rhythm section (drums, bass, piano, guitar) leads a furious pace with a lively and jumpy 4/4 time. It seems that they are in a hurry to get to Milwaukee. There are several notable changes from previous albums. The arrival of trumpeters Glenn Baxter and Bill McElhiney, harmonizing in thirds like mariachis, is surprising. Especially since this duo returns only on "No Reason to Hurry Home," the album's penultimate song. The addition of a ride cymbal to complement the drums, centered on Jerry Carrigan's snare drum, is also an unusual production trick. This is definitely a standout track. The first track of a vinyl being, statistically, the most listened to, it was necessary to have a track that kicked. This was successfully achieved in this case! The session men of Studio B express themselves freely but with a formidable precision, and the themes of each of them follow one another, as in a relay race. The voices of Porter and Dolly are in symbiosis with the backing vocals. In spite of the developments, certain recipes do not change, like the modulation in the middle of the song; this enables an increasingly assured Dolly to make the power of her voice heard.

This Appalachian couple reminds us just how much Dolly loves love and her homeland.

Yours Love

Harlan Howard / 2:23

Vocals: Porter Wagoner, Dolly Parton **Musicians:** Jean Altshuler: harp / David Briggs, Hargus "Pig" Robbins: piano / Jerry Carrigan: drums / Bobby Dyson, Roy "Junior" Huskey: bass / Lloyd Green: pedal steel / Mack Magaha: fiddle / Wayne Moss: guitar / George McCormick: rhythm guitar / Jerry Stembridge: electric guitar **Backing Vocals:** Hurshel Wiginton, June Page, Dolores Edgin, Anita Carter **Recorded:** RCA Studio B, Nashville, December 20, 1968 **Technical Team:** Producer: Bob Ferguson / Sound Engineer: Al Pachucki / Assistant Sound Engineer: Roy M. Shockley **Single:** Side A: Yours Love / Side B: Malena **Release:** RCA Victor, February 3, 1969 (45 rpm ref.: 74-0104) **Best US Chart Ranking:** 9 (ranked for 14 weeks)

Lyrics

This song is an ode to the true, deep, total love of those for whom it lasts until the very last breath, where everything and every action (the fruits of the earth, the food, the children, the words and gestures of affection) reflect this sharing and giving of oneself, which is illustrated by the title and the endings of the lines: "yours love."

Production

With this love ballad, we return to a more classical style. The rhythm guitar has been moved to the left. The banjo and the folk guitar, which provide melodic lines throughout the song, are in the center. Fiddle, pedal steel, and electric guitar alternate themes alongside the vocals. Drummer Jerry Carrigan has taken up the brushes for a much lighter playing style, with little attack, to make room for the harmonic

instruments. The tempo is very slow, and the orchestra is a slightly on a knife edge to maintain a steady pulse; it plays on the back of the beat, meaning that it sounds as though it is going to be late, but it is not. And this produces a haunting effect on the listener. One is not going to dance a waltz, but instead one is going to sway slightly, almost losing one's balance. This is a frequently used effect in reggae. If the band played slightly in front (as opposed to on the back of the beat), as in some very fast rock or funk songs, it would not work. The chorus is always richer (from an instrumental point of view) than the verses. One can detect a recurrent sequence in this type of haunting ballad: The orchestra plays with restraint on the verses and is enriched by solo instruments and backing vocals during the choruses. These instruments remain for a part of the following verse, before pausing then starting again on the next chorus. Dolly Parton's voice always crunches a little. She saturates the accents she puts on certain notes, while Porter Wagoner's is clear. He has less dynamic range (the difference between the lowest and the highest level) than his partner. His control is therefore more sensitive. But one can also notice that, in *The Porter Wagoner Show*, the singer is closer to the microphone, because of their respective sizes and the fact that Porter plays the guitar.

The ending is slightly different from the other songs: Most of the time, it is telegraphed by a repetition of the chorus or a modulation; here, it comes with a slowing down of the tempo through a bar. If ones listens carefully, a bell can be heard before the last chord.

I Don't Believe You've Met My Baby

Autry Inman / 2:11

Vocals: Porter Wagoner, Dolly Parton **Musicians:** David Briggs, Hargus "Pig" Robbins: piano / Jerry Carrigan: drums / Bobby Dyson, Roy "Junior" Huskey: bass / Lloyd Green: pedal steel / Wayne Moss: guitar / George McCormick: rhythm guitar / Jerry Stembridge: electric guitar **Backing Vocals:** Hurshel Wiginton, June Page, Dolores Edgin, Anita Carter **Recorded:** RCA Studio B, Nashville, April 22, 1969 **Technical Team:** Producer: Bob Ferguson / Sound Engineer: Al Pachucki / Assistant Sound Engineer: Roy M. Shockley

A woman dreams of the man she loves, and fears for a moment that he loves another...but no, the narrator really is the one he will marry. The author of this romantic tale is Autry Inman, a country and rockabilly musician from Alabama.

For the intro, the rhythmic setup is a little more elaborate than usual. The rhythm guitar, played using the palm mute technique, gives a dry and contained sound contrasting with the "real" beginning of the song, which starts on an open and lively country shuffle. As with most of the songs on the album, the themes accompanying the verses in counterpoint show some virtuosity. Wayne Moss's torrent of flat-picking notes on folk guitar, Jerry Stembridge's nimble, flowing electric guitar, and Lloyd Green's voluble pedal steel have a field day, but never cut each other off. The instrumental passage before the last verse is another particularity of this song. The two guitars (electric and steel) play the same melody as the vocals with a little embellishment. After giving each other the response, they finish together. Unlike other solos, which are improvised, this one is written out.

Malena

Dolly Parton / 2:21

Vocals: Porter Wagoner, Dolly Parton **Musicians:** Jean Altshuler: harp / David Briggs, Hargus "Pig" Robbins: piano / Jerry Carrigan: drums / Bobby Dyson, Roy "Junior" Huskey: bass / Lloyd Green: pedal steel / Mack Magaha: fiddle / Wayne Moss: guitar / George McCormick: rhythm guitar **Backing Vocals:** Hurshel Wiginton, June Page, Dolores Edgin, Anita Carter **Recorded:** RCA Studio B, Nashville (TN), December 3, 1968 **Technical Team:** Producer: Bob Ferguson / Sound Engineer: Al Pachucki / Assistant Sound Engineer: Roy M. Shockley

As the star recounts in *My Life and Other Unfinished Business*,[1] "Malena" contains an autobiographical element: As a child, Dolly wondered what was on the other side of the mountains and thought that if she could take powder from the wings of butterflies, then maybe she too could fly away. The singer has kept the butterfly as an emblem from her childhood. In this song, the adults explain to Malena that "only in heaven can little girls fly." Then, with a strange gleam in her eyes, Malena makes a wish in secret, before blowing out her last birthday candles...

This song is atypical in many ways. The opening with the backing vocals and the harp creates the atmosphere immediately—we understand then that these are voices of angels. The song is in three time (like many of Dolly Parton's sentimental songs), and the orchestration is fairly sparse. In fact, we hear the piano, which plays short chords on the second beat and resonant chords on the third, which makes the playing bouncier. The guitar is played differently, with the fingers (not flat-picking) for the answers to the song. During the spoken part, only the drums, the bass, and the backing vocals remain. The ensemble is very light in order to leave space for the text, similar to a funeral oration, pronounced by the bereaved father. The harp enters discreetly at the end of the text, the piano restarts, and the singers take up the chorus with more power and emotion. We are definitely in the presence of angels during the last bars, with just the backing vocals and the harp.

1969

The House Where Love Lives

Leona Reese / 2:00

Vocals: Porter Wagoner, Dolly Parton **Musicians:** David Briggs, Hargus "Pig" Robbins: piano / Jerry Carrigan: drums / Bobby Dyson, Roy "Junior" Huskey: bass / Lloyd Green: pedal steel / Mack Magaha: fiddle / Wayne Moss: guitar / George McCormick: rhythm guitar / Jerry Stembridge: electric guitar **Backing Vocals:** Hurshel Wiginton, June Page, Dolores Edgin, Anita Carter **Recorded:** RCA Studio B, Nashville, April 21, 1969 **Technical Team:** Producer: Bob Ferguson / Sound Engineer: Al Pachucki / Assistant Sound Engineer: Roy M. Shockley

In the house where love is present, nothing else matters, not even the bills that pile up in the mailbox. One can survive anything.

In this lightning intro, a pedal steel note is sufficient to launch the theme. The folk guitar assumes the role of a rhythm instrument in arpeggios, while the acoustic guitar plays its chords in strums. From the first verse until the end of the song, the two guitars are content to gently strum along. Each solo instrument has its own melodic line: pedal steel, electric guitar, and violin; the backing vocals harmonize elegantly, always well positioned in the right stereo channel. Good, honest, middle-of-the-road country music, as Dolly and Porter know exactly how to produce again and again.

Why Don't You Haul Off & Love Me

Wayne Raney, Lonnie Glosson / 1:50

Vocals: Porter Wagoner, Dolly Parton **Musicians:** David Briggs, Hargus "Pig" Robbins: piano / Jerry Carrigan: drums / Bobby Dyson, Roy "Junior" Huskey: bass / Lloyd Green: pedal steel / Mack Magaha: fiddle / Wayne Moss: guitar / George McCormick: rhythm guitar / Jerry Stembridge: electric guitar **Backing Vocals:** Hurshel Wiginton, June Page, Dolores Edgin, Anita Carter **Recorded:** RCA Studio B, Nashville, April 22, 1969 **Technical Team:** Producer: Bob Ferguson / Sound Engineer: Al Pachucki / Assistant Sound Engineer: Roy M. Shockley

The narrator proposes that a woman he loves should let herself go in the pleasure of the embrace, and love and hold him until he loses himself. He invites her to physical pleasure, and if she refuses, then he will just have to leave.

This song was first recorded in 1949, by Wayne Raney, and it reached number one on the country and western charts. The beginning of the song is very country, with three folk guitars: the rhythm guitar in the middle of the mix, and the other two surrounding it, playing a harmonized theme. The piano enters discreetly to accompany the rhythm section, as usual. At the beginning of the first chorus, the first notes of Lloyd Green's pedal steel part are doubled in unison by Jerry Stembridge's electric guitar. The result is a stereo effect that emphasizes the words "Why don't you...," to be taken here as a real exhortation. The entire solo that follows, at the end of the first chorus, benefits from the same pedal steel–electric guitar mirrored play. This production device, based on the use of the mimicry (ensured by the flawless technique of the best session men), mixing the timbres of the two instruments, is a relatively common Nashvillian gimmick, but the effect produced is always striking. This instrumental part resolves on the famous tonal modulation. The fiddle comes in for the final chorus, along with the tambourine, for a climactic ending.

Always, Always

Joyce McCord / 2:35

Vocals: Porter Wagoner, Dolly Parton **Musicians:** David Briggs, Hargus "Pig" Robbins: piano / Jerry Carrigan: drums / Bobby Dyson, Roy "Junior" Huskey: bass / Lloyd Green: pedal steel / Mack Magaha: fiddle / Wayne Moss: guitar / George McCormick: rhythm guitar / Jerry Stembridge: electric guitar / Buck Trent: banjo **Backing Vocals:** Hurshel Wiginton, June Page, Dolores Edgin, Anita Carter **Recorded:** RCA Studio B, Nashville, April 23, 1969 **Technical Team:** Producer: Bob Ferguson / Sound Engineer: Al Pachucki / Assistant Sound Engineer: Roy M. Shockley **Single:** Side A: Always, Always / Side B: No Reason to Hurry Home **Release:** RCA Victor, May 19, 1969 (45 rpm ref.: 74-0172) **Best US Chart Ranking:** 16 (ranked for 11 weeks)

The eternal question: Can love last forever, as strong as on the first day, no matter what? Porter and Dolly combine finesse and tenderness in this slow-paced song. The banjo, omnipresent but never featured, has the privilege of playing this intro, and then some more. It is usually assigned to the rhythm section or to small contributions; here it plays the leading roles, as does the fiddle, which we find again when evoking the relationships between men and women. In the verses, the orchestra is very sparse and restrained, to highlight the voices of Porter and Dolly. It is on the choruses that the solo instruments come in, as well as the backing vocals. Finally, just for a change, the piece remains in the same key from beginning to end. One might almost be disappointed...

An evocation of extreme rural poverty with "There Never Was a Time": a dilapidated plantation in the Mississippi Delta in 1971.

There Never Was A Time

Myra Smith, Margaret Lewis / 2:25

Vocals: Porter Wagoner, Dolly Parton **Musicians:** Jean Altshuler: harp / David Briggs, Hargus "Pig" Robbins: piano / Jerry Carrigan: drums / Bobby Dyson, Roy "Junior" Huskey: bass / Lloyd Green: pedal steel / Mack Magaha: fiddle / Wayne Moss: guitar / George McCormick: rhythm guitar / Jerry Stembridge: electric guitar **Backing Vocals:** Hurshel Wiginton, June Page, Dolores Edgin, Anita Carter **Recorded:** RCA Studio B, Nashville, April 23, 1969 **Technical Team:** Producer: Bob Ferguson / Sound Engineer: Al Pachucki / Assistant Sound Engineer: Roy M. Shockley

This is the story of a family so poor that they cannot give their children anything for Christmas. It is a hard life, where the children's grief causes the parents to despair, but a strong love binds them together, and one day things work out. The story suggests that a divine intervention is involved, no doubt because of their love, unwavering even in the trials of life. The lyrics are not by Dolly Parton, but they could have been.

This song is very similar to "Billy Boy," a traditional British song from the beginning of the twentieth century, widely covered, notably by Miles Davis on *Milestones* in 1958 and by Jerry Lee Lewis in 1970. It is rather classical in its structure, with quite a linear progression. The first verse is played with the rhythm section in charge of the intro. Then comes the modulation of a semitone upward. It should be noted that this one is done naturally enough, whereas it is necessary to use some melodic tricks when the key rises by a tone. The second part of the song welcomes a tambourine, which adds a swing feel. This swing is supported by the folk guitar, which plays short phrases, then a little longer, reminiscent of gypsy jazz. It enables the second modulation of the song to pass smoothly. In the third verse, the bass drum adds some hits, then come the backing vocals; the bass plays some long notes (muffled until then); the guitar, which played some themes, reverts to some very prominent chords, until a beautiful tutti (all the instruments). Then the intro is resumed to conclude on a gentle note.

Good As Gold

Paul Martin / 2:20

Vocals: Porter Wagoner, Dolly Parton **Musicians:** David Briggs, Hargus "Pig" Robbins: piano / Jerry Carrigan: drums / Bobby Dyson, Roy "Junior" Huskey: bass / Lloyd Green: pedal steel / Mack Magaha: fiddle / Wayne Moss: guitar / George McCormick: rhythm guitar / Jerry Stembridge: electric guitar **Backing Vocals:** Hurshel Wiginton, June Page, Dolores Edgin, Anita Carter **Recorded:** RCA Studio B, Nashville, December 20, 1968 **Technical Team:** Producer: Bob Ferguson / Sound Engineer: Al Pachucki / Assistant Sound Engineer: Roy M. Shockley

A theme dear to Dolly Parton: love transcends material hardship ("We've got each other and that's as good as gold"). This song, although not in itself of major interest, does however offer some unusual subtleties. The piano, with its honky-tonk playing, is supported by the bass and marks all the beats of the bar, instead of the traditional accent on the first. On drums, Jerry Carrigan's cross-stick playing is in symbiosis with George McCormick's acoustic guitar, which is strummed in a swing style—it is hard to keep your foot from tapping. If one listens closely, on the left channel one can hear a percussion sound resembling claves (two pieces of wood struck against each other, very common in Cuban music). The violin also has a particular way of playing: Usually it plays one note after the other, while here Mack Magaha's bow touches two strings at the same time, a typical playing style in mountain music that is also practiced in traditional Irish music.

My Hands Are Tied

Dolly Parton / 2:31

Vocals: Porter Wagoner, Dolly Parton **Musicians:** David Briggs, Hargus "Pig" Robbins: piano / Jerry Carrigan: drums / Bobby Dyson, Roy "Junior" Huskey: bass / Lloyd Green: pedal steel / Mack Magaha: fiddle / Wayne Moss: guitar / George McCormick: rhythm guitar / Jerry Stembridge: electric guitar **Backing Vocals:** Hurshel Wiginton, June Page, Dolores Edgin, Anita Carter **Recorded:** RCA Studio B, Nashville, April 23, 1969 **Technical Team:** Producer: Bob Ferguson / Sound Engineer: Al Pachucki / Assistant Sound Engineer: Roy M. Shockley

Rumors and fiction both make people believe things that may not be true. The narrator loves a married man, and the ring on her finger cannot allow them to love each other. There have been wild rumors of a love interest between Dolly and Porter. Both have denied it, but perhaps their situation has inspired the songwriter?

In this ballad, for once, the piano takes the solo role. It provides the intro as well as answers during the verse. The very linear arrangement, without extravagance in the structure, enhances the lyrics, which convey a message about the personal situation of the characters embodied here by Dolly Parton and Porter Wagoner. How much do the lyrics evoke their real-life relationship? No one can say. But one thing is certain: In the country music world, choosing the angle of confession, whether true or false, is a proven marketing technique. The end of the song, with its four sustained notes, slowing down the tempo, seems to indicate that the discussion is closed, once and for all.

No Reason To Hurry Home

Dolly Parton / 2:24

Vocals: Porter Wagoner, Dolly Parton **Musicians:** Glenn Baxter, Bill McElhiney: trumpet / David Briggs, Hargus "Pig" Robbins: piano / Jerry Carrigan: drums / Bobby Dyson, Roy "Junior" Huskey: bass / Lloyd Green: pedal steel / Mack Magaha: fiddle / Wayne Moss: guitar / George McCormick: rhythm guitar / Jerry Stembridge: electric guitar **Backing Vocals:** Hurshel Wiginton, June Page, Dolores Edgin, Anita Carter **Recorded:** RCA Studio B, Nashville, April 21, 1969 **Technical Team:** Producer: Bob Ferguson / Sound Engineer: Al Pachucki / Assistant Sound Engineer: Roy M. Shockley

What is worse than a love that has grown tired? When the children are gone, when all that is left is the shadow of love, and the loneliness that fills the house, and the hearts. "No reason to hurry home," as this song says.

In this traditional country waltz, the themes on fiddle, electric guitar, pedal steel, and folk guitar follow one another in turn. It also marks the return of the trumpets. They make three contributions, including the very last notes. Exceptionally, two instruments (pedal steel and fiddle) play the intro—most of the time, only one instrument does this, which facilitates the entrance of the orchestra. The fiddle, slightly out of tune, brings a slight sense of tiredness and drift to this disillusioned piece. Generally, in the songs, there is a balance between the parts sung by two people and the solos. Here, Dolly Parton and Porter Wagoner sing separately at the beginning of the second verse, and all the rest is sung in duet, as a way to show that they agree: This love has no future.

Onstage in 1967, the formidable duo formed by Dolly Parton and Porter Wagoner, in Nudie suits.

Anything's Better Than Nothing

Marie Wilson / 2:21

Vocals: Porter Wagoner, Dolly Parton **Musicians:** David Briggs, Hargus "Pig" Robbins: piano / Jerry Carrigan: drums / Bobby Dyson, Roy "Junior" Huskey: bass / Lloyd Green: pedal steel / Mack Magaha: fiddle / Wayne Moss: guitar / George McCormick: rhythm guitar / Jerry Stembridge: electric guitar **Backing Vocals:** Hurshel Wiginton, June Page, Dolores Edgin, Anita Carter **Recorded:** RCA Studio B, Nashville, April 23, 1969 **Technical Team:** Producer: Bob Ferguson / Sound Engineer: Al Pachucki / Assistant Sound Engineer: Roy M. Shockley

Despite the disappointment and the pain, anything is better than this "nothing," this one-way love: This is the conclusion of the narrator.

We can hear the reverberation effect applied to the voices (lead and backing vocals), giving the impression of being in a large room (a church?), with some imagination. This is a rather linear piece, a country waltz in which the contributions of the soloists (electric guitar, pedal steel, violin, folk guitar) follow one another. In the verses, the bass marks the first beats with the bass drum and the left hand of the piano, while in the chorus and the instrumental bridge, it almost invariably marks the first two eighth notes, to get the pulse going again and invite the audience to dance. The fiddle, as in "Good as Gold," uses its typical mountain music bowing, which always evokes an affiliation with Irish music. The backing vocals harmonically enrich the chorus and bring a feeling of openness, also due to some heavy application of the echo chamber effect. *More reverb*, Phil Spector would have said; but in Nashville, they know how to keep things restrained.

ALBUM

The Fairest of Them All

Daddy Come and Get Me . Chas . When Possession Gets Too Strong .
Before You Make Up Your Mind . I'm Doing This for Your Sake . But You Loved Me Then .
Just the Way I Am . More Than Their Share . Mammie . Down from Dover . Robert

RELEASE DATE
United States: February2, 1970
Reference: RCA Victor—LSP-4288
Best US Chart Ranking: 13 (ranked for 17 weeks)

During the demonstration against the Vietnam War, in Boston, April 15, 1970.

Consecration and Controversy

Dolly's fifth solo album, *The Fairest of Them All*, was released in February 1970. The songwriter delivered an excellent set of compositions, as the critics confirmed. Some of the songs were controversial, but the "fairest of all," who wrote or co-wrote all eleven tracks on the LP, decided to run her own show. While the album was not a huge commercial success, it is of a remarkable quality, which did not escape the attention of either the music industry professionals or the public.

When the Music Is the Subject of Discussion

The Fairest of Them All was released in an effervescent context. In American society, the 1970s shifted the cursor of relationships, of bourgeois morality, of social conventions, and saw the birth of great international movements. The 1970s were synonymous with freedom and change, individual and collective consciousness, as illustrated by the first Earth Day, a major ecological demonstration that took place on April 22, 1970. Opponents of the war in Vietnam did not give up, nor did Richard Nixon. Anger was rising in American homes, where people were tired of seeing their boys killed or coming back completely destroyed.

In the context of sex, drugs, and rock 'n' roll, LSD was still all the rage, both within the Flower Power generation and in neuropsychiatric research. The 1970s was also a decade of great upheaval in psychiatric methods, including the rise of the infamous electroconvulsive therapy. Ken Kesey's novel,[16] *One Flew over the Cuckoo's Nest*, whose 1975 film adaptation by Milos Forman won five Oscars, is an unapologetic plea against the treatment of patients in the psychiatric institution.

The LGBTQIA+ community was in its infancy as far as organization was concerned, but the Stonewall riots (1969)—following the revolt of the clientele of a New York gay bar against frequent police raids—permanently altered the history of the movement. Everywhere, people claimed the right to be exactly who they wanted to be. The desire for modernity in morals, work, culture, consumption, nutrition, choices in loving relationships, and how to raise one's children took hold of young people, while tradition tried to slow down this wave of emancipation. It was a pivotal

The Fairest of Them All
Dolly Parton

When Possession Gets Too Strong/More Than Their Share/Just the Way I Am
Before You Make Up Your Mind/I'm Doing This for Your Sake/Mommie
But You Loved Me Then/Robert/Down from Dover/Daddy Come and Get Me/Chas

RCA · LSP-4288 · VICTOR STEREO

An extravagant fairy dress for Dolly.

For Dolly Addicts

The song "Down from Dover" appeared in the TV series *Heartstrings*. Streaming on Netflix beginning in November 2019, it was co-produced and presented by Dolly herself.

1970

decade for Dolly Parton, who also claimed her own creative freedom.

When Dolly Set the Tone

Throughout her career, Dolly Parton's creativity has been based on a paradox that is permanent and fascinating, as it weaves the rich and complex poetic fabric of her work: glamour meets vulgarity, sweetness and innocence flirt with violence, pink meets blackness, love meets heartbreak, and joy meets pain. Dolly embodies the joy of life, but she takes the ugliness of the world and turns it into unforgettable songs, which is obviously the mark of great artists. "Daddy Come and Get Me" is a powerful example of this, as it is about love and abusive psychiatric confinement.

The whole album resonates with the changes occurring in society. Pregnant, single, or in love with men who walk out on them or are unsuitable, girls and women are misjudged by society, so they might be hidden away from society, supposedly for their own good, or condemned by those who would be moral gatekeepers. Through "Down from Dover," the songwriter takes a sharp look at this situation, which has cost so many young women dearly.

When Heritage Becomes Modernity

For a better understanding of Dolly Parton's writing, we need to go back to the origins of country music and to the star's childhood. Between her mother and her grandfather, the Reverend Jake Owens, in a sense little Dolly was practicing her scales from birth. She was bathed in the melodies and stories of gospel and spirituals, she heard terrible stories sung, a heritage of her distant ancestors from the Highlands of Scotland and Ireland. The stories were impossible in scope, stories of Shakespearean-level

loves, betrayals, murders, abandoned children, boys killed in war; they spoke of sorrow, the particular sadness specific to some secular songs under the reign of Elizabeth I. These subjects bring tears to our eyes, but they are also sublime and they fascinated little Dolly, who loved to sing in church, in the fields, at home, everywhere. So this child, who also had things to say, wrote stories that speak of her experience.

Later, when the songwriter started to emerge, in Nashville, her texts, impregnated with tradition, were nevertheless at the cutting edge of modernity. In 1970, Dolly had just celebrated her twenty-fourth birthday. She was a star on *The Porter Wagoner Show*, and her popularity grew with each of her albums. She had been Porter's partner for three years now, in the middle of a five-year commitment, but she was now considering her future without him. Porter did not want to think about her leaving. He was ambitious, a little possessive, and Dolly was a part of his future plans. As for the singer, while she was gradually earning an aura of a national star, she has only one desire: to move up a gear. "The Fairest of Them All" is one more stone in her edifice, her dream of superstardom.

Album Cover

During her first meeting with the singer Patty Loveless in 1972, Dolly Parton said that this was the funniest album cover she had ever done! She wanted to look like a fairy tale character, even if the aesthetic choice may seem contradictory to the themes of the songs. Facing a golden-framed mirror, adorned in a pink dress with a spectacular collar, Dolly, as in Disney's adaptation of the *Snow White* fairy tale, seems to be interrogating her reflection: "Mirror, mirror, am I the fairest of them all?"

The 1970s are marked by great upheavals in psychiatry, and the use of electroconvulsive therapy is highly controversial and a topic of *One Flew over the Cuckoo's Nest* (1975), starring Jack Nicholson.

Daddy Come And Get Me

Dorothy Jo Hope, Dolly Parton / 3:01

Vocals: Dolly Parton **Musicians:** Jerry Carrigan: drums / Lloyd Green: pedal steel / Roy "Junior" Huskey: bass / Mack Magaha: fiddle / George McCormick: rhythm guitar / Wayne Moss, Jerry Stembridge: guitar / Hargus "Pig" Robbins: piano / Buck Trent: electric banjo
Backing Vocals: Joe Babcock, Dolores Edgin, June Page
Recorded: RCA Studio B, Nashville, October 31, 1969
Technical Team: Producer: Bob Ferguson / Sound Engineer: Al Pachucki / Assistant Sound Engineers: Milton Henderson, Roy Shockley **Single:** Side A: Daddy Come and Get Me / Side B: Chas
Release: RCA Victor, December 1969 (45 rpm ref.: 47-9784)
Best US Chart Ranking: 40

Genesis and Lyrics

The singer wrote this song with her aunt, Dorothy Jo Hope, wife of Bill Owens. How do you get rid of your wife when you love another? By having her involuntarily committed, the song answers. Against this abusive internment—a widespread practice, at the time, in American society as elsewhere—the only recourse for this young woman is her father, who promised her his help in case of need. But, deprived of her freedom, she cannot go to him, so she prays that he will come to her—even though he is probably unaware of her situation.

Production

This album was the first on which Dolly Parton achieved compositional excellence. Using the techniques she learned from Porter Wagoner, she was inspired by the popular duets of Anita Carter and Hank Williams—especially 1952's "I Can't Help It (If I'm Still in Love with You)"—and learned how to put her voice forward for a key word or a short moment, and then tone down her volume. The idea might have come from Porter Wagoner, but the virtuosity with which Dolly modulates her vocals in the upper registers is her own. She had reinvented herself, and listeners appreciated her for who she was. As for the musicians, we find the A-Team from RCA Studios, still with Bob Ferguson on production and Al Pachucki at the controls. Why change a winning team? The sound has even more richness and mellowness. It perfectly suits this piece, whose difficult theme requires some coating, especially in view of a single release. The bass is deeper, and the stereo field is wider; one feels that the studio equipment is evolving, but the recording and mixing techniques remain the same. In the immediate future, the single did not reach the top of the charts—it was ranked fortieth—but with time, the public would realize what Dolly had accomplished artistically, well before the great successes of *9 To 5* or *Coat of Many Colors*.

Chas

Dolly Parton / 2:24

Vocals: Dolly Parton **Musicians:** Jerry Carrigan: drums / Lloyd Green: pedal steel / Roy "Junior" Huskey: bass / Mack Magaha: fiddle / George McCormick: rhythm guitar / Wayne Moss, Jerry Stembridge: guitar / Hargus "Pig" Robbins: piano / Buck Trent: electric banjo **Backing Vocals:** Joe Babcock, Dolores Edgin, June Page **Recorded:** RCA Studio B, Nashville, October 30, 1969 **Technical Team:** Producer: Bob Ferguson / Sound Engineer: Al Pachucki / Assistant Sound Engineers: Milton Henderson, Roy Shockley

The story of an impossible love. She, the lover, takes care of everything concerning Chas…even the woman he loves—an invalid who cannot walk. In silence, the narrator is consumed, but admits that she will never do anything…except love Chas.

We sense that everything is going well in the legendary Studio B. Dolly Parton is back with her favorite session men, and the country waltz is in full swing, delicate and lively. All the musicians are in their respective places, and the music is flowing. Hargus "Pig" Robbins's piano responds with an elegant arpeggio to Mack Magaha's fiddle, which seems to have put on its best waltz costume in a dialogue with Lloyd Green's pedal steel, itself in perfect symbiosis with the choir that moves effortlessly between unison and close harmony.

When Possession Gets Too Strong

Louis Owens, Dolly Parton / 2:04

Vocals: Dolly Parton **Musicians:** Jerry Carrigan: drums / Lloyd Green: pedal steel / Roy "Junior" Huskey: bass / Mack Magaha: fiddle / George McCormick: rhythm guitar / Wayne Moss, Jerry Stembridge: guitar / Hargus "Pig" Robbins: piano / Buck Trent: electric banjo **Backing Vocals:** Joe Babcock, Dolores Edgin, June Page **Recorded:** RCA Studio B, Nashville, October 31, 1969 **Technical Team:** Producer: Bob Ferguson / Sound Engineer: Al Pachucki / Assistant Sound Engineers: Milton Henderson, Roy Shockley

Dolly Parton co-wrote this song with Louis Owens, another member of the Owens clan, who was probably also involved in the arrangements. In this text, which is once again about love, the subject is possessiveness. But, as the narrator says, even a deep love cannot be encumbered by chains. The parallel with Lesley Gore's 1963 hit "You Don't Own Me" is striking, with Dolly writing lyrics like: "I can't live with you if you try to own me"…Also in 1963, Bob Dylan sang "Blowin' in the Wind," and that wind of freedom was still blowing in 1970.

This song sounds quite different from the others. First of all, there is the guitar that doubles the bass in palm mute playing at the octave on the right stereo channel, the famous tick-tock sound. This detail brings a real drive to the ensemble, as well as a certain modernity. On the left channel, the fiddle part is doubled by Mack Magaha himself in overdub, creating a chorus effect that was still very rare in country music in 1970. The extreme clarity of the chorus on the right is also surprising. It is rare to hear the three voices and their respective harmonies so distinctly; their volume exceeds even that of Dolly Parton's voice at times. Their echo chamber treatment is also particularly strong, especially compared to Dolly's voice, whose treatment is here much drier (without or with only very little reverb) and intimate.

Before You Make Up Your Mind

Bill Owens / 3:10

Vocals: Dolly Parton **Musicians:** Jerry Carrigan: drums / Lloyd Green: pedal steel / Roy "Junior" Huskey: bass / Mack Magaha: fiddle / George McCormick: rhythm guitar / Wayne Moss, Jerry Stembridge: guitar / Hargus "Pig" Robbins: piano / Buck Trent: electric banjo **Backing Vocals:** Joe Babcock, Dolores Edgin, June Page **Recorded:** RCA Studio B, Nashville, October 31, 1969 **Technical Team:** Producer: Bob Ferguson / Sound Engineer: Al Pachucki / Assistant Sound Engineers: Milton Henderson, Roy Shockley

The narrator, in love with the man who is about to leave her for another woman, asks him to reflect on it, before walking out of the door and slamming it on their love.

Dolly chooses to develop this *other woman* song on a country shuffle with a very fast tempo. The electric guitars have the main role: The country licks of Jerry Stembridge rain down on the left channel, while on the right, the prodigious pedal steel of Lloyd Green accumulates syncopations and melodic prowess. This duel on the top frames Dolly's voice on both sides, alone in the center with the rhythm section, as if to illustrate the conflict and the tense situation described here: "Before you tell me that it's all over / Let me say what I have to say, it won't take me all day." The very cinematic atmosphere of "Before You Make Up Your Mind" immerses the listener in a scene that is a cross between a spaghetti western and 1920s slapstick saloon decor. Never a dull moment!

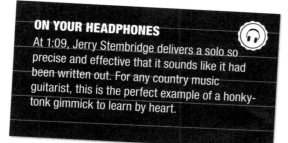

I'm Doing This For Your Sake

Dolly Parton / 2:11

Vocals: Dolly Parton **Musicians:** Jerry Carrigan: drums / Lloyd Green: pedal steel / Roy "Junior" Huskey: bass / Mack Magaha: fiddle / George McCormick: rhythm guitar / Wayne Moss, Jerry Stembridge: guitar / Hargus "Pig" Robbins: piano / Buck Trent: electric banjo **Backing Vocals:** Joe Babcock, Dolores Edgin, June Page **Recorded:** RCA Studio B, Nashville, September 10, 1968 **Technical Team:** Producer: Bob Ferguson / Sound Engineer: Al Pachucki / Assistant Sound Engineers: Milton Henderson, Roy Shockley

With this number the songwriter offers another variation of the story of a young pregnant girl. The man she thought would become her future husband, upon learning that she is expecting a child, abandons her. So, out of love, she entrusts her "beloved little girl" to another, to ensure her a better life—presumably free from want and far from judgment.

What better than a country ballad to illustrate this new "sad ass song"? The pedal steel and the fiddle, both on the right stereo channel, converse in a plaintive tone that only nonfretted instruments are capable of emulating. One can easily imagine the setting of this domestic drama—a little cabin or shack in the heart of the Great Smoky Mountains. In such a context, the choice of this instrumentation seem to make sense.

But You Loved Me Then

Dolly Parton / 1:52

Vocals: Dolly Parton **Musicians:** Jerry Carrigan: drums / Lloyd Green: pedal steel / Roy "Junior" Huskey: bass / Mack Magaha: fiddle / George McCormick: rhythm guitar / Wayne Moss, Jerry Stembridge: guitar / Hargus "Pig" Robbins: piano / Buck Trent: electric banjo **Backing Vocals:** Joe Babcock, Dolores Edgin, June Page **Recorded:** RCA Studio B, Nashville, May 21, 1969 **Technical Team:** Producer: Bob Ferguson / Sound Engineer: Al Pachucki / Assistant Sound Engineers: Milton Henderson, Roy Shockley

When he loved her, they lived in a wonderful world…then he left. Now she wanders alone through the ruins of the sand castles they had built together. She has lost her way and lost the enchantment of those happy days.

To counterbalance the sadness of the subject, the A-Team works on a very groovy and syncopated three time rhythm to weave the backdrop of this song about lost love. Roy "Junior" Huskey's bass and Jerry Carrigan's drums give it their all. On the chorus, with the effect of a sudden passage in 4/4, the tempo even seems to accelerate. The verse turns on a soul-funk pattern whose unstoppable rhythmic figure would be abundantly sampled by the rap scene from the beginning of the 1980s, and then by the initiators of trip hop in England in the 1990s.

Just The Way I Am

Dolly Parton / 2:28

Vocals: Dolly Parton **Musicians:** Jerry Carrigan: drums / Lloyd Green: pedal steel / Roy "Junior" Huskey: bass / Mack Magaha: fiddle / George McCormick: rhythm guitar / Wayne Moss, Jerry Stembridge: guitar / Hargus "Pig" Robbins: piano / Buck Trent: electric banjo **Backing Vocals:** Joe Babcock, Dolores Edgin, June Page **Recorded:** RCA Studio B, Nashville, October 31, 1969 **Technical Team:** Producer: Bob Ferguson / Sound Engineer: Al Pachucki / Assistant Sound Engineers: Milton Henderson, Roy Shockley

Dolly has said and written many times that her biggest job was to be herself. At the beginning of her career, journalists were astonished that a woman so naturally beautiful would use so much artifice, to the point of appearing superficial. She always replied that underneath her legendary breasts, one would find her heart, her authenticity. This song is perhaps a little bit about all of that, but also about the fact that we are all different—"My mind and spirit must be free […] / I don't know why, it's just the way I am"—and that is self-explanatory.

On a fast-paced 4/4, Dolly's voice rises gracefully and lightly above the musical embroidery of the Studio B team.

COUNTRY FUNK

Mac Davis, Bobby Darin, and Tony Joe White are some of the proud representatives of this hybrid yet natural style. As one can hear on "But You Loved Me Then," this marriage flows naturally. Interestingly, one of Dolly Parton's wishes (listen to the podcast *Dolly Parton's America*) is that her music survives her through the use of her isolated vocal tracks for future remixes or other new arrangements.

One of Dolly Parton's themes, that of child mothers and children out of wedlock.

The clawhammer, an Appalachian banjo-playing technique, consists of using the thumb and forefinger while attacking the strings from top to bottom. This technique takes its name from the fact that the hand that strikes the strings, misshapen by agricultural work, assumes the shape of an eagle's claw.

Mammie

Dolly Parton / 3:11

Vocals: Dolly Parton **Musicians:** Jerry Carrigan: drums / Lloyd Green: pedal steel / Roy "Junior" Huskey: bass / Mack Magaha: fiddle / George McCormick: rhythm guitar / Wayne Moss, Jerry Stembridge: guitar / Hargus "Pig" Robbins: piano / Buck Trent: electric banjo **Backing Vocals:** Joe Babcock, Dolores Edgin, June Page **Recorded:** RCA Studio B, Nashville, May 13, 1969 **Technical Team:** Producer: Bob Ferguson / Sound Engineer: Al Pachucki / Assistant Sound Engineers: Milton Henderson, Roy Shockley

"Mammie" was one of the first songs recorded for this album, along with "But You Loved Me Then." Its lyrics bring together three generations: a woman; her mother, who dies after giving birth to her; and her grandmother, who raises her then dies. The passing of time, the love given and received, the learning of right and wrong, and the importance of inter-generational bonds are the driving forces of this song. Dolly Parton also celebrates the strength of the women in her family—in her native Tennessee, the population had to endure the opportunism of the carpetbaggers, profiteers who came from the North in the aftermath of the Civil War to buy up the hillbillies' farms and land at low prices.

The phrasing of Mack Magaha's fiddle evokes the odyssey of Southern families, far beyond the fighting between Confederates and Unionists. The chords played by the guitar and banjo, on the left and right stereo channels respectively, enable Dolly Parton's voice instantly to set the scene for this bluegrass waltz. On the right, Jerry Stembridge plays some sumptuous electric guitar arpeggios, and Buck Trent responds with a typical Appalachian banjo clawhammer; while on the left, Hargus "Pig" Robbins, installed at the back of Studio B, supports George McCormick's acoustic guitar by hammering out beats two and three on a harpsichord that was gathering dust. To highlight the chorus, the choral effect produced by the voices of Babcock, Edgin, and Page is of such power and intensity that one could believe that they were doubled, even tripled, in overdubs, but a high level of echo chamber application could have been enough to create this effect.

More Than Their Share

Dolly Parton / 2:20

Vocals: Dolly Parton **Musicians:** Jerry Carrigan: drums / Lloyd Green: pedal steel / Roy "Junior" Huskey: bass / Mack Magaha: fiddle / George McCormick: rhythm guitar / Wayne Moss, Jerry Stembridge: guitar / Hargus "Pig" Robbins: piano / Buck Trent: electric banjo **Backing Vocals:** Joe Babcock, Dolores Edgin, June Page **Recorded:** RCA Studio B, Nashville, October 31, 1969 **Technical Team:** Producer: Bob Ferguson / Sound Engineer: Al Pachucki / Assistant Sound Engineers: Milton Henderson, Roy Shockley

Double standards…In a couple, is there always one who gives more than the other, who, for the sake of love, always gives in? This song questions the relationship imbalance, the inequality of feelings and behaviors, a theme dear to Dolly Parton.

Porter Wagoner was convinced that the lyrics were too controversial for radio stations, but a few weeks after the record's release, Nashville radio was on board.

Subtly heralding the narrator's distress, Lloyd Green's pedal steel introduction underscores the country-blues atmosphere of this slow ballad, carrying a message that speaks to everyone. Pig Robbins's piano skillfully responds to Dolly's vocals from 1:52, like a second voice, and the singer knowingly plays with this alternation to express the frustration of a love not equally returned.

Down From Dover

Dolly Parton / 3:46

Vocals: Dolly Parton **Musicians:** Jerry Carrigan: drums / Lloyd Green: pedal steel / Roy "Junior" Huskey: bass / Mack Magaha: fiddle / George McCormick: rhythm guitar / Wayne Moss, Jerry Stembridge: guitar / Hargus "Pig" Robbins: piano / Buck Trent: electric banjo **Backing Vocals:** Joe Babcock, Dolores Edgin, June Page **Recorded:** RCA Studio B, Nashville, September 4, 1969 **Technical Team:** Producer: Bob Ferguson / Sound Engineer: Al Pachucki / Assistant Sound Engineers: Milton Henderson, Roy Shockley

Genesis and Lyrics

The society that Dolly describes is not kind to young girls who are pregnant and unmarried or pregnant by a man who their parents consider to be unsuitable. The control exercised over the sexuality, feelings, and future of these women is a very violent one. In "Down from Dover," the young narrator, pregnant and abandoned by her lover—but hoping with all her heart that he will return—is sent away from her parents to hide her "shameful" pregnancy. Even worse, she then gives birth to a lifeless baby girl. An episode of the series *Heartstrings*,[6] also titled "Down from Dover," offers a different scenario: The young girl—white, high school student, and pastor's daughter—loves a young black man who goes to war in Vietnam. She is excluded from society and placed in a hospice for unmarried girls.

One can understand why, despite the beauty of the music and the delicate arrangement, Dolly's tragic story seemed to have no commercial potential. Even in December 1969, with the changes in society that were underway, the song was controversial. Porter Wagoner had warned Dolly that radio stations would not play the song. He was wrong. Nancy Sinatra and her producer, Lee Hazlewood, recorded it the following year; their version was a hit on California stations, and its success instantly spread to the whole country.

Production

This midtempo number written in 4/4 time is an unusual groove for Dolly Parton because it has more than one

string to its bow: On the left, the autoharp chords and the tambourine immersed in reverb bring a real solemnity to the ensemble; they are supported on the right by powerful backing vocals with particularly inspired arrangements. The repetition of the word "Dover" produces an almost supernatural effect and underlines the dramatic scope of the piece. The similarities with Lee Hazlewood's songwriting and universe are such that one would almost wonder if "Down from Dover" had been written directly for Nancy Sinatra. Dolly Parton rerecorded the song for her album *Little Sparrow* (2001), with an extra verse that had been removed from the original version.

Robert

Dolly Parton / 2:39

Vocals: Dolly Parton **Musicians:** Jerry Carrigan: drums / Lloyd Green: pedal steel / Roy "Junior" Huskey: bass / Mack Magaha: fiddle / George McCormick: rhythm guitar / Wayne Moss, Jerry Stembridge: guitar / Hargus "Pig" Robbins: piano / Buck Trent: electric banjo **Backing Vocals:** Joe Babcock, Dolores Edgin, June Page **Recorded:** RCA Studio B, Nashville, September 4, 1969 **Technical Team:** Producer: Bob Ferguson / Sound Engineer: Al Pachucki / Assistant Sound Engineers: Milton Henderson, Roy Shockley

Another thwarted love, with a social background—he is rich, she is poor. The narrator is in love with a boy who does not know they have the same father, a rich man who loved her mother and whose illegitimate child she is, the fruit of a love prevented by the families: "And I am a symbol of the love that they stole."

Wayne Moss's and George McCormick's guitars, and Buck Trent's banjo create the perfect musical backdrop for the unfolding drama. Porter Wagoner is the uncredited producer. Of note: On the right stereo channel, the lead guitar riff is played on nylon strings, instead of the steel strings of the traditional folk guitar. Willie Nelson is one of the few country musicians who played exclusively on nylon strings, on a modified Martin he nicknamed "Trigger," which greatly contributed to the development of his percussive and melodic playing.

ALBUM

As Long As I Love

Why, Why, Why . I Wound Easy . I Don't Want You Around Me Anymore . Hillbilly Willy .
This Boy Has Been Hurt . Daddy Won't Be Home Anymore . As Long As I Love .
A Habit I Can't Break . I'm Not Worth the Tears . I Don't Trust Me Around You .
I Couldn't Wait Forever . Too Lonely Too Long

RELEASE DATE
United States: April 1, 1970
Reference: Monument Records—SLP18136

Revisiting the Past

As Long as I Love was released on April 1, 1970, by former Dolly Parton producer Fred Foster. This compilation of songs recorded at Monument Records contains three tracks released as singles ("Why, Why, Why," "I Couldn't Wait Forever," and "I'm Not Worth the Tears"), but the others were hitherto unreleased, and all the songs are written by Dolly Parton or co-written by Dolly and Bill Owens. The album presents a mix of situations that the songwriter never ceases to explore: feelings of love, broken hearts, the honor of families tainted by shame.

As Long As I Love, though not ranked on sales charts, would nevertheless be appreciated by critics.

New from Old

What stands out in 1970 is Dolly's incredible ability to write and perfect artistic content. As *Billboard* magazine said in praise of its release, the quality of this album could not fail to win over the songwriter's fans.

So it had been a busy year of recordings and album releases, both solo and as a duo. Dolly had gained in maturity, and in studio and stage experience, in particular due to her performances on *The Porter Wagoner Show*. Her professional relationship with Porter was both challenging and difficult, as the two artists did not always see eye to eye on the young woman's career plans. With her show partner, Dolly recorded the albums *Porter Wayne and Dolly Rebecca* and *Once More*, both of which were well received by critics and audiences alike. Dolly also began recording "Mule Skinner Blues (Blue Yodel No. 8)," a country standard covered by many celebrities. The single "Joshua" was released in a tense social, cultural, and political climate, despite the advances in science and the major social movements, essential pivots of this new decade. Culture was buzzing in the circles of cinema, theater, and contemporary art. But it was especially music that, more than ever, seemed to be at the same time a refuge, an escape from too much reality, and a link between people. Cat Stevens released "Lady

D'Arbanville," Simon and Garfunkel thrilled their fans with "Bridge over Troubled Water," and the Rolling Stones went on a European tour.

Dolly Day

In April 1970, as festivals and concerts proliferated in the United States and Europe, Dolly gave a live concert in her childhood town of Sevierville. She received the keys to the city.[1] The concert was recorded and released as her first live album, *A Real Live Dolly*.

Under the aegis of Porter Wagoner and the Wagonmasters, who participated in the event as guests, it was a time for celebration and reunion. Speck Rhodes of The *Porter Wagoner Show* provided humorous interludes and other comedy sequences. Friends and stars were there—including Cas Walker, who introduced the concert, and Bud Wendell, general manager of the Grand Ole Opry—and, of course, the Parton family, as well as 2,500 spectators, which was huge for a town like Sevierville. Among the crowd: those who laughed at Dolly and her teenage ambitions but were now proud of the star, their heroine. Facing her: the girls and boys, now adults, with whom she went to college. Also in front of her: the people whose lives she chronicled, the sad stories of love and sex, the scorned feelings, the violent poverty, representative of the so-called deep America.

Dolly performed songs from her days at Monument Records. Whether it was nostalgia or a need to recharge her batteries, it was in any case through music that she traveled back in time.

The young woman was twenty-four years old. This event would henceforth bear the name Dolly Day, and it has since been celebrated every year in Sevierville.

Album Cover

Photographed by Bill Goodwin, the cover shows Dolly seated, a guitar on her knees, her arms crossed over it, with a bright smile and a radiant face under a flamboyant wig.

Portrait of Dolly by the
famous photographer Harry
Langdon, ca. 1970.

Why, Why, Why

Bill Owens, Dolly Parton / 2:19

Vocals: Dolly Parton **Musicians:** (?) **Backing Vocals:** (?)
Recorded: Monument Records, Hendersonville, Tennessee, date?
Technical Team: Producer: Fred Foster / Sound Engineer: Tommy
Strong **Single:** Side A: I Couldn't Wait Forever / Side B: Why, Why,
Why **Release:** Monument Records, October 1967 (45 rpm ref.:
45-1032) / **Best US Chart Ranking:** Did Not Chart

This catchy song is written in the form of questions asked
by the narrator: She wonders what she did or said to make
her man leave her. Although this song is co-written by Bill
Owens, it takes up a theme dear to Dolly Parton.

The electric piano uses a harpsichord-like sound, reminiscent of the naïve and charming analog sounds of the Vox
Continental or the Farfisa Compact Deluxe, both manufactured before the 1970s. It spices up the rhythm by hammering out beats two and four, or adds phrases in response to
the vocals, like the pedal steel and folk guitar. Its descending melodic part, in unison with the chorus, adds a kind
of synthetic brilliance to the vocals for an effect that is
as strange as it is pleasant. The double bass contributes a
more folk and organic touch than the electric bass. One can
clearly hear the fingerpicking, when the musician's right
hand hits the strings (and the neck with it), producing that
distinctive little "clack" on the attack of the notes.

I Wound Easy

Bill Owens / 2:17

Vocals: Dolly Parton **Musicians:** (?) **Backing Vocals:** (?)
Recorded: Monument Records, Hendersonville, Tennessee, date?
Technical Team: Producer: Fred Foster / Sound Engineer:
Tommy Strong

The wounds of love, and how to get over them, are a recurrent theme in Dolly Parton's work—even though this song
is written by Bill Owens. In this case, the loneliness and
the sorrow of the one who remains waiting for the return
of her man, who has gone elsewhere, once again…The lyrics express the paradoxes inherent in the feeling of love:
With each infidelity, the narrator is easily hurt but quickly
heals, then is hurt again and again, and heals again and

again. An infernal cycle, but it has a resilience that can also
be seen as a strength.

On this country shuffle ballad, Fred Foster opts to bring
out the heavy artillery. We find the electric piano and its
famous harpsichord sound on the notes at the end of the
chorus. The vibraphone lays down enveloping chords on
the first verse, then embellishes the sumptuous strings
arrangements throughout the song. A piano seems to enter
discreetly to support the rhythm section from the second
verse. The violins are very present, almost louder than the
vocals, and add gentleness, when the electric guitar plays
the same notes as the bass, two octaves above. The attack
of the plectrum is precisely audible. The snare drum is well
timed (metal wires stretched under the drum vibrate with
each hit to create the metallic sound). From the second
verse, the chorus and the pedal steel play the same chords,
which is rare enough to warrant emphasis—usually, the
soloists do more or less what they want.

I Don't Want You Around Me Anymore

Bill Owens, Dolly Parton / 2:04

Vocals: Dolly Parton **Musicians:** (?) **Backing Vocals:** (?) **Recorded:**
Monument Records, Hendersonville, Tennessee, date? **Technical Team:**
Producer: Fred Foster / Sound Engineer: Tommy Strong

The lyrics sound like an act of rebellion on the part of the
narrator, who does not care anymore. Her man does as he
pleases; she is no longer blind and sees him as he is—that
is, much less intelligent than he thinks he is.

This song seems to continue the story told in "I Wound
Easy." Relief results from her realization, and it is symbolized by the fast tempo and by the rather joyful, bouncy,
and very assured melody, like the piano chords supported
by the vibraphone and hammered out from the intro in a
very authoritative way. A real buildup of instruments settles
in over the course of the song, until the last verse, where
they are all present. The voice is almost drowned in the
musical abundance, especially the string quartet, which is
well to the fore.

Hillbilly Willy

Dolly Parton / 1:55

Vocals: Dolly Parton **Musicians:** (?) **Backing Vocals:** (?) **Recorded:** Monument Records, Hendersonville, Tennessee, date? **Technical Team:** Producer: Fred Foster / Sound Engineer: Tommy Strong

This is the story of a little guy who came down from the hill. Willy is not very handsome, and especially not very tall, but he knows how to talk to the girls, with the charming drawl of his hillbilly voice that makes them all fall in love…Absolutely, but with all of his five feet in stature,

he had better be a rough, tough guy in the face of the competition!

Back to the 4/4 for this traditional up-tempo country song. The guitars provide the themes in response to the vocals. The sound of the drums and the orchestration suggest that this track was recorded at the same time—or even during the same session—as "Why, Why, Why." We note the presence of the electric guitar in the rhythm section and the nuances applied to the playing, depending on whether the vocals are present. A last amusing detail: the voice of the colossus who was robbed of his sweetheart is very low, almost caricatured. This cartoonish tone underlines perfectly the comical aspect of Hillbilly Willy's adventures. Dolly Parton definitely has a particular gift for painting these Appalachian sketches full of fun.

This Boy Has Been Hurt

Bill Owens, Dolly Parton / 2:15

Vocals: Dolly Parton **Musicians:** (?) **Backing Vocals:** (?) **Recorded:** Monument Records, Hendersonville, Tennessee, date? **Technical Team:** Producer: Fred Foster / Sound Engineer: Tommy Strong

For once in Dolly's songs, it is a man who is heartbroken, a victim of love, as though abandoned by the roadside. The narrator, touched by his distress, feels the desire to save him, and therefore to love him.

The piece begins with an intro on the pedal steel, which continues its meanderings until the end. Then the orchestra makes its entrance, calm and majestic. On the first verse, we notice first the padded sound of the vibraphone, completely on the right (almost behind, when listening on headphones); then, on the second verse, on the left, the backing vocals come in to add to the range of the vibraphone. The alternation provided is very pleasant to the ear, fueled by a lush string ensemble. The song has no real chorus, with the narrator telling a story composed of several stanzas. The title of the song itself is only sung, twice, toward the end, when, as the melody changes, the narrator asserts her intention to save and heal the wounded man.

Daddy Won't Be Home Anymore

Dolly Parton / 2:52

Vocals: Dolly Parton **Musicians:** (?) **Backing Vocals:** (?) **Recorded:** Monument Records, Hendersonville, Tennessee, date ? **Technical Team:** Producer: Fred Foster / Sound Engineer: Tommy Strong

In this song, Dolly expresses the pain common to all women whose husbands have gone to war and to all mothers who have to tell their children the terrible news: "Daddy won't be home anymore." At that time the country was in the middle of the Vietnam War, but the lyrics apply equally to all the conflicts of yesterday and tomorrow.

The beginning of this song is a rarity in Dolly Parton's discography of that time—two whole sections, backing vocals and violins, start together. The three verses are based on the same pattern: a sparse beginning, then the instruments join in little by little until the end of the chorus, and then we start again. On the first verse, the vibraphone and the pedal steel are the first, then the violins come in. The second verse is a little more fleshed out, but the playing is very light, with the piano, folk guitar, and backing vocals. These are in the center of the mix for the first time on the album. This gives a nice spatial balance, with the vibraphone on the right and the string ensemble—the melodic phrasing of the acoustic guitar sometimes played on slide, dobro style—on the left. The string ensemble, always mixed very prominently, creates peaks of intensity, and the piece ends on a tutti with a controlled climax.

As Long As I Love

Dolly Parton / 2:42

Vocals: Dolly Parton **Musicians:** (?) **Backing Vocals:** (?) **Recorded:** Monument Records, Hendersonville, Tennessee, date ? **Technical Team:** Producer: Fred Foster / Sound Engineer: Tommy Strong

The album's title track plunges the listener into the close, and perhaps inescapable, relationship that the feeling of love has with suffering, because as long as the narrator loves this man who knows only how to give pain, she knows that she will suffer because of it. This does not prevent her from continuing to love him.

The beginning of the piece is dissonant (folk guitar and violins with their descending notes), and then becomes stable. The folk guitar plays arpeggios throughout, with drums, bass, and rhythm guitar. One can distinguish a rhythm strummed with the autoharp, Dolly Parton's favorite instrument—it is not impossible that she played this part herself. The instrument is in the center of the mix, as if it had been recorded with the voice. The backing vocals are divided: two voices on the left and two in the center—including the male voice. A particular feature of this song is that the backing vocalists sing only the chorus with Dolly Parton. The piano is moved to the right. The violins are well forward during the song with small runs, which contrast with and complete the downward notes of the pedal steel.

A Habit I Can't Break

Bill Owens / 3:15

Vocals: Dolly Parton **Musicians:** (?) **Backing Vocals:** (?) **Recorded:** Monument Records, Hendersonville, Tennessee, date? **Technical Team:** Producer: Fred Foster / Sound Engineer: Tommy Strong

In this song, too, love is unhappy. The narrator could, however, save herself from grief if she managed to break this habit of loving even when it is not good for her. Love—suffering, as fatal as an addiction.

In this piece that is more than three minutes long—an unusual length for Dolly—it is difficult to know if the harpsichord part is played on the electric piano, by the real instrument, or on the autoharp. Nevertheless, the effect produced finds its place perfectly in the arrangement. On the second verse, one can hear a classical guitar (nylon strings), and a few notes that buzz (a finger of the left hand out of place, with the string touching the fret). The snare drum is played louder, with brushes. The piano is very prominent in the rhythm and plays themes during the third verse. The string quartet casts its satin veil over the whole piece, a play of light and shadow dotted with trills and glissandi. Everyone is there on the last verse, cleverly revived by a repeat of the song's intro.

I'm Not Worth The Tears

Dolly Parton / 2:33

Vocals: Dolly Parton **Musicians:** (?) **Backing Vocals:** (?)
Recorded: Monument Records, Hendersonville, Tennessee, 1964–
1967 **Technical Team:** Producer: Fred Foster / Sound Engineer:
Tommy Strong **Single:** Side A: I'm Not Worth the Tears / Side B: Ping
Pong **Release:** Monument Records, January 1968 (45 rpm ref.:
45-1047) **Best US Chart Ranking:** Did Not Chart

"I'm Not Worth the Tears" is the story of a young girl who admits that she is not worth the tears her parents shed because of her—she is probably pregnant. She had an affair with a man who abandoned her, and feels ashamed that her father can no longer walk with his head held high, ashamed of the grief of his family.

When "I'm Not Worth the Tears" was recorded at Monument Records, the chamber orchestra was absent, which lends a distinctive sound to this song. We find the other instruments, but in the mix of the time: either on the left, or on the right, or both (therefore in the center). All the rhythm section (drums, bass, piano, guitar) is on the right. The piano embroiders a little, and the pedal steel plays some notes, as if placed on the cloud of chords created by the vibraphone. The ensemble is remarkably sober.

I Don't Trust Me Around You

Bill Owens / 2:54

Vocals: Dolly Parton **Musicians:** (?) **Backing Vocals:** (?) **Recorded:**
Monument Records, Hendersonville, Tennessee, date? **Technical Team:**
Producer: Fred Foster / Sound Engineer: Tommy Strong

The narrator's temptation toward infidelity is so strong that she is afraid she may be powerless to stop herself from giving in.

This time, it is Dolly's voice that opens the piece, carried by the carpet of trills played by the string ensemble. If the outtakes were available, one would certainly discover which instrument gives her the opening note. An experienced performer can start on the right note without assistance, but he or she must have a particularly trained ear and could fall just short, which would be enough to require a restart. It is certain that in live performance a player gives Dolly the right note or chord to start with. The trills of the string ensemble raise the tension. The suspense is at its peak…Will the narrator break?

I Couldn't Wait Forever

Bill Owens, Dolly Parton / 2:23

Vocals: Dolly Parton **Musicians:** (?) **Backing Vocals:** (?)
Recorded: Monument Records, Hendersonville, Tennessee, date?
Technical Team: Producer: Fred Foster / Sound Engineer: Tommy
Strong **Single:** Side A: Why, Why, Why / Side B: I Couldn't Wait
Forever **Release:** Monument Records, October 1967 (45 rpm ref.:
45-1032) **Best US Chart Ranking:** Did Not Chart

The narrator explains that she could not wait forever for this man who only offered her promises, because eternity is too long when one is eager to love and be loved in return. Then other arms, other lips, put an end to this agony, to this solitude…Very beautiful lyrics, sensitive and sensual.

Everyone enters the dance at the same time on a mid-tempo country shuffle; only the violins and the backing vocals are missing. It sounds like the opening of a western movie, near the Mexican border. The classical guitar comes in on the second verse, along with the violins. The pedal steel and the electric guitar play a phrase in relay at the end of the first chorus; the pedal steel starts, and the electric guitar is added, which then finishes the phrase by itself. So we have a melody that starts on the right, then goes to the center, and ends on the left in a few bars.

Too Lonely Too Long

Dolly Parton / 2:21

Vocals: Dolly Parton **Musicians:** (?) **Backing Vocals:** (?) **Recorded:**
Monument Records, Hendersonville, Tennessee, date? **Technical Team:**
Producer: Fred Foster / Sound Engineer: Tommy Strong

A woman, alone for too long, begs the man who has rekindled desire in her not to tempt her and not to be tempted. The tension between the desire to be free to love and the idea that it might well be a sin is a torment.

On this country shuffle ballad, the drumming is particularly sparse. A snare drum played with brushes and a light cross stick is enough; it is on the left stereo channel on this piece, whereas it is on the right or in the center on the other tracks. The same applies for the piano. On the right, the electric guitar plays the same part as the bass, two octaves higher—the famous tick-tock. The balance of the mix is strange, because all the soloists are on the left (pedal steel and piano), as well as the backing vocals. Here we have country minimalism in all its splendor, rocked by Dolly's voice, expert in the art of the sweet lament.

The Best of Porter Wagoner & Dolly Parton

Just Someone I Used to Know
Daddy Was an Old Time Preacher Man
Tomorrow Is Forever
Jeannie's Afraid of the Dark
The Last Thing on My Mind
The Pain of Loving You
Better Move It on Home
Holding On to Nothin'
Run That by Me One More Time
We'll Get Ahead Someday

Release Date
United States: July 19, 1971
Reference: RCA Victor—LSP-4556
Best US Chart Ranking: 7

When the Bell Tolls

The Best of Porter Wagoner & Dolly Parton is a compilation of the best songs written and/or performed by the duo. It was released by RCA Victor and produced by Bob Ferguson. *Billboard* and *Cashbox* magazines praised the compilation, but music critic Robert Christgau considered the album syrupy and sentimental. Half the tracks are covers of songs by other artists, and the others are written or co-written by Dolly Parton.

The Best Kept for Last

In September 1967, Dolly Parton signed up with Porter Wagoner and his show for five years. In 1971, their professional relationship was still productive but strained. Dolly knew she owed to Porter the launch of her career because when no one else believed in her, he firmly and solidly did have faith in her. She sold, a lot, and increasingly so. The RCA Victor label, to justify its reservations about Dolly, referred to the unique sound of her voice. But this unique voice, recognizable among thousands, was also an asset. Dolly had to deal with an audience that did not

like change, and it was the duets with Porter Wagoner that finally won people over. Aware that Dolly was not comfortable onstage, as the audience was still clamoring for her predecessor, Norma Jean, Porter suggested that Dolly should sing some duets. They set to work, studied their strengths and weaknesses, and went for it. When they sang together, they alternated verses—she in her high, clear voice, he in his lower tenor voice—in other words, Dolly sang and Porter recited. The singers then declared that their two voices matched in the same way as those of a blood brother and sister. Porter had heard Dolly sing with her sisters and said that they harmonized better than any professional singer in Nashville.[11] They also had a unique way of singing. Both also had a particular way of accenting syllables, emphasizing a letter or pausing between words. Dolly and Porter shared a great bond. It took only a brief glance for each to know where the other was, how they would perform in the songs, the lines, and the jokes that punctuate the songs. It was a performance that appealed to fans of *The Porter Wagoner Show*, and while Miss Norma remained in their hearts, she was now a thing of the past. Biographer Alanna Nash[3] said that the duo was so convincing in their love songs that audiences thought that Dolly and Porter were married, while those who knew them well in Nashville believed they were having an affair. Truth or rumor, it does not matter: In 1971, Dolly Parton was on the rise, walking toward the realization of her dream. When the compilation *The Best of Porter Wagoner & Dolly Parton* was released, Dolly had learned and progressed so much that she had become better than Porter—a fact that was noticed by the specialist press and by some of Dolly's and Porter's friends.

Eclipsing the Mentor

Minnie Pearl, an actor for more than fifty years at the Grand Ole Opry, told Alanna Nash[3] that Porter and Dolly were a great duo, much better than anyone recognized at the time, because everything worked together to make

them winners. From Porter's point of view, Dolly was already a superstar, ready to stand on her own two feet, who could never be satisfied with a dependent relationship, especially not while achieving her dream of becoming an iconic artist. Also speaking to Alanna Nash, Fred Foster of Monument Records, Dolly's former producer and friend, said the songwriter did not need *The Porter Wagoner Show* to become an even bigger star. While Dolly had international ambitions, staying on the show deprived her of a wider audience, as only country fans watched it.

But Dolly was grateful to Porter for giving her a chance, so she waited as their relationship deteriorated. It was time for the parting of ways, and for her, who was faithful in her relationships, it was a heartbreaker. She was about to leave, and she tried to get Porter used to the idea, but he would not listen. He made himself Dolly's manager, overseeing everything, needing to be in control, and

he could even be tyrannical. What she experienced with Porter, Dolly had already experienced with her uncle, who was also an authoritarian man, notes Alanna Nash. However, in the last few shows, Porter seemed to be fading behind Dolly's brilliance. The question arises: Did he refuse to let her go because he sensed that without her he would be the loser?

Album Cover

The cover of this compilation, created by Les Leverett, is in the same vein as the previous albums: Porter Wagoner and Dolly Parton pose side by side, dressed in red and black, on a red background that haloes their faces, as though they are illuminated by a red light, the whole composition giving this image an almost surreal aspect, evoking the aesthetics of science fiction series of the 1960s-1970s. Please note: the musicians who participated in the recording of this album are not listed in the credits.

Just Someone I Used To Know

Jack Clement / 2:21

Vocals: Porter Wagoner, Dolly Parton **Musicians:** (?) **Recorded:** RCA Victor, Nashville, April 21, 1969 **Technical Team:** Producer: Bob Ferguson / Sound Engineers: Al Pachucki, Jim Malloy, Chuck Seitz / Assistant Sound Engineer: Roy Shockley **Single:** Side A: Just Someone I Used to Know / Side B: My Hands Are Tied **Release:** RCA Victor, October 1969 (45 rpm ref.: 74-0247) **Best US Chart Ranking:** 5

This love song dwells in nostalgia. There is a photo of a departed loved one, and to the question "Who is that?" the answer is, "Just someone I used to know." As though it were not a big deal, when obviously it is. And although time has passed since that flame had almost been extinguished, the memory of the tears shed is still vivid.

This version by Porter and Dolly is a cover of the Jack Clement song "A Girl I Used to Know," performed by George Jones in 1962.

The song opens with a duet of trumpets, first in unison, ending in thirds on the last three notes. Unusual in country instrumentation, this arrangement with two trumpets is reminiscent of mariachi music (traditional Mexican music with vocals, strings, and trumpets), as if to evoke not only the time that has passed but also the distance traveled since the end of this love. This arrangement makes the nostalgia palpable, despite the protagonists' refusal to acknowledge the depth of their pain.

Daddy Was An Old Time Preacher Man

Dorothy Jo Hope, Dolly Parton / 2:57

Vocals: Porter Wagoner, Dolly Parton **Musicians:** (?) **Recorded:** RCA Victor, Nashville, April 21, 1970 **Technical Team:** Producer: Bob Ferguson / Sound Engineers: Al Pachucki, Jim Malloy, Chuck Seitz / Assistant Sound Engineer: Roy Shockley / **Single:** Side A: Daddy Was an Old Time Preacher Man / Side B : A Good Understanding **Release:** RCA Victor, July 1979 (45 rpm ref.: 47-9875) **Best US Chart Ranking:** Did Not Chart

Although in this song the preacher is referred to as "Daddy," Dolly (along with her aunt, the co-author) is referring here

to her maternal grandfather, Reverend Jake Owens, a highly respected man in his community, whose sermons were reputed to be hotter than hell. It was with him, in the church he built, that Dolly learned to sing old gospel songs at an early age, and it was there she realized that God and music were inextricably linked. The church was also a place where hope persisted beneath harsh poverty. So believing and singing, looking for God and finding him, allows one to hold on, to hope, to see further.

On a 4/4 rhythm with a lively tempo and communicative energy, Dolly and Porter pay a joyful tribute to the fervor of their favorite old-time preacher man. Like the sermons at the church, the song builds up in waves, reaching a first climax between 1:02 and 1:10, due particularly to the intervention of a bass drum, hammered without restraint with a mallet. On Porter Wagoner's solo verse, the atmosphere calms down before rising gradually, from 2:22, toward a country gospel trance until the end. We imagine the piece continuing and intensifying for many minutes still as it fades out.

Tomorrow Is Forever

Dolly Parton / 2:45

Vocals: Porter Wagoner, Dolly Parton **Musicians:** Glenn Baxter, Danny Davis: trumpet (uncredited) **Recorded:** RCA Victor, Nashville, December 2, 1969 **Technical Team:** Producer: Bob Ferguson / Sound Engineers: Al Pachucki, Jim Malloy, Chuck Seitz / Assistant Sound Engineer: Roy Shockley **Single:** Side A: Tomorrow Is Forever / Side B: Mendy Never Sleeps **Release:** RCA Victor, January 1970 (45 rpm ref.: 47-9799) **Best US Chart Ranking:** 9

Yesterday…we must forget it, because yesterday is gone, it is only a memory. Only tomorrow counts so that this love can live on, unencumbered by the past. Because tomorrow…tomorrow, everything is possible, especially when it comes to love. When one knows the history of the duet, one is tempted to want to read between the lines: Is this song, written by Dolly, a preamble to the separation of her partnership with Porter? A way of saying that whatever happens, even if she leaves, the important things and the feelings will remain intact?

The intro of this country shuffle ballad, carried by a few bluesy piano licks, brings the listener into the heart of this ode in the present time. The chorus literally explodes under the intensity of the low notes of the piano and the fiddle, the latter answering the former in a double note on the second beat of each measure. The trio of backing vocals support Dolly's and Porter's voices, while bass drum stresses the first beat and the snare drum stresses the second beat. On the right, the electric guitar knits some sumptuous lines in response to the softness of the pedal steel, located at the opposite end of the stereo field. In the distance, mainly on the verses, we can hear a duet of trumpets, lining the whole effect with velvet. They are Glenn Baxter and Danny Davis, already present on "Just Someone I Used to Know"—nothing surprising, since "Tomorrow Is Forever" is from the same album: *Porter Wayne and Dolly Rebecca*.

Jeannie's Afraid Of The Dark

Dolly Parton / 2:44

Vocals: Porter Wagoner, Dolly Parton **Backing Vocals:** (?) Anita Carter and Dolores Edgin (uncredited) **Musicians:** George McCormick: guitar (other musicians are uncredited) **Recorded:** RCA Victor, Nashville, May 21, 1969 **Technical Team:** Producer: Bob Ferguson / Sound Engineers: Al Pachucki, Jim Malloy, Chuck Seitz / Assistant Sound Engineer: Roy Shockley

After being picked on by students at her school and locked in a closet for hours, Dolly retained her fear of the dark and slept with the light on. In the song, Jeannie, a little girl, is also terrified of the dark. The darkness of the night, but also the darkness of death, and she would not want to be buried, alone, in the darkness of a grave. A bad omen? The little girl dies, and her parents place an eternal flame on her grave, "cause Jeannie's afraid of the dark"…

Despite the seriousness of the subject matter, this song was a big hit with the *Porter Wagoner Show* audience. It is because of the melodic counterpoints of George McCormick's guitar that we enter this sad ditty with accents of acoustic country waltz, restrained and elegant. From 1:36 on, the voices of Anita Carter and Dolores Edgin plunge the listener into a soft melody to comfort little Jeannie, lulling her with their crystalline and bewitching tones. Two-thirds of the way through the piece, Porter Wagoner's spoken voice as the girl's father reveals the tragic outcome of the story, before Dolly concludes by singing, "Our Jeannie's afraid of the dark."

The Cajun two-step is the traditional Louisiana dance par excellence, danced at any age, notwithstanding its fast rhythm.

The Last Thing On My Mind

Tom Paxton / 2:34

Vocals: Porter Wagoner, Dolly Parton **Musicians:** (?) **Recorded:** RCA Victor, Nashville, October 11, 1967 **Technical Team:** Producer: Bob Ferguson / Sound Engineers: Al Pachucki, Jim Malloy, Chuck Seitz / Assistant Sound Engineer: Roy Shockley

This is one of Dolly Parton's favorite themes—love stories—and this one ends badly. The narrator regrets that she left without a goodbye because of the way he behaved. Did he mistreat her? It is not stated, but he acknowledges that he was mean, even if it was not intentional.

Musically, it starts off strongly: an acoustic guitar riff, joined by the bass on the second bar, and the song starts on an up-tempo 4/4, supported on the drums by a cross stick on the quarter note. Two bars later, Porter launches into his trademark, sober, confident tone: "It's a lesson too late for the learnin'." On the left, the acoustic guitar unrolls a volley of notes in flat-picking (melodic and fast single note playing on the pick, typical of bluegrass): we feel that there is a sense of urgency!

The Pain Of Loving You

Dolly Parton, Porter Wagoner / 2:05

Vocals: Porter Wagoner, Dolly Parton **Musicians:** (?) **Recorded:** RCA Victor, Nashville, December 14, 1970 **Technical Team:** Producer: Bob Ferguson / Sound Engineers: Al Pachucki, Jim Malloy, Chuck Seitz / Assistant Sound Engineer: Roy Shockley

Of course, when the duo performed this song, the rumors were flying. Regardless, this song fits well with their vocal register and their favorite theme: love songs. This one is about a painful love, because to love someone without being loved in return is to adore and hate them at the same time. One remains alone, with one's love in one's heart.

As if to brighten up the subject, the mariachi trumpets open the ball once again. However, this intro is misleading, because never before in Dolly Parton's career has a song sounded so close to Cajun music. This 4/4 shuffle takes the listener straight to the floor, somewhere in Louisiana, in the back room of a bar where the Cajun two-step is in full swing. The fiddle adopts a plaintive and haunting play, while the trumpet duo has fun blurring the lines, skillfully underlining this paradox that we all know: Any love story always entails its share of suffering.

SINGLE

Better Move It On Home

Ray Griff / 2:14

Vocals: Porter Wagoner, Dolly Parton **Musicians:** Dale Sellers, Mack Magaha (uncredited) **Recorded:** RCA Victor, Nashville, December 14, 1970 **Technical Team:** Producer: Bob Ferguson / Sound Engineers: Al Pachucki, Jim Malloy, Chuck Seitz / Assistant Sound Engineer: Roy Shockley **Single:** Side A: Two of a Kind / Side B: Better Move It on Home **Release:** RCA Victor, January 1971 (45 rpm ref.: 47-9958) **Best Chart Ranking:** 7 in the Billboard Hot Country Songs (USA); 7 in the RPM Country 50 (Canada)

Another story of dissatisfaction in a couple's relationship. The woman keeps the dinner prepared for her man warm, who does not see the clock ticking while he is having a good time at the bar. It would be better for him to rush home and put his foot down…

Dale Sellers kicks off the festivities with an amazing chicken-picking demonstration. The Telecaster (a model of electric guitar manufactured and marketed in series by Fender from 1951) slams like never before and contributes to maintaining the tension throughout the song. Mack Magaha's bowing evokes the thundering sound of horns with his trills and double stops in incongruous harmonies. The pedal steel plays along with the electric guitar, using its arsenal of sounds to help set the scene for this skit, which moves from a smoky bar, with the jukebox volume turned up, to a frantic drive through a traffic jam. The duet of Dolly and Porter works wonderfully, even beyond the quality of their singing, and one can commend their acting performance on the dialogue in spoken voice at the end of the piece, both realistic and truculent. As for Dolly, Jane Fonda made no mistake when she recruited her to co-star in the film *9 to 5*.

SINGLE

Holding On To Nothin'

Jerry Chesnut / 2:26

Vocals: Porter Wagoner, Dolly Parton **Musicians:** (?) **Recorded:** RCA Victor, Nashville, January 31, 1968 **Technical Team:** Producer: Bob Ferguson / Sound Engineers: Al Pachucki, Jim Malloy, Chuck Seitz / Assistant Sound Engineer: Roy Shockley

A slightly guilty but realistic and resolute resignation to an ending relationship: Why hang on when there is nothing left to save?

To illustrate this umpteenth "sad ass song," what better than a midtempo country shuffle? As if to counterbalance the eminently Nashville classic character of this Jerry Chesnut composition, some notable changes in the distribution of the stereo field are applied. Firstly, and surprisingly, the backing vocals are on the left. What is it that has bitten Al Pachucki and Bob Ferguson? The drums, played in cross stick, are entirely on the right, as well as the fiddle, while the bass remains in the center. The rhythm provided by the acoustic guitar balances out on the left. A second unusual feature is that the pedal steel swings from one side to the other. At the time, it was generally considered that an instrument should keep a fixed place from the beginning to the end of a song, in order not to disturb the listener's auditory perception. This technique is still widely used in modern mixing studios.

Run That By Me One More Time

Dolly Parton / 2:18

Vocals: Porter Wagoner, Dolly Parton **Musicians:** Dale Sellers: guitar (other musicians are uncredited) **Recorded:** RCA Victor, Nashville, December 3, 1969 **Technical Team:** Producer: Bob Ferguson / Sound Engineers: Al Pachucki, Jim Malloy, Chuck Seitz / Assistant Sound Engineer: Roy Shockley

In this song about the evils of alcohol and poverty, the two narrators tell their sad story: One has spent his rent money on booze and claims that he doesn't smell like alcohol but like aftershave; the other is tired of his prattle and predicts that if he continues to drink his aftershave, it will kill him—with luck…

Dale Sellers's intro is, once again, played with a chicken-picking technique. His precise and voluble Telecaster playing punctuates this fast country shuffle with exquisite solos and syncopated licks, illustrating the deceitful adventures of the character played by Porter Wagoner. At the end of the song, as in "Better Move It on Home," we find them both improvising a quarrel in spoken voice. Nothing could be more natural for these two strong-headed characters!

The winners reunited during the Country Music Association Awards, 1968. From left to right: Roy Clark, Merle Haggard, Dolly Parton, and Porter Wagoner.

We'll Get Ahead Someday

Mack Magaha / 1:55

Vocals: Porter Wagoner, Dolly Parton **Musicians:** Mack Magaha: fiddle / Pete Drake: pedal steel (uncredited) **Recorded:** RCA Victor, Nashville, May 22, 1968 **Technical Team:** Producer: Bob Ferguson / Sound Engineers: Al Pachucki, Jim Malloy, Chuck Seitz / Assistant Sound Engineer: Roy Shockley

Usually Mack Magaha is on the musicians' side of the RCA studio, fiddle in hand. In this song, he writes about the effects of poverty on relationships and daily life.

The pedal steel introduces this fast-paced 4/4. The band rolls out a perfect soundtrack for the voices of Dolly Parton and Porter Wagoner, who, without softening the harsh reality of working-class life, carry a message of hope: "We'll get ahead someday." The bass drum fanfare supports the choruses on the first and third beats with its appealing eighth note. This rhythmic figure inevitably gives the impression that the music is moving forward and creates an almost irresistible desire to enter the dance, to move forward together, despite the difficulties. Far from being merely satisfied with his status as a songwriter, Mack Magaha also graces his audience with a very bluegrass and devilishly catchy solo. To top it all off, Pete Drake's pedal steel interventions bring their dose of light and enthusiasm to this already very positive and unifying set.

ALBUM

The Golden Streets of Glory

I Believe . Yes, I See God . The Master's Hand . Heaven's Just a Prayer Away .
Golden Streets of Glory . How Great Thou Art . I'll Keep Climbing .
Book of Life . Wings of a Dove . Lord, Hold My Hand

RELEASE DATE
United States: February 15, 1971
Reference: RCA Victor—LSP-4398
Best US Chart Ranking: 22

This photo by David Turnley immortalizes the crossgenerational connections, as Dolly likes to sing them.

The Tribute Album

The Golden Streets of Glory is Dolly Parton's sixth solo album, produced by Bob Ferguson. This particular opus pays tribute to her maternal grandfather, the Reverend Jake Owens, who wrote one of the numbers, "Book of Life," and the sleeve notes. It also glorifies the roots of country music by featuring gospel and spirituals. Critically acclaimed, the album was nominated for the Fourteenth Annual Grammy Awards in 1972 for Best Sacred Performance.

1971, a Year of Inspiration

During this year, Dolly Parton recorded a number of singles and albums, both with Porter Wagoner and as a solo artist, including *Coat of Many Colors*, which became a classic. Her relationship with RCA Victor seemed to be more fruitful than ever. In 1970 and 1971, his singles were hits, including "Mule Skinner Blues," which reached number three on the Billboard Hot Country Songs chart, and "Joshua," which reached number one.

Around the world, 1971 was marred by serious political unrest. In Europe, civil war raged on the streets of Belfast, and opponents of Francisco Franco continued to fight in Spain. In the United States, the Pentagon Papers affair challenged the freedom of the press, with the *New York Times* being forced to delay publication of the report on US involvement in the Vietnam War in the name of national defense, which was a first (and which was later overturned). More than 70 percent of Americans believed that this war was a mistake.

In the field of culture, it was also a significant year: French haute couture was in mourning after the death of Coco Chanel; the Beatles received a Grammy Award for the *Let It Be* movie; Jim Morrison, the singer of the Doors, and Louis Armstrong both died…

In this context of desire for freedom, social upheavals, and authority exercised by the powers that be, the people of the Western world indulged in rock 'n' roll, embraced the psychedelic movement, and celebrated miniskirts—a symbol of feminist advocacy—because, despite the tensions, the atmosphere was festive.

As for Dolly Parton, she continued her ascension and treated herself to an album of sacred music: "I don't know if my style has any description, except that it's just me. It's my soul. And my feelings,"[17] said the star, adding that the emotions she felt when singing gospel music were unique and that no other music gave her those feelings. In the album's liner notes, Reverend Jake Owens makes the same point: This album is special because it touches the soul, the essence of all things.

1971

A church in Tennessee, reminiscent of the one where Dolly Parton's grandfather officiated.

Sacred Way, Secular Voice

Whether one is a believer—a little, a lot, to an extreme, or not at all—the music that Dolly Parton loves comes from there, it comes from gospel—to paraphrase the lyrics of "La Musique Que J'aime" [The music I love], recorded by Johnny Hallyday in 1973. Gospel and country music share a common musical lineage. Both draw on ancient songs imported from Europe and excerpts from the Bible that are reworked or adapted by modern songwriters. And country music combines singing, dancing, gospel, and spirituals.

Dolly Parton's culture comes from her childhood, when she sang at home with her family or at the Church of God, where her grandfather was known for his fiery sermons. The church was the vital heart of the community, animating and governing daily life, but in her grandfather's church there was a freedom of worship that the young girl appreciated.

In her autobiography,[1] Dolly reveals that she has three passions in life: God, music, and sex, in that order. She also reports what can only be called a mystical experience, which occurred when she was very young. Feeling the need for privacy to pray, she sought out a place of introspection and found a disused chapel near Caton's Chapel, where the Parton family had recently moved. With its broken windows and dirty floor, the chapel was no longer used for the word of God, but was home to lovemaking and to teenagers who came to drink and pass the time, covering the walls with licentious graffiti. There was also an old piano, abandoned by the congregation. So it was there that she came to pray and play music on her old mandolin. One day, while she was meditating, with the deepest sincerity, she felt herself pass through the wall that separated her from God. As a result of this experience, Dolly asked her mother to baptize her. Since then, her faith in life, in God, and in herself has never left her.

Album Cover

Dolly Parton is at her window, angelic, enveloped in a golden halo and dressed in purple. She seems to be looking at the road to glory, paved with gold, which stretches away toward the horizon. In the background, a red-and-gold setting sun, or perhaps it is the light of God…We owe this photo of religious inspiration, in the form of a diptych, to Les Leverett.

American soldier James Hekman photographed in 1970, at the height of the Vietnam War.

I Believe

Ervin Drake, Jimmy Shirl, Irvin Graham, Al Stillman / 2:17

Vocals: Dolly Parton **Musicians:** (?) **Backing Vocals:** (?)
Recorded: RCA Studio B, Nashville, May 13, 1970 **Technical Team:**
Producer: Bob Ferguson / Sound Engineer: Al Pachucki / Assistant
Sound Engineer: Roy Shockley

"I Believe" was commissioned in the early 1950s by singer and actress Jane Froman and featured on her TV show. Disturbed by the intensity of the war in Korea, which had started in the aftermath of World War II, Jane Froman asked songwriters Ervin Drake, Irvin Graham, Jimmy Shirl, and Al Stillman to write a song that would give hope and support the faith of the people. The song reached number eleven on the Billboard charts.

The song reminds us that God is everywhere, in the raindrop that makes a flower bloom, in the glow of a candle, in the cry of a newborn baby...There is beauty in the world, and it is inherently divine.

In the legendary Studio B, the instrumentation is reduced to a strict minimum: no pedal steel or electric guitar, and very little piano. The beginning of the song, therefore, is inherently restrained; the acoustic guitar plays arpeggios, the drums are very light, and the violins and the backing vocals provide layers of sound. The bass provides a foundation, then comes the second verse, and everything is let loose! The drummer really hits his drums, the bass doubles its pace, and the voices deliver all their energy—and even a little too much, because some of the notes distort. The very end is typical of gospel, with the flights of the lead voice and the backing choir. A small drawback, however: Dolly Parton's voice does not have the power required by this style.

Yes, I See God

Dorothy Jo Hope / 2:15

Vocals: Dolly Parton **Musicians:** (?) **Backing Vocals:** (?)
Recorded: RCA Studio B, Nashville, May 13, 1970 **Technical Team:**
Producer: Bob Ferguson / Sound Engineer: Al Pachucki / Assistant
Sound Engineer: Roy Shockley

Written by Dorothy Jo Hope, Dolly Parton's maternal aunt, "Yes I See God" is a song to the glory of God, visible in all things and beings. Do we hear a real xylophone, or is it a keyboard that reproduces its sound perfectly? Either way, one can recognize the classic formation around Dolly: drums, bass, two folk guitars, piano, electric guitar, pedal steel, fiddle, and backing vocals—a very high-pitched voice, evocative of angels and heaven, reminiscent of "Malena." We also find the same good old recipes, such as the upward modulation to the next semitone, in each verse.

The chord grid of this song is typical of the blues. In addition, a Hammond organ produces the famous blue note (minor seventh). The bass is very prominent and takes some liberties, such as the very fast notes (at 0:07) or the small rises in its melody. The bassist certainly plays very close to the microphones, because the attack of the notes is very audible. The instrumentation is pared down on the verses. A few guitar chords come in further down the neck before the chorus, before the full orchestra comes in. As in "I Believe," Dolly Parton finishes as a gospel lead singer.

The Master's Hand

Dolly Parton / 2:41

Vocals: Dolly Parton **Musicians:** (?) **Backing Vocals:** (?)
Recorded: RCA Studio B, Nashville, May 12, 1970 **Technical Team:** Producer: Bob Ferguson / Sound Engineer: Al Pachucki / Assistant Sound Engineer: Roy Shockley

A great theme of the sacred texts, "The Master's Hand" tells the story of Noah and his ark. Noah obeyed the word of God and was guided by his hand, just like those who walked on the burning thistles.

The mix between religious music and honky-tonk country is successful, although somewhat paradoxical, as honky-tonk was considered immoral by puritans. The tambourine is very present, as it is in the majority of the gospel songs, and is still a mark of this mixture of the genres. The piano intro does not announce the next section. At the end of a rather soft measure, it plays loud notes in unison with the bass. This phrase is repeated after the chorus and proceeds to the modulation, also repeated at the end. The emphasis of the piano gives a very rich rhythmic harmonic, especially since it is accompanied by the notes of the electric guitar, pedal steel, violins, and backing vocals, entering in turn or all together.

Heaven's Just A Prayer Away

Tommy Tomlinson / 2:45

Vocals: Dolly Parton **Musicians:** (?) **Backing Vocals:** (?)
Recorded: RCA Studio B, Nashville, May 12, 1970 **Technical Team:** Producer: Bob Ferguson / Sound Engineer: Al Pachucki / Assistant Sound Engineer: Roy Shockley

"Heaven's just a prayer away…," a prayer that can change everything, as long as you go to church on Sunday and pray with all your heart and soul. This song was originally performed in 1967 by Norma Jean, whom Dolly replaced on *The Porter Wagoner Show*.

SINGLE

Golden Streets Of Glory

Dolly Parton / 2:54

Vocals: Dolly Parton **Musicians:** (?) **Backing Vocals:** (?)
Recorded: RCA Studio B, Nashville, May 11, 1970 **Technical Team:** Producer: Bob Ferguson / Sound Engineer: Al Pachucki / Assistant Sound Engineer: Roy Shockley **Single:** Side A: Comin' For to Carry Me Home / Side B: Golden Streets of Glory **Release:** RCA Victor, March 1971 (45 rpm ref.: 47-9971) **Best US Chart Ranking:** 23

This ode to walking on the golden road leads us to the place where all is abundance, where God is enthroned. This track was taken from the album to be released as a religious music single.

With the backing vocals and the organ, the first intro is similar to the beginning of a liturgical chant. Then a second intro brings us back to Dolly Parton's world, with the entrance of the electric guitar, then of the other instruments, at one- or two-bar intervals. The drummer hits the hi-hat; the bass drum, which sounds a little cardboard-like, stands out. It is the bass that occupies the bottom of the spectrum, as if to signal an important break between the psalms and the orchestral parts.

How Great Thou Art

Stuart K. Hine / 3:34

Vocals: Dolly Parton **Musicians:** (?) **Backing Vocals:** (?)
Recorded: RCA Studio B, Nashville, May 12, 1970 **Technical Team:**
Producer: Bob Ferguson / Sound Engineer: Al Pachucki / Assistant
Sound Engineer: Roy Shockley

1971

This hymn originates from a text written by the Swedish pastor Carl Boberg, at the end of the nineteenth century, in homage to Creation and to God. On his way home after the afternoon church service, the poet was listening to the bells ringing when suddenly furious winds arose, the sky darkened with threatening clouds and was streaked with lightning, and the heavy rain began to fall. Then, after the violence of the storm, a rainbow followed and the calm returned.

In the United States, this song is certainly the most famous in Pentecostal, Baptist, Adventist, Protestant, and Catholic churches. Dolly Parton chooses to interpret it with a great instrumental simplicity, to leave room for her voice and the backing vocals from the intro. Thus, as at the beginning of a film score, the bells open the piece with the backing vocals—including a bass voice, which is unusual on this album. Then, in the manner of a prayer or a sermon, the organ and the backing vocals create layers. A more prominent reverberation effect than on the rest of the album is applied to Dolly's voice, as in a real church. Then comes the chorus, for which the whole orchestra enters, in a rhythm of three beats. The second verse is identical, but a piano plays instead of the organ—which might have sounded too much like a Mass.

I'll Keep Climbing

Dorothy Jo Hope / 2:41

Vocals: Dolly Parton **Musicians:** (?) **Backing Vocals:** (?)
Recorded: RCA Studio B, Nashville, May 12, 1970 **Technical Team:**
Producer: Bob Ferguson / Sound Engineer: Al Pachucki / Assistant
Sound Engineer: Roy Shockley

In this song, the narrator describes her arduous but rewarding ascent to heaven. True to the concept of a religious and family album, Dolly Parton covers another composition by her aunt, Dorothy Jo Hope. Moreover, it is perhaps the piece that most resembles a gospel song, notably in its refrains on a four-beat measure, where the verses are on three beats, but also with the tambourine, which plays on beats two and four, and the bass marks the strong beats (one and three). The hand claps by the choir add a final gospel touch. The electric guitarist plucks chords with the fingers in the choruses, and the pedal steel is played the same way, but its presence is more discreet in the mix.

Book Of Life

Jake Robert Owens / 1:44

Vocals: Dolly Parton **Musicians:** (?) **Backing Vocals:** (?)
Recorded: RCA Studio B, Nashville, May 13, 1970 **Technical Team:**
Producer: Bob Ferguson / Sound Engineer: Al Pachucki / Assistant
Sound Engineer: Roy Shockley

The star's whole family is involved in her music. "Book of Life," written by her maternal grandfather, is a directive not to allow oneself to be diverted from the path that leads to Jesus and God, so that one's name can be written in the book of life.

The tempo here is faster than on the other songs on the album. Unlike some songs, the intro clearly announces the rest of the song. The piano plays a rising crochet motif that is repeated after the chorus. When not playing a theme, the electric guitar plays the bass line two octaves above in a palm mute style, as on "Golden Streets of Glory." The bass voice of the backing vocals is more present than elsewhere in the album; it repeats a single phrase, in the manner of the Temptations in "Since I Lost My Baby" (1965).

Wings Of A Dove

Bob Ferguson / 2:35

Vocals: Dolly Parton **Musicians:** (?) **Backing Vocals:** (?)
Recorded: RCA Studio B, Nashville, May, 11, 1970 **Technical Team:**
Producer: Bob Ferguson / Sound Engineer: Al Pachucki / Assistant
Sound Engineer: Roy Shockley

Written in 1958 by Bob Ferguson, "Wings of a Dove" became popular, two years later, due to the singer Ferlin Husky. This song evokes the doves sent by God, especially in the story of Noah. Dolly Parton and Porter Wagoner, who took turns covering it, added an episode in which Jesus, after his baptism, sees the Spirit of God descending toward him, like a dove.

A beautiful exchange takes place between the electric guitar and the folk guitar before giving way to Dolly's voice. This nice dialogue starts again after the chorus. During the verses, it is between the singer, the fiddle, and the pedal steel. On the last chorus, the drummer hits his cymbal on each beat, and the bass drum is brought forward, unlike at the beginning of the song. The end is a tutti where everyone gives more power to their playing.

Lord, Hold My Hand

Dolly Parton, Ginny Dean / 2:03

Vocals: Dolly Parton **Musicians:** (?) **Backing Vocals:** (?)
Recorded: RCA Studio B, Nashville, May 13, 1970 **Technical Team:**
Producer: Bob Ferguson / Sound Engineer: Al Pachucki / Assistant
Sound Engineer: Roy Shockley **Single:** Side A: When I Sing For Him /
Side B: Lord, Hold My Hand **Release:** RCA Victor, September 4, 1972
(45 rpm ref: 74-0797)

This prayer is addressed to God so that he may always be the guide and protector. Dolly Parton composed this hymn with Ginny Dean, her mother-in-law. She liked Ginny's deep voice, which provided the backing vocals.

As in "How Great Thou Art," a large reverb effect is symbolically applied to Dolly's voice—it could have been applied throughout this album to reflect the glory of God, but it would have taken up significant space and detracted from the intelligibility of the other songs. The song starts with the refrain with the whole orchestra. The verse is more sparse in instrumentation. Here also, the bass, very present and deep, contributes a foundation to the mix. One can clearly distinguish the distribution of the instruments on the frequency spectrum, as on the different planes of a photograph. When several of them occupy the same frequency band, they are spatially distributed in the mix.

ALBUM

Joshua

Joshua . The Last One to Touch Me . Walls of My Mind .
It Ain't Fair That It Ain't Right . J. J. Sneed . You Can't Reach Me Anymore .
Daddy's Moonshine Still . Chicken Every Sunday .
The Fire's Still Burning . Letter to Heaven

RELEASE DATE
United States: April 12, 1971
Reference: RCA Victor—LSP-4507
Best US Chart Ranking: 16

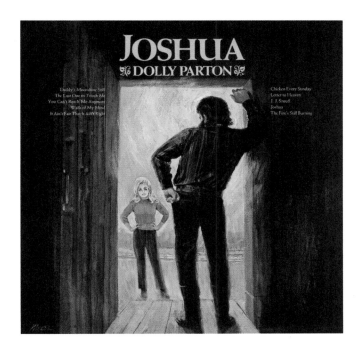

Upon its release in 1970, the single "Joshua" dominated the charts (reaching number one on the Billboard Hot Country Songs).

For Dolly Addicts

The song "Joshua" was nominated at the Fourteenth Annual Grammy Awards for Best Female Country Vocal Performance.

When All You Have Is Love

Joshua is Dolly Parton's seventh solo album, produced by Bob Ferguson. It was released in April 1971, two months after *The Golden Streets of Glory*. Dolly Parton had been very busy—she could write several songs in one day. The single "Joshua," on the other hand, was released in 1970 and made it to the charts: number one on the Billboard Hot Country Songs and 108th on the Billboard 100. The critics applauded: "One of the all-time best country records ever recorded," said *Cashbox* magazine in the same year. It was a way of telling the industry, the media, and anyone else who might still be in doubt that a star was shining higher and higher in the Nashville sky.

Joshua is the album of love, Dolly's favorite subject. It shows the songwriter's undeniable artistic progression as she continues to explore this theme again and again. From song to song, Dolly Parton's world takes shape a little more precisely and seems more complex and deeper. Her creative process was becoming richer.

A Duo Album *Versus* a Solo: Two Different Approaches

Dolly's collaborations with Porter Wagoner—the success of their singles and duet albums—contributed to her personal rise, but the singer-songwriter yearned to be known and recognized in her own right, so she felt the need to refocus on her creativity. She had done this with each of her solo albums, which are all building blocks, especially *Joshua*. Her fans loved "J. J. Sneed," a reference to Bonnie and Clyde, and they cried when listening to "Letter to Heaven," a missive from a little girl who lost her mother.

From one album to the next, fragments of songs revive the listener's recollections, like a perfume whose fragrance awakens the memory. It was as though the listener had heard the story before, felt the emotion before, like a prolonged echo from song to song. This is the other trademark of the songwriter: always the same theme, but never really the same treatment, each new piece adding its own nuance.

After the Sacred, a Return to Love

"Joshua" opens the album, which contains ten tracks, eight of which were written or co-written by Dolly. Happy or unhappy, she likes to tell love stories. Through this opus, she portrays different facets of the feeling of love. Some of the lyrics are dark and remind us of the tragic themes of *The Fairest of Them All*. Dolly claims the right to love, to cry, to renounce an unhappy love, to burn again and again, even for a lover who has run away. Love also enables the star to denounce the condition of women. Writing about hurt or joy in love while using poetry to examine the suffering, and the inequality of treatment of women and men—this is Dolly Parton's special gift.

Broadway, a major road in Nashville, was figuratively paved with the dreams and hopes of so many artists.

Although Dolly Parton did not claim to be a feminist, she was constantly concerned about the condition of women.

Stories of Women and the Conditions of Female Workers

While Dolly Parton does not claim to be a feminist, she is constantly concerned about the condition of women, especially those from the underprivileged classes. She reveals what awaits young women fleeing the poverty of the countryside in hopes of a better life, only to turn to despair when they end up on the city sidewalks. Some songs are about the way they are treated, young or old, lovers for one night or for a lifetime—as in "The Last One to Touch Me." Others tell of rural poverty and the tragedies caused by the lack of means and resources of all kinds, such as education—an important subject in Dolly's eyes.

The wars that involved the United States—and still do—the terrible consequences of the Great Depression, the conditions of life in the American countryside, the situation of the immigrants, those descendants of Europeans who came in search of a promised land, all of this infuses Dolly Parton's lyrics in one way or another. She lived in the Great Smoky Mountains of East Tennessee, where poverty spared almost no one. As a child, then as a teenager, she observed the evils of this poverty, the efforts made to survive, the material discomfort of families, and the pressure—exerted mainly on women—of the prevailing morality, of self-righteousness, often with harmful effects. She has seen misogyny at work and the power of the intransigent laws of patriarchy, she has felt these situations, in her heart and in her flesh, and has acquired a deep knowledge and understanding of them. So what could be more effective and poetic at the same time than a beautiful song, capable of making those who listen to it want to dance and cry at the same time?

Album Cover

The album sleeve illustration, by Nashville artist Bill Myers, might suggest a western or film noir. A tall, shadowy man, seen from behind standing on the threshold of a darkened house, seems to stare at the bright young woman (Dolly) standing outside, hands on hips. Whatever the message of this posture—expectation, determination, or "What's up?"—the light comes from the female side...

SIDE A

Joshua

Dolly Parton / 3:02

Vocals: Dolly Parton **Musicians:** (?) **Recorded:** RCA Studio B, Nashville, October 21, 1970 **Technical Team:** Producer: Bob Ferguson / Sound Engineer: Al Pachucki / Assistant Sound Engineer: Roy Shockley **Single:** Side A: Joshua / Side B: I'm Doing This for Your Sake **Release:** RCA Victor, November 9, 1970 (45 rpm ref.: 47-9928) **Best Chart Ranking:** 1 on the Billboard Hot Country Songs, 2 on the RPM Country 50 (Canada)

Genesis and Lyrics

"Joshua" is the story of a young orphan girl who, ignoring the gossip, visits a reclusive and allegedly wicked man. They get to know each other, become friends, and end up living together. This story, in the form of an Appalachian tale, was undoubtedly inspired by Dolly's experience as a child, as she recounts in her autobiography[1]: As a child, she had made a habit of visiting Sawdust, a hermit who had a well-known reputation as being dirty and perhaps even crazy. In reality, she had discovered a man with a fascinating life story, who had traveled and sailed the seas. The young Dolly had overcome her fears and prejudices about Sawdust when she heard him play music. In his company, she enjoyed herself, singing and learning guitar chords.

In this song, we find a theme dear to Dolly Parton: that of the right to be different, which, when misunderstood, leads to ostracism and violence. The character of Joshua is reminiscent of "Boo" Radley in Robert Mulligan's film *To Kill a Mockingbird* (1962), adapted from Harper Lee's novel (1960). Radley, an invisible neighbor, inspires rumors and superstitions among the neighborhood children, who are both afraid and fascinated.

For this storytelling gem, we start off at a hundred miles an hour on an up-tempo 4/4 that showcases the talent of the session men from Studio B. The song opens with the rhythm section, starting with the drums, all the way to the left—bass drum pulsing on the crochet, a heady ripple on the eighth note, and a nervous cross stick on the second and third sixteenth notes. Then comes the twang guitar, which plays a very surf music line in palm mute in the bass, and the entrance of an electric guitar

theme in chicken-picking. Then come the harmonica, the bass, Dolly's humming vocals, the rhythmic folk guitar and the pedal steel. This extraordinary musical tension holds from the beginning to the end of the piece, enabling Dolly to unfold her rapid narrative flow to tell the tale of the two characters' (and the big black dog's) adventures, the reckless and supposedly perilous approach, then the good understanding, and the hillbilly bonhomie that takes over. At 0:48, the resumption of the intro theme by the drums and the twang guitar reinstates a certain suspense, before the narrator (an orphan, unlike Dolly) overcomes her fear of meeting this gigantic man. The resumption of the instruments indicates this crucial moment: She "swallowed hard," then regains confidence when the colossus speaks. The chorus comes quite late, when he tells her that his name is Joshua. Finally, the key rises a semitone to express the bond with this man and the growing joy of knowing him. The famous final yodel—Dolly also has this (vocal!) string to her bow—comes like a musical firework to celebrate this new and unusual friendship, sincere and, against all odds, perfectly natural. A beautiful lesson in tolerance, Appalachian style.

Recording

The distribution of the instruments in the space is typical of the 1940s, 1950s, and 1960s. Indeed, the consoles were not equipped with panning potentiometers (PanPot). The three-position switch—Left, Center, or Right (LCR)—did not allow for any panning (such as 30 degrees left). Thus, with the Beatles, for example, many songs were either mono, such as "Please Please Me" and "She Loves You," or LCR stereo, such as "I Want to Hold Your Hand." So one must take into account that the consumer listening systems of the time were not as sophisticated as those of today. People did not listen to digital music on computers or cell phones, but with a cassette tape or vinyl player, with an amplifier and built-in speakers, installed on a piece of furniture. In this configuration, it was less "disturbing" to have such a spatial distribution of instruments.

As she shows in "J.J. Sneed,"
Dolly is fond of Westerns,
although she regrets the
absence of strong female
characters in them.

The Last One To Touch Me

Dolly Parton / 3:04

Vocals: Dolly Parton **Musicians:** (?) **Backing Vocals:** (?)
Recorded: RCA Studio B, Nashville, February 11, 1971
Technical Team: Producer: Bob Ferguson / Sound Engineer: Al
Pachucki / Assistant Sound Engineer: Roy Shockley

This ode to true love exalts the passion of the narrator
for her man. He will be the last to touch her, before she
passes away, into a sleep, as eternal as their love, which
will last beyond death. A powerful bond that nothing can
alter—this is a theme dear to Dolly Parton. More than fifty
years after "The Last One to Touch Me," an episode of the
TV series *Heartstrings*[6] entitled "Sugar Hill" evokes these
loves, which never break. It is important to remember that
Dolly grew up with the image of her parents' relationship,
who loved each other deeply and stayed together until their
last day.

This ballad is almost a cliché, so much does it adhere
to the codes: a haunting rhythm that makes you want to
swing, with notably the syncopated bass line, the violins,
the pedal steel and their sliding notes, the simplicity of
the chord grid…Unlike "Joshua," whose structure evolves
over the course of the song, this one is very classic, with
its verse-chorus sequence. Only a bridge in the middle of
the song breaks the monotony. We feel in Dolly's voice
the desire to convey a message. The simple melodic line
gives all the more weight to the words, and the choruses of
the refrain, in the gospel style, confer an almost religious
dimension to the narrator's vow.

Walls Of My Mind

Dolly Parton / 2:32

Vocals: Dolly Parton **Musicians:** (?) **Backing Vocals:** (?)
Recorded: RCA Studio B, Nashville, October 31, 1969
Technical Team: Producer: Bob Ferguson / Sound Engineer: Al
Pachucki / Assistant Sound Engineer: Roy Shockley

The theme of lost love is revisited here with a gentleness
of phrasing as well as in the evocation of the past. The
heartbroken narrator of this story is haunted by the lover
who left her—the cherry blossoms in spring, the walks, the
eyes shining with desire. We feel the painful ambivalence
of these wonderful images, which remain forever on "the
walls of [her] mind."

The intro of this slow ballad subtly announces the
woman's sorrow. All the instruments intervene on themes
throughout the song. The fiddle, in the bratsch style
(Romanian violin played on the offbeats, which gave its
name to the famous French group Bratsch), plays some of
the rhythm in the choruses. The last verse welcomes the
whole orchestra to express the happiness of remembering.

It Ain't Fair That It Ain't Right

Bob Eggers, Janice Eggers / 2:18

Vocals: Dolly Parton **Musicians:** (?) **Backing Vocals:** (?)
Recorded: RCA Studio B, Nashville, April 20, 1970 **Technical Team:**
Producer: Bob Ferguson / Sound Engineer: Al Pachucki / Assistant
Sound Engineer: Roy Shockley

Dolly Parton did not write this number, but it is easy to
understand why she chose to perform it, because it refers,
in part, to "Just Because I'm a Woman." The narrator has
been loved, but since she gave herself away, her lover
no longer desires her and abandons her. Are not women
always considered for their physical charms, and then
immediately discredited because they are reduced to just
that? Dolly denounces this injustice with a wounded sensuality and generosity.

The dobro has a prominent place in this piece. It plays
a theme in harmony with the electric guitar and dialogues
with the violin. This contributes a warm color, despite the
bitterness of the subject. The music creates a real landscape, as in westerns (one could imagine hearing the clip-
clop of a horse with the hi-hat and the rimshot).

J.J. Sneed

Dorothy Jo Hope, Dolly Parton / 2:53

Vocals: Dolly Parton **Musicians:** (?) **Recorded:** RCA Studio B,
Nashville, January 26, 1971 **Technical Team:** Producer: Bob Ferguson
/ Sound Engineer: Al Pachucki / Assistant Sound Engineer: Roy Shockley

With a nod to Bonnie and Clyde, the song "J. J. Sneed" is
quite violent and dramatic, like a good old western, a genre
that Dolly Parton loves—with one drawback—the absence
of strong, armed female figures. Too often, women in these

scenarios are the victims to be saved, as Dolly notes in her *Heartstrings*[6] series on Netflix. The heroine in "J. J. Sneed," however, will not let this happen. To her partner in love and robberies, who abandons her for another, she announces, "But now you have betrayed me, and for that you're gonna die."

In a configuration atypical in the work of Dolly Parton, the instruments are reduced to a minimum: drums, a bass, a folk guitar that plays arpeggios. Even the usual backing vocals are absent. This sobriety makes it possible to hear very well (almost too well) the reverb effect applied to the voice. Each instrument enters in a progressive way: first the guitar, then the bass, and finally the drums (bass drum, snare drum, hi-hat). It is rare to be able to hear all the notes of the bass so well. The bassist also allows himself some small excursions, which makes the music come alive. As is often the case with Dolly, we appreciate the modulation of her voice in the middle of the song. It still cracks, but very little. And her assurance fits perfectly with the strong woman of this story.

You Can't Reach Me Anymore
Dorothy Jo Hope, Dolly Parton / 2:38

Vocals: Dolly Parton **Musicians:** (?) **Backing Vocals:** (?)
Recorded: RCA Studio B, Nashville, October 31, 1969
Technical Team: Producer: Bob Ferguson / Sound Engineer: Al Pachucki / Assistant Sound Engineer: Roy Shockley

In this song, the narrator stands in unwavering indifference to her former lover, who has repented and would like to renew his relationship with her. We find here the complete orchestra (drums, bass, piano, guitars, fiddle, and backing vocals). The intro is played with the drums, with the bass and the violin on a rising scale. The pedal steel plays some lachrymose phrases. The soprano voice of the backing vocals (the highest) accompanies only part of the verse, which is unusual. In the backing vocals mix, this is the voice that is most highlighted. For the rest, the arrangement is typical of Dolly Parton's production standards.

The Dobro, a guitar whose sound is amplified by a resonator, ca. 1970.

Daddy's Moonshine Still

Dolly Parton / 3:29

Vocals: Dolly Parton **Musicians:** (?) **Backing Vocals:** (?)
Recorded: RCA Studio B, Nashville, January 26, 1971
Technical Team: Producer: Bob Ferguson / Sound Engineer: Al Pachucki / Assistant Sound Engineer: Roy Shockley

This dark tale is one of Dolly Parton's songs about a struggle, an ongoing battle to stem the pernicious and often deadly effects of poverty. This time, the violence comes from the father, a drinker and moonshine smuggler, whose attitude and activities lead to the deaths of the narrator's two brothers. The narrator leaves the country for the city, from where she sends money to her mother, money earned in a way that is better left unsaid.

We find on this piece the same formation as on "J. J. Sneed," along with the electric guitar and a very complete set of drums. Indeed, the toms as well as the cymbals are very present. The stereo recording is clearly noticeable: The drums are on the left of the mix, but when the cymbals are played, you can hear them precisely on both sides. This recording is achieved with the microphones positioned overhead, above the drums, and each directed toward one or more cymbals, depending on the drums to be recorded.

The musicians enjoy themselves, taking liberties with their respective playing. The bass knits when it can and holds its ground when it has to (for example, at 3:02). The drummer marks some pauses, and the electric guitar seems to be totally improvisatory. Only the rhythm guitar seems to keep to the rules. The vocal melody is simple, without many notes and with a rather fast pace. It is only in the chorus that Dolly Parton goes very high in her register, which adds emphasis to the lyrics. Contrary to her voice in "J. J. Sneed," this one is quite dry, with very little reverb.

Chicken Every Sunday

Charlie Craig, Betty Craig / 2:35

Vocals: Dolly Parton **Musicians:** (?) **Backing Vocals:** (?)
Recorded: RCA Studio B, Nashville, October 21, 1970
Technical Team: Producer: Bob Ferguson / Sound Engineer: Al Pachucki / Assistant Sound Engineer: Roy Shockley

Focusing on the dramatic effects of poverty, this song by Charlie and Betty Craig is less bleak than "Daddy's Moonshine Still." The young girl in the story has become infatuated with a boy from a wealthy background, who rejects her. Her mother comforts her by reminding her that while their home is modest, they enjoy the simple pleasures of family life.

In bluegrass style, the introduction resonates with ZZ Top's "Brown Sugar," a song contemporary with "Joshua" (1971). The rest is much more faithful to Dolly Parton's country music. As usual, there are many players in the same range: piano, guitars, choir, violin. A dobro with a high and fast phrasing has been invited. The instruments are paired—piano and dobro, fiddle and backing vocals—with the exception of the pedal steel, which, independently, responds to the vocals.

"Letter to Heaven," the darkest story on the album *Joshua*, tells the tragic story of a little girl who has lost her mother.

The Fire's Still Burning

Dorothy Jo Hope, Dolly Parton / 2:49

Vocals: Dolly Parton **Musicians:** (?) **Backing Vocals:** (?)
Recorded: RCA Studio B, Nashville, October 31, 1969
Technical Team: Producer: Bob Ferguson / Sound Engineer: Al
Pachucki / Assistant Sound Engineer: Roy Shockley

In this dramatic, typical country ballad, grief vies with hope. There is pain in "The Fire's Still Burning," as the narrator is alone every night, unable to forget her love, unable to give it up. She strives to do so, but her tears flow over this inner flame that continues to consume her.

Despite the quality of the musicians, the melodic line, the chord grid, and the arrangements are conventional. However, while seeming to want to remain in her comfort zone, she sings once again with a moving precision.

Letter To Heaven

Dolly Parton / 2:29

Lead and Backing Vocals: Dolly Parton **Musicians:** (?) **Recorded:**
RCA Studio B, Nashville, January 26, 1971 **Technical Team:** Producer:
Bob Ferguson / Sound Engineer: Al Pachucki / Assistant Sound Engineer:
Roy Shockley

This is probably the darkest and most poignant story on the album *Joshua*, tragic in the way that Dolly knows how to write (and sing) so well. It is the story of a little girl whose mother has died. She asks her grandfather for help because she wants to write a letter and send it to her in heaven. She wants to tell her mother that she misses her and that she prays to God she will soon be able to find her up there. On the way to mail her letter, the girl is hit by a car and dies. The mailman retrieves the letter and imagines the little girl happy, now in heaven at her mother's side.

The production of this song is interesting because it has only two instruments: a bass and a classical guitar. Dolly Parton provides the backing vocals herself. To do this, the singer overdubbed her voice (also known as "re-re," for "re-record"). To do this, she first recorded her voice with the instruments on tape. There was one track left, so by replaying the tape, she was able to record harmonized vocals on this last track. As on "J. J. Sneed," the reverb effect applied to the voice is clearly audible.

The power of the song lies in its restraint: a simple chord grid, a melody with few notes and which repeats itself, two instruments, and moving lyrics; we are far from the very rich orchestrations with violin, choirs, piano, three guitars…

Unlike "J. J. Sneed" and "Daddy's Moonshine Still," the accompanists stick to their written parts, leaving Dolly to tell this sad and beautiful story.

ON YOUR HEADPHONES

On the headphones, it is possible to hear Dolly Parton's voice at times as a "ghost" on the right. It was apparently captured by the guitar microphone. The musicians must have been a few meters away from each other, because one can perceive a slight time shift. This phenomenon, undoubtedly frequent, is completely masked when a large number of instruments are playing.

ALBUM

Coat of Many Colors

Coat of Many Colors . Traveling Man . My Blue Tears . If I Lose My Mind .
The Mystery of the Mystery . She Never Met a Man (She Didn't Like) .
Early Morning Breeze . The Way I See You .
Here I Am . A Better Place to Live

RELEASE DATE
United States: October 1, 1971
Reference: RCA Victor—LSP-4603
Best US Chart Ranking: 7

The dry cleaning receipt on which the song *Coat of Many Colors* was written, which Porter originally framed, is now on display at Dollywood.

The Album of a Life

In the preface to her autobiography, Dolly Parton states that her whole life has been a kind of patchwork.[1] *Coat of Many Colors* was her eighth solo album; critics and fans alike gave her a standing ovation. *Billboard*, *Cashbox*, and *Rolling Stone* magazines all agreed that Dolly Parton had outdone herself, exploring such diverse themes as death, betrayal, the brutality of love, and the inscrutable ways of God, in a mix of country, pop, and gospel, with even a hint of rock. This opus marks a decisive step in her career, and it would give her international recognition.

The Founding Narrative

Since *Dumb Blonde*, Dolly Parton had been making albums, duets, and singles; performing concerts; and writing. The songwriter says she wrote "Coat of Many Colors" on the back of a dry cleaning receipt for a Porter Wagoner Nudie outfit, in 1969, on their tour bus. Dolly would wait two years before recording this song, which has since become a classic and which would follow her all her life.

But why this delay? The story of "Coat of Many Colors" evokes the past, not far from Sevierville, at the time of the harshest poverty, of the first great joys of childhood, and of the cruelty inflicted by her classmates. Avie Lee Parton, Dolly's mother, was preparing a surprise for her daughter: she spent hours making a wonderful coat for her, a combination of several pieces of fabric of different colors, like Joseph's tunic in the Bible—in poverty, it takes love and imagination to give the best gift. Dolly was impatient, thinking only of the day when she would wear it to school. When the moment arrived, Dolly set off, proud and happy, illuminated by the colors of this coat that made her unique and so loved. On the way, she passed a boy, to whom she pointed out her new coat. With the nastiness of which

children are sometimes capable, he replied: "What? This pile of rags?" Dolly took it in her stride, told herself that he was just a boy, and went on her way. At school, the other kids made fun of her, bullied her, made her feel how despicable she was because she was poor, she who felt so rich dressed in this new coat. Humiliated, deeply wounded in her heart and in her soul, Dolly did not understand this violence that robbed her of one of her most beautiful childhood moments. The cloak of pride became one of shame and sorrow.

This was why Dolly Parton delayed recording this song so long. Now she was ready to sing it in public, which would not be without stirring up memories and emotions. "Coat of Many Colors" thus became the song around which Dolly articulated and built her whole world.

More Than a Song, a Philosophy of Life

Dolly Parton has often spoken about this poignant memory, which she had kept buried inside her for a long time before turning it into a composition. In her previous albums, while the songwriter wrote, recorded, and sang dark songs, the sadness expressed was not necessarily her own. Undoubtedly, even if one is an artist whose fame, in 1971, heralds a future as a superstar, it still takes courage to face one's own pain. In numerous interviews, Dolly has spoken of the impossibility of letting go of the feeling of pain linked to this episode in her life, of the difficulty in performing onstage when one is overwhelmed with emotion. And even more so when her mother was ill, and after her death, singing "Coat of Many Colors" became a difficult thing to do. An experience like this builds character, guides life choices, and develops empathy and compassion.

Dolly and actress Tori Smith dressed in the famous Coat of Many Colors at the Dollywood Theatre, Pigeon Forge, Tennessee, in 2017.

The Artistic Pinnacle

Beyond the story told by the title track, this album is, in its entirety, pure Dolly Parton. Some tracks seem explicitly to reflect the issues and dramas that are troubling or challenging American society: the Vietnam War, the sexual revolution of women, the clash between tradition and modernity. With ten songs, including three written by Porter Wagoner, *Coat of Many Colors* wears its colors proudly. In 2007, John Metzger said on the internet radio program *The Music Box* that the album remains the artistic pinnacle of Dolly Parton's career because it was brave, bold, and emotionally pure. To this day, the superstar's millions of fans remain convinced of this fact.

Time for Sharing

As a philanthropist and seasoned businesswoman, Dolly Parton has made *Coat of Many Colors* an anchor for supporting children who feel devalued, abused, and bullied, turning the song into a book, a film, events, and meetings. We understand Dolly better when she confesses that writing is her therapy: When the experience becomes a work of art that is transmitted between generations, the life story of its author has been transcended.

Album Cover

In this painted portrait, photographed by Les Leverett, Dolly's childlike face, clad in a coat of many colors, expresses both playfulness through her frank smile and bright eyes, and emotion in her misty eyes and the tears rolling down her cheeks.

SIDE A

Coat Of Many Colors

Dolly Parton / 3:05

Vocals: Dolly Parton **Musicians:** Buddy Spicher, Mack Magaha, Johnny Gimble: fiddle / David Briggs, Hargus "Pig" Robbins: piano / Pete Drake: pedal steel / Jerry Carrigan: drums / Bobby Dyson: bass / Bill Sanford, Jerry Shook, George McCormick, Dave Kirby: guitar / Jerry Stembridge: electric guitar / Buck Trent: electric banjo **Backing Vocals:** The Nashville Edition **Recorded:** RCA Studio B, Nashville, April 1971 **Technical Team:** Producer: Bob Ferguson / Sound Engineer: Al Pachucki / Assistant Sound Engineer: Roy Shockley **Single:** Side A: Coat of Many Colors / Side B: Here I Am **Release:** RCA Victor—September 1971 (45 rpm. ref.: 74-0538) **Best Chart Ranking:** Did Not Chart (USA); 15 on the RPM Country 50 (Canada)

Genesis and Lyrics

The song tells the story of the patchwork coat, the "coat of many colors," a testament to a mother's love for her daughter, Dolly, and a father's love for his son, Joseph, in the Bible, as Avie Lee teaches the little girl. Putting her heart into each stitch, assembling the disparate pieces of fabric, she creates, for luck and happiness, a unique, colorful garment in which, on the way to school, the child feels proud, happy, and even rich with all that love. But the mocking cruelty of the other children instantly destroys the beauty of the moment and the joy of Dolly, who is attached to the immense symbolic and maternal value of her coat. This song is a story of tragedy, but it is also an ode to the love between a mother and her daughter.

Production

To introduce this classic among classics, a sumptuous duet of acoustic guitars is provided by Dave Kirby and George McCormick, faithful companions of Dolly since her beginnings at RCA. One plays using a fingerpicking technique, and the other with flat-picking so that they sound like a single instrument, delicate and nuanced. They are soon joined by Bobby Dyson's bass, which picks up the theme of the acoustic guitars an octave lower, high on the neck of his Fender Precision, and Jerry Carrigan's brushes, which introduce the smooth rhythm. Dolly begins to sing "Back through the years / I go wonderin' once again," and we are already straight into the narrative, in the Appalachian cabin home where Avie Lee, rocking in her rocking chair, is sewing the coat out of a patchwork of multicolored rags. In the second verse, at 0:52, it is the turn of Hargus "Pig" Robbins on the pump organ to fill out the ensemble with some partly placed, partly arpeggiated chords in the high midrange of the instrument. The backing vocals on the chorus complete the picture of this timeless ritornello. One should note the remarkable work of Bobby Dyson, who highlights Dolly's voice and supports the whole song, alternating bass notes (between the fifth, third, and octave) and melodic turnarounds of a rare musicality. The clarity of the mix and the presence of the instruments immediately make the listener aware that they are entering a new era of music production. The first signs of it were perceptible on *Blue Ridge Mountain Boy*, but now, here it is: Dolly soars in other spheres, and nothing can stop her.

A Taylor G5 guitar, in the shades of the "Coat of Many Colors," preserved at the Country Music Hall of Fame and Museum, Nashville.

Traveling Man

Dolly Parton / 2:40

Vocals: Dolly Parton **Musicians:** Buddy Spicher, Mack Magaha, Johnny Gimble: fiddle / David Briggs, Hargus "Pig" Robbins: piano / Pete Drake: pedal steel / Jerry Carrigan: drums / Bobby Dyson: bass / Bill Sanford, Jerry Shook, George McCormick, Dave Kirby: guitar / Jerry Stembridge: electric guitar / Buck Trent: electric banjo **Backing Vocals:** The Nashville Edition **Recorded:** RCA Studio B, Nashville, April 16, 1971 **Technical Team:** Producer: Bob Ferguson / Sound Engineer: Al Pachucki / Assistant Sound Engineer: Roy Shockley

In this number, Dolly tackles a thorny subject. A young woman meets a salesman who sells his wares from door to door. Certain that her mother would object to this relationship, she begins to tell lies in order to meet her lover in secret. But he also becomes her mother's lover and runs away with her, leaving the narrator, already abandoned by her father. A mother-daughter relationship in total contrast with that shown in *Coat of Many Colors*!

As for the music, we go full throttle on an up-tempo 4/4 that takes us, once again, on the winding roads of country funk. Bobby Dyson again impresses, performing numerous drums setups, with a fantastic vivacity, an unbridled melodic game often starting high on the neck, with syncopations galore…Bob Ferguson and Dolly are unerring in their judgement: Sensing Bobby Dyson at the top of his art, they decide to leave him alone with Jerry Carrigan to support Dolly's voice on a whole verse. This bass-drums passage is very effective and provides a great boost to the song before the last chorus. It should be noted that the drums are mixed on the left, except for some interventions from the bass drum (probably recorded alone in overdub), remaining in the center, with a lot of low register to inflate the sound—and thus mark the pulse on the choruses and on some setups with the bass. Jerry Stembridge also does a splendid job on the electric guitar, all in chicken-picking technique, syncopations, and dazzling country licks.

SINGLE

My Blue Tears

Dolly Parton / 2:16

Vocals: Dolly Parton **Musicians:** Buddy Spicher, Mack Magaha, Johnny Gimble: fiddle / David Briggs, Hargus "Pig" Robbins: piano / Pete Drake: pedal steel / Jerry Carrigan: drums / Bobby Dyson: bass / Bill Sanford, Jerry Shook, George McCormick, Dave Kirby: guitar / Jerry Stembridge: electric guitar / Buck Trent: electric banjo **Backing Vocals:** The Nashville Edition **Recorded:** RCA Studio B, Nashville, April 1971 **Technical Team:** Producer: Bob Ferguson / Sound Engineer: Al Pachucki / Assistant Sound Engineer: Roy Shockley **Single:** Side A: My Blue Tears / Side B: The Mystery of the Mystery **Release:** RCA Victor, June 1971 (45 rpm ref.: 47-9999) **Best Chart Ranking:** 17 on the Billboard Hot Country Songs (USA); 4 on the RPM Country 50 (Canada)

This is a beautiful and poignant love song, as Dolly Parton knows so well how to write and sing them. The blue of the bird at the window, of the sky, of all that is alive, is also the color of the tears of the woman abandoned by her lover. So, may this singing bird, the shining sun, and the other beauties of the world leave her to her sorrow while she mourns her lost love…The association between nature and feelings is not new to the songwriter, who, as a true daughter of rural Tennessee, has extensively observed this nature, and also human nature. Originally, this song was to be covered by Dolly Parton, Emmylou Harris, and Linda Ronstadt, but it was finally incorporated into the album *Little Sparrow*, released in 2001. What could be better than "blue tears" for a bluegrass album!

Back to the roots with this up-tempo country song with a mountain music feel. The high notes swirl all around; on the right, George McCormick's and Dave Kirby's guitars really go to town, while on the left Buck Trent's electric banjo merges with Hargus "Pig" Robbins's harpsichord, and the backing vocals and fiddle wrap it all up. Dolly doubles her own voice in overdub, moving from thirds to unison, and Bobby Dyson's bass—definitely in great shape on this album—wanders, free as a bird. The hoedown is in full swing!

If I Lose My Mind

Porter Wagoner / 2:29

Vocals: Dolly Parton **Musicians:** Buddy Spicher, Mack Magaha, Johnny Gimble: fiddle / David Briggs, Hargus "Pig" Robbins: piano / Pete Drake: pedal steel / Jerry Carrigan: drums / Bobby Dyson: bass / Bill Sanford, Jerry Shook, George McCormick, Dave Kirby: guitar / Jerry Stembridge: electric guitar / Buck Trent: electric banjo **Backing Vocals:** The Nashville Edition **Recorded:** RCA Studio B, Nashville, April 1971 **Technical Team:** Producer: Bob Ferguson / Sound Engineer: Al Pachucki / Assistant Sound Engineer: Roy Shockley

This song was written by a man (Porter Wagoner) in the early 1970s, when free love and Woodstock-esque orgies were in vogue. The lyrics do not raise any moral issues in themselves, but rather the difficulty a woman faces when confronted with a male desire that is not her own. At the heart of this delicate subject, the love relationship (obviously), vulnerability, incomprehension, resistance to pressure (male, in this case), freedom, and the influence of society. The narrator of this story takes refuge in her mother's house, where she will find a sympathetic ear, comfort, and, above all, a true love.

To illustrate this sad story musically, Dolly chooses the classic country shuffle midtempo. All the ingredients are there: on the right, the fiddle, the backing vocals, and the electric guitar, played essentially in tic-tac mode, but with a few turnarounds in the bass and natural arpeggiated harmonics; on the left: the drums, the acoustic guitar, strumming, and the pedal steel; in the center: the bass and, of course, Dolly's voice, juggling between an in-your-face singing style and powerful and perfectly controlled flights of fancy. Masterful.

The Mystery Of The Mystery

Porter Wagoner / 2:28

Vocals: Dolly Parton **Musicians:** Buddy Spicher, Mack Magaha, Johnny Gimble: fiddle / David Briggs, Hargus "Pig" Robbins: piano / Pete Drake: pedal steel / Jerry Carrigan: drums / Bobby Dyson: bass / Bill Sanford, Jerry Shook, George McCormick, Dave Kirby: guitar / Jerry Stembridge: electric guitar / Buck Trent: electric banjo **Backing Vocals:** The Nashville Edition **Recorded:** RCA Studio B, Nashville, April 1971 **Technical Team:** Producer: Bob Ferguson / Sound Engineer: Al Pachucki / Assistant Sound Engineer: Roy M. Shockley **Single:** Side A: My Blue Tears / Side B: The Mystery of the Mystery **Release:** RCA Victor, June 1971 (45 rpm ref.: 47-9999) **Best Chart Ranking:** 17 on the *Billboard* Hot Country Songs (USA); 4 on the RPM Country 50 (Canada)

This other song written by Porter Wagoner is a radical departure from "If I Lose My Mind." It evokes the great questions of humanity: What is life? Where does it begin, and what comes after it? How can it be explained? For Dolly, the explanation of the "mystery of the mystery," that some people try to elucidate, is known only to God.

This metaphysical reflection, imbued with religious faith, Eastern wisdom, and hillbilly common sense, is set to music in a particularly slow-tempo country shuffle ballad. The pedal steel has rarely sounded so close to its Hawaiian origins, the Hammond organ wanders from left to right, sitting in the high notes, the electric guitar gives its most beautiful tremolo on a few loose chords, while the fiddle, immersed in the reverb, answers Dolly's voice while alternating with the backing vocals. During this time, the rhythm section (acoustic guitar, bass, drums) unwinds quietly. This piece, however classic in its form, is a curiosity: Indeed, country songs rarely address the great existential questions. We can thank Porter Wagoner for having departed from the rule by writing "The Mystery of the Mystery," and Dolly, for having known how to interpret it with serenity and conviction.

She Never Met A Man (She Didn't Like)

Dolly Parton / 2:41

Vocals: Dolly Parton **Musicians:** Buddy Spicher, Mack Magaha, Johnny Gimble: fiddle / David Briggs, Hargus "Pig" Robbins: piano / Pete Drake: pedal steel / Jerry Carrigan: drums / Bobby Dyson: bass / Bill Sanford, Jerry Shook, George McCormick, Dave Kirby: guitar / Jerry Stembridge: electric guitar / Buck Trent: electric banjo **Backing Vocals:** The Nashville Edition **Recorded:** RCA Studio B, Nashville, October 30, 1969 **Technical Team:** Producer: Bob Ferguson / Sound Engineer: Al Pachucki / Assistant Sound Engineer: Roy Shockley

This title seems to presage "Jolene," as if, over time, the songwriter was refining, chiseling, exploring, transforming, becoming an alchemist of words and emotions. This may seem repetitive, even obsessive, but it is not. For exploring even a part of one's imagination, or a part of reality, can take a lifetime.

After "The Mystery of the Mystery," we move on to a new country shuffle ballad. But no existential questions in this case; we go back to the basics with this "other woman" song of classic construction. From 1:23, the piano makes its entrance; the precise and articulate playing of David Briggs embellishes the harmony, first in response to Dolly's voice, then in support of the orchestra, which begins a build from 1:55 to reach its climax at 2:20. In this song—perhaps the only song on the album—the piano and fiddle are front and center; the drums, usually on the left in the stereo field, are mixed here in the center.

Early Morning Breeze

Dolly Parton / 2:54

Vocals: Dolly Parton **Musicians:** Buddy Spicher, Mack Magaha, Johnny Gimble: fiddle / David Briggs, Hargus "Pig" Robbins: piano / Pete Drake: pedal steel / Jerry Carrigan: drums / Bobby Dyson: bass / Bill Sanford, Jerry Shook, George McCormick, Dave Kirby: guitar / Jerry Stembridge: electric guitar / Buck Trent: electric banjo **Backing Vocals:** The Nashville Edition **Recorded:** RCA Studio B, Nashville, January 26, 1971 **Technical Team:** Producer: Bob Ferguson / Sound Engineer: Al Pachucki / Assistant Sound Engineer: Roy Shockley

Dolly later covers this song, an ode to the beauty of nature that gives strength to welcome a new day, in the albums *Jolene* and *Blue Smoke*.

Dare we say it, Bobby Dyson is the star musician of this album. His double-note slider intro is simply fantastic. This is 1971 in the RCA studios. Dyson's lively, melodic playing dialogues beautifully with Dolly's voice, bringing a surprising groove to this kind of song, which otherwise might have sounded typically country folk. By relying on bass-drums setups, the music moves forward as though breaking free. In the verses, the drums keep the tempo with only the hi-hat and provide multiple breaks on very matt-sounding toms (probably covered with a cloth to cut the resonance). The rhythm decides to impose itself only on the choruses and the finale ad lib in fade-out. A fingerpicking guitar on nylon strings acts as the main thread from the beginning to the end of the song. The guitarist's playing, probably by Dave Kirby, is clearly inspired by Dolly Parton's, a straightforward and fast picking perfectly suited to the lightness of the theme; we feel very much "in the early morning breeze." "Early Morning Breeze" is reminiscent of the standard "Early Morning Rain," a classic by Canadian songwriter Gordon Lightfoot, released in 1966 and later covered by many artists, including Elvis Presley.

"Early Morning Breeze" recalls "Early Morning Rain," a classic by Canadian songwriter Gordon Lightfoot (1966), which Elvis Presley would cover.

The Way I See You

Porter Wagoner / 2:46

Vocals: Dolly Parton **Musicians:** Buddy Spicher, Mack Magaha, Johnny Gimble: fiddle / David Briggs, Hargus "Pig" Robbins: piano / Pete Drake: pedal steel / Jerry Carrigan: drums / Bobby Dyson: bass / Bill Sanford, Jerry Shook, George McCormick, Dave Kirby: guitar / Jerry Stembridge: electric guitar / Buck Trent: electric banjo **Backing Vocals:** The Nashville Edition **Recorded:** RCA Studio B, Nashville, April 1971 **Technical Team:** Producer: Bob Ferguson / Sound Engineer: Al Pachucki / Assistant Sound Engineer: Roy Shockley

This is Porter Wagoner's third song on this album, and it is about love, the intimacy between lovers, the way we look at each other.

She and Porter have written and performed dozens of love songs—Dolly's preference—and maybe even hundreds. But there is no sense of the routine, because here Dolly, Bob Ferguson, Al Pachucki, and the musicians outdo themselves. This piano intro, a rotating arpeggio that is very modern in its form and sound, augmented by a delay, creates a romantic depth that was still rare in 1971, but that would frequently be encountered from the mid-1970s onward. The haunting melody of the second parts of the verses, when Dolly goes into the high notes, evokes the Kodachrome films of the late '70s with their bright, saturated colors. "The Way I See You" is a big step away from the traditional Nashville sound and country music. Here Dolly Parton makes her entry into pop, and in the most beautiful way: as a visionary. The musicianship in this adventure is also admirable, the A-Team of Studio B contributing largely to create this new sound, in the same way as the Funk Brothers created the Motown sound.

SINGLE

Here I Am
Dolly Parton / 2:19

Vocals: Dolly Parton **Musicians:** Buddy Spicher, Mack Magaha, Johnny Gimble: fiddle / David Briggs, Hargus "Pig" Robbins: piano / Pete Drake: pedal steel / Jerry Carrigan: drums / Bobby Dyson: bass / Bill Sanford, Jerry Shook, George McCormick, Dave Kirby: guitar / Jerry Stembridge: electric guitar / Buck Trent: electric banjo **Backing Vocals:** The Nashville Edition **Recorded:** RCA Studio B, Nashville, April 1971 **Technical Team:** Producer: Bob Ferguson / Sound Engineer: Al Pachucki / Assistant Sound Engineer: Roy Shockley **Single:** Side A: Coat of Many Colors / Side B: Here I Am **Release:** RCA Victor, September 1971 (45 rpm ref.: 74-0538) **Best Chart Ranking:** Did Not Chart (USA); 15 on the RPM Country 50 (Canada)

This is the song of optimism, of hope. Here, no one suffers (except from too much love), no one dies, no one abandons anyone. On the contrary, the narrator reaches out, opens her heart, calls out: She is there, ready to offer the love she feels the need to share.

After three piano chords, the number starts very strongly, from the beginning, on a chorus: "Here I am," sings Dolly with all the soul we know she is capable of—one remembers in particular the very great "Fresh Out of Forgiveness," on the album *In the Good Old Days (When Times Were Bad)*, where the singer already deployed her arsenal of vibes on a country blues close to the gospel. Here, the soul inspiration is more direct, but the A-Team's playing is closer to the swing that was so particular to the Band.

Impossible not to mention once again the playing of the bassist Bobby Dyson, around which the orchestration seems to be built. The Nashville Edition, for this occasion, transforms into a gospel choir, evoking the powerful backing vocals of Aretha Franklin, no less! The bridges between soul, rock, folk, country, and blues music have always existed.

From 0:42, to expand the second cycle of the first verse, the fiddles of Buddy Spicher, Mack Magaha, and Johnny Gimble create a convincing orchestral effect, contributing their share of solemnity. The beat really kicks in at 1:00 on the second chorus and keeps the pulse going all the way through; by the climax of the last chorus, the gospel trance is not far away.

The swing of the musicians of "Here I Am" is close to that of the Band (in concert in San Francisco, 1976).

A Better Place To Live
Dolly Parton / 2:39

Vocals: Dolly Parton **Musicians:** Buddy Spicher, Mack Magaha, Johnny Gimble: fiddle / David Briggs, Hargus "Pig" Robbins: piano / Pete Drake: pedal steel / Jerry Carrigan: drums / Bobby Dyson: bass / Bill Sanford, Jerry Shook, George McCormick, Dave Kirby: guitar / Jerry Stembridge: electric guitar / Buck Trent: electric banjo **Backing Vocals:** The Nashville Edition **Recorded:** RCA Studio B, Nashville, October 30, 1969 **Technical Team:** Producer: Bob Ferguson / Sound Engineer: Al Pachucki / Assistant Sound Engineer: Roy Shockley

The Band is a Canadian rock, folk, and Americana band, active since the early 1960s, which had long accompanied Ronnie Hawkins, then Bob Dylan. The Band had its heyday with its own albums between 1968 and 1976. Their farewell concert was the subject of *The Last Waltz*, filmed by Martin Scorsese, and it included many prestigious guests, such as Neil Young, Bob Dylan, Eric Clapton, Joni Mitchell, Van Morrison, and Muddy Waters.

In 1971, in the middle of the Vietnam War, reconciliation was still not on Richard Nixon's agenda. This song is a prayer for peace.

Dolly Parton was familiar with gospel singing in her grandfather's church; however, on this sing-along track, praise moves away from the black American gospel influences of "Here I Am" to an up-tempo country tune in 4/4 time. It rolls, it flows; Dolly and her session men are experienced in this kind of thing. On the choruses and instrumental bridges, there is a marked change in rhythmic pulse, whose shifts are reminiscent of the famous Bo Diddley Beat (a rhythmic figure invented by Bo Diddley and popularized by his 1955 song "Bo Diddley"), as a way of calling out to the listener and inviting him to pray with Dolly: "We could make the world we're livin' in a better place to live [...] / Everybody take your brother's hand and sing my song with me."

The Murder Ballads Criminal Laments

Spreading from Scandinavia to Scotland or Ireland, passing through France, before reaching America with the arrival of the first European migrants, the narrative song relates crimes and other sordid events, such as public executions, in order to disseminate information and to impress the minds of people. These are also cases of justice that must be told—robberies and criminal acts, stories of gibbets and hanged men, infanticides, and murders of women.

Two themes became dominant in the twentieth century: ballads that recounted murderous acts committed by men against anyone in general, and those that describe the murder of women.

The Origins of This Singular Genre

Originally transmitted by the troubadours, the criminal lament, or narrative song, describing tragic and criminal events, has crossed the centuries and all of Europe. One of the most repeated and emblematic laments of the genre is "The Maid Freed from the Gallows." It changes title and continent—it is found in America in the nineteenth century—but it still tells the same story, with some variations: that of a girl (or a young man) who must be hanged and tries to be freed by paying the executioner (or judge). In the twentieth century, it metamorphosed into a folk song, "The Gallis Pole," sung by the bluesman Lead Belly, then it was taken up, under the title "Gallows Pole," by the group Led Zeppelin.

In 1924, musician Eva Davis, accompanied by her friend and colleague Samantha Bumgarner, travelled to New York to record, on the banjo, the murder ballad "John Hardy"—a railroad worker and craps player, Hardy was sentenced to death and hanged for killing a man under the influence of alcohol. Then, in 1928, with Maybelle Carter on guitar, the famous Carter Family released the cover "John Hardy Was a Desperate Little Man."

Some outlaw songs had their origins in the Civil War, such as "The Ballad of Casey Jones." Another variation of the genre are the stories of famous serial killers.

The Murder Ballads, Crimes Against Women

Between the nineteenth and early twentieth centuries, American ballads mainly evoke abject murders, mostly committed against women. Moreover, it is not uncommon for the victims to be pregnant, and for the murderers to dispose of them by drowning, stabbing, or some other extreme means. In other cases, when women refuse a man's sexual advances, the reaction is swift: they lose their lives. A good example is the song "Pearl Bryan," which tells the tragic story of a woman who was killed by her lover—the woman was a pregnant twenty-two-year-old who was found decapitated in Fort Thomas, Kentucky, in 1896.

In the mid-1930s, the Coon Creek Girls, a girl group, recorded "Pretty Polly," a bloody ballad from the eighteenth century. A relatively mundane affair, but one that pushed the aspect of premeditation to an extreme: Before their marriage, Polly was stabbed by her man, who had planned for this and already dug her grave—the song's punchline marks Polly's bloody grave. This ballad was included in an episode of the TV series *House of Cards* in 2013. Singer Idy Harper and the Coon Creek Girls have also covered "Omie Wise," a nineteenth-century ballad, retitled "Poor Naomi Wise." The story of Omie, or Naomi, is very similar to that of Pearl Bryan: The pregnant Omie is drowned by her man, who had promised her a new—and beautiful—life. By going back in time to the murderous ballads, we can measure the violence that women were already subjected to, even when pregnant. And one can only be stunned by the capacity of some men to settle matrimonial, social, and sexual issues by resorting to murder...

The 1950s, or Winding Back the Crank Handle

In 1948, Herb Leventhal and Hank Fort wrote "I Didn't Know the Gun Was Loaded," a song covered by Patsy Montana. In this ballad, Miss Effie regularly shoots men, until one day she shoots the sheriff; during the trial, she gives her usual excuse—she did not know the gun was

loaded. She walks free but is killed by the sheriff's wife. It is easy to imagine Miss Effie as a femme fatale—in every sense of the word! From the early 1950s onward, according to Karen Hogg, women artists began to reclaim the murder ballads, writing and recording original music and empowering their heroines. This creative process echoes feminist advocacy. One of the most famous murder ballads, written at the end of the twentieth century, is "Goodbye Earl," by the Chicks: Wanda marries Earl, who almost beats her to death; her childhood friend, Mary Ann, joins her in the hospital, where they decide to finish Earl off. The video is rather jubilant, but the song was controversial and was rejected by about twenty out of 149 country radio stations.

The Art of the Ballad by Dolly Parton

With her first albums, recorded at the end of the 1960s, Dolly Parton immersed the listener in the daily life of women, as few had done before her, and testified to the mistreatment they suffered. During this period, in the United States and in Europe, tensions were high between tradition and modernity, and women were demanding their sexual, marital, and reproductive freedoms.

During her career, Dolly Parton covered several traditional ballads, such as "Banks of the Ohio" (on the album *Blue Smoke*), the terrible story of a man in love who kills the woman of his heart because she will never be his. When Dolly recorded "The Bridge," which was and still is a huge success, she broke with tradition by reversing the point of view in the narrative, just as one changes the camera angle. It is no longer a news item that is reported, but the protagonist of the story who tells it: In love but left by the man who made her pregnant, she returns to the bridge where they met and separated, where everything began and where everything must end...

Dolly Parton reinvents the genre of the murder ballad. From now on, the voices of women are heard; from now on, the way is open for them to escape their role as victims. Dolly Parton chronicles and artistically interprets her times. We see how this ancient tradition of the ballad evolves over the centuries according to the social relationships and violence in societies. Like a lighthouse whose beam flashes in the night and shows us the pitfalls to avoid, murder ballads hold a special place in our culture. Filled with sadness and melancholy, these ballads relate often-terrible events in society, and we, the listeners, find them so beautiful.

ALBUM

Touch Your Woman

Will He Be Waiting? . The Greatest Days of All . Touch Your Woman . A Lot of You Left in Me .
Second Best . A Little at a Time . Love Is Only as Strong (As Your Weakest Moment) .
Love Isn't Free . Mission Chapel Memories . Loneliness Found Me

RELEASE DATE
United States: March 6, 1972
Reference: RCA Victor—LSP-4686
Best US Chart Ranking: 19

On Fifth Avenue in New York City, the National Organization for Women march for women's rights, August 26, 1970.

And God Created Women

Dolly Parton's ninth solo album, *Touch Your Woman*, produced by Bob Ferguson and released on RCA Victor, received rave reviews. Mostly written by Dolly, the songs deal with love relationships from different angles and are all about women. At twenty-six years old, she was not afraid to present an artificial image, with heavy makeup, a voluminous wig, and flashy clothes. She was not afraid to claim her freedom and her ultrafemininity in a world ruled by men, namely that of the record industry. The progressiveness of the sexiest of the country singers upset the censors, and the title song was rejected by several radio stations because of its eroticism.

The Awakening of Eros

Between the end of the 1950s and the beginning of the 1970s, the social climate in the United States was far from serene. In France, which was still recovering from the most recent world war, skirts were getting shorter and men's hair was getting longer. On both sides of the Atlantic, censorship stood in the way of the desire for freedom. Nineteen fifty-three saw the publication of the first issue of *Playboy*, a men's magazine that featured beautiful, naked women, the first of whom was Marilyn Monroe. In 1956, Roger Vadim released his classic film, *Et Dieu…créa la femme (And God Created Woman)*, that starred another scandalizing blonde, Brigitte Bardot. In 1959, Grove Press published *Lady Chatterley's Lover* by D. H. Lawrence and saw the copies confiscated by the U.S. Post Office. A year later, in Great Britain, Penguin Books was sued for the same reasons, with the argument supporting the complaint: "Is it a book that you would even wish your wife or your servants to read?" The legal actions to censor it failed, and the novel

became the huge bestseller that we know. In Nashville, Elvis Presley swayed lasciviously, his fans screamed with uninhibited pleasure, and not everyone liked it. In London, the stylist Mary Quant revolutionized fashion by inventing the miniskirt, thereby attracting the wrath of mothers, who refused to allow their daughters to wear "that thing." The sexual revolution was underway; women came out of their reserve.

Dolly Parton wrote[1] that her great passions were God, music, and sex. It is not a big leap to suggest that all three have a common denominator: the celebration of life. Music is indispensable in that it allows one to experience a whole range of emotions and feelings; sex is also indispensable; and the relationship with God provides a feeling of exaltation that thrills the soul and the body. These elements make up a trilogy: Dolly sings of love and the unfathomable mysteries of God and Creation. With *Touch Your Woman*, Dolly dedicates her new opus to desire, through lyrics that are sometimes erotic, or at least clearly express the specific desires of women—something for men to take note of.

On the Institution of Marriage

In this America in full social crisis, where Flower Power erects its Peace and Love as a flag of freedom, one may like women to be beautiful, but one has less of an appreciation for their demands and even less for questioning institutions such as marriage. In the early 1960s, in France, it was Niki de Saint Phalle who set the tone, shocking the public with her sculpture *La Mariée (The Bride)*, far from any romanticism or the usual perception of this status.

As she had begun to do in 1967, with *Hello, I'm Dolly*, the star is looking at the destiny of wives, the relationship

Left: In the late 1960s, a lot of girls moved to the cities to find a better life, only to end up working as prostitutes.

Right: In a rather conservative country setting, Dolly embraced her glamorous outfit and wig.

with marriage and adultery, and the freedom to love. Dolly Parton's songs evoke waiting, loneliness, the wear and tear on feelings, men who leave and do not return, men who stay but no longer hear that little inner music capable of making them want to break through the walls of silence, boredom, and remoteness.

There is a kind of bridge, a continuity between *Just Because I'm a Woman* and *Touch Your Woman*, through which Dolly Parton explores different facets of women—knowing that, from the artist's point of view, a whole life might not be enough. With songs like "My Blue Ridge Mountain Boy," "Just Because I'm a Woman," or "But You Loved Me Then," talking about love enables Dolly to chronicle American society while dissecting the consequences of the feeling of love. For once married and having become mothers, once passion and desire wither, what is left for the women of the 1960s and 1970s?

Femininity and Feminism— Are They "Country"?

At the beginning of the seventies, there was no doubt that with Dolly the world of country music was haloed by femininity and a wind of freedom for women, with which the traditionalists were perhaps not very comfortable. It is not surprising that feminists have applauded the star, even though she does not in any way claim to be one of them. But the words that carry her work, like the moods that color it, resonate in unison with the aspirations of modernity. At the time *Touch Your Woman* was released, young girls who were pregnant out of wedlock or unmarried were still faced with certain societal expectations. At that time, none of Dolly's songs addressed abortion—a

subject that had already been debated in conjunction with contraception; these girls had no other solution but to commit suicide—as in "The Bridge"—or to abandon their child at birth, so that it could be adopted by others—as in "Down from Dover." Beyond the questions of the feminine and feminism, which challenge Western society as a whole, Dolly's songs support women who are in pain. In a way, these women are no longer alone, because someone—Dolly Parton, in this case—is talking about them, and talking to them. This may seem like a small thing, but it is actually a big thing.

The City Sidewalks

In her lyrics, Dolly often talks about what the city sometimes does with its sidewalks and the women who walk them. Several songs tell the story of the girl who came to the city to find a better life and ended up as a prostitute. In *Touch Your Woman*, the songwriter tackles another social reality, all the more acute in the late 1960s, when a large number of young girls had left their families and homes behind to go to the cities and replace the men who had gone to war in Vietnam.

Album Cover

Glamorous in a deep blue velvet dress, long and full like a voluptuous wave, Dolly is nonchalantly installed in a sea of cushions in seventies colors, between Flower Power and orientalism, which seems to be inviting some kind of erotic dalliance. As the country scene was rather conservative at the beginning of the decade, the choice of this photo, by Les Leverett, was not without significance.

The Byrds spearheaded the California folk–country rock movement in the early 1970s.

enters only at the beginning of the return of the acoustic guitars on the second cycle of the second verse, to support the rhythm and enrich the harmony. It only stops to let one of the two guitars play the final chords on the last phrase of the chorus. "Will he be waiting for me?" sings Dolly on a falling tempo. The question remains an open one.

Will He Be Waiting?

Dolly Parton / 2:31

Vocals: Dolly Parton **Musicians:** (?) **Recorded:** RCA Studio B, Nashville, December 14, 1971 **Technical Team:** Producer: Bob Ferguson / Sound Engineers: Al Pachucki, Tom Pick / Assistant Sound Engineers: Roy Shockley, Mike Shockley

This song echoes "My Blue Ridge Mountain Boy" by again exploring the theme of the woman who leaves, and leaves her love, and then misses him. As the narrator walks home, the songwriter combines the beauty and expressiveness of nature—the shade of the trees, the wind, the scent of laurel—with the narrator's feelings—the shadow cast over her heart…Will her love still be waiting for her?

To develop her story, Dolly opts for an up-tempo 4/4 in D major with particularly pared-down arrangements. Two acoustic guitars, one on the right, the other in the middle, are strummed in the upper part of the neck, probably with a capo at the fifth fret, in an *A* major position (at least on one of the two guitars). The higher the capo, the brighter the sound, which allows for a jangly, energetic sound. The cross stick drums share left field with the piano, and the bass is in the center. The musicians were not credited on this album, but the bass line, fast, melodic, and agile, is very much like Bobby Dyson's playing. The whole arrangement is articulated around this bass and the fast vibrato of Dolly's voice, always powerful, understated, and precise. As is often the case, the Queen of Country doubles her voice in the upper third on the choruses and on the first cycle of the second verse. On this occasion, the jangly guitars are silent, leaving the bass–high hat duet in charge of the main part of Dolly's voice harmonized in overdub. The piano

The Greatest Days Of All

Dolly Parton / 2:41

Vocals: Dolly Parton **Musicians:** (?) **Recorded:** RCA Studio B, Nashville, December 14, 1971 **Technical Team:** Producer: Bob Ferguson / Sound Engineers: Al Pachucki, Tom Pick / Assistant Sound Engineers: Roy Shockley, Mike Shockley

This number has elements of "In the Good Old Days (When Times Were Bad)": the contrast of times, the days of yesteryear compared to today, and the opposition between town and country; the cities, asphalted, deafening, and congested, do not give the blades of grass the slightest chance to grow, and no bird—a recurrent creature in Dolly Parton's songs—comes to sing among the flowers. In the old days in the country, there were, of course, good and bad days, happy and sad days, but these were the best of all.

Another 4/4 with a very fast tempo for this ecological song ahead of its time. After the first measures of strummed guitars, the drummer graces us with an infinite descent of toms—the effect is almost comical—and the bass joins the happy trio on the last measures of this explosive intro. Dolly's voice, very prominent on this track, is surrounded by the two acoustic guitars, which strum to their hearts' content, each on its side of the stereo field. The bass, in the center, is always precise and swirling. The drums are very specialized: The snare and the hi-hat stand out more on the left, the bass drum and the cymbals on the right. This is close to modern mixing techniques, but with a certain exaggeration in the distribution of the elements. At that time, sound engineers were still experimenting, even in mainstream music, which was still very diverse. Still no fiddle, or electric guitar, or pedal steel on the horizon…Even the piano, which contributed on "Will He Be Waiting?" is absent from the arrangement. The complementarity of the respective play of the acoustic guitars, the bass, and the drums is enough to fill the spectrum of this very straightforward and energetic piece.

1972

SINGLE

Touch Your Woman

Dolly Parton / 2:43

Vocals: Dolly Parton **Backing Vocals:** (?) **Musicians:** (?) **Recorded:** RCA Studio B, Nashville, December 14, 1971 **Technical Team:** Producer: Bob Ferguson / Sound Engineers: Al Pachucki, Tom Pick / Assistant Sound Engineers: Roy Shockley, Mike Shockley **Single:** Side A: Touch Your Woman / Side B: Mission Chapel Memories **Release:** RCA Victor, February 14, 1972 (45 rpm ref.: 74-0662) **Best Chart Ranking:** 6 on the Billboard Hot Country Songs (USA); 28 on the RPM Country 50 (Canada)

In this evocation of the relationship of a couple, the message is clear: no longevity in love if the man stops touching his wife. The song reminds him that she needs him, needs to be understood, to be supported on a daily basis, and fulfilled in intimacy, with the one she loves, before falling asleep at his side in peace. No matter the quarrels and worries, an embrace and everything is forgotten. Perhaps this is in praise of monogamy, in these times of sexual turbulence in society, or perhaps it is simply the conviction that love can survive the wear and tear of daily life and the passage of time…It is for listeners to glean from this whatever they are looking for.

The slow pace of this ballad reflects the languor shown on the cover of the record. And this ode to heterosexual female pleasure begins with the delicate sound of a classical guitar arpeggio and some folk guitar chords gently played. From the second cycle of the first verse, the piano mirrors the classical guitar—an octave above it on the arpeggiated parts and often an octave below it on the rhythm parts. This duet—piano on the left, classical guitar on the right—lays the foundations of this ballad in 4/4. It also marks the great return of backing vocals and pedal steel, which perfectly underline the purpose of this sub versive song in spite of itself. The melodic meanders of the pedal steel evoke the caresses and lasciviousness, while the backing vocals, between power and restraint, seem to follow the path of the ecstasy. On the coda of the last chorus, after a generous musical climax at 2:20, one can feel that this ecstasy has been reached, or, failing that, a certain appeasement: "Everything's all right," sings Dolly at the end of each chorus…Has the man understood the message?

A Lot Of You Left In Me

Porter Wagoner, Dolly Parton / 2:31

Vocals: Dolly Parton **Musicians:** (?) **Recorded:** RCA Studio B, Nashville, January 1, 1972 **Technical Team:** Producer: Bob Ferguson / Sound Engineers: Al Pachucki, Tom Pick / Assistant Sound Engineers: Roy Shockley, Mike Shockley

This is the story of a woman abandoned by her love, whom she laments because there is so much of him left in her…A lot of memories, imprints of him on (or in) her body, and it is a suffering. For this archetypal "sad ass song," Dolly did not hesitate: a good old country shuffle with a honky-tonk sauce, or nothing! Everybody is relaxed in Studio B, and the orchestra is complete; one senses a freshness and the pleasure of playing. It is likely that this is a first take for Dolly and her A-Team.

Second Best

Dolly Parton / 2:57

Vocals: Dolly Parton **Musicians:** (?) **Recorded:** RCA Studio B, Nashville, January 12, 1972 **Technical Team:** Producer: Bob Ferguson / Sound Engineers: Al Pachucki, Tom Pick / Assistant Sound Engineers: Roy Shockley, Mike Shockley

What happens when you love a man who still loves his ex? How do you make someone forget the past, if at all possible? With a feeling of helplessness, the narrator describes herself as the eternal second woman in the life of the loved one.

This song could have been performed by Elvis Presley in his Hawaiian period. The intro, especially, but also the rhythm on the chorus sound like a curiosity in Dolly's repertoire. The backing vocals in close harmony, the play of the pedal steel surfing on its authentic Hawaiian origins, the acoustic guitar played at the top of the neck in jerky back-and-forth strokes as if to imitate the sound of the ukulele, the drums in cross stick on a reggae pattern before its time, and the bass spiked in a Caribbean way. The stage is set. One can easily visualize the scene: a groomed handsome man basking in the arms of some wahine in the middle of a pasteboard beach, and Dolly imploring the ingrate, her body swaying gently to the sound of her ukulele.

"A Lot of You Left in Me" could almost be an allusion to the honky-tonk world, from which the singer detaches herself a little more with each album, especially since the end of her collaboration with Porter Wagoner.

A Little At A Time

Dolly Parton / 2:14

Vocals: Dolly Parton **Musicians:** (?) **Recorded:** RCA Studio B, Nashville, January 1, 1972 **Technical Team:** Producer: Bob Ferguson / Sound Engineers: Al Pachucki, Tom Pick / Assistant Sound Engineers: Roy Shockley, Mike Shockley

A little at a time…With gravity but not without humor, Dolly Parton describes in this song the insatiable desire to have more and the dangers of consumerism, especially for the working class, who are offered so many things they cannot afford. This song also evokes the financial solution that a marriage can offer to a modest woman. While waiting to find a rich man, the narrator of the story lives on credit, paying for her life…little by little.

Back to the slapstick saloon skit on this up-tempo 4/4 that goes full steam ahead on the Tennessee River. This is the kind of song where Dolly can let her trashy alter ego and her already legendary hillbilly swagger speak freely. The only solos come from the electric guitar, which slams its best chicken-picking here in a few well-judged salvos. All the musicians contribute to intensify the rhythm; even the pedal steel sticks to it, and also provides us with some melodic counterpoints on the last chorus.

Love Is Only As Strong (As Your Weakest Moment)

Bill Owens / 2:05

Vocals: Dolly Parton **Musicians:** (?) **Recorded:** RCA Studio B, Nashville, January 12, 1972 **Technical Team:** Producer: Bob Ferguson / Sound Engineers: Al Pachucki, Tom Pick / Assistant Sound Engineers: Roy Shockley, Mike Shockley

On a slow country shuffle, Dolly Parton describes the paradox that lies in the strength and vulnerability of each of us when dealing with our loved one. The assertion contained in the title and choruses could be translated as "The strength of love is only measured by our greatest moment of weakness." A whole program in this piece by Bill Owens, Dolly's uncle, whose melody and arrangements recall the slows of the early 1960s, but transformed into early '70s Nashville.

We enter directly into the heart of the subject with a chorus, and we are immediately challenged by the extremely melodic play of the bass, which enriches the harmony of the piece by not consistently playing the fundamental on the first beats of each measure. The chromatic rise of the chorus, between the first chord and the third, is a good example of the rich and inventive playing of the person we can reasonably suspect as being Bobby Dyson. Indeed, all the harmonic instruments play an A major, followed by an F sharp major, followed by a B minor; but to achieve its ingenious chromaticism, the bass starts from the A, passes through the B flat—that is, the major third of the F sharp— to arrive on the B. The harmonic depression thus created gives all its color to the chorus. We will regularly find this type of device in future pop music, but at that time, and within the framework of a country ballad, it was quite audacious.

On this electronic instrument, invented in 1920 by the Russian Lev Sergeyevich Termen, known as Leon Theremin, the right hand controls the pitch of the note by varying its distance from the vertical antenna, while the horizontal antenna, shaped like a loop, is used to vary the volume according to its distance from the left hand. This particularity, which makes it possible to produce music without the instrument being touched by the player, and this vibrating sound, whose glissando is often reminiscent of the human voice, along with the ondes Martenot, made this instrument one of the emblematic sounds of science fiction. Today it remains associated with a certain notion of retrofuturism.

Love Isn't Free

Joe Babcock / 2:34

Vocals: Dolly Parton **Musicians:** (?) **Recorded:** RCA Studio B, Nashville, October 30, 1969 **Technical Team:** Producer: Bob Ferguson / Sound Engineers: Al Pachucki, Tom Pick / Assistant Sound Engineers: Roy Shockley, Mike Shockley

Through this recurrent theme in Dolly Parton's work—the abandoned pregnant girl—we feel the weight of the patriarchal, moralistic, hypocritical archetype, which condemns girls in love with fickle, inconsequential men, too young, engaged elsewhere, or unable to accept responsibility… Why do women pay so high a price for their desire and their love?

As an intro to this mid-tempo 4/4, we hear two acoustic guitars, one playing the rhythm on the left, the other providing a few melodic turnarounds in the bass on the right. In the background in the center, a mysterious layer, probably played on a harmonium or a pump organ, creates a link between the instruments. While the verses are driven by the drummer's sixteenth-note brush playing, the tempo on the chorus seems to both split and accelerate as the brushes go to eighth note while maintaining a very present quarter-note hi-hat (played with the foot). The result is a very pop-sounding chorus, whose melody is reminiscent of the West Coast atmosphere of the Box Tops' 1967 hit "The Letter," and of the 1966 Herman's Hermits megahit "No Milk Today." Dolly's vocal control seems to take a new step forward on this recording; the multiple nuances of interpretation (fortepiano, note holding, modulations, vibrato) seem to be effortless for her.

Mission Chapel Memories

Porter Wagoner, Dolly Parton / 3:09

Vocals: Dolly Parton **Musicians:** (?) **Recorded:** RCA Studio B, Nashville, January 1, 1972 **Technical Team:** Producer: Bob Ferguson / Sound Engineers: Al Pachucki, Tom Pick / Assistant Sound Engineers: Roy Shockley, Mike Shockley **Single:** Side A: Touch Your Woman / Side B: Mission Chapel Memories **Release:** RCA Victor, February 14, 1972 (45 rpm ref.: 74-0662) **Best Chart Ranking:** 6 on the Billboard Hot Country Songs (USA); 28 on the RPM Country 50 (Canada)

It is not clear whether the man the narrator loved has left, or even died. In any case, all that remains are the memories of their wedding—the rice thrown, her veil and dress, the sound of the bells…in this now-deserted and silent chapel. To evoke these memories, the choice of a country ballad in 4/4 time seems to be a natural one. In the purest Nashville tradition, the musicians touch their instruments lightly, in total control of their sound. The slightest rise in intensity of the orchestra creates a real relief, in symbiosis with Dolly's voice, and enables the emphasis to be placed on certain phrases, certain memories. The backing vocals coupled with the pedal steel phrases are, like the choir in Greek tragedy, protagonists in their own right. Their contributions correspond to the emotional climaxes, like so many peaks of nostalgia contained in this homage to the rural marriage ceremony, simple and authentic.

Once married and a mother, and once passion and desire wither, what is left for the women of the 1960s and 1970s?

Loneliness Found Me

Porter Wagoner / 1:56

Vocals: Dolly Parton **Musicians:** (?) **Recorded:** RCA Studio B, Nashville, December 14, 1971 **Technical Team:** Producer: Bob Ferguson / Sound Engineers: Al Pachucki, Tom Pick / Assistant Sound Engineers: Roy Shockley, Mike Shockley

When one toys with a commitment, like a marriage, in the end one ends up alone with one's solitude. To illustrate this bitter observation, the song begins with Dolly's voice, alone on the first word—a stretched out "Loneliness"—then joined by an expressive acoustic guitar whose turnarounds in the bass remain the cornerstone of the song. The guitar is the first and last witness to this loneliness, which the narrator feels she has earned, and punctuates the last phrase, sung a cappella, with "Loneliness found me," over a gracefully played chord. Meanwhile, on the left, the drums with brushes and the acoustic guitar in gentle strumming, largely supported by the walking bass alone in the center, play the discreet secondary roles, restrained and elegant.

ALBUM

Dolly Parton Sings "My Favorite Songwriter, Porter Wagoner"

Lonely Comin' Down . Do You Hear the Robins Sing . What Ain't to Be, Just Might Happen .
The Bird That Never Flew . Comes and Goes . Washday Blues . When I Sing for Him .
He Left Me Love . Oh, He's Everywhere . Still on Your Mind

RELEASE DATE
United States: October 2, 1972
Reference: RCA Victor—LSP-4572
Best US Chart Ranking: 33

The concern on Porter Wagoner's face seems to be an indication of Dolly's impending departure.

Dolly Bows Out

Dolly Parton Sings "My Favorite Songwriter, Porter Wagoner" is Dolly Parton's tenth solo album, and the first without any of her own songs, all of which were written by Porter Wagoner. Produced by Bob Ferguson, it was released by RCA Victor on October 2, 1972. *Billboard* magazine said that with this moving album, Dolly Parton was the hottest country singer in the business. *Cashbox* was also enthusiastic, praising both Dolly's beauty and her voice, and recognizing that the combination of Dolly's singing and Porter's writing was brilliant.

This album marks a shift in the musical approach of the songs, which are closer to rock and pop, in vogue at that time. It peaked at number 33 on the Billboard charts, and "Washday Blues," one of the two singles from it, peaked at number twenty on the charts.

Homage to the Master

In the album liner notes, Dolly Parton states and reaffirms that her favorite author is Porter Wagoner. This, in retrospect, seems unconvincing. Before *Coat of Many Colors* (1971), which contained two songs written by him, and after *Love Is Like a Butterfly* (1974), no Porter Wagoner song appears on Dolly's solo albums.

The star was about to break her commitments to her mentor and his show. This tribute appears to be an elegant way to leave and to indicate that the debt had been paid. In the introduction to chapter 5 of Alanna Nash's Dolly biography,[3] one can read this quotation from Dolly Parton: "We were good for each other in a lot of ways and just a disaster for each other in a lot of ways. I'll always love him, in my own way. You have to follow your own dreams."

The album *The Best of Porter Wagoner & Dolly Parton* heralded the end of a specific period, that of the duo. "My Favorite Songwriter, Porter Wagoner" confirms that an era is over, and the critics were not wrong.

One Step Forward, One Step Backward

In 1972, there was the woman who had never disguised the fact, even from her husband, Carl Dean, that her career and her passion for music came before anything else. There was the artist who was finishing an apprenticeship of sorts and wanted to stand on her own two feet. There was the friend who could not stand the conflicts with Porter. In her autobiography,[1] the star describes her difficulty leaving the show, and thus also Porter, who refused in an almost pathological way to let her go.

Aside from this now untenable relationship, the songwriter was busy working: on the release of *Touch Your Woman*, on tours, on *The Porter Wagoner Show*, on studio recordings of singles and albums, and especially on writing. With this album, Dolly Parton honors the songwriter that Porter Wagoner had become again, the years spent by her side, the one who believed in her. They formed an exceptional duo, in which each one respected the other. The storm that came to overshadow the end of their association did not erase anything from the achievements and the feelings of the singer. The disciple was overtaking the master. Notwithstanding Porter's uncompromising attitude, which she had to deal with, it took a lot of courage for her to leave what nourished her, but also to leave a friend, a brother in music. It takes strength not to bend under authoritarianism, machismo, and selfishness, and to pursue, with her head held high, her own path. In these difficult times, did Dolly think about the pioneers who feminized country music? Did she draw energy from the fortunes of Patsy Montana, Rose Maddox, Kitty Wells, Loretta Lynn, or Patsy Cline? History tells us only that Dolly Parton was grateful to them for opening the doors behind which her own superstar destiny awaited.

Album Cover

Compared to the luminous and warm portraits of the previous album sleeves, these portraits, also created by Les Leverett, seem dark. Porter Wagoner's face, in the background, hovers like a shadow around Dolly Parton's. In a black outfit, illuminated by a white butterfly on a necklace, Dolly shows a less radiant smile than usual, with perhaps even a veil of sadness in the eyes...

Lonely Comin' Down

Porter Wagoner / 3:10

Vocals: Dolly Parton **Musicians:** Jerry Carrigan: drums / Hargus "Pig" Robbins, Jerry Carrigan: piano / Hargus "Pig" Robbins: organ / Buck Trent, Bobby Thompson: banjo / Bobby Dyson, Dave Kirby: electric guitar / Bobby Dyson: bass / Jerry Stembridge, Chip Young: flat top guitar / Billy Sanford, Bobby Thompson: rhythm guitar / Mack Magaha, Johnny Gimble: fiddle / Pete Drake: pedal steel **Backing Vocals:** The Nashville Edition **Recorded:** RCA Studio B, Nashville, May 3, 1972 **Technical Team:** Producer: Bob Ferguson / Sound Engineer: Al Pachucki, Tom Pick / Assistant Sound Engineer: Roy Shockley

This very country ballad recounts the narrator's solitude once his beloved woman has disappeared. A first glance toward the pillow still crumpled by the head of the one who left; a second toward the mirror in which the other is not reflected anymore, in spite of her presence hovering everywhere, and the loneliness that comes and descends on the narrator like a cloud of sadness. Dolly takes up this title in her album *Jolene* (1974).

The percussionist uses all his drums and cymbals. This is one of the first times that the hi-hat is used open (in this case in the intro). The two folk guitars play arpeggios and alternate the lines that a bass would otherwise play, as the bass has not yet come in. During the intro, one of the guitars plays harmonics. The bass waits until 1:45 to introduce high notes with the piano and launch the whole orchestra. Thus begins a pop rhythm the like of which we are not used to hearing from Dolly Parton. The play of the drums is very complete and departs from the country style, in a rather minimalist way.

Do You Hear The Robins Sing

Porter Wagoner / 2:27

Vocals: Dolly Parton **Musicians:** Jerry Carrigan: drums / Hargus "Pig" Robbins, Jerry Carrigan: piano / Hargus "Pig" Robbins: organ / Buck Trent, Bobby Thompson: banjo / Bobby Dyson, Dave Kirby: electric guitar / Bobby Dyson: bass / Jerry Stembridge, Chip Young: flat top guitar / Billy Sanford, Bobby Thompson: rhythm guitar / Mack Magaha, Johnny Gimble: fiddle / Pete Drake: pedal steel **Backing Vocals:** The Nashville Edition **Recorded:** RCA Studio B, Nashville, May 4, 1972 **Technical Team:** Producer: Bob Ferguson / Sound Engineer: Al Pachucki, Tom Pick / Assistant Sound Engineer: Roy Shockley

This ode to nature celebrates life in its simplicity, from the outset contrasting it with the city, which is beautiful, but where robins do not sing. In keeping with the subject matter, this piece is in the folk style, reflecting the hippie movement. The chord grid evokes "Where Have All the Flowers Gone," sung by Peter, Paul and Mary ten years

earlier. One could almost hum "Blowin' in the Wind" or "Don't Think Twice, It's All Right," two Bob Dylan tracks released in 1963. In addition to the folk guitars, which are very present, the lap steel intervenes during the chorus to suggest the robin's song, with its high sliding notes. A guitar also plays the main theme, which can be found in several covers of the song under the same title, notably by Irish performers Sharon in 1976 and Big Tom in 1977.

What Ain't To Be, Just Might Happen

Porter Wagoner / 2:22

Vocals: Dolly Parton **Musicians:** Jerry Carrigan: drums / Hargus "Pig" Robbins, Jerry Carrigan: piano / Hargus "Pig" Robbins: organ / Buck Trent, Bobby Thompson: banjo / Bobby Dyson, Dave Kirby: electric guitar / Bobby Dyson: bass / Jerry Stembridge, Chip Young: flat top guitar / Billy Sanford, Bobby Thompson: rhythm guitar / Mack Magaha, Johnny Gimble: fiddle / Pete Drake: pedal steel **Backing Vocals:** The Nashville Edition **Recorded:** RCA Studio B, Nashville, June 19, 1972 **Technical Team:** Producer: Bob Ferguson / Sound Engineer: Al Pachucki, Tom Pick / Assistant Sound Engineer: Roy Shockley

This rather rhythmic song expresses an optimistic philosophy, inviting the listener to take things as they come—or do not come—to enjoy life, to live a little lighter, without forgetting to laugh. The intro is "Tarantino-esque," with the guitar line and the drums entering from the second bar. The continuation is more in the style of Dolly Parton, even though it belongs with the songs opening up toward other horizons such as rock or soul, with backing vocals sounding very Motown (as well as in "Washday Blues"). As for the arrangements, the verses are more refined than the choruses, with just the guitars, the bass—very prominent in the mix—and the drums. In the chorus, the lap steel and fiddle come in, but they play few notes, leaving the vocals and backing vocals to carry the song.

The Bird That Never Flew

Porter Wagoner / 3:13

Vocals: Dolly Parton **Musicians:** Jerry Carrigan: drums / Hargus "Pig" Robbins, Jerry Carrigan: piano / Hargus "Pig" Robbins: organ / Buck Trent, Bobby Thompson: banjo / Bobby Dyson, Dave Kirby: electric guitar / Bobby Dyson: bass / Jerry Stembridge, Chip Young: flat top guitar / Billy Sanford, Bobby Thompson: rhythm guitar / Mack Magaha, Johnny Gimble: fiddle / Pete Drake: pedal steel **Backing Vocals:** The Nashville Edition **Recorded:** RCA Studio B, Nashville, May 4, 1972 **Technical Team:** Producer: Bob Ferguson / Sound Engineer: Al Pachucki, Tom Pick / Assistant Sound Engineer: Roy Shockley

1972

"Do You Hear the Robins Sing" is in the folk style of Peter, Paul and Mary, photographed in 1962.

This piece, with its gospel feel, is a real curiosity. Dolly begins not in song but in recitation, in a clear and poignant voice, as though whispering in one's ear. The narrator finds a bird without wings, an allegory of her relationship with God. The recitation creates a real intimacy with the listener as the narrator evokes the great mysteries of the Creation. The gospel is underlined by the melody of the Hammond organ, and the lyrics sound like a gospel. Then folk and lap steel guitars replace the organ. The doves are associated with the arrival of violins, then with the backing vocals (unusually in the center of the mix). The organ accompanies the end of the story, with this bird with golden wings, which had never flown until then.

Comes And Goes

Porter Wagoner / 3:15

Vocals: Dolly Parton **Musicians:** Jerry Carrigan: drums / Hargus "Pig" Robbins, Jerry Carrigan: piano / Hargus "Pig" Robbins: organ / Buck Trent, Bobby Thompson: banjo / Bobby Dyson, Dave Kirby: electric guitar / Bobby Dyson: bass / Jerry Stembridge, Chip Young: flat top guitar / Billy Sanford, Bobby Thompson: rhythm guitar / Mack Magaha, Johnny Gimble: fiddle / Pete Drake: pedal steel **Backing Vocals:** The Nashville Edition **Recorded:** RCA Studio B, Nashville, May 2, 1972 **Technical Team:** Producer: Bob Ferguson / Sound Engineer: Al Pachucki, Tom Pick / Assistant Sound Engineer: Roy Shockley

We discover a classic rhythm in this song, a melancholic ballad with which Dolly Parton is perfectly at ease. It is a story of lost love, where memories come and go, sometimes crystal clear, sometimes volatile and elusive. Because time erases everything, even the face of the loved one.

In the album, the main part is taken up by folk guitars, perhaps because this is Porter Wagoner's favorite instrument. The drums are played very lightly, with brushes. The bass is very prominent and is not supported by the bass drum. During the ascents, a strange phenomenon occurs: We hear the vibrations of the brushes' bristles, which produce a shimmering metallic sound, as if the snare drum had been turned over and the drummer was directly striking the snare wires.

"Washday Blues" in Texas in the 1930s.

Washday Blues

Porter Wagoner / 2:04

Vocals: Dolly Parton **Musicians:** Jerry Carrigan: drums / Hargus "Pig" Robbins, Jerry Carrigan: piano / Hargus "Pig" Robbins: organ / Buck Trent, Bobby Thompson: banjo / Bobby Dyson, Dave Kirby: electric guitar / Bobby Dyson: bass / Jerry Stembridge, Chip Young: flat top guitar / Billy Sanford, Bobby Thompson: rhythm guitar / Mack Magaha, Johnny Gimble: fiddle / Pete Drake: pedal steel **Backing Vocals:** The Nashville Edition **Recorded:** RCA Studio B, Nashville, May 3, 1972 **Technical Team:** Producer: Bob Ferguson / Sound Engineer: Al Pachucki, Tom Pick / Assistant Sound Engineer: Roy Shockley **Single:** Side A: Washday Blues / Side B: Just as Good as Gone **Release:** RCA Victor, July 10, 1972 (45 rpm ref.: 74-0757) **Best US Chart Ranking:** 20

This song describes the torment of a woman who has to wash and scrub dirty clothes, hang out the washing, then wash and scrub again...all the while dreaming of a washing machine she cannot afford. Her man could give it to her, but he prefers to dress her like a queen. We sense that Dolly is having fun with this catchy music. Nodding toward the artist's audiovisual past, the narrator confesses that she would like to get a job on television—in a soap commercial, for example.

This song is unusual in many ways. The beginning would not be out of place in a Quentin Tarantino movie. The intro, with the bass line, the drums, and a folk guitar whose strummed strings are muffled by the left hand is reminiscent of the sound of the washboard, a percussive instrument accompanying traditional country music and also very present in Cajun music from Louisiana. It is therefore no coincidence that this sound can be found in the "laundry day blues." The chord grid is typical of the blues, the rhythm swings, the vocals are lively, the violin enriches the melodic parts, and the backing vocalists sing along happily, independent of the main vocal line. The beginning of the third verse breaks the routine of the song, a change that usually involves a key modulation. The rhythm is very funky, with drums, bass, and piano. The bass drum marks the strong beats of the measure, which are the first and third beats, with eighth notes. The snare drum is played on the second and fourth beats, and the hi-hat on sixteenth notes. The rhythm is very binary, on the beats, while the rest of the piece is syncopated, like the blues. This rhythm is used by many artists of all genres—disco, hip-hop, groove—from AC/DC, to Lauryn Hill, to Earth, Wind & Fire. It lasts only four bars, but the device proves very effective in relaunching the end of the song. The last verse is spoken, over the music of the chorus, and repeated until the fade-out.

With this dedication album, Dolly Parton honors the songwriter Porter Wagoner.

When I Sing For Him

Porter Wagoner / 2:58

Vocals: Dolly Parton **Musicians:** Jerry Carrigan: drums / Hargus "Pig" Robbins, Jerry Carrigan: piano / Hargus "Pig" Robbins: organ / Buck Trent, Bobby Thompson: banjo / Bobby Dyson, Dave Kirby: electric guitar / Bobby Dyson: bass / Jerry Stembridge, Chip Young: flat top guitar / Billy Sanford, Bobby Thompson: rhythm guitar / Mack Magaha, Johnny Gimble: fiddle / Pete Drake: pedal steel **Backing Vocals:** The Nashville Edition **Recorded:** RCA Studio B, Nashville, May 4, 1972 **Technical Team:** Producer: Bob Ferguson / Sound Engineer: Al Pachucki, Tom Pick / Assistant Sound Engineer: Roy Shockley **Single:** Side A: When I Sing for Him / Side B: Lord Hold My Hand **Release:** RCA Victor, September 4, 1972 (45 rpm ref.: 74-0797)
Best US Chart Ranking: Did Not Chart

A return to the gospel heritage with "When I Sing for Him," with perhaps a more personal tone, because even though she did not write these lyrics, Dolly sings about her relationship with God, about the emotion she feels when she senses that she is close to him.

As in the other tracks in this opus, the bass occupies a predominant place. It follows the melody of the song almost to the note. Moreover, on this album, this instrument has a much lower, warmer tone than on the previous ones. The music is celestial. The lap steel produces very high, discreet notes; the reverberation applied to the voice is very perceptible, but the reverberation time (decay) is quite short for a religious song—in general, the aim is to suggest the atmosphere of a church, or even a cathedral, with a longer decay.

Dolly's voice on this track has a great dynamic range (the difference between the lowest and the highest levels), and the reverb effect is very noticeable. When an effect is mixed, as is the usual practice, the signal is doubled. This way, one part of the song remains natural, and the other is influenced by the effect. Then, the balance between the two is measured. This enables the direct signal not to be drowned in the reverb if, for example, the singer sings less loudly (this can be heard very clearly at 40 seconds).

As on several other tracks on the album ("Lonely Comin' Down," "Comes and Goes," "Do You Hear the Robins Sing"), the string instruments play polyphonic melodies—whereas usually only one instrument (guitar, lap steel, violin, or other) played a theme in response to the vocals or in support. This is a new development in Dolly Parton's work. Another detail, which is not new but is more prevalent in this album: the alternation of verses and choruses is not consistent. The title of the song comes back regularly, but the rest of the song tells a story, with events, a beginning and an end. From the arrival of the backing vocals and the "Hallelujah!" this is the final bouquet, like the conclusion of a musical, with the last drum notes.

He Left Me Love

Porter Wagoner / 2:57

Vocals: Dolly Parton **Musicians:** Jerry Carrigan: drums / Hargus "Pig" Robbins, Jerry Carrigan: piano / Hargus "Pig" Robbins: organ / Buck Trent, Bobby Thompson: banjo / Bobby Dyson, Dave Kirby: electric guitar / Bobby Dyson: bass / Jerry Stembridge, Chip Young: flat top guitar / Billy Sanford, Bobby Thompson: rhythm guitar / Mack Magaha, Johnny Gimble: fiddle / Pete Drake: pedal steel **Backing Vocals:** The Nashville Edition **Recorded:** RCA Studio B, Nashville, May 2, 1972 **Technical Team:** Producer: Bob Ferguson / Sound Engineer: Al Pachucki, Tom Pick / Assistant Sound Engineer: Roy Shockley

Once again, country music is nostalgia and melancholy, with this song that describes how the narrator deals with the disappearance of her love…who has not truly disappeared, since he lives in her memories. And these are so strong, so sweet, so present, in addition to being eternal, that she has no reason to seek another love.

On this number, the drummer's playing is very pop sounding. Apparently he does not have a crash cymbal, since all the breaks finish on the ride cymbal or are simply played on the snare drum. After the breaks that end on the ride cymbal, one would expect it to replace the hi-hat, as is the usual practice, in order to maintain the effect of the rise of the playing due to the break; but in the end, this does not happen, so that one remains as if in suspense, and then falls back, whereas one would have liked to go to the end of the rise. The bass is always very present, but it has a strange sound, almost synthetic, as though it were produced on a keyboard. In any case, it is not alone, as there is a guitar playing the bass line two octaves above. The sound becomes more natural at the end of the piece. One can hear very clearly the sound of the plectrum playing on the rhythm guitars, especially on the guitar on the left in the mix.

Oh, He's Everywhere

Porter Wagoner / 3:01

Vocals: Dolly Parton **Musicians:** Jerry Carrigan: drums / Hargus "Pig" Robbins, Jerry Carrigan: piano / Hargus "Pig" Robbins: organ / Buck Trent, Bobby Thompson: banjo / Bobby Dyson, Dave Kirby: electric guitar / Bobby Dyson: bass / Jerry Stembridge, Chip Young: flat top guitar / Billy Sanford, Bobby Thompson: rhythm guitar / Mack Magaha, Johnny Gimble: fiddle / Pete Drake: pedal steel **Backing Vocals:** The Nashville Edition **Recorded:** RCA Studio B, Nashville, May 3, 1972 **Technical Team:** Producer: Bob Ferguson / Sound Engineer: Al Pachucki, Tom Pick / Assistant Sound Engineer: Roy Shockley

In the same vein as the previous song, a lost love haunts the narrator, who, even in the heart of darkness, sees the face of the loved one.

We note the development, on this album, of the beginnings of the song. Until this point, in the singer's work, it was almost routine for an instrument to begin alone before being joined by the orchestra. Starting with this album at least three or even four instruments simultaneously start in the intros. The first two verses are in the purest Dolly Parton style. The good old recipe of tonal modulation is used in the third verse; the accompaniment changes: The chords are replaced by arpeggios, enabling the banjo to be heard better—with a very dry attack on the notes.

Still On Your Mind

Porter Wagoner / 2:41

Vocals: Dolly Parton **Musicians:** Jerry Carrigan: drums / Hargus "Pig" Robbins, Jerry Carrigan: piano / Hargus "Pig" Robbins: organ / Buck Trent, Bobby Thompson: banjo / Bobby Dyson, Dave Kirby: electric guitar / Bobby Dyson: bass / Jerry Stembridge, Chip Young: flat top guitar / Billy Sanford, Bobby Thompson: rhythm guitar / Mack Magaha, Johnny Gimble: fiddle / Pete Drake: pedal steel **Backing Vocals:** The Nashville Edition **Recorded:** RCA Studio B, Nashville, January 12, 1972 **Technical Team:** Producer: Bob Ferguson / Sound Engineer: Al Pachucki, Tom Pick / Assistant Sound Engineer: Roy Shockley

"Still on Your Mind" is a moving gospel song that describes the despair of a woman in love with a man who still loves another woman—a one-sided love already evoked in "Second Best" (on the album *Touch Your Woman*).

The track starts with drums, bass, and keyboard. This simplicity of scoring enables the listener to fully appreciate Bobby Dyson's subtle playing. The organ provides the song with its gospel color, while the bass, drums, and electric guitar (which comes in on the second verse) have a very soul-like feel, in the spirit of Aretha Franklin's 1967 song "I Never Loved a Man the Way I Love You." No other instruments come in until the end of the song.

ALBUM

My Tennessee Mountain Home

The Letter . I Remember . Old Black Kettle . Daddy's Working Boots .
Dr. Robert F. Thomas . In the Good Old Days (When Times Were Bad) .
My Tennessee Mountain Home . The Wrong Direction Home . Back Home .
The Better Part of Life . Down on Music Row

RELEASE DATE
United States: April 2, 1973
Reference: RCA Victor—APL1-0033
Best US Chart Ranking: 15

An Album of Memories

My Tennessee Mountain Home, Dolly Parton's eleventh solo album, also produced by Bob Ferguson, was released in April 1973 by RCA. Its title is explicit: Dolly returns to the source of all things—her family, her Tennessee, and its landscapes. The importance of roots—those of the earth as well as those of the heart, the pivot and central axis of life—constitutes the main thread of this opus, which the songwriter wrote entirely herself, and which was praised by the critics. The question of identity has always been addressed in the star's interviews and writings. Here, she revisits her childhood with emotion and nostalgia, and makes it clear that she misses the simple things of her former life as she builds her career in Nashville.

Remembering Where You Come From

In 1973, like Dolly Parton, America was at a crossroads. The Watergate scandal shattered Richard Nixon's government, military conscription was over, and the repatriation of American military equipment marked the end of the ground war in Vietnam. It was also the year of the inauguration, in April, of the World Trade Center in New York. A homecoming for the GIs, a homecoming for Dolly in eleven songs.

Dolly is from Sevier County, Tennessee, which in the 1970s had a population of less than three thousand. At the beginning of the eighteenth century, Cherokee Indians populated this territory along the river. Then came the migrants, mostly from Ireland and Scotland, who began to found small communities in the heart of this wilderness that Dolly loved and sang about regularly. By the mid-eighteenth century, in this part of deepest America, living in fairly peaceful harmony with the Cherokees, migrants from the Old World were mainly engaged in the trade of animal furs, which they exchanged for manufactured goods. Sevier County—where Dolly Parton was born in 1946—was established in 1794. Her ancestors first migrated to Greenbrier, Virginia, around 1850, then settled in Locust Ridge, near Pittman Center, Tennessee.

The songwriter was used to writing lyrics about poverty, the condition of women, and working-class women. In *My Tennessee Mountain Home* she is more pastoral, gentle, or nostalgic, and she defines the issues of the album from the first track, "The Letter." She narrates and sings about her region, all the things that made her feel good when she was little Dolly Rebecca. She sings of her love for her loved ones, for the beauty of the world, God, and simple things, as in "Old Black Kettle."

The writing and release of *My Tennessee Mountain Home*, beyond the memories and a form of homesickness, were for Dolly Parton, at this precise moment of her life, a way of drawing strength and serenity from her roots. To find herself, in order to be whole, and no longer half of someone else as she had been during her professional partnership with Porter Wagoner, which had now lasted for six years. As the album was released, Dolly continued to struggle against Porter's relentless will. For this was no longer a banal contractual breakup for the duo; because of Porter's attitude, the conflict became almost filial, in the sense that he acted like a disappointed and irascible father who, having planned to shape his child's destiny, becomes enraged when his child decides to follow a different path.

1973

Appalachian trails, forests, and mountains as far as the eye can see. This is Dolly's land, the origin of country music.

A Milestone Year

In 1973, tired of not being able to be get Porter to listen to her, short of words and conversations, and probably emotionally exhausted, Dolly did what she knew how to do so well: She wrote the most beautiful love song, "I Will Always Love You," which was released by RCA Victor on April 6, 1974 (45 rpm ref.: APB0-0234). In her autobiography,[1] she recounts that upon hearing it, Porter, with tears in his eyes, made her swear that he would be the producer of what he perceived as a potential hit. He was not mistaken: This song would be a worldwide megahit. Dolly finally won the approval of her friend, mentor, and, frankly, tyrannical boss.

In terms of writing, 1973 was an important year for Dolly Parton, as she also wrote and recorded "Jolene"—which was released as a single by RCA Victor, with the B-side "Love, You're So Beautiful Tonight" (45 rpm ref.: APB0-0145). "Jolene" is one of Dolly Parton's most emblematic songs; not only was it a huge success, but the song and the album marked a turning point in her career in 1974.

For Dolly Addicts

Years later, Dolly used "My Tennessee Mountain Home" as the theme song for her theme park, Dollywood.

Album Cover

A nostalgic moment…on this cover is the cabin in which the Parton family lived when Dolly was a child. The focus is on the home, the subject of the album. In a wooded landscape under a clear sky, there is no one—only the house, surrounded by nature. This picture was taken by Louis Owens, one of Dolly's uncles. Inside the cover are family photos and two notes signed by the songwriter's parents. An album, in its presentation and content, that is 100 percent autobiographical.

The Letter

Dolly Parton / 2:03

Vocals: Dolly Parton **Musicians:** Charlie McCoy (or Jimmy Riddle): harmonica; Bobby Thompson, Dave Kirby, Jerry Stembridge: rhythm guitar **Backing Vocals:** The Nashville Edition **Recorded:** RCA Studio B, Nashville (TN), September 5, 1972 **Technical Team:** Producer: Bob Ferguson / Recording Engineer: Tom Pick / Sound Engineer: Al Pachucki / Assistant Sound Engineer: Roy Shockley

With "The Letter," the album opens with the reading of an original letter that Dolly sent to her parents when she had just moved to Nashville.[1] She tries to reassure her mother and father that she loves them and her siblings, that she is doing well—despite her homesickness—and that she has everything she needs and has even found a job. The beginnings in Music City were rough for the young woman; she did not always have enough to eat, and convincing the studios to be interested in her and her songs was not easy. But this is also the letter of confirmation: She came to Nashville with the goal of becoming a superstar and was determined to make her dreams come true. Little did Dolly Parton know at the time that in 2022 she would publish a novel and album with James Patterson that would tell the story of her determination to become a star. She also did not know that she would become an iconic artist.

It is Charlie McCoy (or possibly Jimmy Riddle; a doubt remains), alone on harmonica, who has the honor of accompanying Dolly's reading. This familiar tune sounds like a traditional Celtic vocal imported by early settlers in the seventeenth century, passed down during long summer evenings spent playing music with the family on the front porch of a southern Appalachian cabin.

I Remember

Dolly Parton / 3:42

Vocals: Dolly Parton **Musicians:** Jerry Carrigan: drums / Hargus "Pig" Robbins: piano / Charlie McCoy: harmonica / Buck Trent: electric banjo / Dolly Parton, Jimmy Colvard, Jimmy Capps, Dave Kirby, Chip Young, Bobby Thompson: guitar / Bobby Dyson: bass / Mack Magaha, Johnny Gimble: fiddle / Don Warden: dobro / Pete Drake: pedal steel / Mary Hoepfinger: harp **Backing Vocals:** The Nashville Edition **Recorded:** RCA Studio B, Nashville (TN), September 5, 1972 **Technical Team:** Producer: Bob Ferguson / Sound Engineer: Al Pachucki / Assistant Sound Engineer: Roy Shockley

"I Remember" takes the listener to golden wheat fields and meadows, to the sweetness of a mountain moment. It is a sentimental journey into childhood, recounting the discoveries of nature and music, the memories of daily life in the shadow of the Smokies. Dolly's parents instilled in their children a strong faith in God, a love of music, and the importance of certain values. In this remote area of East Tennessee—where nature flourishes, where communities gather around the church, around the vocals, around prayers—the poetry of Avie Lee, Dolly's mother, brings comfort to her children. From Nashville, Dolly remembers the childhood, the landscapes, and the family love around which she was built. At the age of twenty-eight, she calls upon her memory and descends each step of her recollections to return home.

After a very solemn opening on the pump organ, each musician plays their own arpeggio on this 4/4 mid-tempo song, well grounded in the country tradition. On the left, the nylon string guitar, whose finger-picking turn is very similar to Dolly's own playing (she is credited here for the first time as a guitarist on one of her albums); on the right, the finger-picking folk guitar (probably played by Dave Kirby), soon joined by Buck Trent's clawhammer banjo and Don Warden's dobro lines. At 2:00, on the second verse, one wonders if it is Mary Hoepfinger arpeggiating on her harp in the high range, or Hargus "Pig" Robbins who has settled in on the harpsichord to counterbalance the folk guitar. Either way, for instruments that are not meant for this kind of exercise or to produce this kind of sound, the imitation of the finger-picking of the guitars is perfect. The song ends with Dolly's voice, first alone with the organ, then joined by the backing vocals in a sumptuous arrangement by the Nashville Edition.

Old Black Kettle

Dolly Parton / 2:32

Vocals: Dolly Parton **Musicians:** Jerry Carrigan: drums / Hargus "Pig" Robbins: piano / Charlie McCoy: harmonica / Buck Trent: electric banjo / Dolly Parton, Jimmy Colvard, Jimmy Capps, Dave Kirby, Chip Young, Bobby Thompson: guitar / Bobby Dyson: bass / Mack Magaha, Johnny Gimble: fiddle / Don Warden: dobro / Pete Drake: pedal steel / Mary Hoepfinger: harp **Backing Vocals:** The Nashville Edition **Recorded:** RCA Studio B, Nashville (TN), September 5, 1972 **Technical Team:** Producer: Bob Ferguson / Sound Engineer: Al Pachucki / Assistant Sound Engineer: Roy Shockley

Genesis and Lyrics

Dolly remembers the simple, pleasant things in life, like the antique kettle that has been used so much on the old wood stove that it has turned black. A nostalgic song of a bygone childhood, which allows the listener to enter the Partons' house, to smell the coffee, the ginger cake, the scent of childhood and family love. But everything has changed with time: The slightly dilapidated stove and the old kettle no longer exist; they survive only through memories,

"Daddy's Working Boots" sounds like a daughter's anthem to her father. Here, fourteen-year-old Dolly is photographed at her school in Sevier, 1960.

Daddy's Working Boots

Dolly Parton / 2:52

Vocals: Dolly Parton **Musicians:** Jerry Carrigan: drums / Hargus "Pig" Robbins: piano / Charlie McCoy: harmonica / Buck Trent: electric banjo / Dolly Parton, Jimmy Colvard, Jimmy Capps, Dave Kirby, Chip Young, Bobby Thompson: guitar / Bobby Dyson: bass / Mack Magaha, Johnny Gimble: fiddle / Don Warden: dobro / Pete Drake: pedal steel / Mary Hoepfinger: harp **Backing Vocals:** The Nashville Edition **Recorded:** RCA Studio B, Nashville (TN), September 1, 1972 **Technical Team:** Producer: Bob Ferguson / Sound Engineer: Al Pachucki / Assistant Sound Engineer: Roy Shockley

This song sounds like a daughter's anthem to her father, proclaiming her gratitude to the man who raised her and made it possible for her to become who she is.

Don Warden, with his finger-picking dobro, sets the bucolic mood for this country ballad in 4/4 time. Supported by Jerry Carrigan's brushes and Bobby Dyson's minimalist bass, the woody yet metallic sound of the dobro allows the song to begin soberly, almost humbly, one might say, in the image of honest Tennessee farmers. After a few notes of harmonica, and eighteen bells later (the exact count!), the chorus comes in, fuller and more powerful, with backing vocals and folk guitar on the right and Buck Trent's banjo as a clawhammer on the left. The courage and dignity of manual laborers is celebrated through the image of their hands, calloused and sore but sturdy, and the image of their work boots, worn but tough and solid, like the fundamentals of their lives. Then comes an elegant bass turnaround that leads to the inevitable modulation of the second verse. After that, the song goes its own way, until the reappearance of the bells, after the second chorus, on an instrumental verse grid to evoke the pickaxes and hammers of American working-class heroes.

because objects are not eternal. As one can see, Dolly is tired of the complications of her new life.

Production

Charlie McCoy's harmonica starts the ball rolling on this fast-paced country shuffle, quickly joined by the bass-and-drums duo (we immediately notice that the tom bass benefits from a surprisingly low and deep tuning) and by the strumming acoustic guitars, which complete the transition to the first verse. Four bars and three chords suffice to complete this well-crafted intro, which reappears with a few variations before the second verse at 1:07, and again at 2:13, before the last four bars of the false verse that serves as a conclusion: "Now, I just mean to say the simple things are gone / The old black kettle's gone."

To emphasize the choruses, the A Team at Studio B opts to go with a rhythmic pattern that is a complete break from the country shuffle of the verses. This unusual pattern gives the impression that the rhythm becomes binary and that the tempo is divided by two. To create contrast and spice things up a bit, Buck Trent's banjo does not enter until the second cycle of the second verse, Bobby Dyson plays a very melodic walking bass high on the neck, and Jerry Carrigan returns to the cross stick playing of the first verse. The resulting restrained playing helps to highlight the second and final chorus.

Dr. Robert F. Thomas

Dolly Parton / 2:36

Vocals: Dolly Parton **Musicians:** Jerry Carrigan: drums / Hargus "Pig" Robbins, Ron Oates: piano / Charlie McCoy: harmonica / Buck Trent: electric banjo / Dolly Parton, Jimmy Colvard, Jimmy Capps, Dave Kirby, Chip Young, Bobby Thompson: guitar / Bobby Dyson: bass / Mack Magaha, Johnny Gimble: fiddle / Don Warden: dobro / Pete Drake: pedal steel / Mary Hoepfinger: harp **Backing Vocals:** The Nashville Edition **Recorded:** RCA Studio B, Nashville (TN), October 2, 1972 **Technical Team:** Producer: Bob Ferguson / Sound Engineer: Al Pachucki / Assistant Sound Engineer: Roy Shockley

Through this recognition of the man who brought her into the world, Dolly Parton pays tribute to the birth, life, dedication, and bravery of the country doctor, who faces bad weather and difficult roads, day and night, to go, on horseback or even on foot, where he is needed. As far as the music is concerned, this is an up-tempo country shuffle without any major particularity. Most of the usual ingredients are there: strummed acoustic guitars, clawhammer banjo, melodic harmonica counterpoints, lightning-fast dobro lines, drums on brushes and cross stick, palm mute bass alternating tonic/third/fifth/octave, backing vocals and fiddles on the choruses, not to mention the modulation on the second verse. All that remains is for the narration and Dolly's impeccable vocals to be placed on top of this custom-made instrumentation, and the job is done. The good doctor Robert F. Thomas will not be forgotten.

In The Good Old Days (When Times Were Bad)

Dolly Parton / 3:25

Vocals: Dolly Parton **Musicians:** Jerry Carrigan: drums / Hargus "Pig" Robbins, Ron Oates: piano / Charlie McCoy: harmonica / Buck Trent: electric banjo / Dolly Parton, Jimmy Colvard, Jimmy Capps, Dave Kirby, Chip Young, Bobby Thompson: guitar / Bobby Dyson: bass / Mack Magaha, Johnny Gimble: fiddle / Don Warden: dobro / Pete Drake: pedal steel / Mary Hoepfinger: harp **Backing Vocals:** The Nashville Edition **Recorded:** RCA Studio B, Nashville (TN), October 2, 1972 **Technical Team:** Producer: Bob Ferguson / Sound Engineer: Al Pachucki / Assistant Sound Engineer: Roy Shockley

While the whole album unveils some rather pleasant memories, Dolly marks a break by rerecording this track,

present on the eponymous album of 1969. Here, no nostalgia for a past that no longer has anything sweet and comforting, because the songwriter says it outright: Nothing in the world would make her want to relive those old times, when life was so hard.

The tempo is slower than on the 1969 version; here, it is the option of a light and twirling country waltz that is chosen by Dolly and her musicians. Arpeggios of dobro, folk guitar, and banjo share the spotlight. Their incessant knitting, punctuated by inspired turnarounds, carries the instrumental part as much as the rhythm section. To lay a solid foundation, Bobby Dyson's bass is particularly strong in the mix, alone in the center with Carrigan's brushes and Dolly's voice, whose sensitive interpretation hits the spot once again. The backing vocals and the fiddle duo of Mack Magaha and Johnny Gimble, as usual, help the choruses to take off.

My Tennessee Mountain Home

Dolly Parton / 3:06

Vocals: Dolly Parton **Musicians:** Jerry Carrigan: drums / Hargus "Pig" Robbins, Ron Oates: piano / Charlie McCoy: harmonica / Buck Trent: electric banjo / Dolly Parton, Jimmy Colvard, Jimmy Capps, Dave Kirby, Chip Young, Bobby Thompson: guitar / Bobby Dyson: bass / Mack Magaha, Johnny Gimble: fiddle / Don Warden: dobro / Pete Drake: pedal steel / Mary Hoepfinger: harp **Backing Vocals:** Rickie Page, Joe Babcock, Dolores Edgin, Hurshel Wiginton **Recorded:** RCA Studio B, Nashville (TN), September 1, 1972 **Technical Team:** Producer: Bob Ferguson / Sound Engineer: Al Pachucki / Assistant Sound Engineer: Roy Shockley **Single:** Side A: My Tennessee Mountain Home / Side B: The Better Part of Life **Released:** RCA Victor, December 4, 1972 (45 rpm ref.: 74-0868) **Best Chart Ranking:** 15 on Billboard Hot Country Songs (US), 10 on RPM Country Tracks (Canada)

This song evokes a time that is no longer but which was good and whose memory is precious for the songwriter, who affirms and embraces her roots, despite the poverty in which her family lived.

To begin this mid-tempo country shuffle, Dolly's voice comes to rest on some folk guitar arpeggios, joined at 0:27 by another finger-picking folk guitar, but playing lower in the neck, then everyone arrives on the first instance of the chorus, at 0:42: the backing vocals with their depth, the banjo, the dobro, and the rhythm section. At 1:17, after a very short second verse, the second chorus comes in with a bang, with the bass drum accentuating each quarter note in a very marked way. The song ends in a fade-out; the melody of the chorus is taken up by the harmonica, then, after some humming by Dolly in counterpoint, by a distant whistling evoking perfectly the sweet wandering in the mountains of the Tennessee of her childhood.

The Wrong Direction Home

Dolly Parton / 2:25

Vocals: Dolly Parton **Musicians:** Jerry Carrigan: drums / Hargus "Pig" Robbins, Ron Oates: piano / Charlie McCoy: harmonica / Buck Trent: electric banjo / Dolly Parton, Jimmy Colvard, Jimmy Capps, Dave Kirby, Chip Young, Bobby Thompson: guitar / Bobby Dyson: bass / Mack Magaha, Johnny Gimble: fiddle / Don Warden: dobro / Pete Drake: pedal steel / Mary Hoepfinger: harp **Backing Vocals:** The Nashville Edition **Recorded:** RCA Studio B, Nashville (TN), September 1, 1972 **Technical Team:** Producer: Bob Ferguson / Sound Engineer: Al Pachucki / Assistant Sound Engineer: Roy Shockley

In this ode to the happiness of a home where love reigns, Dolly's childhood resurfaces as though cleansed of the harshness of former times. What remains is the beauty of nature and the sweetness of a countryside where life was hard but also simpler. The singer evokes her departure for Nashville, the hope for a future so much dreamed of and undoubtedly put to the test at a time when she had to fight to find her independence.

Back to 4/4 for this mid-tempo that moves "in the wrong direction," certainly, but that moves forward. Like most of the tracks on the album, "The Wrong Direction Home" relies a good deal on alternation between contained narrative verses and epic choruses generously supported by the backing vocals. One notices, once again, that Buck Trent's banjo does not appear until the second cycle of the second verse. It must be admitted that this strand of arrangement is effective in relaunching the machine of the song, whose structure, with two verses and one chorus twice repeated, might seem a little linear. The song stops on a climax carried by the backing vocals and by Dolly's voice.

Back Home

Dolly Parton / 2:41

Vocals: Dolly Parton **Musicians:** Jerry Carrigan: drums / Hargus "Pig" Robbins, Ron Oates: piano / Charlie McCoy: harmonica / Buck Trent: electric banjo / Dolly Parton, Jimmy Colvard, Jimmy Capps, Dave Kirby, Chip Young, Bobby Thompson: guitar / Bobby Dyson: bass / Mack Magaha, Johnny Gimble: fiddle / Don Warden: dobro / Pete Drake: pedal steel / Mary Hoepfinger: harp **Backing Vocals:** The Nashville Edition **Recorded:** RCA Studio B, Nashville (TN), October 3, 1972 **Technical Team:** Producer: Bob Ferguson / Sound Engineer: Al Pachucki / Assistant Sound Engineer: Roy Shockley

Continuing in the vein of the previous track, "Back Home" is a somewhat melancholic kind of reverie, in which Dolly evokes her return to her parents while knowing that she will continue on her way, in Nashville, toward her dream of glory.

This mid-tempo country shuffle kicks off with the Nashville Edition's powerful backing vocals, which Dolly's voice beautifully overlays. The "Mission Chapel Memories" of the album *Touch Your Woman*, released a year earlier, is not far away. Because it is indeed a prayer that Dolly addresses here to God—and to whoever wants to hear it. If only for a few moments, being back with her mother and her loved ones is a vital need. The arrangement is in the same spirit as the previous tracks, not surprising for an album centered on the evocation of the mountains of her native Tennessee and recorded in four days, between September 1 and October 3, 1972. This time, Buck Trent's banjo is present from the beginning, and Dolly chooses the option of the spoken voice on the whole second verse to emphasize the intimate, the confidence whispered in the ear: *Just like you, who live a more ordinary life, I sometimes need to go back home.* Surprisingly, the song ends in the same way as "The Wrong Direction Home," on a climax carried by the backing vocals and Dolly's voice on the word "home" at the end of the second chorus.

The Better Part Of Life

Dolly Parton / 3:12

Vocals: Dolly Parton **Musicians:** Jerry Carrigan: drums / Hargus "Pig" Robbins, Ron Oates: piano, organ / Charlie McCoy: harmonica / Buck Trent: electric banjo / Dolly Parton, Jimmy Colvard, Jimmy Capps, Dave Kirby, Chip Young, Bobby Thompson: guitar / Bobby Dyson: bass / Mack Magaha, Johnny Gimble: fiddle / Don Warden: dobro / Pete Drake: pedal steel / Mary Hoepfinger: harp **Backing Vocals:** Rickie Page, Joe Babcock, Dolores Edgin, Hurshel Wiginton **Recorded:** RCA Studio B, Nashville (TN), October 3, 1972 **Technical Team:** Producer: Bob Ferguson / Sound Engineer: Al Pachucki / Assistant Sound Engineer: Roy Shockley **Single:** Side A: My Tennessee Mountain Home / Side B: The Better Part of Life **Release:** RCA Victor, December 4, 1972 (45 rpm ref.: 74-0868) **Best Chart Ranking:** 15 on Billboard Hot Country Songs (US), 10 on RPM Country Tracks (Canada)

The insistence of the star on revisiting the past and evoking her childhood, real or imaginary, conveys the measure of her need to recharge her batteries at this period of her life.

Another mid-tempo country shuffle, rather pared down this time. The instruments politely allow themselves to speak on the different parts of the song. Hargus "Pig" Robbins is back in his organist's seat; we have not heard him play this instrument since "I Remember," the second track on the album. Dolly and her A Team create soft reliefs, contrasts in shades of gray. We are far from the alternation of contained verses/epic choruses that dominates the album. A good way to talk about the simple pleasures of life, the beautiful things that we left behind.

The Ryman Auditorium (on the right) was the home of the Grand Ole Opry in Nashville from 1943 to 1974.

Down On Music Row

Dolly Parton / 2:55

Vocals: Dolly Parton **Musicians:** Jerry Carrigan: drums / Hargus "Pig" Robbins, Ron Oates: piano, organ / Charlie McCoy: harmonica / Buck Trent: electric banjo / Dolly Parton, Jimmy Colvard, Jimmy Capps, Dave Kirby, Chip Young, Bobby Thompson: guitar / Bobby Dyson: bass / Mack Magaha, Johnny Gimble: fiddle / Don Warden: dobro / Pete Drake: pedal steel / Mary Hoepfinger: harp **Backing Vocals:** The Nashville Edition **Recorded:** RCA Studio B, Nashville (TN), September 5, 1972 **Technical Team:** Producer: Bob Ferguson / Sound Engineer: Al Pachucki / Assistant Sound Engineer: Roy Shockley

A change of scenery for this last track, an urban stroll down Music Row, where one has the impression of accompanying Dolly in her peregrinations at the beginning of her career: her arrival in Nashville, her awareness of the harsh reality of the environment, her meeting with RCA, and also her loneliness. Another return to the past, recent this time, while another future is taking shape for Dolly. Undoubtedly, the songwriter is making this souvenir album a focus on herself.

For this grand finale, everyone is invited to the party. Initially the first guests: the folk guitar and its impeccable finger-picking, followed by the rhythm section, then the harmonica, then the dobro, the banjo, the electric guitar in tic-tac and slide mode, and backing vocals…the only thing missing is the duo of fiddles and the organ, surprisingly absent from this commemoration of Dolly's first steps in the ruthless world of show business. After a modulation of a semitone, at the exit of the second verse, the intensity drops again to allow for a spoken voice passage before building even more strongly on the cheerful refrain of this hymn to determination. We notice in passing the fast and atypical placement of the bass drum, sometimes pushing the limits of unbalancing the rhythm. Yet this works, with the pulse of the chorus encouraging the listener to enter the dance "down on Music Row."

ALBUM

Bubbling Over

Bubbling Over . Traveling Man . Alabama Sundown . Afraid to Live and Afraid of Dying .
Love with Me . My Kind of Man . Sometimes an Old Memory Gets in My Eye .
Pleasant as May . The Beginning . Love, You're So Beautiful Tonight

RELEASE DATE
USA: October 14, 1973
Reference: RCA Victor—LSP-0286
Best US Chart Ranking: 14

End of an Era

Produced by Bob Ferguson, Dolly Parton's twelfth solo album, *Bubbling Over*, came out in September 1973 under the RCA label. After her return to her roots with the melancholy *My Tennessee Mountain Home*, Dolly's new album—altogether more cheerful and optimistic—is bursting with professional and emotional excitement combined with her joy in her newfound freedom. Well received by critics, it consists of ten songs, including six written by the singer-songwriter herself.

A Newfound Freedom

During the last year of her partnership with Porter Wagoner, Dolly brought out four albums: two singing solo (*My Tennessee Mountain Home* and *Bubbling Over*) and two duetting with Porter (*We Found It* and *Love and Music*). RCA Victor also brought out a compilation of Dolly's songs, *Mine*, and the single "Jolene," with "Love, You're So Beautiful Tonight" on the B-side.

Paradoxically, Porter wrote to RCA complaining that the record company did not seem, in his view, to take Dolly Parton seriously enough. Intense relationships like this one are strange in that the protagonists are a mass of contradictory feelings. Despite their differences, Porter was clearly prompted by his friendship and respect for Dolly. Despite his intransigence and refusal to consider his show partner's desire for freedom, he believed in her talent.

That same year, 1973, Stevie Wonder sang "You Are the Sunshine of My Life." Americans were beginning to emerge from a difficult period—the Vietnam War would soon be filed away as a bad memory—and William Friedkin's movie *The Exorcist* thrilled and terrified its audience.

Turbulent Emotions

Change was imminent and was officially confirmed in a press conference on February 19, 1974. Dolly was on the point of leaving Porter and *The Porter Wagoner Show*. It symbolized a split between two worlds of country music: that of Porter, older than Dolly not only in years but also musically in his attachment to traditional country music, and that of Dolly, who was part of the revival of this music and belonged to its future. As described in her autography,[1] this departure was rather more drawn out than expected. But, all things considered, those seven years dedicated to *The Porter Wagoner Show*, as intense as they were instructive and as creative as they were exhausting, allowed her to secure a solid start to her career. The credit was due not only to Porter but also to Dolly's talent and her incredible capacity for hard work. Her personality gave her a considerable advantage: Dolly is empathetic, funny, intelligent, and knows how endear herself to others. She was building her career in the way a house is built: foundations, framework, windows with a view of the world, and a space where people who mattered could be invited in. Looking back philosophically, she has compared these seven years to those that Jacob, in Genesis, spent working for Laban in order to earn the right to marry. Dolly was taking a step into a new and decisive stage in her career, although the separation from the past was horribly painful.

About to get into the taxi that was to take her toward this new life, she became aware that leaving for real was something far more complicated than thinking about it in the abstract. She describes[1] how the few yards to the taxi seemed like miles. Her legs would hardly carry her and her heart ached. But if it was a sorrowful and bruised Dolly that got into the taxi, the Dolly that sank into the back seat was quite another—and stronger—person. Obviously, this did not mean that the door was slammed instantly on Porter and their long collaboration—the one-time partners were to meet again one week later to settle matters of joint interest.

1973

By 1973, relations between Dolly and Porter had deteriorated significantly. The breakup was finalized early the following year.

And now, as the taxi carried her away from Porter, it began to rain, and, as if in sympathy with the skies, Dolly wept. She was almost always overcome with sadness when a major change affected her life, even though she would tell herself over and over again that everything would be all right, repeating the words like a mantra. Then the skies cleared and the sun came out. By the time she reached her destination, Dolly had composed "Light of a Clear Blue Morning," a lovely song that would come out in 1977 on her album *New Harvest...First Gathering.* Just one example of the way Dolly worked: Wherever she was, whatever the time of day, her reactions to her feelings often inspired her with words and phrases that were very poetic. With a melody already formed in her mind, she found her themes not only from outside circumstances but also from her innermost self. From tears to a ray of sunlight in the time of a taxi ride, "Light of a Clear Blue Morning" came to symbolize Dolly's newfound freedom.

The Flip Side of Friendship

By the end of 1973, Dolly was getting her new life as singer-songwriter organized. One problem remaining from the official break with Porter continued to cause concern: What would her relationship with the RCA Victor label be? Porter had indicated that without him, RCA would drop her. It was

imperative that this matter be clarified as soon as possible. Dolly traveled to New York to discuss things with RCA, imagining that she would have to do some special pleading to convince them. In fact, RCA's response was entirely positive: The label was staking its all on their new star Dolly Parton, more than ready to continue along the road—from one album to the next—already paved in gold, thanks to her. There were to be no more reservations of the kind they had had when Porter had introduced the young singer seven years earlier.

The approaching new year, 1974, brought with it the new Dolly Parton—alone, free, understandably anxious about how things would go in the future but more determined than ever to be what she had always wanted to be: a superstar.

Album Cover

Designed by Les Leverett, the photo on this extraordinarily kitschy album sleeve was taken by the fountain at the Country Music Hall of Fame in Nashville. In the background, a full-length image of Dolly—in massive blond wig and long flowery yellow and orange skirt—seems almost to merge with the long brick wall of the Music Hall. In the foreground we see her smiling face, which appears to be shooting out of the fountain's foaming jet.

Bubbling Over

Dolly Parton / 2:18

Musicians: (not credited) **Vocals:** Dolly Parton **Recorded:** RCA Studio B, Nashville (TN), May 22, 1973 **Technical Team:** Producer: Bob Ferguson / Sound Engineer: Al Pachucki / Assistant Sound Engineers: Roy Shockley, Mike Shockley

The album's opening track is a bouncy, joyful, fizzing love song in a style relatively rare in Dolly's early catalogue. It explodes and bubbles over a lively country pop rhythm. Tradition and innovation meet here. While we still find the straightforward drumming of the albums from the 1960s, using just a discreet bass drum and the hi-hat played with a pedal, what is notable here is the presence of a percussion section making use of claves, pieces of exotic wood banged rhythmically together, typically in salsa music. The bass is well to the fore, its sound having a subtle resonance. The guitars have parts that are harmonically much more complex than on the preceding albums.

Traveling Man

Dolly Parton / 2:12

Musicians: (not credited) **Vocals:** Dolly Parton **Recorded:** RCA Studio B, Nashville (TN), April 9, 1973 **Technical Team:** Producer: Bob Ferguson / Sound Engineer: Al Pachucki / Assistant Sound Engineers: Roy Shockley, Mike Shockley **Single:** Side A: Traveling Man / Side B: I Remember **Released:** RCA Victor, 1973 (45 rpm ref.: 74-0950) **Best Chart Ranking:** 20 on Billboard Hot Country Songs (US), 12 on RPM Country Tracks (Canada)

Genesis and Lyrics

In "Traveling Man," Dolly uses irony to tackle a tricky subject. The song is about a mother who falls for her daughter's lover, a traveling salesman who moves from town to town selling his cheap wares. Sure that her mother will be against this relationship, the girl lies to her mother before secretly meeting the man, planning to run away with him—but, surprise, surprise, it's her mother the man is leaving with, leaving her all alone. Abandoned again: Many years before, Dolly's father had walked out on his family and home, leaving his daughter behind.

Production

The first version of "Traveling Man" featured on the *Coat of Many Colors* album. It appeared for a second time in a newly recorded version issued first as a single, with "I Remember" on the B-side, and then on the *Bubbling Over* album.

The electric guitars in "Bubbling Over" may have had elaborate parts, but here they go one better. The crashing entry of the rhythm guitars is astonishing. The drummer is clearly enjoying himself alternating breaks, ride cymbals, and simple use of the high-hat cymbals. The tempo is fast and you can feel the musicians' delight in keeping up with the "moving train." Drums stay in the background as the percussion section adds bongos on the first verse—a perfect example of an instrument that is felt more than heard but which is of paramount importance.

The highly varied arrangements of this piece work wonderfully well. First we have the phrase with the three amplified guitars (two electric and one with steel strings), repeated with subtle variations up to the middle of the second verse. The interplay between the percussion and drums section is very successful, both in the music and in the mix. We scarcely notice the transitions, something that helps to carry the audience along. Use is made of rhythmic bridging rather than tonal modulation. One of these bridges can be heard after the first chorus (drums, guitar, and an entry on the bass), and another after the second (drums, bass, entry of the vocals). The drummer frequently makes use of the ride cymbal's bell, the bulge in the center of the cymbal, which has a shorter, sharper sound resembling that of a bell. These two bridging passages bring a richness and variety not seen before in Dolly Parton's repertoire. The rock influence is obvious. The intros of "Little Green Bag" by the George Baker Selection (1970) or Iggy Pop's "Lust for Life" (1977) could reasonably be said to have a similar construction.

There is a big reverb effect applied to Dolly's voice, as in most of the songs on the album (with the exception of "Bubbling Over" and "The Beginning"). The principle of a reverb is to re-create a particular acoustic space by taking into account several criteria: the time between the dry sound and the first audible onset (pre-delay), the time it takes for the reverberation to disappear (decay), and the dry/wet mix (proportion of dry sound and reverberated sound in the resulting signal of the effect).

Alabama Sundown

Dave Kirby, Danny Morrison / 2:31

Musicians: (not credited) **Vocals:** Dolly Parton **Recorded:** RCA Studio B, Nashville (TN), December 14, 1971 **Technical Team:** Producer: Bob Ferguson / Sound Engineer: Al Pachucki / Assistant Sound Engineers: Roy Shockley, Mike Shockley

In this song revisited by the composer of the music and words, Dave Kirby, there is a return to a theme already

Dolly and her great friend Judy Ogle, reunited here in New York.

sung about by Dolly: that of the narrator far from home and ill at ease in the big city, dreaming of the landscape of her birthplace. Although Dolly was not the author of the lyrics, the song has echoes of an episode described in her autography when, with her great friend since childhood, Judy Ogle, she went to New York for the first time.[1] Suddenly they found themselves in the red-light district. Accosted by a man, Dolly went on the attack; the stranger got more than he bargained for. The two friends were not impressed by their stay in the Big Apple, where everything was overpriced and prostitutes walked the streets.

From the orchestral point of view, this number continues along the same lines as the first two on the album: a fairly fast tempo and some groove or even rock passages with a light instrumentation. The chief novelty, however, is the use of an electric guitar with a big reverb (at 1:00) and wah-wah pedal (so called for the sound it makes). This pedal amplifies a band of frequencies in the spectrum around a central frequency. The wah-wah effect is obtained by operating it with the foot, using the heel for the bass and the toe for the treble. The effect can be heard from the guitar to the right side of the mix, but it is not overdone. The playing of the ride cymbal uses the same tricks as in "Traveling Man." Percussion is limited to a snare drum played with brushes.

Afraid To Live
And Afraid Of Dying
Porter Wagoner / 2:02

Musicians: (not credited) **Vocals:** Dolly Parton **Recorded:** RCA Studio B, Nashville (TN), May 19, 1972 **Technical Team:** Producer: Bob Ferguson / Sound Engineer: Al Pachucki / Assistant Sound Engineers: Roy Shockley, Mike Shockley

We are constantly being warned against things that can harm our health and hasten our end: what we eat or drink, what we breathe, what we love, what could hurt us. Result: we are afraid to live because we are afraid of dying before our time. The narrator's philosophy is to enjoy the gift of life with serenity and only worry about being on good terms with God. The big questions of healthy living and pollution were already on people's minds in 1970s America.

The intro is almost identical to that of "The Master's Hand" or "Book of Life" (on the 1971 *Golden Streets of Glory* album), and the chord sequences are very similar to those on "Do You Hear the Robins Sing" (*My Favorite Songwriter, Porter Wagoner*, 1972). Moreover, all the old elements used by singer-songwriter Porter Wagoner appear again here: the violins, the little interjections of pedal steel guitar, the choruses, the modulation in the middle of the song.

Love With Me
Dolly Parton / 2:15

Musicians: (not credited) **Vocals:** Dolly Parton **Recorded:** RCA Studio B, Nashville (TN), February 1, 1973 **Technical Team:** Producer: Bob Ferguson / Sound Engineer: Al Pachucki / Assistant Sound Engineers: Roy Shockley, Mike Shockley

In *Bubbling Over* we have moved on from the period of betrayed, disappointed, or neglected loves. It's time for something sweeter. This song speaks of the possibility of true love—love of the kind Dolly believes in, full of lightness and sincerity. With "Love with Me," she revisits the country-glam style she has made her own.

Dolly's composing style is less florid than Porter Wagoner's and can easily be told apart. Her voice comes in right from the start against a rhythmic backing and guitar arpeggios. The sound is quite gentle. The violins come in for the chorus and then, in a classic progression, the pedal steel guitar. As the song progresses, the reverb effect becomes more prominent.

My Kind Of Man

Dolly Parton / 2:22

Musicians: (not credited) **Vocals:** Dolly Parton **Recorded:** RCA Studio B, Nashville (TN), December 12, 1972 **Technical Team:** Producer: Bob Ferguson / Sound Engineer: Al Pachucki / Assistant Sound Engineers: Roy Shockley, Mike Shockley

The female narrator in Dolly's songs likes a man who will respect her and love her as she is, with no desire to change her. It's quite simple: If a man claiming to love her does not understand this, he can get out of her life, because she will not compromise. For Dolly, to love someone is to respect everything about them. This universal theme is one that Dolly has often sung about. At the end of 1973, however, it has a more personal resonance: Dolly had to fight to get Porter to understand that she had her own path to follow and her own dreams to fulfill. The title of this song also reminds us of her empathy with the position of women. In the 1970s, women, often economically more fragile and dependent, still hesitated to leave a man, even if he did not accept them for themselves.

This track features an instrument that we haven't heard for quite a while—the harmonica. It adds a western movie feel to this syncopated ballad. In the choruses, particularly the last one, Dolly's voice swells to aim for a bluesy sound (in "Find someone who can" and "Being just the way I am"), something only rarely found in her songs up until then.

Sometimes An Old Memory Gets In My Eye

Bill Owens / 2:19

Musicians: (not credited) **Vocals:** Dolly Parton **Recorded:** RCA Studio B, Nashville (TN), February 1, 1973 **Technical Team:** Producer: Bob Ferguson / Sound Engineer: Al Pachucki / Assistant Sound Engineers: Roy Shockley, Mike Shockley

Dolly returns to the past with this number written by Bill Owens, the uncle who was at her side from the earliest days of her career. The lyrics speaks of a lost love, the memory of which can still be seen in the narrator's eyes. She assures us these are not tears, even though it is not easy to hold them back.

As with "Afraid to Live and Afraid of Dying," the identity of the author of the song is a clue to what we are about to hear. The song is in waltz time, the intro being played by a single instrument (a lap steel guitar). The composition develops, however: Some themes appear from the fiddle and the electric guitar playing together—a new departure. Also different is the mix, more spatially balanced than on the Porter Wagoner tracks. The two rhythm guitars and the backing vocals are equally distributed to avoid the impression of going back and forth from right to left, which can disrupt the listening experience.

Pleasant As May

Dolly Parton / 2:34

Musicians: (not credited) **Vocals:** Dolly Parton **Recorded:** RCA Studio B, Nashville (TN), January 26, 1971 **Technical Team:** Producer: Bob Ferguson / Sound Engineer: Al Pachucki / Assistant Sound Engineers: Roy Shockley, Mike Shockley

"Pleasant as May" is a song in which love and the seasons seem in harmony until something changes. If the summer sun struggles to compete with the sun that sets a loving heart on fire, it is powerless to warm a broken heart. A recurring idea in Dolly's writing is this connection with nature, something not always in tune with her feelings and thus intensifying the nostalgic dimension of the evocation. Spring may return each year, but love and happiness do not endure. For this song—a bluegrass number subsequently rerecorded for the album *Trio*—Dolly uses a restricted number of instruments: snare drum, present but discreet, rhythm guitar playing arpeggios, bass, and pedal steel guitar. The sensitive and nuanced playing of this last instrument fits perfectly with Dolly's voice, particularly when used on its own to accompany the singer. The musician uses a volume pedal. You can clearly hear the rise in intensity of the chords, without the attack. The small number of instruments makes the long reverb on the voice even more apparent.

Dolly onstage with an acoustic guitar, in 1974, the year of "I Will Always Love You."

The Beginning

Dolly Parton / 2:32

Musicians: (not credited) **Vocals:** Dolly Parton **Recorded:** RCA Studio B, Nashville (TN), January 11, 1972 **Technical Team:** Producer: Bob Ferguson / Sound Engineer: Al Pachucki / Assistant Sound Engineers: Roy Shockley, Mike Shockley

By any other writer and singer, this song by Dolly Parton would just be the banal story of a banal couple. They love one another, at first a lot and then rather less until the announcement of the birth of a baby turns everything upside down. Two become three and love brings them all together again.

Like the two preceding ballads, this one is in 3/4 time. The rhythm guitars play arpeggios. The piano line is clearly heard here, whereas in the other tracks it gets a bit lost. As well as accompanying the choruses, it interweaves with the singer in the second verse. The song does not have the classic alternation of verse and refrain. As the story unfolds, each paragraph can be seen as a verse. While there are few breaks in the vocals, a beautiful rise in intensity of all the instruments breaks the monotony of the piece.

Love, You're So Beautiful Tonight

Porter Wagoner / 3:08

Musicians: (not credited) **Vocals:** Dolly Parton **Recorded:** RCA Studio B, Nashville (TN), May 19, 1972 **Technical Team:** Producer: Bob Ferguson / Sound Engineer: Al Pachucki / Assistant Sound Engineers: Roy Shockley, Mike Shockley

Far from the world outside, this song is an ode to transcendent love. It describes the serene togetherness of two people and the narrator's passionate love for the beauty of the woman. Dolly sings it with simple clarity, providing a perfect ending to the album: an invitation to a slow dance entwined with your lover.

The new ballad has a very slow tempo. A volume pedal simulation on the bass creates a vibrato effect with rapid alternations of loud and soft. This track marks a departure from the traditional nature of Porter Wagoner's other titles; here he is trying his hand at technical innovations. In many ways the song resembles "The Beginning," with its use of rhythm guitars, drums in the verses, and the progressive introduction of the various instruments.

1973

Twelve Albums and a Separation

1967–1970: A Passionate Partnership

The meeting between Porter Wagoner and Dolly Parton took place in 1967 in Nashville. After seven years of collaboration with Porter and a close friendly and professional relationship, singer Norma Jean had just left *The Porter Wagoner Show*, to the despair of forty-five million TV viewers. Struck by two of Dolly Parton's songs, "Dumb Blonde" and "Something Fishy," Porter contacted Dolly Parton. Dolly had been in Nashville for three years by then and was struggling to make her way in an environment that all too readily took her to be merely a dumb blonde. Porter's offer was more than she could have hoped for. It meant that she would have television and stage work all year round and could at last earn a decent living—no small thing at a time when, several nights a week, she was going to bed hungry and tearful. Porter was to open the way for her, allowing her to establish her career. From Porter's point of view, this encounter would be the saving of his show and an inspiration in his career—he had written nothing for years.

Much has been written about their relationship. There are those who, today, still believe that their relationship was more than platonic. Dolly Parton has always denied that they were lovers,[1] although she has said that they loved one another deeply and shared many things, in particular a love of music. On this subject, she has more than once expressed surprise that a woman can't have a close friendship with a man without people immediately thinking that their relationship must be sexual. Porter, who at that time was successfully performing other people's compositions, never hid his fascination with Dolly's talent for composition, even if he found her imagination excessive and her dreams too crazy.[11]

After they split up, Dolly was to say that those years with Porter represented both some of the best years of her life[5] and also some of the worst. The meeting of two strong personalities, two ambitious people, two creative people, makes sparks fly—in every sense of the word.

Creative Passion

Porter was immediately enthralled by Dolly's energy and enormous capacity for writing anywhere, at any time. What's more, she was ravishing, both fiery and warm, a major asset to his show. The two performers shared a love of music and words, a sense of humor and jokes, and a belief in doing a good job, however long it took.

That said, they did not share the same dreams. Dolly was young, highly motivated, talented, and on the look-out for fame and love. Since the release of *Hello, I'm Dolly*, people were beginning to take some notice of her, but not enough to satisfy her. Porter had already earned his spurs in Nashville and with television viewers who were fans of country music. From this lofty position, the famous forty-year-old appointed himself mentor to the sexiest country singer in the world.

He got things organized very quickly. He got her signed up with his label, RCA Victor, became the producer of both her solo and her duo albums, and signed the checks every month. Since he was the boss he made all the decisions—as he freely admitted in Francis Whately's documentary[7] *Dolly Parton: Here I Am*. Dolly had everything to learn about her trade, find her bearings, and get used to not only Porter but also the audience of *The Porter Wagoner Show*, who made her "pay" for the departure of Norma Jean. Porter was furious at this hostility: He announced to his fans that Norma Jean belonged to the past and Miss Dolly was taking over from her.

Porter and Dolly began bringing out singles in September 1967, and January 1968 saw the launch of their first joint album, *Just Between You and Me*—the title indicative of their closeness. The title of their second album, *Just the Two of Us*, is equally explicit: This insistence on "just you and me" seems to underline the almost exclusive nature of this special relationship. Dolly was well aware, however, that this duo was in fact a trio: There was Porter, Dolly, and then this "us," perhaps rather too closely connected for the young star. Given that Porter Wagoner apparently made all the decisions, it is likely that he was the one to pick the titles. A singer-songwriter knows better than anyone that the words—of a song's title or its lyrics—are a reflection of their life. This was a time when the relationship between Porter and Dolly was at its most intense. Nevertheless, some of the love songs they sang together may be no more than an expression of their creative friendship. Spending half the year on the road, they managed at the same time to record one or two albums and appear on television in *The Porter Wagoner Show*. The reality was that they were

Porter Wagoner's lobby card, in 1966, with his band, as in their hundreds of performances of *The Porter Wagoner Show.*

more "married" to one another than either of them to their respective spouses. Their relationship was intense, each with their own projects to realize, and they spared neither time nor energy to achieve them.

The main thing was that the public came to love this duo, the way they harmonized their voices, and their jokey personalities. The country music audience now conquered, Dolly found herself in the spotlight. The specialist press commented that she had brought a new brilliance to *The Porter Wagoner Show*, sparkling as much as the diamonds—presents from her mentor and manager—that she wore on each of her fingers. The rumor mill went wild.

The Beginning of the End

Dolly might have been young, both in terms of age and experience, but she could stand up for herself. She knew precisely what she wanted to do and what she wanted to be. With or without diamonds, she intended to become a superstar—in other words, a person in her own right, not just half an entity as she saw her position in her partnership with Porter. Her project was not at all to his liking. Porter understood all too clearly that he was dealing with an artist intent on building a career in which he was only a cog, however important.

Dolly wrote a huge number of songs during the years of doing the television show. Another important event in her progress was her admission in 1969 to the Grand Ole Opry as the fifty-fourth member. The singles and albums featuring the Wagoner/Parton duo came out nonstop, but this did not interfere with Dolly's plans as a solo singer. Her contract with Wagoner, however, stipulated that he should be her producer. While the arrangement seemed acceptable at

the time they met, Dolly soon realized that when she made a dollar, Porter made ten. She began to wonder whether she, too, could earn this kind of money. But it was not yet the moment for the break with Porter.

Dolly was working constantly, sustained by her faith, her creative strength, and her dreams. In 1969, she and Porter brought out their third joint album, *Always, Always.* Porter Wagoner was not just the smiling showman in the flashy rhinestone-studded purple suit who appeared on television. He was a man with a complex personality. Highly professional, he was also a perfectionist who needed to control everything. He could be very harsh, something confirmed by Norma Jean,[1] who had often left the studio in tears. As time passed, the harmonious moments began to be interrupted by periods of shouting and quarreling. Dolly was sincerely and profoundly grateful to Porter. But his constant reminder that "It was me that made you a star" did not help matters when arguments broke out. With these two hot-blooded personalities, some days it was more a case of "Never, Never" than "Always, Always."

In 1970, the duo brought out two albums: *Porter Wayne and Dolly Rebecca* and *Once More.* They were spending a good part of each year on the road, traveling from town to town and concert to concert. Dolly used these journeys to write. It was during this period, under the guidance of Porter, that she amassed an enormous fund of songs and learned how to appear on stage. She understood instinctively how to talk to an audience, how to make them laugh, pausing between one song and the next to make jokes and interact with the public. She loved her fans and they loved her. Dolly found this motivating, keen not only to be recognized but also loved by all.

"I Will Always Love You" will remain Dolly's great farewell song to Porter. Here onstage at the Grand Ole Opry, ca. 1990.

1971–1974: From a Duo to a Duel

In an interview given in May 1971 at the underground newspaper the *Great Speckled Bird*,[5] Gene Guerrero asked Dolly how she got on with Porter. The journalist was well aware that the two superstars made up a duo that was as successful musically as it was commercially. But he couldn't have failed to hear or read about the rumors that were circulating. Dolly answered his questions in the way she was to reply throughout her career: Porter was someone amazing. She owed him a lot, starting with her initiation into the music business and subsequently the fame she acquired. But she also confessed that the way in which Porter tried to control her sometimes annoyed her. Although both were people with strong personalities, they were always professional—for the moment.

In the early 1970s, Dolly and Porter were the most popular duo in the world of country music. Perhaps explained by the upheavals in American society or the Vietnam War, whatever the reason, it seemed that country fans were clamoring for "homegrown" music. This demand for authenticity made it easier to gather around the fire, in the kitchen, or at the bar, and to sing and dance together. Country music was evolving to appeal to a wider audience as television and radio became accessible in even the most remote areas.

Porter Wagoner and Dolly Parton had their fingers on the pulse of this changing world. They knew their public, spending time with their fans on and off stage. Porter remained available until every fan had their autograph. These were lessons that Dolly never forgot. She continued her apprenticeship, but in the knowledge that soon she would strike out on her own in a different direction. She planned to conquer the whole world, building her own network of fans. This meant leaving Porter and *The Porter Wagoner Show*.

Tribute Album and a Farewell Song

Many people have written that Dolly owed her career and her fame to Porter. They forget that the opposite is equally true. While Dolly was full of praise for her mentor and friend, releasing a tenth solo album in 1972 entitled *My Favorite Songwriter, Porter Wagoner*, it was meeting Dolly that inspired Porter to start writing songs again—songs that were very much a joint effort. When the time came for Dolly to leave, Porter dug his heels in, unwilling to release his partner. In her autobiography,[1] Dolly Parton describes how Porter closed his ears to the subject both of her departure and of her personal ambitions. For more than two years he refused to listen, even as their relationship soured.

After his official separation from Dolly Parton, Porter Wagoner would host *The Porter Wagoner Show* until 1981.

agreement was conditional, but Dolly was free. She had finally achieved her aim.

Things might have ended here but for the intermingled personal and professional lives of the two singers. Their separation seemed more like an acrimonious divorce. Porter had showered Dolly with presents: diamonds, a Cadillac…if she was going to leave the show, she would owe him years of her earnings to repay the investment and time he had put into her career. Anger, grief, and a refusal to see the end of their outstanding artistic relationship made Porter all too human—a wounded artist unable to accept that the success of their duo owed as much to Dolly as to him.

These arguments came to the fore when they broke up and did not sit well with the coldness of the law, where facts are rationalized and emotions are detached from business. Dolly learned to protect her interests, but the price she had to pay was high. Porter demanded three million dollars, a colossal sum in the mid-1970s. She managed to settle out of court for one million in cash in order to spare herself—and her family—a long and acrimonious trial. The media was agog. The announcement of Dolly's departure traveled around a stunned world.

The Legacy of Porter Wagoner & Dolly Parton

After the separation with its emotional turbulence and legal intricacies, things began to settle down. Tolerance and peace were restored away from the legal circuits and the media frenzy. Dolly became what she had always wanted to be: an international superstar. Porter continued to present *The Porter Wagoner Show* until 1981. They performed again as a duo on several occasions in 1975, recording the album *Say Forever You'll Be Mine*. The record sleeve shows photos of the two singers in oval frames to resemble the kind of old family portraits people kept on their mantelpieces. One more joint album was recorded in 1980, *Porter & Dolly*. In 2014, Bear Family Records brought out *Just Between You and Me: The Complete Recordings, 1967–1976*. This compilation disk brings together all the recordings of duets made by Wagoner and Parton during their partnership.

In her autobiography,[1] published in 1994, Dolly Parton devotes many pages to this period of her life. Ultimately, she has chosen to keep the good things and has come to terms with the rest. When Porter became ill and until he died of lung cancer in October 2007, Dolly was always at his side.

There is no doubt that Porter Wagoner and Dolly Parton had an important impact on country music. Two consummate artists: Dolly's soprano and Porter's tenor, their humor that was so much part of the success of their show, more than a hundred recorded songs—some of which are now "classics" of country music—and a melodic phrasing technique unique to them.

Dolly had signed on for five years; she ended up spending seven years with Porter and his show. In the long run it did her no harm, but when a person is driven by an urgent desire to achieve, two years can seem a long time.

They quarreled, made peace, worked together again; but, well before the official split announced on stage, a number of fans noticed the cracks in their relationship. Behind the scenes the quarrels multiplied. Porter was easily angered and Dolly, who hated any kind of argument, nevertheless raised her voice in response. Doors were slammed. The two exhausted their energy in what had become a kind of duel.

As always when emotions were heightened and words were not enough, Dolly would pick up her pen and write a song. The result this time was one that would become a mega international hit: "I Will Always Love You." A song to tell Porter that she was leaving, that she had decided to pursue her dream. It was something she had to do and she had to do it without him. When Dolly played and sang this song to Porter, he began to cry and said it was the most beautiful song he had ever heard. Dolly could go, but only if he was the one to produce "I Will Always Love You." His

An Important Collaboration

For editorial reasons, as this book is mainly about Dolly Parton, not all the albums from the Porter Wagoner/Dolly Parton period have been covered in detail. Only *Always, Always* and *The Best of Porter Wagoner & Dolly Parton* have been presented as examples of their collaboration. For the other albums, we offer a biographical and musical overview here.

Just Between You and Me

Produced by Bob Ferguson, this first album by the duo came out on January 15, 1968, on the RCA Victor label. The sleeve shows Porter and Dolly, their arms around each other, wearing identical red sweaters. The album went to No. 8 on Billboard Top Country Albums, while "The Last Thing on My Mind," the only single to be taken from *Just Between You and Me*, reached No. 7 on Billboard Hot Country Songs. Five of the songs were written or co-written by Dolly. In retrospect, life turned out to be rather different from that presented by the title of this first album. Porter wanted his partnership with Dolly to be exclusive, with nothing coming between them. Of course, we know what was to happen next: Dolly had already fixed on her ambitious dreams for her future and was going to do everything in her power to make them come true. But for the time being, the Porter/Dolly combination worked well, and both the album and the single were praised, with critics describing the duo as outstanding, joyful, and groovy.

Just the Two of Us

The second joint album came out on September 9, 1968, again on the RCA Victor label with the same Bob Ferguson as producer. The luminosity of the album sleeve comes from the clothes the two singers are wearing—identical again, with cream jackets replacing the red sweaters. Porter, in the foreground, and Dolly, just behind and leaning slightly against him, have their heads turned in the same direction, looking up and smiling. The album appeared at No. 184 on the Billboard 200 and was ranked No. 5 on Billboard Top Country Albums, remaining at that spot for forty-nine weeks. Three singles resulted from this album: "Holding On to Nothin'," which, after seven weeks on Billboard Hot Country Songs, reached No. 7; "We'll Get Ahead Someday," which reached No. 5 after nine weeks being listed; and "Jeannie's Afraid of the Dark," which went to No. 51 after four weeks. For the second time in one year, 1968, an album by Porter and Dolly received a positive response from the critics. Three of the songs are by Dolly Parton: "The Party," "I Can," and "Jeannie's Afraid of the Dark," the latter a very beautiful and very sad ballad of the kind at which Dolly excelled.

Porter Wayne and Dolly Rebecca

The duo's fourth album was issued on March 9, 1970, on the RCA Victor label, produced by Bob Ferguson. The sleeve, designed by photographer Les Leverett, features school photos of Porter Wayne and Dolly Rebecca, inserted into a family photo album placed on a crochet doily and next to a framed embroidered representation of a bird. Although the sleeve looks dated now, at the time the choice of images was very likely dictated by a desire to clarify the relationship between the singers: friends but not lovers. Porter commented once that his and Dolly's voices fitted together even better than if they had been brother and sister. But they belonged to the same family: the family of country music. On this album of eleven songs, five are composed by Dolly Parton, while one was co-written with Dorothy Jo Hope, her aunt.

Once More

The fifth album by the Porter and Dolly duo, *Once More* came out on August 3, 1970, on the RCA Victor label, produced by Bob Ferguson. The color pink dominates on the cover, showing the two smiling artists close to one another. The single taken from the album, "Daddy Was an Old Time Preacher Man," Dolly's tribute to her grandfather, the reverend Jake Owens, was No. 7 on Billboard Hot Country Songs and was nominated for a Grammy Award in the category Best Country Duo/Group Performance. *Once More* was No. 7 on Billboard Top Country Albums and No. 191 on the Billboard 200. The reception from Billboard and *Cashbox* magazines was favorable. The singing duo was on the road to fame.

Two of a Kind

Porter and Dolly brought out their sixth album on February 8, 1971. Unusually, it was not preceded by the issuing of a single. The record sleeve is very dark, with a shaft of light illuminating Dolly and Porter's profiles arranged one above the other. The album was ranked No. 13 on Billboard Top Country Albums and No. 142 on Billboard 200. "Curse of the Wild Weed Flower," one of only a few country songs at that time to mention drugs, condemns the use of marijuana. It is on this album that we first see songs co-written by Dolly and Porter.

The Right Combination— Burning the Midnight Oil

The seventh album of the Porter and Dolly duo, produced by Bob Ferguson and issued by RCA Victor, came out on January 3, 1972. Three out of the ten songs are by Dolly Parton: "I've Been This Way Too Long," "In Each Love Some Pain Must Fall," and "Somewhere Along the Way." This album is characterized by a particular theme: the relationship between lovers over the passage of time. With hindsight, it is tempting to think that it represents the beginning of the end of the relationship between Porter and Dolly. It is interesting that, for the first time, the image on the record sleeve shows the two singers physically separated, like an old couple tiring of one another.

Together Always

The eighth album by the duo came out on September 11, 1972, under the RCA Victor label, produced by Bob Ferguson. Why abandon a winning team? Dolly's extraordinary talent as a songwriter was by now confirmed. Porter and Dolly composed and co-composed the whole of this album and so it does not feature any cover titles. Undiluted Porter and Dolly. It includes the hit "Lost Forever in Your Kiss" and the humorous "Ten Four—Over and Out," referring to the craze for CB radio before it became a major phenomenon in the United States. Another interesting difference from earlier albums is that the notes on the back of the sleeve are written by Porter and Dolly themselves. The design of the sleeve is quite unlike that of *The Right Combination—Burning the*

Midnight Oil: Looking happy and joyful, Porter and Dolly are once more presented like a couple, as if physically welded together. Were they to be "together always"? No one knew. But the desire to sing together was still there, for the moment.

We Found It

The ninth joint Porter Wagoner/Dolly Parton album went on sale on February 12, 1973. Produced by Bob Ferguson for RCA Victor, *We Found It*, like *Together Always*, showcases songs co-authored by the two singers and features no cover items. The album entered the charts but did not do especially well. The cracks in the duo's relationship were becoming more apparent. Dolly was becoming a star in her own right, her career was expanding, and she was increasingly asserting her desire for independence. It could not be long before her departure.

Love and Music

The tenth joint album by Porter Wagoner and Dolly Parton came out on July 2, 1973, on the RCA Victor label with Bob Ferguson as producer. The record sleeve shows a heart-shaped photo of Porter and Dolly supported by a pair of quarter notes and framed with orange scrolls on a pink background, the colors echoing the sugary tone of the album. The title, *Love and Music*, perfectly sums up the relationship between the two singer-songwriters. Because beyond the gossip, disagreements, and arguments, what united them—and what was to separate them—was a love of music, despite their personal differences in feelings and art.

Porter 'n' Dolly

The eleventh album by the duo, *Porter 'n' Dolly* came out on August 19, 1974, produced as always by Bob Ferguson on the RCA Victor label. Ironically, one of the tracks, "Please Don't Stop Loving Me," went to number one on Billboard Hot Country Songs. The album was essentially Dolly's work, and the sleeve, for the first time, shows Dolly in the foreground in front of Porter. Like the songs, the images hint at a story, sometimes echoing that of the two singers.

ALBUM

Jolene

Jolene . When Someone Wants to Leave . River of Happiness .
Early Morning Breeze . Highlight of My Life . I Will Always Love You . Randy .
Living on Memories of You . Lonely Comin' Down . It Must Be You

RELEASE DATE
USA: February 4, 1974
Reference: RCA Victor—APL1-0473
Best US Chart Ranking: 6

The Birth of a Legend

Dolly Parton's thirteenth solo album, *Jolene*, marked an important moment in her career. Produced by Bob Ferguson on the RCA label in February 1974, it included two titles that were to become megahits, "Jolene" and "I Will Always Love You," songs that she says she wrote on the same day. The critics were not yet to know that these two songs would become some of the singer's most well-known—and most frequently covered—numbers, but the magazines *Billboard* and *Cashbox* were already greeting the star's new album with enthusiasm.

In Nashville—and not only there—the name Dolly Parton was on everyone's lips. They discussed her eye-catching outfits, her outrageously blond and inflated wigs, her generously applied makeup, her breakup with Porter Wagoner, but most of all they talked about the fact that, after "Joshua," she now had her second number one in the charts with "Jolene." The single chimed with the times, its themes dealing with the position of women, their view of love, and their place in a couple—but it lasted through time to become a legendary title in Dolly's discography.

New Career, New Team

In 1974, ousted by the Watergate scandal, Richard Nixon made way for Gerald Ford, thirty-eighth president of the United States. The jazz world mourned the passing of pianist and composer Duke Ellington, and, unbeknownst to Hollywood, Leonardo DiCaprio had just been born. For Dolly Parton, February was undoubtedly a month to remember—partly because of the announcement in a press conference of the end of her partnership with Porter Wagoner (who was taking legal action against her), and partly because it was the month when her important album *Jolene* came out. Nineteen seventy-four was a vintage year.

After making sure that she could continue working with the RCA Victor label, Dolly took on Don Warden,[5] the invaluable "Mr. Everything," as she affectionately called him. Singer and musician in the Wagonmasters on *The Porter Wagoner Show* until 1974, he now left to work with Dolly, staying with her for almost fifty years. She was deeply affected by his death in 2017. Don Warden knew all the right phone numbers to help Dolly's dream move forward successfully. He was so well-known in Nashville that there was a range of T-shirts for sale bearing the words "I Know Don Warden." Dolly's many encounters are indicative of her loyalty—in love, to her husband, Carl Dean; in friendship, to Judy Ogle; to her family; and to the music business. She was judicious in her choice of people to surround her, but it is tempting to think that chance—or God, she says—played a role in her life, putting the right people on her path at the right moment. A sensitive woman, Dolly followed both her head and her heart. She became close friends at this time with Ann, Warden's wife, making her responsible for the design of part of Dollywood. Ann also designed the "Dolly Doll," a doll that was launched in 1975. Other names of those sitting round her table among her friends included singer Roy Acuff, comedian at the Grand Ole Opry Minnie Pearl, and producer and guitarist Chet Atkins. She had met Chet through her uncle Bill Owens when she was young and was to meet him again at the RCA studios. Brothers, sisters, cousins, and uncles were all part of the journey and participated in Dolly's first band, the Travelin' Family Band.

On the Road

Bill Rehrig, leader of the Travelin' Family Band and Dolly's friend, took over leading the backing vocals from Richard Dennison. Dennison married Rachel, Dolly's youngest sister, and so was a member of the Parton family twice over. The Travelin' Family Band was short-lived, however. Dolly realized it was a mistake when she found that each member saw her more as a sister or cousin than an artist. And the working conditions were tough. In an interview with *Playboy* in 1978,[5] she described to the journalist Lawrence Grobel how she and her group traveled nonstop, from fairs to rodeos to school gymnasiums. Dolly was on the brink of disaster. Exhausted by her relatives' individual demands to the detriment of discussions about tours and bookings, Dolly regretfully dissolved the band. She had always dreamed of creating a family group, but now her professional rigor told her she should work in a different way, regardless of sentiment. Dolly put together a new band, Gypsy Fever, touring with it in 1977.

Since the time when she had included a cover version of singer-songwriter and actor Mac Davis's "In the

Cher and Sandy Gallin in 1977. Gallin worked as Dolly's manager.

Dolly Parton wrote "I Will Always Love You" for Porter Wagoner.

In New Zealand during the COVID-19 epidemic, a newspaper ran an article on "Essential Things to Know," suggesting that washing your hands with soap should take "as long as it takes to sing 'Happy Birthday' twice, or the chorus of Dolly Parton's hit song 'Jolene.'"

Ghetto" on her 1969 album *My Blue Ridge Mountain Boy*, Dolly had remained in contact with him (she went on to collaborate with him again in 1989 on her album *White Limozeen*). When she told him that she wanted to bring her music to a wider audience, he suggested that she meet Cher's manager, Sandy Gallin, but did not know if she would find him suitable. Gypsy Fever performed all summer on Mac Davis's TV show, and the meeting with Sandy Gallin was to be decisive, leading to an association that lasted for several decades. It was Gallin who persuaded Dolly to record the hit number "Here You Come Again" in 1977.

The Album: Success and Rumors

Rumors have a habit of hanging around for a long time, and Dolly has had to put up with innumerable questions about her appearance, her admirably discreet husband, and her possible extra-conjugal sexual affairs. In 1974, rumor had it that "I Will Always Love You" was a love song dedicated to Porter Wagoner, since it was believed that the singer with the suits embroidered with rhinestone wagon wheels and the famous songwriter had had a passionate love affair. While it is a love song for Porter, it was not written to celebrate a romance. It was a way of leaving this friend and professional partner who had helped her in so many ways. In her autobiography, *Dolly: My Life and Other*

Unfinished Business,[1] Dolly relates how the singer Tammy Wynette, in the course of a conversation, asked her "why Porter goes around saying he has slept with us all." Dolly, already accustomed to this kind of gossip, answered that it didn't matter anyway because only half of Nashville would believe it. Other rumors circulated, including that the relationship between Dolly and her friend Judy Ogle was more than just a friendship because Dolly was a lesbian. The proof, according to certain rumormongers, was that the two women shared a hotel bed. And then there is the tabloid newspapers' fascination with her plastic surgery and her refusal to reveal the darker, more secret side of her life that they were convinced existed.

For decades now, the singer has continued to assert that all people need to do is read and listen to her songs, that she has no mysterious secrets. But the rumors persist. Dolly disregards them, moving onward with her head held high.

The Sleeve

The sleeve, with its photo by Hope Powell against a pale yellow background, gives no hint of the importance of this album. The only touch of bright color is the indigo of the fake fur rug Dolly is sitting on, dressed in a blue and white outfit with sleeves as bouffant as her wig. It does little to cheer her slightly sad expression.

SIDE A

Jolene

Dolly Parton / 2:43

Musicians: Dolly Parton, Jimmy Colvard, Dave Kirby, Bobby Thompson, Chip Young: guitar / Pete Drake, Stu Basore: pedal steel / Bobby Dyson: bass / Jerry Carrigan, Larrie Londin, Kenny Malone: drums / Buck Trent: banjo / Mack Magaha, Johnny Gimble: fiddle / Hargus "Pig" Robbins, David Briggs: piano / Onie Wheeler: harmonica
Vocals: Dolly Parton **Backing Vocals:** The Nashville Edition
Recorded: RCA Studio B, Nashville (TN), May 22, 1973
Technical Team: Producer: Bob Ferguson / Sound Engineer: Al Pachucki / Assistant Sound Engineers: Roy Shockley, Mike Shockley
Single: Side A: Jolene / Side B: Love, You're So Beautiful Tonight
Released: RCA Victor, 1973 (45 rpm ref.: APBO-0145)
Best Chart Ranking: 1 on Billboard Hot Country Songs (US)

Genesis and Lyrics

The song deals with a universal theme: that of a woman's vulnerability when competing with a beautiful rival, a rival who threatens to steal her man. Infatuated, he murmurs the other woman's name in his sleep. The narrator begs her competitor to set her sights on any man but hers.

The story here has a double autobiographical resonance. First, the name Jolene, which was the name of a little girl who asked Dolly for an autograph. Second, at the beginning of the first episode of *Dolly Parton's Heartstrings*,[6] devoted to this song, Dolly describes how one day she caught a beautiful redheaded bank teller flirting with her husband. Dolly combines the two elements in the one song. The heartrending way Dolly pronounces the name Jolene, the threat it represents—that of betrayal in love—the way the singer uses it in the opening of the song, her voice, the music, all contribute to make this a memorable song. Most of all, we hear the narrator's sense of powerlessness, in despair at losing her man, the love of her life, while Jolene can have any man she wants. Who among us has not felt this fear at least once in their life? We can all identify with the character, and the emotional power that the singer brings to the song is more than convincing. All the conditions were there to guarantee a huge hit, not only in the year it was released but to this day, because "Jolene" remains one of Dolly Parton's fans' favorite songs, the ultimate "other woman" song.

Production

First, on the right side of the stereo field, we hear a syncopated guitar riff, played by Dolly Parton on nylon string guitar. On the left, there is a persistent strumming on the steel strings of a folk guitar. This brilliant arrangement idea, almost a production detail, generates all the dramatic tension necessary for the introduction of this classic, whose popularity was soon to spread far beyond the world of folk and country music. A combination of bass and drums makes a forcible entry, quickly supported by the continuous picking of the folk guitar (the one that created the tension on strummed strings in the intro), providing the perfect complement to Dolly's guitar. Next to enter is the pedal steel guitar and fiddle, and, from the second verse, the congas. At the beginning of the third verse, the piano accompanies the ensemble with an insistent arpeggio motif imitating the picking of a guitar an octave lower. Dolly's voice, as if in a state of grace, hovers effortlessly over this arrangement, which is both sober and imbued with a kind of pagan mysticism. This unusual atmosphere is due in particular to the use of the Dorian mode, equivalent to the natural minor scale (or Aeolian mode) but with the sixth note raised by a semitone. Dolly harmonizes her own voice, using two superimposed overdubs, creating a chorus-like effect that adds to the addictive strangeness of the track.

Cover Versions and Reactions

"Jolene" was twice nominated at the Grammy Awards, in 1974 and 1975, in the category of Best Female Country Vocal Performance. The song's success encouraged others to do their own versions: Olivia Newton-John in 1976, the White Stripes in 2004, and in 2016, Pentatonix with Dolly Parton. This excellent a cappella version won the Grammy Award for Best Country Duo/Group Performance.

Several singers, both male and female, have written and performed songs in response to Dolly's song, among them "You Can Have Him Jolene" by the Chapel Hart trio (2021). This version imagines what happens next. The narrator was afraid that her rival would steal her man, but time has passed and now she has really had enough of him—the beautiful redhead can take him away! An energetic and humorous country tribute to the songwriter, who on July 20, 2022, her husband's birthday, tweeted her admiration for the Chapel Hart version.

JOLENE
Dolly Parton

Featuring:
I WILL ALWAYS LOVE YOU

Jolene featured two tracks that would become major hits: "Jolene" and "I Will Always Love You."

Dressed in a rhinestone-covered white pantsuit, Dolly sang in front of over 180,000 people at the 2014 Glastonbury Festival of Contemporary Performing Arts (UK) while, to her surprise, her team behind her did dance moves to "Jolene." Dolly wrote on her official site: "I'm just a country girl and now I feel like a rock star."

When Someone Wants To Leave

Dolly Parton / 2:06

Musicians: Dolly Parton, Jimmy Colvard, Dave Kirby, Bobby Thompson, Chip Young: guitar / Pete Drake, Stu Basore: pedal steel / Bobby Dyson: bass / Jerry Carrigan, Larrie Londin, Kenny Malone: drums / Buck Trent: banjo / Mack Magaha, Johnny Gimble: fiddle / Hargus "Pig" Robbins, David Briggs: piano / Onie Wheeler: harmonica **Vocals:** Dolly Parton **Backing Vocals:** The Nashville Edition **Recorded:** RCA Studio B, Nashville (TN), December 26, 1973 **Technical Team:** Producer: Bob Ferguson / Sound Engineer: Al Pachucki / Assistant Sound Engineers: Roy Shockley, Mike Shockley

This song is about the heartbreak of a couple when one loves more than the other. Dolly puts herself in the shoes of a woman who loves but is aware of losing her man, and also aware that when he has made that decision, he must be let go. The difficult experience with Porter, who refused to let Dolly leave him, may have been a factor in the writing of this song.

To illustrate this "sad situation," as the narrator describes it, Dolly and her musicians opt for the good old 4/4 midtempo. The bass provides a robust line, the drummer pulls out his best country ballroom gear, the dobro converses cheerfully with the acoustic guitar, and on the choruses the pedal steel joins in the debate. At the end of the discussion, everyone seems to agree: Even if it's sad, when someone wants to leave, they have to leave.

River Of Happiness

Dolly Parton / 2:19

Musicians: Dolly Parton, Jimmy Colvard, Dave Kirby, Bobby Thompson, Chip Young: guitar / Pete Drake, Stu Basore: pedal steel / Bobby Dyson: bass / Jerry Carrigan, Larrie Londin, Kenny Malone: drums / Buck Trent: banjo / Mack Magaha, Johnny Gimble: fiddle / Hargus "Pig" Robbins, David Briggs: piano / Onie Wheeler: harmonica **Vocals:** Dolly Parton **Backing Vocals:** The Nashville Edition **Recorded:** RCA Studio B, Nashville (TN), December 26, 1973 **Technical Team:** Producer: Bob Ferguson / Sound Engineer: Al Pachucki / Assistant Sound Engineers: Roy Shockley, Mike Shockley

This track brings together two themes close to Dolly's heart: love and nature. This time, nature welcomes love, makes it grow, makes it flow like a river. The narrator invites the man she loves to come with her to sit on the banks of the river of happiness. Dolly Parton seems to be in a joyful mood. The Queen of Country's voice in this ode to bucolic love is light and relaxed, the song having a slightly faster tempo than "When Someone Wants to Leave." The instrumentation is identical, except that David Briggs gives an extra dose of swing to the catchy chorus with his precise and rhythmical piano playing. It's clear: Independence suits Dolly.

1974

"Highlight of My Life"
marked the return of Mack
Magaha and Johnny Gimble
(shown at left) on fiddle.

1974

Early Morning Breeze

Dolly Parton / 2:45

Musicians: Dolly Parton, Jimmy Colvard, Dave Kirby, Bobby Thompson, Chip Young: guitar / Pete Drake, Stu Basore: pedal steel / Bobby Dyson: bass / Jerry Carrigan, Larrie Londin, Kenny Malone: drums / Buck Trent: banjo / Mack Magaha, Johnny Gimble: fiddle / Hargus "Pig" Robbins, David Briggs: piano / Onie Wheeler: harmonica
Vocals: Dolly Parton **Backing Vocals:** The Nashville Edition
Recorded: RCA Studio B, Nashville (TN), December 26, 1973
Technical Team: Producer: Bob Ferguson / Sound Engineer: Al Pachucki / Assistant Sound Engineers: Roy Shockley, Mike Shockley

This song, taken from the album *Coat of Many Colors*, is a pastoral and bucolic ballad, an ode to nature, Dolly Parton style. It is interesting to compare the two versions, as at the beginning they seem to be identical. The tempo, Bobby Dyson's incredible bass line, Jerry Carrigan's subtle drumming, a Dolly-style nylon string guitar probably played by Dave Kirby, and the smooth and agile vocal performance are all similar in the version recorded on January 26, 1971. Two instruments were added later, on December 26, 1973, as an overdub: the pedal steel, on the right in the stereo field, and the electric guitar, on the left. These fine additions, crafted by expert players and composers, do not in any way detract from this new version and perhaps improve it, though some may prefer the purity of the original, which emphasized Dolly's voice and Dyson's bass as a second voice in counterpoint in the lower part of the spectrum.

Highlight Of My Life

Dolly Parton / 2:18

Musicians: Dolly Parton, Jimmy Colvard, Dave Kirby, Bobby Thompson, Chip Young: guitar / Pete Drake, Stu Basore: pedal steel / Bobby Dyson: bass / Jerry Carrigan, Larrie Londin, Kenny Malone: drums / Buck Trent: banjo / Mack Magaha, Johnny Gimble: fiddle / Hargus "Pig" Robbins, David Briggs: piano / Onie Wheeler: harmonica
Vocals: Dolly Parton **Backing Vocals:** The Nashville Edition
Recorded: RCA Studio B, Nashville (TN), December 3, 1973
Technical Team: Producer: Bob Ferguson / Sound Engineer: Al Pachucki / Assistant Sound Engineers: Roy Shockley, Mike Shockley

This love song, a recognition of the happiness given to her by the loved one, is set to an up-tempo country shuffle that is made for dancing. All the ingredients of the hoedown are there, the most remarkable perhaps being the clear and abundant piano part, to the left of the stereo field, which brings a good dose of swing to the band. It also marks the welcome return of Mack Magaha and Johnny Gimble on fiddles, rather surprisingly mixed separately, one on the left and the other on the right (traditionally, at that time, instruments of the same family were mixed on the same side). The pedal steel duet harmonized in thirds by the legendary Pete Drake and by Stu Basore, panned (placed in the stereo field) in the same way as the fiddles but never playing at the same time, is also surprising. The mood is always one of joy and good humor, as Dolly is determined to celebrate her artistic independence with dignity, not forgetting to pay tribute to her mentor and closest collaborator, Porter Wagoner. But the best tribute is yet to come…

Not long after the release of "I Will Always Love You," Elvis Presley offered to buy the rights to a cover version from Dolly Parton. But Elvis's offer was too mean, and Dolly knew instinctively that, quite apart from it being important to her personally and emotionally, this was a very important song. She was forced to stand up to the King and reject his offer—she related later that she cried all night!

SIDE A

In 1992, Whitney Houston sang her own rendition of "I Will Always Love You," which became a major hit and earned Dolly Parton millions of dollars.

I Will Always Love You

Dolly Parton / 2:56

Musicians: Dolly Parton, Jimmy Colvard, Dave Kirby, Bobby Thompson, Chip Young: guitar / Pete Drake, Stu Basore: pedal steel / Bobby Dyson: bass / Jerry Carrigan, Larrie Londin, Kenny Malone: drums / Buck Trent: banjo / Mack Magaha, Johnny Gimble: fiddle / Hargus "Pig" Robbins, David Briggs: piano / Onie Wheeler: harmonica
Vocals: Dolly Parton **Backing Vocals:** The Nashville Edition
Recorded: RCA Studio B, Nashville (TN), June 12, 1973
Technical Team: Producer: Bob Ferguson / Sound Engineer: Al Pachucki / Assistant Sound Engineers: Roy Shockley, Mike Shockley
Single: Side A: I Will Always Love You / Side B: Lonely Comin' Down
Released: RCA Victor, April 4, 1974 (45 rpm ref.: APBO-0234)
Best Chart Ranking: 1 on Billboard Hot Country Songs (US), 4 on RPM Country Tracks (Canada)

Genesis and Lyrics

Dolly has said that she wrote this song on the same day as "Jolene" (or within a few days of it, depending on the source). This is hard to believe but shows how accomplished a songwriter Dolly had become. Her intention would have been to get Porter to admit that she was leaving the show and that their collaboration was over. When "I Will Always Love You" was released in 1974, people sat up and took notice. This song—a future international megahit—immediately shot to number one in the US charts. The protagonist of the story knows that she is not right for the man she loves and that she must leave him, taking with her bittersweet memories and the certainty that she will always love him. In 1992, Whitney Houston had a huge hit with the song, earning millions for Dolly Parton, who expressed her gratitude to "The Voice," and her amazement at what she had done with the love song. Whitney's spectacular version is on the soundtrack of the film *The Bodyguard*, directed by Mick Jackson. Today, there are countless covers of this hit, a song taken up by innumerable professional and aspiring singers. As for the original version, Dolly's fans will never forget the first time they heard her say "bittersweet memories" in that way that only she could do, with deep emotion, as if whispering a secret in the listener's ear.

Production

This song in a slow 4/4 tempo starts with a sumptuous tangle of electric guitars, both passed through a tremolo circuit to give a sense of openness and depth. On the left, the acoustic guitar and piano embroider a perfect texture over unadorned but perfectly executed arpeggios. Pedal steel and backing vocals get the choruses off the ground, supported by fiddles and the appearance of a cello in the last verse. Placed in the center, the bass and drums play what is needed where it is needed, and Dolly's voice literally takes off. The interpretation is remarkable, going from the most intimate spoken voice on the verses to the holding of the choruses, where Dolly's mastery and strength would melt the toughest heart. How many first kisses have been exchanged when listening to this masterpiece of romantic singing?

"Randy" evokes common themes from Dolly's career: the desire for passion, and the vital need to love and be loved.

Randy

Dolly Parton / 1:53

Musicians: Dolly Parton, Jimmy Colvard, Dave Kirby, Bobby Thompson, Chip Young: guitar / Pete Drake, Stu Basore: pedal steel / Bobby Dyson: bass / Jerry Carrigan, Larrie Londin, Kenny Malone: drums / Buck Trent: banjo / Mack Magaha, Johnny Gimble: fiddle / Hargus "Pig" Robbins, David Briggs: piano / Onie Wheeler: harmonica
Vocals: Dolly Parton **Backing Vocals:** The Nashville Edition
Recorded: RCA Studio B, Nashville (TN), December 26, 1973
Technical Team: Producer: Bob Ferguson / Sound Engineer: Al Pachucki / Assistant Sound Engineers: Roy Shockley, Mike Shockley

This love song, very different from "I Will Always Love You," evokes other themes found in the album: passion, the vital need to love and be loved.

Back to the up-tempo 4/4 and celebration for this track with its rather pronounced soft rock attributes. On the right, the acoustic guitar gives the song its brilliance thanks to the unrestrained strumming, the electric guitar does its best riffs and shares the turnarounds with the pedal steel; while on the left, the piano gives structure to the whole alongside the particularly compressed bass and drums duo mixed in the center of the space. There's no doubt about it: This Randy gives wings to the queen of country music.

Living On Memories Of You

Dolly Parton / 2:47

Musicians: Dolly Parton, Jimmy Colvard, Dave Kirby, Bobby Thompson, Chip Young: guitar / Pete Drake, Stu Basore: pedal steel / Bobby Dyson: bass / Jerry Carrigan, Larrie Londin, Kenny Malone: drums / Buck Trent: banjo / Mack Magaha, Johnny Gimble: fiddle / Hargus "Pig" Robbins, David Briggs: piano / Onie Wheeler: harmonica **Vocals:** Dolly Parton **Backing Vocals:** The Nashville Edition **Recorded:** RCA Studio B, Nashville (TN), December 26, 1973 **Technical Team:** Producer: Bob Ferguson / Sound Engineer: Al Pachucki / Assistant Sound Engineers: Roy Shockley, Mike Shockley

This song tells the story of a despairing love for a lost loved one. The country blues format is not so common with Dolly Parton, yet "Living on Memories of You," with its slow shuffle, is an archetype of the genre. The piano intro immediately sets the mood; on the verses, Onie Wheeler is able to exhibit the full extent of his blues skills on harmonica; the pedal steel soars on the chorus; and the electric guitar alternates between shuffle rhythm and hearty bluesy turnarounds.

Country and blues have always been close cousins, and this track is a perfect illustration of the proximity of the two genres. A country shuffle can take a decidedly bluesy turn in no time at all: a slightly stronger ternary rhythm, an evocation of the famous three chords (first, fourth, and fifth degrees of the scale or key of the song), a freer, more emotional playing by the soloists, and a plaintive soulful singing are enough to switch from one genre to the other. The chorus is not typically bluesy, but it blends perfectly with the twelve-bar blues of the verses. A fine exercise in style, admirably serving the purpose of the song, and perfectly executed by Dolly and her musicians.

Lonely Comin' Down
Porter Wagoner / 3:13

Musicians: Dolly Parton, Jimmy Colvard, Dave Kirby, Bobby Thompson, Chip Young: guitar / Pete Drake, Stu Basore: pedal steel / Bobby Dyson: bass / Jerry Carrigan, Larrie Londin, Kenny Malone: drums / Buck Trent: banjo / Mack Magaha, Johnny Gimble: fiddle / Hargus "Pig" Robbins, David Briggs: piano / Onie Wheeler: harmonica
Vocals: Dolly Parton **Backing Vocals:** The Nashville Edition
Recorded: RCA Studio B, Nashville (TN), May 3, 1973
Technical Team: Producer: Bob Ferguson / Sound Engineer: Al Pachucki / Assistant Sound Engineers: Roy Shockley, Mike Shockley
Single: Side A: I Will Always Love You / Side B: Lonely Comin' Down
Released: RCA Victor, April 4, 1974 (45 rpm ref.: APBO-0234)
Best Chart Ranking: 1 on Billboard Hot Country Songs (US), 4 on RPM Country Tracks (Canada)

Genesis and Lyrics
This is a cover version of a song by Porter Wagoner from the album *My Favorite Songwriter, Porter Wagoner*. This version is identical to the previous one, which is surprising, coming from Dolly, who is so productive and never inclined to take the easy option. One can assume therefore that there is an explanation: The master tape on *My Favorite Songwriter* is entirely saturated as soon as the full orchestra comes in. In addition, the mix is very dark, almost muffled by the lack of high frequencies. This song and its beautiful arrangement deserved much better; it receives its due here on the album *Jolene*.

This ballad, typically country in style, tells of the loneliness of the narrator once her lover has gone. She sees the pillow still creased by his head, and the mirror where his face is no longer reflected. And yet his presence is still felt everywhere. Loneliness descends over the narrator like a cloud of sadness. This track seems even more despairing than the previous one.

Production
An acoustic guitar riff in unison with the bass, natural harmonics, then delicate arpeggios constitute an original and skillful intro. Until the chorus, the two acoustic guitars dominate the arrangement with their right/left mirror picking. The drummer plays cymbals with brushes and some snare breaks, while the piano provides a delightful single descending arpeggio at 0:57. At 1:21 the fiddles make their entry with staccato low notes before raising the tension in held notes. After an agile bass descent as a lead-in, the chorus explodes with the full orchestra. Backing vocals, driving drums with hi-hat and eighth notes, pedal steel, staccato fiddles, powerful rhythmic piano, energetic strumming… it's a real fireworks display. You can feel that the band is on the verge of saturation, but this time the drama is avoided. The track ends with an ostinato and gradual fade-out—as if a lonely Dolly were walking away into the night.

It Must Be You
Blaise Tosti / 1:52

Musicians: Dolly Parton, Jimmy Colvard, Dave Kirby, Bobby Thompson, Chip Young: guitar / Pete Drake, Stu Basore: pedal steel / Bobby Dyson: bass / Jerry Carrigan, Larrie Londin, Kenny Malone: drums / Buck Trent: banjo / Mack Magaha, Johnny Gimble: fiddle / Hargus "Pig" Robbins, David Briggs: piano / Onie Wheeler: harmonica
Vocals: Dolly Parton **Backing Vocals:** The Nashville Edition
Recorded: RCA Studio B, Nashville (TN), January 12, 1972
Technical Team: Producer: Bob Ferguson / Sound Engineer: Al Pachucki / Assistant Sound Engineers: Roy Shockley, Mike Shockley

It is easy to see why Dolly chose this number, one that combines the elements of nature with the strength of love. This love song is well handled by the star but is much less impressive than other tracks on the album. Among the rumors and scandals surrounding Dolly Parton are the allegations made by the writer of this song, Blaise Tosti. It is difficult to find reliable evidence for Tosti's accusation that essentially claimed Dolly had sexually abused and harassed him when he was a teenager. For her part, Dolly has had little to say about this "affair," dismissing it as complete nonsense.

Musically, the number is an up-tempo 4/4 starting off with a bang. Repeated at the beginning of each verse, the little eight-note theme is first stated by the dobro and the piano in unison. Later, the piano takes over this effective gimmick on its own, supporting the voice on the last five notes of the theme. The verses trot merrily along and the choruses gallop; the ride is full of hope: "Must be you by my side the whole way through."

ALBUM

Love Is Like a Butterfly

Love Is Like a Butterfly . If I Cross Your Mind . My Eyes Can Only See You . Take Me Back .
Blackie, Kentucky . Gettin' Happy . You're the One That Taught Me How to Swing .
Highway Headin' South . Once Upon a Memory . Sacred Memories

RELEASE DATE
United States: September 16, 1974
Reference: RCA Victor, Nashville (TN)—APL1-0712
Best US Chart Ranking: 7

Flying Free

Produced by Bob Ferguson for the RCA Victor label, *Love Is Like a Butterfly* was Dolly Parton's fourteenth solo album. It was also the second album she brought out in 1974, having conquered the world of country music and now even the pop world with two songs that were to go down in history: "Jolene" and "I Will Always Love You." The themes tackled in the lyrics of "Love Is Like a Butterfly" are a combination of lightness and darkness: love and memories, recalling things past that were perhaps not perfect but, now they have gone, are missed—the country, her town, her family, her friends. The song was critically acclaimed, and *Billboard* and *Cashbox* magazines were full of admiration for this singer-songwriter who had composed eight of the ten tracks on the album—the other two being by Porter Wagoner.

The Girl Who Chased Butterflies

In 1974, Richard Nixon resigned the presidency following the Watergate political espionage scandal and was replaced by Gerald Ford; thirteen US states were hit by the Super Outbreak, a series of 148 tornadoes of unprecedented violence; the world danced to ABBA's "Waterloo"; and Dolly Parton opened her wings and flew.

Ever since her childhood, Dolly has been fascinated by butterflies. She has made the butterfly her badge, her trademark. Like an animal totem, it has become her signature. She loves this insect for its lightness, brilliance, beauty, and gentleness. When she was small she would chase them over hills and mountains and through forests. She would wander on through the countryside, sometimes going far from home, receiving a punishment when she got back for being late. Seen through adult eyes, a butterfly has a freedom that allows it to do what it wants, making us happy just to look at it. Born from a simple thing—sometimes beautiful, sometimes ugly—it metamorphoses from a caterpillar first to a chrysalis, then to a butterfly.

The butterfly has many symbolic meanings in different cultures and belief systems: freedom, joy, change, creativity. Its ability to mutate from one state to another is seen as representing the evolution of the soul and the change of form. This insect is sometimes seen as a symbol of power or even a message from the other world, whether it appears in dreams or in reality. In some countries, including Japan, it symbolizes love, femininity, and faithfulness. Many of these attributes can be associated with Dolly Parton, an artist who has never stopped reinventing herself and the world around her. Leaving the cocoon—her relationship with Porter Wagoner—she emerged one and indivisible. Like the previous album, *Love Is Like a Butterfly* stands as prelude to the new Dolly Parton, the singer preparing to metamorphose from the state of star to that of superstar.

The Real Dolly Parton

After the break with Porter Wagoner, Dolly found herself much taken up with the financial, legal, and professional fallout resulting from the end of her contract. She was also kept busy by the group she had formed with members of her family. Everything was new and different, even her freedom. But the old jokes and rumors did not go away. Since she had arrived in Nashville in 1964 at the age of eighteen, there were always comments about her clothes, her makeup, her voice—deemed childish by some and unique by others. As she described in an interview with Jerry Bailey,[5] wherever she went, wherever she had lunch, wherever she pushed open the door of a studio to sell a song, there was always someone to make fun of her. People talked of nothing but her breasts or her hair, both too inflated as she heard them say in the RCA studios or in the corridors of that venerable institution the Country Music Association. Dolly was happy to admit that she liked to have her hair piled high on her head, joking that it made up for her short stature. Whether or not she was hurt, she was able to shrug off these comments, not giving in to her detractors and refusing to sacrifice even an inch of hair. She was as she wanted to be and fully intended to stay

1974

At regular intervals, Dolly looks back on her past and her childhood in Tennessee.

In Dollywood, Dolly's emblem, the butterfly, is everywhere: substituted for the "w" on the sign at Dolly's theme park, on the staff's uniforms, and even in the flowerbeds where the flowers are planted in the shape of—what else?—a butterfly.

that way. She had won over her fans and their number was increasing. She was free to write what she wanted, and to construct her life and her career as she wished. But during that year, 1974, not everything was rosy, nor was it as light as a butterfly in flight. Dolly was suffering from nodules on her vocal chords and had to rest her voice. This was a serious problem and it obliged her to work less. It did not, however, stop her from pursuing many of her projects or from touring with her group. The Travelin' Family Band, headed by her brother Randy, was not the perfect group, but while waiting for a better arrangement, Dolly went to meet her public and, just as she had done in the days of *The Porter Wagoner Show*, she wrote songs.

An Album of Love and Memories

Dolly Parton has said, written, and repeated many times that she adores love songs, especially those that end well. This album has several, some of which end badly. When love is going well it is often compared to nature—the beauty of a landscape, for example, reflects the happiness of loving another. Memory and reminiscence appear frequently in Dolly's songs. While their appearance in this album was not something new, the themes take on a

more intimate note relating to this particular moment in her life. Often in the lyrics we find a protagonist regretting a choice made, a choice meaning they had to leave. This alternation of present/past/present is a characteristic of Dolly Parton's songs, detectable from her very first album. She looks back at her own past—Tennessee where she was born, her roots, the countryside she loved and explored as a child. With careful attention to the words, we can find elements that help us understand the songwriter, and perhaps even ourselves. Dolly is able to establish a dialogue with her fans, a very particular relationship that, right from the early days, she conscientiously weaves with her public.

Album Cover

Against a psychedelic turquoise-green background, a huge butterfly with spread multicolored wings envelops the star. Dolly's photo, taken by Hope Powell, shows her smiling face emerging from the halo of an extravagant blond wig. She is dressed in red with a rhinestone butterfly on the sleeve. This dazzling cover—100 percent Dolly Parton—heralds the color of the album: love and metamorphosis, strength and fragility.

A tenderhearted track was needed to open *Love Is Like a Butterfly*, and the title song fit the bill with its tale of love's transformational power.

For Dolly Addicts

The song "Love Is Like a Butterfly" is the opening theme of the 1976–1977 variety show *Dolly*.

Love Is Like A Butterfly

Dolly Parton / 2:22

Musicians: Jimmy Colvard, Dave Kirby, Bruce Osbon, Bobby Thompson: guitar / Bobby Dyson: bass / Larrie Londin: drums / Jerry Smith: piano / Stu Basore: pedal steel guitar **Vocals:** Dolly Parton **Backing Vocals:** The Lea Jane Singers **Recorded:** RCA Studio B, Nashville (TN), July 16, 1974 **Technical Team:** Producer: Bob Ferguson / Sound Engineer: (?) **Single:** A side: Love Is Like a Butterfly / B side: Sacred Memories **Released:** RCA Victor, August 5, 1974 (45 rpm ref. PB-10031) **Best US Chart Ranking:** 1 on Billboard Hot Country Songs

Genesis and Lyrics

As an opening to this album, what was needed was a tender love song about all that is lightest, sweetest, and most precious. Here, love is able to transform those who love one another. In the poetic lyrics, nature is associated with the feelings of love. Dolly finds yet another way of reinventing herself, of saying something she has said before but saying it differently. Her fans are delighted—this is Dolly's third number one album since *Hello, I'm Dolly*. The song also appeals to professionals in the entertainment world. A cover version sung by Clare Torry (singer with Pink Floyd) was used in the 1970s as the theme song for the BBC sitcom *Butterflies*.

Production

The musical arrangement of this song marks a notable development compared with preceding albums. We still find the rhythm guitar arpeggios and the use of the pedal steel guitar, but the beginning of each verse is simplified. The guitars mark the offbeats, as in reggae. The piano interjects little high-pitched downward scales, giving a light, playful atmosphere evoking a butterfly. The pedal steel guitar comes in after this famous piano motif, adding its own high notes, contributing to the feeling of airy flight. All the verses are constructed in the same way, with the first half having the offbeats and backing vocals. In each verse, the backing singers and Dolly Parton invert their respective phrases in something almost resembling a canon. The mix of the backing vocals is wide. The voices are distributed by desk in the sound space, the four voices being easily distinguished from one another, particularly the lowest voice at the end of the phrase of the second verse. The bass and drums are unfailingly correct. The musicians don't have a lot to do, in the sense that the bass plays very few notes throughout and the drummer's playing is restrained. The use of the reverb effect increases from album to album. Here it is strongly applied to Dolly's voice and not at all to the backing vocals.

If I Cross Your Mind

Porter Wagoner / 2:40

Musicians: Jimmy Colvard, Dave Kirby, Bruce Osbon, Bobby Thompson: guitar / Bobby Dyson: bass / Larrie Londin: drums / Jerry Smith: piano / Stu Basore: pedal steel guitar / (?): violin **Vocals:** Dolly Parton **Backing Vocals:** The Lea Jane Singers **Recorded:** RCA Studio B, Nashville (TN), July 18, 1974 **Technical Team:** Producer: Bob Ferguson / Sound Engineer: (?)

Dolly's decision to choose this song by Porter Wagoner can be explained in the context of her relationship with Porter. If the woman who has left ever thinks of him, the narrator asks her to pause and cherish the thought for a moment, for long enough to remember the good times, the happiness, and the shared love. The narrator's wish echoes the words of "I Will Always Love You," where Dolly writes that, as she leaves, she takes with her only bittersweet memories.

Sung to a very slow tempo, although the words express hope, Dolly's voice has, unusually, a note of despair. The intro is *a tutti* (with the full orchestra). Two violins appear with the first words. The drummer intervenes on the ride cymbal and the snare drum with brushes. The backing vocals are prominent, unlike the pedal steel guitar that is confined to short phrases. The piano, used as an accompaniment at the beginning, later enters to support the violins. As with some of last few albums, the bass plays a major role both in the rhythm and in the reiteration of the melodies.

My Eyes Can Only See You

Dolly Parton / 2:48

Musicians: Jimmy Colvard, Dave Kirby, Bruce Osbon, Bobby Thompson: guitar / Bobby Dyson: bass / Larrie Londin: drums / Jerry Smith: piano / Stu Basore: pedal steel guitar **Vocals:** Dolly Parton **Backing Vocals:** The Lea Jane Singers **Recorded:** RCA Studio B, Nashville (TN), July 16, 1974 **Technical Team:** Producer: Bob Ferguson / Sound Engineer: (?)

A return to honky-tonk music and forbidden love. Dolly continues her exploration of marriage, of what it means to be together, and whether or not to give in to temptation. These are issues that Dolly Parton has examined many times, stripping off layer after layer, album after album. The tempo of this binary ballad is very slow. While it might remind us of "If I Cross Your Mind," in fact the style of writing is more classical, with the reappearance of the electric guitar dialoguing with the pedal steel guitar. Dolly Parton moves somewhat outside her comfort zone here as she increases the power of her voice. The reverb applied to her voice is wide and, unlike with "Love Is Like a Butterfly," the instruments attenuate the effect felt by occupying the whole spectrum.

Take Me Back

Dolly Parton / 2:37

Musicians: Jimmy Colvard, Dave Kirby, Bruce Osbon, Bobby Thompson: guitar / Bobby Dyson: bass / Larrie Londin: drums / Jerry Smith: piano / Stu Basore: pedal steel guitar **Vocals:** Dolly Parton **Backing Vocals:** The Lea Jane Singers **Recorded:** RCA Studio B, Nashville (TN), July 16, 1974 **Technical Team:** Producer: Bob Ferguson / Sound Engineer: (?)

The title says it all: The narrator looks back to the past and her family, her mother washing clothes on the washboard, the simple pleasures of a loving family, togetherness, siblings, solidarity in hard times. Although as time goes by we all rearrange our memories of the past, it is clear that Dolly often misses those close to her. She particularly misses her childhood family, the family we all treasure in our memories when present reality with its drudgery and difficulties is hard, or just to feel content. Dolly re-creates some of her memories with a certain melancholy, painting in her song an idyllic picture of country life. And as she understands human nature, Dolly knows that the sentiment of "Take Me Back" will speak directly to the hearts of her fans.

The second half of the chorus acts as an intro, backed by the whole orchestra. The first verse begins with the rhythm instruments (drums, bass, folk guitars). These are gradually joined by the other instruments that enter in turn until they are all playing for the refrain. The same thing happens in the second verse, the only difference being one less guitar at the beginning.

Blackie, Kentucky

Dolly Parton / 3:29

Musicians: Jimmy Colvard, Dave Kirby, Bruce Osbon, Bobby Thompson: guitar / Bobby Dyson: bass / Larrie Londin: drums / Jerry Smith: piano / Stu Basore: pedal steel guitar / (?): violin **Vocals:** Dolly Parton **Backing Vocals:** The Lea Jane Singers **Recorded:** RCA Studio B, Nashville (TN), July 16, 1974 **Technical Team:** Producer: Bob Ferguson / Sound Engineer: (?)

If the song "Blackie, Kentucky" seems long and unrelenting, it is because the text is particularly dense. It deals with the themes of exile—from country to town—and unhappiness brought about by love. Dolly often associates a geographical name with her state of mind, using it to define a place's identity and name what is missing. In "Alabama Sundown" (*Bubbling Over* album), for example, the narrator is remembering her birthplace and its sunsets that she had turned her back on to move to the town where she hoped to make her fortune.

The album's pianist, Jerry Smith (shown third from left) with his band, The Sun Rhythm Section.

"Blackie, Kentucky," a dark ballad of deepest despair, is the flip side of the Dolly fairy tale. The woman in the song has left her native Kentucky to marry an older man in the hope of benefiting from his wealth. Instead, once with him, she encounters nothing but loneliness, sadness, and unkindness. He won't let her family come and visit because they are "country and poor." The singer's despair, alone in the couple's mansion like a ghost imprisoned within its walls, is so great that she sees no other way to return to her home again than to kill herself. Only then will her loved ones see her again—when they gather round her grave.

The song is in a restrained ragtime style with picking on the folk guitars. Larrie Londin plays the bass drum very subtly, alternating left and right foot to use the hi-hat on the offbeats. It would appear that he has his hands free to play the bongos. The arrangement is light and cheerful, in sharp contrast with the darkness of the lyrics. It ends, however, with a blues chord taking the listener back to the nostalgic origins of a genre of music that was originally conceived and played by Black Americans.

Gettin' Happy
Dolly Parton / 2:38

Musicians: Jimmy Colvard, Dave Kirby, Bruce Osbon, Bobby Thompson: guitar / Bobby Dyson: bass / Larrie Londin: drums / Jerry Smith: piano / Stu Basore: pedal steel guitar **Vocals:** Dolly Parton **Backing Vocals:** The Lea Jane Singers **Recorded:** RCA Studio B, Nashville (TN), July 16, 1974 **Technical Team:** Producer: Bob Ferguson / Sound Engineer: (?)

A track that is an ode to love and the happiness it brings. No more loneliness, cold nights, endless days. As is well known, Dolly met the man of her life at the age of eighteen outside a Nashville launderette. They have been together ever since, despite the passing of the years and the many rumors. Is the song a nudge to her fans to show them not to despair—the right person will come along? Whatever the

The audio overdrive effect aims to reproduce the saturation of a guitar amp pushed to its limits. Overdrive had been used since the 1940s, but it quickly damaged the equipment. In the early 1960s, a pedal, placed between the electric guitar and its amplifier, allowed the front sound signal (technically, an electrical signal) to be distorted to avoid this damage.

intention, the title is unambiguous: The narrator is going to be happy at last because she has found true love. The cheerfulness of "Gettin' Happy" contrasts with "Blackie, Kentucky," a variation in mood that Dolly likes to play around with.

The intro is very groovy, in the style of Stevie Wonder's "Superstition" (1972), "Sir Duke" (1976), or "Master Blaster (Jammin')" (1980). It begins with the drums, followed by the entry of the bass and then the first electric guitar with an overdrive. This effect is used for artistic reasons to give the song a rock feel. The combination of the saturated and clean electric guitar sounds (pedal steel) with the bass/drums/folk guitar rhythm is well done. You can feel Larrie Londin's pleasure in playing! The funk verse, the swing chorus, the rock breaks: Everything is there. And he even ends the song with a final break.

You're The One That Taught Me How To Swing

Dolly Parton / 2:07

Musicians: Jimmy Colvard, Dave Kirby, Bruce Osbon, Bobby Thompson: guitar / Bobby Dyson: bass / Larrie Londin: drums / Jerry Smith: piano / Stu Basore: pedal steel guitar **Vocals:** Dolly Parton **Backing Vocals:** The Lea Jane Singers **Recorded:** RCA Studio B, Nashville (TN), July 18, 1974 **Technical Team:** Producer: Bob Ferguson / Sound Engineer: (?)

Gone are the joys of new love and the beating heart; back to difficult, even terrifying love with this track that echoes "Just Because I'm a Woman." The narrator describes how she is no longer the innocent country girl she once was. Experience has turned her into someone else, a woman that would please her husband. He was the one who taught her how to dress, how to look sexy, and she has changed. But now he wants her to go back to being like she was: the dilemma of relationships where one person wants to change the other, then no longer recognizes them or likes them like that.

In terms of rhythm, which remains solid, with effective piano playing at the bass end, this piece is quite traditional. Only the bass allows itself short transitional phrases between the parts, giving a strong swing sound.

Highway Headin' South

Porter Wagoner / 2:05

Musicians: Jimmy Colvard, Dave Kirby, Bruce Osbon, Bobby Thompson: guitar / Bobby Dyson: bass / Larrie Londin: drums / Jerry Smith: piano / Stu Basore: pedal steel **Vocals:** Dolly Parton **Backing Vocals:** The Lea Jane Singers **Recorded:** RCA Studio B, Nashville (TN), July 18, 1974 **Technical Team:** Producer: Bob Ferguson / Sound Engineer: (?)

Life is better in the South—in songs at least, if not in reality. Porter Wagoner's lyrics evoke the warmth and sun of the South. And life is all the sweeter when you come home, because, for the narrator, none of the places she's been through are as good as the one she left behind.

"Highway Headin' South" bears the imprint of Southern music, such as the guitar phrases repeating small three-note upward scales. The contrasting effect between the rather quiet verses and the chorus, which expresses an explosion of joy, also evokes the sunshine of Dixie.

Once Upon A Memory

Dolly Parton / 2:05

Musicians: Jimmy Colvard, Dave Kirby, Bruce Osbon, Bobby Thompson: guitar / Bobby Dyson: bass / Larrie Londin: drums / Jerry Smith: piano / Stu Basore: pedal steel guitar **Vocals:** Dolly Parton **Backing Vocals:** The Lea Jane Singers **Recorded:** RCA Studio B, Nashville (TN), July 16, 1974 **Technical Team:** Producer: Bob Ferguson / Sound Engineer: (?)

Like a mirror image of "Love Is Like a Butterfly," "Once Upon a Memory" depicts the same love, full of joy and tenderness, the difference here being that it is no more than a memory. The theme of time and memory, what someone has or has lost, is one that is clearly close to Dolly's heart.

The song is based on a blues rhythm and a blues chord progression. The electric guitar with overdrive emphasizes the style. The breaks are atypical, allowing for the entry of the violins at 0:57 and 2:24. At 1:26, the mix with the backing vocals is interesting: While the voices are usually placed in front, here it is the electric guitars. One might expect a solo, but they play together in harmony. Two electric guitars are added to the pedal steel. Everything comes together to offer a good old blues, full of nostalgia for the past.

Dolly plays the guitar alongside Burt Reynolds during a 1973 appearance on *Burt Reynolds' Late Show* in Nashville. In 1982, Parton and Reynolds costarred in *The Best Little Whorehouse in Texas*.

Sacred Memories

Dolly Parton / 2:42

Musicians: Jimmy Colvard, Dave Kirby, Bruce Osbon, Bobby Thompson: guitar / Bobby Dyson: bass / Larrie Londin: drums / Jerry Smith: piano / Stu Basore: pedal steel guitar **Vocals:** Dolly Parton **Backing Vocals:** The Lea Jane Singers **Recorded:** RCA Studio B, Nashville (TN), September 1, 1972 **Technical Team:** Producer: Bob Ferguson / Sound Engineer: (?) **Single:** Side A: Love Is Like a Butterfly / Side B: Sacred Memories **Released:** RCA Victor, August 5, 1974 (45 rpm ref.: PB-10031) **Best US Chart Ranking:** 1 on Billboard Hot Country Songs

Reflecting on childhood experiences in church, in relation to family, community, nature, song, and God, the narrator thinks of those who are gone, dead to the living, but who remain eternally in Heaven. Memories are sacred, whether in relation to God or to departed friends. On the ten titles of this album, Dolly has returned once more to all those themes that are most important to her and that have made her the star she is.

The track opens with Dolly Parton's voice alone, unaccompanied, in order to evoke an important memory—that of singing "in that little country church I love so much." The fast tempo alternates with slower sections suggesting the hymns the narrator loved. The backing vocals are provided not only by the four Lea Jane Singers, but also by an entire gospel choir. Some instruments absent from the rest of the album make an appearance on this track (harmonica, banjo, and even a Hammond organ for the very last chord), as if to take a bow.

Kitty Wells and Patsy Cline
The Pioneers of Country

The evolution of the world of country music is partly due to the artistic quality of the musicians and singers, but also to the women who have changed the game. It is striking that in their absence, country stories about everyday life and relationships were almost all written by men. As a result of this one-sided viewpoint, female listeners, despite their love of the music, did not recognize themselves in the songwriters' world view. In 1935, Patsy Montana recorded "I Wanna Be a Cowboy's Sweetheart," a song that clearly claimed a freedom the women of her time did not have. Patsy Montana was the first country singer to sell a million records. She marked the beginning of a slow but inevitable revolution in country music: A female singer had just proved that a woman could have the same financial clout as a man, if not more. Patsy Montana led the way, but the Second World War slowed this development, and it was not until 1952 that another artist made her mark.

When female listeners heard Kitty Wells's "It Wasn't God Who Made Honky Tonk Angels," they thought, *Finally, a song that's really about me.* Loretta Lynn says that she started writing songs by listening to Kitty Wells. It was a small revolution that grew from Kitty Wells to Dolly Parton, Patsy Cline, and Loretta Lynn. Like a baton in a relay race, Tammy Wynette, Emmylou Harris, and many others would pick it up and pass it on. Kitty Wells and Patsy Cline paved the way for Dolly Parton, as she states in her autobiography,[1] and changed the musical tone of country music.

Kitty Wells: From Muriel to Kitty

Muriel Ellen Deason was born in Nashville in 1919 and grew up in a musical family. Her mother sang gospel, her uncle and father played country music, and her father taught her guitar. Everything predestined her to go into music. But in 1934, the economic hardships of the Great Depression forced her to leave school and take a job at the Washington Manufacturing Company, where she ironed shirts for nine dollars a week. With her sisters, she formed a band, the Deason Sisters, which performed on the local radio station WSIX.

At eighteen, she married musician Johnnie Wright and together they performed with Johnnie's sister Louise as Johnnie Wright and the Harmony Girls. The trio then met Jack Anglin, who married Louise and joined the group, which was renamed the Tennessee Hillbillies. It was Johnnie who chose his wife's stage name, in reference to "Sweet Kitty Wells," an old folk ballad sung by Bradley

Kincaid in 1928. In 1942, Jack Anglin went off to war, and the band, in which Kitty Wells sang backing vocals, disbanded.

Prior to her first hit, Kitty signed to RCA Victor and recorded several singles ("Don't Wait for the Last Minute to Pray" and "Death at the Bar"). Her songs did not make the charts, and RCA refused to invest any more money in her. In keeping with the longstanding patriarchal tradition that permeated society, record labels tended to view women as minor economic actors. Between the 1950s and the early 1960s, Kitty Wells proved, after Patsy Montana, that the record industry was wrong: Women could make a lot of money.

Kitty Wells Responds to Hank Thompson

In 1952, Decca Records' Paul Cohen offered Johnnie Wright a song written by producer J. D. Miller, and eventually his wife recorded "It Wasn't God Who Made Honky Tonk Angels," a sort of riposte to singer-songwriter Hank Thompson's hit "The Wild Side of Life" (1952). A common practice in country music, these verbal jousts consisted of recording a song in response to another artist's song. In his text, Hank Thompson talks about a "honky tonk angel" who seduced him and then left him to return to her errant life, implying that it was the fault of God, the creator of these women who meet men who frequent the shady bars alone. In the lyrics sung by Kitty Wells, it is very clear that the responsibility lies not with the divine but with the men. Kitty had just dropped a small bomb into the calm waters of country music. However, there had been a precedent for this in the late nineteenth century: the poet, singer, and songwriter William B. Gray, in "She's More to Be Pitied Than Censured," defended a girl who had fallen into the grips of a "bad life" because of a man.

One might think that in the early 1950s this argument would have been convincing to a wide audience, but this is only partly true. The song performed by Kitty Wells was controversial, and although it became a huge hit, reaching number one on the charts for six weeks, the singer was not allowed to perform at the Grand Ole Opry. NBC refused to broadcast "It Wasn't God Who Made Honky Tonk Angels" on its airwaves and as spokespersons for a tradition that resisted the evolution of morals, several radio stations blocked it, as they would do again to Dolly Parton's "Touch Your Woman" twenty years later. However, no matter what some people say or think, it is the public that decides:

Pioneering country music
singer Kitty Wells, ca. 1965.

QUEEN KITTY'S RECOGNITION AND AWARDS
- Country Music Association's Hall of Fame (1976)
- NARAS Governor's Award for Outstanding
  Achievement in the Recording Industry (1981)
- Academy of Country Music Pioneer Award (1985)
- NARAS Grammy Lifetime Achievement Award
  (1991)
- Music City News Living Legend Award (1993)

The record, No. 1 in the summer of 1952, sold more than 800,000 copies in its original version, and reached No. 27 on the Billboard Pop chart.

Kitty Wells's response to Hank Thompson marked a turning point in the history of country music, especially in the writing of lyrics. From now on, women were telling stories about relationships and love from their own perspective. Kitty Wells opened up a breach in the country music vortex, but, as is often the case in the history of pioneers, the ones that come after shine and overshadow the originator, which is what would happen with the one who was first declared "Queen of Country."

Queen Kitty

In 1953, "Paying for That Back Street Affair" was a huge hit, as were the very popular songs of the Kitty and Red Foley duo, such as "One by One," which reached number one on the Billboard Top Country & Western chart in 1954. Kitty never wrote a song and always performed other people's lyrics, such as "Singing His Praise,"[3] written by Dolly Parton's grandfather, the Reverend Jake Owens. In 1966, she recorded "More Love Than Sense" on Decca, a song by Dolly, which was never released.

Following on from her huge success in 1952, Kitty's recordings adhered to the same principle: Deep emotion and unspoken pain are expressed from the woman's point of view. In her songs, sad lovers narrate their drama through Kitty's plaintive singing, accompanied by the wailing of the pedal steel. Other classic ballads by the original "Queen of Country" include "Release Me" (1954), "Making Believe" (1955), and "I Can't Stop Loving You" (1958). Kitty

Wells's hits tell the stories of women of her time, such as the bride-to-be who throws away her dress after her fiancé runs off with her younger sister; or the man who gives up his girlfriend because she is no longer a virgin; or the men who leave their wives for younger women—themes also addressed by Dolly.

In an interview with Nicholas Dawidoff, Kitty Wells explains that while she writes about the condition of women, and manages to touch their hearts, this situation was never her own. Kitty admits to having lived a simple, risk-free life as a wife and mother, always singing and traveling with her husband, never drinking or taking drugs, never forgetting her Bible. But as a woman, she understood and felt the suffering of her fellow women. On stage the singer was neither glamorous nor extravagant, and wore old-fashioned clothes. Kitty Wells was married all her life to Johnnie Wright, who died a year before her; and their children, Bobby, Ruby, and Carol Sue, became part of the family project in the TV series *The Kitty Wells/Johnnie Wright Family Show*. Like the Parton family, who were also involved in Dolly's projects, the whole Wells-Wright family was involved in Kitty's projects: stage, show, and recording label Ruboca Records.

At the age of sixty, Kitty Wells sang her last big hit, "Thank You for the Roses," before a final appearance in 1997 on the stage of the Fan Fair in Nashville, alongside Hank Thompson. The woman who refuted the preconceived notion that women in country music do not sell and cannot make headlines died in 2012. It was due to her work that record companies opened their doors to other female artists.

The first female solo artist to be inducted into the Country Music Hall of Fame, Patsy Cline has inspired many singers, including her friends Loretta Lynn and Dottie West.

Patsy Cline: From Ginny to Patsy

Unlike Kitty Wells, the future Patsy Cline—born Virginia Patterson Hensley in 1932—not only identifies with the condition of women, she is a little bit each of those women: in mourning, in tears, abandoned, brutalized, or passionate. As a child, she oscillated between two worlds: that of instability and violence—she would later testify that her father sexually abused her—and that of music, with her tremendous aptitude and a mother who pushed her to take advantage of her talents. During her childhood, her family moved almost twenty times as her father, a blacksmith, found work. Eventually they settled in Winchester, Virginia, on South Kent Street, where Virginia lived from age sixteen to twenty. At thirteen, Ginny, as she was known, developed a serious throat infection and rheumatic fever, which at times caused her heart to stop. She was hospitalized and put in an oxygen tent. Once the infection was cured, Ginny discovered that her voice had changed: it was deeper. Once she recovered, she joined a Baptist choir. Mother and daughter participated in local events, and Virginia taught herself to play the piano. At the age of fourteen, she auditioned for WINC radio in Winchester, where she asked disc jockey Joltin' Jim McCoy to sing on his broadcast. This was the beginning of a long period of radio and bar performances.

While Kitty Wells looked old-fashioned on stage, with gingham and lace defining the standard attire for singers, Virginia had her own style, and the physique of a movie star. Hilda Hensley was a seamstress, so her daughter drew patterns, which her mother made into clothes—Patsy Cline did not yet exist, but the young woman was already working on her character. In the meantime, she took part in talent shows, for which she created a cabaret act based on the American singer Helen Morgan—Michael Curtiz's 1957 film *The Helen Morgan Story*, starring Ann Blyth and Paul Newman, seems to echo Patsy Cline's life. While her mother supported her, her father abandoned them in 1947, forcing his daughter to leave school to help support the household.

A Star Is Born

By day, Virginia worked in a drugstore, and by night, she sang with a band whose leader, Bill Peer, was the first to call her Patsy.[2] In 1949, she auditioned for the Grand Ole Opry, but was unsuccessful. As she often did in her life, the singer picked herself up and continued on her way, gradually finding her place in this milieu that was still resistant to women. On March 7, 1953, she married Gerald Cline, an unsatisfactory relationship that ended in divorce four years later. During this period, the young woman made inroads into the thriving Washington, DC, country music scene, run by the famous TV show producer Connie B. Gay.

Starting in the fall of 1954, Gay featured Patsy Cline as a soloist on his show, *Town and Country Time*. The year 1957 was a turning point in Patsy's life: On January 21, she appeared on *Arthur Godfrey's Talent Scouts*, singing "Walkin' After Midnight," which not only thrilled audiences but became her first major hit (ranked No. 2 on the country charts and No. 12 on the pop charts).

In the early spring of 1957, Patsy met the love of her life, Charlie Dick, who had been drafted into the army, forcing them to wait until September to get married. During Charlie's military service, Patsy slowed down her activity both on stage and in the studio. In late summer 1958, she gave birth to Julie, their first daughter, and they moved to Nashville, where Patsy signed with manager and former session guitarist Randy Hughes, who tried to relaunch her. Patsy recorded "I Fall to Pieces," which was to be one of her signature songs and climbed the charts week by week. The Grand Ole Opry inducted her as a member in January 1960.

A year later, their son Randy was born, and then, just when everything seemed to be going well in the best of all possible worlds, Patsy and her brother had a car accident. She was thrown through the windshield and suffered serious injuries to her forehead, arm, and hip. While she was recovering in her hospital bed, "I Fall To Pieces" went to number one on the country charts. From then on, Patsy toured extensively…and discovered wigs, which delighted

Hugely influential country music icon Patsy Cline, ca. 1950.

her because she was constantly on the road, where there were no hairdressers. Suddenly, she was enjoying the freedom of constantly changing her appearance: Goodbye, fringed stage costumes and cowgirl boots; hello, long silk dresses and high heels. Once again, life seemed wonderful. Patsy confirmed her success with the songs "Crazy," written by Willie Nelson, and "She's Got You," as well as the albums *Patsy Cline Showcase* (1961) and *Sentimentally Yours* (1962). She toured with Johnny Cash and George Jones (singer and husband of Tammy Wynette) and played in the Hollywood Hills, on the Hollywood Bowl stage, and in the heart of Manhattan, in the famous Carnegie Hall concert hall. The year 1962 was a vintage year for the artist.

The End of a Star
On March 3, 1963, Patsy and several other members of the Grand Ole Opry performed in Kansas City at Memorial Hall to a huge crowd. On her way home, she died in a plane crash that also claimed the lives of pilot and manager Randy Hughes and two other Opry stars, Cowboy Copas and Hawkshaw Hawkins. Patsy Cline's short life echoes the heartbreaking lyrics of the ballads she recorded and, like the stars, her light still shines through, long after her death at the age of thirty.

The singles "Leavin' on Your Mind" and "Sweet Dreams (of You)" entered the top ten after her death. Many recordings were released posthumously, and Patsy Cline remains one of Universal's most consistently high-selling artists (Decca was bought up by MCA, which was in turn acquired by Universal). The 1980 album *Always*, containing songs from the 1960s, inspired the internationally successful musical *Always...Patsy Cline*, created by Ted Swindley.

Also released posthumously, *Patsy Cline's Greatest Hits* (1967) is listed in the 2005 *Guinness Book of World Records* for selling over ten million copies. She has a street named after her at Universal Studios near Los Angeles, and her star shines on the legendary Hollywood Walk of Fame.

ALBUM

The Bargain Store

The Bargain Store . Kentucky Gambler . When I'm Gone .
The Only Hand You'll Need to Hold . On My Mind Again . I Want to Be
What You Need . Love to Remember . You'll Always Be Special to Me .
He Would Know . I'll Never Forget

RELEASE DATE
United States: February 17, 1975
Reference: RCA Victor, Nashville (TN)—APL1-0950
Best US Chart Ranking: 9

1975

Love, Sex, and Censorship

Produced by Bob Ferguson and Porter Wagoner for RCA Victor, *The Bargain Store* is Dolly Parton's fifteenth solo album. Dolly wrote eight of the ten numbers; the other two are by Porter Wagoner and by the singer, guitarist, and composer Merle Haggard, who was also one of Dolly's friends. The album's title song, "The Bargain Store," was boycotted on the grounds that the artist made reference in it to prostitution and sex. As with *Touch Your Woman* in 1972, Dolly once again suffered the displeasure of radio censorship, but this did not prevent the critics or fans from appreciating this album, nor did it hold back the sales, which really took off.

Censorship and Puritanism

The year 1975 saw the start of the trial of Ronald DeFeo Jr. for the murders committed against his family in Amityville, New York—a complex and gory event that shocked America and which was the inspiration for Stuart Rosenberg's film *The Amityville Horror* (1979). Bob Marley became famous with "No Woman No Cry." And, under the initiative of American secretary of state Henry Kissinger, the first meeting of the G6 summit took place in Rambouillet, France, with the major industrial countries opening up a "North-South" dialogue at the invitation of French president Valéry Giscard d'Estaing.

While music might have a civilizing influence, during the twentieth century the "popular" kind of music was constantly subject to censorship and was one of the domains of moralist and puritanical authority—from the premiere of Igor Stravinsky's *Rite of Spring* in Paris in 1913, which led to riots and numerous arrest; to the jazz clubs where people swung and swayed too much for the self-righteous, who saw them as haunts of the devil; to disco music, which stoked the fury of certain American radio presenters who attacked the genre and launched Disco Demolition Night in Chicago in 1979.

The same went for rock 'n' roll; Flower Power at Woodstock and elsewhere; and, among others, Prince and Beyoncé, who inflamed the censors of their time.

Self-Affirmation

In 1974, the CMA (Country Music Association) asked Dolly Parton to wear less hair, she told Jerry Bailey.[5] Dolly was clear about this: If she could not wear the hair she wanted, the flashy stage clothes she liked—in short, if she could not be herself—she would not appear on the CMA show. In fact, not a year went by without the artist being questioned: Porter's authoritarianism, constraints imposed by certain country music establishments, radio boycotts, insidious rumors and hurtful or sexist remarks…all this was part of the context of an ambivalent America, simultaneously audacious and cautious, which, still firmly subordinated to religious beliefs, did not look favorably on certain developments.

As early as 1974, the country music scene was in a state of turmoil: Is Dolly country or pop? "I Will Always Love You" and "Love Is Like a Butterfly" did well in the pop charts, expanding the songwriter's audience, but country purists saw this as an abandonment on her part. She denies this. Like her emblem, the butterfly, Dolly never stops evolving, changing, and asserting herself. *The Bargain Store* is the "sung" proof of this, with very strong songs that, at the time, certainly shook some people's convictions about marriage, the female condition, and sexuality.

Album Cover

On this album sleeve, which is somewhat more restrained than the previous one, in the foreground, Dolly's face, photographed by Hope Powell, seems to express concern or gravity, contrasting with the comforting pink of the letters, while in the background, a shop window evokes the album title.

Guitarist and songwriter Tony Joe White, a proud representative of country funk, in 1971.

The Bargain Store

Dolly Parton / 2:44

In her time, Kitty Wells wrote about the attitude of men who quickly got tired of their wives and went elsewhere—to the honky-tonks, for example—and of those who blamed their conquest for not being a virgin anymore.

Musicians: (?) **Vocals:** Dolly Parton **Backing Vocals:** The Lea Jane Singers **Recorded:** RCA Studio B, Nashville (TN): December 4, 1974 **Technical Team:** Sound Engineer: Tom Pick / Assistant Sound Engineers: Roy Shockley, Randy F. Kling **Single:** Side A: The Bargain Store / Side B: I'll Never Forget **Release:** RCA Victor, January 13, 1975 (45 rpm ref.: PB-10164) **Best Chart Ranking:** 1 on Billboard Hot Country Songs (US), 3 on RPM Country Tracks (Canada)

Genesis and Lyrics

Dolly was twenty-nine years old and already had a full life behind her. The songwriter knew that a woman of her age in 1970s society, especially in the countryside, was unlikely to have a second love life, because she was considered to be worn out by life, both mentally and physically. Moreover, in those days it was rare for women to wait until later in life to give birth, and one could quickly be labeled an "old maid"—a term as stigmatizing as "single mother." The song tells the story of a woman who knows that she is not a virgin, because she has lived and loved, suffered and been happy. Now that she is alone, she hopes for a new love, the kind that can heal old wounds. She is honest with the man who might want her; she embraces her femininity and her sexuality. Comparing herself to a discount shop where you can get a good deal, she says: "You can easily afford it, at this price,"[2] a phrase considered suggestive by the radio stations, which then censored the song.

Dolly takes her time singing "The Bargain Store," every word of which is full of emotion, sincerity, and sadness, much like the lyrics of "Jolene."

Production

Since *Jolene*, released in February 1974, we feel Dolly moving toward rougher sounds. By embracing folk music, venturing into rock and blues territory (remember "Living on Memories of You" on that same album), and after a few soul/gospel turns (such as "Here I Am" on *Coat of Many Colors* and "But You Loved Me Then" on *The Fairest of Them All*), she freed herself from her country label and opened herself up to a wider audience while succeeding in the stylistic feat of remaining solidly connected to her Tennessee roots.

After a unison guitar/bass intro, set to a bass drum stomp that marks the beat throughout, the session men of Studio B skillfully spice up their score: picking and strumming on the acoustic guitars in full panoramic face-off, minimalist bass on the beats, and backing vocals in Ennio Morricone–style echoes…this is a winning combination. The electric guitar takes care of the sinister atmosphere; its syncopated playing and its lightly distorted bite, with a slightly "dirty" timbre, remind us of the swamp blues sound of JJ Cale or Tony Joe White. The scent of scandal emanating from this "Bargain Store" number did not prevent the deal from going through—it has to be said that Dolly knows how to promote herself.

Dolly Parton onstage in
Los Angeles in 1975.

Kentucky Gambler

Dolly Parton / 2:40

Musicians: (?) **Vocals:** Dolly Parton **Backing Vocals:** The Lea Jane
Singers **Recorded:** RCA Studio B, Nashville (TN): May 23, 1973
Technical Team: Sound Engineer: Tom Pick / Assistant Sound
Engineers: Roy Shockley, Randy F. Kling

A song that is unflattering to the male gender. While the
story Dolly sings is a very sad and tearful one, it was probably a harsh reality for many women at the time.

A poor miner who thought he was lucky at gambling
leaves his wife, children, and Kentucky to seek his fortune.
In a Nevada casino, he gambles and gambles again, forgetting that he has a family and that they need him—and
then remembers this when he no longer has a dollar in his
pocket. But in the meantime, someone else has taken his
place in the home and is now taking care of his family.

This is a classic country song, covered by the famous
Merle Haggard. Obviously, the musical arrangement and
interpretation differ depending on whether he is singing in
the first person or Dolly Parton is singing from the external perspective, but the lyrics deliver the same message: A
gambler has a lot more to lose than to gain.

What better way to tell the story of this "Kentucky
Gambler" than with a honky-tonk tune tailor-made for a
country hoedown? The two electric guitars give it their all
in a delightful chicken-picking duel, the pedal steel has
its question mark–like lines, and the bass drives the nails
into the bass drum, first in an extremely spiky way on the
verses—this total absence of resonance creates an almost
comical effect—then unleashed on the choruses to contribute to the opening effect. A master at crafting tragicomic
hillbilly sketches, Dolly takes an empathetic but never com-
placent look at the social poverty that surrounds her.

When I'm Gone

Dolly Parton / 2:16

Musicians: (?) **Vocals:** Dolly Parton **Backing Vocals:** The Lea Jane
Singers **Recorded:** RCA Studio B, Nashville (TN): December 11, 1974
Technical Team: Sound Engineer: Tom Pick / Assistant Sound
Engineers: Roy Shockley, Randy F. Kling

Dolly continues her exploration of the theme of marriage:
When desire fades, when a love is undermined by wear
and tear and everyday life, when boredom sets in, what
can one do? The narrator's answer is simple: She leaves,
certain that only then will her man realize how much he
loves her and the value of the one he has lost. This weary,
perhaps weak man, although he still has feelings for his
wife, seems unable to satisfy his desire for her, to question
their intimacy, to renew it—a situation that has spoken to
more than one woman, and to feminists. Dolly maintains
her position as an artist and songwriter, as one who writes
and describes the world of human beings: the heart, body,
and soul, the women and men of her time.

As for the music, one feels the urgency of the situation.
This up-tempo 4/4 number takes the listener on a wild
ride along the dusty roads of the southern Appalachians.
There is no time to lose; Dolly's message has to come
through loud and clear: "You say [...] you're bored with
me [...] but you'll love me when I'm gone." The A Team
is in great shape, the acoustic and electric guitars unleash
their best turnarounds, the bass slams in like never before,
and the backing vocals of the Lea Jane Singers exude an
energy rarely equaled in the already long discography of
the Queen of Country. And energy is needed to follow Miss
Parton, always at the top of her game but particularly sharp
and concise on this track in the form of a warning: The ravages of marital weariness will not get past her.

The Only Hand You'll Need To Hold

Dolly Parton / 2:12

Musicians: (?) **Vocals:** Dolly Parton **Backing Vocals:** The Lea Jane Singers **Recorded:** RCA Studio B, Nashville (TN): December 4, 1974 **Technical Team:** Sound Engineer: Tom Pick / Assistant Sound Engineers: Roy Shockley, Randy F. Kling

This love song underlines the importance of the unfailing presence and support that we can give to the one we love. There is a conviction in the songwriter's lyrics, as well as in the singer's voice, that the other person needs that helping hand. Without a doubt, even if she has been hurt in certain relationships, Dolly has within her that strong feeling—loving, filial, friendly—that tells us that we can truly and completely rely on the other, with the other by your side.

This ode to fidelity and trust starts with an up-tempo country shuffle that gives pride of place to the acoustic instruments. The rhythm section aside, strumming acoustic guitars, piano, and backing vocals largely dominate the arrangement. With the exception of the electric guitar, which deploys a solo with exemplary melodic conciseness at 0:51 (plus a few well-judged rhythmic syncopations and its traditional tick-tock), the instrumentation remains remarkably restrained and unplugged. No frills to deliver this simple, sincere, and dedicated message. Dolly shows the authenticity of her personality in this song, and this is the musical setting that enables her to express it with the greatest accuracy.

On My Mind Again

Porter Wagoner / 2:51

Musicians: (?) **Vocals:** Dolly Parton **Backing Vocals:** The Lea Jane Singers **Recorded:** RCA Studio B, Nashville (TN): December 11, 1974 **Technical Team:** Sound Engineer: Tom Pick / Assistant Sound Engineers: Roy Shockley, Randy F. Kling

After their separation, Dolly continued to borrow songs written by Porter Wagoner, who produced some of her albums. The choice of this text is probably not insignificant. Some have seen it as fuel for rumors of a romance between Porter and Dolly; others may see it as the weight of that relationship on Dolly's mind—she was only just beginning to have legal battles with her former show partner. This was not the first time Porter Wagoner had tackled this theme of remembering lost love...as an obsession.

For this mid-tempo 4/4 ballad, we remain with a clear line. Restraint is the order of the day, and the acoustic color is still in the spotlight, except for the bass, a discreet electric guitar, and the traditional pedal steel. This choice perfectly suits the purity of Dolly's interpretation and the message Porter Wagoner wants to convey here. "On My Mind Again," with its theme and narrative structure, could well have appeared on one of Dolly and Porter's duo albums.

I Want To Be What You Need

Dolly Parton / 2:42

Musicians: (?) **Vocals:** Dolly Parton **Backing Vocals:** The Lea Jane Singers **Recorded:** RCA Studio B, Nashville (TN): December 9, 1974 **Technical Team:** Sound Engineer: Tom Pick / Assistant Sound Engineers: Roy Shockley, Randy F. Kling

This song follows the theme, already touched upon in "The Only Hand You'll Need to Hold," of the unparalleled and constant support that love represents.

Finally, here is the first country waltz on the album. The interventions of each musician are as delicate as a caress to the soul. The swirls of the pedal steel, the warm voices of the backing singers and their subtle vibrato, the comforting arpeggios of the electric guitar and the piano, the soft crackling of the snare drum played on brushes, combined with the supple strumming of the acoustic guitar: It's all there. All you need to do is add the magic ingredient: a pinch of fiddle, with a charm that is as discreet as it is indispensable to the rise of the whites. A perfect sound cloud to welcome Dolly and her angelic voice. It's hard not to be bewitched.

Love To Remember

Dolly Parton / 2:33

Musicians: (?) **Vocals:** Dolly Parton **Backing Vocals:** The Lea Jane Singers **Recorded:** RCA Studio B, Nashville (TN): December 11, 1974 **Technical Team:** Sound Engineer: Tom Pick / Assistant Sound Engineers: Roy Shockley, Randy F. Kling

Two country waltzes in a row, and this one is even sweeter—who would have thought it possible?—at a slightly slower tempo. In this sensual ballad, every gesture, every caress, every night, consolidates the present and the memory of this wonderful love. The backing vocals of the Lea Jane Singers once again wreak havoc, benefiting here from particularly elaborate arrangements and breathtaking volume nuances. From 1:16 onward, the fiddles are transformed into a ghostly string ensemble with the superimposition of multiple overdubs and a very advanced reverb delivery. The particularly fine work on this ode to languor and nostalgia for love is meticulous. Dolly's interpretation is more than equal to the task; hanging on every word, every note, the listener can let go, plunging into a deep reverie from which they may not emerge completely unscathed.

You'll Always Be Special To Me

Merle Haggard / 2:23

Musicians: (?) **Vocals:** Dolly Parton **Backing Vocals:** The Lea Jane Singers **Recorded:** RCA Studio B, Nashville (TN): December 11, 1974 **Technical Team:** Sound Engineer: Tom Pick / Assistant Sound Engineers: Roy Shockley, Randy F. Kling

The narrator sings of his love for the woman who will always be unique to him, even though he is now only a friend, and even if he cannot get any closer to her. The succession of three country waltz ballads is a first in Dolly Parton's discography. This is confirmed by the fact that in the last third of the album, Dolly and her producers have decided to sit the listener down in the rocking chair and invite them to meditate. "You'll Always Be Special to Me," composed by the great Merle Haggard, contains the same ingredients as the two previous waltzes, but with a slightly faster tempo and a more distanced tone. This time, Dolly has really taken off, as ever, with the respect and delicacy for which we know her.

He Would Know

Dolly Parton / 2:34

Musicians: (?) **Vocals:** Dolly Parton **Backing Vocals:** The Lea Jane Singers **Recorded:** RCA Studio B, Nashville (TN): December 9, 1974 **Technical Team:** Sound Engineer: Tom Pick / Assistant Sound Engineers: Roy Shockley, Randy F. Kling

The temptation of love...Dolly questions the feelings, desires, and constraints of the marital relationship. The narrator says that it would be so good to love another man, but at home her husband is waiting for her, and she cannot and will not lie to him. She flirts and dreams about this other passion, but she does not taste it.

The instrumentation on this song is still extremely delicate: the nylon string guitar picking on the right, probably

played by Dolly Parton, the folk guitar picking on the left, the electric guitar passed through the mellowness of a tremolo circuit, the electric piano also passed through the tremolo mill (probably a Fender Rhodes, since it has its own tremolo circuit), the pedal steel mixed very deep... The fiddle and the backing vocals that are mixed with the overdubs of Dolly's voice contribute to this lightness, not forgetting the bass and the very soft drums, which almost disappear on the verses. The arrangements and the melody of the chorus are striking: At the beginning of each second cycle, the reprise on "And if I lied" is particularly shimmering, superbly enhanced by the chromatic rise at the end of the previous phrase ("to know me very well"). When the A Team decides to go for gold, there is no compromise.

SINGLE

I'll Never Forget

Dolly Parton / 2:47

Musicians: (?) **Vocals:** Dolly Parton **Backing Vocals:** The Lea Jane Singers **Recorded:** RCA Studio B, Nashville (TN): December 11, 1974 **Technical Team:** Sound Engineer: Tom Pick / Assistant Sound Engineers: Roy Shockley, Randy F. Kling **Single:** Side A: The Bargain Store / Side B: I'll Never Forget **Release:** RCA Victor, January 13, 1975 (45 rpm ref.: PB-10164) **Best Chart Ranking:** 1 on Billboard Hot Country Songs (US), 5 on RPM Country Tracks (Canada)

While the album opens with a broken being who claims to be nothing more than a woman who has seen life, *The Bargain Store* ends with a softer song, reminiscent in its tenderness of "Love Is Like a Butterfly." Through this fervent declaration, Dolly teaches us that love remains, even after the other has gone.

The lightness of the arrangement and the soft touch of the session men from Studio B perfectly suit this country/folk ditty composed by Dolly Parton. The drummer's brushes flutter like butterfly wings, the crisscrossing pickings evoke the happy, bucolic atmosphere of a July in the Smokies, and the intervention of the backing vocals on the first chorus seems to dispel the morning mist.

This pretty B-side offers another approach to the theme of nostalgia, already widely addressed in the previous songs: a delicious nostalgia that we like to cultivate in ourselves and that we will never stop cherishing.

ALBUM

Dolly:
The Seeker / We Used To

We Used To . The Love I Used to Call Mine . My Heart Started Breaking .
Most of All, Why? . Bobby's Arms . The Seeker . Hold Me . Because I Love You .
Only the Memory Remains . I'll Remember You as Mine

RELEASE DATE
United States: September 15, 1975
Reference: RCA Victor, Nashville (TN)—APL1-1221 (stereo)
Best US Chart Ranking: 14

Released in 2011, the film *The Year Dolly Parton Was My Mom*, by Canadian Tara Johns, tells the story of an eleven-year-old girl who, upon learning that her parents adopted her, intertwines her search for her identity (and her journey to find her biological mother) with her admiration for Dolly Parton. The star lent her voice to the film's soundtrack.

Love, Always

Dolly: The Seeker / We Used To, produced and arranged by Porter Wagoner, and released by RCA Victor on September 15, 1975, is the artist's sixteenth solo album, and *Billboard* magazine praised its songwriting. It is an album of repetition and continuity. The exploration of love that Dolly had undertaken since the beginning of her career nevertheless takes a different turn here: In contrast to the previous albums, which appealed to feminists, in this one, through the voices of the narrators that Dolly interprets, one detects manifestations of submission. Between country, ballads, and gospel, this opus was appreciated by the fans, even though the sales were disappointing.

The Love Trilogy: Faith, Joy, Sadness

Written entirely by the songwriter, this new album is dedicated to love: Dolly's love for God, but also love that is so sad it makes you cry, love that makes you despair and feel bad, love that is flowery and romantic, love that gives you comfort. In "Because I Love You," Dolly portrays a woman who feels the desire to surrender herself, at the risk of her lover taking control of their relationship; better still, the narrator demands it, intoxicated by the love she feels. This album equates all forms of love, including devotion to the divine, with the songwriter seeing the "seeker's" relationship with God as a kind of loving surrender of self. One might ask whether God and love are not the same entity in Dolly Parton's work, whether they passionately inhabit us or cruelly elude us.

In All Directions

Dolly was exhausted, and the presence of nodules on her vocal cords was increasingly worrying. If she did not give them a rest, an operation would be necessary, which could have serious consequences for her career. The singer worked hard, moving from the recording studio to concerts (Toronto, Alexandria, Nashville), from writing to planning a sister's wedding, from legal hassles with Porter Wagoner to a relative's birthday party. During 1975, Dolly was approached by Bill Graham, president of Show Biz, Inc., the company that produced *The Porter Wagoner Show*.[2] Graham suggested that she should have her own variety show. The show was called *Dolly* and launched in September 1976. Between 1974 and 1975, Dolly recorded her last two duet albums with Porter: *Porter 'n' Dolly* and *Say Forever You'll Be Mine*—ironic titles in the context of their breakup and the legal battle between them. The star continued to plan her new career and decided to travel to the West Coast to meet Sandy Gallin, the producer of singer Cher and comedian Joan Rivers. Dolly's friend and former manager Don Warden stayed by her side to advise her. Despite her fatigue and frustration—because she did not feel she was at the level she wanted to be—Dolly worked on a tour, her band, improving her management, and already she was preparing her transition to pop. The team that surrounded her—family and friends mainly—although professional, did not enable her to go that far. This was something she would remedy in the months to come.

Album Cover

A close-up of Dolly's face, photographed by Dennis Carney, whose portraits of stars are famous in southeast Tennessee. True to form, the star is wearing a bright smile and a flamboyant wig in very soft shades of golden blonde and blue-green.

The Country Music Awards named Dolly Parton the Female Vocalist of the Year in 1975 and again in 1976.

For Dolly Addicts
Ten years after the release of "We Used To," it reached number forty-nine on the charts in the Netherlands.

SIDE A

We Used To

Dolly Parton / 3:14

Musicians: (?) **Vocals:** Dolly Parton **Backing Vocals:** The Lea Jane Singers **Recorded:** RCA Studio B, Nashville (TN), December 9, 1974 **Technical Team:** Sound Engineer: Tom Pick / Assistant Sound Engineer: Roy Shockley **Single:** Side A: We Used To / Side B: My Heart Started Breaking **Release:** RCA Victor, September 8, 1975 (45 rpm ref.: PB-10396) **Best Chart Ranking:** 9 on Billboard Hot Country Songs (US), 4 on RPM Country Tracks (Canada)

Genesis and Lyrics

As is often the case with Dolly Parton, there is a very strong link in the text between the feeling of love—in this case, the memory of a past love—and nature—loving in the rain, sitting together by a river, walking hand in hand through a flowery meadow—giving this moment of union a very special flavor. The memories endure, oscillating between the sweet and the bitter; memory always recalls what was. It is a song to be danced to slowly, held close to each other, a song to be listened to in solitude when the rain is falling outside while an open fire burns inside.

Production

Following "The Bargain Store," Dolly Parton had to take care of her vocal cords, and her songwriting reflects this. The range of the melodies is sufficiently comfortable that the artist does not have to go high or powerful. The proximity of the microphone is also noticeable.

This gentle, melancholic ballad opens with the intro to Led Zeppelin's 1971 rock monument "Stairway to Heaven" (which Dolly Parton covered in 2002). We also recognize the chords—more or less similar—of "The House of the Rising Sun," a traditional song from the South of the United States whose best-known cover is that of the Animals in 1964. And Dolly goes even further on the main part of the chorus by taking the chords of "Yesterday" by the Beatles (1965). With this song, goodbye to traditional country music, and instead, hello to ballads: The electric guitars play discreet themes, the backing vocals are well highlighted, the string quartet's violins have the place of honor, omnipresent throughout the song and at least as strong as the vocals. The bass, preponderant in the previous albums, is a little less prominent, so as not to "disturb" the playing of the violins; it is unassumingly aligned with the low notes of the guitar arpeggios.

The Love I Used To Call Mine

Dolly Parton / 2:50

Musicians: (?) **Vocals:** Dolly Parton **Backing Vocals:** The Lea Jane Singers **Recorded:** RCA Studio B, Nashville (TN), December 26, 1973 **Technical Team:** Sound Engineer: Tom Pick / Assistant Sound Engineer: Roy Shockley

This piece is comparable to "We Used To," but beyond the nostalgia, with a sadder tone in the writing and in the voice. It should be noted that when Dolly switches from singing to reciting, the song becomes less syrupy. The violins leave more room for the electric guitars, especially the pedal steel. The piano, very much in the background on the previous track, is more prominent here in the accompaniment of the vocals, in addition to the folk and classical guitars. The latter plays the little theme of the intro.

My Heart Started Breaking

Dolly Parton / 3:2

Musicians: (?) **Vocals:** Dolly Parton **Backing Vocals:** The Lea Jane Singers **Recorded:** RCA Studio B, Nashville (TN), April 16, 1971 **Technical Team:** Sound Engineer: Tom Pick / Assistant Sound Engineer: Roy Shockley **Single:** Side A: We Used To / Side B: My Heart Started Breaking **Release:** RCA Victor, September 8, 1975 (45 rpm ref.: PB-10396) **Best Chart Ranking:** 9 on Billboard Hot Country Songs (US), 4 on RPM Country Tracks (Canada)

This other love song plays on emotion to perfection: We move from the description of a wonderful love to a cruel love. The other did not live up to his promises and left, leaving the narrator with a broken heart. A Dolly Parton classic in the category of a sobbing, sad love, one that is even to die for.

The reverb effect is back. On the first two tracks of the album it is more discreet, as many instruments together mask it. On this track, which is more streamlined, it is more perceptible. There is also a significant pre-delay (the time between the direct sound and the first reverb), the simulation of a vast reverberating location, but over a rather short time. The drums are given a more ambitious part, and the violins play pizzicato notes—a first in string quartet part writing.

Most Of All, Why?

Dolly Parton / 3:03

Musicians: (?) **Vocals:** Dolly Parton **Backing Vocals:** The Lea Jane Singers **Recorded:** RCA Studio B, Nashville (TN), May 24, 1974 **Technical Team:** Sound Engineer: Tom Pick / Assistant Sound Engineer: Roy Shockley

Another theme that the songwriter continued to explore was the silent dissolution of marriage, so slow and insidious that we do not see it coming. It is as if reality is slipping away from the narrators, caught up in the monotony of everyday life. Why does the feeling of love disappear? Why does boredom replace passion, and sadness erase joy? Dolly does not provide an answer to this existential question, which is also asked by those who used to believe in God when faith leaves them.

To open this delicate piece, the original intro mixes the melody of the piano with the notes of the guitar, bordering on dissonance; a slapback delay has in fact been applied to them: Each of these notes is heard twice. Throughout the song, almost all the solo instruments (violins, electric guitars, backing vocals) play layers together, creating a thick harmonic carpet under Dolly's voice. The jazzy notes of the piano are also noteworthy.

Bobby's Arms

Dolly Parton / 2:40

Musicians: (?) **Vocals:** Dolly Parton **Backing Vocals:** The Lea Jane Singers **Recorded:** RCA Studio B, Nashville (TN), December 1, 1973 **Technical Team:** Sound Engineer: Tom Pick / Assistant Sound Engineer: Roy Shockley

Unlike the previous songs, this one celebrates the sensual and protective love that is unwavering and helps push away the worries of everyday life.

The melodies of the two electric guitars are very precisely timed, so much so that one can hear a single note at times. The reverb is more discreet, as Dolly gives less power than elsewhere on the album. The backing vocal harmonies are also less "classic," as the chords are enriched, with gaps between the notes.

"The Seeker" seduced gospel lovers and was covered by other popular artists, such as Merle Haggard in 1976.

The Seeker

Dolly Parton / 3:02

Musicians: (?) **Vocals:** Dolly Parton **Backing Vocals:** The Lea Jane Singers **Recorded:** RCA Studio B, Nashville (TN), December 9, 1974 **Technical Team:** Sound Engineer: Tom Pick / Assistant Sound Engineer: Roy Shockley **Single:** Side A: The Seeker / Side B: Love with Feeling **Release:** May 1975 (45 rpm. ref.: PB-10310)

Genesis and Lyrics

The spiritual aspirant is one who seeks a master, a teacher who can guide them on the path to God. Here, the narrator, a poor sinful creature, relies totally on the guardian to absolve her, show her the way, and protect her. This title found its audience, probably because it evokes the doubts that every believer or aspirant to religion experiences in their faith. Like the narrator of "The Seeker," everyone would like to have a helping hand in their quest. This song, which will appeal to gospel music lovers, believers, and atheists alike, was covered by other artists, such as Merle Haggard in 1976, and rerecorded by Dolly in 1995 for her album *Something Special*.

Production

This is the first track on the album that is not a ballad. The bass/drums rhythm section and the two folk guitars make one want to rock out, despite the binary character of the rhythm. Usually, at the very least, the bass adopts a slightly syncopated line to avoid monotony. Here, only the last verse escapes the straightforwardness of the song, with the drummer allowing himself some "fantasies" on the bass drum.

As there are few instruments accompanying Dolly Parton, the violins and the backing vocals are quite distinct, while the drums seem more powerful. These contrasts sharpen the listener's interest by taking them in several directions simultaneously. It is also an opportunity to hear the reverb on the backing vocals, perfectly in the gospel style, and the simulation of a church for the vocals. The backing vocals are mixed at the same level as the lead voice. An anecdotal detail: Two accented notes during a quiet part (1:20) are not repeated at any other time in the song. Finally, one assumes that due to her fragile vocal cords, Dolly could not hold out for long at full power. The song ends in a fade-out, but a little too late, following a sense of anticipation.

Hold Me

Dolly Parton / 2:36

Musicians: (?) **Vocals:** Dolly Parton **Backing Vocals:** The Lea Jane Singers **Recorded:** RCA Studio B, Nashville (TN), February 1, 1973 **Technical Team:** Sound Engineer: Tom Pick / Assistant Sound Engineer: Roy Shockley

If "Hold Me" is reminiscent of "Bobby's Arms," it is because it speaks of the same benevolent love that soothes in the face of life's torments, of the same symbolism of arms that embrace, surround, and protect. However, there is a notable difference in this songwriter's text: The narrator is aware that she is dependent on this love, that she is under the influence and even the control of her man, and declares that she is nothing without him. If, in the twenty-first century, these words may seem to be from another time, there is no doubt that some people can still identify with them.

The writing of this piece is also new. The intro is in binary (the beat is divided into two eighth notes), the first verse is in three time (the beat is divided into three eighth notes), and this changes with each verse or refrain. This alternation exists in other songs, but the arrangements are so subtle that they are imperceptible to the casual listener.

Because I Love You

Dolly Parton / 2:16

Musicians: (?) **Vocals:** Dolly Parton **Backing Vocals:** The Lea Jane Singers **Recorded:** RCA Studio B, Nashville (TN), (date?) **Technical Team:** Sound Engineer: Tom Pick / Assistant Sound Engineer: Roy Shockley

The narrator sings of her love for the one who will always be unique in her eyes, even if he is now just a friend, even if he can no longer get close to her. As strongly as the previous track, "Because I Love You" tells us that being in love induces a dependence on the other. One imagines that feminists would not have applauded these words, but the sentimental and psychic meanderings, the complexity of emotions and feelings, which vary from one person to another, are at the heart of the exploration she is pursuing.

This song differs from the other tracks on this opus in that it has much more of a pop sound, both in its rhythm and in its structure: After an alternating verse/chorus/verse/chorus, the latter is repeated at the end, in the same key. Classically, the verse is calm, while the chorus explodes with backing vocals, the violins playing louder, and the drummer striking the skin of his snare drum.

Only The Memory Remains

Dolly Parton / 2:49

Musicians: (?) **Vocals:** Dolly Parton **Backing Vocals:** The Lea Jane Singers **Recorded:** RCA Studio B, Nashville (TN), (date ?) **Technical Team:** Sound Engineer: Tom Pick / Assistant Sound Engineer: Roy Shockley

Between vocals and recitation, Dolly expresses the torments of a woman who still loves the one who left and still burns with the flame that animated the two of them—a torture, now that she is alone. How long must a broken heart hold out before it no longer cries or suffers, and only the memory remains?

The arrangements of this song are very elaborate, starting with the phrase of the two electric guitars—a feature that was becoming more and more recurrent with Dolly. And above all, when the voices sing "Stop!" in the second part, everyone, musicians and singers, stops at the same time, and the following phrases are played *a tutti*.

I'll Remember You As Mine

Dolly Parton / 2:48

Musicians: (?) **Vocals:** Dolly Parton **Backing Vocals:** The Lea Jane Singers **Recorded:** RCA Studio B, Nashville (TN), August 22, 1972 **Technical Team:** Sound Engineer: Tom Pick / Assistant Sound Engineer: Roy Shockley

This last love song plays on the past. The narrator still loves her man and begs him to act as in the time when their feelings were mutual and she was his. Whatever the reason for the end of their story, the lover does not forget.

This is one of the few times when the backing vocals complete the intro, accompanied by folk guitar and drums. On the piano phrase that follows, an electric guitar note "slides": The musician starts from the low end of the neck and moves up to a higher note. This process is repeated after the first chorus, on the upper fifth, for a very rock or funk effect, even though the song as a whole does not belong to these registers. Dolly closes the album *The Seeker* with a ballad, just a little more percussive than those the listener might be used to.

ALBUM

All I Can Do

All I Can Do . The Fire That Keeps You Warm . When the Sun Goes Down Tomorrow .
I'm a Drifter . Falling Out of Love with Me . Shattered Image . Boulder to Birmingham .
Preacher Tom . Life's like Poetry . Hey, Lucky Lady

RELEASE DATE
United States: August 16, 1976
Reference: RCA Victor, Nashville (TN)—APL1-1665 (stereo)
Best US Chart Ranking: 3

Dolly provided the vocal harmonies in the country rock band Pinmonkey's 2002 cover of *Falling Out of Love with Me*.

For Dolly Addicts

For this album, Dolly was nominated for the 19th Annual Grammy Awards in the category of Best Female Country Vocal Performance.

In 1976, Dolly launched her own televised variety show.

The End of an Era

This was a first: Dolly Parton only released one album in 1976, probably due to the state of her vocal cords, but also to the launch of the variety show *Dolly*. The new album was critically acclaimed, with Dolly writing eight of the ten songs. It was also the first time she had co-produced an album, with Porter Wagoner (who produced her for the last time). Released on RCA Victor on August 16, 1976, *All I Can Do* is the artist's seventeenth solo album, authentically country, albeit with a pop rock edginess. The songwriter's talent as a writer was once again confirmed, as *Billboard* magazine emphasized in a glowing review.

A Very Important Period

While Elton John and Kiki Dee sang "Don't Go Breaking My Heart" and French artist Bernard Quentin, invited to the Chicago International Fair as part of the bicentennial of American independence, floated a monumental inflatable Venus on a tract of water, Dolly's career was evolving. This was the first time, but certainly not the last, that the star was involved in the production of her albums. A turning point had been reached; she had regained her autonomy. Concretely, symbolically, and financially, this was a huge step toward greater freedom to create and prosper. For, as Dolly wrote in her autobiography,[1] during the Porter Wagoner years, when he earned ten dollars, she earned only one. The aspiring businesswoman realized that she could do the same, or even more. Dolly moved forward, sometimes happily, sometimes with difficulty, but she held the thread in her hand that would lead her to the realization of her superstar dream.

All That Dolly Can Do

In 1976, Dolly embarked on a new experience: hosting her own TV show. Bill Graham, the producer of *The Porter Wagoner Show*, offered Dolly her own variety show. The star accepted, but after one season, frustrated at not having a free hand, she did not repeat her performance. Despite the state of her vocal cords and the cumbersome legal proceedings with Porter, the songwriter was developing and, with *All I Can Do*, the message was clear: Dolly Parton was going to widen her audience—keep her country audience and conquer the pop market as well. The AllMusic site columnist Mark Deming points out that during those last few recording sessions with Porter Wagoner, Dolly was a little tense. Her first decade in Nashville thus ends on an album with pop rock arrangements (those of "Shattered Image" and "The Fire Keeps You Warm" in particular). Deming also notes, as does *Billboard* magazine, that Dolly's writing is deep, emotionally charged, and explores a wide range of feelings, from nostalgia to sweetness, from lightness to passion, which feeds everyone's heart and soul.

Album Cover

Dolly looks stunning on this cover by photographer Hope Powell. Very sixties, the star is dressed in red-and-white gingham, a scarf tied in her hair, blond and radiant.

"All I Can Do" tells the story of love at first sight via a joyful mix of country, rock, and gospel.

All I Can Do

Dolly Parton / 2:23

Musicians: (?) **Vocals:** Dolly Parton **Backing Vocals:** The Lea Jane Singers **Recorded:** RCA Studio B, Nashville (TN), February 18, 1976 **Technical Team:** Sound Engineer: Tom Pick / Assistant Sound Engineer: Roy Shockley **Single:** Side A: All I Can Do / Side B: Falling Out of Love with Me **Release:** RCA Victor, July 5, 976 (45 rpm ref.: PB-10730) **Best Chart Ranking:** 3 on Billboard Hot Country Songs (US), 1 on RPM Country Tracks (Canada)

Genesis and Lyrics

This song is about love at first sight. The narrator wants to find the courage to declare herself to the man who makes her heart beat. This cheerful country rock and gospel song is a very "Dolly Parton" mix.

Production

This up-tempo 4/4 number is charged with gospel energy. The Lea Jane Singers double Dolly's voice on the entire chorus and punctuate the end of the verse, even going into praise-like vocals on the last chorus. "All I Can Do" can be considered a Dolly Parton/Lea Jane Singers duet, as the group of backing singers enables the song to keep the pace going until the end on this frantic rhythm. Their precise, dynamic, and powerful voices are, of course, the main contributors, but the importance of the hand claps is not insignificant when it comes to reinforcing the pulse in the second half of the song. On the left side of the stereo field, the springy swing of the harmonica in diabolical syncopations also plays a major role in maintaining the ambient excitement, while on the right side the electric guitar holds the rhythmic line in a pattern sometimes reminiscent of the legendary hit "Proud Mary" (composed by John Fogerty of Credence Clearwater Revival and released in 1969, and then covered many times, notably by Ike & Tina Turner in 1971). Another step aside for Dolly and her musicians, who know how to relish these few infidelities to the traditional Nashville sound. One can say it: It's not bad in the bayou!

The Fire That Keeps You Warm

Dolly Parton / 2:49

Musicians: (?) **Vocals:** Dolly Parton **Backing Vocals:** The Lea Jane Singers **Recorded:** RCA Studio B, Nashville (TN), February 19, 1976 **Technical Team:** Sound Engineer: Tom Pick / Assistant Sound Engineer: Roy Shockley

In this other love song, the narrator declares her passion not in a pleading way but in a light tone. In "The Fire That Keeps You Warm," Dolly explores her love poetry between sweetness, sparkle, and sensuality; her narrator dreams of hiding in the shadow of her beloved's eyes, of being the fire that keeps him warm, always, and again and again. The very Southern sound of this excellent B-side is perfectly consistent with the bayou rock atmosphere of the single and first track of the album, "All I Can Do." The dueling electric guitars are reminiscent of the flamboyant sound of Florida's Lynyrd Skynyrd. This album begins in the style of Old Dixie, in the dust and motor oil, the juke joints—small establishments where you can listen to the blues or a jukebox while eating—and the barns that stand on the horizon…from the Smokies to the bayou, there is only one step. Dolly dares to take that step here, exuberant and uninhibited, determined to provide the fire that will keep us warm. In 1974, Dolly sang this song as a duet with Porter Wagoner.

When The Sun Goes Down Tomorrow

Dolly Parton / 2:05

Musicians: (?) **Vocals:** Dolly Parton **Backing Vocals:** The Lea Jane Singers **Recorded:** RCA Studio B, Nashville (TN) **Technical Team:** Sound Engineer: Tom Pick / Assistant Sound Engineer: Roy Shockley

In this song, Dolly returns to a much-discussed theme: the return to the place of origin, to the childhood home. This time it is a rather cheerful return. The narrator hitchhikes home, with both light and deep feelings at the idea of returning to her loved ones and her "home sweet home." Again, the contrast that the songwriter often emphasizes between the countryside and the city is observed, the latter being depicted as dangerous, cold, and inhospitable.

This up-tempo country shuffle starts off with a delightful Nashville-style Bo Diddley beat, which returns at the end of each chorus. Dolly and the A Team of Studio B have decided to have fun, to celebrate life in rock without looking back—except when it comes to the essential

imperative of returning to her family and her native countryside, a much-needed break from a life of constant touring, promotion, and studio sessions, where one can quickly become dizzy. But if there is one thing Dolly has understood, it is how to keep her feet on the ground. The "Queen of Country" has no intention of losing her crown anytime soon.

I'm A Drifter

Dolly Parton / 2:53

Musicians: (?) **Vocals:** Dolly Parton **Backing Vocals:** The Lea Jane Singers **Recorded:** RCA Studio B, Nashville (TN), February 17, 1976 **Technical Team:** Sound Engineer: Tom Pick / Assistant Sound Engineer: Roy Shockley

This text about wandering tells the story of a vagabond who is on the road and feels a deep inner emptiness. He has no home or relatives to care for him and he does not know where he is going, but he continues on his way because he has to survive. It does not matter if he goes in one direction or another, because no one is waiting for him. In the course of the twentieth century, many men and women wandered around America in this way, in the hope of finding odd jobs at random. A socioeconomic wandering often suffered rather than chosen, and sung with energy and empathy by the songwriter. To contrast with the tragic character of the theme, this is a funny and unique song in Dolly Parton's oeuvre. Somewhere between marching, a Mardi Gras band sound, and rocksteady, "I'm a Drifter" takes us into uncharted territory. This stylistic mix, as jubilant as it is disconcerting, perfectly illustrates the subject of drifting and wandering. Some banjo clawhammer playing over a rocksteady backbeat boosted with blues harmonica…we have never heard that before! The placement of the backing vocals on the verses also seems to be inspired by Jamaican music, whereas the rhythm section has obviously not been briefed, and the pedal steel, because of its Hawaiian origins, does not bother with this kind of stylistic consideration. Nor does Dolly, for that matter. If the feeling is right, everything is right. Hats off to the hobos of the world.

Rocksteady is a Jamaican music style that emerged in 1966. It's derived from ska and is classified as a subgenre of reggae despite its earlier origin.

Falling Out Of Love With Me

Dolly Parton / 2:47

Musicians: (?) **Vocals:** Dolly Parton **Backing Vocals:** The Lea Jane Singers **Recorded:** RCA Studio B, Nashville (TN), February 18, 1976 **Technical Team:** Sound Engineer: Tom Pick / Assistant Sound Engineer: Roy Shockley **Single:** Side A: All I Can Do / Side B: Falling Out of Love with Me **Release:** RCA Victor, July 5, 1976 (45 rpm ref.: PB-10730)

This love song is about leaving before love burns out and dies. Although this is a universal theme, some have seen it as a more personal story inspired by the relationship between Porter and Dolly.

A return to a certain classicism for this mid-tempo country shuffle. However, in this new version, the Jamaican influence is still perceptible in the verses, where the piano backbeat and the split drum pattern are enough to evoke the "sway" of reggae. The sumptuous work of the Lea Jane Singers alternates with the vocal harmonies of Dolly, who doubles her own voice in overdubs with all the finesse and precision with which we are familiar. We glide gently through Studio B.

Shattered Image

Dolly Parton / 2:23

Musicians: (?) **Vocals:** Dolly Parton **Backing Vocals:** The Lea Jane Singers **Recorded:** RCA Studio B, Nashville (TN), February 17, 1976 **Technical Team:** Sound Engineer: Tom Pick / Assistant Sound Engineer: Roy Shockley

The narrator of "Shattered Image" says that as a child she used to throw stones to break her reflection in the water or in the windows that reflected her image. Now that she is an adult, it is people who throw stones at her. She bears witness to the coldness and cruelty of others and advises them to look at themselves before judging her, to keep their own front yards clean before hurling trash at her. Tenacious, insistent, and almost painful—there is the repetition of the essential phrase, with the transition from "they" to "you": "They shatter my image with the rocks they throw / Shatter my image with the rocks they throw / Don't shatter my image with the stones you throw / Shatter my image with the stones you throw."

This strong, poetic text describes the phenomenon of rejection of the other or of oneself. Even though Dolly Parton shows a certain sense of humor and self-mockery about her appearance in her interviews, the mockery and malice, especially in the tabloids, are projectiles that hurt her.

The song begins with a sophisticated bluegrass acoustic guitar riff, then moves into a 4/4 tune that is tailor-made for country hoedown. As usual, Dolly, who likes to say things straightforwardly but tends to shy away from belaboring the point, manages to counterbalance the harshness of the theme with a particularly upbeat and danceable arrangement. The congas contribute the exotic touch that seems to be the order of the day in February 1976 in Studio B, while the electric guitar astonishes with the thickness of its grain and its rock/swamp blues licks. Gone is the traditional chicken-picking, usually de rigueur in this kind of musical environment.

Dolly covered "Shattered Image" on the album *Halos & Horns* (2002)

Boulder To Birmingham

Emmylou Harris, Bill Danoff / 4:13

Musicians: (?) **Vocals:** Dolly Parton **Backing Vocals:** The Lea Jane Singers **Recorded:** RCA Studio B, Nashville (TN), February 19, 1976 **Technical Team:** Sound Engineer: Tom Pick / Assistant Sound Engineer: Roy Shockley

This iconic Emmylou Harris song, released in 1975 on the album *Pieces of the Sky*, tells of her grief over the death of American singer-songwriter Gram Parsons (in 1973, at the age of twenty-six), with whom she had recorded two albums. The song suits Dolly Parton's voice perfectly, and this cover marks the new friendship between the two singers.

The first ballad on the album, this is a bittersweet slow song of the kind that only the mid-1970s and its disillusionment could produce. Woodstock and its wild promises seem far away. Emmylou Harris wrote this song as she watched the daybreak over a burning canyon, taking her hopes with it. Dolly performs this mourning song full of grandeur and possibility in a masterful way. No drums. Piano, acoustic guitars, harmonica/electric guitar dialogue, enveloping backing vocals…everything here evokes the grace of the great outdoors, the implacable force of nature. It is difficult not to think of Jackson Browne's song "Late for the Sky," released two years earlier in 1974, and used by Martin Scorsese in a memorable scene of his film *Taxi Driver,* released in 1976. A sign of the times, surely, the correlation is strong; the party is over, and the hangover painful, but life goes on—the show and the dream, too. We are in America, somewhere on Highway 95.

Preacher Tom

Dolly Parton / 3:40

Musicians: (?) **Vocals:** Dolly Parton **Backing Vocals:** The Lea Jane Singers, The Nashville Edition **Recorded:** RCA Studio B, Nashville (TN), February 17, 1976 **Technical Team:** Sound Engineer: Tom Pick / Assistant Sound Engineer: Roy Shockley

This country song about faith and the story of Preacher Tom begins with a recitation by Dolly over a chord played in clawhammer style by two banjos on either side of the stereo field, joined by an acoustic guitar and a pedal steel drone, before the piano announces the entrance of the band. It is then punctuated by a rousing gospel tune where we learn that Preacher Tom is a beacon in the night for anyone who crosses his path. The Lea Jane Singers once again work wonders to instill the spirit of praise; the tambourine, omnipresent from the second verse onward, is joined by claps on the reprise of the chorus ad lib; the piano burbles but still swings impeccably; the minimalist bass/drums duo gently builds; the incursion of pedal steel on the first verse, and the banjo that comes in and out of the dance…everything is right for encouraging the audience to get up from their pews and join in this country/gospel trance. The fiddle is totally absent, and the guitar seems to have been put aside. Apart from a discreet strumming of acoustic guitar on the right, for once the six-strings are not in the spotlight in Studio B.

Life's Like Poetry

Merle Haggard / 1:48

Musicians: (?) **Vocals:** Dolly Parton **Backing Vocals:** The Lea Jane Singers **Recorded:** RCA Studio B, Nashville (TN), (date?) **Technical Team:** Sound Engineer: Tom Pick / Assistant Sound Engineer: Roy Shockley

This song, which is perfect for Dolly, was written by her friend Merle Haggard and teaches us that life rhymes with poetry and so does love, especially when it knocks on the narrator's door and fills a void in his life. The country shuffle flows freely on this mid-tempo song with a clever groove that is as light as a swirling leaf in the heart of the Appalachian autumn. On the chorus, the soft touch of the A Team reaches its paroxysm; the sound texture created by

the mix of backing vocals/pedal steel/electric guitar is of an unparalleled smoothness. All it takes is Dolly's exquisitely smooth voice to make the rapture complete. "Life's like poetry": We can take her word for that.

Hey, Lucky Lady

Dolly Parton / 2:20

Musicians: (?) **Vocals:** Dolly Parton **Backing Vocals:** The Lea Jane Singers **Recorded:** RCA Studio B, Nashville (TN), December 9, 1974 **Technical Team:** Sound Engineer: Tom Pick / Assistant Sound Engineer: Roy Shockley **Best Chart Ranking:** 19 on Billboard Hot Country Songs (US), 11 on RPM Country Tracks (Canada)

The narrator has been lucky: She has found love. But now she turns to another woman, who is also lucky, because she has replaced the narrator in the arms of her love. The narrator implores the woman: If she thinks it is just a fling and does not really appreciate the value of her prize, then let her man come back to her so that the narrator can be the happy lover she was when he loved her.

This classic song by the songwriter evokes, in its writing, the same story told in "Jolene." The fans enjoyed this song, which ranked highly. Yet another "other woman" song in the modest setting of an up-tempo 4/4 designed for dancing. The ironic tone, quite common in Dolly Parton's music, is underlined by the sharp and lively playing of the two electric guitars. Their sharp country licks rain down on this "lucky lady" who didn't ask for so much, while nothing seems to be able to stop the hellish train led by the incisive bass and the percussive cross stick of a drummer whose metronomic rigor would make even the shiniest of drum machines of the 1980s green with envy. One can feel that the luck of this "other woman" is likely to change soon… at the corner of the street, Dolly patiently waits for him, perched on her Buffalo Springfield steamroller (a famous American manufacturer's steamroller), scarf tied in her hair and sleeves rolled up. The album cover already displayed the colors: A smile on her lips and a confident look in her eyes, Dolly was born ready; she was always ready.

ALBUM

New Harvest... First Gathering

Light of a Clear Blue Morning . Applejack . My Girl (My Love) .
Holdin' On to You . You Are . How Does It Feel . Where Beauty Lives in Memory .
(Your Love Has Lifted Me) Higher and Higher . Getting in My Way . There

RELEASE DATE
United States: February 11, 1977
Reference: RCA Victor—APL1-2188
Best US Chart Ranking: 1

Dolly Parton and pop artist Andy Warhol both rose from humble backgrounds before going on to dominate the worlds of music and art.

In 1977, Dolly met the icon of pop art, Andy Warhol, for the first time. The artist and music producer was the toast of Greenwich Village, both underground and in more exclusive circles. Dolly noticed that the prince of the New York art scene was at least as strange and extravagant as she was, especially in his fashion, which he embraced just as much as she did. With humor, she was amused by this brilliant man because of his complexion, as she joked, whose pallor might well be indicative of illness.[2]

New Harvest

Dolly Parton's eighteenth solo album is the album of change. For the first time, Dolly was a producer, with Gregg Perry assisting her on some of the tracks, and the recording sessions were held in Nashville, but the album was mixed in Los Angeles. *New Harvest...First Gathering* was released on February 11, 1977, by RCA Victor. It is an album that stands out not only because of its position in the charts, but also because it clearly announces the new direction taken by the artist. The songwriter wrote eight of the ten songs that opened the doors to an international pop audience. Three years after leaving *The Porter Wagoner Show*, the star was consolidating her position; she was on her way to becoming a superstar.

The Direction of Pop

Dolly Parton won over a huge audience with *New Harvest...First Gathering*, even though some saw it as a betrayal of her country roots. This was not the case, however—Dolly Parton wanted to expand her popularity. In a radio interview, she told Mike Harrison that she had written several songs for this album years earlier but did not have the freedom to record them as she wished. Dolly was now at another turning point in her career, and this album sounded like a dress rehearsal before the premiere. Many of the tracks are more pop than country, but in the Dolly Parton way, with gospel, soul, and even disco influences.

The songwriter put together a band, Gypsy Fever, with which she toured the usual country circuit, but also elsewhere—at the Boarding House in San Francisco, the Ivanhoe in Chicago, and the Bottom Line in Greenwich Village in New York.[2] These venues were more geared toward the pop rock scene, with Bruce Springsteen and Mick Jagger playing there. Dolly was soon everywhere,

Opposite: Dolly
attends a reception
after a concert in
San Francisco.

Above: While on tour in Europe, Dolly Parton meets Queen Elizabeth II after a concert in Glasgow, Scotland.

known by everyone, at the same time popular and admitted into the VIP circles of showbiz.

The star spent half of her time on the road with her faithful childhood friend Judy Ogle. Dolly's unfailing confidante, adviser, protector, and assistant was always at her side. Although the songwriter was completely independent, Judy supported her in the development of her career. Alanna Nash[3] says in her biography of the artist that if Dolly had told her friend about her decision to become president of the United States of America, Judy would have trusted her and helped her to make it happen. But for now, the star was setting out to conquer Europe.

The Roads to Freedom

A series of concerts in Germany and England awaited Dolly Parton, who already had a good fan club there, since she was nominated for best female voice of the year in a poll conducted by several British country music associations. In 1977, in Glasgow, Scotland, at the Royal Variety Performance, the songwriter sang in the presence of Queen Elizabeth II, whom she met with some emotion. Western Europe and, above all, England were in the midst of a punk period, so Dolly's spectrum of looks was vast. This did not prevent the media from seizing on her image and commenting on her clothes and makeup.

In Dolly's life, her career and her marriage are separate. The singer enjoyed a great deal of personal freedom while being able to count on the support of her husband as well as that of Judy. Alanna Nash recounts that when she was

at Dolly's house to interview her,[3] Carl kept to himself and rarely showed up. The moment he sets eyes on his wife, no one else in the world exists for him.

By the end of the seventies, Dolly Parton had consolidated her personal and professional environment, the Gypsy Fever Band was a better fit than the Travelin' Family Band, and she was now just one album away from superstardom. A decade had passed since *Hello, I'm Dolly*, and the harvest was good.

Album Cover

In David Gahr and Nick Sangiamo's photograph, Dolly, dressed in jeans, her blond curls under a navy scarf, sits in the passenger seat of a vintage car, smiling, relaxed, and serene. You can see that something in her has changed. Of note: the interior mural illustrating the harvest, credited to Acy Lehman—a designer who also worked with Andy Warhol on record sleeves—and Richard Sparks.

For Dolly Addicts

There is a rare recording of an interview given by Dolly Parton with radio journalist Mike Harrison: *A Personal Music Dialogue with Dolly Parton*, on vinyl, released in 1977 by RCA Victor (ref: DJL1-2314).

Dolly with Alanna Nash, the author of a 1978 biography on the singer.

For Dolly Addicts

On the May 8, 2008, episode of *Saturday Night Live*, Miley Cyrus covered "Light of a Clear Blue Morning" as a tribute to Dolly, her actual godmother.

ON YOUR HEADPHONES

It is safe to say that on "Light of a Clear Blue Morning," some vocals have been added. Before the gospel, with the backing vocals, at 3:10, the "ghost sound" of Dolly Parton's headphones can be heard—as they are heard in the center, while the backing vocals are in stereo. Totally isolating headphones did not yet exist.

Side A

Light Of A Clear Blue Morning

Dolly Parton / 4:53

Musicians: Stu Basore, Jimmy Crawford, Joe McGuffee: pedal steel / Mark Casstevens, Dolly Parton, Bobby Thompson: banjo / Charlie Chappelear, Bobby Dyson: bass / Ralph Childs: tuba / Jimmy Colvard: acoustic and electric guitar / Shane Keister: electronic organ and organ / Dave Kirby, Bobby Thompson: acoustic guitar / Jerry Kroon, Larry Londin: drums / Jerry Kroon, Farrell Morris: percussion / Joe McGuffee: dobro / Terry McMillan: harmonica / The Nashville Horns: brass / Jamie Nichol: congas / John Pell: classical and acoustic guitar / Gregg Perry: piano, keyboards, tambourine, strings arrangements / Billy Puett: flute, piccolo, brass / Jimmy Riddle: Jew's harp / Don Roth: electric guitar / Rod Smarr: electric and acoustic guitar, slide guitar / Buddy Spicher: fiddle **Vocals:** Dolly Parton **Backing Vocals:** (?) **Recorded:** RCA Studio B, Nashville (TN), August 19, 1976 **Technical Team:** Sound Engineers: Rich Adler, Brent Maher / Mixing: Armin Steiner / **Single:** Side A: Light of a Clear Blue Morning / Side B: There **Release:** RCA Victor, April 21, 1977 (45 rpm ref.: PB-10935) **Best Chart Ranking:** 11 on Billboard Hot Country Songs (US), 1 on RPM Country Tracks (Canada)

Genesis and Lyrics

As she recounts in her autobiography,[1] having just left Porter Wagoner and his show in 1974, Dolly climbed into a taxi with a broken heart. Her emotional state fluctuated between relief at regaining her freedom and immense grief at the breakup after seven years of a professional relationship rich in experiences. That day, it was raining. In the back of the taxi, she was crying. She repeated to herself that everything would be all right, like a mantra or a prayer. When she arrived home, the sun came out and a sense of joy came over her. She was free to fly with her own wings, like the eagle in the song. In the taxi she wrote *Light of a Clear Blue Morning*.

Production

Farewell to country music—Dolly had taken a step forward on all levels: writing, sound recording, mixing. Some elements remain, like the omnipresence of the bass, but the playing is different: It has moved into pop mode, and the number of notes played has tripled since *All Can I Do*. At least one microphone picks up the sound of each instrument; there are two on the piano (one for the bass, one for the treble) and between eight and ten for the drums, depending on the number of instruments in the drum kit. This configuration allows each source to be treated independently, on all levels: dynamics, equalization, effects, level in the mix, and stereo sound panorama. Reverb can be heard throughout the track. The typical pop drum sound, in which there is generally more bass, especially due to the bass drum and the use of larger drums, is still not heard.

Musically, there is a nice progression. The beginning is a piano ballad, which has never had so much space before. It almost turns into a rock ballad from the chorus onward—the only thing missing is the distortion on the guitars. Then we come to a hybrid section, between pop and gospel. This comes after the part in which the backing vocals are alone; characteristic of the genre are the presence of the tambourine, the claps, and especially the doubling of the snare drum rhythm at the end of the song.

Applejack

Dolly Parton / 3:20

Musicians: Stu Basore, Jimmy Crawford, Joe McGuffee: pedal steel / Mark Casstevens, Dolly Parton, Bobby Thompson: banjo / Charlie Chappelear, Bobby Dyson: bass / Ralph Childs: tuba / Jimmy Colvard: acoustic and electric guitar / Shane Keister: electronic organ and organ / Dave Kirby, Bobby Thompson: acoustic guitar / Jerry Kroon, Larry Londin: drums / Jerry Kroon, Farrell Morris: percussion / Joe McGuffee: dobro / Terry McMillan: harmonica / The Nashville Horns: brass / Jamie Nichol: congas / John Pell: classical and acoustic guitar / Gregg Perry: piano, keyboards, tambourine, strings arrangements / Billy Puett: flute, piccolo, brass / Jimmy Riddle: Jew's harp / Don Roth: electric guitar / Rod Smarr: electric and acoustic guitar, slide guitar / Buddy Spicher: fiddle / The Kelly Kirkland Strings: strings **Vocals:** Dolly Parton **Backing Vocals:** Roy Acuff, Chet Atkins, Anita Ball, Bashful Brother Oswald, Lea Jane Berinati, Clyde Brooks, Charlie Chappelear, Jimmy Crawford, Richard Dennison, Bob Ferguson, Mary Fielder, Janie Fricke, Hubert Gregory & the Fruit Jar Drinkers, Joe & Rose Lee Maphis, Kirk McGee, Avie Lee Parton, Lee Parton, Randy Parton, Minnie Pearl, Johnny Pearl, John Pell, Debbie Joe Puckett, Dwight Puckett, Rod Smarr, Ernest Tubb, Ray Walker, The Willis

Brothers, Wilma Lee & Stoney Cooper, Casey Worden, Kelly Worden, Mickie Worden, Johnny Wright, Kitty Wells **Recorded:** RCA Studio B, Nashville (TN), December 10, 1976 **Technical Team:** Sound Engineers: Rich Adler, Brent Maher / Mixing: Armin Steiner **Single:** Side A: You Are / Side B: Applejack **Release:** RCA Victor, March 25, 1977 (45 rpm ref.: PB-9059) **Best Chart Ranking:** Did Not Chart (US), 1 in the Netherlands in 1983

In this song, the narrator recalls her childhood friendship with an old man nicknamed Applejack because he made cider, who played the banjo while she sang. This story resonates with a memory from Dolly Parton's youth, recounted in her autobiography:[1] When a lonely man inspired fear in the locals (unlike Applejack, who was loved by all), Dolly, then a little girl, faced her fear, went to meet him, and sang and played the banjo with him.

With the characteristic presence of the banjo and harmonica, this is the most country track on the album. Although the backing vocals include many of the celebrities of the time (Roy Acuff, Chet Atkins, Kitty Wells), it was only released as a single in the UK. The beautiful stereo ambience recorded at the beginning seems to be staged by the backing vocals, which are very numerous on this track—indeed, a slight reverb can be discerned. There is strength in numbers, and everyone is in unison.

My Girl (My Love)

William Robinson, Ronald White / 3:44

Musicians: Stu Basore, Jimmy Crawford, Joe McGuffee: pedal steel / Mark Casstevens, Dolly Parton, Bobby Thompson: banjo / Charlie Chappelear, Bobby Dyson: bass / Ralph Childs: tuba / Jimmy Colvard: acoustic and electric guitar / Shane Keister: electronic organ and organ / Dave Kirby, Bobby Thompson: acoustic guitar / Jerry Kroon, Larry Londin: drums / Jerry Kroon, Farrell Morris: percussion / Joe McGuffee: dobro / Terry McMillan: harmonica / The Nashville Horns: brass / Jamie Nichol: congas / John Pell: classical and acoustic guitar / Gregg Perry: piano, keyboards, tambourine, strings arrangements, Billy Puett: flute, piccolo, brass / Jimmy Riddle: Jew's harp / Don Roth: electric guitar / Rod Smarr: electric and acoustic guitar, slide guitar / Buddy Spicher: fiddle **Vocals:** Dolly Parton **Backing Vocals:** Janie Fricke, Lea Jane Berinati, Richard Dennison **Recorded:** RCA Studio B, Nashville (TN), December 3, 1976 **Technical Team:** Sound Engineers: Rich Adler, Brent Maher / Mixing: Armin Steiner

"My Girl" is a cover of a classic soul/R & B number by the Temptations, which was released as a single in December 1964 and was a big hit on the Motown label. Dolly uses this love song, but the arrangement is completely reworked. The bass line, one of Motown's most famous, is replaced by a guitar phrase. The melody of the vocals is more or less the same, but the backing vocals, which were the signature of the Detroit band, seem to have been rewritten. There is a profusion of instruments compared to the original and to Otis Redding's 1965 cover, which also caused a stir.

Holdin' On To You

Dolly Parton / 2:46

Musicians: Stu Basore, Jimmy Crawford, Joe McGuffee: pedal steel / Mark Casstevens, Dolly Parton, Bobby Thompson: banjo / Charlie Chappelear, Bobby Dyson: bass / Ralph Childs: tuba / Jimmy Colvard: acoustic and electric guitar / Shane Keister: electronic organ and organ / Dave Kirby, Bobby Thompson: acoustic guitar / Jerry Kroon, Larry Londin: drums / Jerry Kroon, Farrell Morris: percussion / Joe McGuffee: dobro / Terry McMillan: harmonica / The Nashville Horns: brass / Jamie Nichol: congas / John Pell: classical and acoustic guitar / Gregg Perry: piano, keyboards, tambourine, strings arrangements / Billy Puett: flute, piccolo, brass / Jimmy Riddle: Jew's harp / Don Roth: electric guitar / Rod Smarr: electric and acoustic guitar, slide guitar / Buddy Spicher: fiddle **Vocals:** Dolly Parton **Backing Vocals:** Charlie Chappelear, Dwight Puckett, Randy Parton, Richard Dennison **Recorded:** RCA Studio B, Nashville (TN), August 22, 1976 **Technical Team:** Sound Engineers: Rich Adler, Brent Maher / Mixing: Armin Steiner

Another love song, more rhythmic than the previous one but negative in this case, with this one addressing a recurring theme in the songwriter's stories: one-sided love. The opening line seems to have inspired the German singer Nena in her 1983 album *99 Luftballons*. The backing vocals are all male, a first for Dolly, who has always mainly surrounded herself with women's voices.

You Are

Dolly Parton / 5:14

Musicians: Stu Basore, Jimmy Crawford, Joe McGuffee: pedal steel / Mark Casstevens, Dolly Parton, Bobby Thompson: banjo / Charlie Chappelear, Bobby Dyson: bass / Ralph Childs: tuba / Jimmy Colvard: acoustic and electric guitar / Shane Keister: electronic organ and organ / Dave Kirby, Bobby Thompson: acoustic guitar / Jerry Kroon, Larry Londin: drums / Jerry Kroon, Farrell Morris: percussion / Joe McGuffee: dobro / Terry McMillan: harmonica / The Nashville Horns: brass / Jamie Nichol: congas / John Pell: classical and acoustic guitar / Gregg Perry: piano, keyboards, tambourine, strings arrangements / Billy Puett: flute, piccolo, brass / Jimmy Riddle: Jew's harp / Don Roth: electric guitar / Rod Smarr: electric and acoustic guitar, slide guitar / Buddy Spicher: fiddle **Vocals:** Dolly Parton **Backing Vocals:** Dolly Parton, Janie Fricke, Lea Jane Berinati, Richard Dennison **Recorded:** RCA Studio B, Nashville (TN), August 20, 1976 **Technical Team:** Sound Engineers: Rich Adler, Brent Maher / Mixing: Armin Steiner **Single:** Side A: You Are / Side B: Applejack **Release:** RCA Victor, March 25, 1977 (45 rpm ref.: PB-9059) **Best Chart Ranking:** Did Not Chart (US), 1 in the Netherlands in 1983

This song is a beautiful tribute to the man who means everything to the narrator and whom she loves as he is— another principle dear to the songwriter: to respect the loved one without wanting to change him.

There is a huge reverb on Dolly Parton's voice, with a long pre-delay. Usually, reverb simulates a space, but here the usage is outdated. The instruments come in very gradually: classical guitar, violins, backing vocals, bass, and drums with a break. This break comes after the second guitar solo, which is even more overplayed than the first one because it comes after a perfect cadence, which leads us to believe that the song is coming to an end. Although this may seem kitschy today, it was fashionable at the time, when a playing effect was exploited to the full—and sometimes to excess.

Dolly with fans at Dinner with Dolly, a publicity event sponsored by KSAN radio and the RCA label at the Paramount Theatre in Oakland, California.

How Does It Feel

Dolly Parton / 3:13

Musicians: Stu Basore, Jimmy Crawford, Joe McGuffee: pedal steel / Mark Casstevens, Dolly Parton, Bobby Thompson: banjo / Charlie Chappelear, Bobby Dyson: bass / Ralph Childs: tuba / Jimmy Colvard: acoustic and electric guitar / Shane Keister: electronic organ and organ / Dave Kirby, Bobby Thompson: acoustic guitar / Jerry Kroon, Larry Londin: drums / Jerry Kroon, Farrell Morris: percussion / Joe McGuffee: dobro / Terry McMillan: harmonica / The Nashville Horns: brass / Jamie Nichol: congas / John Pell: classical and acoustic guitar / Gregg Perry: piano, keyboards, tambourine, strings arrangements / Billy Puett: flute, piccolo, brass / Jimmy Riddle: Jew's harp / Don Roth: electric guitar / Rod Smarr: electric and acoustic guitar, slide guitar / Buddy Spicher: fiddle **Vocals:** Dolly Parton **Backing Vocals:** Janie Fricke, Lea Jane Berinati, Ray Walker, Richard Dennison **Recorded:** RCA Studio B, Nashville (TN), November 21, 1976 **Technical Team:** Sound Engineers: Rich Adler, Brent Maher / Mixing: Armin Steiner

Another variation on love, in this song where the narrator questions the feelings of the other: "How does it feel to know that someone loves you […] always thinkin' of you […] puts no one above you?" It is noticeable that the love songs on this album are lighter, more confident, than some of the earlier ones.

This song is somewhat similar in its progression to "Light of a Clear Blue Morning." The beginning is played by the whole orchestra; there is a note with a flanger effect (obtained by adding to the original signal the same signal but slightly delayed) on the electronic keyboard and a tom hit. The latter is strange; usually a gate is applied, a treatment that suppresses the resonance of the drum after the impact, and which seems to be applied to it for the rest of the piece. The toms' descent after the second verse, slightly overplayed, sums up the musical style of this period quite well. Dolly Parton's vocal cord problems seem to be behind her and her singing voice has regained its power.

For the record, the low voice at the end of the song is incomprehensible. It undoubtedly adds to the harmonic richness, but because of its range and its place in the mix, its intelligibility is lost.

Dolly performing on NBC in 1977.

Dolly adds her handprints to the sidewalk outside Peaches Records in Atlanta, Georgia, on May 3, 1977.

Where Beauty Lives In Memory

Dolly Parton / 3:50

Musicians: Stu Basore, Jimmy Crawford, Joe McGuffee: pedal steel / Mark Casstevens, Dolly Parton, Bobby Thompson: banjo / Charlie Chappelear, Bobby Dyson: bass / Ralph Childs: tuba / Jimmy Colvard: acoustic and electric guitar / Shane Keister: electronic organ and organ / Dave Kirby, Bobby Thompson: acoustic guitar / Jerry Kroon, Larry Londin: drums / Jerry Kroon, Farrell Morris: percussion / Joe McGuffee: dobro / Terry McMillan: harmonica / The Nashville Horns: brass / Jamie Nichol: congas / John Pell: classical and acoustic guitar / Gregg Perry: piano, keyboards, tambourine, strings arrangements / Billy Puett: flute, piccolo, brass / Jimmy Riddle: Jew's harp / Don Roth: electric guitar / Rod Smarr: electric and acoustic guitar, slide guitar / Buddy Spicher: fiddle **Vocals:** Dolly Parton **Backing Vocals:** Dolly Parton, Janie Fricke, Lea Jane Berinati, Richard Dennison **Recorded:** RCA Studio B, Nashville (TN), December 10, 1976 **Technical Team:** Sound Engineers: Rich Adler, Brent Maher / Mixing: Armin Steiner

This anticipation of a Prince Charming seems to come from a fairy tale—or rather, from a tragedy. A woman prepares and admires herself in her mirror, and asks it: "Who is the most beautiful of all?" Once she was, in the eyes of all, until that handsome prince stole her heart and mind forty years ago…Remaining in that cherished and longed-for time, because "beauty lives in memory," she dies instantly in the hallucination of his return.

Pure Dolly Parton, authentic in the songwriting as in the vocals. We return to the style of the ballads of previous albums, with a restrained drumming, a very present bass, an arpeggiated guitar accompaniment, and pizzicato violins. However, the star has not deprived herself of several additions, such as the metal chimes on the intro, or what seems to be a slide on an autoharp at 3:34. The harmonica plays fewer than ten notes in the whole track. The backing vocals are, spatially, very widely distributed, so that every time they come in there is a sudden broadening of the stereo. Depending on the listener, this sound effect can be disturbing or, on the contrary, very pleasing. This track is one of only two on the album (along with "Applejack") to have an ending, with all the others ending in a fade-out.

The Funk Brothers were Motown studio musicians from 1959 to 1972. Their ranks included Melvin "Wah Wah Watson" Ragin, the originator of the wah-wah pedal. According to Paul Justman's documentary *Standing in the Shadows of Motown* (2002), "The Funk Brothers played on more number one hits than the Beatles, Elvis, the Rolling Stones, and the Beach Boys combined."

A woman of many talents, Dolly Parton plays guitar, banjo, and mandolin.

(Your Love Has Lifted Me) Higher And Higher

Gary Jackson, Carl Smith / 2:52

Musicians: Stu Basore, Jimmy Crawford, Joe McGuffee: pedal steel / Mark Casstevens, Dolly Parton, Bobby Thompson: banjo / Charlie Chappelear, Bobby Dyson: bass / Ralph Childs: tuba / Jimmy Colvard: acoustic and electric guitar / Shane Keister: electronic organ and organ / Dave Kirby, Bobby Thompson: acoustic guitar / Jerry Kroon, Larry Londin: drums / Jerry Kroon, Farrell Morris: percussion / Joe McGuffee: dobro / Terry McMillan: harmonica / The Nashville Horns: brass / Jamie Nichol: congas / John Pell: classical and acoustic guitar / Gregg Perry: piano, keyboards, tambourine, strings arrangements / Billy Puett: flute, piccolo, brass / Jimmy Riddle: Jew's harp / Don Roth: electric guitar / Rod Smarr: electric and acoustic guitar, slide guitar / Buddy Spicher: fiddle **Vocals:** Dolly Parton **Backing Vocals:** Anita Ball, Gregg Perry, Mary Fielder, Richard Dennison **Recorded:** RCA Studio B, Nashville (TN), December 16, 1976 **Technical Team:** Sound Engineers: Rich Adler, Brent Maher / Mixing: Armin Steiner

The original version of this song, "(Your Love Keeps Lifting Me) Higher and Higher," was written in 1967 for entertainer and showman Jackie Wilson and earned him the number one spot on the US Billboard Hot R&B Songs chart. The narrator of this story praises the man whose love heals her wounds and lifts her higher and higher. It is understandable that Dolly Parton was inspired to record this cover, for which she was nominated in the category of Best Female Country Vocal Performance at the 20th Annual Grammy Awards.

The Motown touch is undeniable, and with good reason: The musicians are members of the Funk Brothers, who performed as extras on weekends. Dolly Parton kept the soulful spirit of the song, especially with the bass/drums rhythm, while adding her own country touch (fiddle and banjo).

Getting In My Way

Dolly Parton / 2:40

Musicians: Stu Basore, Jimmy Crawford, Joe McGuffee: pedal steel / Mark Casstevens, Dolly Parton, Bobby Thompson: banjo / Charlie Chappelear, Bobby Dyson: bass / Ralph Childs: tuba / Jimmy Colvard: acoustic and electric guitar / Shane Keister: electronic organ and organ / Dave Kirby, Bobby Thompson: acoustic guitar / Jerry Kroon, Larry Londin: drums / Jerry Kroon, Farrell Morris: percussion / Joe McGuffee: dobro / Terry McMillan: harmonica / The Nashville Horns: brass / Jamie Nichol: congas / John Pell: classical and acoustic guitar / Gregg Perry: piano, keyboards, tambourine, strings arrangements / Billy Puett: flute, piccolo, brass / Jimmy Riddle: Jew's harp / Don Roth: electric guitar / Rod Smarr: electric and acoustic guitar, slide guitar / Buddy Spicher: fiddle **Vocals:** Dolly Parton **Backing Vocals:** Dolly Parton, Janie Fricke, Lea Jane Berinati, Richard Dennison **Recorded:** RCA Studio B, Nashville (TN), August 21, 1976 **Technical Team:** Sound Engineers: Rich Adler, Brent Maher / Mixing: Armin Steiner

A recurring theme in Dolly's work: the memory of a loved one who is no longer there, which becomes so obsessive that it prevents one from eating, sleeping, or moving on.

This is the first time on the album that we hear an electric guitar rhythm so clearly, in the funk style. Similarly, it is the first time in Dolly's work that we hear a guitar theme with a saturated blues sound, a sound that will never really become outdated, because it is still heard today. The drums give way to the percussion section without losing their groove, especially due to the hi-hat playing.

Phil Donohue presenting Dolly's record *New Harvest… First Gathering* during a taping of his show on April 30, 1977.

There

Dolly Parton / 5:32

Musicians: Stu Basore, Jimmy Crawford, Joe McGuffee: pedal steel / Mark Casstevens, Dolly Parton, Bobby Thompson: banjo / Charlie Chappelear, Bobby Dyson: bass / Ralph Childs: tuba / Jimmy Colvard: acoustic and electric guitar / Shane Keister: electronic organ and organ / Dave Kirby, Bobby Thompson: acoustic guitar / Jerry Kroon, Larry Londin: drums / Jerry Kroon, Farrell Morris: percussion / Joe McGuffee: dobro / Terry McMillan: harmonica / The Nashville Horns: brass / Jamie Nichol: congas / John Pell: classical and acoustic guitar / Gregg Perry: piano, keyboards, tambourine, strings arrangements / Billy Puett: flute, piccolo, brass / Jimmy Riddle: Jew's harp / Don Roth: electric guitar / Rod Smarr: electric and acoustic guitar, slide guitar / Buddy Spicher: fiddle **Vocals:** Dolly Parton **Backing Vocals:** Anita Ball, Casey Worden, Dolly Parton, Gregg Perry, Janie Frick, Kelly Worden, Lea Jane Berinati, Mickie Worden, Richard Dennison **Recorded:** RCA Studio B, Nashville (TN), December 17, 1976 **Technical Team:** Sound Engineers: Rich Adler, Brent Maher / Mixing: Armin Steiner **Single:** Side A: Light of a Clear Blue Morning / Side B: There **Release:** RCA Victor, March 21, 1977 (45 rpm ref.: PB-10935) **Best Chart Ranking:** 11 on Billboard Hot Country Songs (US), 1 on RPM Country Tracks (Canada)

This hymn to the divine, to faith, to absolute love, and to God will appeal to both country and gospel fans. One might legitimately wonder if this song was written for the B-side of "Light of a Clear Blue Morning" or if it was chosen for its similarities to it, as the beginnings are so alike, with the guitar arpeggios, bass, and violins. The chord patterns are also similar.

The backing vocals are a very important part of the song, which has a gospel feel. Some children are singing, in groups or solo, probably to underline the universality of the text. There are several styles of voices in the backing vocals, in addition to the children: the choir, the quartet, the solo. There is a strong vibrato on the quartet phrases. The arrival of the chorus is announced by the drums, which mark a call with the toms, and the guitars abandon the arpeggios for placed chords. On the second verse, pedal steel, violins, and piano join in the prayer. The Hammond organ comes in on the third verse. Everyone is there.

To bring the ending into gospel *ad libitum*—which can go on indefinitely; the ending is decided between the musicians at the time or after a set number of rounds—a passage in the major key is very well executed on the first chord of the initial grid. Then everyone does a little of what they want, notably some of the backing singers, who are capable of contributing some powerful high notes; and the drummer, who slightly modifies his rhythm, provides breaks, and does not spare the cymbals, which seem very compressed. It should be noted that the cymbals are mixed less loudly than the hi-hat.

Dolly, the show, premiered in 1974, and it lasted for one season.

Dolly: The Dolly Parton Television Show Has a Price

In 1975, Bill Graham, producer of *The Porter Wagoner Show* (on which Dolly sang for seven years), and president of Show Biz, Inc., convinced the artist to launch her own variety show. Conceived as a series, with a cost of $100,000 per thirty-minute episode—all twenty-six were filmed in Opryland, the studios of the Grand Ole Opry—*Dolly* was the most expensive show in Nashville at the time, in syndication (i.e., sold to several broadcasters simultaneously) and scheduled by 130 television stations. Dolly Parton was the first female country star to have her own TV show.

Key Meetings

The program starts with the notes of "Love Is Like a Butterfly" (released in 1974) and a focus on a huge, glittering, very girly butterfly—the artist's emblem—and then Dolly, wearing a voluminous wavy blond wig and a pretty gray dress with white scalloping, descends from the studio "sky" on a swing, singing, for example, "Knock Three Times" (a song by Irwin Levine and L. Russell Brown, from 1970). Suddenly, the camera shows us a man from behind, enclosed in a tall box, knocking three times on the wood

with a wrench. Dolly opens the mysterious package and pulls out the famous Kenny Rogers, dressed in turquoise satin, the guest star of this episode. They continue the song together, joking with each other. The two stars developed a great friendship, which led to their duet "Islands in the Stream," a megahit in 1983 (written by the Bee Gees).

Other meetings were essential for Dolly, such as those with singers and guitarists Emmylou Harris and Linda Ronstadt. It was during an episode of the show that the three women laid the foundation for the *Trio* album. Dolly would also have liked to feature Bob Dylan, but he eventually declined the invitation. At the end of the program, Dolly wished her audience joy and love and sang "I Will Always Love You" (1974). In another episode, with her entire family on set—a rare occurrence—Dolly sang "Old Black Kettle," written for the album *My Tennessee Mountain Home* (1973).

All the ingredients seemed to be in place for the show to be a success, with a strong audience from Nashville to New York, but Dolly was not satisfied, and the show lasted only one season.

Dolly on the set of her television show in 1976.

History Repeats Itself

The *Dolly* show was a real success and, in this context, the star made contacts that would be decisive for the rest of her career, but, working eighteen hours a day, the songwriter maltreated her vocal cords, became exhausted, and put on weight. And above all, Dolly was deeply disturbed by having to endure and support a program that did not suit her. During the last few years with Porter Wagoner, the young woman was not in charge; Porter was the boss and decided everything for everyone, forcing Dolly to comply with his decisions, regardless of her own opinions. The star relived the same situation with her own show, as she confided to the writer Alanna Nash[3] in 1977. She admitted that she liked each of her guests, some of whom became great friends, but if she had had a free hand, she would have made different choices. Thus, when in 1976 she was asked to sing "My Funny Valentine"—a popular jazz standard from the 1937 Broadway musical *Babes in Arms*—Dolly felt out of place, out of her vocal range, and out of step with the guests. To Nash, the star recounted that her audience no longer recognized her and that her friends wondered if she had gone

mad. As for the viewers who saw her perform, the artist feared that they would get the wrong impression of her. For Dolly Parton, not being her true self was painful. This feeling led her to terminate her contract with Show Biz, Inc., as she had done with Porter Wagoner.

In 2007 a DVD was released by Show Biz, Inc., entitled *Dolly Parton & Friends*, that included six episodes of the series. But, as Freddie Mercury sang, "the show must go on," and Dolly Parton returned to television later, and in her own way.

For Dolly Addicts

In 2020, Time Life released a nineteen-disc box set of the star's music, *Dolly: The Ultimate Collection—Deluxe Edition*, which contains many episodes of the show.

ALBUM

Here You Come Again

Here You Come Again . Baby, Come Out Tonight . It's All Wrong, but It's All Right .
Me and Little Andy . Lovin' You . Cowgirl & the Dandy . Two Doors Down .
As Soon as I Touched Him . God's Coloring Book . Sweet Music Man

RELEASE DATE
United States: October 3, 1977
Reference: RCA Victor, Nashville (TN)—APL1-2544
Best US Chart Ranking: 1

Platinum Blonde

Here You Come Again was released on October 3, 1977, by RCA Victor. The star's nineteenth solo album was produced by producer and songwriter Gary Klein. The critics were enthusiastic and praised the ease with which Dolly Parton crossed the bridge between country and pop, while a few voices protested against what they considered to be a betrayal of country music, a fallacy that Dolly does not hesitate to dismantle with her characteristic plain speaking: She is not abandoning anything or anyone; she loves country, gospel, pop, soul, everything that constitutes her musical identity. In the US, *Here You Come Again* reached No. 1 on the Billboard Top Country Albums chart and No. 20 on the Billboard 200, and in Canada, it reached No. 12 on the RPM Top Albums chart.

The Year of Success

In January 1977, Democrat Jimmy Carter won the presidential election. America trembled as it read Stephen King's terrifying *The Shining*, a best-selling novel that confirmed the writer's talent. Still in the realms of fiction, the conquest of space continued with George Lucas's *Star Wars*, while in reality, the *Voyager 2* probe was heading out toward Jupiter, Saturn, Uranus, and Neptune. A small revolution began with the arrival on the market of the VHS video recorder, which enabled Americans to watch Steven Spielberg's *Close Encounters of the Third Kind* and Martin Scorsese's *New York, New York* (starring the unforgettable Liza Minnelli and Robert De Niro), films released that same year. The end of the 1970s was marked by a creative effervescence in a multitude of fields, including culture, science and technology, the evolution of morals and sexual liberation, and space conquest.

On earth—but in full ascension!—Dolly Parton was making a name for herself in the charts. The songwriter was already popular, and she became even more so: Already a star on the country planet, she was conquering the whole world, indulging in a fully developed pop style. She sold over a million copies of *Here You Come Again*, which went platinum. It was a personal and professional triumph. Her detractors' only argument was that she was moving away from her country audience. The star denied this; she loved her audience and, wherever she went and whatever she did, she never forgot her roots. Still, crossing the border between country and pop confirmed that Dolly Parton was spreading her wings to fly even higher.

The Dolly Parton Genre

Ten years after the release of her first solo album, *Hello, I'm Dolly*, Dolly Parton was now everywhere: in the media and onstage, in America and Europe. Her records were sold in more countries than ever before: in New Zealand, the United Kingdom, Holland, Germany, Japan, and especially in Australia and Canada, where her album of the fall of 1977 went gold. While *New Harvest...First Gathering* had clearly given Dolly access to the pop charts, *Here You Come Again* testifies to the infatuation of a vast public with her songs and her voice. Whether they were pop, rock, or country fans, the fans loved the singer, past and present. So the question was not where she belonged musically—she has always mixed genres—but who she was: Dolly Parton, singer-songwriter, and now superstar.

Album Cover

We notice right away, in white on a black background, imagined by the designer and photographer Michael Manoogian, Dolly's logo-signature, which she would keep forever. Below, in jeans and red shirt, perched on high heels, three blond Dollys seem to be dancing, visibly happy. Created by illustrator and photographer Ed Caraeff, this photo condenses several influences: pop art, disco, and cowgirl style. Inside the cover, we discover another Dolly: Both glamorous and romantic, the star is as though shrouded in a kind of floral mist. This contrast of images, which reconcile softness and energy, tenderness and strength, femininity and dynamism, rurality and urbanity, echoes the artist's musical diversity.

The cover of the album *Here You Come Again*, released in 1977.

SIDE A

Here You Come Again
Barry Mann, Cynthia Weil / 2:48

Musicians: Ben Benay, Jay Graydon: guitar / Al Perkins, Dave Wolfert: pedal steel / Nick DeCaro: accordion, vocal and strings arrangements / Harry Bluestone: first violin / David Foster: keyboards, synthesizer / Ed Greene: drums / David Hungate: bass / Jim Keltner: percussion / David Lindley: slide guitar / Dean Parks: lead guitar, banjo **Vocals:** Dolly Parton **Backing Vocals:** Nick DeCaro, Jan Gassman, Myrna Matthews, Marti McCall, Gene Morford, Zedrick Turnbough **Recorded:** Sound Labs Studios, Los Angeles (CA), June 15, 1977 **Technical Team:** Producer: Gary Klein / Sound Engineer: Armin Steiner / Assistant Sound Engineers: Don Henderson, Linda Tyler / Mixing: Armin Steiner **Single:** Side A: Here You Come Again / Side B: Me and Little Andy **Release:** RCA Studio B, September 26, 1977 (45 rpm ref.: PB-11123) **Best Chart Ranking:** 1 on Billboard Hot Country Songs (US), 3 on Billboard Hot 100 (US), 2 on Billboard Adult Contemporary (US), 7 on Cashbox Top 100 (US), 1 on RPM Country Tracks (Canada)

Genesis and Lyrics

When Barry Mann and Cynthia Weil wrote "Here You Come Again," they intended it for the singer Brenda Lee, to whom we owe "I'm Sorry," a huge hit in 1960. In the end, Brenda Lee did not record it, and producer Gary Klein retrieved the song and took advantage of it to launch the country star into her conquest of the pop charts. Dolly would have begged Klein to include a pedal steel so that there was a little country tonality in the song. Covered forty years later in the 2018 film *Dumplin'*, directed by Anne Fletcher, the song has not aged a bit, as one might say. The story tells of a flashback. The narrator sees an old love return and her heart races. Dolly's energy is a perfect match for *Here You Come Again*, the song with which she won her first Grammy at the 21st Grammy Awards, in the category of Best Female Country Vocal Performance.

The Yamaha CP80 is an 88-key electro-acoustic piano, amplified by microphones similar to those on an electric guitar. It was developed in 1978 by Yamaha as a successor to the CP70, which had only 73 keys.

Production

Since her previous album, *New Harvest…First Gathering*, released in February 1977, Dolly's life had changed: Her collaboration with Porter Wagoner had ended, and she had left the legendary Studio B, which meant new producers (in this case Gary Klein), new musicians, and a new sound. For *New Harvest…*, Dolly was keen to make a transition—her crown as queen of country music had become too restrictive—but there was still some hesitation. On "Here I Come Again," she is uninhibited: We enter straight into mainstream pop; nothing will stop her anymore. It starts with a piano part played on a Yamaha CP80, the standard of the late 1970s pop sound. The addition of a light chorus brings this shimmering color that anchors the song in its time from the first bars. The sound of the electric guitar lead also benefits from this "modern" treatment: chorus, a larger-than-life reverb, and compression are in order. The presence and definition of the bass/drums sound goes a step further: For the first time on a Dolly album, the bass drum and the bass can reproduce frequencies below 50 Hz. Nick DeCaro's string arrangement, with Harry Bluestone at the forefront, is very representative of a sound that would characterize the 1980s. *Brilliance*, *depth*, and *precision* are the key words here. This contemporary romanticism, full of optimism and insouciance, was to rock the planet for more than a decade. As always, Dolly Parton knew how to jump onto a bandwagon.

Dolly waves to fans outside the Peaches Records store in Atlanta after leaving her handprints in the sidewalk (May 3, 1977).

Baby, Come Out Tonight

Kathy McCord / 3:27

Musicians: Ben Benay, Jay Graydon: guitar / Al Perkins, Dave Wolfert: pedal steel / Nick DeCaro: accordion, vocal and strings arrangements / Harry Bluestone: first violin / David Foster: keyboards, synthesizer / Ed Greene: drums / David Hungate: bass / Jim Keltner: percussion / David Lindley: slide guitar / Dean Parks: lead guitar, banjo **Vocals:** Dolly Parton **Backing Vocals:** Nick DeCaro, Jan Gassman, Myrna Matthews, Marti McCall, Gene Morford, Zedrick Turnbough **Recorded:** Sound Labs Studios, Los Angeles (CA), June 15, 1977
Technical Team: Producer: Gary Klein / Sound Engineer: Armin Steiner / Assistant Sound Engineers: Don Henderson, Linda Tyler / Mixing: Armin Steiner

The narrator tries to convince a married man to meet her in the moonlight. Dolly sings *Baby Come Out Tonight* in a smooth, quiet voice, but with an extraordinary groove.

This 4/4 ballad sways like a bittersweet Paul Simon song performed by Rickie Lee Jones. The flashy colors alternate with the darkness of an apartment on the seventeenth floor of a Manhattan tower, blinds half-open on the night lights. The rhythmic artifices, claves dipped in reverb and other ethnic percussion instruments, are played by the legendary Jim Keltner (collaborator of Neil Young, Leon Russell, Harry Nilsson, John Lennon…). The rhythm, completely fragmented, propels the listener into reveries full of romanticism and hope. The Rhodes piano full of chorus, the glossy sound of the strings, the syncopated play of the acoustic guitar and the bass: Everything contributes to create this sensual and enveloping atmosphere. We would like time to stand still, "clingin' to each other in the soft mornin' light."

It's All Wrong, But It's All Right

Dolly Parton / 3:19

Musicians: Ben Benay, Jay Graydon: guitar / Al Perkins, Dave Wolfert: pedal steel / Nick DeCaro: accordion, vocal and strings arrangements / Harry Bluestone: first violin / David Foster: keyboards, synthesizer / Ed Greene: drums / David Hungate: bass / Jim Keltner: percussion / David Lindley: slide guitar / Dean Parks: lead guitar, banjo **Vocals:** Dolly Parton **Backing Vocals:** Nick DeCaro, Jan Gassman, Myrna Matthews, Marti McCall, Gene Morford, Zedrick Turnbough **Recorded:** Sound Labs Studios, Los Angeles (CA), July 22, 1977 **Technical Team:** Producer: Gary Klein / Sound Engineer: Armin Steiner / Assistant Sound Engineers: Don Henderson, Linda Tyler / Mixing: Armin Steiner **Single:** Side A: Two Doors Down / Side B: It's All Wrong, but It's All Right **Release:** RCA Studio B, February 27, 1978 (45 rpm ref.: PB-11240) **Best Chart Ranking:** 1 on Billboard Hot Country Songs (US), 1 on RPM Country Tracks (Canada)

Even though everything about this love is wrong, it will be all right, says the narrator. For she is so lonely that she is willing to accept an artificial relationship as long as the sweet lies and hugs warm her heart.

This is the second ballad in a row with this third track (and second single) from the album. But Ed Greene's drums, with his semiquaver hi-hat playing on the choruses, offer us, this time, the triumphant version of the romantic slow song, another great classic of the early 1980s. Surrounded by her orchestra—lush backing vocals and strings arrangements, epic electric guitar licks followed by cascades of natural harmonics, crunchy Fender Rhodes with plenty of backing vocals—Dolly can indulge in a night of love without thinking about tomorrow: "Just close your eyes and hold me tight." We remain in a state of extrovert sensuality.

Me And Little Andy

Dolly Parton / 2:40

Musicians: Ben Benay, Jay Graydon: guitar / Al Perkins, Dave Wolfert: pedal steel / Nick DeCaro: accordion, vocal and strings arrangements / Harry Bluestone: first violin / David Foster: keyboards, synthesizer / Ed Greene: drums / David Hungate: bass / Jim Keltner: percussion / David Lindley: slide guitar / Dean Parks: lead guitar, banjo **Vocals:** Dolly Parton **Backing Vocals:** Nick DeCaro, Jan Gassman, Myrna Matthews, Marti McCall, Gene Morford, Zedrick Turnbough **Recorded:** Sound Labs Studios, Los Angeles (CA), August 2, 1977 **Technical Team:** Producer: Gary Klein / Sound Engineer: Armin Steiner / Assistant Sound Engineers: Don Henderson, Linda Tyler / Mixing: Armin Steiner **Single:** Side A: Here You Come Again / Side B: Me and Little Andy **Release:** RCA Victor, September 26, 1977 (45 rpm ref.: PB-11123) **Best Chart Ranking:** Did Not Chart

One stormy night, a little girl, Sandy, with her puppy, Andy, in her arms, knocks on the narrator's door. In rags and starving, she asks for candy and cakes, and a bed—her mother has run away, and her father is drunk. The man welcomes them, but the girl and the dog die in their sleep. This drama, inspired by a report on child abuse, evokes the song "Gypsy, Joe and Me," released on the album *My Blue Ridge Mountain Boy* in 1969, where Dolly sings in a childish voice, close to recitation at times, which may seem annoying but works well—she regularly re-created this effect in concert. On April 4, 1980, the song was released as a single in the United Kingdom but did not chart.

The arrangement of this tragic story—the third single from the album—is very cinematic. The song is in the tradition of Dickensian playlets that Dolly Parton takes a strange pleasure in writing and interpreting. The creepy atmosphere makes it hard to imagine why this song was chosen as a European single in September 1977; even the distorted American perception of British gothic culture was barely a justification for the hope of a resounding success in the UK—despite the quality of Dolly's orchestration and interpretation.

John Sebastian, founder of the Lovin' Spoonful, at a 1975 concert in New York City's Central Park.

A gifted songwriter, solo performer, and leader of the Lovin' Spoonful, John B. Sebastian had been a central figure in the West Coast folk/rock scene since 1964. His many hits, including *Darling Be Home Soon, Daydream, Summer in the City*, and *You Didn't Have to Be So Nice*, as well as his solo performance at the 1969 Woodstock Festival, have bequeathed an enduring impression.

Lovin' You

John Benson Sebastian / 2:24

Musicians: Ben Benay, Jay Graydon: guitar / Al Perkins, Dave Wolfert: pedal steel / Nick DeCaro: accordion / David Foster: keyboards, synthesizer / Ed Greene: drums / David Hungate: bass / Jim Keltner: percussion / David Lindley: slide guitar / Dean Parks: lead guitar, banjo
Vocals: Dolly Parton **Backing Vocals:** Nick DeCaro, Jan Gassman, Myrna Matthews, Marti McCall, Gene Morford, Zedrick Turnbough
Recorded: Sound Labs Studios, Los Angeles (CA), June 16, 1977
Technical Team: Producer: Gary Klein / Sound Engineer: Armin Steiner / Assistant Sound Engineers: Don Henderson, Linda Tyler / Mixing: Armin Steiner

While her man sleeps, the narrator is right there, eyes closed, loving him. But she also thinks about what she would do if she were not sleeping. If she had not found him, she would be out looking for him. Previously, she could barely imagine this man; now she imagines being able to leave him. But, with her eyes still closed, she continues to love him. This shuffle-like little song with country-blues accents is typical of John B. Sebastian's songwriting. As far as arrangements are concerned, one might imagine one was back in Studio B: folk guitar picking, slide guitar, electric guitar, banjo, honky-tonk piano, no excessive reverb or strings—Dolly Parton is at home and her musicians are, too. Their enjoyment of the playing is palpable.

Cowgirl & The Dandy

Bobby Goldsboro / 3:46

Musicians: Ben Benay, Jay Graydon: guitar / Al Perkins, Dave Wolfert: pedal steel / Nick DeCaro: accordion, vocal and strings arrangements / Harry Bluestone: first violin / David Foster: keyboards, synthesizer / Ed Greene: drums / David Hungate: bass / Jim Keltner: percussion / David Lindley: slide guitar / Dean Parks: lead guitar, banjo **Vocals:** Dolly Parton **Backing Vocals:** Nick DeCaro, Jan Gassman, Myrna Matthews, Marti McCall, Gene Morford, Zedrick Turnbough **Recorded:** Sound Labs Studios, Los Angeles (CA), August 5, 1977 **Technical Team:** Producer: Gary Klein / Sound Engineer: Armin Steiner / Assistant Sound Engineers: Don Henderson, Linda Tyler / Mixing: Armin Steiner

This is the unlikely meeting between a cowgirl, in her boots and rhinestones, and a dandy who likes to sip his 1959 Chablis on some Parisian terrace in the summer, or ski down the slopes of Aspen, Colorado, in the winter. Their sociocultural backgrounds should have kept them apart, but on that rainy night in Tennessee, they are united despite their differences. Dolly asked the author, Bobby Goldsboro, to rework the original text ("The Cowboy and the Lady") to replace the protagonists with the cowgirl and the dandy. In 1980, Brenda Lee successfully covered this song.

A rather rootsy intro for this ballad in 4/4, whose arrangement finally uses all the tricks available at the time, makes this number work to brilliant effect. Yamaha CP80 pianos and Fender Rhodes in chorus style, grandiloquent string arrangement, drums with brushes and hi-hat playing, melodic electric guitar counterpoints harmonized in overdubs, and acoustic guitar arpeggios...could it be that Dolly had found the formula for the new sound of the Grand Ole Opry, Nashville, Tennessee? In August 1977, many people thought so.

Two Doors Down

Dolly Parton / 3:07

Musicians: Ben Benay, Jay Graydon: guitar / Al Perkins, Dave Wolfert: pedal steel / Nick DeCaro: accordion / David Foster: keyboards, synthesizer / Ed Greene: drums / David Hungate: bass / Jim Keltner: percussion / David Lindley: slide guitar / Dean Parks: lead guitar, banjo **Vocals:** Dolly Parton **Backing Vocals:** Nick DeCaro, Jan Gassman, Myrna Matthews, Marti McCall, Gene Morford, Zedrick Turnbough **Recorded:** Sound Labs Studios, Los Angeles (CA), August 1, 1977 **Technical Team:** Producer: Gary Klein / Sound Engineer: Armin Steiner / Assistant Sound Engineers: Don Henderson, Linda Tyler / Mixing: Armin Steiner **Single:** Side A: Two Doors Down / Side B: It's All Wrong, but It's All Right **Release:** RCA Studio B, February 27, 1978 (45 rpm ref.: PB-11240) **Best Chart Ranking:** 12 on Billboard Contemporary (US), 7 on RPM Adult Contemporary Tracks (Canada)

Sometimes, when one is crying out of despair, loneliness, and grief, all one has to do is walk down two flights of stairs to find a festive air, life in full swing, smiles, and maybe even love, just two doors down from home. This catchy song, one of the songwriter's best, has been transposed into *Dolly Parton's Heartstrings*, the 2019 Dolly Parton co-produced series.

The country shuffle, unceremoniously passed through the modernist mill of Sound Labs Studios, is an invitation to party, which lifts the protagonist out of her drama. In the verses, the sound of a modified organ is intriguing; it is difficult to determine the exact origin of this instrument, especially since it is quickly overtaken by the Fender Rhodes and joined by the Yamaha CP80. The real novelty here is the appearance of a brass section from the second chorus. This dynamic and sharp sound is typical of the big productions intended for the clubs of the time. People must have danced a lot to this number, at the end of the disco era.

God's Coloring Book

Dolly Parton / 3:10

Musicians: Ben Benay, Jay Graydon: guitar / Al Perkins, Dave Wolfert: pedal steel / Nick DeCaro: accordion / David Foster: keyboards, synthesizer / Ed Greene: drums / David Hungate: bass / Jim Keltner: percussion / David Lindley: slide guitar / Dean Parks: lead guitar, banjo **Vocals:** Dolly Parton **Backing Vocals:** Nick DeCaro, Jan Gassman, Myrna Matthews, Marti McCall, Gene Morford, Zedrick Turnbough **Recorded:** Sound Labs Studios, Los Angeles (CA), August 1, 1977 **Technical Team:** Producer: Gary Klein / Sound Engineer: Armin Steiner / Assistant Sound Engineers: Don Henderson, Linda Tyler / Mixing: Armin Steiner

This ode to the beauty of the world is a Dolly Parton classic: God is in every detail of nature, every day is like a new page in "God's coloring book." It is the most uncluttered song of the album and maybe also—together with "The Letter" (the first song on *My Tennessee Mountain Home*, spoken voice and harmonica)—of Dolly's entire discography. Perhaps it is a way of saying: "I want to become a pop star, but I have not forgotten my roots or God."

Over a beautiful recording of the folk guitar, played with a perfect finger-picking technique, Dolly Parton's interpretation is superb, with a light and assured voice that pirouettes like a multicolored butterfly in the purple light of the Smokies at sunset. "Though God doesn't speak to me / I see him everywhere" says Dolly. Either way, grace certainly goes with her here.

As Soon As I Touched Him

Norma Helms, Ken Hirsch / 3:09

Musicians: Ben Benay, Jay Graydon: guitar / Al Perkins, Dave Wolfert: pedal steel / Nick DeCaro: accordion, vocal and strings arrangements / Harry Bluestone: first violin / David Foster: keyboards, synthesizer / Ed Greene: drums / David Hungate: bass / Jim Keltner: percussion / David Lindley: slide guitar / Dean Parks: lead guitar, banjo **Vocals:** Dolly Parton **Backing Vocals:** Nick DeCaro, Jan Gassman, Myrna Matthews, Marti McCall, Gene Morford, Zedrick Turnbough **Recorded:** Sound Labs Studios, Los Angeles (CA), August 1, 1977 **Technical Team:** Producer: Gary Klein / Sound Engineer: Armin Steiner / Assistant Sound Engineers: Don Henderson, Linda Tyler / Mixing: Armin Steiner

Another love story, that of love at first sight, of a moment of fusion. When the narrator touches her man, she immediately feels more of a woman than ever, as though reborn in herself.

This sensual song is introduced by David Foster and his big piano arpeggios, loose and majestic. The piano recording is extremely spatialized; the width of the stereo field (bass on the left, treble on the right) is striking. Another step forward in the production technique. Then the vocals come in, accompanied by a bass playing at the top of the neck, an array of cymbals played with finesse, and a hi-hat on the foot pedal that introduces the slow pulse as if to create suspense, the expectation of an intense and orchestrated piece. The listener is not disappointed. The arrangement builds through until the end, to finish on a last chorus

whose magnitude borders on the symphonic: strings, backing vocals, piano, strummed guitars, all carried by an epic bass/drums play. One finds oneself regretting that the fade-out, although unusually long, so soon shortens the coda of the chorus.

Sweet Music Man

Kenny Rogers / 3:08

Musicians: Ben Benay, Jay Graydon: guitar / Al Perkins, Dave Wolfert: pedal steel / Nick DeCaro: accordion, vocal and strings arrangements / Harry Bluestone: first violin / David Foster: keyboards, synthesizer / Ed Greene: drums / David Hungate: bass / Jim Keltner: percussion / David Lindley: slide guitar / Dean Parks: lead guitar, banjo **Vocals:** Dolly Parton **Backing Vocals:** Nick DeCaro, Jan Gassman, Myrna Matthews, Marti McCall, Gene Morford, Zedrick Turnbough **Recorded:** Sound Labs Studios, Los Angeles (CA), June 5, 1977 **Technical Team:** Producer: Gary Klein / Sound Engineer: Armin Steiner / Assistant Sound Engineers: Don Henderson, Linda Tyler / Mixing: Armin Steiner

Dolly Parton met Kenny Rogers on her variety show, *Dolly*. *Sweet Music Man* tells the story of a musician-singer's rise and fall. Dolly Parton sang *Sweet Music Man* as a duet with Alison Krauss on April 10, 2010, at the MGM Grand Theater at Foxwoods Resort Casino in Connecticut, during a concert event celebrating fifty years of Kenny Rogers's songs.

This "tension and release" ballad is a nice way to close the album. During the first third of the piece, the orchestration plays with subtlety on contrasts and false starts. After the acoustic guitar arpeggio and CP80 cascades in the intro, Dolly's voice escorted by the bass drum and the bass, the CP80 returns on a seismic low note, with Dolly's overdubbed harmonies, guitar tremolo volleys, and a cloud of strings on the horizon. Then the play with the brushes starts on the first chorus, taking the band with it. The strings return only at the end of the chorus and only settle definitively from the second cycle of the second verse until the end, in a gradient leading toward a very pared-down guitar/vocal ensemble. A final return of the strings solemnly punctuates the final chord. The loop is closed. The listener, a little groggy, just has to get up, turn over their LP, and put it on again.

Linda Ronstadt and Dolly Parton at the Coliseum in Oakland, California, in 1977. The *Trio* album with Emmylou Harris took several years to percolate before finally seeing the light of day.

ALBUM

Heartbreaker

I Really Got the Feeling . It's Too Late to Love Me Now . We're Through Forever ('Til Tomorrow) . Sure Thing . With You Gone . Baby I'm Burnin' . Nickels and Dimes . The Man . Heartbreaker . I Wanna Fall in Love

RELEASE DATE
United States: July 17, 1978
Reference: RCA Victor, Nashville (TN)—AFL1-2797
Best US Chart Ranking: 1

A photograph taken for the cover of *Heartbreaker* in 1978.

For Dolly Addicts

For the release of *Heartbreaker*, the production launched a major publicity campaign, with, notably, a huge neon "Dolly" sign on the Sunset Strip in Hollywood, and hundreds of pink satin shorts stamped "Dolly" on one leg and "Heartbreaker" on the other, distributed to record shops and radio stations.[5]

Affairs of the Heart

After the success of the album *Here You Come Again*, Dolly Parton continued her ascent with her twentieth solo album, *Heartbreaker*, which was released by RCA Victor on July 17, 1978. It would be a mistake to imagine that the artist could be satisfied with just one success. In this new opus, hailed by the critics, Dolly sings about love, with pop-disco music tinged with rock.

At the end of November 1978, at the legendary Carnegie Hall in New York, another star appeared: Dalida, a singer born in Egypt, adopted by France, and celebrated in the United States. From one continent to another, from one blonde to another, the same motto: "When we sing, we want people to love us," confided Dalida. There is no doubt that Dolly Parton would agree.

The Media Watershed

Heartbreaker entered the pop, country, and disco charts in a year dominated by John Badham's film *Saturday Night Fever*. Dolly Parton was more than in tune with the spirit of the times with a number such as *Baby I'm Burnin'*. But she had to wait until 1977 and *Here You Come Again* to be invited onto the set of major TV shows, such as *The Tonight Show Starring Johnny Carson*. She had gained some weight, so for a while the tabloids would shift their focus from gossiping about her and Porter to her extra pounds. During her appearance at Johnny Carson's house on her birthday, Dolly showed that she was finally in control of her image and communications message. She joked a lot, and it is clear that Carson was under the spell—and hypnotized by her chest size. Ten years after her first long interview, with Everett Corbin,[5] Dolly was no longer the young woman newly arrived from the countryside to make her fortune in Nashville. At thirty-one, the artist knew better than anyone what it means to build an image, and she had resisted all those who tried to remodel her. She had embraced her ultra-visible outfits, her outrageous makeup, and the dizzying height of her wigs. She embraced her roots and her cowgirl image even more, and ended up winning over everyone who crossed her path, without too much resistance on their part. The queen of country music had knocked over the boundaries that ghettoize every genre, whether human or musical.

From *Rolling Stone* to *Playboy*

The same year, in August, the magazine *Rolling Stone*, the bible of rock, published a long interview with Dolly Parton conducted by journalist Chet Flippo. They met while the star was on tour in Connecticut with singer Mac Davis.

Chet and Dolly were driving in a sky-blue Mustang; he was driving and Dolly was singing along to the radio. When the reporter suggested that she find a suitable place to interview him, Dolly replied that the cemetery would be perfect; she liked to write in the shade of the silent alleys, she confided to him. When Flippo asked her about country music, Dolly explained that she was not giving it up; she just needed to dare to do something different, to be brave and go for the music that best embodied it—"I just want to dream free,"[5] she added. In March 1978, she was approached by Lawrence Grobel for an interview, which ran for more than a dozen pages in *Playboy* magazine. Both Flippo and Grobel were won over by Dolly's temperament. The two writers took the time to discover her, to follow her in concert with her band in the tour bus; they accompanied Dolly and she confided in them.[5]

Love Stories

Through the reading of Chet Flippo's and Lawrence Grobel's articles, one can see how Dolly Parton was now an integral part of the musical landscape and the star system. But Dolly remained true to herself, authentic, frank, funny, sometimes seemingly naïve, though she was certainly not naïve when it came to her dreams and creativity. We better perceive her sensitivity and the wounds caused by those who mistreated her in the media. If one looks at all this closely, one can often sense a form of sexism, because it is certain that if the artist had been a man, the attacks against her looks, her weight, and her alleged extramarital affairs would have been less virulent. With time, an aspect of her personality emerges clearly: Dolly wants to be loved, and that makes her deeply lovable. It is a way of being, which is not just related to her religious convictions, and which motivates her refusal to position herself politically, in order not to hurt anyone. She dedicates herself to joy, passion, music, equality, and freedom for women and men. The creative artist works for herself, but always with others and toward others.

Album Cover

For this second cover produced for RCA Victor, photographer Ed Caraeff was able to capture two facets of the artist's personality: In the background, a joyful Dolly passes, with burlesque humor, through a romantic painted decor, literally bursting through the screen; in the foreground, another Dolly stands out, more posed but with a deliberately sexy attitude, a leg revealed and a look full of promise. Swathed in a vaporous pink, sometimes playfully, sometimes glamorously, the songwriter accordingly announces the tone of this album dedicated to seduction, to love found, lost, missed, found again—a love that rhymes with sensuality and sexuality.

The album *Heartbreaker* went gold in the United States, selling over 500,000 copies, and in Canada with 50,000 copies.

1978

Musician Jeff Baxter (left), guitar legend and Dolly collaborator, posing with The Doobie Brothers in 1978.

I Really Got The Feeling

Billy Vera / 3:09

Musicians: Jeff Baxter: guitar synthesizer / Paulinho da Costa: congas / Nick DeCaro: strings arrangements / Joe McGuffee: steel guitar/ David Foster, Mac Rebennack, David Paich, Gregg Perry, Michael Omartian: piano / Bill Reichenbach: trombone / Larry Williams: tenor saxophone, flute / Jerry Hey, Steve Madaio: trumpet / David Hungate: bass / Jim Keltner: drums, special effects / Joe McGuffee: pedal steel / David Wolfert: acoustic and electric guitar / Kim Hutchcroft: soprano, tenor, and baritone saxophone **Vocals:** Dolly Parton **Backing Vocals:** Anita Ball, Richard Dennison, Jim Gilstrap, Augie Johnson, Myrna Matthews, Stephanie Spruill, Angela Winbush **Recorded:** Sound Labs Studios, Los Angeles (CA), March 7, 1978 **Technical Team:** Producers: Gary Klein, Dolly Parton / Sound Engineer: Armin Steiner / Assistant Sound Engineers: Don Henderson, Linda Tyler / Mixing: Armin Steiner **Single:** Side A: Baby I'm Burnin' / Side B: I Really Got the Feeling **Release:** RCA Victor, November 1978 (45 rpm ref.: PB-11420) **Best Chart Ranking:** 1 on Billboard Hot Country Songs (US), 25 on Billboard Hot 100 (US), 11 on Billboard Adult Contemporary (US), 1 on RPM Country Tracks (Canada)

Genesis and Lyrics

The single, released on November 6, 1978, confirms that country and pop fans are on the same page. *I Really Got the Feeling* is a love song with a hint of disco to dance to, which Dolly performs in a beautiful, clear, and confident voice.

Production

Over the years and through her work, the star asserts herself in the music world in the United States. The recording sessions in Los Angeles enabled Dolly Parton to meet musicians from other worlds. The guitar synthesizer and keyboard intro is played by Jeff Baxter, a guitar legend who has toured with rock bands Steely Dan and the Doobie Brothers. David Paich, who also contributed to the album, was one of the founding members of the band Toto.

On this track, the sound is radically different from the Nashville recordings. The drums are much more rocking, and Jim Keltner does not overdo it on his breaks—usually the bass is rounder, warmer, and not as pervasive. Here, the mix is more subtle. The reverb effects are less exaggerated, despite the length of the decay; they are more natural. One can hear the stereo output of the effect, especially on headphones. Level variations are perceptible in Dolly's voice. Allowing her to express herself, not touching her dynamics too much, was a deliberate choice. Thus, the singer manages her nuances, with her voice but also with the distance between her and the microphone. The keyboard plays a major role in the melodic accompaniment. All the other solo instruments (violins, backing vocals) or rhythmic instruments (folk guitars) are on the right or left side of the mix (except drums and bass). On the other hand, the violins (first and second) play almost louder than the vocals—this is the least subtle part. These violins, with the drums pattern, evoke the credits of the TV series *Little House on the Prairie*, written by David Rose, who also composed several film scores under the MGM label in California. It is also the sound of the West Coast, with its beaches, its promenades, and its luxury villas, that reaches us.

Emmylou Harris, Dolly Parton, and tailor Nudie Cohn, who made multiple costumes for Dolly, 1978.

We're Through Forever ('Til Tomorrow)

Blaise Tosti / 3:50

Musicians: Jeff Baxter: guitar synthesizer / Paulinho da Costa: congas / Nick DeCaro: strings arrangements / Joe McGuffee: steel guitar/ David Foster, Mac Rebennack, David Paich, Gregg Perry, Michael Omartian: piano / Bill Reichenbach: trombone / Larry Williams: tenor saxophone, flute / Jerry Hey, Steve Madaio: trumpet / David Hungate: bass / Jim Keltner: drums, special effects / Joe McGuffee: pedal steel / David Wolfert: acoustic and electric guitar / Kim Hutchcroft: soprano, tenor, and baritone saxophone **Vocals:** Dolly Parton **Backing Vocals:** Anita Ball, Richard Dennison, Jim Gilstrap, Augie Johnson, Myrna Matthews, Stephanie Spruill, Angela Winbush **Recorded:** Sound Labs Studios, Los Angeles (CA), March 7, 1978 **Technical Team:** Producers: Gary Klein, Dolly Parton / Sound Engineer: Armin Steiner / Assistant Sound Engineers: Don Henderson, Linda Tyler / Mixing: Armin Steiner

Even after his separation from Dolly Parton's younger sister Rachel, the faithful Richard Dennison remained with Dolly; sometimes he sang, but more often than not he was in the backing vocals and led them. He is here in duet with Dolly on a very pop-soul love song that evokes the inevitable state of war between lovers: the arguments, at the end of which everything is finished "forever," then the reconciliation and the excuses, before making love, a very "sweet revenge."

It is the only duet of the album, and the first one since the last opus with Porter Wagoner. The intro is led by the piano, the two folk guitars, then the bass. The piano and the bass stop to leave the space for the vocals and the two guitars. And the song could go on like this, because the two guitar parts work very well, but it is the orchestra that gradually enters until the chorus in *a tutti*.

It's Too Late To Love Me Now

Rory Bourke, Gene Dobbins, Jay Wilson / 3:02

Musicians: Jeff Baxter: guitar synthesizer / Paulinho da Costa: congas / Nick DeCaro: strings arrangements / Joe McGuffee: steel guitar/ David Foster, Mac Rebennack, David Paich, Gregg Perry, Michael Omartian: piano / Bill Reichenbach: trombone / Larry Williams: tenor saxophone, flute / Jerry Hey, Steve Madaio: trumpet / David Hungate: bass / Jim Keltner: drums, special effects / Joe McGuffee: pedal steel / David Wolfert: acoustic and electric guitar / Kim Hutchcroft: soprano, tenor, and baritone saxophone **Vocals:** Dolly Parton **Backing Vocals:** Anita Ball, Richard Dennison, Jim Gilstrap, Augie Johnson, Myrna Matthews, Stephanie Spruill, Angela Winbush **Recorded:** Sound Labs Studios, Los Angeles (CA), March 7, 1978 **Technical Team:** Producers: Gary Klein, Dolly Parton / Sound Engineer: Armin Steiner / Assistant Sound Engineers: Don Henderson, Linda Tyler / Mixing: Armin Steiner

A love story in which each one missed the other: When she loved him, it was not the right time; when he loved her, it was too late, she loved another. A single was released in South Africa at the end of 1978, but it did not chart. With this song, we return to the usual sound of Dolly Parton, especially with the pedal steel, present since the beginning of her career. The play of the violins is still just as pronounced. With the star's pop direction, the vocals are more in the mix. During her country period, the orchestra was there to serve the vocals; it has become more important since *New Harvest…First Gathering.*

1978

David Paich (second from the right) poses with the group Toto in 1982. He was a pianist who worked with Dolly on *Heartbreaker*.

Side B

Sure Thing

Dolly Parton / 3:33

Musicians: Jeff Baxter: guitar synthesizer / Paulinho da Costa: congas / Nick DeCaro: strings arrangements / Joe McGuffee: steel guitar / David Foster, Mac Rebennack, David Paich, Gregg Perry, Michael Omartian: piano / Bill Reichenbach: trombone / Larry Williams: tenor saxophone, flute / Jerry Hey, Steve Madaio: trumpet / David Hungate: bass / Jim Keltner: drums, special effects / Joe McGuffee: pedal steel / David Wolfert: acoustic and electric guitar / Kim Hutchcroft: soprano, tenor, and baritone saxophone **Vocals:** Dolly Parton **Backing Vocals:** Anita Ball, Richard Dennison, Jim Gilstrap, Augie Johnson, Myrna Matthews, Stephanie Spruill, Angela Winbush **Recorded:** Sound Labs Studios, Los Angeles (CA), March 7, 1978 **Technical Team:** Producers: Gary Klein, Dolly Parton / Sound Engineer: Armin Steiner / Assistant Sound Engineers: Don Henderson, Linda Tyler / Mixing: Armin Steiner **Single:** Side A: Heartbreaker / Side B: Sure Thing **Release:** RCA Victor, July 1978 (45 rpm ref.: PB-11296) **Best Chart Ranking:** Did Not Chart

It is rare for the songwriter to write about dancing and preparing for a party (makeup, hair, outfit). In this song, the narrator looks at herself in the mirror, rehearses her steps, and then goes out dancing all night in order, perhaps, to find love (and take him home with her, to dance in intimacy).

This is a very funk, even rock piece. The intro is reminiscent, in the construction and the insertion of the vocals, of "Kashmir" by Led Zeppelin (1975), even though the guitar line is very different. The small notes of guitar in the air during the first verse produce an undeniable groove. The horn section, finally complete in this album, contributes a soulful touch. An important detail, mentioned in connection with the albums *Hello, I'm Dolly* or *In the Good Old Days*, is the placing and the presence of the tambourine, which also contributes to the structure of the groove. All the power of the piece lies in the tempo, rather slow—a groove that is even more difficult to express at a slower pace.

As in *I Really Got the Feeling*, the level of Dolly's voice varies, especially at the beginning, where she stays behind the orchestra and then resumes her place. At the end of the word "sure" in the title phrase, Dolly Parton breaks her voice, producing either a very rapid rise in pitch, bordering on yodeling, or a rasp. This effect, not very usual for her—we heard it previously in *Applejack*, on the album *New Harvest...First Gathering*, in 1977—is very much used today by Duffy or by Joss Stone, for example. The trumpet does a similar thing in the note just after the chorus.

Each instrument contributes its rock or groove touch, and it works. An electric guitar plays phrases with a saturated sound, without hiding the rest. The bass is a slap: David Hungate pulls on a string perpendicular to the instrument, then releases it; the string then hits a microphone on the instrument with a percussive sound; at the same time, the thumb taps the strings to create a percussive melody.

Dolly Parton in 1978. Her European tour included stops in England, the Netherlands, France, and Sweden.

With You Gone

Dolly Parton / 3:07

Musicians: Jeff Baxter: guitar synthesizer / Paulinho da Costa: congas / Nick DeCaro: strings arrangements / Joe McGuffee: steel guitar/ David Foster, Mac Rebennack, David Paich, Gregg Perry, Michael Omartian: piano / Bill Reichenbach: trombone / Larry Williams: tenor saxophone, flute / Jerry Hey, Steve Madaio: trumpet / David Hungate: bass / Jim Keltner: drums, special effects / Joe McGuffee: pedal steel / David Wolfert: acoustic and electric guitar / Kim Hutchcroft: soprano, tenor, and baritone saxophone **Vocals:** Dolly Parton **Backing Vocals:** Anita Ball, Richard Dennison, Jim Gilstrap, Augie Johnson, Myrna Matthews, Stephanie Spruill, Angela Winbush **Recorded:** Sound Labs Studios, Los Angeles (CA), March 7, 1978 **Technical Team:** Producers: Gary Klein, Dolly Parton / Sound Engineer: Armin Steiner / Assistant Sound Engineers: Don Henderson, Linda Tyler / Mixing: Armin Steiner

In *With You Gone*, Dolly returns to themes already explored: One leaves, the other stays, with their love still very much alive. The narrator sings about what will become of her and the uncertainty as to whether her heart will one day heal.

The beginning, with drums, piano, and bass, recalls the 1975 song "December, 1963 (Oh, What a Night)" by the Four Seasons, This is the first track on the album in which the percussion section is featured. The congas, and a bell (on the right in the mix) after the pedal steel solo, are noticeable. A solo of more than four bars is noteworthy because, in general, the phrases extend over a grid length. The trombone is the only instrument in the wind section to play on the track, in a rather low range. Listening through headphones, one can tell that there are two snare drums. The main drum is slightly spatialized on the right, to coexist better with the congas; the second is completely on the left.

Left: A ticket for a Dolly Parton concert given at Théâtre Mogador in Paris on November 13, 1978.

ON YOUR HEADPHONES
Since *New Harvest…First Gathering's* initial release, this track has gained about a minute in length.

Baby I'm Burnin'

Dolly Parton / 2:37

Musicians: Jeff Baxter: guitar synthesizer / Paulinho da Costa: congas / Nick DeCaro: strings arrangements / Al Perkins: pedal steel / David Foster, Mac Rebennack, David Paich, Gregg Perry, Michael Omartian: piano / Bill Reichenbach: trombone / Larry Williams: tenor saxophone, flute / Jerry Hey, Steve Madaio: trumpet / Ed Greene: drums / David Hungate: bass / Jim Keltner: drums, special effects / Joe McGuffee: pedal steel / David Wolfert: acoustic and electric guitar / Dean Parks: soprano, tenor, and baritone saxophone **Vocals:** Dolly Parton **Backing Vocals:** Anita Ball, Richard Dennison, Jim Gilstrap, Augie Johnson, Myrna Matthews, Stephanie Spruill, Angela Winbush **Recorded:** Sound Labs, Los Angeles (CA), March 8, 1978 **Technical Team:** Producers: Gary Klein, Dolly Parton / Sound Engineer: Armin Steiner / Assistant Sound Engineers: Don Henderson, Linda Tyler / Mixing: Armin Steiner **Single:** Side A: Baby I'm Burnin' / Side B: I Really Got the Feeling **Release:** RCA Victor, November 1978 (45 rpm ref.: PB-11420) **Best Chart Ranking:** 1 on Billboard Hot Country Songs (US), 25 on Billboard Hot 100 (US), 11 on Billboard Adult Contemporary (US), 1 on RPM Country Tracks (Canada)

This sensual song describes the fire of desire that nothing can extinguish, because—and the metaphor may seem strange—it is like a gun that burns with an ardent desire. All this on a rather disco-rock rhythm. *Cashbox* magazine compared this track to Elvis Presley's "Way Down" (1977).

This is a track with multiple influences: disco, rather fast, but also rock, with its saturated guitars, and soul. Everyone becomes, as Dolly Parton sings, "out of control." Ed Greene plays a typical disco rhythm: the bass drum on all beats, and the snare drum on beats 2 and 4 of the bar. The hi-hat does a little of what it feels like with its cymbals. Greene could just as well have played it offbeat, but the effect would have been less rocking, supported by the saturated guitars. In any case, the bass drum does not move, except on a break before the fade-out. And Jeff Baxter sends battle sounds into space. Since the arrival of all these new toys, everything was tried out. And it works, as long as it is done wholeheartedly!

The brass melody is almost identical to the keyboard line of "I Can't Help Myself" by the Four Tops (Motown, 1965), and one also thinks of "Uptight" by Stevie Wonder (Tamla, 1965).

The modulation of Dolly's voice a semitone higher makes its return. On the chorus, Dolly sings the notes of the perfect chord, suggesting that she wants to make *Baby I'm Burnin'* last longer. The fade-out reinforces this impression (fade-outs are particularly significant on this album: about 25 seconds per song). Despite these two devices, the song duration is only 2:37.

Dolly appears alongside Johnny Cash, June Carter Cash, Chet Atkins, and Merle Haggard while onstage during the 1978 Country Music Awards ceremony.

Nickels And Dimes

Dolly Parton, Floyd Estel / 3:24

Musicians: Jeff Baxter: guitar synthesizer / Paulinho da Costa: congas / Nick DeCaro: strings arrangements / Al Perkins: pedal steel / David Foster, Mac Rebennack, David Paich, Gregg Perry, Michael Omartian: piano / Bill Reichenbach: trombone / Larry Williams: tenor saxophone, flute / Jerry Hey, Steve Madaio: trumpet / Ed Greene: drums / David Hungate: bass / Jim Keltner: drums, special effects / Joe McGuffee: pedal steel / David Wolfert: acoustic and electric guitar / Dean Parks: soprano, tenor, and baritone saxophone **Vocals:** Dolly Parton **Backing Vocals:** Anita Ball, Richard Dennison, Jim Gilstrap, Augie Johnson, Myrna Matthews, Stephanie Spruill, Angela Winbush
Recorded: Sound Labs, Los Angeles (CA), March 8, 1978
Technical Team: Producers: Gary Klein, Dolly Parton / Sound Engineer: Armin Steiner / Assistant Sound Engineers: Don Henderson, Linda Tyler / Mixing: Armin Steiner

The narrator explains that she owes a debt to everyone who gave her a few cents when she was singing on the street, dreaming of becoming famous. Dolly writes in her autobiography[1] that in the early days in Nashville, she had to wait until she had enough money to go to her uncle's house, so she would strum her guitar and sing in the street, people would stop, a woman would give her a few coins…

Back to country with this song, which also has a pronounced blues side to it. What could be more coherent, when Dolly is inspired by her past and sings to the past?

The Man

Dolly Parton / 3:16

Musicians: Jeff Baxter: guitar synthesizer / Paulinho da Costa: congas / Nick DeCaro: strings arrangements / Al Perkins: pedal steel / David Foster, Mac Rebennack, David Paich, Gregg Perry, Michael Omartian: piano / Bill Reichenbach: trombone / Larry Williams: tenor saxophone, flute / Jerry Hey, Steve Madaio: trumpet / Ed Greene: drums / David Hungate: bass / Jim Keltner: drums, special effects / Joe McGuffee: pedal steel / David Wolfert: acoustic and electric guitar / Dean Parks: soprano, tenor, and baritone saxophone **Vocals:** Dolly Parton **Backing Vocals:** Anita Ball, Richard Dennison, Jim Gilstrap, Augie Johnson, Myrna Matthews, Stephanie Spruill, Angela Winbush
Recorded: Sound Labs, Los Angeles (CA), March 8, 1978
Technical Team: Producers: Gary Klein, Dolly Parton / Sound Engineer: Armin Steiner / Assistant Sound Engineers: Don Henderson, Linda Tyler / Mixing: Armin Steiner

A homage to the "man," who is none other than the father of the songwriter, in a form of intimacy with his interiority. Musically, this is a concept piece. A sound effect resembles the opening of a bottle. The words of the chorus are a little strange, seeming to end on an inspiration. The drums are limited to the hi-hat, a little bass drum, and the tom, played with mallets. One can also make out a shaker, probably played by the percussionist Paulinho da Costa. In the choruses, Dolly supplements the backing vocals, standing far from the microphone and singing loudly, with a big reverb.

1978

Dolly during a 1978 concert at the Hammersmith Odeon in London.

SINGLE

Heartbreaker
Carole Bayer Sager, David Wolfert / 3:35

Musicians: Jeff Baxter: guitar synthesizer / Paulinho da Costa: congas / Nick DeCaro: strings arrangements / Al Perkins: pedal steel / David Foster, Mac Rebennack, David Paich, Gregg Perry, Michael Omartian: piano / Bill Reichenbach: trombone / Larry Williams: tenor saxophone, flute / Jerry Hey, Steve Madaio: trumpet / Ed Greene: drums / David Hungate: bass / Jim Keltner: drums, special effects / Joe McGuffee: pedal steel / David Wolfert: acoustic and electric guitar / Dean Parks: soprano, tenor, and baritone saxophone **Vocals:** Dolly Parton **Backing Vocals:** Anita Ball, Richard Dennison, Jim Gilstrap, Augie Johnson, Myrna Matthews, Stephanie Spruill, Angela Winbush **Recorded:** Sound Labs, Los Angeles (CA), March 8, 1978 **Technical Team:** Producers: Gary Klein, Dolly Parton / Sound Engineer: Armin Steiner / Assistant Sound Engineers: Don Henderson, Linda Tyler / Mixing: Armin Steiner **Single:** Side A: Heartbreaker / Side B: Sure Thing **Release:** RCA Victor, July 1978 (45 rpm ref.: PB-11296) **Best Chart Ranking:** 37 on Billboard Hot 100 (US), 12 on Billboard Adult Contemporary (US), 1 on RPM Adult Contemporary (Canada)

The narrator, who has fallen under the spell of a heartbreaker, regrets that love blinds her to the point of masking reality: She has a lover who does not keep his promises.

The return of the violins is welcome in this love song. After a long piano intro, then a piano/voice duet, the song is constructed in the same way as "I Will Always Love You," from the album *Jolene* (1974). It is also reminiscent of the second piano part of "Layla," performed by Derek and the Dominos in 1970, written by Jim Gordon (the beginning was composed by Eric Clapton). With the exception of the vocals, the same ingredients are present, with the drums played in rock ballad, folk guitars, and piano as accompaniment. The backing vocals that repeat "lovers" and "kissed me" just before the chorus are very kitschy. Dolly added a second voice on the verses.

I Wanna Fall In Love
Dolly Parton / 2:26

Musicians: Jeff Baxter: guitar synthesizer / Paulinho da Costa: congas / Nick DeCaro: strings arrangements / Al Perkins: pedal steel / David Foster, Mac Rebennack, David Paich, Gregg Perry, Michael Omartian: piano / Bill Reichenbach: trombone / Larry Williams: tenor saxophone, flute / Jerry Hey, Steve Madaio: trumpet / Ed Greene: drums / David Hungate: bass / Jim Keltner: drums, special effects / Joe McGuffee: pedal steel / David Wolfert: acoustic and electric guitar / Dean Parks: soprano, tenor, and baritone saxophone **Vocals:** Dolly Parton **Backing Vocals:** Anita Ball, Richard Dennison, Jim Gilstrap, Augie Johnson, Myrna Matthews, Stephanie Spruill, Angela Winbush **Recorded:** Sound Labs, Los Angeles (CA), March 8, 1978 **Technical Team:** Producers: Gary Klein, Dolly Parton / Sound Engineer: Armin Steiner / Assistant Sound Engineers: Don Henderson, Linda Tyler / Mixing: Armin Steiner

A different lover every day, with the same story repeated over and over again, does not satisfy the narrator. What she longs for is to fall in love, to have a man just for her, with her, in her home, for life. The guitars, the piano, the bass, the drums, the horns: All the ingredients are combined to create a pure funk track. The horn section is the most extensive on the album, but also the most present. It is possible that this song inspired Diana Ross's "Upside Down," released in 1980—one can feel the spirit at the beginning. The same is true in an even more obvious way when listening to "Celebration" by Kool & the Gang, also released in 1980.

Dolly at Day on the Green in Oakland, California—an annual festival that took place for almost 30 years, stopping in 1992 and then resuming in 2015.

Dolly in *Playboy*
A Public-Facing, Modest Woman

Founded in 1953 by Hugh Hefner, *Playboy* magazine made its way around the world with its signature rabbit in a bow tie. This glamour magazine, aimed at the contemporary man—preferably single, cultured, and living in an ultramodern penthouse—celebrated the art of living and fashion and beautiful naked women. Marilyn Monroe was Hefner's first Playmate, and Pamela Anderson was the one who accumulated fourteen *Playboy* covers over a period of twenty-five years.

In 1978, Dolly Parton agreed to an interview orchestrated by the writer Lawrence Grobel, and, playing the game, she agreed to be photographed as a "bunny" by the very glamorous Harry Langdon. *Playboy* articles were known for their quality, and Lawrence Grobel was known for taking the time to study his subjects seriously. Publication in the pages of this magazine represented a significant communications strategy for Dolly, precisely at the time of her shift in the direction of pop. Between the journalist and the singer an almost intimate conversation took place, as though between friends, and, in fact, Grobel and Dolly did become friends. He was won over by the frankness, the ease, and humor of the songwriter; on her side, the artist had a sense of trust.

The fifteen-page article was published in the October issue, and Dolly felt a certain degree of pride in this.

Between Freedom and Restraint

Lawrence Grobel and Dolly Parton met on March 13, 1978. The writer admits that he was completely taken aback. While he was expecting a little woman, he witnessed the arrival of an impressive personality.[5] Grobel was immediately touched by Dolly's open-mindedness, honesty, and professionalism. Two months later, he joined her in Virginia, where she was touring, and shared time with the star and her team, from bus to hotel or concert. From the start, Dolly took control of the interview and put the writer at ease by providing him with the first question: Why did she choose such an extravagant appearance? Grobel answered that he would prefer to receive her impressions of the photo shoot with Harry Langdon first. Dolly frankly admitted that she had not found this a particularly amusing experience. At the beginning, she was even a little worried. The star refused to pose naked, especially out of respect for her entourage, who might take umbrage—her chest size had already caused a lot of ink to flow. This did not prevent her from answering another question about nudity: Does she sleep naked or in nightclothes? It depends, answered Dolly. She did not simply evade; she gave an answer that was in character with her: changeable and adaptive. Aspects of the chameleon, just like her.

Reading this interview today reveals in retrospect the great modernity and freedom of Dolly Parton at the end of this decade. Her depth and generosity, too.

Self-Portrait: Simple and Sincere

Whether it is her childhood, her outfits, her private or professional life, talking about sex, or her artistic choices, Dolly Parton is wholehearted in what she says, what she does, and what she dreams about. Throughout the interview, the singer questioned herself, trying to define her identity as well as possible, to explain her actions with a mixture of seriousness, honesty, and humor that is typical of her. When Grobel asked her if her look could become a model for women, Dolly burst out laughing, as though it were unthinkable, and concluded that it spices up life a bit, dressing up like that. From question to question, we discover that the star is far from perceiving herself as a sex symbol or a great beauty. If people find her sexy, she respects their point of view, but she keeps it to herself. If she really wanted to please men, she would dress differently, she says. Anyway, as Dolly points out, she is married, and Carl loves her whether she is extravagant or not. The interview goes on to talk about her amazing maturity and seriousness as a little girl, her life in Tennessee, her family. Dolly talks about how she used her mental resources to write and think intensely, and to dream.

On the Importance of Being Oneself

In 1978, the thirty-two-year-old star was at a turning point in her life—the album *Here You Come Again* was a chart-topper and gave her her first million sales. When Grobel asked her how she saw herself, Dolly replied that she was proud to be an honest person, free, and curious enough to venture into new experiences. She loves change and novelty, as well as creative, professional, relational, and personal discoveries; and is not afraid to challenge herself. She considers herself sentimental, very emotional, and courageous, and says she is in love with life, which she is not afraid of. Another characteristic of the star is that she is very determined, and although she embraces her femininity, she thinks "like a man" when it comes to work. Finally, she is loyal and dedicated...and full of flaws, she assures Grobel. Dolly prefers to be appreciated for her talent as a songwriter rather than for her performance as a singer-songwriter, stating that she doesn't believe she has a beautiful voice but a different voice that she can use to achieve what others will never achieve.

During a 1978 interview with Lawrence Grobel from *Playboy*, Dolly confides that she thinks of herself as immortal because dreamers do not die!

When asked about her political and feminist stance, she remains consistent, the course she has kept to all her life, saying she is apolitical and not a feminist. Dolly is an artist who has many friends, relations, and fans; she does not want to upset anyone, so her convictions remain a private matter.

Desire and Creativity

Dolly states that neither she or her husband is plagued by jealousy. When asked how Dolly would feel about the possibility of being cheated on during his long absences, she replies that she would not want to know about it, but Carl would not do so, and if he did, it would be the end of the world for her. And, conversely, it would be the same for him. No one can take Carl's place in the songwriter's life. Dolly confides that she likes sex, has always had good experiences, and was interested in it at an early age. The young woman was surrounded by aunts and uncles not much older than her, who taught her what she needed to know about sex. For her, sex is neither shameful nor degrading; on the contrary, it is an intimate and authentic experience that she has never been afraid of. She does not talk about her fantasies but agrees that she has them, and she admits that she likes to flirt because life is all about seduction. Dolly says she goes on her way with open arms and heart. The star withholds the age of her first intimacy, deftly casting a modest veil over Grobel's question and thus preserving the boundaries she has long set on her privacy.

When Lawrence Grobel asks her what she will have carved on her tombstone, Dolly replies that she is immortal, because dreamers don't die!

ALBUM

Great Balls of Fire

Star of the Show . Down . You're the Only One . Help! . Do You Think
That Time Stands Still . Sweet Summer Lovin' . Great Balls of Fire . Almost in Love .
It's Not My Affair Anymore . Sandy's Song

RELEASE DATE
United States: May 28, 1979
Reference: RCA Victor, Nashville (TN)—AHL1-3361
Best US Chart Ranking: 4

Fire in the Belly

Great Balls of Fire, Dolly Parton's twenty-first solo album, produced by Dean Parks and Gregg Perry, was released on May 28, 1979, by RCA Victor. Although it sold less than the two previous albums, it was well received by the critics, notably by *Billboard* and *Cashbox* magazines, and by the reviewer of the AllMusic website, Mark Deming. Dolly Parton wrote four of the ten songs on this pop-disco album, which peaked at number 40 on the Billboard 200 and was reissued on CD in February 2007 and digitally in March 2007.

With "Star of the Show," the first track on the album, Dolly sets the tone: She will not be anyone's shadow. She had made the transition from country to pop without losing her country audience and was about to put on her stage clothes to make her first steps in the movie industry. Nothing could stop her on the highway of her dreams, and because of her determination, even when she faltered or fell, she still had fire in her belly and never gave up.

The Focus of All Attention

At the time of the release of *Great Balls of Fire*, Dolly Parton was professionally successful. Since 1977, the star had been on the covers of *Life*, *People*, *Cosmopolitan*, *Rolling Stone*, *Playboy*, and many other magazines, which contributed to her popularity. In 1977, facing the journalist Barbara Walters, a pioneer of female television, who had a reputation for not mincing her words—the artist's entourage predicted the worst—Dolly remained herself, and it worked very well between them. During her performance on *The Barbara Walters Summer Special*, she surprised her interviewer with her authenticity and depth. Barbara Walters could not help but ask her why a beautiful and intelligent woman like her chose such an artificial appearance. It was a question often asked of Dolly, who explained, among other reasons, that it was her thing, her way of differentiating herself, and that this appearance did not in any way detract from what makes up the real Dolly Parton: her values and her qualities.

In 1979, all eyes were on the songwriter—including those of 20th Century Fox, which offered her a contract. Was it this newfound fame that fueled jealousy, envy, or regret? The fact was that Porter Wagoner was on the attack again, even more than before.

The Burden of the Past

Sandy Gallin, the man who transformed Dolly's career and image, was looking out for her, but he was unable to prevent the past from catching up with her in the person of Porter Wagoner, who was more confrontational and litigious than ever. As reported by journalist Gerri Hirshey[5] in an interview with the singer for *Family Circle* magazine, Porter Wagoner demanded $3 million, arguing that he had given Dolly two cars, rings, and a diamond necklace. His lawyer went on to demand 15 percent of Dolly's net income from June 1974 to June 1979 and 15 percent of her future royalties. The songwriter realized how angry Porter was with her. According to Stephen Miller,[2] 1979 was a festival of backbiting and settling of scores: Porter said he would never trust someone like Dolly because, he said, she would not hesitate to turn her back on anyone to satisfy her interests. He disapproved of anything she did, even the cover of *Rolling Stone* magazine, on which she posed with Arnold Schwarzenegger. Dolly responded through the press, first calmly, and then without concealing her anger. In the end, through complaints and recriminations, Porter obtained $1 million, the conclusion of an amicable settlement between the parties, because Dolly had had enough and wanted to spare those close to her.

Album Cover

On this third cover by photographer Ed Caraeff, Dolly, more beautiful and smiling than ever, appears in a sort of fireworks display of colored neon lights, in a pink-white swirl, under her name bursting out in letters of fire. Inside the sleeve, a photo taken during a live show frames the star from behind, onstage, after nightfall, dressed all in white.

1979

Since 1977 the star has been much courted by the press, and she has appeared on the covers of *Life*, *People*, *Cosmopolitan*, *Rolling Stone*, *Playboy*, and many other magazines.

In "Star of the Show," the metronomic movement revolves around 129 bpm (beats per minute), whereas, traditionally, the disco tempo is around 120 bpm. A difference of about 10 bpm on the same song considerably changes the listener's perception and the associated feeling (the kind of dancing, for example). This metronomic excitement can be attributed to Dolly Parton's enthusiasm for her first disco song. After all, especially in pop music, rules are made to be broken.

Star Of The Show

Dolly Parton / 3:56

Musicians: Lenny Castro: congas / Quitman Dennis, Chuck Findley, Gary Herbig, Jim Horn: brass / Earl Dumler: English horn / David Grisman: mandolin / Dean Parks: guitar, alto flute, synthesizer / David Foster: keyboards / Joe McGuffee: pedal steel / Gregg Perry: piano / Abraham Laboriel: bass / Jim Keltner: drums, percussion / Dorothy Remsen: harp / Stephanie Spruill: tambourine **Vocals:** Dolly Parton **Backing Vocals:** Anita Ball, Richard Dennison, Roy Galloway, Stephanie Spruill, Julia Waters, Maxine Waters **Recorded:** Sound Labs, Los Angeles (CA), December 1978 **Technical Team:** Producers: Dean Parks, Dolly Parton, Gregg Perry / Executive Producers: Dolly Parton, Charles Koppelman / Sound Engineer: Eric Prestidge / Assistant: Linda Tyler / Mixing: Bernie Grundmann

In this energetic song, one can clearly hear the determination in Dolly's voice. It is difficult not to think of what she had been through professionally and was still going through legally with Porter Wagoner in 1979, because this song sounds like a declamation, even a declaration of inviolable principle: She is the star who shines, the first one at the top of the bill, and she will never again play anyone's second fiddle. In 1979, the song was also released as a single in Australia, New Zealand, and the Netherlands.

While the glory days of this style were already a thing of the past, this was Dolly Parton's first disco song, composed and written by her. Better late than never for Dolly, who seems to have fun and to give it her all on this track made for big stages and heavy turnover in the nightclubs. The "dumb blonde" from southern Appalachia had definitely come a long way since her first steps onstage. Strangely, the only thing missing is the strings, so present on one of the previous albums (*Here You Come Again*, released in October 1977), to complete the disco picture offered here by Dean Parks, Gregg Perry, Dolly, and her musicians. One can appreciate the octave bass pedals and the tonal ascents of Abraham Laboriel, the drums of the great Jim Keltner—bass drum on the quarter note, snare drum on beats 2 and 4, and hi-hat in sixteenth notes played with two hands. Lenny Castro's congas, Stephanie Spruill's tambourine, funk electric guitar effects, Dean Parks's synthesizer programming, and Gregg Perry's placed CP80 chords are all noteworthy, not to mention the energetic backing vocals in unison. "If, after all that, the dance floor does not catch fire, nothing makes sense any more," Dolly and her producers must have been saying to themselves.

1979

Down

Dolly Parton / 3:35

Musicians: Lenny Castro: congas / Quitman Dennis, Chuck Findley, Gary Herbig, Jim Horn: brass / Earl Dumler: English horn / David Grisman: mandolin / Dean Parks: guitar, alto flute, synthesizer / Joe McGuffee: pedal steel / Gregg Perry: synthesizer / Bill Payne: keyboards / Abraham Laboriel: bass / Jim Keltner: drums, percussion / Dorothy Remsen: harp / Stephanie Spruill: tambourine **Vocals:** Dolly Parton **Backing Vocals:** Anita Ball, Roy Galloway, Stephanie Spruill, Julia Waters, Maxine Waters **Recorded:** Sound Labs, Los Angeles (CA), May 14, 1979 **Technical Team:** Producers: Dean Parks, Dolly Parton, Gregg Perry / Executive Producers: Dolly Parton, Charles Koppelman / Sound Engineer: Eric Prestidge / Assistant: Linda Tyler / Mixing: Bernie Grundmann **Single:** Side A: You're the Only One / Side B: Down **Release:** RCA Victor, May 14, 1979 (45 rpm ref.: PB-11577) **Best Chart Ranking:** 1 on Billboard Hot Country Songs (US), 1 on RPM Country Tracks (Canada)

A woman tells the story of how, having given her money without considering the cost, she finds herself lower than dirt. She cannot help but give to everyone, including the man she loves, who used her. This title also echoes Dolly's direct experience; the similarities are there. As the song says, the narrator has learned her lesson and will do things differently the next time she is "down," because there will be a next time.

In a change of mood for this 4/4 mid-tempo number, the warm and crunchy sound of the Hammond organ is immediately striking. Its phrasing mixes with that of the Fender Rhodes to create an extremely shimmering, bluesy anthology. Thus the keyboards steal the show from Dean Parks's electric guitar, which is content to play the rhythm, with a few turnarounds. Rhythmic restraint is de rigueur here; Parks plays straight and furiously "in the pocket" (very solid and rhythmically in place). Dolly can unfold her narration with all the clarity and sense of nuance that we know well. Her character's dismay and determination not to repeat the mistakes of the past are palpable. Alas, in the face of unreasonable love, this is not always enough.

You're The Only One

Carole Bayer Sager, Bruce Roberts / 3:23

Musicians: Quitman Dennis, Chuck Findley, Gary Herbig, Jim Horn: brass / Earl Dumler: English horn / David Grisman: mandolin / Dean Parks: guitar, alto flute, synthesizer / Joe McGuffee: pedal steel / Gregg Perry: synthesizer / Abraham Laboriel: bass / Jim Keltner: drums, percussion / Michael Omartian: keyboards / Dorothy Remsen: harp **Vocals:** Dolly Parton **Backing Vocals:** Anita Ball, Carol Carmichael Parks **Recorded:** Sound Labs, Los Angeles (CA), May 14, 1979 **Technical Team:** Producers: Dean Parks, Dolly Parton, Gregg Perry / Executive Producers: Dolly Parton, Charles Koppelman / Sound Engineer: Eric Prestidge / Assistant: Linda Tyler / Mixing: Bernie Grundmann **Single:** Side A: You're the Only One / Side B: Down **Release:** RCA Victor, May 14, 1979 (45 rpm ref.: PB-11577) **Best Chart Ranking:** 1 on Billboard Hot Country Songs (US), 1 on RPM Country Tracks (Canada)

The narrator declares her love, again and again, to the man she left but ardently desires to find again. She has a better realization afterward of what she left behind, and now she is coming back, hoping that he will want to reconnect as well. This very early 1980s pop ballad charmed the fans. A slide guitar line and we fly away on this piece that is conducive to romantic dreams. The production trick that makes all the difference here—characteristic of the eighties—is the exaggerated sending of the snare drum in a long reverb (here with the addition of a subtle gate). This is particularly noticeable on the verses played in cross stick. This effect plunges the listener into an extremely enveloping supernatural sound environment, a bubble in which to take refuge, to cry for lost love or to exalt romantic passions.

1979

Dolly poses alongside Carol Burnett to promote their show, which CBS aired on February 14, 1979.

Help!

John Lennon, Paul McCartney / 2:45

Musicians: Quitman Dennis, Chuck Findley, Gary Herbig, Jim Horn: brass / Earl Dumler: English horn / David Grisman: mandolin / Dean Parks: guitar, alto flute, synthesizer / Joe McGuffee: pedal steel / Gregg Perry: synthesizer / Bill Payne: keyboards / Herb Pedersen: banjo / Abraham Laboriel: bass / Jim Keltner: drums, percussion / Dorothy Remsen: harp **Vocals:** Dolly Parton **Backing Vocals:** Anita Ball, Herb Pedersen, Ricky Skaggs **Recorded:** Sound Labs, Los Angeles (CA), December 1978 **Technical Team:** Producers: Dean Parks, Dolly Parton, Gregg Perry / Executive Producers: Dolly Parton, Charles Koppelman / Sound Engineer: Eric Prestidge / Assistant: Linda Tyler / Mixing: Bernie Grundmann

The famous Beatles song is treated to a cover version by Dolly Parton. The narrator tells how he needs help, how he feels bad, and if someone else—and not just anyone—can help him get back on his feet, then he will leave his door open.

We may not have imagined the futuristic bluegrass potential of this global hit…Dolly and her musicians saw it, and the result makes it sound like an obvious choice. The almost frenetic pickings of the acoustic guitar and the frailing banjo (a technique halfway between clawhammer and picking), the spinning of the drums with brushes, the bass that unwinds on the beat, and the virtuoso riffs of David Grisman's mandolin contribute to the traditional bluegrass part. The futuristic aspect comes from the addition, very unusual in this context, of a Fender Rhodes with a very elaborate sound (extensive reverb and subtle chorus) and an electric guitar with an essentially textural role.

Do You Think That Time Stands Still

Dolly Parton / 3:56

Musicians: Lenny Castro: congas / Quitman Dennis, Chuck Findley, Gary Herbig, Jim Horn: brass / Earl Dumler: English horn / David Grisman: mandolin / Dean Parks: guitar, alto flute, synthesizer / Joe McGuffee: pedal steel / Gregg Perry: synthesizer / Abraham Laboriel: bass / Jim Keltner: drums, percussion / Michael Omartian: keyboards / Dorothy Remsen: harp **Vocals:** Dolly Parton **Backing Vocals:** Anita Ball, Richard Dennison **Recorded:** Sound Labs, Los Angeles (CA), December 1978 **Technical Team:** Producers: Dean Parks, Dolly Parton, Gregg Perry / Executive Producers: Dolly Parton, Charles Koppelman / Sound Engineer: Eric Prestidge / Assistant: Linda Tyler / Mixing: Bernie Grundmann

The narrator asks the man who returns thinking he will find things and feelings as they were when he left: "Do you think that time stands still?" The answer of the wounded but reconstructed woman is, irrefutably: It cannot, because she did not stop living but continued without him.

The piece begins with an acoustic guitar arpeggio given a chorus effect of the kind that is "good for the slow song," in the 1980s version. Here, no half measures: syrupy strings, lacy piano, emphatic backing vocals, heroic drum breaks, rumbling bass, and crystalline synth layers. Instead of the electric guitar, it is the grand resurrection of the pedal steel, which blends perfectly in this neo-romantic glossy/existentialist decorum of the late 1970s.

Sweet Summer Lovin'

Bud Reneau, Blaise Tosti / 3:17

Musicians: Quitman Dennis, Chuck Findley, Gary Herbig, Jim Horn: brass / Earl Dumler: English horn / David Grisman: mandolin / Dean Parks: guitar, alto flute, synthesizer / Joe McGuffee: pedal steel / Gregg Perry: synthesizer / Abraham Laboriel: bass / Jim Keltner: drums, percussion / Dorothy Remsen: harp **Vocals:** Dolly Parton **Backing Vocals:** Anita Ball, Carol Carmichael Parks **Recorded:** Sound Labs, Los Angeles (CA), August 6, 1979 **Technical Team:** Producers: Dean Parks, Dolly Parton, Gregg Perry / Executive Producers: Dolly Parton, Charles Koppelman / Sound Engineer: Eric Prestidge / Assistant: Linda Tyler / Mixing: Bernie Grundmann **Single:** Side A: Sweet Summer Lovin' / Side B: Great Balls of Fire **Release:** RCA Victor, August 6, 1979 (45 rpm ref.: PB-11705) **Best Chart Ranking:** 7 on Billboard Hot Country Songs (US), 6 on RPM Country Tracks (Canada)

In this love song, feelings are in unison with nature. This text by Bud Reneau and Blaise Tosti could have been written by Dolly, who loves love as much as nature, especially when she can bring the two together.

Sweetness and positivity are, indeed, the watchwords of this 4/4 up-tempo number. The old school of Nashville is confronted with the avant-garde of the Sound Labs of Los Angeles…and it works. As in "Help!" the banjo unrolls its frailing technique on a carpet of synthesizer, the Rhodes, the flute. Dolly Parton's voice benefits from the first digital treatments, the electric guitar is filled with choruses, and the backing vocals juggle between unison and aerial humming, everything driven by a rhythm section as light as it is imperturbable. The sound texture of "Sweet Summer Lovin'" is almost addictive, like the scent of dandelions and the heady taste of candy wine. One might wish to never leave this state: the bliss, however ephemeral, of summer romances.

1979

For Dolly Addicts

"Sweet Summer Lovin'" is the star's eleventh song to be ranked number one in the charts.

The slap delay (a very short delay) on Dolly's voice is as much a reminder of the rock 'n' roll sound of the 1950s as it is of the glam rock of the mid-1970s, which brought this effect back into fashion. Today, the application of a slap delay on the voice or the electric guitar is a classic production technique, always appropriate when the musical context allows it.

Great Balls Of Fire

Otis Blackwell, Jack Hammer / 3:51

Musicians: Quitman Dennis, Chuck Findley, Gary Herbig, Jim Horn: brass / Earl Dumler: English horn / David Grisman: mandolin / Dean Parks: guitar, alto flute, synthesizer / Joe McGuffee: pedal steel / Gregg Perry: synthesizer / Bill Payne: keyboards / Abraham Laboriel: bass / Jim Keltner: drums, percussion / Dorothy Remsen: harp **Vocals:** Dolly Parton **Backing Vocals:** Anita Ball **Recorded:** Sound Labs, Los Angeles (CA), August 6, 1979 **Technical Team:** Producers: Dean Parks, Dolly Parton, Gregg Perry / Executive Producers: Dolly Parton, Charles Koppelman / Sound Engineer: Eric Prestidge / Assistant: Linda Tyler / Mixing: Bernie Grundmann **Single:** Side A: Sweet Summer Lovin' / Side B: Great Balls of Fire **Release:** RCA Victor, August 6, 1979 (45 rpm ref.: PB-11705) **Best Chart Ranking:** Did Not Chart

The narrator is very clear: This love drives her crazy, in a good way and in a bad way. A classic rock 'n' roll love song! It is a fair bet that Jerry Lee Lewis himself would not have disowned this version, which oscillates between glam rock and proto-punk, with its electric guitars turned up to 11 and its sharp and tight brass section. The dry and tense drums, the roaring toms, the supercharged piano, and the unflappable eighth-note bass are also remarkable. Dolly's fast vibrato and the natural swagger of her voice work wonders on this honky-tonk rock number on steroids boosted by the studio techniques of the time.

Dolly with her manager, Sandy Gallin, to whom she paid tribute on "Sandy's Song."

Following spread: Dolly and the Mandrell Sisters—(from left) Irlene, Louise, and Barbara—who hosted their own TV show on NBC between 1980 and 1982.

Dolly arrived in Sydney, Australia, on July 11, 1979, while *Great Balls of Fire* was ranked in the top 100.

Almost In Love

Dean Parks, Doug Thiele / 3:15

Musicians: Quitman Dennis, Chuck Findley, Gary Herbig, Jim Horn: brass / Earl Dumler: English horn / David Grisman: mandolin / Dean Parks: guitar, alto flute, synthesizer / David Foster: keyboards / Joe McGuffee: pedal steel / Gregg Perry: piano, synthesizer / Abraham Laboriel: bass / Jim Keltner: drums, percussion / Dorothy Remsen: harp **Vocals:** Dolly Parton **Backing Vocals:** Anita Ball, Carol Carmichael Parks **Recorded:** Sound Labs, Los Angeles (CA), December 1978 **Technical Team:** Producers: Dean Parks, Dolly Parton, Gregg Perry / Executive Producers: Dolly Parton, Charles Koppelman / Sound Engineer: Eric Prestidge / Assistant: Linda Tyler / Mixing: Bernie Grundmann

The narrator asks her mother to let her go, because she feels that she is "almost" falling in love. More and more, the man she is beginning to love is bowling her over, so it is time for her to go and live her life as a woman with him.

This is the third syrupy slow song of the album, and although they all have their particularities, we find this enveloping sound using the same production techniques. The parallel with "Do You Think That Time Stands Still" is especially striking, even though the tempo here is slower. Produced during the same recording session, the instrumentation is identical, and the sound recording, arrangement, and mixing have been approached in a very similar way. One can sense that the Sound Labs team had done a lot of this kind of work before.

It's Not My Affair Anymore

Jeanne French / 3:17

Musicians: Lenny Castro: congas / Quitman Dennis, Chuck Findley, Gary Herbig, Jim Horn: brass / Earl Dumler: English horn / David Grisman: mandolin / Dean Parks: guitar, alto flute, synthesizer / Joe McGuffee: pedal steel / Gregg Perry: synthesizer / Abraham Laboriel: bass / Jim Keltner: drums, percussion / Michael Omartian: keyboards / Dorothy Remsen: harp **Vocals:** Dolly Parton **Backing Vocals:** Anita Ball, Richard Dennison, Carol Carmichael Parks **Recorded:** Sound Labs, Los Angeles (CA), 1978 **Technical Team:** Producers: Dean Parks, Dolly Parton, Gregg Perry / Executive Producers: Dolly Parton, Charles Koppelman / Sound Engineer: Eric Prestidge / Assistant: Linda Tyler / Mixing: Bernie Grundmann

In the vast palette of love songs that the songwriter is fond of, this one tells what a woman experiences and feels when she sees the man she loved on the arm of another, with the same sparkle in his eyes that he had when he looked at her…before.

With this groovy mid-tempo 4/4 number, full of contrasts, composed by the blues singer Jeanne French, we find the carefree spirit, the joy of living, and resilience. The electric guitar has a well-judged funk sound; on bass, Abraham Laboriel—aware of the rich sound of his bass—has no need to overdo it; Jim Keltner on drums and Lenny Castro on congas play as one. The acoustic guitar energizes the chorus with impeccable strumming and is mixed very forward; the backing vocals envelop the chorus and

1979

call out to Dolly on the verse ("Remember…"). All that remains is to fill in the frequency spectrum and to slip into the few rhythmic gaps still vacant; this is the role of Michael Omartian on Fender Rhodes. This seemingly simple track is reminiscent of the quality and sophistication of the productions of Steely Dan (founded in 1971 by the duo of New York musicians and producers Donald Fagen and Walter Becker, to whom we owe the soft rock hits "Rikki Don't Lose That Number," "Do It Again," and "Reelin' in the Years." Dolly can express all her soul and the extraordinary quality of her phrasing.

Sandy's Song
Dolly Parton / 3:17

Musicians: Quitman Dennis, Chuck Findley, Gary Herbig, Jim Horn: brass / Earl Dumler: English horn / David Grisman: mandolin / Dean Parks: guitar, alto flute, synthesizer / Joe McGuffee: pedal steel / Gregg Perry: synthesizer / Bill Payne: keyboards / Abraham Laboriel: bass / Jim Keltner: drums, percussion / Dorothy Remsen: harp **Vocals:** Dolly Parton **Backing Vocals:** Anita Ball **Recorded:** Sound Labs, Los Angeles (CA), 1978 **Technical Team:** Producers: Dean Parks, Gregg Perry / Executive Producers: Dolly Parton, Charles Koppelman / Sound Engineer: Eric Prestidge / Assistant: Linda Tyler / Mixing: Bernie Grundmann

Through this song, Dolly pays tribute to her manager, Sandy Gallin, the one who had faith in her to go further and who enabled the artist to become herself. She feels love and gratitude for him, but she tells him that one day she will leave him and their story will end—however, not before the "green grass turns lavender blue / And all the stars fall from heaven and vanish like dew," which, we must agree, may take some time.

As for the music, we start in an Irish-medieval atmosphere, with a touch of new age. Progressively, the piece evolves toward a very cinematographic orchestral arrangement, scored by Gregg Perry himself. The duo of Dean Parks on acoustic guitar and Dorothy Remsen on harp is quickly joined by Earl Dumler's English horn, then by Bill Payne's piano. At 0:40, the strings discreetly enter on the second verse before the first flight at 1:12, on the chorus. Then follows an instrumental part whose main theme is carried by the English horn before the sublime flight of strings and winds that follows on the second and last chorus. Then the storm calms down to give way to the coda of the guitar/harp intro. "I'll love you 'til then," sings Dolly, and we then understand that this love is eternal. Very beautiful work, refined and inspired. It is difficult to imagine a better conclusion for this album, whose diversity was still without equal in Dolly Parton's discography in 1979.

ALBUM

Dolly, Dolly, Dolly

Starting Over Again . Same Old Fool . Old Flames Can't Hold a Candle to You .
You're the Only One I Ever Needed . Say Goodnight . Fool for Your Love .
Even a Fool Would Let Go . Sweet Agony . I Knew You When . Packin' It Up

RELEASE DATE
United States: April 14, 1980
Reference: RCA Victor—AHL1-3546
Best US Chart Ranking: 7

Swings and Roundabout

Dolly Parton's twenty-second solo album, *Dolly, Dolly, Dolly*, was released on the RCA Victor label on April 14, 1980. Reviews from both fans and critics were mixed, although they were all impressed by two of the songs—"Starting Over Again" and "Old Flames Can't Hold a Candle to You"—sending them to the top of the charts. None of the numbers on this album was written by Dolly—the first time this had happened—and this perhaps explained the album's only moderate success. Nevertheless, it provided Dolly with the chance to experiment in a new musical environment at a time when she was preparing to become a movie star.

The Price of Fame

The years 1979 and 1980 were difficult for the United States. The Shah of Iran took refuge there and, as a result, Jimmy Carter had to deal with the consequences of this asylum: the "Canadian Caper" (aka Argo Affair) and the taking of American hostages by the Ayatollah Ruhollah Khomeini's men as revenge for America's political stance.

At the Fan Fair, the most important country music event in Nashville, crowds of people desperate to see their favorite star pressed round the RCA Victor stand where Dolly was signing autographs. In the confusion, people were being pushed and knocked down, and one young boy suffered injuries that made headlines.[2] Dolly was well looked after, escorted and protected by bodyguards. As Stephen Miller comments in *Smart Blonde*, this kind of fame was considered normal for Hollywood stars. In one of life's ironies, it was also the year in which the last joint album with Porter Wagoner, *Porter & Dolly*, was released. On the record sleeve, the two artists, just then in the middle of a legal battle, pose as a happy couple. In reality, the shots were taken separately by two different photographers.

In June 1980, Dolly was engaged to do a six-week stint at the Riviera Hotel in Las Vegas—the city famous for its unique atmosphere and ability to make money change hands. According to Stephen Miller,[2] the weekly takings amounted to about $350,000. But Dolly was suffering from health problems. The effects of the air-conditioning in the tour coach and the cigarette smoke in the venues (smoking was still allowed at the time) were affecting her overused vocal cords. As a result, Dolly was obliged to slow down and even take some time off, and some concerts were postponed. Despite a few more canceled shows, things improved and Dolly gave her best, bringing some of her biggest hits to the Riviera's stage. Nevertheless, problems with her weight and nodules on her vocal cords were beginning to haunt her; she was paying the price for fifteen years of stress, emotional hurt, and overwork.

Straight Thinking

Nineteen eighty marked a change in Dolly Parton's life: It was the year when she starred with Jane Fonda and Lily Tomlin in the movie *9 to 5*, which led to a soundtrack album with the same name. In an interview with the magazine *Family Circle*, Gerri Hirshey[5] asked Dolly what secret let her realize all her dreams—was it her love for Carl Dean, fame…? Dolly replied that she was a positive person who rejected negativity in order to concentrate on her objectives. She described how she and her husband designed their house: On each wedding anniversary they took a trip in the car and stopped to photograph items—a porch, a roof—that appealed to them. Assembling these images, they used them to fire up their imaginations until the day they could build their dream house. The recipe seems all too simple, but it seems to have worked wonderfully well in Dolly's life. But it does require total faith in oneself, in the world, and in God—a star tip!

Album Cover

Sitting on a carousel horse, Dolly looks radiant and fresh in her embroidered skirt, seemly exhilarated by the movement of the carousel. The title of the album over her head consists of her signature repeated three times in bright colors.

Donna Summer and her husband, Bruce Sudano, at an event in New York ca. 1980.

Starting Over Again

Donna Summer, Bruce Sudano / 3:55

The song "Starting Over Again," jointly written by the singer Donna Summer and songwriter Bruce Sudano, was inspired by the latter's parents' divorce.

Vocals: Dolly Parton **Musicians:** Jay Graydon: acoustic guitar / Neil Stubenhaus: bass / Jeff Porcaro: drums / Buzzy Feiten: electric guitar / Tommy Morgan: harmonica / Michael Omartian: keyboard / Nick DeCaro : synthesizer and arrangements **Backing Vocals:** Denise Maynelli, Jim Gilstrap, Marti McCall, Myrna Matthews **Recorded:** Sound Lab Studios, Los Angeles, December 1979 **Technical Team:** Producer: Gary Klein / Executive Producer: Charles Koppelman / Sound Engineer: John Arrias / Assistants: Don Henderson, Sheridan Eldridge / Mixing: Mike Reese **Single:** Side A: Starting Over Again / Side B: Sweet Agony **Release:** RCA Victor, February 25, 1980 (45 rpm ref.: PB-11926) **Best Chart Ranking:** 1 on the Billboard Hot Country Songs (USA); 2 on the RPM Country 75 Singles (Canada)

Genesis and Lyrics

The narrator tells of her parents' separation after thirty years together. Her mother has left, her father has sold their house, and they have divided up their money. The child has failed to reconcile them and wonders how they are going to manage. Her parents will have to build their lives again from scratch. Where do they start? The mother looks back over her past; the father tries to make some money in business deals. The child hears the whole town gossiping about the separation. Dolly Parton's voice expresses a genuine sadness, bringing emotional energy to the words.

Production

The 1980s influenced Dolly Parton's kind of popular music. Electronic drum kits had not yet appeared, but synthesizers certainly had. Several can be heard in this long piano intro, being used to "enrich" the piano sound. One of them, in piano mode, plays chords while another adds unaccented layers of sound. The folk guitar is there, of course. Around 1:21, at the end of the first refrain, we can hear notes that seem to be played on an electric guitar in such a way as to give the impression of a keyboard as well. The last instrument to come in is a slightly saturated synth, which appears after the bridging passage with the backing vocals. These notes completely cover the sound of the actual bass guitar.

There is not much space for the "traditional" instruments (guitar, bass, drums, violin) in this frenzy of synthesizers and special effects. Dolly's voice is more or less natural, with only a touch of reverb. Another reverb effect is used for the backing vocals that come in just once after the second refrain. The male voices alternate (left/right), either by a time lag with a single repeat or by the singing of the vocals during the recording. This Ping-Pong-like effect is achieved with a stereo output, the signal being sent alternately to the left and right.

The queen of disco—
posing here in Los
Angeles in 1980—
wrote the first single
from the album *Dolly,
Dolly, Dolly.*

Dolly poses for a photo shoot before taking the stage at Caesars Palace in South Lake Tahoe, California, 1980.

Same Old Fool

Greg Sutton, Gregg Leroy, Jim Helmer / 3:20

Vocals: Dolly Parton **Musicians:** Neil Stubenhaus: bass / Jeff Porcaro: drums / Buzzy Feiten, Jeff Baxter: electric guitar / Michael Omartian: keyboards / Lenny Castro: percussion / Michael Omartian: arrangements **Backing Vocals:** Denise Maynelli, Marti McCall, Myrna Matthews **Recorded:** Sound Lab Studios, Los Angeles, December 1979 **Technical Team:** Producer: Gary Klein / Executive Producer: Charles Koppelman / Sound Engineer: John Arrias / Assistants: Don Henderson, Sheridan Eldridge / Mixing: Mike Reese

The woman narrator complains that her man loves to hate her and hates to love her. She begs for a second chance… Although there are as many keyboards used here as in the album's first track, the writing and the notes come through more clearly. The bass is doubled by a synthesizer. The final rendering is modified, but the result is more appropriate than the multilayered "Starting Over Again." The drummer plays a pattern that is frequently found in the pop music of this decade. It is very straight, with the bass drum on all beats and little syncopation. One example is Cyndi Lauper's 1983 hit "Girls Just Want to Have Fun," a cover of a song by Robert Hazard released in 1979.

Old Flames Can't Hold A Candle To You

Pebe Sebert, Hugh Moffatt / 3:28

Vocals: Dolly Parton **Musicians:** Jay Graydon: acoustic guitar / David Hungate: bass / Jeff Porcaro: drums / Al Perkins: pedal steel guitar / Jai Winding: keyboards / Nick DeCaro: arrangements **Backing Vocals:** Herb Pedersen, Randy Parton **Recorded:** Sound Lab Studios, Los Angeles, December 1979 **Technical Team:** Producer: Gary Klein / Executive Producer: Charles Koppelman / Sound Engineer: John Arrias / Assistants: Don Henderson, Sheridan Eldridge / Mixing: Mike Reese **Single:** Side A: Old Flames Can't Hold a Candle to You / Side B: I Knew You When **Release:** RCA Victor, June 23, 1980 (45 rpm ref.: PB-12040) **Best US Chart Ranking:** 1

The narrator tells the man she loves now that the "old flames" of her past—the men she had known before him—are definitely extinguished and do not compare with him. This is a ballad in the country music style, featuring drums, bass, pedal steel, and folk guitars. Set among the album's artificial-sounding disco-style tracks, this song marks a return to the roots of country music. The writing is much more restrained. But there are, nevertheless, new effects; for example, reverb is used on the snare drum—a technique still used today—giving the sound more body by suppressing the "box-like" effect noticeable when the sound is too dry. The drumming here reveals a radical departure from previous albums, with a change in recording technique that gives it a more rock feel. A lot of rock ballads use this sound and pattern, the most famous including "Still Loving You" by the Scorpions (1984) and "Knockin' on Heaven's Door," the cover by Guns N' Roses (1987) of the song by Bob Dylan (1973).

In the first refrain, Dolly Parton sings with one man and then with two. In the second refrain the three of them can be heard from the start—unprecedented in terms of the number of singers and the absence of a female voice among the backup singers. This track is one of the few that ends without a fade-out—there are four like this on *Dolly, Dolly, Dolly*, unlike on *Heartbreaker*, where there were none—and they are all ballads. It is probably less complicated to compose an ending for a ballad with a final chord than it is to end a punchier piece. The fade-out was not only a fashion at the time, but also an easy solution. It didn't work in concerts, however, so something different had to be devised for live performances.

You're The Only One I Ever Needed

Robbie Patton, Linda Mallah / 2:57

Vocals: Dolly Parton **Musicians:** Jay Graydon: acoustic guitar / David Hungate: bass / Jeff Porcaro: drums / Ben Benay, Jeff Baxter: electric guitar / Michael Omartian: keyboards, synthesizer / Lenny Castro: percussion / Nick DeCaro: arrangements **Backing Vocals:** Denise Maynelli, Jim Gilstrap, Marti McCall, Myrna Matthews **Recorded:** Sound Lab Studios, Los Angeles, December 1979 **Technical Team:** Producer: Gary Klein / Executive Producer: Charles Koppelman / Sound Engineer: John Arrias / Assistants: Don Henderson, Sheridan Eldridge / Mixing: Mike Reese

In this love song, the narrator tells a man that she loves only him, that she needs no one but him. The song, ternary in structure, may be part of the 1980s scene, but it is clearly more concerned with content than with effects and new technologies. The rhythmic pattern is unprecedented for a Dolly Parton song, with keyboards and guitars on every beat of the verse and drums filling in the bars with some nice breaks. This number is reminiscent of Stevie Wonder's "Isn't She Lovely" (on his 1976 album *Songs in the Key of Life*), notable for the quality of its composition.

Say Goodnight

Gary Portnoy, Sue Shendan / 4:04

Vocals: Dolly Parton **Musicians:** Jay Graydon: acoustic guitar / David Hungate: bass / Jeff Porcaro: drums / Ben Benay: electric guitar / Michael Omartian: keyboards / Nick DeCaro: arrangements **Backing Vocals:** Denise Maynelli, Marti McCall, Myrna Matthews **Recorded:** Sound Lab Studios, Los Angeles, December 1979 **Technical Team:** Producer: Gary Klein / Executive Producer: Charles Koppelman / Sound Engineer: John Arrias / Assistants: Don Henderson, Sheridan Eldridge / Mixing: Mike Reese

The city is still under the gentle light of dawn as the narrator stands with a man she has let into her life. She dreams of tomorrow, which she will share with him. But now he has to go. She hopes he will always remember this perfect night of love and, if he is to say good night, let it not be goodbye.

Following on from "You're the Only One I Ever Needed," but more in the style of a dynamic ballad, this track is also ternary in construction. The arrangements are a bit sugary, in keeping with the lyrics. The piano chords on each eighth note in the choruses, in particular, express the innocence of this fervent new love.

Fool For Your Love

Michael Omartian, Leo Sayer / 3:05

Vocals: Dolly Parton **Musicians:** Jay Graydon: acoustic guitar / David Hungate: bass / Jeff Porcaro: drums / Ben Benay: electric guitar / Michael Omartian: keyboards, synthesizer, arrangements **Backing Vocals:** Denise Maynelli, Jim Gilstrap, Marti McCall, Myrna Matthews **Recorded:** Sound Lab Studios, Los Angeles, December 1979 **Technical Team:** Producer: Gary Klein / Executive Producer: Charles Koppelman / Sound Engineer: John Arrias / Assistants: Don Henderson, Sheridan Eldridge / Mixing: Mike Reese

Love seemed impossibly hard to find, but now at last the narrator is madly in love with someone, more and more each day, until she feels she's losing her mind in a whirl of ecstasy and happiness…Clapping is added to the snare drum beats in this pure pop song—something typical of this period as, for example, in "Ladies Night" by Kool and the Gang (1979). The effect—still relevant today—is to give more attack and slightly modify the timbre of the electronic snare drum.

Even A Fool Would Let Go

Tom Snow, Kerry Chater / 3:18

Vocals: Dolly Parton **Musicians:** Jay Graydon: acoustic guitar / Neil Stubenhaus: bass / Jeff Porcaro: drums / Buzzy Feiten, Jeff Baxter: electric guitar / Michael Omartian: keyboards, synthesizer, arrangements **Backing Vocals:** Anita Ball, Alexandra Brown, Denise DeCaro, Richard Dennison, Roy Galloway, William "Bill" Greene, Gene Morford, Jim Salestrom, Stephanie Spruill **Recorded:** Sound Lab Studios, Los Angeles, December 1979 **Technical Team:** Producer: Gary Klein / Executive Producer: Charles Koppelman / Sound Engineer: John Arrias / Assistants: Don Henderson, Sheridan Eldridge / Mixing: Mike Reese

Another take on love. Here, the narrator knows full well that the relationship will not work, but she and the man both feel trapped in it. Even a fool would let go, but she cannot, knowing that love is not rational.

On the model of "Starting Over Again," a long piano intro precedes the entry of the bass and the electric guitar, which imitate the same phrases, adding little slides on the neck. The rest of the ballad is true to form. The only notable element is the particularly strong keyboard entry at 2:35.

Sweet Agony

David Wolfert, Sue Sheridan / 3:40

Vocals: Dolly Parton **Musicians:** Jay Graydon: acoustic guitar / David Hungate: bass / Jeff Porcaro: drums / Ben Benay, Jeff Baxter: electric guitar / Bill Payne: keyboards / Michael Omartian: synthesizer, arrangements / Tom Saviano: saxophone / Lenny Castro : percussion **Backing Vocals:** Denise Maynelli, Jim Gilstrap, Marti McCall, Myrna Matthews **Recorded:** Sound Lab Studios, Los Angeles, December 1979 **Technical Team:** Producer: Gary Klein / Executive Producer: Charles Koppelman / Sound Engineer: John Arrias / Assistants: Don Henderson, Sheridan Eldridge / Mixing: Mike Reese **Single:** Side A: Starting Over Again / Side B: Sweet Agony **Release:** RCA Victor, February 25, 1980 (45 rpm ref.: PB-11926) **Best Chart Ranking:** 1 on the Billboard Hot Country Songs (USA); 2 on the RPM Country 75 Singles (Canada)

The singer begs her lover to free her from the grip of a sweet agony. She had dreamed of finding this kind of love, but she is now frightened by the intensity of her feelings. Is it just a sensual dream, something in her imagination, or a real loving relationship? She leaves it to the listener to decide…

This song has a funky rhythmic feel, especially on the keyboards. The verses are not cluttered with an abundance of harmonic instruments (sometimes found in the excessive use of synthetic sounds). It seems very likely that Stevie Wonder was an influence in the composition of some of the numbers on this album, including this one. For example, the piano intro brings to mind "Superstition" (*Talking Book*, 1972) or "I Wish" (*Songs in the Key of Life*, 1976). Other examples are "Light My Fire" by the Doors (*The Doors*, 1967) and the Who's "Baba O'Riley" (*Who's Next*, 1971). Guitars are added to the keyboard, and the latter plays continuously throughout the track. These provide a rhythmic base of very effective funky patterns—known as "cocottes"—on either side of the mix, leaving the keyboard, backed by the bass, in the spotlight. The use of wind instruments reminds us of another of Stevie Wonder's numbers: "Sir Duke" (also on *Songs in the Key of Life*) or "My Old School" by Steely Dan. The center of the mix is "open," which allows the percussion section to come through, particularly the timbales, a Latin instrument with a very resonant timbre used a lot in salsa. This piece owes its charm to the simplicity of the vocal treatment, without an exaggerated use of reverb. Simplicity is the best recipe for sincerity and authenticity.

1980

Dolly Parton photographed in Los Angeles in March 1980.

Dolly Parton has always worked with her family. Here she is with her brother David during a concert at the Royal Lyceum Theatre in Edinburgh, Scotland, on October 30, 1980.

SINGLE

I Knew You When

Rupert Holmes / 3:10

Vocals: Dolly Parton **Musicians:** Jay Graydon: acoustic guitar / David Hungate: bass / Jeff Porcaro: drums / Ben Benay: electric guitar / Jai Winding: keyboards / Michael Omartian: synthesizer / Nick DeCaro: arrangements **Backing Vocals:** Anita Ball, Alexandra Brown, Denise DeCaro, Richard Dennison, Roy Galloway, William "Bill" Greene, Gene Morford, Jim Salestrom, Stephanie Spruill **Recorded:** Sound Lab Studios, Los Angeles, December 1979 **Technical Team:** Producer: Gary Klein / Executive Producer: Charles Koppelman / Sound Engineer: John Arrias / Assistants: Don Henderson, Sheridan Eldridge / Mixing: Mike Reese **Single:** Side A: Old Flames Can't Hold a Candle to You / Side B: I Knew You When **Release:** RCA Victor, June 23, 1980 (45 rpm ref.: PB-12040) **Best US Chart Ranking:** 1

The singer remembers the year when she and the man she still loves danced center stage at the school prom.

This nostalgia-filled ballad is seemingly traditional in style, but some elements nevertheless stand out: a wah-wah pedal on the guitar and a keyboard that plays from time to time with a sound similar to the clarinet. But most notable are the piano harmonies, a few notes that seem to clash and sound dissonant at first hearing, but which arouse the listener's interest and are perfectly integrated, as at 0:20 and at 1:06, and again at 1:34.

Packin' It Up

Sandy Farina, Lisa Ratner / 3:30

Vocals: Dolly Parton **Musicians:** Jay Graydon: acoustic guitar / David Hungate: bass / Jeff Porcaro: drums / Jeff Baxter: electric guitar / Jai Winding: keyboards / Michael Omartian: synthesizer / Lenny Castro: percussions / Nick DeCaro: arrangements **Backing Vocals:** Anita Ball, Alexandra Brown, Denise DeCaro, Richard Dennison, Roy Galloway, William "Bill" Greene, Gene Morford, Jim Salestrom, Stephanie Spruill **Recorded:** Sound Lab Studios, Los Angeles, December 1979 **Technical Team:** Producer: Gary Klein / Executive Producer: Charles Koppelman / Sound Engineer: John Arrias / Assistants: Don Henderson, Sheridan Eldridge / Mixing: Mike Reese

The lyrics describe the excitement of waiting for the moment when the couple shut up shop and leave their everyday life in the country, putting on their fancy clothes and going to the city and the bright lights. They'll go to the movies or a show and then dance all night before returning to make love in their hotel suite.

"Packin' It Up" is unapologetically rock. The guitarists have brought out their overdrive pedals and the breaks are well-thought-out, giving the song a good boost. The drummer is enjoying himself, hitting harder than on the previous tracks. Here, the voice is treated not with a reverb but a delay, with only one repetition and a rather short time lag (200–300 ms). It's time to go out dancing!

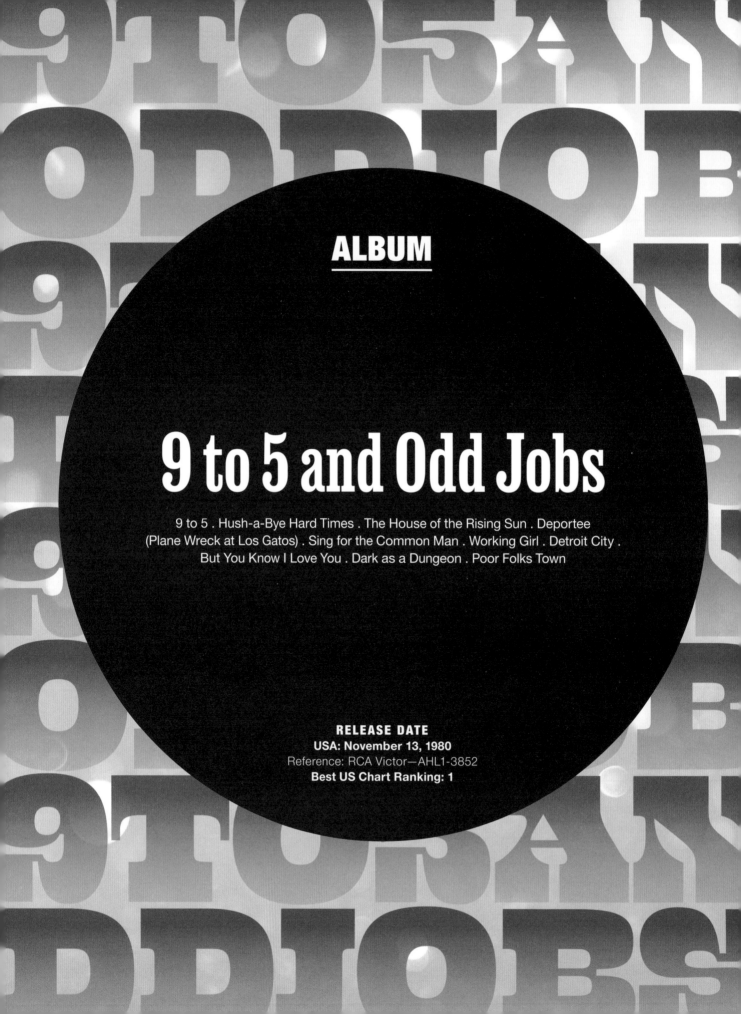

ALBUM

9 to 5 and Odd Jobs

9 to 5 . Hush-a-Bye Hard Times . The House of the Rising Sun . Deportee (Plane Wreck at Los Gatos) . Sing for the Common Man . Working Girl . Detroit City . But You Know I Love You . Dark as a Dungeon . Poor Folks Town

RELEASE DATE
USA: November 13, 1980
Reference: RCA Victor—AHL1-3852
Best US Chart Ranking: 1

In *9 to 5*, Dolly Parton plays an employee working for a sexist boss, played by Dabney Coleman.

A Hymn to Working Women

9 to 5 and Odd Jobs was released by RCA Victor on November 13, 1980, and it was Dolly Parton's twenty-third solo album. On this new album, five out of ten songs are composed by her, if we include one cowritten with Mike Post, who produced the album (apart from the track "9 to 5," produced by Gregg Perry). The disk went to number one on the Billboard Hot Country Albums chart, number eleven on the Billboard 200 in the United States, and number three in Canada.

There is nothing sexist about this work. Women's voices are heard every bit as clearly as those of men.

An (Almost) Endless Story

Let's rewind Dolly's life back to the beginning…fourth child of twelve, Dolly Rebecca Parton grew up in one of the poorest parts of America, East Tennessee. In 1964, at the age of eighteen, with her high school diploma in her pocket, she jumped on a bus to Nashville with the intention of becoming a country music star. She achieved her ambition; in 1977 she increased fan base by moving into pop music with her album *Here You Come Again*, which went gold and platinum in the United States. Dolly set both the charts and the public on fire. Despite her problems with Porter Wagoner and, even more worrying, the state of her vocal cords, she managed in just a few years to realize another of her dreams: to be an actor. Actor and political

activist Jane Fonda helped her get a foot on the ladder by casting her as Doralee Rhodes in the movie *9 to 5*. Hugely successful, the movie's script, written by Patricia Resnick, revolves around the daily working lives of three women played by the famous Jane Fonda, Lily Tomlin, and Dolly Parton. They play employees in a business run by a sexist, selfish, and hypocritical boss (Dabney Coleman). This comedy looks at working women and the harassment they suffer in the office; it culminates in the moment when Fonda, Tomlin, and Parton begin to fantasize about getting their revenge on the boss.

The movie confirmed Dolly's talents as an actor. The following decades saw her adapt and continue acting in various ways: in a TV series of more than eighty episodes that featured her youngest sister, Rachel, in the role of Doralee Rhodes; in a musical staged at the Marquis Theatre on Broadway in 2009, with twenty new songs written specially for it by Dolly; and in a documentary, *Still Working 9 to 5*. The documentary, receiving many nominations from all around the world, was directed by John Lavin, who also made the much-garlanded *Hollywood to Dollywood* (2011).

New Decade, New Chapter

Nineteen eighty opened a new decade for North America. It was marked by the eruption of Mount St. Helens, which

For Dolly Addicts

The Recording Industry Association of America awarded "9 to 5" a gold certification on March 6, 1981. The song has since gone multiplatinum.

A few months before Dolly's song and the movie came out, the Scottish singer Sheena Easton brought out a single in the UK with the title "9 to 5." The following year, when Easton's song came out in the United States, it was retitled "Morning Train (Nine to Five)" so as to avoid confusion. Despite the similarities in their titles, the two songs are very different. Dolly Part on describes the life of a working woman, while Sheena Easton tells of a woman waiting for her husband to return from work.

affected the entire state of Washington; the death of actor Steve McQueen from pleural mesothelioma; and the murder of John Lennon. The Canadian Caper (Operation Argo), undertaken jointly by Canada and the United States, succeeded in smuggling six American diplomats out of Iran but did not save President Jimmy Carter; he lost his bid for reelection and was succeeded by Ronald Reagan. America needed a break from all this. The movie *9 to 5* concerned discrimination against women in the workplace, but nevertheless it was a comedy loved by an enthusiastic public. The movie confirmed that Dolly Parton was genuinely multitalented. From this point on, whether on the big or the small screen, Dolly Parton was not to be ignored. The album was very well received, and several of its tracks entered the charts. But the title song "9 to 5" had the most impact. Just on its own, it was able to sum up all the tensions and contradictions endured by office workers, be they men or women.

As in her preceding albums, Dolly Parton turns a light on the problems of married women, of unmarried pregnant girls banished by their families, and of violence against woman. This star, the embodiment of the American dream, thinks not of herself but of those men and women who have no control over their own lives.

Album Cover

Dolly is depicted against a neutral background, balanced on high heels but wearing a helmet. She is dressed in overalls and is surrounded by every kind of work tool: typewriter, hose, paint roller, work boots…She is leaning forward as if weighed down by all these chores. On the back cover, we see her sitting in an armchair, relaxed but alluring, pink-feathered mules on her feet, nonchalantly reading a magazine. The image on the inner sleeve shows Dolly busy in the office, mischievous and sexy. The photos were taken by Ron Slenzak.

The Power Behind The Throne

JANE FONDA   LILY TOMLIN   DOLLY PARTON

9 TO 5

AN IPC FILMS PRODUCTION OF A COLIN HIGGINS PICTURE

NINE TO FIVE

DABNEY COLEMAN · ELIZABETH WILSON
and STERLING HAYDEN as The Chairman of the Board
Produced by BRUCE GILBERT   Directed by COLIN HIGGINS
Screenplay by COLIN HIGGINS and PATRICIA RESNICK   Story by PATRICIA RESNICK

PG PARENTAL GUIDANCE SUGGESTED
SOME MATERIAL MAY NOT BE SUITABLE FOR CHILDREN
Music by CHARLES FOX   COLOR BY DELUXE®

READ THE BANTAM BOOK   ©1980 TWENTIETH CENTURY-FOX

It was *9 to 5* co-producer and actress Jane Fonda who entrusted Dolly with the role of Doralee Rhodes.

Recording Sessions: "9 to 5" was released on the RCA Victor label, and it was recorded at three different studios: Sound Lab Studios in Hollywood, Audio Media in Nashville, and Western Recorders in Los Angeles. In the interest of simplicity, we list only the primary studio in the single's credits.

9 To 5

Dolly Parton / 2:45

Vocals: Dolly Parton **Musicians:** Jeff Baxter, Marty Walsh: guitar / Lenny Castro: percussion / Jerry Hey: trumpet / Kim Hutchcroft: baritone saxophone / Abraham Laboriel: bass / Larry Knechtel: piano / Joe McGuffee: pedal steel / Sonny Osborne: banjo / Ron Oates: keyboards / Bill Reichenbach: trombone / Ian Underwood: synthesizer / Tom Saviano: saxophone / Rick Shlosser: drums / Sid Sharp: first violin **Backing Vocals:** Anita Ball, Denise Maynelli, Stephanie Spruill **Recorded:** Sound Lab Studios, Hollywood: April–September 1980 **Technical Team:** Producer: Gregg Perry / Sound Engineers: Chuck Britz, Doug Parry, Larry Carlton, Marshall Morgan, Paul Dobbe / Assistant Sound Engineers: Pat McMakin, Rick Romano / Mixing: Mike Reese **Single:** Side A: 9 to 5 / Side B: Sing for the Common Man **Release:** RCA Victor, November 3, 1980 (45 rpm ref.: PB-12133) **Best US Chart Ranking:** 1 on the Billboard Hot Country Songs, 1 on the Billboard Hot 100, and 1 on the Billboard Adult Contemporary.

Genesis and Lyrics

Is this the first time the sound of a typewriter featured in a country pop number? The words penned by Dolly, the tap-tap of her acrylic false nails, and the song's liveliness all contribute to making this song timeless. Dolly sings of the emptiness people feel when their work is unrewarding and done only to earn a living. All you can do is dream of something better.

Production

Before accepting the offer to act in the movie *9 to 5*, Dolly made one condition: She must be the one to compose the signature song. Today, we can see that she was absolutely right. Her intuition was evidence once again of her acute business sense together with the quality of her songwriting, which was always in touch with the times. From the opening piano chords with staccato eighth notes, we can tell things are going to be humming in the offices of this business symbolizing corporate America. In the background, patterns from palm-muted electric guitars, stabs from the brass, and a typewriter create the ambience for this ode to the heroes and heroines of the working class. While the Sound Lab Studios' session guitarist adheres strictly to Gregg Perry's score, the magnificent rhythms of Rick Shlosser on drums and Abraham Laboriel on bass bring a feeling of freedom that is still quite new in Dolly Parton's work. One thing for sure—the eighties wouldn't have been the eighties without her.

Hush-A-Bye Hard Times

Dolly Parton / 3:48

Vocals: Dolly Parton **Musicians:** Eddie Bayers: drums / Reggie Young: guitar / Leland Sklar: bass / Joe McGuffee: pedal steel / Sonny Osborne: banjo / Ron Oates: keyboards / Ian Underwood: synthesizer / Sid Sharp: first violin **Backing Vocals:** Anita Ball, Richard Dennison, Bobby Osborne, Sonny Osborne, Joey Scarbury **Recorded:** Sound Lab Studios, Hollywood, April–September 1980 **Technical Team:** Producer: Mike Post / Associate Producer: Gregg Perry / Sound Engineers: Chuck Britz, Doug Parry, Larry Carlton, Marshall Morgan, Paul Dobbe / Assistant Sound Engineers: Pat McMakin, Rick Romano / Mixing: Mike Reese

Being a mother is another job performed by women, but one for which they receive no pay. It is a heavy, unceasing responsibility. This title takes Dolly's fans back to the time when she was writing about growing up in poverty. The song tells of the struggle faced by a mother who does not have enough money to feed her crying child. She knows the wolves are at the cabin door, yet she still hangs on to hopes for a better future.

The song begins with a cappella voices quoting the well-known song "Hard Times Come Again No More" (1854) by Stephen Foster (the "father of American music"), to mention but one of his compositions. It then takes off in a midtempo 4/4, ideal for country ballrooms. Bass drum and bass guitar stress the quarter notes, an ultrasyncopated rhythm from the piano, killer licks from the great Larry Carlton on the electric guitar (sometimes doubled in thirds) echo Dolly's voice, and powerful and spiky backing vocals, nothing more is needed to communicate the openhearted optimism of the South to three generations of country music lovers. Even when times are hard, they can still smile. Here, as also in "9 to 5," we encounter one of Dolly's trademark themes: her desire to make her listeners dance to anthems of struggle and resilience.

The sound of the typewriter, the songwriter's lyrics, and the tap-tap of her fake nails all mix with Dolly's inimitable voice to make the song "9 to 5" a timeless classic.

The House Of The Rising Sun

Arrangement by Dolly Parton and Mike Post / 4:02

Vocals: Dolly Parton **Musicians:** Eddie Bayers: drums / Reggie Young, Larry Carlton: guitar / John Goux: slide guitar / Joe McGuffee: pedal steel / Sonny Osborne: banjo / Ron Oates: keyboards / Ian Underwood: synthesizer / Sid Sharp: first violin **Backing Vocals:** Anita Ball, Richard Dennison, Stephanie Spruill **Recorded:** Sound Lab Studios, Hollywood, November 1980 **Technical Team:** Producer: Mike Post / Associate Producer: Gregg Perry / Sound Engineers: Chuck Britz, Doug Parry, Larry Carlton, Marshall Morgan, Paul Dobbe / Assistant Sound Engineers: Pat McMakin, Rick Romano / Mixing: Mike Reese **Single:** Side A: The House of the Rising Sun / Side B: Working Girl **Release:** RCA Victor, August 3, 1981 (45 rpm ref.: PB-12282) **Best US Chart Ranking:** 14

The narrator of this song, a prostitute, warns mothers all over the world to protect their daughters from sin and shame. She describes herself as having been a "good girl" before she sold her body for money in the "house of the Rising Sun" in New Orleans.

This traditional song, made famous worldwide in 1964 by the English group the Animals, is given an unexpected disco backing as recorded in Sound Lab Studios. But perhaps that was inevitable in the early 1980s. The opening chords of the synthesizers set the tone. It is not so much a rejection of tradition as an updating. Peroxide mullets, epaulets, and rolled-up sleeves: You're either modern or you're not. John Goux makes much of the slide guitar, the only surviving element of the Nashville sound, which Dolly was keen to preserve. A way of satisfying both her more conservative critics and her more recent fans while at the same time remaining true to her roots. Dolly is well aware of the need to keep anchored.

Singer-songwriter and musician Woody Guthrie has produced hundreds of political and traditional songs, as well as songs for children.

Deportee
(Plane Wreck At Los Gatos)

Woody Guthrie, Martin Hoffmann / 4:41

Vocals: Dolly Parton **Musicians:** Eddie Bayers: drums / Reggie Young: guitar / Leland Sklar: bass / Joe McGuffee: pedal steel / Sonny Osborne: banjo / Ron Oates: keyboards / Ian Underwood: synthesizer / Sid Sharp: first violin **Backing Vocals:** Anita Ball, Richard Dennison, Joey Scarbury **Recorded:** Sound Lab Studios, Hollywood, April–September 1980 **Technical Team:** Producer: Mike Post / Associate Producer: Gregg Perry / Sound Engineers: Chuck Britz, Doug Parry, Larry Carlton, Marshall Morgan, Paul Dobbe / Assistant Sound Engineers: Pat McMakin, Rick Romano / Mixing: Mike Reese

This ballad describes the condition of migrant workers, Mexican men and women; once their seasonal work is finished, they are loaded into airplanes and sent home. They become nameless; they are simply deportees.

This protest song was written by Woody Guthrie and Martin Hoffman after the plane crash at the Los Gatos Canyon in 1948. Four Americans and twenty-eight deported Mexican agricultural workers died. Versions of this song have been recorded by numerous artists, including Joan Baez (1971) (and with Bob Dylan in 1976), Judy Collins (1972), and Bruce Springsteen (2000). This track is the second cover song on this album.

Dolly knows where to find the standard versions on which to base her songs. Woody Guthrie was the model and unchallenged master for Bob Dylan. Dolly's ability to manage her own artistic direction was already clear but, from the date of the album *Here You Come Again* (1977), it was officially confirmed: She is the boss. Transforming this protest song into a ballad was a wise choice. Up to 1:49, Dolly's voice is accompanied only by exquisitely intermingled arpeggios on piano and guitar. At this point, when the strings enter, the song takes on a bigger, more dramatic sound that tugs at our heartstrings. Once again, Dolly brilliantly gives us a protest song with a tragic ending, this one to the rhythm of a gentle waltz.

The star is surprised while on the set of *9 to 5* in Beverly Hills, California, on March 18, 1980.

Sing For The Common Man

Freida Parton, Mark Andersen / 3:47

Vocals: Dolly Parton **Musicians:** Eddie Bayers: drums / Reggie Young: guitar / Leland Sklar: bass / Joe McGuffee: pedal steel / Sonny Osborne: banjo / Ron Oates: keyboards / Ian Underwood: synthesizer / Rick Shlosser: drums / Sid Sharp: first violin **Backing Vocals:** Anita Ball, Richard Dennison, Joey Scarbury **Recorded:** Sound Lab Studios, Hollywood, April–September 1980 **Technical Team:** Producer: Mike Post / Associate Producer: Gregg Perry / Sound Engineers: Chuck Britz, Doug Parry, Larry Carlton, Marshall Morgan, Paul Dobbe / Assistant Sound Engineers: Pat McMakin, Rick Romano / Mixing: Mike Reese
Single: Side A: 9 to 5 / Side B: Sing for the Common Man **Release:** RCA Victor, November 3, 1980 (45 rpm ref.: PB-12133)
Best US Chart Ranking: 1 on the Billboard Hot Country Songs, 1 on the Billboard Hot 100, and 1 on the Billboard Adult Contemporary.

Cowritten by Mark Andersen and Freida Parton, one of Dolly Parton's sisters, this number pays homage to those men who toiled hard all their lives. In its subject, "Sing for the Common Man" is not unlike "Daddy's Working Boots," a track on Dolly's album *My Tennessee Mountain Home*.

This midtempo 4/4 number oscillates between a ballad style with a split tempo on the verses and the more pop-sounding choruses. This ambiguity fits perfectly with the chiaroscuro picture painted by the composers to express both the strength of these honest workers and their almost unbearable living conditions. Once again, Dolly speaks up for the working-class heroes. The epic intro, with its four bass notes flying over the staccato eighth notes in the synthesizer chords, is reminiscent of "Baba O'Riley," also known as "Teenage Wasteland" (1971), by the English band the Who. Their song was an ode to working-class teenagers, while "Sing for the Common Man" is dedicated to American workers. Dolly has always been much more rock 'n' roll than we realize.

Working Girl

Dolly Parton / 3:17

Vocals: Dolly Parton **Musicians:** Eddie Bayers: drums / Larry Carlton: guitar / Joe McGuffee: pedal steel / Sonny Osborne: banjo / Ron Oates: keyboards / Ian Underwood: synthesizer / Sid Sharp: first violin **Backing Vocals:** Anita Ball, Richard Dennison, Stephanie Spruill **Technical Team:** Producer: Mike Post / Associate Producer: Gregg Perry / Sound Engineers: Chuck Britz, Doug Parry, Larry Carlton, Marshall Morgan, Paul Dobbe / Assistant Sound Engineers: Pat McMakin, Rick Romano / Mixing: Mike Reese **Recorded:** Sound Lab Studios, Hollywood, November 1980 **Single:** Side A: The House of the Rising Sun / Side B: Working Girl **Release:** RCA Victor, August 3, 1981 (45 rpm ref.: PB-12282) **Best US Chart Ranking:** 14

This song celebrates all working women, wherever they are on the professional and salaried ladder, mothers and wives, or single and free. They all have style and courage and are proud that they work.

The intro of this 4/4 midtempo track is played on a CP80 piano and synthesizers. Larry Carlton gives us some stabbing licks on the electric guitar, very different from the standard country-rock sound, while Ian Underwood creates a liquid bass line on a synthesizer, producing a remarkably sophisticated sound very much ahead of its time. The absence of a hi-hat gives the impression that the song is standing still; Eddie Bayers was apparently instructed to hit the snare drum as hard as possible on the third beat and the bass drum on the first and second beats. The effect is to express the strength of the single women who bring up their children on their own, true heroines of modern times, confident and sexy.

Detroit City

Danny Dill, Mel Tillis / 3:35

Vocals: Dolly Parton **Musicians:** Eddie Bayers: drums / Reggie Young: guitar / Leland Sklar: bass / Joe McGuffee: pedal steel / Sonny Osborne: banjo / Ron Oates: keyboards / Ian Underwood: synthesizer / Rick Shlosser: drums / Sid Sharp: first violin **Backing Vocals:** Anita Ball, Richard Dennison, Joey Scarbury **Recorded:** Sound Lab Studios, Hollywood, April–September 1980 **Technical Team:** Producer: Mike Post / Associate Producer: Gregg Perry / Sound Engineers: Chuck Britz, Doug Parry, Larry Carlton, Marshall Morgan, Paul Dobbe / Assistant Sound Engineers: Pat McMakin, Rick Romano / Mixing: Mike Reese

This cover of "Detroit City" suits Dolly Parton's voice perfectly. First recorded in 1962 by Billy Grammer under the title "Detroit City (I Wanna Go Home)," the song was made famous by Bobby Bare (1963) and then by Tom Jones (1967). As in "Alabama Sundown" on Dolly's *Bubbling Over* album, the narrator tells how he longs to go home, to the cotton fields, to his family, where he would feel happier than in Detroit. There, he works hard all day and spends the evening drinking in bars.

Known as the "Motor City," Detroit was thriving in 1980. From 0:48 to 0:56 on this track, the very metallic sound of the electric guitar played with the pick very close to the bridge (where the tension of the string is greatest) evokes the sound of the stamping of sheet metal in the car factories. Apart from that, this is a standard ballad in 4/4. There are many elements of the Nashville sound: pedal steel, piano, strummed acoustic guitar, drums played cross stick, bass provided by the bass drum, and country licks on the electric guitar. The string arrangement brings a touch of modernity to a piece originally made for the road.

1980

"But You Know I Love You" was
sung by Kenny Rogers (foreground)
and the First Edition in 1968.

But You Know I Love You

Mike Settle / 3:17

Vocals: Dolly Parton **Musicians:** Eddie Bayers: drums / Joe McGuffee: pedal steel / Sonny Osborne: banjo / Ron Oates: keyboards / Mike Post: synthesized flute / Ian Underwood: synthesizer / Tom Saviano: saxophone / Rick Shlosser: drums / Sid Sharp: first violin **Backing Vocals:** Anita Ball, Richard Dennison, Stephanie Spruill **Recorded:** Sound Lab Studios, Hollywood, April–September 1980 **Technical Team:** Producer: Mike Post / Associate Producer: Gregg Perry / Sound Engineers: Chuck Britz, Doug Parry, Larry Carlton, Marshall Morgan, Paul Dobbe / Assistant Sound Engineers: Pat McMakin, Rick Romano / Mixing: Mike Reese **Single:** Side A: But You Know I Love You / Side B: Poor Folks Town **Release:** RCA Victor, March 16, 1981 (45 rpm ref.: PB-12200) **Best US Chart Ranking:** 1

Dolly makes this title, previously recorded by Kenny Rogers in 1968, all her own—and it's a hit. The subject deals again with one of the problems caused by the need to find work: the distance that separates a couple in love. The narrator is constantly on the road, earning money to pay the rent. But the price is distance and loneliness. Life like this seems to have no sense if it means seeing loved ones so rarely.

In the intro, as well as in the arpeggios from the acoustic guitar, we hear a flute, probably created by a synthesizer either imitating or sampling the sound. It expresses perfectly the literal romanticism of the song. Dolly sings of the need and the hope that the flame of love will continue to burn bright, come what may, despite the distance and time that keep the lovers apart. After the intro the song launches into a midtempo ballad with a very cinematic arrangement. The breadth brought in by the long reverb on the drums, the strings, and especially the voice gives a feeling of the wide-open spaces, of the traveler crossing the vast American plains to find their loved one. Another track to be listened to at full volume in a Ford Mustang.

Dark As A Dungeon

Merle Travis / 3:25

Vocals: Dolly Parton **Musicians:** Eddie Bayers: drums / Reggie Young: guitar / Leland Sklar: bass / Joe McGuffee: pedal steel / Sonny Osborne: banjo / Ron Oates: keyboards / Ian Underwood: synthesizer / Rick Shlosser: drums / Sid Sharp: first violin **Backing Vocals:** Anita Ball, Richard Dennison, Joey Scarbury **Recorded:** Sound Lab Studios, Hollywood, April–September 1980 **Technical Team:** Producer: Mike Post / Associate Producer: Gregg Perry / Sound Engineers: Chuck Britz, Doug Parry, Larry Carlton, Marshall Morgan, Paul Dobbe / Assistant Sound Engineers: Pat McMakin, Rick Romano / Mixing: Mike Reese

This song's lyrics speak of the hard life of a miner and the darkness of the mine. The song has become a rallying anthem for miners.

Up to the point where the synthesizer chords enter at 0:41, the acoustic guitar, drowned in the chorus, is the soloist here. At 1:15, the strings enter and the texture fills out; the sound becomes denser and resonates through the whole. Next, at 1:30, the bass section comes into play: double bass and cello expand the sound spectrum. At 1:49 the high strings take advantage of a lull to pierce through the texture, joining the pedal steel. The arrangement develops as the song progress, but always with restraint, just like Dolly Parton's beautifully expressive voice—sometimes fragile, sometimes powerful, giving life to this song by guitarist and songwriter Merle Travis. A dignified and realistic evocation of the mine and the miner.

1980

Poor Folks Town

Dolly Parton / 2:57

Vocals: Dolly Parton **Musicians:** Eddie Bayers: drums / Reggie Young: guitar / Gregg Perry: organ / Leland Sklar: bass / Joe McGuffee: pedal steel / Sonny Osborne: banjo / Ron Oates: keyboards / Ian Underwood: synthesizer / Rick Shlosser: drums / Sid Sharp: first violin
Backing Vocals: Anita Ball, Richard Dennison, Joey Scarbury
Recorded: Sound Lab Studios, Hollywood, April–September 1980
Technical Team: Producer: Mike Post / Sound Engineers: Chuck Britz, Doug Parry, Larry Carlton, Marshall Morgan, Paul Dobbe / Assistant Sound Engineers: Pat McMakin, Rick Romano / Mixing: Mike Reese **Single:** Side A: But You Know I Love You / Side B: Poor Folks Town **Release:** RCA Victor, March 16, 1981 (45 rpm ref.: PB-12200)
Best US Chart Ranking: 1

The singer invites us to come and discover the riches of a poor town where the only fortune the people possess is love. While others may have big cars, fashionable clothes, and everything that money can buy, these people have love to spare. In the brash intro of this midtempo 4/4, the electric guitar and synthesizer leads mix together, sometimes merging into one. The rhythm section supporting the tempo consists of a minimalist bass working with the bass drum, the snare drum—present only on the choruses to give additional drive—a syncopated piano, and electric guitar playing the afterbeat. All this works perfectly on the last track of this album that is dedicated to work and its heroes. Dolly and her musicians leave the listener with a joyful hoedown spiced with a sauce of Californian "after work." We are reminded that happiness, friendship, and love count for more than all the gold in the world.

Dolly Parton playing the banjo onstage in 1981—note the length of her fingernails.

ALBUM

Heartbreak Express

Heartbreak Express . Single Women . My Blue Ridge Mountain Boy . As Much as Always .
Do I Ever Cross Your Mind . Release Me . Barbara on Your Mind . Act Like a Fool .
Prime of Our Love . Hollywood Potters

RELEASE DATE
United States: March 29, 1982
USA reference: RCA Victor—AHL1-4289
Best US Chart Ranking: 5

In *The Best Little Whorehouse in Texas*, Dolly appeared alongside her friend Burt Reynolds.

Inspired by Tai Uhlmann's 2006 documentary *For the Love of Dolly*, Rhymes with Opera staged an opera called *Heartbreak Express* at the Bank Street Theater in New York's West Village in November 2015. The opera told the story of four Dolly Parton superfans' encounter with their idol, reflecting her impact on their lives. Between the two acts, in an intermezzo, "Jolene" and "Heartbreak Express" were performed.

A Broken Heart

Heartbreak Express is Dolly Parton's twenty-fourth solo album, released by RCA Victor on March 29, 1982. It was coproduced by Dolly and Gregg Perry. More than a year had passed since the release of *9 to 5*. The break was a first for the star, who, since her arrival in Nashville, usually offered her public at least one album, if not two or three, every year! The new album reached 106 on the Billboard 200.

The Descent into Hell

In the United States, 1982 also saw the releases of Michael Jackson's *Thriller* and Ridley Scott's film *Blade Runner*, starring Harrison Ford, but also the first use of the AIDS acronym, following the appearance of the disease, and the first transplant of a permanent artificial heart. Dolly Parton's heart failed and broke. As Dolly recounts in her autobiography, she was accused of having stolen the song "9 to 5": Neil and Jan Goldberg, the authors of the song "Money World," accused her of plagiarism, but their claim was unsuccessful…and then they asked her to write for them! Dolly, whose integrity had been questioned during this affair, thought their request to be the height of audacity. Gregg Perry, leader of Dolly's band and producer of the song "9 to 5," distanced himself from Dolly, frustrated and disillusioned at not having been entrusted with producing the new album. It had been given to Mike Post, a friend of

the star and a producer that the label and the studios had asked for.

Dolly was living in Los Angeles, where she suffered from loneliness. Her husband, Carl, had stayed at home. Her good friend Judy Ogle was also in a bad way—she was trying to save her marriage—and the two women hardly saw each other anymore. A vicious circle began: Dolly was sad, so she ate and put on weight; she was on edge, wracked by stress. Her vocal cords were still damaged, and she was put on cortisone. She was once a rock, but her body was failing her, her legendary energy was disappearing, and her thoughts were darkening. Professionally, while the filming of *9 to 5* was great from all points of view, the filming of *The Best Little Whorehouse in Texas* did not look so good. The departure of Gregg Perry—who had left the business to finish medical school—was the last straw for Dolly. Dejected, she did what she does best: She wrote a song, "What a Heartache." The songwriter reproached herself a thousand times: for not being good enough, for not being generous enough, for not being present enough, for not being this or that… Devoured by guilt, on the edge of nervous depression, she started to drink. Between doubts and questioning, Dolly Parton assessed how much she depended on others. The little girl who dreamed of becoming a huge star looked in the mirror and saw a huge, exhausted, desperate

A promotional image taken during filming of *The Best Little Whorehouse* in Texas, 1982. After *9 to 5*, this was Dolly's second film.

After a descent into hell, Dolly wrote eight of the ten songs that appeared on *Heartbreak Express*, putting all of her talent into a rich expression of emotion.

thirty-four-year-old woman. For the first time in her life, Dolly contemplated suicide.

Rising from the Ashes

Naturally, the tabloids commented on this bad patch, some even predicting that Dolly Parton was finished. She had reached the bottom of the abyss. She lived a nightmare, waking up every day feeling like the living dead—she stopped writing, singing, and playing the guitar for months. Then she decided to return to life—to *her* life. The album *Heartbreak Express* is one of the outcomes of this: Dolly wrote eight of the ten songs and put all of her talent into expressing a rich palette of emotions, which captivated both her audience and the critics. The other outcome was that she came back stronger than ever, aware of her near-death experience.

Sandy Gallin, the friend and manager who made her a superstar, took charge. He sent her to all the mind and body specialists to get her back on track and booked her a holiday in Australia. The first few hours of Dolly's break were filled with thousands of fans waiting for her at the Sydney airport. The press, intrigued by the man she was with, invented a new romance for her, unaware that Sandy Gallin was gay. Then the manager and the star were caught in a storm, Cyclone Abigail, which threatened to break up the boat they had hired to escape the journalists. Sandy saved Dolly from drowning, which brought them even a little closer together. If they survived this, they would survive anything. It was time for Dolly to rebuild.

Album Cover

Wrapped in a fur-collared coat, Dolly looks pensively through the window of the train in which she is sitting, the *Heartbreak Express*, symbolized by a cracked red heart; the fans have no doubt that their star's heart is broken. The back cover photo shows the same carriage but empty; a black-and-white shot on the inner sleeve shows the singer on the platform, sadly alone, surrounded only by her luggage. The photos are by Herb Ritts.

For Dolly Addicts

The compilation *The Winning Hand*, released on November 1, 1982, on Monument Records and produced by Fred Foster (one of Dolly's first producers), features Dolly Parton, Willie Nelson, Brenda Lee, and Kris Kristofferson. The sleeve notes are by Johnny Cash, who in March 1985 hosted the TV show inspired by the album.

At the premier of their film, which was held at the Paramount Theatre in Austin, Texas, on July 11, 1982, Dolly Parton nearly eclipsed Burt Reynolds (standing and facing away from the camera).

The year 1982 was one of rebuilding for Dolly Parton.

Heartbreak Express
Dolly Parton / 3:13

Vocals: Dolly Parton **Musicians:** Jeff Baxter, Albert Lee, Fred Tackett, Mike Severs, Steve Cropper: guitar / Eddy Anderson: drums / Lenny Castro: congas / Abe Laboriel, Leland Sklar, Nathan East: bass / Joe McGuffee: pedal steel / Buddy Spicher: fiddle / Gregg Perry: dulcimer / Red Young, Ron Oates: keyboards / Chuck Findley, Gary Grant, Gary Herbig, George Bohanon, Jim Horn, Slide Hyde, Tom Saviano, Tom Scott: brass **Backing Vocals:** Anita Ball, Denise Maynelli DeCaro, Gene Morford, Jim Salestrom, Richard Dennison, Roy Galloway, Willie Greene Jr., Stephanie Spruill **Recorded:** RCA Victor, Nashville, December 1981–January 1982 **Technical Team:** Producers: Dolly Parton, Gregg Perry / Sound Engineers: Chuck Britz, Doug Parry, Larry Carlton, Marshall Morgan, Paul Dobbe / Assistant Sound Engineers: Pat McMakin, Rick Romano / Mixing: Mike Reese **Single:** Side A: Heartbreak Express / Side B: Act Like a Fool **Release:** RCA Victor, May 3, 1982 (45 rpm ref.: PB-13234) **Best Chart Ranking:** 7 on the Billboard Hot Country Songs (USA); 1 on the RPM Country 50 Singles (Canada)

Genesis and Lyrics

Bringing a failed relationship to a close, the narrator boards the *Heartbreak Express*, hoping to forget her unfaithful man. Dolly Parton's life experiences are obviously the ferment of many of her songs; this sentence therefore resonates as a synthesis of her uncertainties and regrets, and of the nervous and physical exhaustion in which she lived through 1981: "It hurts to know it ain't enough when you give your best."

Production

Launched with a sax intro, this track has no syncopation but a very straight country rhythm, on four-beat measures, that approaches the boogie-woogie style. It is a dance track: The lowest voice of the backing vocals supports the song, and the bass offers a nice complement to the drums. With the percussion slightly set back, the drums sound lower, less bright, with less cymbal and a reduced reverb of the vocals. The overall sound differs from that of the Los Angeles studio period. The wind instruments are very present, contrasting with the trumpet and trombone—spatialized on the left and right—while the alto, tenor, and baritone saxes are located in the center. The tessitura of the piano seems to be that of an upright piano. Note: The vast majority of the pieces are played on wooden pianos, the best material in terms of sound absorption and reflection.

The breaks are played by the whole orchestra, including the voices. The pedal steel does not intervene much, unusual for Dolly Parton. The electric guitar is rather restrained, its chords being well integrated into the rhythm section, with a clear sound. The saxophonist has to blow hard, because one can hear the vibrations of the reed (when blowing more softly, the sound is closer to that of the clarinet). Finally, the harmonica intervention is modestly limited to the imitation of the train throughout the piece.

Chief sound engineer Pat McMakin, shown at right in this photograph taken at music publisher Tree International, has worked on several Dolly Parton albums.

SINGLE

Single Women

Michael O'Donoghue / 3:44

Vocals: Dolly Parton **Musicians:** Jeff Baxter, Albert Lee, Fred Tackett, Mike Severs, Steve Cropper: guitar / Eddy Anderson: drums / Lenny Castro: congas / Abe Laboriel, Leland Sklar, Nathan East: bass / Joe McGuffee: pedal steel / Buddy Spicher: fiddle / Gregg Perry: dulcimer / Red Young, Ron Oates: keyboards / Chuck Findley, Gary Grant, Gary Herbig, George Bohanon, Jim Horn, Slide Hyde, Tom Saviano, Tom Scott: brass **Recorded:** RCA Victor, Nashville, December 1981–January 1982 **Technical Team:** Producers: Dolly Parton, Gregg Perry / Sound Engineers: Chuck Britz, Doug Parry, Larry Carlton, Marshall Morgan, Paul Dobbe / Assistant Sound Engineers: Pat McMakin, Rick Romano / Mixing: Mike Reese **Single:** Side A: Single Women / Side B: Barbara on Your Mind **Release:** RCA Victor, February 1, 1982 (45 rpm ref.: PB-13057) **Best Chart Ranking:** 8 on the Billboard Hot Country Songs (USA); 1 on the RPM Country 50 Singles (Canada)

"Single Women" is a song about women who go to bars to find love, even for one night. Their discussions are as long as the night spent flirting, dancing, and drinking, looking for the one who opens the door to love. Interestingly, the song was originally written for *Saturday Night Live* (Michael O'Donoghue was a writer on the show), and it was sung on the show by cast member Christine Ebersole. Parton used an abbreviated version of the song on her album.

In this three-quarter time piece with a caustic tone and a touch of black humor, we immediately dive into the atmosphere of a night spot (reminiscent of "Applejack" on *New Harvest...First Gathering*) with the intro bars of the piano and the alto sax. A piano-vocal duet is the first verse. The entry of the pedal steel announces the arrival of the bass, the drums in rim shot, and the folk guitar. The drummer resumes a pop-playing style by hitting the skin of the snare drum while the violins reappear at the same time as the sax. It then alternates between these two types of playing. The reverb on the voice and the snare drum is strong and stands out all the more as the instrumentation is light. To this restraint is added the absence of backing vocals (as in other tracks of the album), a rarity for Dolly until then.

Dolly Parton,
photographed in 1983.

My Blue Ridge Mountain Boy

Dolly Parton / 3:49

Vocals: Dolly Parton **Musicians:** Jeff Baxter, Albert Lee, Fred Tackett, Mike Severs, Steve Cropper: guitar / Eddy Anderson: drums / Lenny Castro: congas / Abe Laboriel, Leland Sklar, Nathan East: bass / Joe McGuffee: pedal steel / Buddy Spicher: fiddle / Gregg Perry: dulcimer / Red Young, Ron Oates: keyboards / Chuck Findley, Gary Grant, Gary Herbig, George Bohanon, Jim Horn, Slide Hyde, Tom Saviano, Tom Scott: brass **Backing Vocals:** Anita Ball, Denise Maynelli DeCaro, Gene Morford, Jim Salestrom, Richard Dennison, Roy Galloway, Willie Greene Jr., Stephanie Spruill **Recorded:** RCA Victor, Nashville, December 1981–January 1982 **Technical Team:** Producers: Dolly Parton, Gregg Perry / Sound Engineers: Chuck Britz, Doug Parry, Larry Carlton, Marshall Morgan, Paul Dobbe / Assistant Sound Engineers: Pat McMakin, Rick Romano / Mixing: Mike Reese

This lament of a woman who left for the city to earn a living at any cost—including her honor—and who misses her countryside and her lost love, had already been recorded in 1969 for the album of the same name. This time, it is a pop ballad in which Dolly Parton shows off her voice, despite the state of her vocal cords. While the drums remain in the background, leaving room for the harmonic instruments, this traditional song features the harmonica, the fiddle, and the pedal steel, back in full strength.

As Much As Always

Dolly Parton / 3:01

Vocals: Dolly Parton **Musicians:** Jeff Baxter, Albert Lee, Fred Tackett, Mike Severs, Steve Cropper: guitar / Eddy Anderson: drums / Lenny Castro: congas / Abe Laboriel, Leland Sklar, Nathan East: bass / Joe McGuffee: pedal steel / Buddy Spicher: fiddle / Gregg Perry: dulcimer / Red Young, Ron Oates: keyboards / Chuck Findley, Gary Grant, Gary Herbig, George Bohanon, Jim Horn, Slide Hyde, Tom Saviano, Tom Scott: brass **Backing Vocals:** Anita Ball, Denise Maynelli DeCaro, Gene Morford, Jim Salestrom, Richard Dennison, Roy Galloway, Willie Greene Jr., Stephanie Spruill **Recorded:** RCA Victor, Nashville, December 1981–January 1982 **Technical Team:** Producers: Dolly Parton, Gregg Perry / Sound Engineers: Chuck Britz, Doug Parry, Larry Carlton, Marshall Morgan, Paul Dobbe / Assistant Sound Engineers: Pat McMakin, Rick Romano / Mixing: Mike Reese

The narrator is still thinking about the one who has gone, the one who remains in her mind and in her heart, the one she misses and cannot replace. For she still loves him and needs him. Beautifully expressed by Dolly, this pain is perceptible in her voice, which is well to the fore, and in the beautiful presence of the keyboard. The discretion of the bass drum blends perfectly with the percussion, which regains some impact even though the drummer uses only the foot pedals (bass drum and hi-hat) and the cymbals, forsaking the other skins.

Dolly is surrounded by guitar legends: Les Paul (left), who gave his name to the famous Gibson guitar, Chet Atkins (right), and Freddy Fender (far right).

Do I Ever Cross Your Mind

Dolly Parton / 4:01

Vocals: Dolly Parton **Musicians:** Jeff Baxter, Albert Lee, Fred Tackett, Mike Severs, Steve Cropper: guitar / Eddy Anderson: drums / Lenny Castro: congas / Abe Laboriel, Leland Sklar, Nathan East: bass / Joe McGuffee: pedal steel / Buddy Spicher: fiddle / Gregg Perry: dulcimer / Red Young, Ron Oates: keyboards / Chuck Findley, Gary Grant, Gary Herbig, George Bohanon, Jim Horn, Slide Hyde, Tom Saviano, Tom Scott: brass **Backing Vocals:** Gene Morford, Jim Salestrom, Richard Dennison, Roy Galloway, Willie Greene Jr. **Recorded:** RCA Victor, Nashville, December 1981–January 1982 **Technical Team:** Producers: Dolly Parton, Gregg Perry / Sound Engineers: Chuck Britz, Doug Parry, Larry Carlton, Marshall Morgan, Paul Dobbe / Assistant Sound Engineers: Pat McMakin, Rick Romano / Mixing: Mike Reese **Single:** Side A: I Will Always Love You / Side B: Do I Ever Cross Your Mind **Release:** RCA Victor, July 12, 1982 (45 rpm ref.: PB-13260) **Best US Chart Ranking:** 1

Genesis and Lyrics

This love song written by Dolly Parton is the cover of a duet she sang with the king of country music, Chet Atkins, for his album *The Best of Chet Atkins & Friends*, released in 1976. Dolly also performed it in a trio with Linda Ronstadt and Emmylou Harris in 1994. The narrator thinks of a former love that was strong but still exists, albeit only through her memories. She wonders if, like him, the one he loved is still thinking about him. This song would be covered many times subsequently by professional musicians such as Australian Tommy Emmanuel but also by amateurs, as evidenced by the many videos online.

Production

On this hit song, considered by many to be one of the most beautiful country songs ever written, Chet Atkins's picking guitar playing is recognizable among all the others. The keyboard assumes a prominent place, especially on the changes in the chord grid. On the rhythmic parts, the playing contributes to the groove, perhaps reflecting Stevie Wonder's influence. Here too, the drumming is very simple: The bass drum is on the beat, the snare drum is in rim shot, and the hi-hat is played on the foot pedal against the beat. The backing vocals—exclusively male— are brought well forward, and the bass voice of the singers is distinctive, especially on the choruses and part of the verses. For once, the folk guitar performs a solo, while the pedal steel remains discreet. The tessitura of Dolly Parton, rather low (the singer is very close to the microphone), gives to the listener the impression of someone whispering in their ear. Logically so, for these rather intimate lyrics.

Release Me

Eddie Miller, Dub Williams, Robert Yount / 3:27

Vocals: Dolly Parton **Musicians:** Jeff Baxter, Albert Lee, Fred Tackett, Mike Severs, Steve Cropper: guitar / Eddy Anderson: drums / Lenny Castro: congas / Abe Laboriel, Leland Sklar, Nathan East: bass / Joe McGuffee: pedal steel / Buddy Spicher: fiddle / Gregg Perry: dulcimer / Red Young, Ron Oates: keyboards / Chuck Findley, Gary Grant, Gary Herbig, George Bohanon, Jim Horn, Slide Hyde, Tom Saviano, Tom Scott: brass **Backing Vocals:** Anita Ball, Denise Maynelli DeCaro, Gene Morford, Jim Salestrom, Richard Dennison, Roy Galloway, Willie Greene Jr., Stephanie Spruill **Recorded:** RCA Victor, Nashville, December 1981–January 1982 **Technical Team:** Producers: Dolly Parton, Gregg Perry / Sound Engineers: Chuck Britz, Doug Parry, Larry Carlton, Marshall Morgan, Paul Dobbe / Assistant Sound Engineers: Pat McMakin, Rick Romano / Mixing: Mike Reese

Another version of love that no longer works, a theme already addressed by the songwriter: The narrator asks to be set free so that she can love again. But this time, Dolly adds the notion of sin—living with someone for whom one no longer feels anything.

The tempo of this song, in the style of "Heartbreak Express," is not so fast. The drums are still in the background compared to the rest of the band. It should be noted that the bass and an electric guitar play the same line throughout the song; this line consists of going up and down a few key notes of the scale of the chord they are in. The instrumental intro is one of the longest in Dolly's repertoire—thirty seconds. Finally, a last detail, rare enough to warrant emphasis: The electric guitar and then the harmonica play two consecutive solos, for a smooth modulation.

Barbara On Your Mind

Dolly Parton / 3:27

Vocals: Dolly Parton **Musicians:** Jeff Baxter, Albert Lee, Fred Tackett, Mike Severs, Steve Cropper: guitar / Eddy Anderson: drums / Lenny Castro: congas / Abe Laboriel, Leland Sklar, Nathan East: bass / Joe McGuffee: pedal steel / Buddy Spicher: fiddle / Gregg Perry: dulcimer / Red Young, Ron Oates: keyboards / Chuck Findley, Gary Grant, Gary Herbig, George Bohanon, Jim Horn, Slide Hyde, Tom Saviano, Tom Scott: brass **Recorded:** RCA Victor, Nashville, December 1981–January 1982

Technical Team: Producers: Dolly Parton, Gregg Perry / Sound Engineers: Chuck Britz, Doug Parry, Larry Carlton, Marshall Morgan, Paul Dobbe / Assistant Sound Engineers: Pat McMakin, Rick Romano / Mixing: Mike Reese **Single:** Side A: Single Women / Side B: Barbara on Your Mind **Release:** RCA Victor, February 1, 1982 (45 rpm ref.: PB-13057) **Best Chart Ranking:** 8 on the Billboard Hot Country Songs (USA); 1 on the RPM Country 50 Singles (Canada)

Genesis and Lyrics

Betrayal in love, or when the one you love looks at you, embraces you, and caresses you while thinking of another. The narrator finds small traces of Barbara on her man—a hair, the mark of a kiss on his skin—and in his sleep, he utters the name of his mistress instead of hers. We think back to the story of "Jolene."

Production

For this song about a disappointed love, violin, piano, keyboard, and big reverb are back. However, some melodic passages that are jazzy, with plenty of seventh chords, come as a surprise to the listener. After an intro played by the violin, the first verse consists of a piano-vocal duet, with the keyboard coming in for the jazzy melodies. The chorus creates a very interesting point of articulation, due to a very high note from the violin that attracts attention, masking the arrival of the folk guitar. The instruments are gradually inserted in the second verse: the bass, then the violin, and finally the drums and the pedal steel in the second chorus. We also notice a big difference in level between the beginning and the end of the song. One may think that this is natural, as many instruments have entered the game, but it is the strength of the mix and the arrangements. Finally: the absence of backing vocals and the "real" musical ending—not a fade-out, as in "Single Women." The "ease" of writing an off-tempo ending to a slow song with dragging chords was evoked earlier.

Act Like A Fool

Dolly Parton / 3:24

Vocals: Dolly Parton **Musicians:** Jeff Baxter, Albert Lee, Fred Tackett, Mike Severs, Steve Cropper: guitar / Eddy Anderson: drums / Lenny Castro: congas / Abe Laboriel, Leland Sklar, Nathan East: bass / Joe McGuffee: pedal steel / Buddy Spicher: fiddle / Gregg Perry: dulcimer / Red Young, Ron Oates: keyboards / Chuck Findley, Gary Grant, Gary Herbig, George Bohanon, Jim Horn, Slide Hyde, Tom Saviano,

Tom Scott: brass **Backing Vocals:** Anita Ball, Denise Maynelli DeCaro, Stephanie Spruill **Recorded:** RCA Victor, Nashville, December 1981—January 1982 **Technical Team:** Producers: Dolly Parton, Gregg Perry / Sound Engineers: Chuck Britz, Doug Parry, Larry Carlton, Marshall Morgan, Paul Dobbe / Assistant Sound Engineers: Pat McMakin, Rick Romano / Mixing: Mike Reese **Single:** Side A: Heartbreak Express / Side B: Act Like a Fool **Release:** RCA Victor, May 3, 1982 (45 rpm ref.: PB-13234) **Best Chart Ranking:** 7 on the Billboard Hot Country Songs (USA); 1 on the RPM Country 50 Singles (Canada)

This song, performed with passion by Dolly Parton, exposes the evils of a destructive, controlling relationship. Helplessly, the narrator wonders why she lets her lover do this and why he is so cruel and malicious toward her.

This piece seems musically inspired by "(You Make Me Feel Like) A Natural Woman," sung by Aretha Franklin in 1967. Composed by Carole King, it has become an anthem for many women, and probably also for Dolly. Everything is there: the piano part, very important, played by Aretha, the brass parts, the drums that subdivide the tempo, and the backing vocals, female this time, that take up the refrain. The resemblance continues up to these three words, "You make me," in the intro. Perceptibly, the chords are placed, then cut dryly to restart the song at 0:55. Finally, we note the "You" in a head voice starting the chorus.

Recorded fifteen years later, Dolly's song is certainly a musical tribute to the Queen of Soul. As such, the quality of the recordings and the sounds of the instruments are in tune with the times. For example, the sound of the drums with the big reverb on the snare drum was non-existent in the 1960s. The bass and the brass have a very soulful playing style, while the Hammond organ adds a nostalgic touch.

Prime Of Our Love

Dolly Parton / 3:46

Vocals: Dolly Parton **Musicians:** Jeff Baxter, Albert Lee, Fred Tackett, Mike Severs, Steve Cropper: guitar / Eddy Anderson: drums / Lenny Castro: congas / Abe Laboriel, Leland Sklar, Nathan East: bass / Joe McGuffee: pedal steel / Buddy Spicher: fiddle / Gregg Perry: dulcimer / Red Young, Ron Oates: keyboards / Chuck Findley, Gary Grant, Gary Herbig, George Bohanon, Jim Horn, Slide Hyde, Tom Saviano, Tom Scott: brass **Backing Vocals:** Anita Ball, Denise Maynelli DeCaro, Gene Morford, Jim Salestrom, Richard Dennison, Roy Galloway, Willie Greene Jr., Stephanie Spruill **Recorded:** RCA Victor, Nashville,

December 1981–January 1982 **Technical Team:** Producers: Dolly Parton, Gregg Perry / Sound Engineers: Chuck Britz, Doug Parry, Larry Carlton, Marshall Morgan, Paul Dobbe / Assistant Sound Engineers: Pat McMakin, Rick Romano / Mixing: Mike Reese

When a lover departs and leaves behind a broken heart... By linking feelings to natural elements—a flower, a willow tree—this song poetically evokes the grief of the one who remains, alone, bruised, and incredulous.

Here, the dulcimer, a traditional instrument of the zither family, which produces metallic high notes, is an Appalachian dulcimer. The folk guitars play arpeggios, reminiscent of the hippie period of the 1960s and 1970s. The percussion has a traditional character, too, provided by an instrument difficult to identify but close to the Irish bodhran.

Hollywood Potters

Dolly Parton / 3:55

Vocals: Dolly Parton **Musicians:** Jeff Baxter, Albert Lee, Fred Tackett, Mike Severs, Steve Cropper: guitar / Eddy Anderson: drums / Lenny Castro: congas / Abe Laboriel, Leland Sklar, Nathan East: bass / Joe McGuffee: pedal steel / Buddy Spicher: fiddle / Gregg Perry: dulcimer / Red Young, Ron Oates: keyboards / Chuck Findley, Gary Grant, Gary Herbig, George Bohanon, Jim Horn, Slide Hyde, Tom Saviano, Tom Scott: brass **Backing Vocals:** Anita Ball, Denise Maynelli DeCaro, Gene Morford, Jim Salestrom, Richard Dennison, Roy Galloway, Willie Greene Jr., Stephanie Spruill **Recorded:** RCA Victor, Nashville, December 1981–January 1982 **Technical Team:** Producers: Dolly Parton, Gregg Perry / Sound Engineers: Chuck Britz, Doug Parry, Larry Carlton, Marshall Morgan, Paul Dobbe / Assistant Sound Engineers: Pat McMakin, Rick Romano / Mixing: Mike Reese

In this realist song, which has its roots in Dolly's first film experience, the star evokes the multitude of extras who flock to Hollywood hoping to find fame and fortune. But, as she sings it, Hollywood is the "center of sorrow, city of schemes"; one is filled with expectations, and we leave disappointed or broken, having been chewed up and spat out by the dream industry.

The piece is constructed like a musical, with an a cappella beginning (rare, even unique in Dolly Parton's work), then a powerful tutti. A faster, three-beat part is played by the organ, the instrument that, according to the codes of the musical, traditionally belongs to the villain (in this case, the city). Then a tutti closes the piece in apotheosis.

ALBUM

Burlap & Satin

Ooo-Eee . Send Me the Pillow You Dream On . Jealous Heart . A Gamble Either Way .
Appalachian Memories . I Really Don't Want to Know . Potential New Boyfriend .
A Cowboy's Ways . One of Those Days . Calm on the Water

RELEASE DATE
United States: June 18, 1983
Reference: RCA Victor—AHL1-4691
Best US Chart Ranking: 5

"Islands in the Stream" was written by the Bee Gees (including Robin and Maurice Gibb, shown here) and became a major hit in 1983.

An Album of Paradoxes

Dolly Parton's twenty-fifth solo album, *Burlap & Satin*, coproduced by Dolly and Gregg Perry, was released by RCA Victor on June 18, 1983. Although the reviews were positive for the songwriter, some reviewers, such as on the music blog *Highway Queens*, found Gregg Perry's arrangements disappointing. The title evokes the two worlds in which the star moves. This album, which ranked 127th on the Billboard 200, reflects the search for a balance between pop and country, and a return to the roots of the songwriter, who wrote six of the ten songs.

The Flip Side of Celebrity

In 1983, American president Ronald Reagan declared January 15, which was Martin Luther King Jr.'s birthday, a public holiday; Michael Jackson's moonwalk excited fans, and Al Pacino dazzled the big screen in Brian De Palma's *Scarface*. At the beginning of the year, the Nashville press reported on death threats against Dolly Parton. Police had been tipped off by an anonymous caller: A man, motivated by revenge, claimed that he had been married to Dolly and that she had betrayed him by marrying Carl Dean. The December 1980 assassination of John Lennon was still very present in people's memories. The star and her family were placed under protection. The tabloids were making a big deal out of it, linking the breakup of Gypsy Fever and the cancellation of Dolly's concerts to these threats. But Gypsy Fever had been at a standstill while the artist was recovering from her injuries, both physical and mental. Dolly needed to rest her vocal cords, her body, and her mind.

At a Crossroads

Dolly Parton may have hit rock bottom in 1981, but in 1983, she was still there, more determined than ever. The title of this new album, *Burlap & Satin*, sums up part of the star's universe at that time of her life: the rough side, the one that scratches, the one of her origins, the depths of her native Tennessee countryside, but which is authentic and stands the test of time; and the satin side, with its shiny, refined, elegant surface, its sensual softness, and its suppleness, but also its fragility. This title also sums up the paradox of the superstar, who lives these two sides of fame: on the one hand, the professional recognition, the fortune, the burgeoning of human relations, the glamour, the celebrity, the people who adore you; on the other hand, the burden all this brings, the constraints, the solitude, the difficulty in keeping private what is personal and intimate, or in protecting one's entourage from rumors and death threats. Being a superstar is as soft and light as satin, and as rough and heavy as burlap. Finally, satin perhaps symbolizes pop, and burlap symbolizes country, to which Dolly Parton invariably returns, in her own way.

Album Cover

A change of atmosphere with this album sleeve created by Ed Caraeff. Against a dark background we see Dolly's face, with its satin pink complexion, soft and luminous. On the jacket's back cover, the star, very beautiful—and slimmed down—is comfortably installed on a sofa covered with garnet satin; she seems to be looking toward a new horizon, with a serenity tinged with melancholy, but also with a newfound determination.

BRITAIN'S BESTSELLER **24p** **June 11ᵗʰ 1983**

WOMAN'S OWN

Cool,
casual 'n' cotton
—the best
summer fashion

YOUR HEALTH AND WELFARE

That shocking headache
—you tell us
about migraine

Lessons to learn from the rape that shocked the world

Acne agony
—a cure in sight?

DOLLY

'It costs a lot to look this cheap!'

WHAT GOES ON AT A SEANCE WITH MEDIUM DORIS FISHER STOKES

AUSTRALIA $1   NEW ZEALAND $1 25   CANADA $1 60 GG70302   IR 35p (inc. VAT)

The July 11, 1983, cover
of British magazine
Woman's Own.

Where do some of the rumors
that make the front page of
the tabloids come from?
Partly from one of Dolly
Parton's aunts—whom the
star barely knew as a child.
For the money, and to satisfy
a need for recognition, she
sold to the press stories
invented from scratch. As the
artist confides in her
autobiography,[1] she was both
amused and horrified when
she found out about this.

Ooo-Eee

Annie McLoone / 3:38

Vocals: Dolly Parton **Musicians:** Hugh McCracken, Marty Walsh, Mike Severs, Pete Bordonali, Tom Rutledge: guitar / Eddy Anderson, Rick Marotta: drums / Eddy Anderson: percussion / Michael Rhodes, Tommy Cogbill, Leland Sklar: bass / Joe McGuffee: pedal steel / Dolly Parton, Gregg Perry, Mitch Humphries, Robbie Buchanan, Ron Oates: keyboards / Ron Oates: synthesizer / Denis Solee: saxophone, flutes / Dewayne Pigg: English horn / Nashville String Machine: strings **Backing Vocals:** Anita Ball, Donna McElroy, Judy Rodman, Karen Taylor-Good, Lea Jane Berinati, Lisa Silver, Michael Black, Ray Walker, Richard Dennison **Handclaps:** Anita Ball, Dolly Parton, Ernie Winfrey, Judy Ogle, Judy Rodman **Recorded:** RCA Studio B, Nashville (TN), February 1983 **Technical Team:** Producers: Dolly Parton, Gregg Perry / Sound Engineers: Ernie Winfrey, Phil Jamtaas / Assistant Sound Engineers: Fran Overall, Jim Scott / Mixing: Ernie Winfrey

In this lighthearted song, in every sense of the word, the narrator cheerfully proclaims her love. We wondered when the "full on reverb" saxophone—a true sound standard of the eighties—was going to make its appearance in Dolly Parton's discography. This is now a reality with Denis Solee's performance on this very upbeat 4/4 track. In addition to the saxophone runs, we find the ingredients of the time: stabs and leads on synthesizer, electric guitar molded in chorus, bass and drums hyper-disciplined, choruses in thirds and fifths perfectly synchronized (probably provided by Dolly herself, in overdubs) and glossy mixing close to drowning, so much is each instrument bathed in reverb and delay.

Dolly arrives in London circa March 1983.

Send Me The Pillow You Dream On

Hank Locklin / 3:10

Vocals: Dolly Parton **Musicians:** Hugh McCracken, Marty Walsh, Mike Severs, Pete Bordonali, Tom Rutledge: guitar / Eddy Anderson, Rick Marotta: drums / Eddy Anderson: percussion / Michael Rhodes, Tommy Cogbill, Leland Sklar: bass / Joe McGuffee: pedal steel / Dolly Parton, Gregg Perry, Mitch Humphries, Robbie Buchanan, Ron Oates: keyboards / Ron Oates: synthesizer / Denis Solee: saxophone, flutes / Dewayne Pigg: English horn / Nashville String Machine: strings **Backing Vocals:** Anita Ball, Donna McElroy, Judy Rodman, Karen Taylor-Good, Lea Jane Berinati, Lisa Silver, Michael Black, Ray Walker, Richard Dennison **Handclaps:** Anita Ball, Dolly Parton, Ernie Winfrey, Judy Ogle, Judy Rodman **Recorded:** RCA Studio B, Nashville, February 1983 **Technical Team:** Producers: Dolly Parton, Gregg Perry / Sound Engineers: Ernie Winfrey, Phil Jamtaas / Assistant Sound Engineers: Fran Overall, Jim Scott / Mixing: Ernie Winfrey

The narrator asks the man she loves to send her the pillow on which he sleeps and dreams, so that she, too, can dream on it, as if she were next to him. The dreamy decorum is well there, in the 1980s version; the ethereal and deep sound of the synthesizer contributes largely to the musical atmosphere. We are in the digital era: Apart from the mixing desk and the tapes on which the tracks are recorded, there is not much left of the analog roundness of yesteryear. The warmth of acoustic instruments and valves has been replaced by the definition and brilliance, sometimes a little icy, of digital and transistors. One can regret it or, like Dolly Parton and Gregg Perry, choose to enjoy it. The use of these new technologies has clearly inspired the arrangement of this country classic (performed by Dean Martin, Loretta Lynn, Johnny Tillotson, and Hank Locklin himself), which is a far cry from the traditional Nashville sound. Everything here is conducive to reverie. A dive into a comforting sound universe that is also much more harmonious than life; in this sense, it is a total success.

Dolly Parton happily indulges in local customs, donning a Scottish scarf.

Jealous Heart

Dolly Parton / 3:25

Vocals: Dolly Parton **Musicians:** Hugh McCracken, Marty Walsh, Mike Severs, Pete Bordonali, Tom Rutledge: guitar / Eddy Anderson, Rick Marotta: drums / Eddy Anderson: percussion / Michael Rhodes, Tommy Cogbill, Leland Sklar: bass / Joe McGuffee: pedal steel / Dolly Parton, Gregg Perry, Mitch Humphries, Robbie Buchanan, Ron Oates: keyboards / Ron Oates: synthesizer / Denis Solee: saxophone, flutes / Dewayne Pigg: English horn / Nashville String Machine: strings **Backing Vocals:** Anita Ball, Donna McElroy, Judy Rodman, Karen Taylor-Good, Lea Jane Berinati, Lisa Silver, Michael Black, Ray Walker, Richard Dennison **Handclaps:** Anita Ball, Dolly Parton, Ernie Winfrey, Judy Ogle, Judy Rodman **Recorded:** RCA Studio B, Nashville, February 1983 **Technical Team:** Producers: Dolly Parton, Gregg Perry / Sound Engineers: Ernie Winfrey, Phil Jamtaas / Assistant Sound Engineers: Fran Overall, Jim Scott / Mixing: Ernie Winfrey

In a sorry mea culpa, the narrator describes the mechanism of her jealous heart, this almost obsessive curse, which is fed by an imagination that is unleashed as if from nowhere, is stronger than reason, and is a source of unbearable torments. We find here the preoccupations of the songwriter, her reflections, both personal and universal, on the subject of love. Musically, this midtempo country ballad is not far from a return to the roots. With the exception of the vocal descent on the lyrics "for the fool you are"—typical of the eighties—the arrangement and Dolly's songwriting are very traditional. As for the playing, only the acoustic guitar, strummed with the accent on the offbeat, modernizes the whole effect to some extent by adding a reggae touch. For the coherence of the album, the mixing of Ernie Winfrey and the production of Gregg Perry take care of the rest.

A Gamble Either Way

Dolly Parton /3:34

Vocals: Dolly Parton **Musicians:** Hugh McCracken, Marty Walsh, Mike Severs, Pete Bordonali, Tom Rutledge: guitar / Eddy Anderson, Rick Marotta: drums / Eddy Anderson: percussion / Michael Rhodes, Tommy Cogbill, Leland Sklar: bass / Joe McGuffee: pedal steel / Dolly Parton, Gregg Perry, Mitch Humphries, Robbie Buchanan, Ron Oates: keyboards / Ron Oates: synthesizer / Denis Solee: saxophone, flutes / Dewayne Pigg: English horn / Nashville String Machine: strings **Backing Vocals:** Anita Ball, Donna McElroy, Judy Rodman, Karen Taylor-Good, Lea Jane Berinati, Lisa Silver, Michael Black, Ray Walker, Richard Dennison **Handclaps:** Anita Ball, Dolly Parton, Ernie Winfrey, Judy Ogle, Judy Rodman **Recorded:** RCA Studio B, Nashville, February 1983 **Technical Team:** Producers: Dolly Parton, Gregg Perry / Sound Engineers: Ernie Winfrey, Phil Jamtaas / Assistant Sound Engineers: Fran Overall, Jim Scott / Mixing: Ernie Winfrey

Dolly Parton wrote this song thinking it would be part of the soundtrack of the movie *The Best Little Whorehouse in Texas*. It is the story of an orphan, born into loneliness and abandonment, who hits the road at fifteen. She hitchhikes, feels free, but this road leads her to prostitution. Whatever our background, we must play the hand that life has dealt us, as in cards—this is the lesson the narrator draws from it.

With the piano, the acoustic guitar arpeggios, the big comeback of the pedal steel, and the bass, it is difficult to date this elegant and airy production before 2:23—this piece could have been recorded and produced in 1975. But when the first sound of synthesized backing vocals ("Aaah") arrives, on the last third of the song, the 1970s are long gone, even though the problems of the working class remain unchanged, especially for the women—"A 15-year-old girl don't have no trouble hitching rides"...This should be classified in the "sad ass songs" of the "reality check" category, a genre that Dolly masters and loves particularly. The final climax is striking, backing vocals, pedal steel, and synthesizer mixing to form a dense, deep, and harmonious sound cloud. The production sticks perfectly to the temporality of the narration, from the protagonist's birth to her sixteen years, from acoustic piano to the synthesizer. The intention of Dolly Parton and Gregg Perry is clearly read on this point. High art.

Appalachian Memories

Dolly Parton / 4:15

Vocals: Dolly Parton **Musicians:** Hugh McCracken, Marty Walsh, Mike Severs, Pete Bordonali, Tom Rutledge: guitar / Eddy Anderson, Rick Marotta: drums / Eddy Anderson: percussion / Michael Rhodes, Tommy Cogbill, Leland Sklar: bass / Joe McGuffee: pedal steel / Dolly Parton, Gregg Perry, Mitch Humphries, Robbie Buchanan, Ron Oates: keyboards / Ron Oates: synthesizer / Denis Solee: saxophone, flutes / Dewayne Pigg: English horn / Nashville String Machine: strings **Backing Vocals:** Anita Ball, Donna McElroy, Judy Rodman, Karen Taylor-Good, Lea Jane Berinati, Lisa Silver, Michael Black, Ray Walker, Richard Dennison **Handclaps:** Anita Ball, Dolly Parton, Ernie Winfrey, Judy Ogle, Judy Rodman **Recorded:** RCA Studio B, Nashville, February 1983 **Technical Team:** Producers: Dolly Parton, Gregg Perry / Sound Engineers: Ernie Winfrey, Phil Jamtaas / Assistant Sound Engineers: Fran Overall, Jim Scott / Mixing: Ernie Winfrey

In the form of an existential questioning, this song summons the memory of origins, of the place where one comes from. The narrator and her family, farmers, left her place in the South for the North in the hope of escaping poverty. But in this North which has none of the characteristics of a "promised land," only the reminiscence of their Appalachian Mountains and an unshakable faith help them to remain strong.

The intro, with its ensemble with flutes, sounds like an ancient chant, then the voice makes its entrance, and the piano and strings of the Nashville String Machine take over. The musicians' playing and the dynamic arrangement enable Dolly to reach the stratosphere, to soar above the Appalachians and to cast a benevolent eye over the memory of a difficult but courageous and dignified life. The solemn tone, the gratitude, the strength drawn from roots and faith—all of this is made palpable by the interpretation of Dolly and her session men, until the flutes return to conclude this introspective journey in fervor and contemplation.

1983

I Really Don't Want To Know

Howard Barnes, Don Robertson / 3:02

Vocals: Dolly Parton, Willie Nelson **Musicians:** Hugh McCracken, Marty Walsh, Mike Severs, Pete Bordonali, Tom Rutledge: guitar / Eddy Anderson, Rick Marotta: drums / Eddy Anderson: percussion / Michael Rhodes, Tommy Cogbill, Leland Sklar: bass / Joe McGuffee: pedal steel / Dolly Parton, Gregg Perry, Mitch Humphries, Robbie Buchanan, Ron Oates: keyboards / Ron Oates: synthesizer / Denis Solee: saxophone, flutes / Dewayne Pigg: English horn / Nashville String Machine: strings **Backing Vocals:** Anita Ball, Donna McElroy, Judy Rodman, Karen Taylor-Good, Lea Jane Berinati, Lisa Silver, Michael Black, Ray Walker, Richard Dennison **Handclaps:** Anita Ball, Dolly Parton, Ernie Winfrey, Judy Ogle, Judy Rodman **Recorded:** RCA Studio B, Nashville, February 1983 **Technical Team:** Producers: Dolly Parton, Gregg Perry / Sound Engineers: Ernie Winfrey, Phil Jamtaas / Assistant Sound Engineers: Fran Overall, Jim Scott / Mixing: Ernie Winfrey

An understandable dilemma: The narrator cannot help but wonder how many women the man she loves has known before her...but she prefers never to know.

Apart from her long collaboration with Porter Wagoner, Dolly Parton does not usually perform duets on her solo albums. But here is one, and not the least of them, either, sung with the country giant Willie Nelson. A year earlier, Dolly had already recorded the song "Everything's Beautiful (In Its Own Way)" with him for the collaborative album *The Winning Hand*. Willie returned the favor in 2013 by inviting Dolly to sing with him "From Here to the Moon and Back" on his duets album *To All the Girls...* In 2020, Dolly repeated the experience by inviting her old friend to sing "Pretty Paper," written by Willie, on her Christmas album *A Holly Dolly Christmas*. "I Really Don't Want to Know" is reminiscent of Paul Simon's "Still Crazy After All These Years" (1975), in the melody and the chord progression first, but also in the sound, of the Fender Rhodes type, with a light chorus (more flashy here), and the strings arrangement. The sweet nostalgia that emanates from these two pieces evokes a very similar feeling: a sadness mixed with comfort.

Potential New Boyfriend

Steve Kipner, John Lewis Parker / 3:39

Vocals: Dolly Parton **Musicians:** Hugh McCracken, Marty Walsh, Mike Severs, Pete Bordonali, Tom Rutledge: guitar / Eddy Anderson, Rick Marotta: drums / Eddy Anderson: percussion / Michael Rhodes, Tommy Cogbill, Leland Sklar: bass / Joe McGuffee: pedal steel / Dolly Parton, Gregg Perry, Mitch Humphries, Robbie Buchanan, Ron Oates: keyboards / Ron Oates: synthesizer / Denis Solee: saxophone, flutes / Dewayne Pigg: English horn / Nashville String Machine: strings **Backing Vocals:** Anita Ball, Donna McElroy, Judy Rodman, Karen Taylor-Good, Lea Jane Berinati, Lisa Silver, Michael Black, Ray Walker, Richard Dennison **Handclaps:** Anita Ball, Dolly Parton, Ernie Winfrey, Judy Ogle, Judy Rodman **Recorded:** RCA Studio B, Nashville, 1983 **Technical Team:** Producers: Dolly Parton, Gregg Perry / Sound Engineers: Ernie Winfrey, Phil Jamtaas / Assistant Sound Engineers: Fran Overall, Jim Scott / Mixing: Ernie Winfrey **Single:** Side A: Potential New Boyfriend / Side B: One of Those Days **Release:** RCA Victor, April 11, 1983 (45 rpm ref.: PB-13514) **Best US Chart Ranking:** 20 on the Billboard Hot Country Songs, 14 on the Billboard Dance Club Songs.

The narrator warns all the other women: this attractive man is potentially her new boyfriend, so don't touch him...not until she knows if she really wants him. This song gave Dolly her first video, directed by Steve Barron, who also directed Michael Jackson's 1982 video for "Billie Jean." Another song very far from the roots of the Queen of Country. We find ourselves swimming in full eighties-pop mode, with all the gimmicks already mentioned: full reverb, chorus on the keyboards and electric guitars. The gated reverb applied to the snare drum is particularly pronounced on the verses: a guaranteed "whiplash" effect, a real tonic validated by the DJs of the time, which ensured the song multiple broadcasts on mainstream radios and in clubs. The result: a well-deserved fourteenth place in the Billboard Dance Club Songs chart.

A Cowboy's Ways

Dolly Parton / 4:17

Vocals: Dolly Parton **Musicians:** Hugh McCracken, Marty Walsh, Mike Severs, Pete Bordonali, Tom Rutledge: guitar / Eddy Anderson, Rick Marotta: drums / Eddy Anderson: percussion / Michael Rhodes, Tommy Cogbill, Leland Sklar: bass / Joe McGuffee: pedal steel / Dolly Parton, Gregg Perry, Mitch Humphries, Robbie Buchanan, Ron Oates: keyboards / Ron Oates: synthesizer / Denis Solee: saxophone, flutes / Dewayne Pigg: English horn / Nashville String Machine: strings **Backing Vocals:** Anita Ball, Donna McElroy, Judy Rodman, Karen Taylor-Good, Lea Jane Berinati, Lisa Silver, Michael Black, Ray Walker, Richard Dennison **Handclaps:** Anita Ball, Dolly Parton, Ernie Winfrey, Judy Ogle, Judy Rodman **Recorded:** RCA Studio B, Nashville, February 1983 **Technical Team:** Producers: Dolly Parton, Gregg Perry / Sound Engineers: Ernie Winfrey, Phil Jamtaas / Assistant Sound Engineers: Fran Overall, Jim Scott / Mixing: Ernie Winfrey

Another song written during the filming of *The Best Little Whorehouse in Texas,* for actor Burt Reynolds (it was not used in the final film). However much he may be in love, a cowboy does not know how to say "I love you" or "Forgive me," being too clumsy with the words, but also too proud. Despite this shortcoming, his lover loves him nonetheless. Thematically, this country pop ballad is rather like Tammy Wynette's 1968 hit "Stand by Your Man." The syrupy production does not do nuance, and the heavy artillery is out in force: English horn for the exposition of the theme and for the counterpoints, crystalline acoustic guitar arpeggios, piano and Fender Rhodes, minimalist bass-drums duet, although swollen with larger-than-life reverb, strings arrangements flirting with the symphonic. The whole allows Dolly to exploit her chest voice in the high notes. The power of her interpretation on the choruses equals that of the greatest singers of the time—a way to remind us all that Dolly is a fine vocal technician, with an outstanding array of capabilities.

One Of Those Days

Dolly Parton / 3:59

Vocals: Dolly Parton **Musicians:** Hugh McCracken, Marty Walsh, Mike Severs, Pete Bordonali, Tom Rutledge: guitar / Eddy Anderson, Rick Marotta: drums / Eddy Anderson: percussion / Michael Rhodes, Tommy Cogbill, Leland Sklar: bass / Joe McGuffee: pedal steel / Dolly Parton, Gregg Perry, Mitch Humphries, Robbie Buchanan, Ron Oates: keyboards / Ron Oates: synthesizer / Denis Solee: saxophone, flutes / Dewayne Pigg: English horn / Nashville String Machine: strings **Backing Vocals:** Anita Ball, Donna McElroy, Judy Rodman, Karen Taylor-Good, Lea Jane Berinati, Lisa Silver, Michael Black, Ray Walker, Richard Dennison **Handclaps:** Anita Ball, Dolly Parton, Ernie Winfrey, Judy Ogle, Judy Rodman **Recorded:** RCA Studio B, Nashville, 1982 **Technical Team:** Producers: Dolly Parton, Gregg Perry / Sound Engineers: Ernie Winfrey, Phil Jamtaas / Assistant Sound Engineers: Fran Overall, Jim Scott / Mixing: Ernie Winfrey **Single:** Side A: Potential New Boyfriend / Side B: One of Those Days **Release:** RCA Victor, April 11, 1983 (45 rpm ref.: PB-13514) **Best US Chart Ranking:** 20 on the Billboard Hot Country Songs, 14 on the Billboard Dance Club Songs

It is one of those days when the narrator remembers this happiness, this love. This beautiful love that has vanished: She maintains a deep nostalgia for it, and the painful certainty of never getting over it.

We were expecting it—here is the album's country shuffle ballad. The production seems hardly dated today, the pedal steel is prominent once more, the drummer picks up the brushes again, the bass nails the rhythm of the bass drum and provides some nice turnarounds, the gentle strumming of the acoustic guitar works wonders, combined with the fine articulations of the Fender Rhodes keyboard, and the arrangement of the strings remains understated, like a shadow cast over the orchestra, warm and enveloping. Dolly can then overlay her vocals, with restraint and delicacy, close to a whisper on the spoken passages at the end: "It's been one of those days / That reminded me in many ways / Of when we were happy, still in love." A piece full of tenderness, a caress.

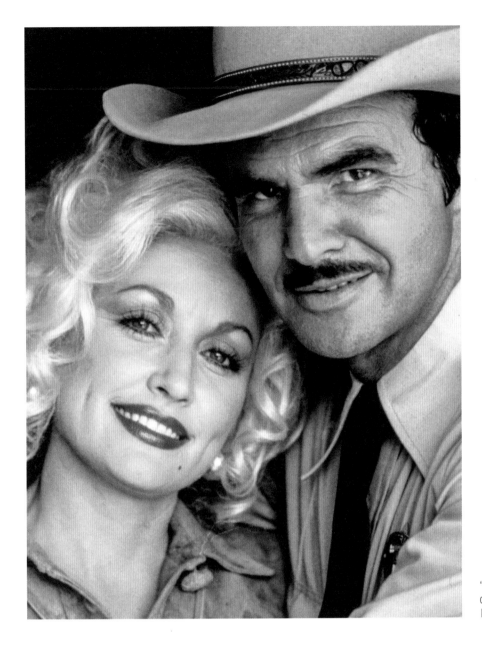

"A Cowboy's Ways" was written during filming for *The Best Little Whorehouse in Texas.*

Calm On The Water

Dolly Parton / 3:59

Vocals: Dolly Parton **Musicians:** Hugh McCracken, Marty Walsh, Mike Severs, Pete Bordonali, Tom Rutledge: guitar / Eddy Anderson, Rick Marotta: drums / Eddy Anderson: percussion / Michael Rhodes, Tommy Cogbill, Leland Sklar: bass / Joe McGuffee: pedal steel / Dolly Parton, Gregg Perry, Mitch Humphries, Robbie Buchanan, Ron Oates: keyboards / Ron Oates: synthesizer / Denis Solee: saxophone, flutes / Dewayne Pigg: English horn / Nashville String Machine: strings **Backing Vocals:** Anita Ball, Donna McElroy, Judy Rodman, Karen Taylor-Good, Lea Jane Berinati, Lisa Silver, Michael Black, Ray Walker, Richard Dennison **Handclaps:** Anita Ball, Dolly Parton, Ernie Winfrey, Judy Ogle, Judy Rodman **Recorded:** RCA Studio B, Nashville, February 1983 **Technical Team:** Producers: Dolly Parton, Gregg Perry / Sound Engineers: Ernie Winfrey, Phil Jamtaas / Assistant Sound Engineers: Fran Overall, Jim Scott / Mixing: Ernie Winfrey

This is a gospel song in praise of Jesus, about personal uplift through love. As is often the case with the Queen of Country, it ends on a bright and cheerful note. The bass-drums groove, supported by an Afro–Caribbean sounding electric guitar, is unusual for Dolly and her musicians, but it works perfectly. The bass gives us some supersonic flights of fancy, the backing singers blaze away to their hearts' content, and the acoustic guitar strumming it all answer one another on both sides of the stereo field in a duel of syncopations with a communicative energy. This unifying and dancing piece is the exotic cherry on the cake of this dense and joyfully varied album.

ALBUM

The Great Pretender

Save the Last Dance for Me . I Walk the Line . Turn, Turn, Turn
(To Everything There Is a Season) . Downtown . We Had It All . She Don't Love You
(Like I Love You) . We'll Sing in the Sunshine . I Can't Help Myself
(Sugar Pie, Honey Bunch) . Elusive Butterfly . The Great Pretender

RELEASE DATE
United States: January 23, 1984
Reference: RCA Victor—AHL1-4940
Best US Chart Ranking: 7

Pure Interpretation

The Great Pretender is Dolly Parton's twenty-sixth solo album, released by RCA Victor on January 23, 1984, and produced by Val Garay. The star performs ten songs written by others. In 1984, Dolly continued her return to fitness and was about to film *Rhinestone*, a movie directed by Bob Clark and costarring Sylvester Stallone. Before filming, the artist allowed herself a few days in Hawaii, where she took care of her body, with a diet and sports, and took the time to read scripts to honor her contract with 20th Century Fox.

The choice of songs on *The Great Pretender* seems to be logical for this interim period: less personal involvement, since none of the songs are hers. (She would write several songs for the *Rhinestone* soundtrack.) A reissue in 1999 contained six bonus tracks, three of which were past hits—"I Will Always Love You," "Jolene," and "9 to 5." The album reached number 73 on the Billboard 200.

Renewal

In 1984, the worlds of culture and sports were in mourning after the murder of Marvin Gaye by his father, the death of jazz pianist Count Basie, the death of author Truman Capote, and the death of Olympic swimmer (and five-time gold medalist) Johnny Weissmuller, famous for having played Tarzan more than ten times in the movies. On November 6, President Ronald Reagan was reelected with 58.8 percent of the vote.

As always when she sings what others have written, Dolly Parton is less affected by the critics and the public. Another explanation: Gregg Perry was no longer producing. In an interview given in 1982 to Cliff Jarrh,[5] she admitted that she was heartbroken when Perry told her that he was ending their collaboration. In her autobiography, the songwriter said she felt very close to him.[1] The tabloids obviously concocted a story of the heart and sex—some newspapers did not hesitate to attribute romances or other stories to the stars, to fill their pages and sell copy. However, beyond the fantasies, it seems natural and understandable that between artists the time spent together creating is a special time, intense and fruitful, heightening feelings and emotions.

The Crowning Moment in Nashville

In 1984, an exhibition on the life and work of Dolly Parton was arranged for the first time at the Country Music Hall of Fame in Nashville, the temple of country music. Until then, few artists—Johnny Cash and Willie Nelson, in particular—had had this illustrious honor. The exhibition chronicled Dolly's childhood and upbringing, and it showcased the singer-songwriter with archival documents that celebrated Dolly's songwriting, including "Two Doors Down," while also including costumes worn at concerts in 1983 and featuring clips of Dolly as an actress. During this decade, more than thirty exhibitions around the world presented photos, videos, wigs, and stage outfits of the superstar.

Another distinction saluting the artist and her work: This same year, the star's name was added to the Hollywood Walk of Fame.

Album Cover

On both sides of album jacket, in photos by Richard Avedon, we notice how much Dolly has slimmed down. In a three-quarter pose highlighting her figure, with her legs uncovered and her waist hugged in both black (on the front) and white (on the back) embroidered dresses or revealing her impressive cleavage in a pretty black-and-white portrait (on the inside sleeve), Dolly seems to be in the best shape of her life, seductive and sure of herself.

A scene from the 1984 movie *Rhinestone*, starring Dolly Parton and Sylvester Stallone.

The Jupiter-8, manufactured by Roland from 1981, is an analog polyphonic synthesizer with eight channels.

SINGLE

Save The Last Dance For Me

Doc Pomus, Mort Shuman / 3:50

Vocals: Dolly Parton **Musicians:** David Platshon: drums / Leland Sklar: bass / Brian Glascock: percussion / Graig Hull, Ron Elliott: electric guitar / Steve Goldstein: drum machine, synthesizers / Jeff Colella: synthesizer **Backing Vocals:** The Jordanaires / Steve Goldstein: arrangements **Recorded:** RCA Studio B, Nashville, October 24–December 5, 1983 **Technical Team:** Producer: Val Garay / Sound Engineers: Val Garay, Niko Bolas / Assistant Sound Engineers: Richard Bosworth, Denny Densmore, Scott Hendricks, Danny Mundhenk, Paul Goldberg, Billy Miranda, David Leonard **Single:** Side A: Save the Last Dance for Me / Side B: Elusive Butterfly **Release:** RCA Victor, November 28, 1983 (45 rpm ref.: PB-13703) **Best Chart Ranking:** 3 on the Billboard Hot Country Songs (USA); 2 on the RPM Country 50 Singles (Canada)

In this cover of the Drifters' 1960 hit song, written by Doc Pomus and Mort Shuman (who performed it in French in 1976), the narrator tells the man she loves that he can dance, drink, laugh, and flirt, as long as he gives her the last dance. Lou Reed, who collaborated with Doc Pomus, says Pomus wrote the song in his wheelchair on the day of his wedding to singer and actress Willi Burke. Pomus, who had polio, was watching her dance with others, knowing that she would be going home with him.

The song begins with a Jupiter-8 synthesizer layer in the bass before Dolly's voice is heard. On the second cycle of the first verse, Steve Goldstein launches his drum machine programming, a DMX model (manufactured by Oberheim since 1980), producing the iconic, percussive sound of the 1980s. Apart from the bass and the electric guitar, whose sound is so elaborate that it could be mistaken for keyboards, this track relies almost entirely on the synthesizers and the famous drum machine. The musical atmosphere is an invitation to the solitary reverie at the heart of the bustling cities, to the sound of a Walkman or the trendy clubs of the time, lulled by the promise of a last love dance.

"Turn, Turn, Turn (To Everything There Is a Season)" is a cover of a song by Pete Seeger, the godfather of the folk revival that took place in the 1960s.

I Walk The Line

Johnny Cash / 3:34

Vocals: Dolly Parton **Musicians:** David Platshon: drums / Leland Sklar: bass / Brian Glascock: percussion / Craig Hull, Ron Elliott: electric guitar / Steve Goldstein: synthesizer / Jeff Colella: organ, strings **Recorded:** RCA Studio B, Nashville, October 24–December 5, 1983 **Technical Team:** Producer: Val Garay / Sound Engineers: Val Garay, Niko Bolas / Assistant Sound Engineers: Richard Bosworth, Denny Densmore, Scott Hendricks, Danny Mundhenk, Paul Goldberg, Billy Miranda, David Leonard

In this song written by Johnny Cash, the narrator declares to his girlfriend that he is going straight because he loves her. The cover is put through the 1980s mill: hypersaturated electric guitar rhythm; drums imitating the drum machine and leaving all the groove to Brian Glascock's percussion; a monochord bass; Jupiter-8 synthesizer layers; and, at the end, always the promise of love. In 1983, it was difficult to bypass this type of production if one wanted to remain in the mainstream. There are even a few guitar hero shots deep in the mix. Although the synths were adopted without restraint, Dolly and Val Garay cautiously handle the mainstream hard rock clichés in vogue at the time.

Turn, Turn, Turn (To Everything There Is A Season)

Pete Seeger / 4:24

Vocals: Dolly Parton **Musicians:** David Platshon: drums / Leland Sklar: bass / Brian Glascock: percussion / Craig Hull, Ron Elliott: electric guitar / Jeff Colella: synthesizer / Waddy Wachtel: electric guitar (solo) / Russell Kunkel: congas / Steve Goldstein: electric grand piano **Recorded:** RCA Studio B, Nashville, October 24–December 5, 1983 **Technical Team:** Producer: Val Garay / Sound Engineers: Val Garay, Niko Bolas / Assistant Sound Engineers: Richard Bosworth, Denny Densmore, Scott Hendricks, Danny Mundhenk, Paul Goldberg, Billy Miranda, David Leonard

Life, which is in essence fluctuating, is presented in all its facets, and if one wants to see a rainbow, as Dolly often says in her writings, one must first accept the rain. This is a perpetual dance of emotions and experiences, sometimes contradictory—like building and destroying—because there is a time for everything.

The Byrds' cover version of this song by Pete Seeger, the legendary godfather of the 1960s folk revival, was number one on the US charts in 1965. The lyrics, written in the late

1950s, are taken almost entirely from chapter 3 of the biblical book of Ecclesiastes, which suits Dolly Parton perfectly.

As far as the musical direction is concerned, modernity remains the watchword here. However, the arrangement essentially revolves around the piano part played by Steve Goldstein on a Kawai Electric Grand (a large electric piano with eighty-eight keys, direct competitor of the already famous CP80 by Yamaha), the percussion of Brian Glascock, and the bass of Leland Sklar. Waddy Wachtel on electric guitar and Jeff Colella on synthesizers add subtle arpeggios and backing vocals until David Platshon's crashing entry break on electronic drums at 2:14. At this point, the listener is propelled into an epic score that could be described, not without a certain audacity, as neosymphonic. Each element of the orchestra brings a considerable amplitude to the whole before falling back, then starting again, a few seconds later, at 3:08, on a doubled tempo very favorable to the stadium rock genre. The lift is total, a long way from Pete Seeger's banjo and the Byrds' twelve-string Rickenbacker.

Downtown

Tony Hatch / 3:19

Vocals: Dolly Parton **Musicians:** David Platshon: drums / Leland Sklar: bass / Brian Glascock: percussion / Craig Hull, Ron Elliott: electric guitar / Jeff Colella: synthesizers / Waddy Wachtel: electric guitar (solo) / Russell Kunkel: congas / Steve Goldstein: keyboards / Chuck Findley, Slide Hyde, Don Menza, Tom Scott, Gary Grant, Bill Reichenbach: brass / Steve Goldstein: brass arrangement **Recorded:** RCA Studio B, Nashville, December 1983 **Technical Team:** Producer: Val Garay / Sound Engineers: Val Garay, Niko Bolas / Assistant Sound Engineers: Richard Bosworth, Denny Densmore, Scott Hendricks, Danny Mundhenk, Paul Goldberg, Billy Miranda, David Leonard **Single:** Side A: Downtown / Side B: The Great Pretender **Release:** RCA Victor, March 12, 1984 (45 rpm ref.: PB-13756) **Best Chart Ranking:** 36 on the Billboard Hot Country Songs (USA); 20 on the RPM Country Singles (Canada)

A huge hit performed by Petula Clark in 1964, "Downtown" is an ode to downtown, where everything glitters, where everything can help you forget your worries, and where there is always something going on somewhere. And it certainly makes a glittering impact! Saturated guitars, synth stabs, drums fills (rolls placed to fill the sound space and boost the rhythm), and a tempo dangerously reminiscent of "Jump," the hit by the band Van Halen, released the same year. It is difficult to know if either artist was influenced by the other, since these two tracks were recorded in the same year. In any case, these sounds were in the spirit of the times; glitz, grandiloquence, and insouciance were the order of the day in the materialistic and uncomplicated America of Ronald Reagan. To complete the picture, the epic brass section, the palm mute electric guitar shots, the disco-style bass playing in octaves, and Dolly Parton's extremely energetic voice propel the arrangement toward the heights of the genre.

We Had It All

Donnie Fritts, Troy Seals / 3:51

Vocals: Dolly Parton **Musicians:** Ron Elliott: acoustic guitar / Steve Goldstein: acoustic piano, strings arrangement **Recorded:** RCA Studio B, Nashville, October 24–December 5, 1983 **Technical Team:** Producer: Val Garay / Sound Engineers: Val Garay, Niko Bolas / Assistant Sound Engineers: Richard Bosworth, Denny Densmore, Scott Hendricks, Danny Mundhenk, Paul Goldberg, Billy Miranda, David Leonard

The narrator remembers that perfect love, that time when they had everything, and even though it is now over, she cherishes this undying memory. Dolly covers this song in 1986 in the compilation "Think About Love." For this nostalgic ballad, a duo of musicians and a string arrangement suffice: Ron Elliott's acoustic guitar arpeggios and Steve Goldstein's clear and uncluttered piano playing carry Dolly's voice effortlessly. Her performance, at once fragile and confident, powerful and nuanced, takes the listener into a sunset among the Georgia pines. Like a dream, it is the reminiscence of a feeling that had all the makings of true love.

"Downtown" is a 1964 classic sung by Petula Clark and covered by Dolly (pictured here in 1984) on *The Great Pretender*.

She Don't Love You (Like I Love You)

Jerry Butler, Calvin Carter, Curtis Mayfield / 3:41

Vocals: Dolly Parton **Musicians:** David Platshon: drums / Leland Sklar: bass / Brian Glascock: congas / Ron Elliott: acoustic guitar / Craig Hull: electric guitar, slide guitar / Steve Goldstein: electric grand piano / Jeff Colella: ARP strings **Backing Vocals:** Rosemary Butler, Arnold McCuller, Mary Ellen Quinn **Recorded:** RCA Studio B, Nashville, October 24–December 5, 1983 **Technical Team:** Producer: Val Garay / Sound Engineers: Val Garay, Niko Bolas / Assistant Sound Engineers: Richard Bosworth, Denny Densmore, Scott Hendricks, Danny Mundhenk, Paul Goldberg, Billy Miranda, David Leonard

Dolly Parton covers Tony Orlando and Dawn's song "He Don't Love You (Like I Love You)" (1975), reversing the gender of the protagonists: This pretty girl doesn't love the narrator's man the way she loves him. When this flirt breaks his heart—a foregone conclusion—the narrator will be there for him, because her love for him is stronger. In terms of orchestration, Dolly Parton and Val Garay decided, once again, to focus on energy and the flashy side of strength. The saturated guitars, the synthesizers, the crystalline arpeggios of acoustic guitar, the drums that slam (we feel the compression in parallel, a technique that was still very cutting-edge at the time, which skims the attacks of the snare drum to give it this *smashed* sound that is so recognizable), and the bass in symbiosis with the bass drum are present here. The touch of groove—which makes all the difference here—is provided by Brian Glascock, doctor of congas. An effective track that sails through elegantly and blends perfectly with the color of the album.

"We'll Sing in the Sunshine" is a cover of a song by Gale Garnett, shown here soon after the track was originally released in 1966.

Gale Garnett is a New Zealand–born Canadian singer, songwriter, and actress. She began her career in the early 1960s, notably with the band the Gentle Reign, and retired from the music scene in the early 1980s.

I Can't Help Myself (Sugar Pie, Honey Bunch)

Brian Holland, Eddie Holland, Lamont Dozier / 2:50

Vocals: Dolly Parton **Musicians:** David Platshon: drums / Leland Sklar: bass / Brian Glascock: percussion / Ron Elliott, Craig Hull: electric guitar / Waddy Wachtel: electric guitar (solo) / Steve Goldstein: electric grand piano, keyboards, strings arrangement / Jeff Colella: synthesizer / Bill Cuomo: synthesizer **Backing Vocals:** Oren and Luther Waters **Recorded:** RCA Studio B, Nashville, October 24–December 5, 1983 **Technical Team:** Producer: Val Garay / Sound Engineers: Val Garay, Niko Bolas / Assistant Sound Engineers: Richard Bosworth, Denny Densmore, Scott Hendricks, Danny Mundhenk, Paul Goldberg, Billy Miranda, David Leonard

We'll Sing In The Sunshine

Gale Garnett / 3:25

Vocals: Dolly Parton **Musicians:** David Platshon: drums / Leland Sklar: bass / Brian Glascock: congas / Ron Elliott: acoustic guitar / Craig Hull: electric guitar / Steve Goldstein: keyboards / Jeff Colella: synthesizer / Lee Dresser: harmonica **Recorded:** RCA Studio B, Nashville, October 24–December 5, 1983 **Technical Team:** Producer: Val Garay / Sound Engineers: Val Garay, Niko Bolas / Assistant Sound Engineers: Richard Bosworth, Denny Densmore, Scott Hendricks, Danny Mundhenk, Paul Goldberg, Billy Miranda, David Leonard

This is an invitation to experience love without commitments, because being really in love is too expensive. This cover of Gale Garnett's 1966 hit begins in the manner of Peggy Lee's famous "Fever" (composed by Otis Blackwell and Eddie Cooley, and first recorded by Little Willie John in 1956). A walking bass line in the foreground, hi-hat on beats 2 and 4, congas, light percussion, a Fender Rhodes keyboard with a shimmering chorus, delicate strumming of acoustic guitar...The string arrangement, limited to the high notes, covers the whole with an acidulous harmonic cloud, an echo of 1966 and hippie reminiscences. In this waking dream, we literally float, caressed by Dolly's voice, in a country where love and the sweetness of life reign in unison and weave the threads of perfect harmony.

This song tells of the strength and weakness of the feeling of love, which makes you stupid and against which you cannot really fight. This Tamla Motown hit—which has been recorded by the Four Tops (1965), the Supremes (1966), and Donnie Elbert (1972), among others—has been given a neat production face-lift here, but the arrangement remains very close to the original version. Val Garay and Dolly Parton know that it is necessary to keep the pulse going, and to retain the essence of this title. The famous Detroit beat is preserved, the bass turn is identical, the strings part is played with the synthesizer, and the syncopated piano is played on a Kawai Electric Grand. Dolly, perfectly in her element and decidedly very much on form, allows herself a few well-judged variations. A nice tribute to the heroes of Motown.

Dolly at a March 1984 album signing for *The Great Pretender*, held at the Hyatt hotel in Chicago.

Bob Lind is an American singer-songwriter whose influence on the sixties folk-rock scene was considerable. He is the author of four albums released between 1966 and 1971; the song "Elusive Butterfly" (1966) was his biggest hit.

Elusive Butterfly

Bob Lind / 2:47

Vocals: Dolly Parton **Musicians:** David Platshon: drums / Leland Sklar: bass / Brian Glascock: percussion / Ron Elliott, Craig Hull: electric guitar / Waddy Wachtel: electric guitar (solo) / Steve Goldstein, Jeff Colella: synthesizer / Bill Cuomo: synthesizer / Lee Dresser: harmonica **Recorded:** RCA Studio B, Nashville, October 24–December 5, 1983 **Technical Team:** Producer: Val Garay / Sound Engineers: Val Garay, Niko Bolas / Assistant Sound Engineers: Richard Bosworth, Denny Densmore, Scott Hendricks, Danny Mundhenk, Paul Goldberg, Billy Miranda, David Leonard **Single:** Side A: Save the Last Dance for Me / Side B: Elusive Butterfly **Release:** RCA Victor, November 28, 1983 (45 rpm ref.: PB-13703) **Best Chart Ranking:** 3 on the Billboard Hot Country Songs (USA); 2 on the RPM Country 50 Singles (Canada)

In her dreams, the narrator with a net in her hand chases the elusive butterfly that embodies love. This great Bob Lind hit is simply reinterpreted by Dolly Parton and her musicians. The arrangement and the production remain remarkably classical compared to the rest of the album. It must be said that the words and the melody are enough on their own; Dolly Parton and Val Garay know this well, so there is no question of bringing out the heavy artillery. The mistake would have been to try to compete with the prestigious production and the sumptuous string arrangement of Jack Nitzsche at the Sunset Sound studio in 1965 (a session with Bob Lind that included a legendary line-up: Hal Blaine on drums, Carole Kaye on bass, and Leon Russell on piano, to name a few). Clean-sounding electric guitar picking, an ascetic bass-drums tandem, a trickle of synthetic violins, and Lee Dresser's harmonica do most of the work here, fluid and light like a butterfly flying over the current of a Smokies river.

The Great Pretender

Buck Ram / 3:41

Vocals: Dolly Parton **Musicians:** Steve Goldstein: organ **Backing Vocals:** The Waters Family (Maxine, Julia, Oren, and Luther Waters) **Recorded:** RCA Studio B, Nashville, October 24–December 5, 1983 **Technical Team:** Producer: Val Garay / Sound Engineers: Val Garay, Niko Bolas / Assistant Sound Engineers: Richard Bosworth, Denny Densmore, Scott Hendricks, Danny Mundhenk, Paul Goldberg, Billy Miranda, David Leonard **Single:** Side A: Downtown / Side B: The Great Pretender **Release:** RCA Victor, March 12, 1984 (45 rpm ref.: PB-13756) **Best Chart Ranking:** 36 on the Billboard Hot Country Songs (USA); 20 on the RPM Country 50 Singles (Canada)

This song is about pretending to be someone you are not, about leading a false trail for others and for yourself. On the subject of pretenses, the synthesizer—which, from the intro, pretends to imitate the old Compton Static Organs of the big halls and cinemas of the 1930s—is a nice touch. To provide the backing vocals on this song originally performed by the Platters in 1955, and to give her cover the gospel soul she was so fond of, Dolly called on the Waters Family. Her version of "Elusive Butterfly" was already surprisingly understated, but to close this colorful album—sometimes excessively so—Dolly dons her Queen of Country costume and offers an (almost) uncovered interpretation. In 1987, Freddie Mercury took over this song—included on his posthumous album *The Great Pretender* (1992)—the sobriety giving way, on that occasion, to exuberance, which was a tremendous success.

A Dolly-themed exhibit from the CMA Music Festival, held in 2013 at the Music City Convention Center in Nashville, Tennessee.

Country Style: A Diamond Called Dolly Parton

After superstars die, their closets are frequently opened and the clothes that helped shape their image are displayed—or sold. In February–March 2019, the Grammy Museum in Los Angeles paid tribute to Dolly Parton with the exhibition *Diamond in a Rhinestone World: The Costumes of Dolly Parton*, which presented her most iconic outfits (as well as her records, covers, etc.). The title of the event perfectly summed up this facet of the artist, which is not just about appearance: Dolly sparkles like a diamond in a rhinestone world.

A Memory of Rhinestone

Dolly has told the story many times: As a child, she saw a woman dressed and made up in an outrageous way, according to the prevailing standards of the American South at that time. Literally dazzled, she asked her mother who this woman was. "A tramp," answered Avie Lee Parton. So be it, said the little girl—later, she would be a "tramp"!

The star has often been asked about the reasons for so much makeup, vertiginous wigs, and ultra-vivid clothes—in a word, artifices. Dolly Parton has always answered that she loves the glitter, the flamboyance, the light, and the colors. The singer even stated that if she had been born a boy, she would have been a drag queen, just for the fun of dressing up like that, with all that pomp.

It may seem paradoxical to wear so many rhinestones, to show herself to the world as deliciously superficial, while at the same time remaining authentically herself. Like the butterfly, her emblem, and the diamond, a carbon crystal becoming the most precious of stones, Dolly has this extraordinary capacity for transmutation: Once poor and unknown, she has become rich and universally recognized.

In 2019, the exhibition at the Grammy Museum sublimated this aspect of Dolly. According to Michael Sticka, the museum's executive director, these unique items—for the first time on view outside of Dollywood—transported the public through several decades of the career of an infinitely beloved and respected artist.

Another celebration, the same year: Three days after the exhibition's opening, at a gala as sumptuous as it was prestigious, the MusiCares Foundation honored Dolly Parton for her philanthropic work. The star shone brightly with both heart and sequins.

A Fashion Icon

Record sleeves, live performance videos, and photo shoots inspired the design of the exhibition. Of course, the designers were also honored, including Lucy Adams, who created many of the outfits for the star's first album covers, such as this pink, lace-trimmed ruffled dress for *Heartbreaker*. Here, we admire the white dress sewn with sparkling black pearls that Dolly wore in 1984 for the premiere of *Rhinestone*, her film with Sylvester Stallone. Here, it is the white pantsuit—from the Glastonbury (England) concert, adorned with rhinestones, or the pink dress created for the album *Backwoods Barbie*, released in 2008. Long dresses, high wigs, bright colors, short pants, fringes, bustiers set with rhinestones: a festival of materials, colors, and memories provided by this retrospective at the Grammy Museum, a fairy-tale tribute to the universe and personality of Dolly Parton.

Right: Dolly Parton's outfit worn on the cover of *Together Always*, on display at the Grammy Museum (Los Angeles, 2022).

Following spread: Dolly gets a star on the Hollywood Walk of Fame as her *Rhinestone* costar, Sylvester Stallone, looks on.

ALBUM

Once Upon a Christmas

I Believe in Santa Claus . Medley: Winter Wonderland / Sleigh Ride . Christmas Without You .
The Christmas Song . A Christmas to Remember . With Bells On . Silent Night .
The Greatest Gift of All . White Christmas . Once Upon a Christmas

RELEASE DATE
United States: October 29, 1984
Reference: RCA Victor—ASL1-5307
Best US Chart Ranking: 12

The cover of *Once Upon a Christmas,* Dolly's holiday album made with Kenny Rogers (1984).

On December 2, 1984, CBS broadcast a special, *Kenny & Dolly: A Christmas to Remember.* The star couple, Santa Claus / Kenny and Mrs. Claus / Dolly, charmed 30 million viewers with sketches and songs.

Merry Christmas!

Once Upon a Christmas, an album by Dolly Parton and Kenny Rogers, was produced by the latter and David Foster and was released by RCA Victor on October 29, 1984. Dolly wrote four of the ten songs, plus one cowritten with Steve Goldstein (who also wrote and played for Diana Ross and Kim Carnes, among others). This album, on which Kenny and Dolly alternate solos and duets, went double platinum in 1989 and reached number 31 on the Billboard 200, but few singles made it to the charts, despite its overall success. It was nevertheless reissued in 1997.

Long Live the Spirit of Winter!

After some difficulties with scheduling the recording sessions due to the full schedules of both artists, the album was ready in September 1984. Dolly and Kenny had both been raised religiously, and Christmas was a very special time, as it was for many American families. This time of year, dedicated to family, sharing meals, and exchanging gifts, still inspires TV movies, films, and songs in the United States. Unlike Dolly, Kenny Rogers had already released a Christmas album (*Christmas,* in 1981). A break in the middle of winter, this holiday should be a warm moment during which everyone puts aside their problems to devote themselves to their loved ones. The album reflects the importance of this celebration, and we know, as Dolly often stated, how much this holiday—the expectation, the surprises—meant to her as a child. Although very poor, the Partons were, at Christmas, richer for that happiness.

This album also cemented the friendship and respect that bound the two artists together, as evidenced by an article published in *Cashbox* magazine's November 3, 1984, issue. Kenny Rogers confided that when they were together, they were greater than when they were apart, and Dolly went on to confirm that the current between them was really good! They continued to demonstrate this through each of their collaborations, winning over their respective fans.

Album Cover

In this photo by Gene Trindl—who was a prolific photographer of magazine covers—Dolly and Kenny, appearing as Mother and Father Christmas, emerge from a wreath, complicit and playful, next to a reindeer. The back cover shows Dolly behind her little round glasses and Kenny smoking a pipe in his armchair in their "workshop" filled with toys. Both of them look delightfully vintage, mischievous, and welcoming.

DOLLY PARTON ALL THE SONGS **327**

Recording Sessions: Probably due to the team's geographical and scheduling constraints, the recording sessions for the album took place at different studios in August 1984: Lion Share (Los Angeles), Sunset Sound (Hollywood), Evergreen (Nashville), Cecca Sound (Dallas), and Lighthouse Recorders (Los Angeles). The technical team consisted of the following members: Humberto Gatica, Tommy Vicari (sound engineers); Humberto Gatica (mixing), and Wally Traugott (mastering).

Technical Team: Humberto Gatica, Tommy Vicari (sound engineers); Humberto Gatica (mixing); and Wally Traugott (mastering).

For Dolly Addicts

The song "Medley: Winter Wonderland / Sleigh Ride" did not make the charts when it was released in 1984 but reached number 70 on the Billboard Hot Country Songs chart in 1999.

I Believe In Santa Claus

Dolly Parton / 3:30

Vocals: Dolly Parton, Kenny Rogers **Musicians:** Erich Bulling, Jimmy Cox, David Foster, John Hobbs, Randy Waldman: keyboards / Erich Bulling: synthesizer / David Foster: rhythm arrangements / John Goux, Michael Landau, Fred Tackett, Kin Vassy, Billy Joe Walker Jr.: guitar / Dennis Belfield, Joe Chemay, Neil Stubenhaus: bass / Ed Greene, Paul Leim, John Robinson: drums / Paul Leim, Victor Feldman: percussion / Jeremy Lubbock: strings and rhythm arrangements **Backing Vocals:** (?) **Recorded:** August 1984 **Technical Team:** Producers: David Foster, Kenny Rogers / Production Assistant: Debbie Caponetta **Single:** Side A: I Believe in Santa Claus / Side B: Christmas Without You **Release:** RCA Victor, November 23, 1984 (45 rpm ref.: 5352-7-R)

Christmas goes *country*! This song contains everything Dolly Parton believes in: love, hope, God, dreams, miracles...and Santa Claus.

It blows a wind of modernity (for that period) on this number. Witness, from the intro, the pedal steel, the electric guitar, and especially the sound of the eighties snare drum: a big attack, and a lot of reverb, sounding almost synthetic on the chorus. For the verse, back to the traditional country sound with a very classic drums pattern: bass drum and rim shot. The chorus is more pop; keyboards are used to imitate bells. A piano is inserted in the guitar melodies and the sound of the organ, in a teeming mixture, in which children's choirs cheerfully contribute. Kenny Rogers takes the upper voice while Dolly Parton remains in the background, probably to preserve her vocal cords.

Medley: Winter Wonderland / Sleigh Ride

Dick Smith, Felix Bernard / Mitchell Parish, Leroy Anderson / 3:43

Vocals: Dolly Parton **Musicians:** Erich Bulling, Jimmy Cox, David Foster, John Hobbs, Randy Waldman: keyboards / Erich Bulling: synthesizer / David Foster: rhythm arrangements / John Goux, Michael Landau, Fred Tackett, Kin Vassy, Billy Joe Walker Jr.: guitar / Dennis Belfield, Joe Chemay, Neil Stubenhaus: bass / Ed Greene, Paul Leim, John Robinson: drums / Paul Leim, Victor Feldman: percussion / Jeremy Lubbock: strings and rhythm arrangements **Recorded:** August 1984 **Technical Team:** Producers: David Foster, Kenny Rogers / Production Assistant: Debbie Caponetta **Single:** Side A: Medley: Winter Wonderland / Sleigh Ride / Side B: The Christmas Song **Release:** RCA Victor, November 26, 1984 (45 rpm ref.: PB-13944) **Best US Chart Ranking:** 70

This Christmas medley is about how wonderful winter is when we hug each other by the fire or in a sleigh, sliding on the snow, while the bells ring.

Sung by Dolly, it makes extensive use of synthetic keyboards. The rhythm, always very pop, starts on a rather quiet drums pattern with bass drum, rim shot snare, and hi-hat. Then it goes into overdrive during the medley. A break at 2:06 throws the listener into the atmosphere of a musical. The ending seems to be inspired by Stevie Wonder's "Isn't She Lovely" (1976), with the syncopated turning of the keyboard and bass line that has been building up throughout the track.

Once Upon a Christmas is a joyous celebration, though it does also stop to consider people who have a hard time around the holidays.

Christmas Without You

Dolly Parton, Steve Goldstein / 3:55

Vocals: Dolly Parton, Kenny Rogers **Musicians:** Erich Bulling, Jimmy Cox, David Foster, John Hobbs, Randy Waldman: keyboards / Erich Bulling: synthesizer / David Foster: rhythm arrangements / John Goux, Michael Landau, Fred Tackett, Kin Vassy, Billy Joe Walker Jr.: guitar / Dennis Belfield, Joe Chemay, Neil Stubenhaus: bass / Ed Greene, Paul Leim, John Robinson: drums / Paul Leim, Victor Feldman: percussion / Jeremy Lubbock: strings and rhythm arrangements **Recorded:** August 1984 **Technical Team:** Producers: David Foster, Kenny Rogers / Production Assistant: Debbie Caponetta **Single:** Side A: I Believe in Santa Claus / Side B: Christmas Without You **Release:** RCA Victor, November 23, 1984 (45 rpm ref.: 5352-7-R)

In this sad and nostalgic song, the loved one is so badly missed on this Christmas Day that there could be no more wonderful gift than his return.

The introduction provides the first saturated guitar sound of the album. The rhythm section is largely inspired by Stevie Wonder—the beginning of the vocal melody is almost identical to that of "Isn't She Lovely"; the electric guitar melody is reminiscent of Chic guitarist Nile Rodgers. Add to that a percussion section and congas, and the whole piece becomes a testimony to the considerable amount of work that went into writing this song. The chord attacks of the folk guitar with the pick can be heard distinctly, unlike the chords themselves, which are not very perceptible. They stand out more when there is an instrumental "hollow," as at the beginning of the first verse sung by Kenny Rogers.

The old recipe of the semitone upward modulation returns for our maximum enjoyment at 2:33, introduced subtly by a drums break. The two artists answer each other, then alternate singing parts. Dolly Parton gives more power on this track than on the first ones on the album and rises well up in her chest voice. The contrast between the purity of her tone and the slightly hoarse character of Kenny Rogers works wonderfully. A change of rhythm of the keyboards and the electric guitar at 3:05 is maintained until the end. From then on, Kenny Rogers is doubled with a little delay, which produces a slight robotic effect. A very long fade-out, twenty-five seconds long, ends the piece.

1984

John Lithgow in the film *Santa Claus*, which was released in 1985 and directed by Jeannot Szwarc.

SINGLE

The Christmas Song

Mel Tormé, Robert Wells / 3:23

Vocals: Kenny Rogers **Musicians:** Erich Bulling, Jimmy Cox, David Foster, John Hobbs, Randy Waldman: keyboards / Erich Bulling: synthesizer / David Foster: rhythm arrangements / John Goux, Michael Landau, Fred Tackett, Kin Vassy, Billy Joe Walker Jr.: guitar / Dennis Belfield, Joe Chemay, Neil Stubenhaus: bass / Ed Greene, Paul Leim, John Robinson: drums / Paul Leim, Victor Feldman: percussion / Jeremy Lubbock: strings and rhythm arrangements **Recorded:** August 1984 **Technical Team:** Producers: David Foster, Kenny Rogers / Production Assistant: Debbie Caponetta **Single:** Side A: Medley: Winter Wonderland / Sleigh Ride / Side B: The Christmas Song **Release:** RCA Victor, November 26, 1984 (45 rpm ref.: PB-13944) **Best US Chart Ranking:** 70

This sweet and tender song evokes the smell of roasting chestnuts, noses frozen by the cold, turkey on the table, and children from one to ninety-two years old with bright eyes, in eager anticipation of Santa's arrival.

Like "Silent Night," another track on the album sung solo by Kenny Rogers, this one begins with the keyboard only, before the violins enter, followed by the whole orchestra. The profusion of information in the same range, with violins, keyboards, guitar, and voice, makes for a very busy effect.

A Christmas To Remember

Dolly Parton / 3:41

Vocals: Dolly Parton, Kenny Rogers **Musicians:** Erich Bulling, Jimmy Cox, David Foster, John Hobbs, Randy Waldman: keyboards / Erich Bulling: synthesizer / David Foster: rhythm arrangements / John Goux, Michael Landau, Fred Tackett, Kin Vassy, Billy Joe Walker Jr.: guitar / Dennis Belfield, Joe Chemay, Neil Stubenhaus: bass / Ed Greene, Paul Leim, John Robinson: drums / Paul Leim, Victor Feldman: percussion / Jeremy Lubbock: strings and rhythm arrangements **Backing Vocals:** (?) **Recorded:** August 1984 **Technical Team:** Producers: David Foster, Kenny Rogers / Production Assistant: Debbie Caponetta

The song tells of a brief but wonderful Christmas romance. This encounter has made the winter as sweet as spring. The narrator would so much like to repeat the experience again, the following year, for another unforgettable Christmas!

Although they are very discreet, there are backing vocals on this track (they can also be heard in "The Greatest Gift of All"). This is a pop song, with only a few instruments: keyboards; a percussion section, including congas; a strings ensemble; a guitar playing chords; and bells. During the intro, before the drums enter, there is something that sounds like a finger click—or a rim shot snare hit?—with little direct sound and a lot of reverb. Also noteworthy: a bridge with delay and reverb on the vocals at 2:25, and a false ending at 2:55. The song ends with a reprise of the chorus ad lib.

The year 1984 was a prolific one for Dolly, shown here in New York. She released an album and starred in the movie *Rhinestone*, for which she also wrote the soundtrack.

With Bells On

Dolly Parton / 2:42

Vocals: Dolly Parton, Kenny Rogers **Musicians:** Erich Bulling, Jimmy Cox, David Foster, John Hobbs, Randy Waldman: keyboards / Erich Bulling: synthesizer / David Foster: rhythm arrangements / John Goux, Michael Landau, Fred Tackett, Kin Vassy, Billy Joe Walker Jr.: guitar / Dennis Belfield, Joe Chemay, Neil Stubenhaus: bass / Ed Greene, Paul Leim, John Robinson: drums / Paul Leim, Victor Feldman: percussion / Jeremy Lubbock: strings and rhythm arrangements **Recorded:** August 1984 **Technical Team:** Producers: David Foster, Kenny Rogers / Production Assistant: Debbie Caponetta

After a long absence, the narrator is happy to return home, where the whole family is preparing for Christmas. A heart-warming occasion.

The piece begins with the melody of the chimes of Big Ben. The arrival of Santa Claus is announced by the tambourine, which reproduces the sound of the sleigh bells, and the synthesizer, which imitates the sound of the bells. Apart from a pedal steel solo, the codes of the simplest and most effective country music are exploited here: drums pattern, bass on all the beats, funk guitar strums, and piano accompaniment. A sprinkling of Christmas sounds, a good mix...and the result is Christmas *country*!

Silent Night

Joseph Mohr, Franz Gruber / 3:18

Vocals: Kenny Rogers **Musicians:** Erich Bulling, Jimmy Cox, David Foster, John Hobbs, Randy Waldman: keyboards / Erich Bulling: synthesizer / David Foster: rhythm arrangements / John Goux, Michael Landau, Fred Tackett, Kin Vassy, Billy Joe Walker Jr.: guitar / Dennis Belfield, Joe Chemay, Neil Stubenhaus: bass / Ed Greene, Paul Leim, John Robinson: drums / Paul Leim, Victor Feldman: percussion / Jeremy Lubbock: strings and rhythm arrangements **Recorded:** August 1984 **Technical Team:** Producers: David Foster, Kenny Rogers / Production Assistant: Debbie Caponetta

Sung by Kenny Rogers solo, "Silent Night" glorifies, for all believers, the coming into the world of the baby Jesus. The keyboard accompanies him on the first verse, then the violins and a very minimalist bass-drums combination come in. The crescendo continues on the third verse before ending gently.

When you listen through headphones, the sound of the keyboard moves from left to right and back again in waves (one of them is clearly audible in the intro). This is the effect of the Leslie cabinets, consisting of a rotating speaker in a separate module from the keyboard, and two microphones placed in the path of the speaker.

Pictured are three common ingredients to a Christmas in New York: Santa Claus, a Salvation Army volunteer, and the famous Rockefeller Center Christmas tree.

SINGLE

The Greatest Gift Of All

John Jarvis / 3:46

Vocals: Dolly Parton, Kenny Rogers **Musicians:** Erich Bulling, Jimmy Cox, David Foster, John Hobbs, Randy Waldman: keyboards / Erich Bulling: synthesizer / David Foster: rhythm arrangements / John Goux, Michael Landau, Fred Tackett, Kin Vassy, Billy Joe Walker Jr.: guitar / Dennis Belfield, Joe Chemay, Neil Stubenhaus: bass / Ed Greene, Paul Leim, John Robinson: drums / Paul Leim, Victor Feldman: percussion / Jeremy Lubbock: strings and rhythm arrangements **Backing Vocals:** (?) **Recorded:** August 1984 **Technical Team:** Producers: David Foster, Kenny Rogers / Production Assistant: Debbie Caponetta **Single:** Side A: The Greatest Gift of All / Side B: White Christmas **Release:** RCA Victor, November 26, 1984 (45 rpm ref.: PB-13945) **Best US Chart Ranking:** 53 on the Billboard Hot Country Songs; 40 on the Billboard Adult Contemporary

On this Christmas Eve, the most beautiful gift is that he is in love with her, and she with him. This song is, more generally, a message of peace and love for everyone, everywhere in the world.

Back to pop with this ballad. The instrumentation is restrained at the beginning, with a keyboard intro, to which are added folk guitar arpeggios, then the bass and drums intervene, with a lot of reverb on the snare. On the second verse, for Dolly's vocals, violins enter with a flute melody. This is the third song on the album with backing vocals. They are a little more prominent than on "A Christmas to Remember," but remain discreet. We hear them more when the text becomes a prayer, and then we return to the gospel spirit. The voices of the two singers seem to be doubled (i.e., recorded twice or more and mixed together) from the third verse, in the tutti part, which begins with a drums break enabling the modulation. The pedal steel, which had a prominent place in all Dolly Parton's albums, is more unusual here. This is a real turning point in the style of the songwriter, who has become more deeply involved in pop.

White Christmas, starring Bing Crosby, was released in 1954.

Irving Berlin, successful songwriter and musical comedy pioneer.

White Christmas
Irving Berlin / 3:06

Vocals: Dolly Parton **Musicians:** Erich Bulling, Jimmy Cox, David Foster, John Hobbs, Randy Waldman: keyboards / Erich Bulling: synthesizer / David Foster: rhythm arrangements / John Goux, Michael Landau, Fred Tackett, Kin Vassy, Billy Joe Walker Jr.: guitar / Dennis Belfield, Joe Chemay, Neil Stubenhaus: bass / Ed Greene, Paul Leim, John Robinson: drums / Paul Leim, Victor Feldman: percussion / Jeremy Lubbock: strings and rhythm arrangements **Recorded:** August 1984 **Technical Team:** Producers: David Foster, Kenny Rogers / Production Assistant: Debbie Caponetta **Single:** Side A: The Greatest Gift of All / Side B: White Christmas **Release:** RCA Victor, November 26, 1984 (45 rpm ref.: PB-13945) **Best US Chart Ranking:** 53 on the Billboard Hot Country Songs; 40 on the Billboard Adult Contemporary

"White Christmas," written in the early 1940s, is *the one.* These lyrics, by the great Irving Berlin, focus on the essential elements: the joys of a snowy Christmas, as in childhood. Here, Dolly Parton is discreetly accompanied by the violins, a reverb, and the keyboards. One of them plays this accompaniment with an electronic timbre while the synthesizer intervenes, at 0:58 in particular. A clarinet can be heard at 1:55, although the instrument is not credited; the perception of the vibrations of the wood of the reed and the very soft attacks of the notes seem, however, to confirm its presence—if produced by a synthesizer, the sound would have been more metallic. No Kenny Rogers on this piece; his voice was probably not suited to this kind of instrumentation.

Once Upon A Christmas
Dolly Parton / 4:21

Vocals: Dolly Parton, Kenny Rogers **Musicians:** Erich Bulling, Jimmy Cox, David Foster, John Hobbs, Randy Waldman: keyboards / Erich Bulling: synthesizer / David Foster: rhythm arrangements / John Goux, Michael Landau, Fred Tackett, Kin Vassy, Billy Joe Walker Jr.: guitar / Dennis Belfield, Joe Chemay, Neil Stubenhaus: bass / Ed Greene, Paul Leim, John Robinson: drums / Paul Leim, Victor Feldman: percussion / Jeremy Lubbock: strings and rhythm arrangements **Recorded:** August 1984 **Technical Team:** Producers: David Foster, Kenny Rogers / Production Assistant: Debbie Caponetta

This Christmas classic celebrates the birth of the Savior in Bethlehem.

Musically, too, it is a classic piece. After a powerful intro played by the strings and punctuated by the timpani, the story begins softly, spoken by Kenny Rogers. Then Dolly Parton's singing announces the event, in which everyone rejoices: Jesus is born. A major key passage for the duet singing expresses the general enthusiasm; it precedes the orchestral part, with the repetition of the theme of the intro, then the apotheosis of the communal prayer. This piece is played by a symphony orchestra, with piano, string ensemble (double basses, cellos, violas, violins), brass (trumpets, trombones, horns), woodwinds (clarinets, oboes, bassoons), and harmonic percussion (timbales), complemented by a choir elegantly singing, "Hosanna." "Once Upon a Christmas" concludes beautifully.

IRVING BERLIN'S
White Christmas

VISTA VISION

STARRING **BING CROSBY · DANNY KAYE**
ROSEMARY CLOONEY
VERA-ELLEN

COLOR BY
TECHNICOLOR

A PARAMOUNT PICTURE

with DEAN JAGGER · Lyrics and Music by IRVING BERLIN
Produced by Robert Emmett Dolan · Directed by MICHAEL CURTIZ
Dances and Musical Numbers Staged by Robert Alton
Written for the screen by Norman Krasna, Norman Panama and Melvin Frank

(L to R) Kenny Rogers, Dolly Parton, and Barry Gibb promoting *Islands in the Stream* in 1983.

Kenny Rogers: "Magic Man"

Among the friends and artists close to Dolly Parton, both personally and professionally, the one who has particularly counted is Kenny Rogers ever since their meeting on the set of the *Dolly* show in 1976. Singer, composer, and bass player, he entered the world of music at the end of the 1950s, then the world of cinema. Popular with country music fans, the artist did not limit himself to this musical genre, and touched on jazz, pop, folk, and rock. As a multidisciplinary artist, he also moved from singing and songwriting to acting in television and film.

Inducted into the Country Music Hall of Fame in 2013, the singer in his own right has sold over 120 million records, one diamond album, twenty platinum albums, and eleven gold albums, as well as having numerous awards to his name.

An Artistic Spirit, a Taste for Work

The young Texan Kenneth Ray Rogers (1938–2020)—who is believed to have had Irish and American Indian origins on his father's side—was one of eight children, but he did not experience the same poverty as Dolly Parton. With a mother who was a caregiver and a father who was a carpenter, the family was simply broke, and a peanut butter sandwich was often served as a meal.

As a young man, Kenny got his first taste of show business when he won a talent show at the Texan Theatre in 1949. He worked odd jobs as a hotel restaurant clerk and hat store sweeper before attending the University of Houston, graduating in 1956. In the late 1950s, he began his career with the Houston-based group the Scholars and a debut track, "The Poor Little Doggie." After releasing a few solo songs, including "That Crazy Feeling" in 1958, Rogers joined the band of jazz singer Bobby Doyle. In 1966, he joined the folk ensemble New Christy Minstrels, in which he sang and played bass and double bass. In 1967, he and other members of this group founded First Edition. His first hit, "Just Dropped In (To See What Condition My Condition Was In)," a psychedelic rock song, climbed to number 5 on the Billboard Hot 100 chart. Led by Rogers, the band gradually evolved into a more country-oriented group before breaking up in the mid-1970s. Rogers then began a long and fruitful solo career marked by major collaborations, including duets with singers Dottie West, Dolly Parton, and Sheena Easton, and writing lyrics with Lionel Richie.

A Star Is Born

While his single "Lucille," released in 1977, sold more than 5 million copies, his signature song, "The Gambler," earned

Dolly and Kenny onstage at Nassau Coliseum in New York on August 29, 1985.

him a Grammy Award in 1980. *The Gambler* also became a series of TV movies, three of which were Emmy-nominated. Like Dolly Parton, Rogers appeared in several films—including the title role of a racing driver in Daniel Petrie's *Six Pack* (1982)—and appeared on numerous television shows.

In 1985, along with Harry Belafonte, Michael Jackson, Lionel Richie, and others, he joined a group of forty-five artists, USA for Africa, whose hit single "We Are the World" went on to sell more than 20 million copies worldwide. Rogers did not stop there: He composed for the films *Convoy* by Sam Peckinpah (1978), *Urban Cowboy* by James Bridges (1980), and *The Big Lebowski* by Joel and Ethan Coen (1998). Barry, Maurice, and Robin Gibb wrote "Islands in the Stream" for Kenny's 1983 album *Eyes That See in the Dark*, which he sang as a duet with Dolly Parton and which became a hit. In 1991, Rogers also cofounded the Kenny Rogers Roasters restaurant chain with the former CEO of Kentucky Fried Chicken.

Alter Ego, Loyal Friend

Throughout their fifty-year friendship, Dolly Parton and Kenny Rogers combined their talents by singing together, thrilling audiences, and climbing the charts. Both were captivating through their optimism, their radiance, and their ability to give back what they received from the public, through love and support for charity. On the other hand, there are no similarities with Dolly's personal life, as the singer's life was an eventful one, with five marriages and five children.

After almost seven decades of music, singing and performing, sports, and photography, the artist Kenny Rogers, who was suffering from cancer, retired. In a video tweeted on March 20, 2020, Dolly expressed her emotion, moving her fans and those of Kenny in mourning the passing of her friend, that "magical man," as she called him, and pointing out, "You never know how much you love somebody until they're gone."

ALBUM

Real Love

Think About Love . Tie Our Love (In a Double Knot) . We Got Too Much .
It's Such a Heartache . Don't Call It Love . Real Love . I Can't Be True .
Once in a Very Blue Moon . Come Back to Me . I Hope You're Never Happy

RELEASE DATE
United States: January 21, 1985
Reference: RCA Victor—AHL1-5414
Best US Chart Ranking: 9

Can Love Ever Be Real?

A very eighties opus, *Real Love* is Dolly Parton's twenty-seventh solo album, produced by David Malloy and released by RCA Victor on January 21, 1985. Dolly wrote four of the ten songs and sang "Real Love" as a duet with Kenny Rogers. A double CD reissue with *Burlap & Satin* was released during her European tour in 2007.

Flashback

We are in 1985 and the star had just come back from a personal hell, both physical and emotional. Getting herself back on track, she discovered a new determination to live better. Since her arrival in Nashville, she did not stop for one second until she became a superstar as a songwriter, a singer, and an actress.

Going back in time...Dolly Parton's strategy to reach her goals entailed taking some risks. So in 1967 she left her friend and producer Fred Foster of Monument Records, with whom she had one of her first hits, "Dumb Blonde," to sign with RCA Victor under the guidance of Porter Wagoner. Dolly worked extensively for *The Porter Wagoner Show*, and the recording of their albums as a duo lasted seven long, intensive years. In 1974, instead of sticking with a now-familiar process, the star decided to go solo and do her own thing. She kept her contract with RCA Victor, hosted her own show, *Dolly!*, and then called a halt to the TV adventure after one season because it was not what she wanted to do. She started her own band and set out to conquer the pop audience.

Flying on Her Own Wings

As she confided in March 1983 to Terry Wogan, who hosted a BBC talk show, Dolly had been dreaming about Dollywood for a few years. She knew that there was a place in the Great Smoky Mountains National Park where she would build an imaginary town that would offer many attractions, shows, and concerts, and would house hotels and restaurants and even a Dolly Parton museum. The name of the park came to her one day when she was in Hollywood and had the idea of replacing the *H* with the *D* in *Dolly*. Simple and effective. Dolly was not content with dreaming: She was making this project a reality, which would see the light of day in 1986 and continue to develop. In July 1984, an interview was published, jointly conducted by the writer Maura Moynihan and the prince of pop art, Andy Warhol,[5] in which the star answered with sincerity—she recalled her childhood, the beginning of her career, and admitted to having lost her footing, but was in full reconstruction mode. Dolly has this incredible capacity to change, to know how to give up what is comfortable, known, mastered, in order to go further down the road of her dreams and ambitions. Nineteen eighty-five sounded the death knell of her relationship with RCA Victor, putting an end to a collaboration of almost twenty years. Wishing to have a total independence, Dolly thought about creating her own label—Blue Eye Records, which she later founded in 1994, with Steve Buckingham.

Album Cover

On the front-cover photo by Richard D'Amore, the Hollywood touch is undeniable: the focus on Dolly Parton's face and eyes, ultrablond, and shrouded in a pinkish opalescence, gives the star an image that is both evanescent and glamorous. The back cover displays the same ambience in a full-length photo, but the "young bride in a long dress in front of a marble fireplace" pose seems rather conventional.

The sonic production of "Tie Our Love (In a Double Knot)" recalls Paul Simon's classic album *Graceland*, which was recorded in 1985, and famously included vocals from Ladysmith Black Mambazo.

Think About Love

Richard "Spady" Brannan, Tom Campbell / 3:26

Vocals: Dolly Parton **Musicians:** Billy Joe Walker Jr., Dean Parks: guitar / Bob Glaub: bass / Paul Leim: drums / Bobby Hall, Lenny Castro: percussion / Randy McCormick, Steve Goldstein: keyboards, strings arrangements / Tom Scott: saxophone **Backing Vocals:** Gene Morford, Jennifer Kimball, Richard Marx, Terry Williams **Recorded:** Rumbo Recorders, Hollywood, January 1985 **Technical Team:** Producer: David Malloy **Single:** Side A: Think About Love / Side B: Come Back to Me **Release:** RCA Victor, November 11, 1985 (45 rpm ref.: PB-14218) **Best Chart Ranking:** 1 on the Billboard Hot Country Songs (USA); 1 on the RPM Country Singles (Canada)

The narrator sings to tell the one she loves that he must think of her when he thinks of love, because only she can love him as much. On the production side, we remain on the clear line of the 1980s: The synthesizers, crystalline and percussive, are out in front, while the electric guitar rhythm is played in palm mute with a clean sound, chorused as it should be, and embellished with a light delay to establish its position well in the mix. With the robotic drums a very pronounced gated reverb is applied on the snare drum; we can distinguish some electronic pad sounds, the restrained and contractual bass, the keyboard playing with a stab on the eighth note on the choruses and the synth lead (a Hammond-type organ, set on its high harmonics range), reverberated, discreetly positioned at the bottom right. The overall feel, airy and bouncy, still has a certain freshness to it; it is therefore not difficult to imagine the effect it produced on the public in 1985. Another hit for Dolly Parton and her team.

Tie Our Love (In A Double Knot)

Jeff Silbar, John Reid / 3:27

Vocals: Dolly Parton **Musicians:** Billy Joe Walker Jr., Dean Parks:
guitar / Bob Glaub: bass / Paul Leim: drums / Bobby Hall, Lenny
Castro: percussion / Randy McCormick, Steve Goldstein: keyboards,
strings arrangements / Tom Scott: saxophone **Backing Vocals:**
Gene Morford, Jennifer Kimball, Richard Marx, Terry Williams
Recorded: Rumbo Recorders, Hollywood, October–November
1984 **Technical Team:** Producer: David Malloy **Single:** Side A:
Tie Our Love (In a Double Knot) / Side B: I Hope You're Never Happy
Release: RCA Victor, April 7, 1986 (45 rpm ref.: PB-14297)
Best Chart Ranking: 17 on the Billboard Hot Country Songs
(USA); 20 on the RPM Country Singles (Canada)

The narrator of this song suggests to her lover that they
tie together their feelings for each other so that they last
forever, because she doesn't want a single night but an
eternal love.

This 4/4 number with a fast tempo once again features
synthesizers and a clean, chorused electric guitar sound.
This time, the bass's role is more important: It provides
a large part of the rhythmic drive, with the drums, of
course, whose snare drum now seems to be unable to do
without its trademark gated reverb. The choruses, successively in thirds and in response on the chorus "Tie
our love in a double knot," contribute largely to its catchy
feeling. The production is reminiscent of Paul Simon's
Graceland (recorded in 1985 and released in 1986) and
Johnny Clegg and Savuka's *Third World Child* (recorded
between 1986 and 1987, and released in 1987). Without
falling into the world music genre, very much in vogue at
the time, by recruiting David Malloy, Dolly acquired the
services of a producer at the cutting edge.

We Got Too Much

Dolly Parton / 3:16

Vocals: Dolly Parton **Musicians:** Billy Joe Walker Jr., Dean Parks:
guitar / Bob Glaub: bass / Paul Leim: drums / Bobby Hall, Lenny Castro:
percussion / Randy McCormick, Steve Goldstein: keyboards, strings

Conga drum player Lenny Castro (right) and pianist Joe Sample in 1985.

arrangements / Tom Scott: saxophone **Backing Vocals:** Gene
Morford, Jennifer Kimball, Richard Marx, Terry Williams **Recorded:**
Rumbo Recorders, Hollywood, October–November 1984
Technical Team: Producer: David Malloy **Single:** Side A: Don't Call It
Love / Side B: We Got Too Much **Release:** RCA Victor, January 1985
(45 rpm ref.: PB-13987) **Best Chart Ranking:** 3 on the Billboard Hot
Country Songs (USA); 5 on the RPM Country Singles (Canada)

This is a classic Dolly Parton love song, with the narrator
trying to convince her lover that this other woman who has
been messing with his head will never love him as well
as she does. Even though they feel they are losing themselves in their relationship, they share too much to make
it worthwhile to look elsewhere. It had been a while since
Dolly had graced us with a good "other woman" song, a
gap filled with "We Got Too Much"—in an optimistic and
upbeat version, however. It's not world music, but the percussion of Lenny Castro and the syncopated electric guitar
rhythm give it a pleasant, exotic perfume. The synthesizers
are present, of course, merging at times with the electric
guitar in grainy stabs, arpeggios, cottony leads, or organ-
like chord layers. Another carefully produced track that
would surely hit the charts. Dolly Parton, David Malloy, and
the session musicians of Rumbo Recorders can congratulate
themselves for this number.

In 1985, Dolly Parton had just left RCA Victor, and she was thinking of founding her own label—Blue Eye Records—which would eventually happen in 1994.

"Don't Call It Love" is a cover of a song recorded by Kim Carnes in 1981.

It's Such A Heartache

Even Stevens, Hillary Kanter / 3:25

Vocals: Dolly Parton **Musicians:** Billy Joe Walker Jr., Dean Parks: guitar / Bob Glaub: bass / Paul Leim: drums / Bobby Hall, Lenny Castro: percussion / Randy McCormick, Steve Goldstein: keyboards, strings arrangements / Tom Scott: saxophone **Backing Vocals:** Gene Morford, Jennifer Kimball, Richard Marx, Terry Williams **Recorded:** Rumbo Recorders, Hollywood, October–November 1984 **Technical Team:** Producer: David Malloy

In this sad song, the narrator, in the grip of a huge heartbreak, cannot stop her heart from breaking or her hands from shaking, so great is her pain. This is the first real "sad-ass song" on the album, but sad as the lyrics are, the production of the time still gives an upbeat, hopeful, and combative feel to the most tragic songs—Dolly did not wait until the 1980s to become an expert in handling this kind of paradox. The fireworks of the synthesizers, the punch of a gated reverb on the snare, or the shimmering sound of a clean electric guitar played in a palm mute and passed through a chorus effect are not equal to the energy contained in Dolly's voice and her sometimes sensitive but never self-indulgent interpretation. Even with a broken heart, Dolly Parton is always moving forward.

Don't Call It Love

Dean Pitchford, Tom Snow / 3:16

Vocals: Dolly Parton **Musicians:** Billy Joe Walker Jr., Dean Parks: guitar / Bob Glaub: bass / Paul Leim: drums / Bobby Hall, Lenny Castro: percussion / Randy McCormick, Steve Goldstein: keyboards, strings arrangements / Tom Scott: saxophone **Backing Vocals:** Gene Morford, Jennifer Kimball, Richard Marx, Terry Williams **Recorded:** Rumbo Recorders, Hollywood, October–November 1984 **Technical Team:** Producer: David Malloy **Single:** Side A: Don't Call It Love / Side B: We Got Too Much **Release:** RCA Victor, January 1985 (45 rpm ref.: PB-13987) **Best Chart Ranking:** 3 on the Billboard Hot Country Songs (USA); 5 on the RPM Country Singles (Canada)

"Don't call it love / 'Cause that ain't enough," the narrator tells her man, in this song originally recorded by Kim Carnes in 1981. Another very upbeat midtempo number, still in 4/4. There is an interesting key change on the bridge at 1:41 that leads into a single tone modulation (not the traditional semitone above); this accommodates the first saxophone solo on the album, played by Tom Scott, and ends the song with an extra degree of intensity.

Dolly Parton and Kenny Rogers always drew a crowd whenever they appeared together in public.

Real Love

David Malloy, Richard "Spady" Brannan, Randy McCormick / 3:54

Vocals: Dolly Parton, Kenny Rogers **Musicians:** Billy Joe Walker Jr., Dean Parks: guitar / Bob Glaub: bass / Paul Leim: drums / Bobby Hall, Lenny Castro: percussion / Randy McCormick, Steve Goldstein: keyboards, strings arrangements / Tom Scott: saxophone **Backing Vocals:** Gene Morford, Jennifer Kimball, Richard Marx, Terry Williams **Recorded:** Rumbo Recorders, Hollywood, October–November 1984 **Technical Team:** Producer: David Malloy **Single:** Side A: Real Love / Side B: I Can't Be True **Release:** RCA Victor, April 29, 1985 (45 rpm ref.: PB-14058) **Best Chart Ranking:** 1 on the Billboard Hot Country Songs (USA); 1 on the RPM Country Singles (Canada)

During the February 1985 tour, HBO filmed a Dolly Parton concert with Kenny Rogers and extracted a video clip for the single "Real Love." Dolly might have written some of the lyrics of this song herself: powerful, authentic love, lovers who dream, who struggle sometimes but love each other deeply.

An ode to love for a charming duo, even though the song did not meet with the same success as "Islands in the Stream." It is a midtempo ballad in a rather classical style. The voices of Kenny Rogers and Dolly Parton blend perfectly, especially on the choruses, where Kenny harmonizes at the fifth. The result, which is especially catchy, enables him to find the slightly saturated grain at the top of his register in his chest voice. For the rest, as always: the army of synthesizers, a strings arrangement confined to the unison in the high register, an ascetic bass-drums combination, and an electric guitar solo after the second chorus, followed by a modulation of a semitone (this time, the tradition is respected). Nothing was left to chance by Dolly Parton and David Malloy: All the ingredients are brought together for "Real Love" to be a chart-topping hit at that time.

I Can't Be True

Dolly Parton / 3:18

Vocals: Dolly Parton **Musicians:** Billy Joe Walker Jr., Dean Parks: guitar / Bob Glaub: bass / Paul Leim: drums / Bobby Hall, Lenny Castro: percussion / Randy McCormick, Steve Goldstein: keyboards, strings arrangements / Tom Scott: saxophone **Backing Vocals:** Gene Morford, Jennifer Kimball, Richard Marx, Terry Williams **Recorded:** Rumbo Recorders, Hollywood, October–November 1984 **Technical Team:** Producer: David Malloy **Single:** Side A: Real Love / Side B: I Can't Be True **Release:** RCA Victor, April 29, 1985 (45 rpm ref.: PB-14058) **Best Chart Ranking:** 1 on the Billboard Hot Country Songs (USA); 1 on the RPM Country Singles (Canada)

The narrator confesses to her lover that she has a weakness for men, that she can become inflamed for the pleasure of feeling the first emotions of a new love, again and again. He has nothing to do with it; it comes from her.

Musically, this Dolly Parton composition is a real recreational indulgence for her and her musicians. Back to basics: Everyone seems to appreciate the exercise, and one can hear it. After the first chorus, the electric guitar riffs rain down and showcase thirty years of rock 'n' roll. Bob Glaub's unstoppable walking bass clings to Paul Leim's drums, which drive straight ahead. The old-fashioned doo-wop choirs impart their syncopated energy, and Dolly does an Elvis Presley–like tremolo, showing once again the full extent of her vocal range. A tribute to the rock 'n' roll of the 1950s plus a touch of honky-tonk, with a production at the cutting edge of its time.

Once In A Very Blue Moon

Pat Alger, Gene Levine / 3:45

Vocals: Dolly Parton **Musicians:** Billy Joe Walker Jr., Dean Parks: guitar / Bob Glaub: bass / Paul Leim: drums / Bobby Hall, Lenny Castro: percussion / Randy McCormick, Steve Goldstein: keyboards, strings arrangements / Tom Scott: saxophone **Backing Vocals:** Gene Morford, Jennifer Kimball, Richard Marx, Terry Williams **Recorded:** Rumbo Recorders, Hollywood, October–November 1984 **Technical Team:** Producer: David Malloy

The narrator receives a letter from her departed love, who wants to know if she is well and if she misses him. The song's idiomatic title provides an explicit answer: as rarely as the appearance of a second full moon in a single month. This is the first slow song on the album, introduced by Steve Goldstein on piano (probably a Kawai Electric Grand or Yamaha CP-80) and a flutelike lead played on a synthesizer. To create the announcement effect, the first wave of strings arrives at the end of the intro, then disappears immediately and reappears at the second cycle of the first verse. One can feel immediately that the arrangement will unashamedly embrace the syrupy mode, and indeed, all the ingredients are there: piano playing full of romantic emphasis, cheesy synth lead, strings perched in the high end of the spectrum, clean and discreet electric guitar, bass, and drums not making a fuss, and velvety backing vocals. Generally restrained in her interpretation, Dolly plays the game to the full, and we hear the actress in this number: with many plaintive inflections and throat effects for the intimate part and amplitude modulations (volume) for the choruses in chest voice, but always with a certain reserve. A successful exercise in style perfectly mastered by Dolly. It should be said that this is, of course, far from her first outing in this genre.

Come Back To Me

Dolly Parton / 3:36

Vocals: Dolly Parton **Musicians:** Billy Joe Walker Jr., Dean Parks: guitar / Bob Glaub: bass / Paul Leim: drums / Bobby Hall, Lenny Castro: percussion / Randy McCormick, Steve Goldstein: keyboards, strings arrangements / Tom Scott: saxophone **Backing Vocals:** Gene Morford, Jennifer Kimball, Richard Marx, Terry Williams **Recorded:** Rumbo Recorders, Hollywood, October–November 1984 **Technical Team:** Producer: David Malloy **Single:** Side A: Think About Love / Side B: Come Back to Me **Release:** RCA Victor, November 11, 1985 (45 rpm ref.: PB-14218) **Best Chart Ranking:** 1 on the Billboard Hot Country Songs (USA); 1 on the RPM Country Singles (Canada)

This poetic song evokes a separation, the time needed to get over it, the heartbreak, the memories, the lack of the other. All this in a different kind of slow song. With its keyboard chords in sixteenth-note Motown style and its doo-wop–inspired chorus, we are in the middle of a sixties bubblegum–pop–rhythm & blues pastiche, coated with an eighties sauce. We can see in this song, written by Dolly Parton, a wink to the mainstream scene of the early 1960s (much as "I Can't Be True" was her tribute to the rock 'n' roll of the 1950s). Dolly had, in fact, relatively little involvement in this scene as a solo artist—apart from a handful of singles, including "Puppy Love" / "Girl Left Alone" (released in 1959, the year she turned thirteen)—until her first solo album, the classic *Hello, I'm Dolly*, released in 1967.

I Hope You're Never Happy

Dolly Parton / 3:55

Vocals: Dolly Parton **Musicians:** Billy Joe Walker Jr., Dean Parks: guitar / Bob Glaub: bass / Paul Leim: drums / Bobby Hall, Lenny Castro: percussion / Randy McCormick, Steve Goldstein: keyboards, strings arrangements / Tom Scott: saxophone **Backing Vocals:** Gene Morford, Jennifer Kimball, Richard Marx, Terry Williams **Recorded:** Rumbo Recorders, Hollywood, October–November 1984 **Technical Team:** Producer: David Malloy

The narrator makes it clear: She is not like those heroines in novels or movies who accept the departure of the other person and wish him good luck. On the contrary, with the humor of a songwriter, she wishes him nothing but trouble and, above all, that he will never know happiness in the arms of another.

Since the early 1980s, Dolly liked to end her albums with more traditional material. This one could have been recorded in Nashville during the great RCA Studio B era, except for a few playing and production details. On the mixing side, the sound of the drums gives away its period most; on the instrumentation side, the synthesizer for the strings arrangement, of course; and on the playing side, the electric guitar syncopations in a style specific to the eighties and their opening on African music (and its derivatives) in particular. A perfect setting for this gently vengeful piece, where Dolly can give free rein to her hillbilly guile. An elegant snub to conclude this resolutely eighties album.

On July 16, 1986, Dolly Parton cut the ceremonial ribbon and officially opened her amusement park, Dollywood.

From Hollywood to Dollywood: Dolly Celebrates Her Native Tennessee

The American nation has a long history of creating amusement parks, but it does not have a monopoly on the creation of these places of entertainment. The oldest in the world is the Gingerbread Fair, ancestor of the Foire du Trône (France), founded in 957, followed in 1133 by the Bartholomew Fair (United Kingdom) and in 1810 by the Oktoberfest (Germany). In the United States, it was not until 1846 that the Lake Compounce Park (Connecticut) opened. These old fairs and brand-new parks offer attractions, food, drink, sleep, and fun based on a theme, and intense sensations on the roller coaster or Ferris wheel, among other things.

In 1961, the future Dollywood, whose theme was inspired by the Civil War, was called Rebel Railroad. In 1970, it changed hands for the first time and was renamed Goldrush Junction; then in 1976, for its final season, it was simply called Goldrush before becoming the Silver Dollar City Tennessee in 1977. In a little more than two decades, the inhabitants of the Pigeon Forge (Tennessee) area had seen several types of parks, until Dolly Parton arrived in 1986, determined to make Dollywood a permanent success.

Creating and Re-creating Her World

The theme is clear in the title: Dollywood stages Dolly Parton's world, promoting her native region, the heritage and talents of Tennessee, and country music with a museum and many platforms for the artists. The park contributed a significant economic breath of fresh air to the region: From the first year, more than one million visitors came to Dollywood. Some took the *Dollywood Express*, an authentic old steam engine that crossed the Great Smoky Mountains for five miles—enough to escape. Others attended performances at the Back Porch Theater or took a stroll through the park. At the Showstreet Palace Theater, Dolly, as hostess, presented her TV series *Heartstrings*, which featured eight of her most famous songs. The park naturally provides accommodation: in cabins in the heart of the Smokies, luxury chalets inspired by the star's childhood cabin, or in comfortable hotels, such as the family-friendly DreamMore Resort. For a quiet and warm evening, you can enjoy a typically American feast at Dolly Parton's Stampede, or regional specialties in an attractive mill, the Grist Mill, or even opt for the *Pirates Voyage Dinner & Show*, a show based on Blackbeard, with pirate battles, set to music by Dolly Parton and Mark Bryner.

Between tradition and modernity, Dollywood expands and evolves according to the imagination and creations of the star and her team, which includes her close circle.

A Dreamer and a Businesswoman

Dolly Parton is not the 100 percent owner of the location, still owned and operated by the Herschend family, who owned the former Silver Dollar City park and owns more than twenty parks in the United States. After buying shares from them, the businesswoman developed her world around its reputation. In 2010, the star won the most prestigious industry prize, the Liseberg Applause Award, before receiving many other awards.

Dollywood illustrates the multiple facets of the star. Each area of the park represents an imaginary world, a character trait of the artist, from her relationship with Tennessee to her personal, family, or collective history. By investing in both land and entertainment, Dolly Parton emphasizes the importance of shared moments, fun, and meals together, in a place that allows one to forget reality. In her autobiography,[1] we learn that in the Parton family the only leisure activities were playing music, singing, and telling stories...while the young Dolly dreamed of a bright and glorious future. We also discover to what extent these meetings, in the family or in church, around a meal, at Christmas, or on any other occasion, are the fabric of daily life. Dollywood thus appears as a concrete extension of the artist's life, the dream of the young Dolly Rebecca Parton come true. Of course, it glorifies Dolly Parton as a superstar, a singer-songwriter, an actress, a media personality, and a philanthropist, but it also demonstrates the strength and the conviction that she has when it comes to transcending her roots while honoring and sharing them with the whole world.

A dream that seems to have no end. In 2023, the fiftieth anniversary of the megahit "I Will Always Love You," Dollywood celebrates the song as well as the songwriter. For this occasion, the park welcomes other artists in the Songwriters' Showcase, on the stage of the Showstreet Palace Theater—a way of expanding the audience and supporting young talents while paying homage to the creator of this venue. Thus, when the star affirms the importance of believing in something bigger than oneself, she is demonstrating here that these are not empty words.

ALBUM

Trio

The Pain of Loving You . Making Plans . To Know Him Is to Love Him . Hobo's Meditation .
Wildflowers . Telling Me Lies . My Dear Companion . Those Memories of You .
I've Had Enough . Rosewood Casket . Farther Along

RELEASE DATE
USA: March 2, 1987
Ref: Warner Bros Records—9 25491-2 (CD)
Best US Chart Ranking: 1

The *Trio* album cover features Dolly Parton, Linda Ronstadt, and Emmylou Harris.

A Musical Sisterhood

Critically acclaimed and loved by fans, *Trio* was the first album to bring together Dolly Parton, Emmylou Harris, and Linda Ronstadt. Produced by George Massenburg, it came out on the Warner Bros. Records label on March 2, 1987. It was a huge commercial and artistic success for the three singers. More than four million copies of *Trio* were sold, earning it platinum certification. It was listed on all the charts, reaching number six on the Billboard 200 chart.

Musical Flexibility

In no more than twenty years, Dolly Parton had worked in a wide range of musical registers and experimented with various "formulas" (country, gospel, soul, pop). As a songwriter, composer, and performer, Dolly is known as one of the most prolific creators of songs of her time, and she is also an artist who regularly joins forces with other singers. In her first country music period, between 1967 and 1977, there were the duos with Porter Wagoner. In the mid-seventies, up to the time when *Trio* was recorded, she sang with numerous artists, including Willie Nelson and Kris Kristofferson. These singers would often invite one of the others to take part in the recording of an album or to join them onstage, such as when Dolly and Kenny Rogers got together to record and tour behind the album *Real Love* (1985). For Dolly, *Trio* represented a necessary and important step in reconnecting with her roots as she returned to the music that made her the Queen of Country in Nashville. In this album, everything works together to make a harmonious blend. The musicians on the album are some of the best, but they never try to overshadow the three women, whose trio has inspired a cultlike following.

Together at Last

In the late 1970s, Emmylou invited Dolly to visit her in Los Angeles, and Linda joined them soon afterward. They began harmonizing together, loving the sound they produced. And thus began the idea of *Trio*. All three of them shared the same love of music and, as Linda told journalist David Zimmerman from *USA Today*, they were happy to sing and play for days at a time. A first recording session was embarked on in 1975 but did not lead to an album. Some of the numbers, however, were released:

Trio offered Dolly a chance to reunite with Emmylou Harris and Linda Ronstadt, shown here harmonizing together in 1979.

"Mister Sandman" appeared on Emmylou Harris's album *Evangeline*; "My Blue Tears" on Linda Ronstadt's *Get Closer*; and the ballad "I Never Will Marry," recorded by Dolly and Linda, was included on Ronstadt's 1977 album *Simple Dreams*. This first collaboration made it clear to the three singers that they could work very well together.

Dolly celebrated her forty-first birthday in 1987 while the three were working on the project they had all so much longed for. Why did they wait for more than ten years to do it? There are many reasons: the impossibility of finding time in their busy schedules; difficulties with the recording companies; personal problems (Emmylou's fight to get custody of her child, Dolly's and Linda's health problems). Finally in 1987, they were able to realize their dream of singing together. The result was *Trio*, each one of the singers having set aside her ego without ever sacrificing her individuality. Perhaps this is what makes *Trio* such an inspired album. While giving their various solos their full weight, when they sing together their voices—three of the best of this period—fit together in magical harmony. Two years later, Dolly Parton was to say that, along with *9 to 5*, this was one of the most meaningful collaborations she had been involved in. She observed that she must really like working with women.[2]

Album Cover

This 100 percent country, or even country and western, sleeve is the work of photographer Robert Blakeman. From left to right, we see Dolly, Linda, and Emmylou dressed in boots and country-style clothes decorated with rhinestones and embroidery designed by Manuel Cuevas, couturier to the stars. To underline the rural origins of country music, they are shown standing in a corral, with a view of rock formations in the background. On the inside of the CD booklet, in a reference to the long history of this kind of music, is a sepia photo of the three singers dressed in vintage long, embroidered white dresses from the end of the nineteenth or beginning of the twentieth century. Also included with the disk is a playful drawing that depicts the three singers alongside their underwear and clothes in the style of cut-out dress-up paper dolls.

For Dolly Addicts

When Emmylou Harris met Linda Ronstadt in 1973, the two rising stars found they had at least one thing in common: Their favorite female singer was Dolly Parton!

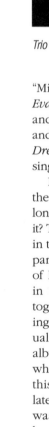

The Pain Of Loving You

Dolly Parton, Porter Wagoner / 2:32

Vocals: Dolly Parton, Linda Ronstadt, Emmylou Harris **Musicians:** Emmylou Harris: acoustic guitar / Albert Lee: acoustic guitar (solo) / Steve Fishell: pedal steel / David Lindley: mandolin / Mark O'Connor: viola / Kenny Edwards: acoustic bass / Russ Kunkel: drums **Recorded:** The Complex, Los Angeles; Woodland Sound Studios, Nashville; Ocean Way Recording, Los Angeles; January–November 1986 **Technical Team:** Producer: George Massenburg / Sound Engineer: George Massenburg / Assistant Sound Engineer: Sharon Rice / Mixing: Doug Sax

This revival of a 1971 song—originally titled "Oh the Pain of Loving You," written by Dolly Parton and Porter Wagoner for their album *Two of a Kind*—tells of the pain of loving someone that you hate as much as you love and who you cannot bring yourself to leave. The three singers give this song about the pain of love a depth that is both beautiful and heartrending.

This opening number on the album starts with the three voices combining perfectly together as if to announce what is to come. The voices of Dolly Parton and Linda Ronstadt are slightly spaced out, Dolly on the left and Linda on the right, on either side of Emmylou Harris. In this way, their different voices can be identified. Dolly has the highest voice and takes the top line, while the bottom line is sung by Linda. The arrangement is restrained, reminiscent of the country music of the 1960s, with nothing more than guitar, viola, pedal steel, drums, and even acoustic bass.

Making Plans

Johnny Russell, Voni Morrison / 3:36

Vocals: Dolly Parton, Linda Ronstadt, Emmylou Harris **Musicians:** Albert Lee: acoustic guitar, high-strung guitar / David Lindley: mandolin / Mark O'Connor: viola, fiddle / Kenny Edwards: acoustic bass / Russ Kunkel: drums **Recorded:** The Complex, Los Angeles; Woodland Sound Studios, Nashville; Ocean Way Recording, Los Angeles; January–November 1986 **Technical Team:** Producer: George Massenburg / Sound Engineer: George Massenburg / Assistant Sound Engineer: Sharon Rice / Mastering: Doug Sax

Dolly originally sang this song with Porter Wagoner on the *Porter & Dolly* album (1980). Her man plans to leave her tomorrow, and the narrator sings of what will follow: the pain she will feel, the tears that will flow, the emptiness and the loneliness she will experience.

Dolly Parton takes the main line, and her voice is given a wide reverb. She stands a little in front of the others of the trio and occasionally sings on her own. The violin appears several times, answering the voices; it is given a short solo before the last verse.

To Know Him Is To Love Him

Phil Spector / 3:48

Vocals: Dolly Parton, Linda Ronstadt, Emmylou Harris **Musicians:** Albert Lee: acoustic guitar / David Lindley: mandolin, Kona Hawaiian guitar / Kenny Edwards: acoustic bass / Russ Kunkel: drums / Ry Cooder: tremolo guitar **Recorded:** The Complex, Los Angeles; Woodland Sound Studios, Nashville; Ocean Way Recording, Los Angeles; January–November 1986 **Technical Team:** Producer: George Massenburg / Sound Engineer: George Massenburg / Assistant Sound Engineer: Sharon Rice / Mastering: Doug Sax **Single:** Side A: To Know Him Is to Love Him / Side B: Farther Along **Release:** Warner Bros. Records, January 26, 1987 (45 rpm ref.: 7-28492 and 9 28492-7) **Best Chart Ranking:** 1 on the Billboard Hot Country Songs (USA); 1 on the RPM Country Singles (Canada)

To know him is to love him. Just one smile from him makes life worth living. Can't he see that she's the one for him? Here Emmylou Harris takes the lead line, to which is added a wide reverb. The fast notes of the mandolin give a feel of Italian folk music. There is a key change after the guitar solo—a classic trick! The drummer's brush sweeps are beautifully delicate, but we can also hear the impact on the snare drum enhanced by a judicious amount of reverb. The guitar intro and solo are played by Ry Cooder, an American singer-songwriter-musician perhaps best known for his slide guitar work.

Dolly Parton photographed in Los Angeles in September 1987.

Trio was produced by Warner Bros. Records out of Nashville, Tennessee's famed Music Row.

Hobo's Meditation

Jimmie Rodgers / 3:17

Vocals: Dolly Parton, Linda Ronstadt, Emmylou Harris **Musicians:** Steve Fishell: dobro / John Starling: acoustic guitar / Herb Pedersen: banjo, vocal arrangements / Leland Sklar: acoustic bass **Recorded:** The Complex, Los Angeles; Woodland Sound Studios, Nashville; Ocean Way Recording, Los Angeles; January–November 1986 **Technical Team:** Producer: George Massenburg / Sound Engineer: George Massenburg / Assistant Sound Engineer: Sharon Rice / Mastering: Doug Sax **Single:** Side A: Wildflowers / Side B: Hobo's Meditation **Release:** Warner Bros. Records, March 14, 1987 (45 rpm ref.: 7-27970) **Best Chart Ranking:** 6 on the Billboard Hot Country Songs (USA); 8 on the RPM Country Singles (Canada)

Genesis and Lyrics

The narrator is the hobo himself, reflecting on his life and death. What will happen when he dies? Is there a heaven for hobos? Implicit in the song are questions about freedom of movement, work, money, poverty, and life's end. This melancholy piece could have been written by Dolly Parton.

Linda Ronstadt here takes her turn as lead. Her voice is recognizable by its deeper timbre and singing style: more powerful with vibrato on the held notes. The orchestration is pared down, in line with traditional folk music, using instruments such as dobro and banjo—sounds that had disappeared from Dolly's recordings when she turned to pop. Each of these two instruments has a solo, the sound projection of the dobro being particularly noticeable. A beautiful acoustic sound accompanies the hobo's meditation.

Production

This deliberately acoustic album marks a return to the roots of country music. The majority of the songs can be played as they are, without amplification, as in "Hobo's Meditation." In the 1930s and '40s, the sound would have been recorded with a pair of microphones (for stereo) in front of the musicians who would be arranged in a half circle. In 1987, only one microphone is used. This configuration, somewhat arranged for the cinema, is illustrated in the movie *O Brother, Where Art Thou* (2000). During the radio recording scene, the three protagonists approach the microphone in turn, depending which particular voice is to be emphasized. More recently, a number of groups have begun to use this technique—for example, the Franco-American group Moriarty for "Jimmy," one of their best-known tracks from their album *Gee Whiz but This Is a Lonesome Town* (2007).

Written more than fifteen years before the album's release, "Wildflowers" evokes Dolly's younger days.

Wildflowers

Dolly Parton / 3:33

Vocals: Dolly Parton, Linda Ronstadt, Emmylou Harris **Musicians:** Emmylou Harris: acoustic guitar / Albert Lee: mandolin / David Lindley: autoharp, harpolek / Mark O'Connor: viola, acoustic guitar / Kenny Edwards: acoustic bass / Russ Kunkel: drums **Recorded:** The Complex, Los Angeles; Woodland Sound Studios, Nashville; Ocean Way Recording, Los Angeles; January–November 1986 **Technical Team:** Producer: George Massenburg / Sound Engineer: George Massenburg / Assistant Sound Engineer: Sharon Rice / Mastering: Doug Sax **Single:** Side A: Wildflowers / Side B: Hobo's Meditation **Release:** Warner Bros. Records, March 14, 1987 (45 rpm ref.: 7-27970) **Best Chart Ranking:** 6 on the Billboard Hot Country Songs (USA); 8 on the RPM Country Singles (Canada)

In this poetic song, Dolly Parton compares the situation of a woman who uproots herself from her birthplace, in a search for freedom, with a wildflower. Wild roses don't care where they grow and similarly the narrator hits the road to follow her dreams. Written more than fifteen years before *Trio* was recorded, "Wildflowers" has a personal feel relating to Dolly's early years.

The intro, first verse, and refrain are played on an autoharp. This instrument is a kind of small traditional Appalachian portable harp. The rest of the instruments come in at the second verse. Dolly Parton is the lead singer. It is noticeable that when she has the main line she is generally singing on her own. Here the singers only come in together for the refrains, either singing words or vocables. The beautifully composed subtle melody on violin brings a note of sweetness that is all too short. The instrument provides a bridge between the different sections, although it gets a bit lost in the mixing. The drums are sober and restrained. Unembellished playing on bass drum, hi-hat, and rim shot on snare drum feature, just enough to serve the needs of the song, which ends without any exaggerated breaks, only the sober sound of the drums. Another instrument contributing to this traditional sound is the acoustic bass, which has a lower range than an electric bass. The resonance box of the acoustic bass, situated halfway between the electric bass and the double bass, is prominent.

Telling Me Lies

Linda Thompson, Betsy Cook / 4:26

Vocals: Dolly Parton, Linda Ronstadt, Emmylou Harris **Musicians:** Bill Payne: acoustic and electric piano / Albert Lee: acoustic guitar / Steve Fishell: pedal steel / David Lindley: acoustic guitar / Herb Pedersen: vocal arrangements / Kenny Edwards: electric bass / Russ Kunkel: drums / David Campbell: orchestration / Charles Veal: concert master **Recorded:** The Complex, Los Angeles; Woodland Sound Studios, Nashville; Ocean Way Recording, Los Angeles; January–November 1986 **Technical Team:** Producer: George Massenburg / Sound Engineer: George Massenburg / Assistant Sound Engineer: Sharon Rice / Mastering: Doug Sax **Single:** Side A: Telling Me Lies / Side B: Rosewood Casket **Release:** Warner Bros. Records, May 1987 (45 rpm ref.: 7-28371) **Best Chart Ranking:** 3 on the Billboard Hot Country Songs (USA); 6 on the RPM Country Singles (Canada)

This song, written by one of Linda Ronstadt's friends, expresses the narrator's pain and bitterness as she realizes the man she loved so blindly is a smooth-talking liar. Perfect lyrics for Dolly Parton, who has specialized in songs about women's unhappy love affairs. "Don't put your life in the hands of a man": just the kind of advice Dolly would give.

In this song the voices don't necessarily harmonize on the same melody. On the refrain, where the word *lies* is held, Linda Ronstadt and Dolly Parton stay on the same note while Emmylou Harris sings three different notes. The same thing happens elsewhere, as, for example, at 1:50. If you compare this song with "Wildflowers," where an acoustic bass is used, the difference in sound between that and the electric bass used here is clear. This number has more of a pop feel with amplified instruments like the bass and the piano, with the full range of the drum kit, and with a heavy reverb applied to the voices. The piano is now heard for the first time on the album, occupying a dominant place not only in the accompaniment, but also at the bridges and transitions. These details suggest that it is no accident Linda Ronstadt was chosen as lead singer; the song fits exactly into the musical repertoire where she feels most at home.

My Dear Companion

Jean Ritchie / 2:55

Vocals: Dolly Parton, Linda Ronstadt, Emmylou Harris **Musicians:** Emmylou Harris: acoustic guitar / Albert Lee: mandolin / David Lindley: autoharp / Mark O'Connor: viola, lead acoustic guitar / Kenny Edwards: acoustic bass **Recorded:** The Complex, Los Angeles; Woodland Sound Studios, Nashville; Ocean Way Recording, Los Angeles; January–November 1986 **Technical Team:** Producer: George Massenburg / Sound Engineer: George Massenburg / Assistant Sound Engineer: Sharon Rice / Mastering: Doug Sax **Single:** Side A: Those Memories of You / Side B: My Dear Companion **Release:** Warner Bros. Records, August 31, 1987 (45 rpm ref.: 7-28248) **Best Chart Ranking:** 5 on the Billboard Hot Country Songs (USA); 1 on the RPM Country Singles (Canada)

In deep distress, the narrator seeks her lost companion, who may have walked out on her. The lyrics look back to a happy relationship but also describe a descent into a hell of sorrow and loneliness. The song's style evokes the Appalachian folk songs of the late nineteenth century.

On the *Trio* album, the lead vocal part is taken by whichever singer is most appropriate for a particular song. Here, the singer is Emmylou Harris, in the style of the folk music with which she—and Dolly, too—was most familiar. Linda Ronstadt, by contrast, came from a more pop-inspired tradition. We don't know how the three singers divided up the numbers: Was the lead singer chosen first and then the accompaniment arranged accordingly? Or did each singer choose which songs she wanted to sing?

The intro, played on a folk guitar, stays on the chord before the entry of the voice. The same chord is played over two bars, giving Emmylou Harris her starting note. Linda Ronstadt and Dolly Parton come in one after the other with their evocative harmonizing. After the first refrain, the rest of the instruments are added in. Solos for mandolin and guitar follow one another in typical folk style. The only thing that seems out of place is the wide reverb on the voices.

Those Memories Of You

Alan O'Bryant / 3:58

Vocals: Dolly Parton, Linda Ronstadt, Emmylou Harris **Musicians:**
Albert Lee: lead acoustic guitar / Steve Fishell: Kona Hawaiian guitar /
John Starling: rhythm acoustic guitar / David Lindley: mandolin / Mark
O'Connor: fiddle / Kenny Edwards: acoustic bass / Russ Kunkel: drums /
David Campbell: orchestration **Recorded:** The Complex, Los Angeles;
Woodland Sound Studios, Nashville; Ocean Way Recording, Los
Angeles; January–November 1986 **Technical Team:** Producer:
George Massenburg / Sound Engineer: George Massenburg / Assistant
Sound Engineer: Sharon Rice / Mastering: Doug Sax **Single:** Side A:
Those Memories of You / Side B: My Dear Companion **Release:**
Warner Bros. Records, August 31, 1987 (45 rpm ref.: 7-28248)
Best Chart Ranking: 5 on the Billboard Hot Country Songs (USA); 1
on the RPM Country Singles (Canada)

Another song of lost love. The narrator is haunted by a
thousand memories of a love that was once happy. Now it
has gone, and the singer cannot sleep or even go on living.

The intro theme is played on a Hawaiian guitar, a type
of lap steel from the American archipelago. For this track it
replaces the "classical" lap steel and stands out by the range
of its playing: While the notes and chords of a lap steel are
usually rather high, this one stays in the mid- or even low
range. It is a very bluesy piece: Almost all the chords are
enriched with the minor seventh, the blue note, which gives
its bluesy color to the song. The melodies and guitar and violin solos on this song all inevitably contain this note.

Rarely used by Dolly Parton and just heard in passing in
a few themes or chords, the mandolin, on this song, belongs
to the rhythm section; it produces dry, muffled chords on the
offbeats along with the snare drum played with brushes. The
bass emits a simple but effective melodic line. Together with
the drums, it supports the other musicians.

There is nothing particularly unusual about the singing.
Dolly, the lead voice, is placed in the center in the mixing.
Linda Ronstadt's lower voice is slightly to the left, while
Emmylou Harris's voice is on the right.

As she did with Kenny Rogers, Dolly Parton maintained her links to
Emmylou Harris and Linda Ronstadt. They recorded their second
collaborative album, *Trio II*, in 1999.

I've Had Enough

Kate McGarrigle / 3:30

Vocals: Dolly Parton, Linda Ronstadt, Emmylou Harris **Musicians:** Bill
Payne: piano / Marty Krystall: clarinet / Brice Martin: flute / Jodi Burnett:
cello / Dennis Karmazyn: cello (solo) / Ilene "Novi" Novog: viola / David
Campbell: orchestration **Recorded:** The Complex, Los Angeles;
Woodland Sound Studios, Nashville; Ocean Way Recording, Los
Angeles; January–November 1986 **Technical Team:** Producer:
George Massenburg / Sound Engineer: George Massenburg / Assistant
Sound Engineer: Sharon Rice / Mastering: Doug Sax

This song tells of how difficult it is to separate from someone and to adopt the right behavior during this delicate
transition.

It is a very atypical track, having no percussion or
plucked strings. The main accompaniment is played on the
piano, to which are added one violin, two cellos, a clarinet,
and a flute. The instrumental section at 1:40 could have
been taken from a piece of another era's music. The lead
voice is Linda Ronstadt's. Dolly Parton adds a very high
line after the first instrumental passage, this being the only
moment she appears on this track.

On the set of ABC's *Dolly*, with (L to R) country musician Johnny Russell, Dolly's faithful uncle Bill Owens, and producer Fred Foster in 1987.

Rosewood Casket

Traditional / 2:59

Vocals: Dolly Parton, Linda Ronstadt, Emmylou Harris **Musicians:** David Lindley: dulcimer / Mark O'Connor: mandolin / Albert Lee: acoustic guitar / Kenny Edwards: acoustic bass / Avie Lee Parton: arrangements **Recorded:** The Complex, Los Angeles; Woodland Sound Studios, Nashville; Ocean Way Recording, Los Angeles; January–November 1986 **Technical Team:** Producer: George Massenburg / Sound Engineer: George Massenburg / Assistant Sound Engineer: Sharon Rice / Mastering: Doug Sax **Single:** Side A: Telling Me Lies / Side B: Rosewood Casket **Release:** Warner Bros. Records, May 1987 (45 rpm ref.: 7-28371) **Best Chart Ranking:** 3 on the Billboard Hot Country Songs (USA); 6 on the RPM Country Singles (Canada)

The narrator finds a box containing old love letters that she had never felt able to reread. She asks her sister to read them for her. She has just seen her man out walking with another woman at his side, and she tells her sister that when she dies she wants to be buried with the letters on her heart, but the gold ring he gave her will never leave her finger. The author of this song is not known, but it has been performed by many singers since the beginning of the twentieth century, including Jean Ritchie, Hank Thompson, and Marty Robbins. The version here was arranged by Dolly's mother.

Already used on the *Heartbreak Express* album, the dulcimer plays an important part on this track. It provides the accompaniment on its lower strings while playing the melodies in the higher register. Its tone resembles that of the mandolin, and their respective ranges complement each other perfectly; the mandolin's range being quite high, it supplies the top end of the music that the dulcimer does not play. When not playing the melody, the mandolin is used as a rhythm instrument, marking the offbeats with rather dry chords. The small number of instruments used allows their individual characters to come through clearly. In the absence of drums, the bass keeps the rhythm going throughout the song. The folk guitar plays chords or arpeggios and has its own short solo just before the end of the piece and the last mandolin solo. Dolly Parton is the lead singer while Emmylou Harris contributes an impressive high descant.

Emmylou Harris plays at the Country Music Festival in London in April 1987.

Farther Along

Traditional / 4:10

Vocals: Dolly Parton, Linda Ronstadt, Emmylou Harris **Musicians:** Bill Payne: acoustic piano, Hammond organ, harmonium / Albert Lee: high-strung guitar, acoustic guitar / John Starling, Emmylou Harris: arrangements **Recorded:** The Complex, Los Angeles; Woodland Sound Studios, Nashville; Ocean Way Recording, Los Angeles; January–November 1986 **Technical Team:** Producer: George Massenburg / Sound Engineer: George Massenburg / Assistant Sound Engineer: Sharon Rice / Mastering: Doug Sax **Single:** Side A: To Know Him Is to Love Him / Side B: Farther Along **Release:** Warner Bros. Records, January 26, 1987 (45 rpm ref.: 7-28492 and 9 28492-7) **Best Chart Ranking:** 1 on the Billboard Hot Country Songs (USA); 1 on the RPM Country Singles (Canada)

This gospel song speaks of the believer's dismay at observing how the wicked seem to prosper with impunity while the righteous suffer. But the singer is comforted by the knowledge that "farther along"—in heaven—everything will become clear and make sense.

The arrangement of this track dispenses with drums but makes much use of keyboards: piano, Hammond organ (for the first time on this album), and harmonium. Also present is a high-strung guitar. Its unusual tuning (an octave up on six of the twelve strings, achieved by using lighter-gauge strings that can withstand the higher tension), confers a particular color. If the strings are sounded from top to bottom, it will be found that the notes do not simply rise from low to high. Audible particularly at the beginning of the song, the effect is not unlike that of a mandolin. The piano is the most important of the instruments, and the other keyboards contribute layers of sound. Dolly Parton takes the lead in this gospel song before passing it over to Linda Ronstadt. All three then sing together, their voices equally mixed in the prayerlike harmonies. The voice of Emmylou Harris can be heard at the end of the song, concluding the album with her soaring soprano voice.

Emmylou Harris: The Queen of Harmony

In 2018, the Country Music Hall of Fame in Nashville mounted an exhibition celebrating the singer-songwriter Emmylou Harris, showing many of her personal documents and items. Feminist, animal rights activist, and advocate for victims of war around the world, Emmylou Harris is an accomplished artist and one of the most influential voices of the past fifty years.

Early Years

Born on April 2, 1947, in Birmingham, Alabama, Emmylou's father was a career soldier. The military life meant frequent moves, and she found it difficult to know where her roots were. Introverted and academically bright, Emmylou learned the guitar and began studies at the School of Music, Theatre and Dance at the University of North Carolina. Abandoning her studies, she moved to New York, working as a waitress and performing in the bars of Greenwich Village. In 1969, she married singer-songwriter Tom Slocum and recorded her first album, *Gliding Bird*. These years marked the height of the folk music revival—with, among others, Woody Guthrie—but New York was a difficult place to live and Emmylou earned very little money. Shortly after her daughter Hallie was born, she and Slocum divorced. With not a penny to her name, Linda returned to live with her family in Clarksville, Maryland, an unincorporated community lying between Baltimore and Washington, DC. During this period she began exploring the power of words to express in song what she was otherwise unable to say.

First Influences

Moving away from folk music, Emmylou met the brilliant musician Gram Parsons. Through him she developed a greater musical complexity at the same time as she did the simplicity of images and conciseness of country music. In January 1973, Gram invited Emmylou to tour with his group, the Fallen Angels. The tour was cut short on September 19 when Parsons suddenly died at the age of twenty-six after an all-too-short career. Their version of "Love Hurts" (written by Felice and Boudleaux Bryant) marked a turning point for a singer who would be later nicknamed "the Queen of Harmony." It was with Parsons that Emmylou Harris discovered and appreciated the synergy of a duo, when voices mingle, combine, and echo one another. With his fine musical understanding, Gram Parsons leads the way, but Emmylou provides the energy of the duo. Their partnership resulted in an album, *Grievous Angel*, issued in 1974 after Parsons's death. Emmylou was devastated by this loss and mourned him for a long time. It was not until 2011 and her album *Hard Bargain* that she was able to express what she owed to Parsons and his importance in her personal and musical life.

While she was living in New York, Emmylou was often the opener for more famous performers at the famous folk and rock venue Gerde's Folk City. Here she met singer-songwriter Townes Van Zandt, many of whose songs she was to interpret.

The other important and life-changing person she met was Rodney Crowell, singer-songwriter and guitarist. *Elite Hotel*, Emmylou's third solo album, released in 1975, included "Amarillo" and "Till I Gain Control Again," both written by Crowell. New horizons beckoned.

Finding Fame

Emmylou Harris forged ahead, singing her intimate and poetic songs in duos and trios like the one she formed with her friends Linda Ronstadt and Dolly Parton. In 1987, the three singers had a huge success with their album *Trio*. Throughout her career, Emmylou chose to interpret—as a duo or as solos—songs by artists she liked. One such example is "Across the Border" by Bruce Springsteen, which she sang in 1999 with Linda Ronstadt. Her voice can be heard on Bob Dylan's 1976 album *Desire*, and in 2006 she appeared onstage with Mark Knopfler of the group Dire Straits. As she told Stan Cuesta of *Rolling Stone* magazine in 2021, she has sung with all the artists she knows, including Bob Dylan and Roy Orbison, to mention but a few. She has expressed her admiration and esteem for Joan Baez and also Neil Young, who makes an appearance on her 1995 album *Wrecking Ball*.

Over a career of fifty years, Emmylou Harris has amassed more than thirty solo albums, over a dozen Grammy Awards, numerous contributions and collaborations, three marriages, two children, and grandchildren. Warm, funny, open, and, as Emmylou says of herself, slow, she appears in Ken Burns's 2019 documentary *Country Music*. It paints a beautiful picture of an artist who has created a musical universe that is both profound and varied, leaving an indelible mark on the vast world that is country music.

Linda Ronstadt: A Unique Voice

It has been said of Linda Ronstadt's voice that it seems to come from another world. This singer-songwriter, producer, and actress is one of those women born after the Second World War who succeeded in a very male music scene. Over the course of her extraordinary and unusual career she has explored every kind of musical genre, ranging from rock music with Mick Jagger to singing Mimi in the opera *La Bohème*.

Cultural and Musical Influences Combine

Linda (born in Tucson, Arizona, in 1946) and her three siblings inherited their taste for music from their father. Half Mexican and half German, by day he worked in his hardware store and in the evening he sang in bars. His daughter's 1987 album *Canciones de Mi Padre* was her tribute to him. It was to have one of the highest sales of any non-English-language album. When she was little, Linda would listen to the radio for hours, to programs that offered her an open window onto the world's musical diversity. (She, too, is a mixture of several different ethnicities, inherited from her father and her American mother's European roots.) Listening to the radio, she was able to hear the finest voices of singers, from the 1920s to the 1950s, in every kind of music—jazz, blues, Mexican music, opera, country, and rock. Everything she heard fed into the eclectic mix that has characterized her career. In the early years she sang mainly in Spanish but, after discovering folk music and Bob Dylan in her adolescence, she began singing in English.

Rebelling against the strictness of Catholic schools, when Linda was eighteen she abandoned her studies and left for Los Angeles. In 1964, she settled in Laurel Canyon, the avant-garde hippie district of LA, where she made several decisive contacts. The city was full of bars and music clubs, and agents and producers came to spot future talents. One such place was the Troubadour, a cult venue for folk and rock until the 1970s. Linda worked for a while with singer-songwriters and guitarists Bobby Kimmel and Kenny Edwards. She was the lead singer for their group, the Stone Poneys, and brought out three albums with them. Her voice, evoking both the softness of velvet and the power of fire, was immediately noticed.

An Otherworldly Voice and a Taste for Cover Songs

When the Stone Poneys broke up, Linda Ronstadt continued singing and bringing out songs with Kenny Edwards for some ten more years. In 1973, she linked up with Emmylou Harris and then with Dolly Parton; in 1987 the three women brought out the album *Trio*. But long before *Trio*, Linda toured with many other artists, including particularly Jackson Browne and the Eagles. She enjoyed singing other people's numbers, from Buddy Holly's "It's So Easy" (1958) to Roy Orbison's "Blue Bayou" (1963). In 1973, "You're No Good," originally sung by Dee Dee Warwick in 1963, was to be one of Linda's first hits to reach number one in the charts. Not yet twenty-eight, she was a star.

Although somewhat lacking in self-confidence in the early years of her career, Linda was nevertheless clear about what she wanted and never hesitated to assert her musical choices, especially country. As so it was that in 1974 she recorded *Heart Like a Wheel*, one of her first solo albums. That same year she performed with Johnny Cash in the Behind Prison Walls concert given in the Tennessee State Prison, Nashville, before an audience of prisoners. Linda also loved jazz—and particularly Ella Fitzgerald—enjoying especially the lyrics and compositions of the 1920s and '30s. Interviewed in July 1985 by Steve Bloom for the jazz and blues magazine *Down Beat*, she spoke at length about her influences and career. Bloom describes her as vivacious, funny, and determined.

Shown here in Los Angeles in the 1980s, Linda Ronstadt explored other musical styles outside of country, including comedy and opera.

Following spread: The Queen of Country on her eponymous show, *Dolly*, in 1987.

A Versatile Artist

Linda stepped onto a new kind of stage in 1980, performing the role of Mabel in the musical comedy *Pirates of Penzance*, based on the comic opera of the same name by Gilbert and Sullivan. In 1984, as part of the New York Shakespeare Festival, she sang the role of Mimi in Puccini's *La Bohème*, delighting her fans with her beautiful mezzo-soprano voice. Linda loved opera, admiring Maria Callas just as much as she admired Tina Turner. Her highly successful 1983 album *What's New* consisted of cover versions of the great American songs of the 1950s with arrangements by bandleader Nelson Riddle. Linda also sang numbers with lullaby arrangements, worked with the famous composer Philip Glass, and covered Elvis Costello numbers.

The diversity of these styles and eras demonstrates her amazing vocal agility, though she defines herself as just a ballad singer. While she didn't write all the songs that have brought her fame, she has put so much of herself into them that they become part of her.

Into the Twenty-First Century

A politically committed artist, Linda Ronstadt publicly supported Michael Moore's 2004 movie *Fahrenheit 9/11*, an indictment against the war in Iraq declared by President George W. Bush. In 2019, interviewed by Anderson Cooper on CNN, she drew a parallel between Donald Trump's America and Hitler's Germany. An independent woman, Linda Ronstadt has more than once hit the headlines with her tumultuous love life—she has never married but has had relationships with filmmaker George Lucas, actor Jim Carrey, and California governor Jerry Brown.

Talking about her friend in Rob Epstein and Jeffrey Friedman's 2019 documentary *Linda Ronstadt: The Sound of My Voice*, Dolly Parton summed her up perfectly: Linda possessed a rare talent that meant she could sing anything. Sadly, since the onset of Parkinson's disease (which was later diagnosed as progressive supranuclear palsy), Linda can no longer sing and has difficulty getting about. In 2011, she announced her retirement. Her legacy to her fans is some twenty solo albums, compilations, hits, unforgettable concerts, and equally remarkable memories.

ALBUM

Rainbow

The River Unbroken . I Know You by Heart . Dump the Dude . Red Hot Screaming Love .
Make Love Work . Everyday Hero . Two Lovers . Could I Have Your Autograph .
Savin' It for You . More Than I Can Say

RELEASE DATE
United States: November 25, 1987
Reference: Columbia Records, Nashville (TN)—CK-40968
Best US Chart Ranking: 18

Alternating Between Rain and Sun

Rainbow is Dolly Parton's twenty-eighth solo album. Produced by Steve "Golde" Goldstein, it was released by Columbia Records on November 25, 1987. The songwriter wrote only two of the ten songs, and the critics were not very enthusiastic: Everyone considered this opus—dedicated to love, once again—one of the star's least good.

A Change of Direction

The year 1987 was rich in events, and between Madonna who, during her Who's That Girl world tour, threw her pants into the audience in front of 130,000 spectators at the Parc de Sceaux in Paris, and George Michael, who caused a scandal with "I Want Your Sex," it was, musically speaking, a hot year. While Michael Jackson started his first solo world tour, Bad, in Detroit, techno was booming. In England, the beginning of the first raves also marked the arrival of the drug ecstasy in nightclubs. The dancer Fred Astaire died in June, and with him passed a whole era of cinema and musical comedy.

Having ended her contract with the RCA Victor label, Dolly Parton did not release any albums in 1986. In January of that year, the star performed at the Grand Ole Opry to celebrate her seventeenth anniversary as a member and sang some of her best songs, including "Coat of Many Colors." As an actress, she played Lorna in the TV movie *A Smoky Mountain Christmas*—directed by Henry Winkler and broadcast on ABC on December 14, 1986—for which she also wrote six songs. It had been ten years since Dolly had crossed the line from country to pop, and ten years since she had tried to stay on top of the pop charts. Was it necessary to leave RCA Victor to achieve this goal?

A Difficult Balance

When she signed with Columbia Records, the star imagined that she would be able to produce and release one album each year that blended country and pop, instead of two: one country, the other pop. Despite some setbacks, Dolly did not give up her pop audience, conquered in 1977 with the album *Here You Come Again*, a resounding but never repeated pop success.

The Dollywood amusement park immediately found its public, that much was certain. In July 1986, its doors had only just opened, but the album *Rainbow* was a disappointment, even though country fans remained loyal to the songwriter. The album's promotion involved, among other things, the artist's new TV show, *Dolly*, broadcast on the ABC channel. Ten years after her first TV experience, Dolly was back on camera, but despite the resources invested, the reception was, again, mixed. Dolly Parton was still looking for her equilibrium, still guided and driven by this ultimate goal since childhood: to become a huge star.

Album Cover

In front of the lens of Annie Leibovitz, Dolly Parton, under a cascade of blond curls, very femme fatale in her strapless dress and her long black-and-gold gloves, like Rita Hayworth, poses, on the front cover as well as on the back, lying on her side in an attitude that emphasizes her figure. Inside the cover, a series of shots shows another Dolly, certainly still ultra-feminine but also joyfully mutinous, somewhat in a Cyndi Lauper style.

The recording sessions for this album took place in three studios: Record One, in Los Angeles (CA), and Ocean Way Recording and A&M Studios, both in Hollywood (CA). Neither the studio nor the members of the technical team were specified for each song in the credits of the record; the sound engineer was Richard Bosworth and assistant sound engineers were Brian Scheuble, Bob Loftus, Brett Swain, and Rail Rogut.

Dolly Parton and Lee Majors on the set of the TV movie *A Smoky Mountain Christmas* in 1986.

The River Unbroken

David Batteau, Darrell Brown / 4:33

Musicians: Waddy Wachtel: acoustic guitar / Kevin Dukes: slide guitar, electric guitar / Al Perkins: pedal steel / Danny Kortchmar: 12-string acoustic guitar / Bob Glaub, Leland Sklar, Abraham Laboriel: bass / Steve Goldstein: keyboard, synthesizer / Bill Cuomo: synthesizer, electric organ / Robert O'Hearn: synthesizer / Patricia Mabee: harpsichord / John Vigran: drum machine programming / Craig Krampf: drums overdubs, drum machine programming / Jim Keltner: drums, percussion / Buck Trent: electric banjo / Bobby Bruce: violin / Tom Scott: saxophone / David Campbell: chromatic harmonica **Vocals:** Dolly Parton **Backing Vocals:** Julia Waters, Maxine Waters, Richard Dennison **Recorded:** July 1985 **Technical Team:** Producer: Steve "Golde" Goldstein / Executive Producer: Dolly Parton **Single:** Side A: The River Unbroken / Side B: More Than I Can Say **Release:** Columbia Records, November 23, 1987 (ref.: 38-07665) **Best Chart Ranking:** 63 on Billboard Hot Country Songs (USA); 23 on RPM Adult Contemporary Singles (Canada)

The narrator looks forward to the train of deliverance, to their ultimate rendezvous with the one who lives in all things: a metaphor for life and death, and the daily struggle for joy, love, and forgiveness to prevail over weariness and sadness. Master of ceremonies on keyboards (pianos and synthesizers), guitars, and strings arrangements on Dolly's albums during the first half of the 1980s, the faithful Steve Goldstein takes on the role of producer for this opus—a well-deserved promotion. From the first track, we feel that the sound tends more toward a mix of electronic sounds (drum programming, pad, synthesizers) and Americana. The slide guitar of Kevin Dukes, with a resolutely organic sound and mixed very forward on this track, prefigures the sound of the mainstream country music to come: big hybrid productions with a very wide and airy sound, with acoustic and electric guitars in front. The atmosphere of "The River Unbroken" is somewhat reminiscent of Bruce Springsteen's albums of the same period, with a desire to speak to the greatest number of people, to shape a sound, and to move toward a style of songwriting made for stadiums.

1987

Smokey Robinson onstage in 1987, the year of his hit duet with Dolly, "I Know You by Heart."

I Know You By Heart

George Merrill, Shannon Rubicam, Dean Pitchford / 4:20

Musicians: Waddy Wachtel: acoustic guitar, electric guitar / Kevin Dukes, Rick Vito: slide guitar, electric guitar / Dann Huff, Michael Landau: electric guitar / Al Perkins: pedal steel / Danny Kortchmar: 12-string acoustic guitar / Bob Glaub, Leland Sklar, Abraham Laboriel: bass / Steve Goldstein: keyboard, synthesizer / Bill Cuomo: synthesizer, electric organ / Robert O'Hearn: synthesizer / Patricia Mabee: harpsichord / John Vigran: drum machine programming / Craig Krampf: drums overdubs, drum machine programming / Jim Keltner: drums, percussion / Buck Trent: electric banjo / Bobby Bruce: violin / Tom Scott: saxophone / David Campbell: chromatic harmonica
Vocals: Dolly Parton, Smokey Robinson **Backing Vocals:** Julia Waters, Maxine Waters, Richard Dennison, Carmen Twillie, Mike Chapman, Blaise Tosti, Anita Ball **Recorded:** July 1985 **Technical Team:** Producer: Steve "Golde" Goldstein / Executive Producer: Dolly Parton **Single:** Side A: I Know You by Heart / Side B: Could I Have Your Autograph **Release:** Columbia Records, February 8, 1988 (ref.: 38-07727) **Best Chart Ranking:** 1 on Billboard Hot Country Songs (USA); 1 on RPM Country Singles (Canada)

The Dolly and Smokey Robinson duo sing of a love where each knows the other so well that they can finish each other's sentences, read each other's minds, anticipate each other's needs, communicate by look or touch. It is an ode to fusional love, of a very eighties pop variety, although the songwriter comes from country origins, and Smokey Robinson from soul and R&B. The only (subtle) concession to Americana lies in the few interventions by David Campbell on the chromatic harmonica. For the rest, it is the desire to make a hit that dominates: cascades of synthesizers; a mix of acoustic drums, electronic pad, and programming; crystalline electric guitars generously coated with chorus; long reverb on each instrument; and the duet with a legendary singer. Surprisingly, Smokey Robinson sings the first vibes on the intro and the first verse. We can imagine behind this a possible contractual negotiation, so contrary is this to the usual, especially on a Dolly Parton solo album. Anyway, Dolly plays the game, the two stars give the best of themselves, and success is duly delivered.

Dump The Dude

Steve Dorff, Allan Rich / 3:52

Musicians: Waddy Wachtel: acoustic guitar, electric guitar / Kevin Dukes, Rick Vito: slide guitar, electric guitar / Dann Huff, Michael Landau: electric guitar / Al Perkins: pedal steel / Danny Kortchmar: 12-string acoustic guitar / Bob Glaub, Leland Sklar, Abraham Laboriel: bass / Steve Goldstein: keyboard, synthesizer / Bill Cuomo: synthesizer, electric organ / Robert O'Hearn: synthesizer / Patricia Mabee: harpsichord / John Vigran: drum machine programming / Craig Krampf: drums overdubs, drum machine programming / Jim Keltner: drums, percussion / Buck Trent: electric banjo / Bobby Bruce: violin / Tom Scott: saxophone / David Campbell: chromatic harmonica **Vocals:** Dolly Parton **Backing Vocals:** Julia Waters, Maxine Waters, Richard Dennison, Carmen Twillie, Mike Chapman, Blaise Tosti, Anita Ball **Recorded:** July 1985 **Technical Team:** Producer: Steve "Golde" Goldstein / Executive Producer: Dolly Parton

In this song about manipulation, lies, and abuse in love, the narrator talks as a friend to a woman who is being abused by her lover, a man who is taciturn and perhaps even cruel. Her advice: Because the woman deserves much better, she should dump this guy as soon as possible and finally find someone nice. With nervous percussion programming, jerky rhythmic sequences, and icy synthesizers in the lead, Steve "Golde" Goldstein relies on a very tense score as well as a lavish arrangement and a Prince-like sharp production. The sequenced sounds come from either an Emulator III sampler (from the American firm E-mu Systems) or a Fairlight CMI; there were no real alternatives, as these machines were then state-of-the-art (but expensive, especially the Fairlight). After the second chorus, Dolly's faithful collaborator Tom Scott gives us the first reverberated saxophone solo on the album. This instrument could pop up at any time in the mainstream music of the time, so we were waiting for it. The alliterations on the lyrics "Dump the dude / You know he's got a rotten attitude" make the chorus particularly dynamic and catchy. It is surprising that this song was not selected for release as a single, as it would have definitely hit the charts.

Red Hot Screaming Love

Mike Chapman / 4:11

Musicians: Waddy Wachtel: acoustic guitar, electric guitar / Kevin Dukes, Rick Vito: slide guitar, electric guitar / Dann Huff, Michael Landau: electric guitar / Al Perkins: pedal steel / Danny Kortchmar: 12-string acoustic guitar / Bob Glaub, Leland Sklar, Abraham Laboriel: bass / Steve Goldstein: keyboard, synthesizer / Bill Cuomo: synthesizer, electric organ / Robert O'Hearn: synthesizer / Patricia Mabee: harpsichord / John Vigran: drum machine programming / Craig Krampf: drums overdubs, drum machine programming / Jim Keltner: drums, percussion / Buck Trent: electric banjo / Bobby Bruce: violin / Tom Scott: saxophone / David Campbell: chromatic harmonica **Vocals:** Dolly Parton **Backing Vocals:** Julia Waters, Maxine Waters, Richard Dennison, Carmen Twillie, Mike Chapman, Blaise Tosti, Anita Ball **Recorded:** July 1985 **Technical Team:** Producer: Steve "Golde" Goldstein / Executive Producer: Dolly Parton

Disregarding the general opinion, the narrator cannot and will not stop loving this man who makes her crazy with love. On the production side, we are back to Springsteenian Americana. Kevin Dukes has put on his bottleneck for a well-judged slide part; the sound of the legendary Jim Keltner on drums is full and polished but natural enough; the synthesizers are a little more discreet; and the backing vocals give an organic depth to the whole. A simple and effective track in the form of an ode to passion.

1987

Make Love Work

Eric Kaz / 3:26

Musicians: Waddy Wachtel: acoustic guitar, electric guitar / Kevin Dukes, Rick Vito: slide guitar, electric guitar / Dann Huff, Michael Landau: electric guitar / Al Perkins: pedal steel / Danny Kortchmar: 12-string acoustic guitar / Bob Glaub, Leland Sklar, Abraham Laboriel: bass / Steve Goldstein: keyboard, synthesizer / Bill Cuomo: synthesizer, electric organ / Robert O'Hearn: synthesizer / Patricia Mabee: harpsichord / John Vigran: drum machine programming / Craig Krampf: drums overdubs, drum machine programming / Jim Keltner: drums, percussion / Buck Trent: electric banjo / Bobby Bruce: violin / Tom Scott: saxophone / David Campbell: chromatic harmonica **Vocals:** Dolly Parton **Backing Vocals:** Julia Waters, Maxine Waters, Richard Dennison, Carmen Twillie, Mike Chapman, Blaise Tosti, Anita Ball **Recorded:** July 1985 **Technical Team:** Producer: Steve "Golde" Goldstein / Executive Producer: Dolly Parton **Single:** Side A: Make Love Work / Side B: Two Lovers **Release:** Columbia Records, July 25, 1988 (ref.: 38-07995)

As an echo to some of Dolly's lyrics, this is about the value of love, and trust in the other person and in oneself, because loving is not simple and requires some effort, but it is worth it. The first syrupy ballad of the album, the recipe is perfect: crystalline keyboards, electric guitars bathed in chorus and reverb, larger-than-life drums, a thick and humming bass, velvet backing vocals, and, to coat the whole thing, Steve Goldstein gratifies us with a very cinematographic string arrangement at the extreme of the grandiose "pompier" style. One feels that all this is done with great ease. It must be said that "Golde" is experienced in this type of exercise and that Dolly does not have to force anything to instill the necessary emphasis into this type of song. The craft and quality of her vocal technique project her effortlessly to the forefront of this dense orchestration. "Make Love Work" is a perfect song for a lascivious slow dance to open or close the ball.

Everyday Hero

Blaise Tosti, Robert O'Hearn / 4:35

Musicians: Waddy Wachtel: acoustic guitar, electric guitar / Kevin Dukes, Rick Vito: slide guitar, electric guitar / Dann Huff, Michael Landau: electric guitar / Al Perkins: pedal steel / Danny Kortchmar: 12-string acoustic guitar / Bob Glaub, Leland Sklar, Abraham Laboriel: bass / Steve Goldstein: keyboard, synthesizer / Bill Cuomo: synthesizer, electric organ / Robert O'Hearn: synthesizer / Patricia Mabee: harpsichord / John Vigran: drum machine programming / Craig Krampf: drums overdubs, drum machine programming / Jim Keltner: drums, percussion / Buck Trent: electric banjo / Bobby Bruce: violin / Tom Scott: saxophone / David Campbell: chromatic harmonica **Vocals:** Dolly Parton **Backing Vocals:** Julia Waters, Maxine Waters, Richard Dennison, Carmen Twillie, Mike Chapman, Blaise Tosti, Anita Ball **Recorded:** July 1985 **Technical Team:** Producer: Steve "Golde" Goldstein / Executive Producer: Dolly Parton

In these lyrics, we find a theme dear to Dolly Parton (although she did not write this song): The real treasure is marital and family love, and difficulties should not tarnish the diamond that is love. Those who manage to overcome life's everyday adversities while preserving their feelings are the true heroes of ordinary life.

The intro is eminently modern: With the sound of the synthesizers, the slide guitar with its round and very clean sound, and the bass drum on the crochets, one could almost expect to be setting off on a contemporary electro/dance track. But the illusion stops there, because as soon as Dolly's voice and the rest of the orchestra make their entrance, we immediately encounter the archetypal sounds of the 1980s. Mid-tempo and flashy, the rhythm section drives the ensemble with authority. The synths slam; the ultra-saturated electric guitar gives its rhythmic palm mute and its guitar hero solo on the modulation that follows the second chorus. The backing vocals add extra soul. A production that Cyndi Lauper would not have disowned.

Dolly Parton in full communion with her adoring Australian fans during a performance at the Sydney Entertainment Center in 1987.

Dennison, Carmen Twillie, Mike Chapman, Blaise Tosti, Anita Ball **Recorded:** July 1985 **Technical Team:** Producer: Steve "Golde" Goldstein / Executive Producer: Dolly Parton **Single:** Side A: Make Love Work / Side B: Two Lovers **Release:** Columbia Records, July 25, 1988 (ref.: 38-07995)

Two Lovers

William "Smokey" Robinson / 3:22

Musicians: Waddy Wachtel: acoustic guitar, electric guitar / Kevin Dukes, Rick Vito: slide guitar, electric guitar / Dann Huff, Michael Landau: electric guitar / Al Perkins: pedal steel / Danny Kortchmar: 12-string acoustic guitar / Bob Glaub, Leland Sklar, Abraham Laboriel: bass / Steve Goldstein: keyboard, synthesizer / Bill Cuomo: synthesizer, electric organ / Robert O'Hearn: synthesizer / Patricia Mabee: harpsichord / John Vigran: drum machine programming / Craig Krampf: drums overdubs, drum machine programming / Jim Keltner: drums, percussion / Buck Trent: electric banjo / Bobby Bruce: violin / Tom Scott: saxophone / David Campbell: chromatic harmonica **Vocals:** Dolly Parton **Backing Vocals:** Julia Waters, Maxine Waters, Richard

This is the story of a woman who loves two men: The first is tender, thoughtful, and loving; the second makes her sad and makes her cry. But these two men are really one, and she cannot help but love both facets. And it is Tom Scott who opens the ball with the sensual sound of his saxophone, treated to a long reverb and a delay regulated on the tempo of the piece. After the intro, he comes back only at the first chorus to place his counterpoints between Dolly's phrases and echoes her until the end. This Smokey Robinson composition—probably an elegant return of a favor for Dolly having agreed to play the duet game on "I Know You by Heart"—is an ode to the ambivalence of love, a swaying mid-tempo number suggestive of the extent of the pleasures of love.

Dolly Parton during an appearance on Oprah Winfrey's talk show in 1987.

Could I Have Your Autograph

Dolly Parton / 3:20

Musicians: Waddy Wachtel: acoustic guitar, electric guitar / Kevin Dukes, Rick Vito: slide guitar, electric guitar / Dann Huff, Michael Landau: electric guitar / Al Perkins: pedal steel / Danny Kortchmar: 12-string acoustic guitar / Bob Glaub, Leland Sklar, Abraham Laboriel: bass / Steve Goldstein: keyboard, synthesizer / Bill Cuomo: synthesizer, electric organ / Robert O'Hearn: synthesizer / Patricia Mabee: harpsichord / John Vigran: drum machine programming / Craig Krampf: drums overdubs, drum machine programming / Jim Keltner: drums, percussion / Buck Trent: slide guitar / Bobby Bruce: violin / Tom Scott: saxophone / David Campbell: chromatic harmonica **Vocals:** Dolly Parton **Backing Vocals:** Julia Waters, Maxine Waters, Richard Dennison, Carmen Twillie, Mike Chapman, Blaise Tosti, Anita Ball **Recorded:** July 1985 **Technical Team:** Producer: Steve "Golde" Goldstein / Executive Producer: Dolly Parton **Single:** Side A: I Know You by Heart / Side B: Could I Have Your Autograph **Release:** Columbia Records, February 8, 1988 (ref.: 38-07727)

This is a flirty story in which the woman takes the lead in trying to get a man's contact information (autograph, name, and phone number) written on a small photo of him, because even if he is not Elvis Presley—and she is not Marilyn Monroe—he is as handsome as a star.

It is almost strange to hear this kind of production on such typical country songwriting. Only the melody and harmony of the bridge sound more in tune with the arrangement. Double entendre lyrics, charm, and light humor: We recognize Dolly's style. The slide guitar and the pedal steel are the only elements really reminiscent of the Nashville sound. It seems that the slide guitar part, extremely minimalist, is played by Buck Trent, an old friend of the singer and faithful collaborator usually on the banjo. Indeed, at 2:17 we can clearly hear Dolly say "Kick it, Buck!" to launch the almost naïve slide solo that follows. It is likely that Dolly was trying to find a place for him on this album; his mainstream pop style is hardly compatible with the frailing banjo technique, Buck Trent's preferred playing style. Times are hard for session men from bluegrass…

Savin' It For You

Dino Fekaris, David Loeb / 4:18

Musicians: Waddy Wachtel: acoustic guitar, electric guitar / Kevin Dukes, Rick Vito: slide guitar, electric guitar / Dann Huff, Michael Landau: electric guitar / Al Perkins: pedal steel / Danny Kortchmar: 12-string acoustic guitar / Bob Glaub, Leland Sklar, Abraham Laboriel: bass / Steve Goldstein: keyboard, synthesizer / Bill Cuomo: synthesizer, electric organ / Robert O'Hearn: synthesizer / Patricia Mabee: harpsichord / John Vigran: drum machine programming / Craig Krampf: drums overdubs, drum machine programming / Jim Keltner: drums, percussion / Buck Trent: electric banjo / Bobby Bruce: violin / Tom Scott: saxophone / David Campbell: chromatic harmonica **Vocals:** Dolly Parton **Backing Vocals:** Julia Waters, Maxine Waters, Richard Dennison, Carmen Twillie, Mike Chapman, Blaise Tosti, Anita Ball **Recorded:** July 1985 **Technical Team:** Producer: Steve "Golde" Goldstein / Executive Producer: Dolly Parton

In this song, more erotic than the other love songs of the album, the narrator has a little present for her lover, which we imagine to be a torrid night of love, to make him forget all his worries. This is a very upbeat track: The production is flashy, the tempo is made for dancing, and the songwriting is elaborate. The structure (verse/pre-chorus/chorus x 2/bridge/chorus/half-tone modulation) is particularly sophisticated. The electric guitar and pedal steel turnarounds, and even a twirling fiddle part played by Bobby Bruce at the end in fade-out, bring to the song a country pop side (on the way to becoming a genre in its own right), while the synthesizers and the rhythm section take care of the sounds of the moment. A winner for Dolly and Steve Goldstein.

More Than I Can Say

Dolly Parton / 4:06

Musicians: Waddy Wachtel: acoustic guitar / Kevin Dukes: slide guitar, electric guitar / Al Perkins: pedal steel / Danny Kortchmar: 12-string acoustic guitar / Bob Glaub, Leland Sklar, Abraham Laboriel: bass / Steve Goldstein: keyboard, synthesizer / Bill Cuomo: synthesizer, electric organ / Robert O'Hearn: synthesizer / Patricia Mabee: harpsichord / John Vigran: drum machine programming / Craig Krampf: drums overdubs, drum machine programming / Jim Keltner: drums, percussion / Buck Trent: electric banjo / Bobby Bruce: violin / Tom Scott: saxophone / David Campbell: chromatic harmonica **Vocals:** Dolly Parton **Backing Vocals:** Julia Waters, Maxine Waters, Richard Dennison **Recorded:** July 1985 **Technical Team:** Producer: Steve "Golde" Goldstein / Executive Producer: Dolly Parton **Single:** Side A: The River Unbroken / Side B: More Than I Can Say **Release:** Columbia Records, November 23, 1987 (ref.: 38-07665) **Best Chart Ranking:** 63 on Billboard Hot Country Songs (US); 23 on RPM Adult Contemporary Singles (Canada)

With this song, the songwriter returns to one of her trademarks, associating nature with the feeling of love, a love as infinite as eternity. For this final bouquet, Dolly Parton and Steve Goldstein offer us a fireworks display in the form of a symphonic ballad. The arrangement, a very cinematographic work of art, unfolds a landscape of mountains and great plains that is difficult to describe in words: "More than I can say," Dolly sings or whispers, while oboe, English horn, French horn, harpsichord, harp, and glockenspiel share the sound space with a rich and vibrant string ensemble. A conclusion like a solemn confession that leaves the listener on a tender note, a breath of exalted romanticism.

ALBUM

White Limozeen

Time for Me to Fly . Yellow Roses . Why'd You Come in Here Lookin' Like That .
Slow Healing Heart . What Is It My Love . White Limozeen . Wait 'Til I Get You Home .
Take Me Back to the Country . The Moon, the Stars and Me . He's Alive

RELEASE DATE
United States: May 30, 1989
Reference: Columbia Records, Nashville (TN)—C-44384
Best US Chart Ranking: 3

Back to Her Roots in Style

White Limozeen is Dolly Parton's twenty-ninth solo album. Produced by the singer-songwriter and Ricky Skaggs, a friend of the star's, it was released by Columbia on May 30, 1989. Out of ten songs, the songwriter wrote two and co-wrote two others with songwriter Mac Davis, also a friend of hers. But above all, she returned to the source of her first successes with a country or even country rock record. The album remained on the charts for one hundred weeks and ended up as a certified gold album. If the star surrounded herself with friends on this opus, it was probably because of her last experiences: the relative failure of *Rainbow* and, before it, the huge success of *Trio*, made with her talented friends Linda Ronstadt and Emmylou Harris.

Flashback

In 1989, the AIDS virus was ravaging the planet. George H. W. Bush succeeded Ronald Reagan to the presidency on January 20. Ecological and climatic disasters followed in quick succession, with the *Exxon Valdez* oil spill on the Alaskan coast, then Tropical Storm Allison, which hit Texas and Louisiana hard. Madonna sang "Like a Prayer," and Simply Red hit the charts with "If You Don't Know Me by Now."

In 1988, Dolly Parton had not released any albums, only singles from *Rainbow* and *Trio*. At the end of the 1970s, for a long interview in *Playboy* magazine, the songwriter met the writer Lawrence Grobel, with whom she became friends. Grobel saw her again ten years later and again Dolly confided in him. For a while, the tabloids were talking about her extra pounds; now, since she had lost weight, they were speculating about anorexia. The first thing that struck Grobel when he met her again was her slenderness, but, as at their first meeting, he was captivated by her beauty, her energy, and her determination, still intact at forty-two after a few hard years, both morally and physically. They discussed *Dolly*, the star's show on

ABC, which had not lived up to her expectations. Then Grobel asked her how she managed everything: writing and composing her songs, preparing an autobiography, the successful Dollywood theme park, filming the TV show, and her personal life. The star replied that if she was happy, then she had all the energy she needed to pursue her many projects—in other words, the realization of her dreams.

Back to Country

In 1989, Dolly was about to play Truvy Jones in *Steel Magnolias*, which tells the story of the friendship and solidarity of a group of women in a small town in Louisiana. No doubt stimulated by the success of the collaborative album *Trio*, the star reconnects with her first love, country music, and offers an album that was appreciated by critics and fans alike. Some of the songs are close to pop, however; perhaps Dolly was still trying to find a balance between the two genres. The album closes with a blazing gospel song, "He's Alive," which Dolly sang with the Christ Church Choir of Nashville at the 1989 CMA Awards—a performance that received a standing ovation. "White Limozeen" encompasses virtually all of the songwriter's favorite musical genres, everything that makes up the Dolly Parton sound.

Album Cover

On this Hollywood-style cover by Robert Blakeman, Dolly, in a tailored white dress embroidered with rhinestones, a white fox fur around her shoulders, having just stepped out of a white limousine, triumphs under the cheers and flashes on the red carpet of a cinema or theater whose marquee announces "Dolly Parton in White Limozeen." The other mood: Just as seductive, Dolly shines in a typical country outfit—in black and white inside the cover, in red on the back.

1989

On this album, the technical team is numerous, and the credits are not detailed for each track. We note the presence of: Sound Engineers: Tom Harding, Scott Hendricks, Pat Hutchinson, Doug Johnson, George Massenburg, Mike Pool, Ed Seay / Mixing: Doug Johnson / Mastering: Denny Purcell

Kevin Cronin, the songwriter behind "Time for Me to Fly" and the front man of REO Speedwagon, onstage in 1990.

Time For Me To Fly

Kevin Cronin / 2:53

Musicians: Eddie Bayers: drums / Farrell Morris, Ricky Skaggs: percussion / Mike Brignardello, Craig Nelson: bass / Barry Beckett, David Huntsinger, John Jarvis: keyboard, piano / Mark Casstevens, Steven A. Gibson, Vince Gill, Albert Lee, Mac McAnally, Ricky Skaggs, Reggie Young: guitar / Stuart Duncan, Ricky Skaggs: fiddle / Paul Franklin: pedabro / Terry Crisp, Lloyd Green, John Hughey, Paul Franklin: pedal steel / Béla Fleck: banjo / Ricky Skaggs: mandolin
Vocals: Dolly Parton **Backing Vocals:** Curtis Young, Liana Young, Lisa Silver, Bernard Peyton, Kim Morrison, Vicki Hampton, Yvonne Hodges, Richard Dennison **Recorded:** Treasure Isle Recorders and the Lawrence Welk "Champagne" Studio (Nashville, TN), February 1989
Technical Team: Producer: Ricky Skaggs **Single:** Side A: Time for Me to Fly / Side B: The Moon, the Stars and Me **Released:** Columbia, January 1, 1990 (ref.: 38-73226) **Best US Chart Ranking:** 39 on Billboard Hot Country Songs

"Time for Me to Fly" is a song released in 1978 by the American rock band REO Speedwagon, which its lead singer, Kevin Cronin, reportedly took ten years to write. In 2020, it enjoyed a resurgence after being used in episode 3 of season 3 of the Netflix series *Ozark*. In this song, Dolly offers a bluegrass take on the story, expressing the weariness of a couple in which one laughs while the other cries. A nice text on the wearying of feelings.

The banjo is given prominence in this piece. The playing of Béla Fleck, a virtuoso musician who knows how to take the banjo beyond traditional American music, is remarkably fluid and rich, with a great flow to it. Unlike the albums of the early 1980s, on which the voice was sometimes lost in the profusion of instruments, here the instruments do not play simultaneously, and the tessituras are well distributed, as is the sound space. The bass drum is very rocking, with plenty of attack and roundness. The other drums are played with brushes. It is interesting to observe that, every second bar or so, the drummer adds a sixteenth note on the snare drum to get the rhythm going again. The mandolin is the banjo's counterpart in the mix. It plays melodic lines like the banjo in the first verse and a kind of palm mute in the second. A pedal steel is slightly set back on the whole track, but it is definitely there. As for the electric guitar and the pedal steel, they play two solos in the same vein as the banjo, with lots of notes.

1989

The intro seems to be played on the pedabro. The credits are not detailed for each song, so there is still some doubt as to whether this is a pedal steel or a pedabro, a hybrid instrument between the dobro—a metal guitar with a cone to project the sound—and the pedal steel. It is the inventor of the pedabro himself, Paul Franklin, who plays on the album.

Dolly Parton wearing black leather during a 1989 performance on *The Tonight Show*, in Los Angeles. Her look here says it all: Her rise to fame is still not over.

Yellow Roses

Dolly Parton / 3:56

Musicians: Eddie Bayers: drums / Farrell Morris, Ricky Skaggs: percussion / Mike Brignardello, Craig Nelson: bass / Barry Beckett, David Huntsinger, John Jarvis: keyboard, piano / Mark Casstevens, Steven A. Gibson, Vince Gill, Albert Lee, Mac McAnally, Ricky Skaggs, Reggie Young: guitar / Stuart Duncan, Ricky Skaggs: fiddle / Paul Franklin: pedabro / Terry Crisp, Lloyd Green, John Hughey, Paul Franklin: pedal steel / Béla Fleck: banjo / Ricky Skaggs: mandolin / Bob Mason: cello / Bobby Taylor: oboe / Jo-El Sonnier: Cajun accordion / Nashville String Machine: strings / Bergen White: strings arrangement **Vocals:** Dolly Parton **Backing Vocals:** Curtis Young, Liana Young, Lisa Silver, Bernard Peyton, Kim Morrison, Vicki Hampton, Yvonne Hodges, Richard Dennison **Recorded:** Treasure Isle Recorders and the Lawrence Welk "Champagne" Studio (Nashville, TN), February 1989 **Technical Team:** Producer: Ricky Skaggs **Single:** Side A: Yellow Roses / Side B: Wait 'Til I Get You Home **Release:** Columbia, July 31, 1989 (ref.: 38-69040) **Best Chart Ranking:** 1 on Billboard Hot Country Songs (US); 1 on RPM Country Singles (Canada)

This sweet and melancholic ballad written by Dolly Parton is a return to her roots, and therefore also to the love song. The narrator falls in love with a stranger who gives her a yellow rose, the color of the sun. They love each other for a while and then he leaves, after giving her another yellow rose.

The song is very similar to "Mama Say a Prayer" on the album *In the Good Old Days* (1969). The tempo is slightly faster, but the chord grid is almost identical, the structure too. The melody of the chorus can be found at the end of the verses. The beginning is quite busy: All the rhythmic forces are there, the pedabro and the strings ensemble (a collective called the Nashville String Machine). The verse, on which only the bass, drums, guitar, and vocals intervene, is rather pared down. The strings are mixed sparingly and remain discreet (generally, the string ensemble is the starring section). Finally, the subtlety of the mix despite the large number of instruments is worthy of mention.

Dolly looking glamorous on the set of her television show in 1989. Her radiant smile and velvet gloves pair perfectly with her role as the boss on a major network show.

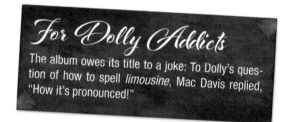

For Dolly Addicts

The album owes its title to a joke: To Dolly's question of how to spell *limousine*, Mac Davis replied, "How it's pronounced!"

SINGLE

Why'd You Come In Here Lookin' Like That

Bob Carlisle, Randy Thomas / 2:33

Musicians: Eddie Bayers: drums / Farrell Morris, Ricky Skaggs: percussion / Mike Brignardello: bass / Barry Beckett: piano / Mark Casstevens, Steven A. Gibson, Albert Lee: guitar / Béla Fleck: banjo / David Huntsinger: piano / Ricky Skaggs: mandolin, acoustic guitar, triangle, fiddle, vocal harmonies / Jo-El Sonnier: Cajun accordion
Vocals: Dolly Parton **Vocal Harmonies:** Curtis Young **Recorded:** Treasure Isle Recorders and the Lawrence Welk "Champagne" Studio (Nashville, TN), February 1989 **Technical Team:** Producer: Ricky Skaggs **Single:** Side A: Why'd You Come in Here Lookin' Like That / Side B: Wait 'Til I Get You Home **Release:** Columbia, April 1989 (ref.: 38-68760) **Best Chart Ranking:** 1 on Billboard Hot Country Songs (US); 2 on RPM Country Singles (Canada)

This catchy song is accompanied by a humorous video clip in which Dolly auditions men for the song's title role, who come to her in the most outlandish outfits. She did not write the lyrics, but her strong and heartfelt performance earned her a Grammy nomination for Best Female Country Vocal Performance.

The song begins with the refrain and the full band—fewer instruments are used than on previous tracks, but they all come in from the start. On the verses, themes are played by the electric guitar, the piano, and the folk guitar. The sense of enjoyment of the musicians and the team is perceptible and is translated in particular by the spontaneous call of a backing singer at 0:43. After the a cappella part, before the last refrains, the attack of Dolly's voice is surprising, especially since it is done in anacrusis (before the first beat of the measure), and the beginning of the refrain is also sung a cappella. The voices do not limit themselves to singing the text, the bass simulates the rhythm (percussion and bass), and the very energetic reentry of the singer is all the more effective. The playing of the banjo and the Cajun accordion give the song its traditional feel. Listening on headphones, one can hear the tinkling of a bell on the choruses—an instrument that is essential for keeping the tempo in Latin music.

Drummer Eddie Bayers sitting behind his drum kit, perhaps getting ready for recording sessions on *White Limozeen*.

A guitar paired with sequins became a standard Dolly Parton stage outfit in 1989.

Slow Healing Heart

Jim Rushing / 3:57

Musicians: Eddie Bayers: drums / Farrell Morris, Ricky Skaggs: percussion / Mike Brignardello, Craig Nelson: bass / Barry Beckett, David Huntsinger, John Jarvis: keyboard, piano / Mark Casstevens, Steven A. Gibson, Vince Gill, Albert Lee, Mac McAnally, Ricky Skaggs, Reggie Young: guitar / Stuart Duncan, Ricky Skaggs: fiddle / Paul Franklin: pedabro / Terry Crisp, Lloyd Green, John Hughey, Paul Franklin: pedal steel / Béla Fleck: banjo / David Huntsinger: piano / Ricky Skaggs: mandolin **Vocals:** Dolly Parton **Backing Vocals:** Curtis Young, Liana Young, Lisa Silver, Bernard Peyton, Kim Morrison, Vicki Hampton, Yvonne Hodges, Richard Dennison **Recorded:** Treasure Isle Recorders and the Lawrence Welk "Champagne" Studio (Nashville, TN), February 1989 **Technical Team:** Producer: Ricky Skaggs **Single:** Side A: Slow Healing Heart / Side B: Take Me Back to the Country **Release:** Columbia, September 1990 (ref.: 38-73498) **Best Chart Ranking:** 1 on Billboard Hot Country Songs (US); 1 on RPM Country Singles (Canada)

In this song, the narrator wonders how to heal her broken heart and love again. A question that the songwriter has addressed many times. A universal question, to which the title answers: "A heart heals slowly."

This sentimental ballad is beautifully performed by the artist. The instruments enter gradually: first, all the pizzicato strings to support the song, then the piano, and finally the other musicians. On the first chorus, the harmonized voice of a man in the background in the mix accompanies the main song of Dolly Parton. The backing singer provides just the necessary support. This voice remains in front of the other backing vocalists on the subsequent refrains. The electric guitar, often found in modern country music, reminds us here of Keziah Jones, in a completely different style of music. Its tone has a big attack, with some overdrive and reverb. Equalized with a slight dip in the midrange, the sound is slightly aggressive, in a good way. For a gigantic effect, the snare drum, played along with a tambourine on the choruses, sounds immense, with a nice attack, bass tones, and huge reverb effect; it is played in rim shot on the verses. "Slow Healing Heart" is a fine example of a successful marriage of traditional and modern sound.

Dolly and Ricky Skaggs, her producer and friend, in the studio for Columbia Records and CBS Records in 1989.

SINGLE

What Is It My Love

Dolly Parton / 4:14

Musicians: David Huntsinger: piano / Bob Mason: cello / Stuart Duncan, Ricky Skaggs: fiddle / Bobby Taylor: oboe / Bergen White: strings arrangement **Vocals:** Dolly Parton **Backing Vocals:** Curtis Young, Liana Young, Lisa Silver, Bernard Peyton, Kim Morrison, Vicki Hampton, Yvonne Hodges, Richard Dennison **Recorded:** Treasure Isle Recorders and the Lawrence Welk "Champagne" Studio (Nashville, TN), February 1989 **Technical Team:** Producer: Ricky Skaggs **Single:** Side A: He's Alive / Side B: What Is It My Love **Release:** Columbia, November 1989 (ref.: 38-73200) **Best US Chart Ranking:** 39 on Billboard Hot Country Songs

This love song, very different from the previous one, reviews the defects of a man, the long list of which does not prevent the narrator from loving him. What kind of love is it? One imagines it to be sensual and sexual, because perhaps only passion can incite indulgence—an inexhaustible theme that the songwriter continually explores. Musically, it is a quartet that accompanies her: piano, cello, violin, and oboe. The latter, rarely played in modern music and more usually found in classical symphonic orchestras, blends perfectly here with the violin.

The ambitious young country girl described in "White Limozeen" dreams of one day having her portrait on the side of a jukebox, just like Dolly Parton.

White Limozeen

Dolly Parton, Mac Davis / 4:19

Musicians: Eddie Bayers: drums / Mike Brignardello, Craig Nelson: bass / Barry Beckett, David Huntsinger, John Jarvis: keyboard, piano / Mark Casstevens, Steven A. Gibson, Vince Gill, Albert Lee, Mac McAnally, Ricky Skaggs, Reggie Young: guitar / Paul Franklin: pedabro **Vocals:** Dolly Parton **Backing Vocals:** Curtis Young, Liana Young, Lisa Silver, Bernard Peyton, Kim Morrison, Vicki Hampton, Yvonne Hodges, Richard Dennison **Recorded:** Treasure Isle Recorders and the Lawrence Welk "Champagne" Studio (Nashville, TN), February 1989 **Technical Team:** Producer: Ricky Skaggs **Single:** Side A: White Limozeen / Side B: The Moon, the Stars and Me **Release:** Columbia, April 9, 1990 (ref.: 38-73341) **Best Chart Ranking:** 29 on Billboard Hot Country Songs (US); 47 on RPM Country Singles (Canada)

Co-written with Mac Davis, the song is about an ambitious country girl who arrives in Hollywood with stars in her eyes—no doubt echoing Dolly's own experience of leaving her native Smoky Mountains for Nashville to fulfill her

dream of becoming a star. A difficult journey toward success, but Daisy Mae has not lost her soul along the way: her name at the top of the bill, the diamonds, the long-coveted white limousine—none of this has changed who she really is.

For the first time on this album, in this fairly rocking track, the drums are brought to the fore. As on *Slow Healing Heart*, the bass drum and snare drum play together to produce a very rich sound often used in reggae. The bass drum, the bass, and the snare complement each other. The bass plays each beat without adding any beat to it, like the bass drum, thus ensuring a solid rhythmic base. The toms share the sound space, which produces a particular effect during the breaks. The pedabro also has a prominent role: It plays all the solos, especially the intro, which is quite powerful. The keyboard, with a very groovy rhythm, reinforces the impression of the power of sound, especially since it is underlined by the bass voice of the backing vocals. The bass naturally suggests power, as our ears have been trained to expect.

1989

Mac Davis, songwriter and friend of Dolly Parton, had two co-writing credits on *White Limozeen*, including the title track.

Wait 'Til I Get You Home

Dolly Parton, Mac Davis / 2:58

Musicians: Eddie Bayers: drums / Farrell Morris, Ricky Skaggs: percussion / Mike Brignardello: bass / Barry Beckett: piano / Mark Casstevens, Steven A. Gibson, Albert Lee: guitar / Béla Fleck: banjo / David Huntsinger: piano / Ricky Skaggs: mandolin, acoustic guitar, triangle, fiddle **Vocals:** Dolly Parton, Mac Davis **Vocal Harmonies:** Curtis Young, Ricky Skaggs **Recorded:** Treasure Isle Recorders and the Lawrence Welk "Champagne" Studio (Nashville, TN), February 1989 **Technical Team:** Producer: Ricky Skaggs **Single:** Side A: Why'd You Come in Here Lookin' Like That / Side B: Wait 'Til I Get You Home **Release:** Columbia, April 1989 (ref.: 38-68760) **Best Chart Ranking:** 1 on Billboard Hot Country Songs (US); 2 on RPM Country Singles (Canada)

Here are some explicitly sensual lyrics that evoke a perfect and intimate love chemistry, intact from the first night, since the first look. Back to pure country with this track: a lap steel playing the theme, the drums providing a syncopated rhythm with the bass, and a folk guitar accompanying—everything is there. Although Mac Davis sings this text in duet with Dolly, she has the main voice in this song.

Take Me Back To The Country

Karen Staley / 2:35

Musicians: Eddie Bayers: drums / Farrell Morris, Ricky Skaggs: percussion / Mike Brignardello, Craig Nelson: bass / Barry Beckett, David Huntsinger, John Jarvis: keyboard, piano / Mark Casstevens, Steven A. Gibson, Vince Gill, Albert Lee, Mac McAnally, Ricky Skaggs, Reggie Young: guitar / Stuart Duncan, Ricky Skaggs: fiddle **Vocals:** Dolly Parton **Backing Vocals:** Curtis Young, Liana Young, Lisa Silver, Bernard Peyton, Kim Morrison, Vicki Hampton, Yvonne Hodges, Richard Dennison **Recorded:** Treasure Isle Recorders and the Lawrence Welk "Champagne" Studio (Nashville, TN), February 1989 **Technical Team:** Producer: Ricky Skaggs

As she has done before, on this number Dolly sings about the city—teeming and frenetic, polluted, distressing, and wearing—and about missing her native countryside, and the desire to get back to what matters: the treetops touching the sky, the flight of an eagle, the calm, the stars eclipsing the city lights, the simple life. The intro is played by two folk guitars placed on each side of the mix. Then the phrase is taken up by the bass and by the electric guitar. On the verse, with a very rock feel, the bass plays in slap mode, and the song is answered by the piano and/or the electric guitar. Suddenly, the chorus takes us back to a very catchy country music, with a fiddle even making an incursion in the second half of the song.

Dolly in a rock-inspired outfit while accepting a CMA gospel award in 1989.

Reggie Young (left) in the studio with Merle Haggard. Young was one of the guitarists who appeared on *White Limozeen*.

The Moon, The Stars And Me

Wayland Patton, Diana Rae / 3:19

Musicians: Eddie Bayers: drums / Farrell Morris, Ricky Skaggs: percussion / Mike Brignardello, Craig Nelson: bass / Barry Beckett, David Huntsinger, John Jarvis: keyboard, piano / Mark Casstevens, Steven A. Gibson, Vince Gill, Albert Lee, Mac McAnally, Ricky Skaggs, Reggie Young: guitar / Terry Crisp, Lloyd Green, John Hughey, Paul Franklin: pedal steel / Ricky Skaggs: mandolin **Vocals:** Dolly Parton **Backing Vocals:** Curtis Young, Liana Young, Lisa Silver, Bernard Peyton, Kim Morrison, Vicki Hampton, Yvonne Hodges, Richard Dennison **Recorded:** Treasure Isle Recorders and the Lawrence Welk "Champagne" Studio (Nashville, TN), February 1989 **Technical Team:** Producer: Ricky Skaggs **Single:** Side A: White Limozeen / Side B: The Moon, the Stars and Me **Release:** Columbia, April 9, 1990 (ref.: 38-73341) **Best Chart Ranking:** 29 on Billboard Hot Country Songs (US); 47 on RPM Country Singles (Canada)

The narrator takes the moon and the stars as her witness: Her lover has betrayed her promise of eternal love. The very soft intro of this slow ballad, which resembles a Christmas song, is played by the folk guitar and the mandolin. A big reverb is applied to the voice, as on most ballads. A folk guitar plays transitional melodies with a lot of attack, the musician playing as close to the bridge as possible to produce a sound similar to that of the electric guitar. We note the absence of the violin.

He's Alive

Don Francisco / 4:39

Musicians: Eddie Bayers: drums / Farrell Morris, Ricky Skaggs: percussion / Mike Brignardello, Craig Nelson: bass / Barry Beckett, David Huntsinger, John Jarvis: keyboard, piano / Mark Casstevens, Steven A. Gibson, Vince Gill, Albert Lee, Mac McAnally, Ricky Skaggs, Reggie Young: guitar / Ricky Skaggs: mandolin / Nashville String Machine: strings / Bergen White: strings arrangement **Vocals:** Dolly Parton **Backing Vocals:** Curtis Young, Liana Young, Lisa Silver, Bernard Peyton, Kim Morrison, Vicki Hampton, Yvonne Hodges, Richard Dennison **Recorded:** Treasure Isle Recorders and the Lawrence Welk "Champagne" Studio (Nashville, TN), February 1989 **Technical Team:** Producer: Ricky Skaggs **Single:** Side A: He's Alive / Side B: What Is It My Love **Release:** Columbia, November 1989 (ref.: 38-73200) **Best US Chart Ranking:** 39 on Billboard Hot Country Songs

For a beautiful conclusion to this opus, this is a gospel cover of a song by Don Francisco (the album *Forgiven*, released in 1977), dedicated to the disappearance of the body of Christ and his resurrection. Dolly's interpretation is spectacular. Like the eponymous song from the album *Once Upon a Christmas*, this one is almost like an UFO in the *White Limozeen* context. And, logically, the treatment of the subject is connected: We are not far from the rock opera, like *Starmania*. The lightness of the beginning comes from the strings, which enter alone, gradually. Three minutes forty seconds pass before the first chorus, the time to increase the pressure.

ALBUM

Home for Christmas

First Noel . Santa Claus Is Coming to Town . I'll Be Home for Christmas .
Rudolph the Red-Nosed Reindeer . Go Tell It on the Mountain . The Little Drummer Boy .
We Three Kings . Jingle Bells . O Little Town of Bethlehem . Joy to the World

RELEASE DATE
United States: September 11, 1990
Reference: Columbia Records, New York (NY)—CK-46796
Best US Chart Ranking: 29

Christmas Spirit

Home for Christmas is Dolly Parton's second Christmas album. Produced by Gary Smith, with Dolly as executive producer, it was released by Columbia Records on September 11, 1990. From the point of view of the critics, it was not Dolly's best album, which revisited standard numbers, but they judged it pleasant nevertheless. It was certified gold in 1994.

The Confectioners' Truce

In the summer of 1990, the Gulf War began, in which George W. Bush's United States led a coalition of some thirty nations against Iraq; by November, more than 500,000 soldiers were deployed in the Persian Gulf. Also that year, the movie stars Barbara Stanwyck, Ava Gardner, Greta Garbo, and Paulette Goddard died. The American population took advantage of the Christmas festivities to find some peace and human warmth, singing "Thank God It's Christmas" by the group Queen (1984) or watching *Edward Scissorhands* by Tim Burton.

In 1989, during her meeting with the writer William Stadiem for the magazine *Interview*—created by Andy Warhol in 1969—we learn that Dolly Parton was writing her autobiography. Untiring, the artist had been working on many projects since she regained her zest for life. A special program was broadcast on December 21 on ABC, *Dolly Parton: Christmas at Home*. It featured footage shot in the studio during the recording of the album, some of which showed Dolly singing with her family in her childhood home, and other sequences that showed the places of her native Tennessee. *Home for Christmas* was also an opportunity for the star to invite viewers into the heart of the Smoky Mountains, her home, to spend Christmas with her.

A Long Religious Tradition

Dolly Parton, like many artists, released *Home for Christmas* in the Christmas songs tradition. The star covers some classics, all celebrating the birth of the Christ child. The carol services, as they are called in the Anglo-Saxon world, have their origins in Europe, some of them dating back to the Middle Ages. Among Catholics, these early songs were joyful, rhythmic, and even danceable. In medieval times, the mysteries of the Nativity were staged as a kind of popular theater where people sang playlets to celebrate the birth of the Divine Child. It is not surprising, therefore, that Dolly should pick up on this, as she attended her grandfather's church as a child and thought of becoming a missionary if she did not become a star! We sometimes forget that Dolly is also a gospel singer and that she lives in faith, driven by a spiritual quest.

Album Cover

In the photos by Dennis Garney, Dolly, on the front cover, is like a snow queen, dressed in white and driving a white sleigh in a pristine landscape, against which the carmine color of the velvet upholstered seat stands out, along with the title of the album and the name of the artist. On the back and inside the cover, in contrast, she is dressed as Mrs. Claus.

1990

"First Noel" is a traditional English Christmas carol celebrating the birth of Christ. Here, a few British revelers celebrate the tallest Christmas tree in England, in December 1976.

First Noel

Traditional / 4:03

Musicians: The Mighty Fine Band: Michael Davis: keyboards / Gary Smith: piano / Steve Turner: drums / Paul Uhrig: acoustic bass / Kent Wells: acoustic guitar / Carl Jackson: acoustic guitar **Vocals:** Dolly Parton **Backing Vocals:** Richard Dennison, Jennifer O'Brien, Howard Smith, The New Salem Methodist Church Congregation **Recorded:** Nightingale Studio, Nashville (TN), July 1990 **Technical Team:** Producer: Gary Smith / Executive Producer: Dolly Parton / Production Assistant: Mark Kiracofe / Sound Engineer: Gary Paczosa / Assistant Sound Engineers: Michael Davis, Chrissy Follmar, Brad Jones, John Kunz / Mixing: Gary Paczosa / Mastering: Denny Purcell

"The First Noel" is a traditional English song, of Cornish origin, which celebrates the birth of Christ. Dolly Parton introduces it with a few words evoking the precious memories of her childhood, and especially of Christmas in the Smoky Mountains with family, neighbors, and friends in that little church where she already loved to sing those old, beautiful songs. As if to put the listener in the mood, there follows a recording of a pastor's voice announcing, "The First Noel," which the congregation then begins to sing. Then comes the studio version of the album, with Gary Smith's piano. The voice of Dolly intones, "The first Noel…," then the acoustic guitar enters in arpeggio, at the same time as a layer of synthesizer-like strings. The bass and drums enter in turn, followed by the cello and backing vocals, with the

intensity rising progressively until the climax at 3:41, before the gentle conclusion: "Born is the King of Israel."

Santa Claus Is Coming To Town

J. Fred Coots, Haven Gillespie / 1:52

Musicians: The Mighty Fine Band: Jimmy Mattingly: fiddle / Steve Turner: percussions / Paul Uhrig: acoustic bass / Kent Wells, Carl Jackson: acoustic guitar / **Vocals:** Dolly Parton **Recorded:** Nightingale Studio, Nashville (TN), July 1990 **Technical Team:** Producer: Gary Smith / Executive Producer: Dolly Parton / Production Assistant: Mark Kiracofe / Sound Engineer: Gary Paczosa / Assistant Sound Engineers: Michael Davis, Chrissy Follmar, Brad Jones, John Kunz / Mixing: Gary Paczosa / Mastering: Denny Purcell

Originally aired at the height of the Great Depression, the song encouraged listeners to be charitable and help the less fortunate at Christmas. Dolly's version is country, with a touch of humor—which she masters. We move from solemnity with "First Noel" to the cheerfulness of this up-tempo country shuffle: a staccato backbeat piano, country licks of electric guitar passed through a slap delay, a bass and drums in cross stick with a bouncy play, enveloping backing vocals, Jimmy Mattingly's invigorating touch of fiddle, and Dolly's mischievous voice. There is no doubt: Santa Claus is coming to town!

Tom T. Hall was the writer behind "Harper Valley PTA" and known in the industry as "The Storyteller." Here he poses with his wife, Dixie, in front of the family Christmas tree.

I'll Be Home For Christmas

Kim Gannon, Walter Kent / 3:13

Musicians: The Mighty Fine Band: Michael Davis: keyboards / Gary Smith: piano / Steve Turner: drums / Paul Uhrig: bass / Kent Wells: electric guitar / Carl Jackson: acoustic guitar / Michael Johnson: gut string guitar / Jack Smith: pedal steel **Vocals:** Dolly Parton **Backing Vocals:** Richard Dennison, Jennifer O'Brien, Howard Smith **Recorded:** Nightingale Studio, Nashville (TN), July 1990 **Technical Team:** Producer: Gary Smith / Executive Producer: Dolly Parton / Production Assistant: Mark Kiracofe / Sound Engineer: Gary Paczosa / Assistant Sound Engineers: Michael Davis, Chrissy Follmar, Brad Jones, John Kunz / Mixing: Gary Paczosa / Mastering: Denny Purcell

Originally written in the 1940s as a tribute to soldiers who dreamed of being home for the holidays, the song "I'll Be Home for Christmas" has become a classic. "I'll be home for Christmas, if only in my dreams…": Such is the melancholy wish that concludes a soldier's letter to his family, all the more poignant if one considers those sons, husbands, fathers, and friends on the front lines in this year of 1990, when the war was raging in Iraq.

This is the jazzy version of this Christmas song: a cozy, hushed atmosphere, drums played on brushes, a round and minimalist bass, piano chords and acoustic guitar softly arpeggiated. Of note: the pedal steel and the silky string arrangement for an ethereal aspect, the fiddle solo as soft as a yule log, the electric guitar with its clear and warm sound, the airy backing vocals like the caressing breath of a winter breeze, and Dolly's voice, so comforting. We listen to this piece as we put on a big wool sweater and warm up by the fire.

The score of *Rudolph the Red-Nosed Reindeer* was inspired by a poem written by Robert L. May in 1939. Johnny Marks, a songwriter famous for his Christmas carols, used the poem as inspiration for the classic Christmas song.

Rudolph The Red-Nosed Reindeer

Johnny Marks / 3:25

Musicians: The Mighty Fine Band: Jimmy Mattingly: fiddle / Steve Turner: percussions / Robert Williams: dobro / Carl Jackson: acoustic guitar / Stuart Duncan: mandolin **Vocals:** Dolly Parton **Backing Vocals:** Our Kids **Recorded:** Nightingale Studio, Nashville (TN), July 1990 **Technical Team:** Producer: Gary Smith / Executive Producer: Dolly Parton / Production Assistant: Mark Kiracofe / Sound Engineer: Gary Paczosa / Assistant Sound Engineers: Michael Davis, Chrissy Follmar, Brad Jones, John Kunz / Mixing: Gary Paczosa / Mastering: Denny Purcell

Inspired by a poem by Robert L. May (1939), this song was written by Johnny Marks, a songwriter famous for his Christmas songs. Many singers have interpreted it, including Harry Belafonte. To begin this song, Dolly addresses some children (her nieces and nephews, in the ABC show), then she sings, soon joined by the backing vocals. Back to festive cheerfulness for this nursery rhyme in the form of an acoustic up-tempo country shuffle. We find the traditional bluegrass instruments (fiddle, acoustic guitars, mandolin) but also those of country (pedal steel and dobro). The mountain music atmosphere of the modest cabin homes of the southern Appalachians, when the whole family is gathered to share a fire and human warmth, is perfectly rendered. One can almost imagine that one is really there!

Go Tell It On The Mountain

Traditional / 2:50

Musicians: The Mighty Fine Band: Gary Smith: piano, Hammond B3 organ / Steve Turner: drums / Paul Uhrig: bass / Kent Wells: electric guitar / Carl Jackson: acoustic guitar / Jack Smith: pedal steel **Vocals:** Dolly Parton **Backing Vocals:** Richard Dennison, Jennifer O'Brien, Howard Smith, Bob Bailey, Bobby Jones & Nashville **Recorded:** Nightingale Studio, Nashville (TN), July 1990 **Technical Team:** Producer: Gary Smith / Executive Producer: Dolly Parton / Production Assistant: Mark Kiracofe / Sound Engineer: Gary Paczosa / Assistant Sound Engineers: Michael Davis, Chrissy Follmar, Brad Jones, John Kunz / Mixing: Gary Paczosa / Mastering: Denny Purcell

"Go Tell It on the Mountain" is an African American spiritual probably dating from 1865, recorded by John Wesley Work Jr., and since then has been sung and recorded by many artists. Dolly and Gary Smith decided to make a big production of it. It starts with a solemn piano, then goes into a country ballad with an ultra-traditional Nashville sound, and ends with a vibrant gospel song with a frenetic tempo. Another great vocal performance from the Queen of Country, who also earns a few more stripes as a soul and gospel performer.

Jo Walker-Meador created the first Country Music Hall of Fame and Museum. Here she poses with Johnny Marks in front of a sign for the "This Is Country Music" exhibition at the museum.

The Little Drummer Boy

Katherine Kennicott Davis, Henry Onorati, Harry Simeone / 4:34

Musicians: The Mighty Fine Band: Michael Davis: keyboards / Gary Smith: piano, keyboards / Paul Uhrig: bass / Carl Jackson: acoustic guitar **Vocals:** Dolly Parton **Backing Vocals:** Richard Dennison, Jennifer O'Brien, Howard Smith, Bobby Jones & Nashville **Recorded:** Nightingale Studio, Nashville (TN), July 1990 **Technical Team:** Producer: Gary Smith / Executive Producer: Dolly Parton / Production Assistant: Mark Kiracofe / Sound Engineer: Gary Paczosa / Assistant Sound Engineers: Michael Davis, Chrissy Follmar, Brad Jones, John Kunz / Mixing: Gary Paczosa / Mastering: Denny Purcell

The story tells how a very poor boy is invited to come and see the baby Jesus, who has just been born. Having no gift to offer, the boy plays his drum. It is Steve Turner's drum, or rather his snare drum, that launches the piece with some masterful rolls—which we hear until the end. The orchestration grows and rises in power until 3:31, continues on a long intro in ad lib, then on to a progressive fade-out. Dolly and Gary Smith offer us a very literal and pictorial arrangement in this number. The sound of tubular bells played by Michael Davis on the synthesizer imitates that of church bells, the male backing vocalists evoke the reassuring voices of the three kings, and the snare drum suggests the boy's drum, with the other instruments wrapping the whole piece very theatrically. All of this to better immerse the listener in this pious Christmas playlet. In the genre, it is successfully done.

John Henry Hopkins Jr. was a former journalist and rector of Christ Episcopal Church in Willamsport, Pennsylvania. He was also the author of "We Three Kings."

We Three Kings

Traditional / 2:44

Musicians: The Mighty Fine Band: Jimmy Mattingly: mandolin / Paul Uhrig: acoustic bass / Kent Wells: electric guitar / Carl Jackson: acoustic guitar / Jack Smith: pedal steel / Alisa Jones Wall: hammered dulcimer **Vocals:** Dolly Parton **Backing Vocals:** The Mighty Fine Band, Carl Jackson **Recorded:** Nightingale Studio, Nashville (TN), July 1990 **Technical Team:** Producer: Gary Smith / Executive Producer: Dolly Parton / Production Assistant: Mark Kiracofe / Sound Engineer: Gary Paczosa / Assistant Sound Engineers: Michael Davis, Chrissy Follmar, Brad Jones, John Kunz / Mixing: Gary Paczosa / Mastering: Denny Purcell

The author of this carol, written in 1857, is John Henry Hopkins Jr., a former New York journalist and rector of Christ Episcopal Church in Williamsport, Pennsylvania. "We Three Kings" was the first carol from the United States to become popular. Echoes of traditional Celtic music can be heard. The addition of a hammered dulcimer part (a string instrument struck by sticks, with Eastern European origins), played by Alisa Jones Wall, evokes the sound of the Celtic harp. Its brilliant sonority is supported by the arpeggios of Carl Carson on acoustic guitar, Kent Wells on electric guitar, Jack Smith on pedal steel, and Jimmy Mattingly's mandolin. The rhythm section supports the ensemble with precise and nuanced playing, while the backing vocals—as at the beginning, immersed, from 0:05 to 0:11, in a very deep reverb to produce a strange and mystical effect—bring a kind of ancient quality to this arrangement, subtly chiseled by the Mighty Fine Band. The soul of the early settlers is very much present in this song in the form of a biblical tale.

The Queen of Country turns into a queen of snow and ice while posing in front of a Christmas tree in Lake Tahoe, ca. 1992.

Jingle Bells

James Lord Pierpont / 1:55

Musicians: The Mighty Fine Band: Michael Davis, Steve Turner: percussions / Steve Turner: drums / Robert Williams: dobro / Carl Jackson: acoustic guitar / Alisa Jones Wall: hammered dulcimer **Vocals:** Dolly Parton **Backing Vocals:** Our Kids **Recorded:** Nightingale Studio, Nashville (TN), July 1990 **Technical Team:** Producer: Gary Smith / Executive Producer: Dolly Parton / Production Assistant: Mark Kiracofe / Sound Engineer: Gary Paczosa / Assistant Sound Engineers: Michael Davis, Chrissy Follmar, Brad Jones, John Kunz / Mixing: Gary Paczosa / Mastering: Denny Purcell

This song, originally written by James Lord Pierpont for the American Thanksgiving holiday, was recorded for the first time on October 30, 1889, on a phonographic cylinder of the Edison Records label, founded by Thomas Edison. From Ella Fitzgerald to the Beatles, from Luciano Pavarotti to Johnny Cash, from Duke Ellington to Dolly Parton, the interpretations are countless—and who, more generally, has not hummed "Jingle Bells" at least once in their life? We encounter the famous hammered dulcimer, again played by Alisa Jones Wall. This time, it does not imitate the Celtic harp but rather constitutes a percussive, childlike, and joyful counterpart to the bells, which are naturally de rigueur here. The arrangement of this up-tempo jingle is in the same spirit as that of "Rudolph the Red-Nosed Reindeer," without fiddle or mandolin, but with a children's choir and the dobro of Robert Williams—probably the two pieces were recorded during the same session. An amusing detail: A flanger is applied to the percussion cymbals, creating a spinning effect, as if to evoke the joyful atmosphere of children's rides. When it comes to producing a Christmas album, one can definitely say that Dolly knows how to motivate her little world. Her legendary drive and good humor are unmistakable.

O Little Town Of Bethlehem

Traditional / 2:39

Musicians: The Mighty Fine Band: Jimmy Mattingly: mandolin / Steve Turner: percussions / Carl Jackson: acoustic guitar / Stuart Duncan: fiddle **Vocals:** Dolly Parton **Backing Vocals:** The Mighty Fine Band **Recorded:** Nightingale Studio, Nashville (TN), July 1990 **Technical Team:** Producer: Gary Smith / Executive Producer: Dolly Parton / Production Assistant: Mark Kiracofe / Sound Engineer: Gary Paczosa / Assistant Sound Engineers: Michael Davis, Chrissy Follmar, Brad Jones, John Kunz / Mixing: Gary Paczosa / Mastering: Denny Purcell

Written in 1868 by Phillips Brooks, Episcopal priest and rector of Holy Trinity Church in Philadelphia, this poem was inspired by his visit to the village of Bethlehem three years earlier, and organist Lewis Redner composed the music. This country ballad, with its very traditional instrumentation, takes us back to the fireside, somewhere in the Smokies, safe from the cold. Smooth acoustic guitar strumming, an expressive fiddle, mandolin arpeggios and tremolos, a warm and full bass sound. It does not take much to set the scene of this song from another time and the context for Dolly to position her angelic voice, so clear and so present.

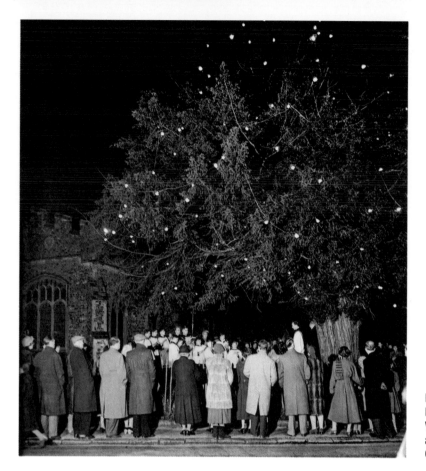

Mass under the Christmas tree at Martins Church in 1952. "Joy to the World" was most likely sung there, as it is one of the most popular Christmas carols in North America.

Joy To The World

Traditional / 4:23

1990

Musicians: The Mighty Fine Band: Michael Davis: keyboards / Gary Smith: piano / Steve Turner: drums / Paul Uhrig: bass / Kent Wells, Carl Jackson: acoustic guitar **Vocals:** Dolly Parton **Backing Vocals:** Richard Dennison, Jennifer O'Brien, Howard Smith, The New Salem Methodist Church Congregation, The Christ Church Pentecostal Choir **Recorded:** Nightingale Studio, Nashville (TN), July 1990 **Technical Team:** Producer: Gary Smith / Executive Producer: Dolly Parton / Production Assistant: Mark Kiracofe / Sound Engineer: Gary Paczosa / Assistant Sound Engineers: Michael Davis, Chrissy Follmar, Brad Jones, John Kunz / Mixing: Gary Paczosa / Mastering: Denny Purcell

"Joy to the World" is the most widely sung Christmas hymn in North America. Written in 1719 by the English pastor and poet Isaac Watts, this hymn is an interpretation of Psalm 98, which celebrates the birth of Jesus Christ.

Back to the big production with this progressive and lavish orchestral arrangement. First the piano and that inspired, twirling acoustic guitar arpeggio, then the bass, strings, backing vocals, brass, and orchestral percussion to give Steve Turner's drums more scope. At 2:27, the climax is reached with the powerful voices of the New Salem Methodist Church Congregation, joined by the Christ Church Pentecostal Choir. From 3:17, a clever transition, very well edited and mixed by Gary Paczosa, enables the piece to slip into another recording, made outside the walls of Nightingale Studio, in the heart of a church, probably with a pair of ambient microphones. In the place of worship, in the middle of a celebration, everyone is singing "Joy to the World" in chorus. Maybe it is the Christ Church Pentecostal Choir and its church, the same as on "First Noel," the first track of the album. In any case, this is a nice way to bring the album full circle, as Dolly assures us that wherever she is, her heart is always with her family at this time of year, and she wishes everyone a Merry Christmas and all the best. A Christmas album well handled by Dolly Parton and her team.

ALBUM

Eagle When She Flies

If You Need Me . Rockin' Years . Country Road . Silver and Gold .
Eagle When She Flies . Best Woman Wins . What a Heartache . Runaway Feelin' .
Dreams Do Come True . Family . Wildest Dreams

RELEASE DATE
United States: March 7, 1991
References: Columbia Records, New York (NY) – CK-46882
Best US Chart Ranking: 1

The Royal Flight

Eagle When She Flies is Dolly Parton's thirtieth solo album. Produced by Steve Buckingham and Gary Smith, with Dolly Parton as executive producer, it was released by Columbia Records on March 7, 1991. This ability to constantly renew herself is one of the artist's many talents, returning to country music in her own way and modernizing it through the sound of the 1990s. The album was met with critical acclaim: It reached number twenty-four on the Billboard 200 chart, stayed on the charts for forty-seven weeks, sold 74,000 copies in its first week of release, and went on to sell over a million copies.

Current Events at the Heart of Artistic Concerns

The year 1991 provided plenty of material for the imagination of screenwriters and writers, with Operation Desert Storm, which ended the Gulf War under President George H. W. Bush, and the Halloween Storm (a meteorological one), which inspired Wolfgang Petersen's 2000 film *The Perfect Storm*.

In 1989, Sandy Gallin, Dolly Parton's manager and friend, co-produced *Common Threads: Stories from the Quilt*, a film that highlighted the ravages of AIDS, which won the Oscar for Best Documentary. Dolly was not personally involved in this project, but she knew the gay community well, starting with her manager, with whom she co-founded Sandollar, one of the film's co-producing companies. This documentary contributed to the greater awareness of the American population and, while normally Dolly avoided public controversy, in 1991 she and the biggest country stars were mobilizing to raise public awareness of the AIDS epidemic. In 1994, Dolly rerecorded the George Jones song "You Gotta Be My Baby" (*A Real Live Dolly*, 1970) for the AIDS album *Red Hot + Country* (or *RH + C*) and took part in the campaign against the HIV virus launched in 1993, alongside Tammy Wynette, Willie Nelson, and many others.

Country Music: The Parton Style

In the early 1960s, Dolly began her career in country music, then in 1977 she turned to pop. In the early 1990s, she returned to country music and enriched it with her pop experience. For *Eagle When She Flies*, the songwriter took up her pen once more, writing five songs on the album and co-writing three others. Another particularity of this opus: She brought together members of her family, by blood and adoption (Floyd Parton, Bill Owens, Mac Davis…). Finally, she recorded in Nashville (at the Nightingale and Doghouse studios) and no longer in Hollywood. This album enabled her country audience to see the artist confident in herself, serene, and more determined than ever in the pursuit of her goals, because, as she confided to the writer William Stadiem in 1989,[5] she was not yet a superstar, at least in her own eyes. Between neotraditional country and bluesy country, ballads, and gospel songs, *Eagle When She Flies* is an album that is 100 percent Dolly Parton.

Album Cover

Photographer Randee St. Nicholas created this undeniably country cover, much more understated than the previous ones. Dolly, looking particularly beautiful, in jeans and a white laced-up ruffled blouse, more blond than the wheat in the background, is standing, smiling on the front cover, pensive on the back, framed by a blurred mountain landscape.

1991

Dolly Parton and her band sing onstage with Kenny Rogers during a 1990 performance at the Target Center in Minneapolis.

On this album, the technical team was quite large, and the credits are not detailed for each track. We note the presence of: Sound Engineer: Gary Paczosa / Strings Arrangement: Ray Bunch / Strings Recording: Javelina East Recording Studio / Digital Editing: Carlos Grier / Vocal Arrangements: Richard Dennison / Mixing: Gary Paczosa / Mastering: Denny Purcell.

1991

If You Need Me

Dolly Parton / 2:44

Musicians: The Mighty Fine Band: organ, piano, keyboards, drums, bass, electric guitar, acoustic guitar, fiddle, mandolin / Sam Bacco: percussion / Romantic Roy Huskey: double bass / Mark Casstevens: acoustic guitar / Glen Duncan: fiddle / Mark Casstevens, Steven A. Gibson: mandolin / Paul Franklin: steel guitar, dobro / Carl Jackson, Paddy Corcoran: acoustic guitar, vocal harmonies / Alison Krauss: vocal harmonies **Vocals:** Dolly Parton **Backing Vocals:** Richard Dennison, Vicki Hampton, Jennifer O'Brien, Howard Smith, Lea Jane Berinati, Louis Nunley, John Wesley Ryles, Lisa Silver, Dennis Wilson, Curtis Young **Recorded:** Nightingale Studios and the Doghouse (Nashville, TN), January 1991 **Technical Team:** Producers: Steve Buckingham, Gary Smith / Executive Producer: Dolly Parton

In this country ballad, the songwriter's sharp pen explores once more the theme of unhappy love affairs: The narrator expresses her weariness with her lover's unreliability, so she leaves, worn out by this unstable and painful relationship in which she is only of interest to him when he needs her. In addition to the bass and drums, all types of stringed instruments (strummed, plucked, struck) make up the orchestra in this piece. Somewhat like James Brown and the J.B.'s, or Sly and the Family Stone, Dolly Parton is accompanied by the Mighty Fine Band, which became famous through playing (exclusively) with her. Rather on the right in the mix, we recognize the dobro, which is back after the pedabro (derived from the former) on "White Limozeen." The harmonies of the choruses differ slightly from those of the other albums, and the intervals between the voices are unusual, which lends a jazzy feel to the piece.

Country singer Ricky Van Shelton, wearing a Stetson and a Batman shirt, posing backstage at the Farm Aid benefit concert in 1993, two years before his "Rockin' Years" duet with Dolly Parton.

Ricky Van Shelton can be considered a "crooner." This word originated in the early days of the use of microphones for singers (as a crooner whispers), which enabled them to be heard by the entire audience, even while whispering.

Rockin' Years

Floyd Parton / 3:25

Musicians: The Mighty Fine Band: organ, piano, keyboards, drums, bass, electric guitar, acoustic guitar, fiddle, mandolin / Sam Bacco: percussion / Mark Casstevens: acoustic guitar / Glen Duncan: fiddle / Mark Casstevens, Steven A. Gibson: mandolin / Paul Franklin: steel guitar, dobro **Vocals:** Dolly Parton, Ricky Van Shelton **Backing Vocals:** Richard Dennison, Vicki Hampton, Jennifer O'Brien, Howard Smith, Lea Jane Berinati, Louis Nunley, John Wesley Ryles, Lisa Silver, Dennis Wilson, Curtis Young **Recorded:** Nightingale Studios and the Doghouse (Nashville, TN), November 8, 1990 **Technical Team:** Producers: Steve Buckingham, Gary Smith / Executive Producer: Dolly Parton **Single:** Side A: Rockin' Years / Side B: What a Heartache **Release:** Columbia Records, February 4, 1991 (ref.: 38-73711) **Best US Chart Ranking:** 1 on Billboard Hot Country Songs, 1 on RPM Country Singles

In this ballad written by Dolly's brother and sung by the star in duo with Ricky Van Shelton, a man and a woman promise to love each other throughout their "rock" years—whatever the circumstances and vicissitudes—to love each other always. The two singers are treated equally in the mix; this is a true duet (we find the codes of the pop ballad present here). A country atmosphere with the bass drum rather low but very present in the attack, the snare drum very reverberated, the cymbals rather discreet, and the hi-hat light, so there is room for the accompanying guitars and piano. At 2:33, during an a cappella passage, the only intervention of the backing vocals is remarkable.

Dolly attends the Country Music
Christmas Spectacular in support of
the charity Love Is Feeding Everyone
(LIFE) in December 1989.

Country Road

Dolly Parton, Gary Scruggs / 3:27

Musicians: The Mighty Fine Band: organ, piano, keyboards, drums, bass, electric guitar, acoustic guitar, fiddle, mandolin / Mark Casstevens: acoustic guitar / Glen Duncan: fiddle / Mark Casstevens, Steven A. Gibson: mandolin / Paul Franklin: steel guitar, dobro / Emmylou Harris, Patty Loveless: vocal harmonies **Vocals:** Dolly Parton **Recorded:** Nightingale Studios and the Doghouse (Nashville, TN), January 1991 **Technical Team:** Producers: Steve Buckingham, Gary Smith / Executive Producer: Dolly Parton **Single:** Side A: Country Road / Side B: Best Woman Wins **Release:** Columbia Records, January 1992 (ref.: 38-74183) **Best US Chart Ranking:** 39 on Billboard Hot Country Songs

In this song co-written with Gary Scruggs, Dolly spins a metaphor by comparing the narrator to a country road, far too slow for the man by whom she would like to be loved, who uses only the fast lane. The graphic contrasts between country and city, slow and fast, poverty and luxury are supported by the backing vocals of Emmylou Harris and Patty Loveless.

The syncopated rhythm of the drums puts this song in the pure country style. Its discretion is noticeable on the verses, while the bass provides the rhythmic foundation. The drums take over on the chorus with the power of the bass drum, with the snare drum and the electric guitars playing a theme in harmony. On one of them, slightly to the left in the mix, note that a volume pedal produces a sound wave effect, the "tremolo." (Nancy Sinatra's "Bang Bang" on the album *How Does That Grab You?*, 1966, originally sung by Cher, is one of the best-known examples of its use, especially in Quentin Tarantino's film *Kill Bill: Volume 1*, 2003, for which it is the main theme.) Folk guitars and piano accompany all of them, joined by steel guitar and fiddle on the first chorus. The backing singers were not invited on this song, leaving the vocal harmonies to Patty Loveless and Emmylou Harris, whose voice we were previously able to admire on *Trio* (1987), produced with Dolly Parton and Linda Ronstadt.

Silver And Gold

Carl Perkins, Greg Perkins, Stan Perkins / 3:54

Musicians: The Mighty Fine Band: organ, piano, keyboards, drums, bass, electric guitar, acoustic guitar, fiddle, mandolin / Sam Bacco: percussion / Mark Casstevens: acoustic guitar / Glen Duncan: fiddle / Mark Casstevens, Steven A. Gibson: mandolin / Paul Franklin: steel guitar, dobro / Harry Stinson, Vince Gill: vocal harmonies **Vocals:** Dolly Parton **Recorded:** Nightingale Studios and the Doghouse (Nashville, TN), January 1991 **Technical Team:** Producers: Steve Buckingham, Gary Smith / Executive Producer: Dolly Parton **Single:** Side A: Silver and Gold / Side B: Runaway Feelin' **Release:** Columbia Records, May 20, 1991 (ref.: 38-73826) **Best US Chart Ranking:** 15 on Billboard Hot Country Songs

The narrator of this song meets an old man in rags—Christ—whom she helps and who, in return, gives her wisdom: Gold and money buy only the material things of this humdrum world, which do not last, but not the time that passes and makes us grow old; fortunately, the time will come for us all to go and live in another world, where we have no more age and where value is not material—the eternal kingdom of God. This ballad is all about strings, with an intro of folk and steel guitars accompanying the vocals. The mandolin, played in the Italian tremolo style (each note is played several times very quickly), at 2:42, and the dobro make their contribution to the structure. Finally, the violin enters to complete the picture on the second verse. The orchestra leans on the rhythm provided by the bass and the drums.

1991

In 2021 Dolly recorded a duet of "Eagle When She Flies" with José Feliciano, the well-known musician, singer, and composer hailing from Puerto Rico.

Eagle When She Flies

Dolly Parton / 3:11

Musicians: The Mighty Fine Band: organ, piano, keyboards, drums, bass, electric guitar, acoustic guitar, fiddle, mandolin / Sam Bacco: percussion / Romantic Roy Huskey: upright bass / Mark Casstevens: acoustic guitar / Glen Duncan: fiddle / Mark Casstevens, Steven A. Gibson: mandolin / Paul Franklin: steel guitar, dobro **Vocals:** Dolly Parton **Backing Vocals:** Richard Dennison, Vicki Hampton, Jennifer O'Brien, Howard Smith, Lea Jane Berinati, Louis Nunley, John Wesley Ryles, Lisa Silver, Dennis Wilson, Curtis Young **Recorded:** Nightingale Studios and the Doghouse (Nashville, TN), January 1991 **Technical Team:** Producers: Steve Buckingham, Gary Smith / Executive Producer: Dolly Parton **Single:** Side A: Eagle When She Flies / Side B: Wildest Dreams **Release:** Columbia Records, October 19, 1991 (ref.: 38-74011) **Best US Chart Ranking:** 33 on Billboard Hot Country Songs

"Eagle When She Flies" pays tribute to women, at once vulnerable and fragile but also incredibly strong and enduring, pillars of strength in the lives of others. This ballad—in which we find the codes of the genre with the violins, and a lot of reverb on the voices and the drums—beautifully sung by Dolly Parton, begins with a guitar tremolo. The softness of the folk guitar arpeggios leads progressively to the powerful playing of the piano and the drums. Grandiloquent passages, especially in the last chorus, support this tribute to women, like a hymn gaining in power. After a very soft first verse with guitar and voice, the rhythm increases little by little with the drums, the violin, and the backing vocals, which enter gradually from the second verse, the play of each instrument rising in power, notably that of the toms. An unusual feature: The lyrics of the first verse, half spoken, half sung, seem to be read out, like a declaration. This solemnity is underlined by the straight playing of the rhythmic instruments (drums, bass, piano), without syncopation or swinging. This play on the beats accentuates the ceremonious, almost military aspect. No room for fantasy on this piece!

There is a version of "Eagle When She Flies" with a Latin color, created by Dolly Parton and the Puerto Rican musician José Feliciano, available since September 2021 on Dolly's website.

Dolly invited country singer Lorrie Morgan to sing a duet about a rivalry between two women on the track "Best Woman Wins."

SINGLE

Best Woman Wins

Dolly Parton / 3:08

Musicians: The Mighty Fine Band: organ, piano, keyboards, drums, bass, electric guitar, acoustic guitar, fiddle, mandolin / Sam Bacco: percussion / Mark Casstevens: acoustic guitar **Vocals:** Dolly Parton, Lorrie Morgan **Recorded:** Nightingale Studios and the Doghouse (Nashville, TN), January 1991 **Technical Team:** Producers: Steve Buckingham, Gary Smith / Executive Producer: Dolly Parton **Single:** Side A: Country Road / Side B: Best Woman Wins **Release:** Columbia Records, January 1992 (ref.: 38-74183) **Best US Chart Ranking:** 39 on Billboard Hot Country Songs

The duo of Lorrie Morgan and Dolly Parton gives expression to a woman's determination to defend her love story against a rival—and may the best woman win. Although lacking the timeless power of "Jolene," "Best Woman Wins" addresses the same theme. Another similarity is that both singers have the same type of voice, with the same range, a similar timbre, and little air in the sound. On first hearing, it is not easy to distinguish them. Lorrie Morgan, however, puts more percussion on the consonants—this is clearly audible on the last stanza of the first verse, at 0:43. Unlike all the early tracks on the album, the guitars here remain in the background, with the piano leading the accompaniment.

What A Heartache

Dolly Parton / 3:32

ON YOUR HEADPHONES
At 2:28, we notice a chord substitution, a process that consists of replacing a chord with another one using essentially the same notes but in a different order. Thus, the tonality is unchanged but the color is slightly modified.

1991

Musicians: The Mighty Fine Band: organ, piano, keyboards, drums, bass, electric guitar, acoustic guitar, fiddle, mandolin / Sam Bacco: percussion / Mark Casstevens: acoustic guitar / Glen Duncan, Mark O'Connor: fiddle / Mark Casstevens, Steven A. Gibson: mandolin / Joey Miskulin: accordion / Alisa Jones Wall: hammer dulcimer **Vocals:** Dolly Parton **Backing Vocals:** Richard Dennison, Vicki Hampton, Jennifer O'Brien, Howard Smith, Lea Jane Berinati, Louis Nunley, John Wesley Ryles, Lisa Silver, Dennis Wilson, Curtis Young **Recorded:** Nightingale Studios and the Doghouse (Nashville, TN), January 1991
Technical Team: Producers: Steve Buckingham, Gary Smith / Executive Producer: Dolly Parton **Single:** Side A: Rockin' Years / Side B: What a Heartache **Release:** Columbia Records, February 4, 1991 (ref.: 38-73711) **Best US Chart Ranking:** 1 on Billboard Hot Country Songs, 1 on RPM Country Singles

In the grip of deep heartache, the narrator expresses her pain and sorrow at having been betrayed and deceived by empty promises. It is in this moving ballad that the dulcimer intervenes. It plays small chords on the intro with the piano and some notes of melody. Recognizable by its very metallic, crystalline tone, it suggests a landscape of great spaces, notably on the chorus, supported by the violin and the electronic keyboard, whose sound resembles that of the bagpipes. The choirs remain in the background. The drums play few strokes, but these are very marked, and accentuated by a reverb, as in a rock ballad—such as, for example, Aerosmith's "I Don't Want to Miss a Thing," theme of the movie *Armageddon* (1998). As in "Best Woman Wins," the piano is the instrument most prominent in the accompaniment. We also hear a folk guitar and a mandolin, but no electric guitar. With the piano on the left in the mix and the strings on the right, the listener experiences a swinging effect in the music of the verses. The accordion completes the collection of traditional acoustic instruments—on a short passage, in layers, played on a bridge with the piano, violin, and voice, after the second chorus.

Runaway Feelin'

Dolly Parton / 2:56

Musicians: The Mighty Fine Band: organ, piano, keyboards, drums, bass, electric guitar, acoustic guitar, fiddle, mandolin / Sam Bacco: percussion / Mark Casstevens: acoustic guitar / Glen Duncan: fiddle / Paul Franklin: steel guitar, dobro **Vocals:** Dolly Parton
Backing Vocals: Richard Dennison, Vicki Hampton, Jennifer O'Brien, Howard Smith, Lea Jane Berinati, Louis Nunley, John Wesley Ryles, Lisa Silver, Dennis Wilson, Curtis Young **Recorded:** Nightingale Studios and the Doghouse (Nashville, TN), January 1991 **Technical Team:** Producers: Steve Buckingham, Gary Smith / Executive Producer: Dolly Parton **Single:** Side A: Silver and Gold / Side B: Runaway Feelin' **Release:** Columbia Records, May 20, 1991 (ref.: 38-73826) **Best US Chart Ranking:** 15 on Billboard Hot Country Songs

In this catchy song, the narrator becomes enamored with a man she feels ready to leave everything behind to run off with, driven by a powerful and perhaps completely new feeling.

This is the fastest track on the album. The drummer, who maintains a steady rhythm throughout, is diabolically precise. We also hear small percussion sonorities, such as castanets or woodblocks, to support the snare drum pattern. The question-and-answer game between the electric guitar and the folk guitar returns regularly.

Dolly Parton looking very glamorous on the set of the TV movie *Wild Texas Wind* in 1991.

Dreams Do Come True

Bill Owens / 3:26

Musicians: The Mighty Fine Band: organ, piano, keyboards, drums, bass, electric guitar, acoustic guitar, fiddle, mandolin / Sam Bacco: percussion / Mark Casstevens: acoustic guitar / Glen Duncan: fiddle / Mark Casstevens, Steven A. Gibson: mandolin / Paul Franklin: steel guitar, dobro **Vocals:** Dolly Parton **Backing Vocals:** Richard Dennison, Vicki Hampton, Jennifer O'Brien, Howard Smith, Lea Jane Berinati, Louis Nunley, John Wesley Ryles, Lisa Silver, Dennis Wilson, Curtis Young **Recorded:** Nightingale Studios and the Doghouse (Nashville, TN), January 1991 **Technical Team:** Producers: Steve Buckingham, Gary Smith / Executive Producer: Dolly Parton

This song about a dream of love come true is by Bill Owens, Dolly's uncle. This ballad, less codified than "Eagle When She Flies," marks a return to pop, with its usual ingredients: breaks that are slightly overplayed, reverb, and almost a saturation of the frequency space with many instruments in the same range (violins, guitar, piano, even the backing vocals), mainly on the refrains. It still works, thanks to the mix, which manages to highlight the voice.

Family

Dolly Parton, Carl Perkins / 3:47

Musicians: The Mighty Fine Band: organ, piano, keyboards, drums, bass, electric guitar, acoustic guitar, fiddle, mandolin / Sam Bacco: percussion / Mark Casstevens: acoustic guitar / Glen Duncan: fiddle / Mark Casstevens, Steven A. Gibson: mandolin / Paul Franklin: steel guitar, dobro / Joey Miskulin: accordion / The Kid Connection: vocal harmonies **Vocals:** Dolly Parton **Backing Vocals:** Richard Dennison, Vicki Hampton, Jennifer O'Brien, Howard Smith, Lea Jane Berinati, Louis Nunley, John Wesley Ryles, Lisa Silver, Dennis Wilson, Curtis Young **Recorded:** Nightingale Studios and the Doghouse (Nashville, TN), January 1991 **Technical Team:** Producers: Steve Buckingham, Gary Smith / Executive Producer: Dolly Parton

The lyrics of this song evoke with lucidity but tenderness the complexity of family relationships: We love each other and we hate each other, we receive and we give, we tolerate (more than anyone else!), and we support each other, because that is how the family works. The chord progression is similar to that of "Dreams Do Come True," as is the tempo, though slightly slower. As in "What a Heartache," the accordion and mandolin play only a few notes, to bring diversity to the instrumentation of the verses—from the second, in the case of the mandolin; and the third, in the case of the accordion.

Wildest Dreams

Dolly Parton, Mac Davis / 4:30

Musicians: The Mighty Fine Band: organ, piano, keyboards, drums, bass, electric guitar, acoustic guitar, fiddle, mandolin / Sam Bacco: percussion / Mark Casstevens: acoustic guitar / Glen Duncan: fiddle / Paul Franklin: steel guitar, dobro **Vocals:** Dolly Parton **Backing Vocals:** Richard Dennison, Vicki Hampton, Jennifer O'Brien, Howard Smith, Lea Jane Berinati, Louis Nunley, John Wesley Ryles, Lisa Silver, Dennis Wilson, Curtis Young **Recorded:** Nightingale Studios and the Doghouse (Nashville, TN), January 1991 **Technical Team:** Producers: Steve Buckingham, Gary Smith / Executive Producer: Dolly Parton **Single:** Side A: Eagle When She Flies / Side B: Wildest Dreams **Release:** Columbia Records, October 19, 1991 (ref.: 38-74011) **Best US Chart Ranking:** 33 on Billboard Hot Country Songs

The final song on the album, co-written by Dolly Parton with her great friend Mac Davis, is in some ways an ideal, gentle breakup in the name of love and the pursuit of the wildest dreams—saying goodbye to the past so that the future can begin.

The piano plays a beautiful duo introduction with Dolly, whose voice is very reverberated. We note the return of the synthesizer, in layers, and the theatrical dimension of the piece. Some passages are indeed directly borrowed from the genre of the musical, as at 1:05, for example, or at 3:00, where the sequence of eighth notes is typical. The song ends on a tonic chord, like most of the tracks of the album, and with a fade-out.

ALBUM

Slow Dancing with the Moon

Full Circle . Romeo . (You Got Me Over) a Heartache Tonight . What Will Baby Be .
More Where That Came From . Put a Little Love in Your Heart . Why Can't We .
I'll Make Your Bed . Whenever Forever Comes . Cross My Heart .
Slow Dancing with the Moon . High and Mighty

RELEASE DATE
United States: February 23, 1993
Reference: Columbia Records, New York (NY) — CSK-53199
Best US Chart Ranking: 4

When the Moon Is High

Slow Dancing with the Moon is Dolly Parton's thirty-first solo album. Produced by Steve Buckingham and Dolly, it was released by Columbia Records on February 23, 1993. This opus, of which the songwriter wrote half of the songs and co-wrote two others, is about eternal love, female flirting, sexuality, dating, and separation, but also about the responsibility of adults in raising children and, more broadly, about the possibility for everyone to live in peace.

After the highly acclaimed *Eagle When She Flies*, the reviews were mixed. However, the album reached number sixteen on the Billboard 200, stayed on the charts for twenty-five weeks, and went platinum.

A Good Use of Time

The year 1993 was marked by the arrival in the White House of Bill Clinton, who appointed Janet Reno as attorney general, the first woman to hold the position. The American public was shocked in February by a bombing at the World Trade Center in New York and, from late February to mid-April, by the siege of Waco, Texas, which resulted in the deaths of several police officers and more than eighty followers of the Branch Davidian cult, as well as their guru, David Koresh.

In the cinema, Steven Spielberg's *Schindler's List* stunned audiences, and the music of the 1990s hit the airwaves: techno, dance, and house. The 1992 romantic comedy *Straight Talk* was Dolly's fourth film as Shirlee Kenyon.

Every shoot, however, felt like a waste of time, especially when she had to be on set early in the morning and sometimes wait for her scene until mid-afternoon. For a woman like Dolly, who is both an artist and a businesswoman, time was precious.

Musical Friendships

For this new album, Dolly Parton called upon her family (Rachel Dennison, Randy Parton) and her songwriter and singer friends to work with her. The title track was written by her longtime friend Mac Davis—the singer-songwriter and actor first collaborated with Dolly in 1969 on "In the Ghetto" (on the album *My Blue Ridge Mountain Boy*), which was originally written for Elvis Presley.

Slow Dancing with the Moon resulted in three singles, including "Romeo," performed with Dolly's friend, singer and comedian Billy Ray Cyrus, father of the singer Miley Cyrus, to whom she is godmother.

Also in 1993, *Honky Tonk Angels* was released, a collaborative album featuring Dolly, Loretta Lynn, and Tammy Wynette. By returning to country music, Dolly Parton also reorganized her family and her projects.

Album Cover

Delicately lit by the full moon, Dolly, dressed in an elegant satin dress, holds some flowers in her hands, in an attitude both wise and seductive. Inside the cover, we discover a beautiful portrait of the star, with a dreamy appearance.

Romeo
Dolly Parton / 3:34

Musicians: Paul Uhrig: bass / Paul Franklin: dobro, pedabro, steel guitar / Steve Turner: drums / Alisa Jones Wall: dulcimer / Jimmy Mattingly: fiddle, mandolin / Kent Wells, Steve A. Gibson: guitar, mandolin / Terry McMillan: harmonica / Michael Davis: keyboards / Bruce Watkins: acoustic guitar / Mitch Humphries, Paul Hollowell, John (Barlow) Jarvis: piano / Sonny Garrish: pedal steel **Vocals:** Dolly Parton, Mary Chapin Carpenter, Pam Tillis, Billy Ray Cyrus, Kathy Mattea, Tanya Tucker **Backing Vocals:** Richard Dennison, Alison Krauss, Carl Jackson, Chuck Cannon, Darrin Vincent, Emmylou Harris, Jennifer O'Brien, Lari White, Maura O'Connell, Michael English, Rhonda Vincent, Ricky Skaggs, Rodney Crowell, Vince Gill **Recorded:** (studio?), October 1992 **Technical Team:** Producers: Steve Buckingham, Dolly Parton / Sound Engineer: (?) **Single:** Side A: Romeo / Side B: High and Mighty **Release:** Columbia, January 25, 1993 (ref.: 38-74876) **Best US Chart Ranking:** 27 on Billboard Hot Country Songs

This choral piece brings together contemporary country stars including Billy Ray Cyrus, a close friend of Dolly Parton, the godmother of his daughter, singer Miley Cyrus—with whom Dolly has sung "Jolene" on several occasions. It is the story of a happy girls' night out in a bar, until Romeo, aka Billy Ray Cyrus, appears. The game of seduction is led by the women, leaving no doubt as to its purpose. The song was nominated for a Grammy Award in the category of Best Country Collaboration with Vocals.

At the crossroads between country, blues, and rock, this song has a fairly classical structure: a verse/chorus set, followed by a bridge passage sung by the famous Romeo. The beginning is interpreted by the singers in a festive atmosphere. It is very likely that this track was recorded live (everyone plays at the same time), because a powerful synergy is released between the singers and the musicians. The lyrics, however, could not have been improvised, because, at precise moments, the song is punctuated with spoken interventions and sound effects (for example, a "tigress" at 1:15), and in the music video, the labial is perfectly calibrated. When the female stars sing together, it is in unison, none of them dominating in the mix, but all are very noticeable.

Full Circle
Dolly Parton, Mac Davis / 3:56

Musicians: Paul Uhrig: bass / Paul Franklin: dobro, pedabro, steel guitar / Steve Turner: drums / Alisa Jones Wall: dulcimer / Kent Wells, Steve A. Gibson: guitar / Michael Davis: keyboards / Joey Miskulin: accordion / Bruce Watkins: acoustic guitar / Mitch Humphries, Paul Hollowell, John (Barlow) Jarvis: piano / Sonny Garrish: pedal steel / Paddy Corcoran: bagpipes **Vocals:** Dolly Parton **Backing Vocals:** Richard Dennison, Alison Krauss, Carl Jackson, Chuck Cannon, Darrin Vincent, Emmylou Harris, Jennifer O'Brien, Lari White, Maura O'Connell, Michael English, Rhonda Vincent, Ricky Skaggs, Rodney Crowell, Vince Gill **Recorded:** (studio?), October 1992 **Technical Team:** Producers: Steve Buckingham, Dolly Parton / Sound Engineer: (?) **Single:** Side A: Full Circle / Side B: What Will Baby Be **Release:** Columbia, June 21, 1993 (ref.: 38-77083)

The chord progression and guitar arpeggios on the verses are very much inspired by the Police's hit "Every Breath You Take" (1983). The backing vocals are mostly two people, reminiscent of the configuration of the superb album *Trio* (1987) with Linda Ronstadt and Emmylou Harris, whose voice is recognizable on the choruses, on the left side of the mix. The orchestra is composed of pop instruments—drums, bass, all kinds of guitars and keyboards—except for the dulcimer, a traditional instrument from the Appalachian region, already heard in Dolly Parton's work, and whose brilliance of sound is perceptible especially at the end of the song, on the words "We come." This ending is worthy of the great pop songs, with this repetition of the chorus over and over again—one thinks of "We Are the World," a hit written by Lionel Richie and Michael Jackson, which brought together many stars in 1985 to support the victims of the famine in Ethiopia, or of "Heal the World," also by Michael Jackson, in 1992.

Songwriter and singer Billy Dean was invited to collaborate with Dolly on "(You Got Me Over) a Heartache Tonight."

SINGLE

What Will Baby Be
Dolly Parton / 3:24

Musicians: Paul Uhrig: bass / Paul Franklin: dobro, pedabro, steel guitar / Steve Turner: drums / Jimmy Mattingly: fiddle, mandolin / Kent Wells, Steve A. Gibson: guitar, mandolin / Terry McMillan: harmonica, percussions / Michael Davis: keyboards / Joey Miskulin: accordion / Bruce Watkins: acoustic guitar / Gove Scrivenor: autoharp / Mitch Humphries, Paul Hollowell, John Barlow Jarvis: piano / Sonny Garrish: pedal steel / Paddy Corcoran: bagpipes **Vocals:** Dolly Parton **Backing Vocals:** Richard Dennison, Alison Krauss, Carl Jackson, Chuck Cannon, Darrin Vincent, Emmylou Harris, Jennifer O'Brien, Lari White, Maura O'Connell, Michael English, Rhonda Vincent, Ricky Skaggs, Rodney Crowell, Vince Gill **Recorded:** (studio?), October 1992 **Technical Team:** Producers: Steve Buckingham, Dolly Parton / Sound Engineer: (?) **Single:** Side A: Full Circle / Side B: What Will Baby Be **Release:** Columbia, June 21, 1993 (ref.: 38-77083)

The text of this song warns of the consequences for a baby, and the child he or she will become, of the behaviors of a dysfunctional family. The bagpipes and the autoharp, two unusual traditional instruments, are brought together here. The autoharp, which was popularized in Appalachia, has enjoyed more limited use than the bagpipes; however, this instrument of the zither family, like the dulcimer, is very popular in American music. In this piece, while the bagpipes play layers with the accordion, the autoharp plays very high melodies as well as chords; the attack of the plectrum on the strings can be heard distinctly. The mixture of the two sounds creates a somewhat synthetic atmosphere. Whereas the previous album favored pop or pop/rock drums with drumsticks and powerful strokes, the playing on this track is very soft and the touch is subtle. The folk guitar contributes to the traditional sound of the song, playing arpeggios but also blues phrases (as at 0:56). The piano is also part of the piece; it contributes to the rhythmic accompaniment with chords placed on the strong beats, but also with short high notes to fill a gap and break the possible monotony of the sound.

(You Got Me Over) A Heartache Tonight
Dolly Parton, Larry Weiss / 3:04

Musicians: Paul Uhrig: bass / Paul Franklin: dobro, pedabro, steel guitar / Steve Turner: drums / Kent Wells, Steve A. Gibson: guitar / Michael Davis: keyboards / Bruce Watkins: acoustic guitar / Mitch Humphries, Paul Hollowell, John Barlow Jarvis: piano / Sonny Garrish: pedal steel **Vocals:** Dolly Parton, Billy Dean **Recorded:** (studio?), October 1992 **Technical Team:** Producers: Steve Buckingham, Dolly Parton / Sound Engineer: (?)

In this duet ballad, the narrator sweeps away a heartache with the help of a transient man. This new encounter will probably be short-lived—or maybe it will last, who knows…but, for now, it comforts her. The songwriter continues to explore this theme: How to repair a broken heart?

The instrumentation here is more classical and restrained than on "Romeo," with the bare minimum for a country band: drums, bass, folk guitar, piano, and pedal steel. Dolly Parton's and Billy Dean's vocals alternate in a rather traditional way, then blend on the choruses, where we hear the addition of a voice harmonized by Dolly.

Alison Krauss, the talented country bluegrass singer and fiddler, was invited to contribute to "More Where That Came From." Krauss often shows up on Dolly's later albums.

More Where That Came From

Dolly Parton / 3:14

Musicians: Paul Uhrig: bass / Paul Franklin: dobro, pedabro, steel guitar / Steve Turner: drums / Jimmy Mattingly: fiddle, mandolin / Kent Wells, Steve A. Gibson: guitar / Michael Davis: keyboards / Joey Miskulin: accordion / Bruce Watkins: acoustic guitar / Mitch Humphries, Paul Hollowell, John Barlow Jarvis: piano / Sonny Garrish: pedal steel **Vocals:** Dolly Parton **Backing Vocals:** Alison Krauss, Emmylou Harris, Jennifer O'Brien, Lari White, Maura O'Connell, Rhonda Vincent, (?) **Recorded:** (studio?), October 1992 **Technical Team:** Producers: Steve Buckingham, Dolly Parton / Sound Engineer: (?) **Single:** Side A: More Where That Came From / Side B: I'll Make Your Bed **Release:** Columbia, April 19, 1993 (ref.: 38-74954)

The narrator of this song declares to her lover that she wants to be everything to him and that she can fulfill all of his needs. On a fast tempo, in a very country style, the regularity of the electric guitar and its rhythmic syncopation, with a superb groove, are particularly remarkable. The themes of the second electric guitar, which answers the singer, could have been played by Mark Knopfler of Dire Straits, notably the rise at the very beginning of the song—in fact, this playing evokes that of "Sultans of Swing," the band's flagship song, released in 1977. The rhythm of the violin and accordion is played on the offbeat during the refrain, before Dolly's "Dee dee dee, dee dee yoo…," which is close to country yodeling, a rarity. In this woman's statement, only one male backing vocalist can be discerned. Also noteworthy: a modulation of a semitone higher at 1:58, during the brief guitar solo; it had been a long time since this trick was used, with Dolly, to extend a song.

Dolly Parton and her manager, Sandy Gallin, celebrating Gallin's fiftieth birthday in Los Angeles.

Dolly Parton on the Ferris wheel during opening week of the Dollywood amusement park in 1993.

Put A Little Love In Your Heart

Jackie DeShannon, Jimmy Holiday, Randy Myers / 2:27

Musicians: Paul Uhrig: bass / Paul Franklin: dobro, pedabro, steel guitar / Steve Turner: drums / Jimmy Mattingly: fiddle / Steve A. Gibson: guitar, mandolin / Terry McMillan: harmonica, percussions / Michael Davis: keyboards / Bruce Watkins: acoustic guitar / Mitch Humphries, Paul Hollowell, John Barlow Jarvis: piano / Sonny Garrish: pedal steel **Vocals:** Dolly Parton, The Christ Church Choir **Backing Vocals:** Richard Dennison, Alison Krauss, Carl Jackson, Chuck Cannon, Darrin Vincent, Emmylou Harris, Jennifer O'Brien, Lari White, Maura O'Connell, Michael English, Rhonda Vincent, Ricky Skaggs, Rodney Crowell, Vince Gill **Recorded:** (studio?), October 1992 **Technical Team:** Producers: Steve Buckingham, Dolly Parton / Sound Engineer: (?)

The rhythm of this song, which invites us to share love to make the world a better place, makes us want to dance. With the Christ Church Choir accompanying Dolly Parton, the song ends in a climax with claps, backing vocals, and a full brass section—horns certainly produced by the synth because, despite the quality of the attacks, the sequence of notes seems too perfect.

Why Can't We

Chuck Cannon, Austin Cunningham, Allen Shamblin / 3:48

Musicians: Paul Uhrig: bass / Paul Franklin: dobro, pedabro, steel guitar / Steve Turner: drums / Jimmy Mattingly: fiddle / Kent Wells, Steve A. Gibson: guitar, mandolin / Terry McMillan: percussion / Michael Davis: keyboards / Bruce Watkins: acoustic guitar / Mitch Humphries, Paul Hollowell, John Barlow Jarvis: piano / Sonny Garrish: pedal steel **Vocals:** Dolly Parton **Backing Vocals:** Richard Dennison, Alison Krauss, Carl Jackson, Chuck Cannon, Darrin Vincent, Emmylou Harris, Jennifer O'Brien, Lari White, Maura O'Connell, Michael English, Rhonda Vincent, Ricky Skaggs, Rodney Crowell, Vince Gill **Recorded:** (studio?), October 1992 **Technical Team:** Producers: Steve Buckingham, Dolly Parton / Sound Engineer: (?)

Following on from "Put a Little Love in Your Heart," the narrator is convinced, and wants to convince us, that, as in nature, where harmony reigns, it is possible to love the other person and to live in peace with them. This three-time ballad offers us a beautiful dialogue between the mandolin and the violin. However, this tandem leaves room for the pedal steel, which here finds itself in a melody role, a little lost on the other tracks of the album. One could also mention a dialogue involving the folk guitars: They play chords on the same rhythm but with different accents; as they are placed on the left and on the right in the mix, the playing of the soloists is thus delimited and preserved.

Dolly surrounded by her band during an intimate concert performance.

I'll Make Your Bed

Dolly Parton / 3:17

Musicians: Paul Uhrig: bass / Paul Franklin: dobro, pedabro, steel guitar / Steve Turner: drums / Jimmy Mattingly: fiddle, mandolin / Kent Wells, Steve A. Gibson: guitar, mandolin / Terry McMillan: harmonica, percussions / Michael Davis: keyboards / Joey Miskulin: accordion / Bruce Watkins: acoustic guitar / Gove Scrivenor: autoharp / Mitch Humphries, Paul Hollowell, John Barlow Jarvis: piano / Sonny Garrish: pedal steel **Vocals:** Dolly Parton **Backing Vocals:** Richard Dennison, Alison Krauss, Carl Jackson, Chuck Cannon, Darrin Vincent, Emmylou Harris, Jennifer O'Brien, Lari White, Maura O'Connell, Michael English, Rhonda Vincent, Ricky Skaggs, Rodney Crowell, Vince Gill **Recorded:**

(studio ?), October 1992 **Technical Team:** Producers: Steve Buckingham, Dolly Parton / Sound Engineer: (?) **Single:** Side A: More Where That Came From / Side B: I'll Make Your Bed **Release:** Columbia, April 19, 1993 (ref.: 38-74954)

Better a passionate lover in bed than a sad cook or seamstress, says the narrator to her lover, with fervor and mischievousness, because sensuality and sexuality form part of the bonds of love and of the couple. In this song, Dolly Parton goes back to traditional country music: The drummer plays only the bass drum, the hi-hat, and the snare drum, with brushes; the bass carefully follows the bass drum, and the guitar picking reminds us of the time of the collaborations with the great Chet Atkins. The dual level of humor, in the lyrics and the music, gives this number its charm.

Dolly's sister Rachel Dennison (pictured) co-wrote "Cross My Heart" along with Dolly's brother Randy Parton and Frank Dycus.

Whenever Forever Comes

Dolly Parton / 3:26

Musicians: Paul Uhrig: bass / Paul Franklin: dobro, pedabro, steel guitar / Steve Turner: drums / Alisa Jones Wall: dulcimer / Jimmy Mattingly: fiddle / Kent Wells, Steve A. Gibson: guitar / Michael Davis: keyboards / Bruce Watkins: acoustic guitar / Gove Scrivenor: autoharp / Mitch Humphries, Paul Hollowell, John Barlow Jarvis: piano / Sonny Garrish: pedal steel **Vocals:** Dolly Parton, Collin Raye **Backing Vocals:** Richard Dennison, Alison Krauss, Carl Jackson, Chuck Cannon, Darrin Vincent, Emmylou Harris, Jennifer O'Brien, Lari White, Maura O'Connell, Michael English, Rhonda Vincent, Ricky Skaggs, Rodney Crowell, Vince Gill **Recorded:** (studio?), October 1992 **Technical Team:** Producers: Steve Buckingham, Dolly Parton / Sound Engineer: (?)

This is a poetic song about love being stronger and even more enduring than eternity. This other three-beat ballad is built on a similar model to "Why Can't We," notably in the instrumentation. Many instruments play off each other, sometimes overloading the frequency space, but the fine and subtle mixing enables the voices to stand out without blurring the melodies of the different artists together.

Cross My Heart

Rachel Dennison, Frank Dycus, Randy Parton / 3:31

Musicians: Paul Uhrig: bass / Paul Franklin: dobro, pedabro, steel guitar / Steve Turner: drums / Jimmy Mattingly: fiddle / Kent Wells, Steve A. Gibson: guitar / Michael Davis: keyboards / Bruce Watkins: acoustic guitar / Mitch Humphries, Paul Hollowell, John Barlow Jarvis: piano / Sonny Garrish: pedal steel **Vocals:** Dolly Parton **Backing Vocals:** Richard Dennison, Alison Krauss, Carl Jackson, Chuck Cannon, Darrin Vincent, Emmylou Harris, Jennifer O'Brien, Lari White, Maura O'Connell, Michael English, Rhonda Vincent, Ricky Skaggs, Rodney Crowell, Vince Gill **Recorded:** (studio?), October 1992 **Technical Team:** Producers: Steve Buckingham, Dolly Parton / Sound Engineer: (?)

Co-written by Randy Parton and Rachel Dennison, Dolly's brother and sister, and by the songwriter Frank Dycus, this love song is a country ballad first performed by Stella Parton in 1987 on a single released by Luv Records.

As on the album as a whole, where the voices are particularly highlighted, the backing vocals occupy a very important position in this song: Almost the entire song is supported by two of them. They are mixed almost louder than Dolly's voice on some passages. Slightly broadened, they are less clogged in the center of the mix.

Dolly, forever on the move, walks between two planes on the tarmac in New York, 1993.

Dolly during a 1993 photo shoot in New York.

Slow Dancing With The Moon

Mac Davis / 3:28

Musicians: Paul Uhrig: bass / Paul Franklin: dobro, pedabro, steel guitar / Steve Turner: drums / Jimmy Mattingly: fiddle / Kent Wells, Steve A. Gibson: guitar, mandolin / Michael Davis: keyboards / Bruce Watkins: acoustic guitar / Mitch Humphries, Paul Hollowell, John Barlow Jarvis: piano / Sonny Garrish: pedal steel **Vocals:** Dolly Parton **Backing Vocals:** Richard Dennison, Alison Krauss, Carl Jackson, Chuck Cannon, Darrin Vincent, Emmylou Harris, Jennifer O'Brien, Lari White, Maura O'Connell, Michael English, Rhonda Vincent, Ricky Skaggs, Rodney Crowell, Vince Gill **Recorded:** (studio ?), October 1992 **Technical Team:** Producers: Steve Buckingham, Dolly Parton / Sound Engineer: (?)

In this beautiful text by Mac Davis, Dolly sees in herself the fifteen-year-old girl who had already sung and danced with the moon, with stars in her eyes and her mind filled with wonderful dreams, in which she still believes. The mandolin, in the traditional Italian mode, plays the same note very quickly and several times in tremolo style, depending on the melody. The intro is played on the dobro, which has a very metallic and midrange sound that is clearly recognizable. The drums are absent—usually, a bass drum or a hi-hat introduces Dolly's songs.

High And Mighty

Dolly Parton / 3:09

Musicians: Paul Uhrig: bass / Paul Franklin: dobro, pedabro, steel guitar / Steve Turner: drums / Kent Wells, Steve A. Gibson: guitar / Terry McMillan: percussions / Michael Davis: keyboards / Bruce Watkins: acoustic guitar / Mitch Humphries, Paul Hollowell, John Barlow Jarvis: piano / Sonny Garrish: pedal steel **Vocals:** Dolly Parton, The Christ Church Choir **Backing Vocals:** Richard Dennison, Alison Krauss, Carl Jackson, Chuck Cannon, Darrin Vincent, Emmylou Harris, Jennifer O'Brien, Lari White, Maura O'Connell, Michael English, Rhonda Vincent, Ricky Skaggs, Rodney Crowell, Vince Gill **Recorded:** (studio ?), October 1992 **Technical Team:** Producers: Steve Buckingham, Dolly Parton / Sound Engineer: (?) **Single:** Side A: Romeo / Side B: High and Mighty **Release:** Columbia, January 25, 1993 (ref.: 38-74876) Best ranking: 27 on Billboard Hot Country Songs

To close this album, the songwriter chose to sing a gospel song of her own composition, to the glory of the love of God, with the bass and the piano as the main instruments. With its high tempo, rhythmic changes, and stops, this is not a traditional religious song. A modulation is played on the word "higher," very appropriately! Even though Dolly Parton does not have the power of the gospel singers, she has succeeded in writing a song in the most advantageous key to enable her to give her best.

The legendary trio of (L to R) Loretta Lynn, Dolly Parton, and Tammy Wynette onstage at the Country Music Awards in 1993.

Honky Tonk Angels:
An Album of Three Modern, Nostalgic Women

It Wasn't God Who Made Honky Tonk Angels *(J. D. Miller / 2:51)*
Put It Off Until Tomorrow *(Dolly Parton, Bill Owens / 2:38)*
Silver Threads and Golden Needles *(Jack Rhodes, Dick Reynolds / 3:04)*
Please Help Me I'm Falling (In Love with You) *(Don Robertson, Hal Blair / 2:35)*
Sittin' on the Front Porch Swing *(Buddy Sheffield / 2:34)*
Wings of a Dove *(Bob Ferguson / 2:54)*
I Forgot More Than You'll Ever Know *(Cecil Null / 2:12)*
Wouldn't It Be Great *(Loretta Lynn / 3:03)*
That's the Way It Could Have Been *(Tammy Wynette / 2:55)*
Let Her Fly *(Dolly Parton / 3:04)*
Lovesick Blues *(Cliff Friend, Irving Mills / 2:18)*
I Dreamed of a Hillbilly Heaven *(Hal Southern, Eddie Dean / 3:32)*

Release Date
United States: November 2, 1993
Reference: Columbia Records, Nashville (TN)—CK-53414
Best US Chart Ranking: 6

Honky Tonk Angels is a collaborative album in the same vein as *Trio*, bringing together Dolly Parton, Loretta Lynn, and Tammy Wynette. Produced by Steve Buckingham and Dolly Parton, it was released by Columbia Records on November 2, 1993. It sings mainly about love, its hopes and disappointments, but also about the passing of time and death. It reached number forty-two on the Billboard 200 chart and was certified gold in January 1994.

Flashback
Since she began her shift from pop to country, and with the rise of Dollywood, the star had been very involved in her home region. In 1988, she created the Dollywood Foundation, a nonprofit organization, to help educate young people and encourage them to continue their education. In 1990, the Dollywood Broadcasting Company, a privately held company with multiple shareholders including Dolly Parton, purchased the radio station WSEV and its smaller FM sister station. Dolly participated in numerous charity concerts, in particular in support of scientific and medical research. Although Dolly did not release a solo

THE SINGLE

The narrator of "Silver Threads and Golden Needles" does not care about her lover's money or taking his name; what she wants is the love he promised her. For even "silver thread and a golden needle" could not mend the heart he had wounded by his deceptions. As for "Let Her Fly," this poetic text evokes the passing of time and the death of those we love—the narrator's mother, in this case—with the fervent and comforting thought that they become angels, whom we will one day be joining.

The cheekily suggestive movie poster for *Honky Tonk Girl*, released in 1937.

album in 1992, she was honored by Whitney Houston, who gave new life to one of the major hits of the songwriter's career, "I Will Always Love You." With the release of the film *The Bodyguard*, the song conquered the globe, becoming the world's best-selling song by a woman. In 1993, Dolly appeared briefly in the film *The Beverly Hillbillies*, then, in the film *Beethoven's 2nd*, performed a duet of the song "The Day I Fall in Love" with soul singer James Ingram. She also performed at the prestigious Carnegie Hall in New York. Finally, her autobiography, *Dolly: My Life and Other Unfinished Business*, would be published the following year.

A Feminine Perspective on Country Music

Like *Trio* before it, this new opus had waited more than a decade to be released. Dolly wanted to bring together the women artists who, like her, broke through on the music scene in the 1960s: Patsy Cline, Kitty Wells, Loretta Lynn, and Tammy Wynette enabled country music to evolve, both in its subject matter and musically. Whatever the similarities and differences in their respective careers, Dolly, Loretta,

and Tammy had become legends, with all the responsibility that comes with that status.

A wide range of songwriters and performers are present throughout the twelve tracks of this album. Chosen to open the album, "It Wasn't God Who Made Honky Tonk Angels," first performed by Kitty Wells in 1952, explains that the angels who frequent the seedy bars were not created by God, but by married men who still believe they are single. With humor and tenderness, "I Dreamed of a Hillbilly Heaven" imagines a hillbilly heaven and quotes all the most famous voices in the country world. By making changes to the text recorded by Tex Ritter in 1961, Dolly pays tribute to all these great figures, living or dead.

Among the covers from Dolly Parton's earlier albums, "Put It Off Until Tomorrow," co-written with her uncle, Bill Owens, was the artist's first hit as a songwriter with singer Bill Phillips in 1966 (see *Hello, I'm Dolly*, her first album, released in 1967). There is also "Wings of a Dove," originally released on *Golden Streets of Glory* (1971). Finally, Dolly "resurrects" Patsy Cline—who died in 1963—with "Lovesick Blues," which includes Cline's 1960 recording.

The poster for the 1929 film *Honky Tonk*, starring Ukrainian-born American singer, comedian, actress, and radio personality Sophie Tucker.

Steve Buckingham (center), Dolly's regular producer as of 1991, poses with Dolly and a guest during the 2008 Songwriters Hall of Fame ceremony.

With an Air of Joyful Nostalgia

This is an album with an extremely homogeneous production. It's the Nashville sound of the 1990s at its best: clear, broad, and detailed. Steve Buckingham, originally a studio guitarist, began his career as a producer in 1977 at Studio One in Doraville, Georgia—producing singer/songwriter Alicia Bridges's hit "I Love the Night Life (Disco 'Round)." In 1991, on the album *Eagle When She Flies*, he became Dolly Parton's new producer. Buckingham was one of the most prominent professionals in the Nashville of that decade, with successes with, among others, Tammy Wynette, Shania Twain, Mary Chapin Carpenter, Dionne Warwick, Garth Brooks, and Linda Ronstadt. This collaboration between Dolly, Loretta, and Tammy, so long awaited, was almost inevitable, because this record seemed easy to produce and its success assured. However, the single "Silver Threads and Golden Needles" (with B-side "Let Her Fly") reached only number sixty-eight on the Billboard Hot Country Songs chart. It does not have the same spontaneity as the *Trio* album (1987), which featured Dolly Parton, Emmylou Harris, and Linda Ronstadt, and on which the joy of their harmonizing voices was palpable (incidentally, they would repeat the experience on the *Trio II* album, in 1999). *Honky Tonk Angels* is nevertheless an excellent traditional country album. "Lovesick Blues" stands out somewhat, with its dry and rough production, a nod to the sound of fifties rock 'n' roll, on which Dolly, Tammy, and Loretta seem to have a lot of fun.

Although *Honky Tonk Angels* did not enjoy the same success as *Trio*, it nevertheless found its audience, perhaps more traditional or nostalgic for a country era that the young generation was in the process of transforming.

Album Cover

For this album with its dated aesthetic, Bruce Wolfe painted the faces of Loretta, Dolly, and Tammy on a background of a blue and gold sky.

For Dolly Addicts

Honky Tonk Angels was nominated for the 1994 TNN/Music City News Country Awards, in the Album of the Year category. The song "Silver Threads and Golden Needles" was nominated for the 37th Annual Grammy Awards in the category of Best Country Collaboration with Vocals, and the 28th Annual Country Music Association Awards in the category of Vocal Event of the Year.

Loretta Lynn performing on an episode of *The Ed Sullivan Show*, which was filmed at the Tennessee State Fair in Memphis on October 7, 1970.

Loretta Lynn (center) poses with her mother, Clara Butcher, and her sister, Crystal Gayle, at the Country Music Awards in 1980.

Loretta Lynn: A Pioneering Voice

A major figure in women's country music passed away on October 4, 2022, following a successful career. The world of country music lost not only one of its most prestigious representatives, but also an artist who never ceased to be concerned about the status of women.

Wife, Mother, and Performing Artist

She was named after the actress Loretta Young, who was the film partner of Clark Gable and Orson Welles, among others. Loretta Webb, born in Kentucky in 1932, daughter of a miner, grew up in a family of eight children. She married at fifteen, becoming Loretta Lynn, and moved to Custer, Washington, when she was pregnant with the first of her six children. Her husband gave her a Harmony guitar, and over the next three years she taught herself to play. With her brother Jay Lee Webb, a guitarist, she created her band Loretta and the Trailblazers, and performed in bars with the Pen Brothers or the Westerneers. In early 1960, she recorded "I'm a Honky Tonk Girl," and just after winning a television contest, she signed a contract with Zero Records, launching her career as a country artist. In 1966, with "You Ain't Woman Enough (To Take My Man)," she became the first woman to reach number one as a songwriter. In 1967, at the age of thirty-five, she released her first album, *Don't Come Home a Drinkin' (With Lovin' on Your Mind)*.

An Heiress and a Pioneer

In 1980, the film *Coal Miner's Daughter*, based on George Vecsey's biography of Loretta, was a huge success at the American box office and established the artist. Very early on, she considered Patsy Cline to be her mentor and felt she belonged to the young family of the most famous women in country music. In 1993, Tammy Wynette, Dolly Parton, and Loretta Lynn formed a trio for the album *Honky Tonk Angels*. Loretta wrote and sang about women's freedom and respect for their rights with an outspokenness that, at the time, was disturbing. Her hit song "Rated X" caused controversy when it was released in 1972; the lyrics denounce gender inequality in marriage and after divorce. The ups and downs of her own life coupled with Oliver Vanetta Lynn were a source of inspiration. In addition to the issues of marriage, fickle men, and their conquests, Loretta Lynn also addressed the status of widows in the aftermath of the Vietnam War in "Dear Uncle Sam" in 1966; repeated childbirth in "One's on the Way" in 1971; and birth control in "The Pill" in 1975.

A Bygone Era

The country radio scene was traditionalist and sexist at the time, and stations boycotted some of Loretta Lynn's—and Dolly's—songs. This did not prevent Loretta from enjoying immense success, being regularly invited to the White House, and, above all, being inducted into the prestigious Country Music Hall of Fame in 1988. At the end of the 1990s, the guitarist and singer Jack White from the White Stripes (a "garage rock" style duo, who covered Dolly Parton's "Jolene" in 2000) expressed his admiration for Loretta Lynn, regularly covered "Rated X" in concert, and collaborated on her album *Van Lear Rose*, released in 2004. In 2021, a year and a half before her death at the age of ninety, Loretta Lynn released her fiftieth studio album, *Still Woman Enough*. Thus ended more than sixty years of an unforgettable career.

Tammy Wynette in character as Darlene Stankowski on the CBS television series *Capitol*.

Tammy Wynette shops at Nudie's Rodeo Tailor in Los Angeles on May 26, 1973.

Tammy Wynette: From Cotton Fields to Fame

Singer, actress, and writer Tammy Wynette, many times the recipient of awards and honored by her peers, is one of the great names of the country music that emerged from the 1960s, in the tradition of Loretta Lynn and Dolly Parton, who lost "a sister" upon her death in 1998.

Youth and Early Career

Virginia Wynette Pugh, known as Tammy Wynette, born in 1942 in a village in Mississippi, was the only daughter of a schoolteacher mother and an aspiring musician father who had no time to make a career or to raise his daughter, because he died when Tammy was nine months old. Her mother moved to Memphis, Tennessee, and worked in the US Department of Defense during World War II. Little Tammy was raised by her grandparents in Mississippi, where she dreamed of becoming a singer as she grew to hate working in the cotton fields on the family farm. She began singing in public at the age of ten and learned to play the piano by ear, then got married at seventeen, won a country music contest on television, separated from her first husband, moved to Nashville, met her second husband, and was noticed by Epic Records. She released singles starting in 1966, including "Apartment No. 9," and in 1968 she co-wrote the huge hit "Stand by Your Man" with her producer, Billy Sherrill.

A Stunning Voice

"Stand by Your Man" opened up the doors of the Grand Ole Opry and brought her massive recognition. Tammy Wynette was now a country star. In the 1970s, as her popularity grew, she met and married songwriter and singer George Jones. Tammy had always liked this artist, who was already one of her favorites when she was young. Together they produced several hits, but their tumultuous relationship ended in divorce in 1975. Jones suffered from alcoholism, and Tammy became addicted to tranquilizers due to health problems. However, nothing seemed to hold back the singer's success, because when she was on stage, both the public and the critics saw her as a true diva. All were unanimous: It was enough to hear her whispering poignant lyrics to feel like crying with her. Her texts honor the hardworking women of the working class and of the backbreaking rural environment. Mother of several children, she married for the fifth time to composer George Richey, who soon became her full-time manager.

More Than One Talent

In addition to having a singing career, Tammy Wynette was also a writer and an actress. She published her autobiography with author Joan Dew in 1979. In 1986–1987, she played Darlene Stankowski on the soap *Capitol*. In 1993, she joined Dolly Parton and Loretta Lynn for the album *Honky Tonk Angels*. The following year, she appeared on the sitcom *Evening Shade* with Burt Reynolds.

In poor health all her life, Tammy Wynette died at the age of fifty-five, of uncertain and controversial causes. One thing is certain: The world of country music—and, more broadly, the world of music—not only lost a great voice but also a female artist who was as talented as she was endearing in so many ways.

ALBUM

Something Special

Crippled Bird . Something Special . Change . I Will Always Love You .
Green-Eyed Boy . Speakin' of the Devil . Jolene . No Good Way
of Saying Good-Bye . The Seeker . Teach Me to Trust

RELEASE DATE
United States: August 22, 1995
References: Columbia Records, New York (NY);
Blue Eye Records, Nashville (TN)—CK 67140
Best US Chart Ranking: 10

Dolly Parton performs during the tenth-anniversary celebrations at Dollywood, in Pigeon Forge, Tennessee.

1995

A Musical Pause

Something Special is Dolly Parton's thirty-second solo album. Produced by Steve Buckingham, it was released on August 22, 1995, under two labels: Columbia, in New York, and Blue Eye Records, in Nashville. It reached number fifty-four on the Billboard 200 chart.

Women's Stories

Against the backdrop of racial issues, two trials of African American athletes divided and fascinated America: that of football player O.J. Simpson, accused of murdering his ex-wife, and that of boxer Mike Tyson, convicted of rape, who was released from prison in 1995, at the same time Simpson was acquitted. The Million Man March was the highlight of the year. This large but controversial event, due in part to the personality of one of its organizers—Louis Farrakhan of the Nation of Islam—brought together hundreds of thousands of African American men in Washington, DC, to fight for better living conditions and to defend their rights. The controversy also stemmed from the fact that women were not invited to attend. They responded two years later with a Million Woman March in Philadelphia.

While other countries were trying to keep certain disturbing episodes of their history under wraps, America was confronting its paradoxes, displaying and commenting on them, and turning them into fiction—like Stephen King's *Rose Madder*, the story of a battered woman trying to escape her torturer—or into songs.

It is in this context that Dolly Parton released *Something Special*, for which she wrote seven songs, plus three reinterpretations, which portray women in love who are unloved or afraid of not being loved. This album, which does not innovate but equally does not disappoint, received a mixed critical reception.

An Obsessive Character

One thing is obvious when one follows Dolly Parton's exceptional career: She knows how to explore endlessly the register of the love song, in all of its aspects and in all its layers. While one may sometimes have the impression that this genre is recurrent with her, even obsessive, it is because we do not listen carefully enough to the songwriter's lyrics. Indeed, we must acknowledge her particular talent in seeming to write the same story over and over again...which is, in fact, never really the same, because with each new song her writing evolves and Dolly unfolds a whole universe, sometimes producing masterpieces. Thus, the songs that please without becoming historical hits also contribute fully to this artistic construction. This is precisely what listening to *Something Special* provokes: a moment of pleasure, a familiar feeling, somewhat like rediscovering someone who matters.

Album Cover

An elegant sobriety seems to be the artistic decision of these photos, both on the cover and inside, where Dolly, in portrait, full length, or sitting in a red padded armchair, is highlighted in a black pencil dress.

Dolly onstage at the Nashville Fan Fair in 1995.

Dolly Parton in "puppy love" circa 1993.

Crippled Bird

Dolly Parton / 3:44

Musicians: Stuart Duncan, Jimmy Mattingly: fiddle / Paul Hollowell, Steve Nathan, Matt Rollings: piano **Vocals:** Dolly Parton
Backing Vocals: Bob Bailey, Margie Cates, Suzanne Cox, Richard Dennison, Vicki Hampton, Yvonne Hodges, Carl Jackson, Alison Krauss, Louis Nunley, Chris Rodriguez, Duawne Starling, Pam Tillis **Recorded:** Nightingale Studio, Sound Emporium, The Doghouse, Woodland Digital Studios (Nashville, TN), 1995 **Technical Team:** Producer: Steve Buckingham / Strings Arrangements: Dale Oehler / Sound Engineers: (?)

This poetic song compares the fragility of a heart to that of a sparrow's wing, easy to break, slow to heal—before it can fly away again. As is often the case in her words and songs, Dolly connects nature, especially birds, to human feelings. Here, to express the pain of the narrator, the range of her voice is very soft, almost airy. The arrangement, mainly piano/voice or a cappella voices, contributes to this softness. The backing vocals seem to be suspended in the air. Then the entry of the fiddles gives the song a certain solemnity, without being heavy.

Something Special

Dolly Parton / 3:06

Musicians: Steve Buckingham, Steve A. Gibson, Brent Mason, Don Potter, Steuart Smith: acoustic guitar / Brent Mason, Brent Rowan, Reggie Young: electric guitar / Terry McMillan: percussions, shaker
Vocals: Dolly Parton **Backing Vocals:** Bob Bailey, Richard Dennison, Carl Jackson, Louis Nunley, Chris Rodriguez, Duawne Starling
Recorded: Nightingale Studio, Sound Emporium, The Doghouse, Woodland Digital Studios (Nashville, TN), 1995 **Technical Team:** Producer: Steve Buckingham / Sound Engineers: (?)

On this classic songwriter's description of an exceptional and transcended love, one feels like joining in the finger clicks that accompany the melody. The instrumentation is one of the most restrained in the work of Dolly Parton. And it is perhaps the most effective and most appropriate to serve the text: two guitars (folk and electric), a shaker, and snaps (finger clicks). Another electric guitar comes in to play a solo. The backing vocals, exclusively male, play a predominant role. The bass voices are particularly highlighted, due to the arrangement without bass or drums. Note: Dolly Parton added a second voice in re-re (rerecord) on some passages.

Shortly after recording their duet rendition of "I Will Always Love You," Dolly Parton and Vince Gill walked the red carpet at a Nashville event in 1995.

Change

Dolly Parton / 3:41

Musicians: Stuart Duncan, Jimmy Mattingly: fiddle / Paul Hollowell, Steve Nathan, Matt Rollings: piano **Vocals:** Dolly Parton **Recorded:** Nightingale Studio, Sound Emporium, The Doghouse, Woodland Digital Studios (Nashville, TN), 1995 **Technical Team:** Producer: Steve Buckingham / Strings Arrangements: Dale Oehler / Sound Engineers: (?)

This song exposes the essential and saving character of separation: When the love paradise turns into hell, it is time to leave, at the risk of otherwise dying by degrees every day in a slow fire.

We find here the same formation as in "Crippled Bird," the first song of the album: piano/vocal arrangements, but without backing vocals. However, the effect of the reverb is such, with a significant pre-delay, that Dolly Parton's voice sounds as if it is doubled. Although this range is relatively low for the singer, it enables her to speak as she sings.

I Will Always Love You

Dolly Parton / 3:17

Musicians: Eddie Bayers, Steve Turner, Owen Hale: drums / Steve Buckingham, Steve A. Gibson, Brent Mason, Don Potter, Steuart Smith: acoustic guitar / Stuart Duncan, Jimmy Mattingly: fiddle / Paul Franklin: steel guitar / Paul Hollowell, Steve Nathan, Matt Rollings: piano / David Hungate, Paul Uhrig: bass / Brent Mason, Brent Rowan, Reggie Young: electric guitar **Vocals:** Dolly Parton, Vince Gill **Backing Vocals:** Bob Bailey, Margie Cates, Suzanne Cox, Richard Dennison, Vicki Hampton, Yvonne Hodges, Carl Jackson, Alison Krauss, Louis Nunley, Chris Rodriguez, Duawne Starling, Pam Tillis **Recorded:** Nightingale Studio, Sound Emporium, The Doghouse, Woodland Digital Studios (Nashville, TN), 1995 **Technical Team:** Producer: Steve Buckingham / Strings Arrangements: Dale Oehler/ Sound Engineers: (?) **Single:** Side A: I Will Always Love You / Side B: Speakin' of the Devil **Release:** Columbia, September 1995 (ref.: 38-78079) **Best US Chart Ranking:** 15 on Billboard Hot Country Songs

The story remains the same as the original version, released in 1974 on the album *Jolene*: Unable to find the words to leave Porter Wagoner and his show, Dolly writes this song as a farewell. The duet she forms here with Vince Gill nevertheless gives the text a different emotional color. Musically, no major change either. The arrangement is created with the instruments that are present on the rest of the album, with the song being simply updated; for example, the tremolos on the guitars, now outdated, have been removed. We note, however, that the key at the beginning is a semitone lower; this enables a modulation at 2:20, with fiddles ascending, to reach the original key, in which Dolly Parton can demonstrate her power. Vince Gill is particularly comfortable with this key, slightly high for his chest voice; he masters the passage in a head voice. Note: The most famous cover of this song, Whitney Houston's 1992 version for the movie *The Bodyguard*, is in the original key. "I Will Always Love You" remains one of the most listened-to songs in the world.

1995

SINGLE

Singer-songwriter Van Morrison wrote the song "Brown Eyed Girl" in 1967.

Green-Eyed Boy

Dolly Parton / 3:17

Musicians: Eddie Bayers, Steve Turner: drums / Steve Buckingham, Steve A. Gibson, Brent Mason, Don Potter, Steuart Smith: acoustic guitar / Stuart Duncan, Jimmy Mattingly: fiddle / Paul Franklin: steel guitar / Owen Hale: drums / David Hungate, Paul Uhrig: bass / Brent Mason, Brent Rowan, Reggie Young: electric guitar **Vocals:** Dolly Parton **Backing Vocals:** Bob Bailey, Margie Cates, Suzanne Cox, Richard Dennison, Vicki Hampton, Yvonne Hodges, Carl Jackson, Alison Krauss, Louis Nunley, Chris Rodriguez, Duawne Starling, Pam Tillis **Recorded:** Nightingale Studio, Sound Emporium, The Doghouse, Woodland Digital Studios (Nashville, TN), 1995 **Technical Team:** Producer: Steve Buckingham / Strings Arrangements: Dale Oehler / Sound Engineers: (?)

In the spirit of "My Blue Ridge Mountain Boy," Dolly sings of the love that is left behind. Unable to go back, she cherishes once more the memory of that "green-eyed boy" who gives her joy. Does she miss him as much as he misses her? As is often the case, songwriters associate their birthplaces with first loves—and with nostalgia, this time for a man, in Dolly's answer to the song "Brown Eyed Girl" (1967) by the Northern Irish singer-songwriter Van Morrison.

After a pop ballad, we return to the country tradition: drums played with brushes, folk and electric guitars, especially the slide with an overdrive, fiddles, and a syncopated rhythm. The band also includes a mandolin (the musician is uncredited).

Stéphane Grappelli plays the violin during the Cheltenham Jazz Festival on April 13, 1996.

Speakin' Of The Devil

Dolly Parton / 3:15

Musicians: Eddie Bayers, Steve Turner, Owen Hale: drums / Steve Buckingham, Steve A. Gibson, Brent Mason, Don Potter, Steuart Smith: acoustic guitar / Stuart Duncan, Jimmy Mattingly: fiddle / Paul Franklin: steel guitar / Paul Hollowell, Steve Nathan, Matt Rollings: piano / David Hungate, Paul Uhrig: bass / Brent Mason, Brent Rowan, Reggie Young: electric guitar **Vocals:** Dolly Parton **Backing Vocals:** Bob Bailey, Margie Cates, Suzanne Cox, Richard Dennison, Vicki Hampton, Yvonne Hodges, Carl Jackson, Alison Krauss, Louis Nunley, Chris Rodriguez, Duawne Starling, Pam Tillis **Recorded:** Nightingale Studio, Sound Emporium, The Doghouse, Woodland Digital Studios (Nashville, TN), 1995 **Technical Team:** Producer: Steve Buckingham / Sound Engineers: (?) **Single:** Side A: I Will Always Love You / Side B: Speakin' of the Devil **Release:** Columbia, September 1995 (ref.: 38-78079) **Best US Chart Ranking:** 15 on Billboard Hot Country Songs

When an angel in appearance turns out to be a seductive devil...This is a foray into Western swing–style jazz, directly inspired by the Andrews Sisters. In the 1940s, this trio of sisters relied on a rather simple but ultra-effective orchestration, and especially on vocal harmonies, which they mastered to perfection. On this Dolly Parton track, we find the same spirit in the choruses, with the difference that Dolly is slightly to the fore of the other backing vocals.

One can imagine having a drink in a cabaret or a trendy bar of the time while soaking up the playing of violinist Stéphane Grappelli—one of the most famous of his generation, having made a career in France, playing with Django Reinhardt among others, as well as across the Atlantic, with Oscar Peterson, Paul Simon, and David Grisman, and others. The piano is also characteristic, in particular when it plays its short melodies on the high notes. One can recognize the sound of the Les Paul electric guitar—he revolutionized both the design of the instrument and the way of playing it (one of the most famous being the Gibson). The theme played by the fiddle and guitars, without embellishments, is a marvel of efficiency, with reprise gimmicks, such as the chromatic descents (descents in semitones). Beautiful, and without ever stealing Dolly's thunder.

Jolene

Dolly Parton / 3:42

Musicians: Eddie Bayers, Steve Turner: drums / Steve Buckingham, Steve A. Gibson, Brent Mason, Don Potter, Steuart Smith: acoustic guitar / Stuart Duncan, Jimmy Mattingly: fiddle / Paul Franklin: steel guitar / Owen Hale: drums / Paul Hollowell, Steve Nathan, Matt Rollings: piano / David Hungate, Paul Uhrig: bass / Brent Mason, Brent Rowan, Reggie Young: electric guitar **Vocals:** Dolly Parton **Backing Vocals:** Bob Bailey, Margie Cates, Suzanne Cox, Richard Dennison, Vicki Hampton, Yvonne Hodges, Carl Jackson, Alison Krauss, Louis Nunley, Chris Rodriguez, Duawne Starling, Pam Tillis **Recorded:** Nightingale Studio, Sound Emporium, The Doghouse, Woodland Digital Studios (Nashville, TN), 1995 **Technical Team:** Producer: Steve Buckingham / Sound Engineers: (?) / Mixing: (?)

A huge hit for the songwriter, almost a trademark, "Jolene" has inspired so many other artists. A timeless song, whatever the orchestration, because the story of "Jolene" is a timeless one: The narrator begs her rival to stop trying to steal her man. The rerelease of this piece only involved some slight instrumental changes, due to the need to update it. The tonality is a little more bass-oriented, and the tempo is slower, to give the story a stronger dramatic effect. But the guitar riff is still present, as well as the long notes on fiddle and steel guitar.

No Good Way Of Saying Good-Bye

Dolly Parton / 2:57

Musicians: Eddie Bayers, Steve Turner, Owen Hale: drums / Steve Buckingham, Steve A. Gibson, Brent Mason, Don Potter, Steuart Smith: acoustic guitar / Stuart Duncan, Jimmy Mattingly: fiddle / Paul Franklin: steel guitar / Paul Hollowell, Steve Nathan, Matt Rollings: piano / David Hungate, Paul Uhrig: bass / Sonny Landreth: slide guitar / Brent Mason, Brent Rowan, Reggie Young: electric guitar / Randy McCormick, Matt Rollings: organ **Vocals:** Dolly Parton **Backing Vocals:** Bob Bailey, Margie Cates, Suzanne Cox, Richard Dennison, Vicki Hampton, Yvonne Hodges, Carl Jackson, Alison Krauss, Louis Nunley, Chris Rodriguez, Duawne Starling, Pam Tillis **Recorded:** Nightingale Studio, Sound Emporium, The Doghouse, Woodland Digital Studios (Nashville, TN), 1995 **Technical Team:** Producer: Steve Buckingham / Sound Engineers: (?) / Mixing: (?)

Dolly sings once again on the subject of the breakup: It is not pleasant to say goodbye, and having to resign oneself to it does not spare the pain, especially when you still love each other.

This piece includes a new instrument: the organ, whose layers contribute additional cohesion to the piece. Much used in the 1960s and 1970s, the organ was then abandoned in favor of synthesizers and their numerous sound possibilities.

The Seeker

Dolly Parton / 3:03

Musicians: Eddie Bayers, Steve Turner, Owen Hale: drums / Steve Buckingham, Steve A. Gibson, Brent Mason, Don Potter, Steuart Smith: acoustic guitar / Paul Franklin: steel guitar / Paul Hollowell, Steve Nathan, Matt Rollings: piano / David Hungate, Paul Uhrig: bass / Brent Mason, Brent Rowan, Reggie Young: electric guitar **Vocals:** Dolly Parton **Backing Vocals:** Bob Bailey, Margie Cates, Suzanne Cox, Richard Dennison, Vicki Hampton, Yvonne Hodges, Carl Jackson, Alison Krauss, Louis Nunley, Chris Rodriguez, Duawne Starling, Pam Tillis **Recorded:** Nightingale Studio, Sound Emporium, The Doghouse, Woodland Digital Studios (Nashville, TN), 1995 **Technical Team:** Producer: Steve Buckingham / Sound Engineers: (?) / Mixing: (?)

The third and final cover, this version of "The Seeker," a gospel song examining the relationship between the spiritual aspirant and the master teacher of the mysteries of the divine, seems more energetic than the previous version, which appeared on the 1975 album *Dolly*. However, the tempo and tone are identical. There is also a greater dynamic between the verses and choruses, and more nuanced arrangements.

Teach Me To Trust

Dolly Parton, Gene Golden / 3:27

Musicians: Steve Buckingham, Steve A. Gibson, Brent Mason, Don Potter, Steuart Smith: acoustic guitar / Stuart Duncan, Jimmy Mattingly: fiddle **Vocals:** Dolly Parton **Backing Vocals:** Bob Bailey, Margie Cates, Suzanne Cox, Richard Dennison, Vicki Hampton, Yvonne Hodges, Carl Jackson, Alison Krauss, Louis Nunley, Chris Rodriguez, Duawne Starling, Pam Tillis **Recorded:** Nightingale Studio, Sound Emporium, The Doghouse, Woodland Digital Studios (Nashville, TN), 1995 **Technical Team:** Producer: Steve Buckingham / Strings Arrangements: Dale Oehler / Sound Engineers: (?) / Mixing: (?)

This song, co-written with singer-songwriter and musician Gene Golden, gives Dolly the opportunity to dramatize her emotional range to perfection, as the narrator learns to trust, while jealousy threatens her happiness.

This album ends as it began, with only two instrument sections, except that the guitar replaces the piano in accompanying the fiddles, with the backing vocals matching their playing with layers of harmonies. The guitar's melody scrupulously follows that of the vocals. This makes for a very fusional duet, as though expressing the strength of the couple, despite their jealousy.

A view of the Country Music Hall of Fame in Nashville, Tennessee.

Period-appropriate stagewear in a window display at the Country Music Hall of Fame.

The Country Music Hall of Fame and Museum: The Pantheon of Country Music

Located in the heart of Nashville, Tennessee, the Country Music Hall of Fame and Museum, a veritable pantheon of country music, is renowned for its cultural impact, educational mission, and unparalleled collection of historical artifacts. On September 22, 1999, Dolly Parton was inducted into the Hall of Fame at an emotional event hosted by her friend Kenny Rogers. Ten years later, she took part in the exhibition *American Currents: State of the Music*. In addition to her ten Grammy Awards, Dolly has won (as of April 2022) thirteen Academy of Country Music Awards and nine Country Music Awards.

Memory and Modernity

The Country Music Hall of Fame and Museum is both an institution and a remarkable museum (officially established in 1964) documenting the history of country music, celebrating its artists, housing a library, and offering exhibits, performances, and concerts. The Country Music Foundation (CMF) develops educational programs (including workshops courses such as Words & Music, an introduction to songwriting), involving schools, students, and families from Tennessee and elsewhere. It also manages the historic RCA Studio B. This research and study center reels out the thread of country music's memory and continuity, supporting emerging talent and honoring legendary pioneers—including Jimmie Rodgers, Fred Rose, and Hank Williams—immortalized on bronze plaques inside the rotunda, which is decorated on the outside with a musical stave featuring the melody of the Carter Family's "Will the Circle Be Unbroken."

Installed, since its opening in 1967, on Nashville's Music Row, the historical heart of country, in 2001 the Country Music Hall of Fame and Museum opened at its current downtown location. After several phases of expansion, the architectural complex now covers more than 140,000 square feet, forming, from the air, the shape of a bass clef. The arc of the majestic museum, whose facade represents a piano keyboard and one end of which imitates a Cadillac wing, is a setting for the rotunda, whose shape is just as symbolic. This rotunda evokes both a railroad water tower and a grain silo. Capped with the four record shapes, pierced and surmounted by a needle similar to the transmission antenna of the famous WSM radio station but also suggesting a church steeple, it perfectly synthesizes the rural origin, the cultural history, and the technological evolution of country music.

An Immersion in Country Music

Inside the museum, the permanent exhibition *Sing Me Back Home—A Journey Through Country Music* immerses visitors in the history of country music through the many records covering entire walls, the vast aisles of display cases containing costumes (1,900 garments and accessories), guitars and other instruments (about 500), and various cult objects that belonged to the artists, as well as 500,000 photos, 40,000 videos and films, 250,000 sound recordings (radio broadcasts, live performances, etc.), manuscripts, periodicals, and even old vehicles. Each year, *American Currents: State of the Music* showcases the major achievements and events of the past year, along with temporary exhibitions.

ALBUM

Treasures

Peace Train / Isitimela Sokuthula . Today I Started Loving You Again .
Just When I Needed You Most . Something's Burning . Before the Next Teardrop Falls .
After the Goldrush . Walking on Sunshine . Behind Closed Doors . Don't Let Me
Cross Over . Satin Sheets . For the Good Times

RELEASE DATE
United States: September 24, 1996
References: Rising Tide Records / Blue Eye Records,
Nashville (TN)—CSK-53414
Best US Chart Ranking: 21

For the release of the remix of "Peace Train" in 1997, Christopher Ciccone, Madonna's brother, directed the video. The single reached number twenty-three on the Billboard Dance Club Songs chart.

A Treasure Trove of Cover Songs

Treasures is Dolly Parton's thirty-third solo album. Produced by Steve Buckingham, it was released on September 24, 1996, by Rising Tide Records and Blue Eye Records—the artist's contract with the Columbia label having expired in 1995. It reached number 122 on the Billboard 200 chart.

Business and Labels
In 1994, the year of creation of the Blue Eye Records label by Dolly Parton and Steve Buckingham, producer of her latest albums, the artist gave a concert at Dollywood and released *Heartsongs*, a live album mixing bluegrass and country. In 1996, as she celebrated her fiftieth birthday—and thirty years of marriage—she joined forces with the Rising Tide label (linked to Universal Records) for the release of *Treasures*. To promote this new album, she appeared in a special TV show, *Dolly Parton: Treasures*, broadcast on CBS on November 30, of which she was the executive producer with her manager, Sandy Gallin. The show included an interview with Cat Stevens (now Yusuf Islam since his religious conversion), with whom she sings on the album, and archive footage from the 1960s related to each cover. Between songs, the star answered questions from the audience with humor.

The Price of Independence
Some fans or critics wondered: Why this album of covers? On her official website, the star answered that she simply had the desire to do it, but also that the radio stations did not play enough of her latest songs, either because of a lack of receptiveness or because of a taste for more traditional music. Her absence from the airwaves was one of the reasons Dolly invested in 1990 in the purchase of WSEV, the famous station in Sevierville, Tennessee, on which she started out with Cas Walker when she was young. Although Dolly Parton has always refused to commit herself politically to one side or another, in her artistic work she has never ceased to spread a clear message of peace and harmony, to write lyrics that resonate with women—as well as men—and to support causes such as literacy, minority rights, access to schooling, and health care. The star continued to rise, despite mixed reviews for some of her latest albums. Perhaps Dolly, at this point in her life and career, was still searching for herself, personally and musically.

Album Cover
In this photo by David LaChapelle, the star, dressed in a long white dress, bathes in the powder pink atmosphere of what looks like a young girl's room. Looking angelic, a mirror in her hands and a porcelain doll at her feet, Dolly poses sitting on a large chest, doubtless filled with treasures...

For Dolly Addicts
On the *Rosie O'Donnell Show* of November 27, 1996, Dolly sang "Walking on Sunshine," which did not rank on any chart (but which she later released a remix of in August 1999).

Ladysmith Black Mambazo contributed music and lyrics to the critically acclaimed *Song of Jacob Zulu*, which was produced by the Steppenwolf Theatre in 1993.

The South African choral group Ladysmith Black Mambazo onstage with Paul Simon at the Warner Theater in Washington, DC, where Simon received the Library of Congress Gershwin Prize for Popular Song.

Peace Train / Isitimela Sokuthula

Cat Stevens, Joseph Shabalala / 4:40

Musicians: Eddie Bayers: drums / Steve Buckingham, Dean Parks: acoustic guitar, slide guitar / Mark Casstevens: high string guitar / David Hungate: bass / Matt Rollings: keyboards / Reggie Young: electric guitar **Vocals:** Dolly Parton, Ladysmith Black Mambazo **Backing Vocals:** Bob Bailey, Matraca Berg, Crystal Bernard, Kim Carnes, Andy Landis, Darci Monet, Louis Nunley, Chris Rodriguez, Duawne Starling, Chris Willis **Recorded:** Nightingale Studio, Masterfonics, The Doghouse (Nashville, TN), February 1993 **Technical Team:** Producer: Steve Buckingham / Production Assistant: Jennie Carey / Strings Arrangements: Steve Dorff / Sound Engineers: Marshall Morgan, Gary Paczosa, Alan Schulman, Toby Seay / Assistant Sound Engineers: Jeff DeMorris, Mel Jones, Ken Ross, Michelle Shelly, Ed Simonton / Editing: Don Cobb / Mixing: Denny Purcell **Single:** CD (ref.: RT5P-1006) **Release:** Rising Tide Records/Blue Eye Records, July 1, 1997 **Best US Chart Ranking:** 7 on Billboard Hot Country Songs

Genesis and Lyrics

This cover of a Cat Stevens song, which he first sang in September 1971, reflects the diverse universe of the songwriter and above all, as she emphasized during the special show broadcast on CBS on November 30, 1996, her desire for peace and harmony. A particular feature of the single release in 1997: Twenty tracks devoted to this title were gathered together on a single CD.

Production

To take the sound of this recording where she wanted it to go, Dolly asked Steve Buckingham to call in the South African choral group Ladysmith Black Mambazo, after hearing them sing in a TV ad—unaware of the identity of the singers at the time, the star left it to Buckingham to investigate. It was certainly one of the most surprising, spontaneous, and daring artistic choices Dolly Parton had made in her long career. And we can also say that it was successful: The depth contained in these rich and vivid vocal arrangements brings a new color to Dolly's palette. She has always liked to take a step to one side, to shake up the country tradition, to enrich the recipe of the Nashville sound with exotic elements, and to play with the codes of mainstream pop. The complementary strumming of the acoustic guitars (respectively on the right and left of the stereo field), played by Steve Buckingham and Dean Parks in a precise and syncopated way, is the backbone of this luxuriant orchestration. The strings mingle with African vocals, a modern rhythm section, expressive slide guitar playing, and compelling electric guitar funk strumming. This arrangement and question-and-answer game with the South African choir is reminiscent of Paul Simon's song "Homeless" (a sumptuous a cappella number on the 1986 album *Graceland*), and for good reason: The choir Paul Simon hired at the time was none other than Ladysmith Black Mambazo.

John Popper, the co-founder and vocalist behind the band Blues Traveler, played the harmonica on "Today I Started Loving You Again."

Today I Started Loving You Again

Merle Haggard, Bonnie Owens / 3:57

Musicians: Eddie Bayers: drums / Steve Buckingham: acoustic guitar / John Popper: harmonica / Matt Rollings: Wurlitzer B3 organ / Reggie Young: electric guitar **Vocals:** Dolly Parton, John Popper **Recorded:** Nightingale Studio, Masterfonics, The Doghouse (Nashville, TN), February 1993 **Technical Team:** Producer: Steve Buckingham / Production Assistant: Jennie Carey / Sound Engineers: Marshall Morgan, Gary Paczosa, Alan Schulman, Toby Seay / Assistant Sound Engineers: Jeff DeMorris, Mel Jones, Ken Ross, Michelle Shelly, Ed Simonton / Editing: Don Cobb / Mixing: Denny Purcell

In this cover of a Merle Haggard song, a woman explains that she tried to get over her heartbreak, but as soon as she recovered, she realized that she was still in love and that the worst was yet to come for her. Immediately one feels that we have entered the second half of the 1990s. The richness of the production, the low frequencies contained in each instrument, the roundness and presence of the acoustic guitars, and a more controlled reverb are all markers of a new era in the world of music production. On this very bluesy 4/4 number, the performance of John Popper (American musician and songwriter, co-founder and lead singer of the band Blues Traveler, formed in 1987), first on harmonica, then on vocals—and again on harmonica on the ad lib at the end—is breathtaking. There is no doubt that Dolly knows how to choose her collaborators, her musicians, and her featuring stars.

A frequent Dolly collaborator, Dan Tyminski is a composer, singer, and bluegrass musician as well as being a member of the band Alison Krauss and Union Station.

SINGLE

Just When I Needed You Most

Randy Van Warmer / 4:36

Musicians: Eddie Bayers: drums / Mark Casstevens, Dean Parks: acoustic guitar / Alison Krauss: violin / Farrell Morris: shaker / Matt Rollings: keyboards / John Sebastian: autoharp / Reggie Young: electric guitar **Vocals:** Dolly Parton **Vocal Harmonies:** Alison Krauss, Dan Tyminski **Backing Vocals:** Steve Buckingham (reprise), Don Potter (reprise) **Recorded:** Nightingale Studio, Masterfonics, The Doghouse (Nashville, TN), February 1993 **Technical Team:** Producer: Steve Buckingham / Production Assistant: Jennie Carey / Sound Engineers: Marshall Morgan, Gary Paczosa, Alan Schulman, Toby Seay / Assistant Sound Engineers: Jeff DeMorris, Mel Jones, Ken Ross, Michelle Shelly, Ed Simonton / Editing: Don Cobb / Mixing: Denny Purcell **Single:** Side A: Just When I Needed You Most / Side B: For the Good Times
Release: Rising Tide Records/Blue Eye Records, September 23, 1996 (ref.: RTS7 56041) Best ranking: 62 on Billboard Hot Country Songs

Crushed by the pain of separation, the narrator has not found the strength to convince the man she loves to stay. Alone now, she reflects on the fact that he left her when she needed him most.

By enlisting the talents of singer and fiddler Alison Krauss and the legendary singer and songwriter John Sebastian (notably the originator of the folk-rock band the Lovin' Spoonful, which had been active since 1965), Dolly ensures continuity in the world of quality modern country roots music. This delightful ballad radiates silky, shimmering sounds. The arpeggios of the acoustic guitars, the cascades of autoharp strummed by John Sebastian, the lightness of the percussion, the precise and airy backing vocals of Alison Krauss and Dan Tyminski, the combined swells of the electric guitar and fiddle and the Fender Rhodes of Matt Rollings bind it all together. The arrangement of "Just When I Needed You Most" is a real delight.

David Hidalgo on stage with his band, Los Lobos, in 1996. Dolly invited Hidalgo to duet on "Before the Next Teardrop Falls."

Texan singer-songwriter Freddy Fender on stage at the Aragon Ballroom in Chicago. Fender took the song "Before the Next Teardrop Falls" to the top of the charts in 1975.

Something's Burning
Mac Davis / 3:59

Musicians: Eddie Bayers: drums / Steve Buckingham: baritone guitar, mandolin, 12-string electric guitar / David Hidalgo: accordion / Dean Parks: acoustic guitar / Matt Rollings: Wurlitzer B3 organ / Reggie Young: electric guitar **Vocals:** Dolly Parton, David Hidalgo **Backing Vocals:** Matraca Berg, Kim Carnes, Liana Manis, Darci Monet, Chris Rodriguez, John Wesley Ryles **Recorded:** Nightingale Studio, Masterfonics, The Doghouse (Nashville, TN), February 1993 **Technical Team:** Producer: Steve Buckingham / Production Assistant: Jennie Carey / Sound Engineers: Marshall Morgan, Gary Paczosa, Alan Schulman, Toby Seay / Assistant Sound Engineers: Jeff DeMorris, Mel Jones, Ken Ross, Michelle Shelly, Ed Simonton / Editing: Don Cobb / Mixing: Denny Purcell

This sensual love song, written by Dolly's close friend, songwriter Mac Davis, describes the burning fire of passion that makes you want to love forever. It is a surprisingly rocking mid-tempo 4/4 number, built on a loud/quiet/loud pattern, typical of 1990s rock and much used in grunge music in particular. It seems that Kim Carnes, the singer with a husky voice, interpreter of the worldwide hit "Bette Davis Eyes" (1981), is hidden in the armada of backing singers. A wise choice for an arrangement that leans toward the heavy side of powerful, and a first for Dolly Parton, who seeks here to make the sacred fire of stadium rock burn on the choruses: "Something's burning…"

> The loud/quiet/loud pattern, usually credited to the Pixies, defines the structure of a song. Usually, it connects quiet beats on the verses and loud beats on the chorus in an abrupt way, in order to create very marked reliefs and to accentuate the dynamics of the song.

Before The Next Teardrop Falls
Ben Peters, Vivian Keith / 4:07

Musicians: Eddie Bayers: drums / Steve Buckingham: acoustic guitar / David Hidalgo: accordion / Farrell Morris: marimba / Don Potter: gut string guitar / Matt Rollings: Wurlitzer / Reggie Young: electric guitar **Vocals:** Dolly Parton, David Hidalgo **Backing Vocals:** Steve Buckingham (reprise), Liana Manis, Don Potter (reprise) Chris Rodriguez **Recorded:** Soundstage and the Doghouse (Nashville, TN), The Hit Factory (New York), Oceanway (Los Angeles), June 1996 **Technical Team:** Producer: Steve Buckingham / Production Assistant: Jennie Carey / Sound Engineers: Marshall Morgan, Gary Paczosa, Alan Schulman, Toby Seay / Assistant Sound Engineers: Jeff DeMorris, Mel Jones, Ken Ross, Michelle Shelly, Ed Simonton / Editing: Don Cobb / Mixing: Denny Purcell

The first time Dolly heard this song on the radio, she was driving and had to pull over because she was so moved. The narrator promises the man she loves, but who lives with another woman, that if she ever makes him unhappy, she'll come running before he has even shed a second tear. The original version of this Latin country song was performed by singer and guitarist Freddy Fender—who in the late 1990s joined the band Los Super Seven, as did David Hidalgo, who performs this duet with Dolly. The hybrid between country and Tex-Mex music works perfectly. The accordion, the melodic solos of Don Potter on the nylon string guitar, with an ideal level of reverb, and the gentle sway of the marimba trills played by Farrell Morris take the listener on a cruise-control road trip to the Mexican border.

The author of *Walking on Sunshine*, Kimberly Rew (left), was also the guitarist of the English rock group Katrina and the Waves, the band who won the Eurovision Song Contest in 1997.

After The Goldrush

Neil Young / 3:45

Musicians: Eddie Bayers: drums / Alison Krauss: violin / Viktor Krauss: aero bass / Pat McInerney: bodhran / Dean Parks: acoustic guitar / Matt Rollings: piano / Reggie Young, Dean Parks: electric guitar **Vocals:** Dolly Parton **Vocal Harmonies:** Alison Krauss **Recorded:** Soundstage and the Doghouse (Nashville, TN), The Hit Factory (New York), Oceanway (Los Angeles), June 1996 **Technical Team:** Producer: Steve Buckingham / Production Assistant: Jennie Carey / Sound Engineers: Marshall Morgan, Gary Paczosa, Alan Schulman, Toby Seay / Assistant Sound Engineers: Jeff DeMorris, Mel Jones, Ken Ross, Michelle Shelly, Ed Simonton / Editing: Don Cobb / Mixing: Denny Purcell

This Neil Young song, written in 1970, is the story of a dream with a rather impenetrable meaning—it is about knights in armor and flying saucers, about Mother Nature, about an environmental catastrophe, and about leaving the planet. Whether it is Linda Ronstadt's version—on *Trio II*, released in 1999—or Dolly's version, one just has to let oneself be carried away by the mystery of it all.

With the help of a very cinematic and cutting-edge production, Steve Buckingham, Dolly Parton, and Alison Krauss manage to plunge us into a fabulous daydream. Viktor Krauss's low-pitched aero bass throbs until it takes us by storm, while the crystalline acoustic guitar arpeggios mingle with the piano chords. The electric guitars, Alison Krauss's violin, the backing vocals, and the percussion seem to rise slowly, ending in total weightlessness. An unexpected and particularly successful rereading of a classic by the man known as "the Loner."

Walking On Sunshine

Kimberley Rew / 3:11

Musicians: Eddie Bayers: drums / Steve Buckingham: electric guitar, baritone guitar / Dean Parks: electric guitar, 12-string guitar / Matt Rollings: keyboards, B3 organ / Reggie Young: electric guitar **Vocals:** Dolly Parton **Vocal Harmonies:** Jennifer O'Brien **Backing Vocals:** Richard Dennison, Vicki Hampton, Louis Nunley **Recorded:** Soundstage and the Doghouse (Nashville, TN), The Hit Factory (New York), Oceanway (Los Angeles), June 1996 **Technical Team:** Producer: Steve Buckingham / Production Assistant: Jennie Carey / Sound Engineers: Marshall Morgan, Gary Paczosa, Alan Schulman, Toby Seay / Assistant Sound Engineers: Jeff DeMorris, Mel Jones, Ken Ross, Michelle Shelly, Ed Simonton / Editing: Don Cobb / Mixing: Denny Purcell

This lively and optimistic love song—in which the narrator walks in the sunshine, happy because her lover is coming back to town—is a cover of the text written by Kimberley Rew, guitarist of the English rock band Katrina and the Waves, at that time little known when their song was released in 1983. Dolly gives a rather cheerful and up-tempo country version. Eddie Bayers's drums, bass drum and snare drum in the foreground, roll out in a breathless gallop, and the guitar tangles (two standard electric guitars, a baritone, and a rhythmic 12-string acoustic guitar) shoot out from all sides. Arpeggios, turnarounds, solos: The entire arsenal of the Nashville studio guitarist of the 1990s is on display! Meanwhile, Matt Rollings maintains his clear and tense line, posted behind his Hammond B3 organ, amply supported by the harmonies of Jennifer O'Brien, Richard Dennison, Vicki Hampton, and Louis Nunley. This driving, fast-paced track takes the listener by the hand and draws them into its whirlwind of positive injunctions—"It's time to feel good…"

American singer, musician, and songwriter Charlie Rich was the first person to record "Behind Closed Doors," a country hit in 1973.

Behind Closed Doors

Kenny O'Dell / 2:59

Musicians: Eddie Bayers: drums / Farrell Morris: vibes / Hargus "Pig" Robbins: piano / Matt Rollings: Wurlitzer / Reggie Young: electric guitar
Vocals: Dolly Parton **Vocal Harmonies:** Loretta Lynn
Backing Vocals: Liana Manis, Louis Nunley, John Wesley Ryles
Recorded: Soundstage and the Doghouse (Nashville, TN), The Hit Factory (New York), Oceanway (Los Angeles), June 1996
Technical Team: Producer: Steve Buckingham / Production Assistant: Jennie Carey / Strings Arrangements: Steve Dorff / Sound Engineers: Marshall Morgan, Gary Paczosa, Alan Schulman, Toby Seay / Assistant Sound Engineers: Jeff DeMorris, Mel Jones, Ken Ross, Michelle Shelly, Ed Simonton / Editing: Don Cobb / Mixing: Denny Purcell

No one knows what happens behind the door when it closes on passionate lovers…this country classic, written by Kenny O'Dell and originally performed by Charlie Rich in 1973, retains its traditional country form here. Only Farrell Morris's vibraphone stands out slightly from the crowd, perfectly matched with Matt Rollings's Wurlitzer. Surprisingly, it was the great Hargus "Pig" Robbins, Dolly Parton's loyal collaborator and comrade from the early days, who played on Charlie Rich's version in 1973. Twenty-three years later, on this new version, he plays almost note for note the same score, with his characteristic clear and articulate playing, and it works just as well. Dolly, comfortably installed in her range and in a style that she masters to perfection, is particularly energetic in this version. The quality of her interpretation, so natural and dynamic, reaches new heights. Unquestionably, even though Dolly waited more than two decades to make it her own, this song was made for her. Note the discreet presence of Loretta Lynn in the harmonies.

Raul Malo, from the band the Mavericks, performing onstage at the Guildford Festival. Dolly invited him to duet on "Don't Let Me Cross Over."

Don't Let Me Cross Over

Penny Jay / 3:03

Musicians: Eddie Bayers: drums / Dan Dugmore: lap steel / Hargus "Pig" Robbins: piano / Joe Spivey: fiddle / Adam Steffey: mandolin / Reggie Young: electric guitar **Vocals:** Dolly Parton **Vocal Harmonies:** Raul Malo **Backing Vocals:** Louis Nunley, John Wesley Ryles **Recorded:** Soundstage and the Doghouse (Nashville, TN), The Hit Factory (New York), Oceanway (Los Angeles), June 1996 **Technical Team:** Producer: Steve Buckingham / Production Assistant: Jennie Carey / Sound Engineers: Marshall Morgan, Gary Paczosa, Alan Schulman, Toby Seay / Assistant Sound Engineers: Jeff DeMorris, Mel Jones, Ken Ross, Michelle Shelly, Ed Simonton / Editing: Don Cobb / Mixing: Denny Purcell

In this duet sung with Raul Malo, leader of the Mavericks—a group founded in Miami in 1989—the narrator tries to resist temptation. Desire that leads to infidelity is a recurring theme in Dolly's discography.

In this first country waltz of the album, Hargus "Pig" Robbins's precise playing once again works wonders. He shares the first desk with Dan Dugmore on lap steel (whose Hawaiian origins are clearly evident here, thanks to Dugmore's inspired and expressive performance) and Adam Steffey on mandolin. The playing of the three musicians is of rare understatement and class. This is perhaps the most rootsy track on the album. In terms of playing and arrangements, this has everything that was done in the late 1960s in the big studios of Nashville. Raul Malo harmonizes perfectly with Dolly, apparently effortlessly; everything flows.

Satin Sheets

John E. Volinkaty / 3:21

Musicians: Eddie Bayers: drums / Paul Franklin: steel guitar / David Hungate: bass / Farrell Morris: vibes / Hargus "Pig" Robbins: piano / Dean Parks, Reggie Young: electric guitar **Vocals:** Dolly Parton, Loretta Lynn, Tammy Wynette **Backing Vocals:** Liana Manis, Louis Nunley, John Wesley Ryles **Recorded:** Soundstage and the Doghouse (Nashville, TN), The Hit Factory (New York), Oceanway (Los Angeles), June 1996 **Technical Team:** Producer: Steve Buckingham / Production Assistant: Jennie Carey / Sound Engineers: Marshall Morgan, Gary Paczosa, Alan Schulman, Toby Seay / Assistant Sound Engineers: Jeff DeMorris, Mel Jones, Ken Ross, Michelle Shelly, Ed Simonton / Editing: Don Cobb / Mixing: Denny Purcell

Neither money, Cadillacs, nor satin sheets can make up for the lack of love the narrator suffers in her relationship, so she wants to be free of her attachment so she can love another man.

This is the first ternary track of *Treasures*, a country blues number with an orchestration similar to that of "Don't Let Me Cross Over," the previous track. Here, however, Dan Dugmore's lap steel is replaced by Paul Franklin's steel guitar, Farrell Morris's vibraphone makes a comeback, and Adam Steffey's mandolin is replaced by the electric guitars of Reggie Young and Dean Parks. Hargus "Pig" Robbins, meanwhile, had no time to get up from his stool: Dolly's big sisters at heart, Loretta Lynn and Tammy Wynette, were passing by and came over to harmonize on the choruses. Even though this is not a good enough reason to be locked into an unhappy relationship, it must be admitted that everyone seems to be at ease in these soft satin sheets!

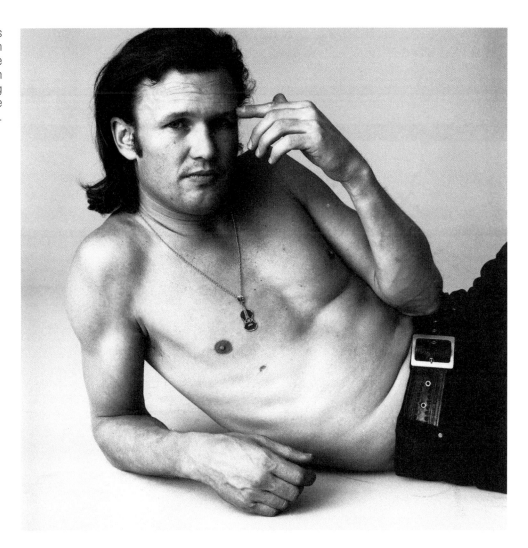

Singer-songwriter Kris Kristofferson strikes a pose in 1970, the same year he wrote "For the Good Times." In 1996, he rerecorded the song as a duet with Dolly for the *Treasures* album.

SINGLE

For The Good Times

Kris Kristofferson / 4:16

Musicians: Eddie Bayers: drums / David Hungate: upright bass / Farrell Morris: vibes / Dean Parks: acoustic guitar / Matt Rollings: piano / Reggie Young: electric guitar **Vocals:** Dolly Parton **Vocal Harmonies:** Liana Manis **Backing Vocals:** Richard Dennison, Vicki Hampton, Louis Nunley, Jennifer O'Brien **Recorded:** Soundstage and the Doghouse (Nashville, TN), The Hit Factory (New York), Oceanway (Los Angeles), June 1996 **Technical Team:** Producer: Steve Buckingham / Production Assistant: Jennie Carey / Strings Arrangements: Steve Dorff / Sound Engineers: Marshall Morgan, Gary Paczosa, Alan Schulman, Toby Seay / Assistant Sound Engineers: Jeff DeMorris, Mel Jones, Ken Ross, Michelle Shelly, Ed Simonton / Editing: Don Cobb / Mixing: Denny Purcell **Single:** Side A: Just When I Needed You Most / Side B: For the Good Times **Release:** Rising Tide/Blue Eye Records, September 23, 1996 (ref.: RTS7 56041) **Best US Chart Ranking:** 62 on Billboard Country Songs

To close this album and for a gentle parting of the ways, here is one last love song, in memory of all "the good times" spent together, as the narrator wishes. A lounge and jazzy atmosphere emanates from this arrangement, which seems to be cut from thick velvet with burgundy tones. As if to say to the listener, "We are so good together...why leave each other so quickly?" "There'll be time enough for sadness..." A beautiful tribute to the song by songwriter, singer, and actor Kris Kristofferson, released in 1970. The strings arrangements hover over Matt Rollings's typical piano bar playing. We can imagine Dolly nonchalantly leaning on the piano, interpreting this ballad in a smoky, Prohibition-era speakeasy atmosphere, her heart tight, full of a bittersweet nostalgia, a glass in one hand and her gaze lost in the middle distance, while a few embracing couples take a few last steps on the dance floor...Dolly always knew how to say her goodbyes to her audience.

ALBUM

Hungry Again

Hungry Again . The Salt in My Tears . Honky Tonk Songs . Blue Valley Songbird .
I Wanna Go Back There . When Jesus Comes Calling for Me . Time and Tears .
I'll Never Say Goodbye . The Camel's Heart . I Still Lost You .
Paradise Road . Shine On

RELEASE DATE
United States: August 25, 1998
Reference: Decca Records/Blue Eye Records,
Nashville (TN)—DRND-70041
Best US Chart Ranking: 23

Reviving the Sacred Fire

Hungry Again is Dolly Parton's thirty-fourth solo album. Produced by Dolly and Richie Owens, it was released on Decca Records/Blue Eye Records on August 25, 1998, and reached number 167 on the Billboard 200 chart.

Radio Rejection

In 1997, Dolly recorded "Silent Night" and "Something Bigger Than Me" for the movie *Annabelle's Wish*, a Christmas story. When *Hungry Again* was released, the reviews from Jana Pendragon on the AllMusic website and *Billboard* magazine were glowing. They noted the return of the star to a writing and singing style more like her debut and concluded that it was one of the best solo albums produced by Dolly Parton in many years. This did not stop country radio stations from condemning and dismissing the first, self-titled single, claiming that listeners no longer wanted to hear this type of song from a woman who "drinks and dances." This probably explains the only moderate enthusiasm for the singles from *Hungry Again* (and their average positions in the charts). The traditionalists refused to see the singer evolve, to recognize that a woman occupied a major position on the country planet. So they kept the star in a paradoxical position: She was acclaimed in Nashville and by her fans all over the world, but rejected on the specialized radio circuit.

Hungry for More Change?

Dolly went into seclusion for three months to write thirty-seven songs, including ten for *Hungry Again*, and

delivered some deep, poetic lyrics. The star went on a retreat, between creation, prayer, and fasting, far from the noise of the city, dividing her time between her cottage by the lake and her house, both at the foot of the Smoky Mountains. In contact with nature, she remembered being hungry as a child, and then in Nashville, and felt the need to remember that feeling in order to go further. In the sleeve notes, she outlines her artistic process, explains the intense desire and strength that drove her to become a star, and admits to still being hungry for producing hits, for writing, and for being a superstar.

Hungry Again is built around Dolly's favorite themes—this is a hallmark of the songwriter, who explores the same topics over and over again, not for lack of inspiration but in order to do better and better, to amaze her audience and surprise herself. As she writes in the booklet that accompanies her record: "Sometimes to know just how far you've traveled, you've gotta go back to where you began."

Album Cover

The front photo shows a very "natural" Dolly, her hair braided, dressed simply in denim overalls and a long-sleeved T-shirt, sitting cross-legged on a garden swing, gazing into the distance. Inside the cover, numerous black-and-white shots of the star and her team offer an intimate view of her musical world. The shots are by J. R. Rabourn, Jason Pirro, Jim Herrington, and Matt Barnes.

Singer Rhonda Vincent's backing vocals are omnipresent on *Hungry Again*.

Hungry Again

Dolly Parton / 3:24

Musicians: Gary Davis: acoustic guitar / Gary Mackey: mandolin / Richie Owens: dobro, acoustic guitar **Vocals:** Dolly Parton
Backing Vocals: Darrin Vincent, Rhonda Vincent **Recorded:** Train Traxx (Nashville, TN), House of Prayer (Locust Ridge, TN), February 1998 **Technical Team:** Producers: Dolly Parton, Richie Owens / Sound Engineers: Richie Owens, J. Allen Williams Jr. / Mixing: Marshall Morgan / Mastering: Denny Purcell **Single:** Side A: The Salt in My Tears / Side B: Hungry Again **Release:** Decca Records/Blue Eye Records, November 9, 1998 (ref.: DRNS7-72080)

The narrator deplores the comfortable but bland routine into which long-term love settles almost ineluctably. She would like to relive with her lover the spark, the desire, even the hunger for each other—in short, the passion that animated them at the beginning of their relationship. On another level of reading, this text perhaps also evokes the artist's need to take stock to find what stirred her and pushed her further toward success.

Musically, after the craziness and sound experimentations (of uneven quality) of the 1980s, the star gradually returned to restraint. She increasingly wrote songs with one or two categories of instruments. We remember, for example, on the album *Something Special*, "Crippled Bird" with piano and violin, or "Teach Me to Trust" with guitars and violin. This piece is interpreted by the plucked strings that are often found in country music (folk guitar, dobro, mandolin), supported by two backing singers. The result of this traditional folk arrangement is very pleasant—only the campfire is missing! Dolly's composition also seems to be more ambitious. For the first time, the dobro and the mandolin are combined—accompanied by the folk guitar—producing a very interesting mix of wood and metal tones.

Richie Owens is a singer, songwriter, and musician who is also a member of Dolly's family and one of her most faithful collaborators.

Richie Owens was very involved in this album, both as a musician and in the production.

The Salt In My Tears

Dolly Parton / 3:54

Musicians: Richie Owens: acoustic guitar, electric guitar / Bob Ocker: electric guitar lead, rhythm guitar / Johnny Lauffer: piano, organ / Eric Rupert: bass / Bob Grundner: drums, percussions **Vocals:** Dolly Parton **Backing Vocals:** Richard Dennison, Jennifer O'Brien, Joy Gardner, Rhonda Vincent, Darrin Vincent, Richie Owens, Brian Waldschlager **Recorded:** Train Traxx (Nashville, TN), House of Prayer (Locust Ridge, TN), February 1998 **Technical Team:** Producers: Dolly Parton, Richie Owens / Sound Engineers: Richie Owens, J. Allen Williams Jr. / Mixing: Marshall Morgan / Mastering: Denny Purcell **Single:** Side A: The Salt in My Tears / Side B: Hungry Again **Release:** Decca Records/Blue Eye Records, November 9, 1998 (ref.: DRNS7-72080)

The narrator has given herself body and soul to her man, who in return has not kept his promises, has only deceived her, lied to her, and hurt her. Conclusion: He is not even worth the salt in the tears she sheds. A classic by the songwriter, tinged with rock.

As for the previous piece, but in a different style, Dolly Parton chooses instrumental simplicity to emphasize the scope of the words. In the past, in a frenzy of synths and reverb, the deep meaning of the lyrics could be partly hidden. Here, almost no effects are applied to the drums and the voice, and the orchestra is a classic country formation—we note the overdrive effect on the guitar, a little louder but perfectly fitting in the mix. The choice of instruments is judicious, in particular that of the organ, whose very soft tone enriches the harmonies of the rhythm of the guitars and contributes to cohesion of the sound. The effects obtained by Johnny Lauffer are particularly successful, such as the descent on the keyboard at 2:05. These features in common (simplicity and a brilliant combination of instruments) certainly explain why "Hungry Again" and "The Salt in My Tears" were included together on the same single.

Honky Tonk Songs

Dolly Parton / 4:32

Musicians: Richie Owens: acoustic guitar, electric guitar, slide guitar / Bob Ocker: electric guitar / Johnny Lauffer: piano / Mark Brooks: bass / Bob Grundner: drums, percussions **Vocals:** Dolly Parton
Backing Vocals: The Honky Tonk Women: Jennifer O'Brien, Joy Gardner, Rhonda Vincent, Rachel Dennison, Judy Ogle, Teresa Hughes, Ira Parker, Lois Baker **Recorded:** Train Traxx (Nashville, TN), House of Prayer (Locust Ridge, TN), February 1998 **Technical Team:** Producers: Dolly Parton, Richie Owens / Sound Engineers: Richie Owens, J. Allen Williams Jr. / Mixing: Marshall Morgan / Mastering: Denny Purcell **Single:** Side A: Honky Tonk Songs / Side B: Paradise Road **Release:** Decca Records/Blue Eye Records, May 5, 1998 (ref.: DRNDS-72061)
Best US Chart Ranking: 74 on Billboard Hot Country Songs

Genesis and Lyrics

In a honky tonk bar, the narrator, left by her man for someone younger than her, asks the bartender for a refill while listening to the songs played on the jukebox. Why are there not more women singing honky tonk songs, about their misfortunes and sorrows when men mistreat them? Rachel Dennison, Dolly's sister, and Judy Ogle, her great friend, are part of the Honky Tonk Women backing vocalists—not to be confused with the *Honky Tonk Angels* (single women who frequent bars), the collaborative album released in 1993 by Dolly Parton, Loretta Lynn, and Tammy Wynette.

Production

Following on from the two previous tracks, this long one (over four minutes), which is very coherent in its writing and its realization, places the emphasis on the voice and the text. Despite the powerful guitar riffs, the verses are very refined—in particular the first one, on which the drums play very little before entering fully with a timbre close to the acoustic. Through subtle proportioning, the drums are not oversized in the mix, which is therefore aerated, with very little reverb. The bass drum and the bass complement each other well, providing a nice foundation for the rhythm section. The folk and electric guitars, as well as the upright piano, contribute this "local" rock sound, which immediately enables the scene to be located geographically.

Behind an apparent lightness, the lyrics of this song address the problem of the place of women in the music industry. It must be said that honky tonks have inspired many artists. In 1996, two years before the release of Dolly Parton's single, George Jones's "Honky Tonk Song" tells the story of a man who has just been handcuffed and who badly needs to go to a bar to relax. And long before that, in 1969, "Honky Tonk Women" by the Rolling Stones was a hit.

The upright piano, easier to install in a saloon than a grand piano, even though it is heavy, is in the medium range. A piano supports 25 tons of tension with 264 strings (three strings per key, 88 keys).

Dolly Parton is all smiles as her limo leaves her hotel in New York City.

Blue Valley Songbird

Dolly Parton / 4:23

Musicians: Richie Owens: guitar / Gary Davis: acoustic guitar / Gary Mackey: mandolin / Mark Brooks: double bass / Bob Grundner: drums **Vocals:** Dolly Parton **Backing Vocals:** Rhonda Vincent, Darrin Vincent **Recorded:** Train Traxx (Nashville, TN), House of Prayer (Locust Ridge, TN), February 1998 **Technical Team:** Producers: Dolly Parton, Richie Owens / Sound Engineers: Richie Owens, J. Allen Williams Jr. / Mixing: Marshall Morgan / Mastering: Denny Purcell

This is the unfortunate story of a young girl from Tennessee, abused by her father physically and psychologically. Her mother urges her to run away while she can, so, at the age of fifteen, she escapes and tries to make a living with music, because, like Dolly, she sings like a bird and writes like a poetess—the comparison ends there. But success does not heal all wounds…the TV movie *Blue Valley Songbird*, released in 1999, starring Dolly Parton, was inspired by this song. Like "Honky Tonk Songs," this song is over four minutes long, with few pauses and few repetitions in the

singing. This shows how inspired the songwriter was by the subject matter. As with "Hungry Again," the matching of all the plucked strings together (even the double bass) makes for a happy marriage. The mandolin plays in the style of tarantella, a traditional dance music from southern Italy (believed to cure spider bites).

ON YOUR HEADPHONES
For all those who have difficulty distinguishing between the bass and the double bass: In "Blue Valley Songbird" the entry of the double bass at 0:54 is very clearly identifiable.

I Wanna Go Back There

Dolly Parton / 3:06

Musicians: Richie Owens: acoustic guitar, dobro / Bob Ocker: electric guitar / Johnny Lauffer: piano / Mark Brooks: bass / Bob Grundner: drums **Vocals:** Dolly Parton **Backing Vocals:** Richard Dennison, Jennifer O'Brien, Joy Gardner, Rhonda Vincent, Darrin Vincent, Richie Owens **Recorded:** Train Traxx (Nashville, TN), House of Prayer (Locust Ridge, TN), February 1998 **Technical Team:** Producers: Dolly Parton, Richie Owens / Sound Engineers: Richie Owens, J. Allen Williams Jr. / Mixing: Marshall Morgan / Mastering: Denny Purcell

The narrator is nostalgic for the time when they were happy as a couple, when the love they shared was tender and serene, and life was perfect. It is rare in Dolly Parton's work that the accompaniment to the song is so heavily driven by bass and drums; here they are omnipresent—the discreet chords of two acoustic guitars are muted during the verses. Harmonically, with the electric guitar playing quite similar melodies throughout the song, there is room for a second voice provided again by Dolly, in overdub, and for those of the backing singers.

When Jesus Comes Calling For Me

Dolly Parton / 2:49

Musicians: Richie Owens: acoustic guitar, harmonica / Bob Ocker: electric guitar / Johnny Lauffer: piano, organ, strings / Mark Brooks: bass / Bob Grundner: drums, percussions **Vocals:** Dolly Parton **Backing Vocals:** Rhonda Vincent, Darrin Vincent **Recorded:** Train Traxx (Nashville, TN), House of Prayer (Locust Ridge, TN), February 1998 **Technical Team:** Producers: Dolly Parton, Richie Owens / Sound Engineers: Richie Owens, J. Allen Williams Jr. / Mixing: Marshall Morgan / Mastering: Denny Purcell

The narrator remembers an old man, known in her childhood, who awaited death serenely, almost with joy, imbued in his faith. Dolly introduces her character by reciting, and then she allows herself to be carried away by her text to the catchy rhythm of gospel music. Musically, it is undoubtedly the piece on the album that is the most refined in postproduction and with the most effects on the instruments. We notice a volume pedal on the electric guitar and a reverb on the drums (even on the bass drum), which intervenes only on the low drums (bass drum and two toms) and the hi-hat. Thus, the drums remain discreet, both harmonically and in the mix, and enhance the vocals and the other instruments particularly well.

Time And Tears

Dolly Parton / 2:56

Musicians: Richie Owens: acoustic guitar / Gary Davis: banjo / Gary Mackey: mandolin, fiddle / Mark Brooks: double bass / Bob Grundner: drums **Vocals:** Dolly Parton **Backing Vocals:** Darrin Vincent, Paul Brewster **Recorded:** Train Traxx (Nashville, TN), House of Prayer (Locust Ridge, TN), February 1998 **Technical Team:** Producers: Dolly Parton, Richie Owens / Sound Engineers: Richie Owens, J. Allen Williams Jr. / Mixing: Marshall Morgan / Mastering: Denny Purcell

Healing from this heartbreak was long and painful, but the narrator managed it, and she did not endure all of that just to agree to her former lover's return. Time and tears—and a new encounter—have helped her get over it; the page is turned. "Time and Tears" is the only song on the album that starts out *a tutti* (in the others, one to three instruments, even on four single notes, are called upon to play). All the traditional instruments emblematic of popular country music are brought together here: the banjo, the mandolin, and the fiddle—a formation that requires no amplification, a rarity in contemporary mainstream music production. The banjo, which plays continuously and without ever slackening the pace, brings an additional country touch to the piece.

I'll Never Say Goodbye

Dolly Parton / 3:14

Musicians: Richie Owens: acoustic guitar, pedal steel, mandolin / Bob Ocker: acoustic guitar lead / Mark Brooks: double bass / Bob Grundner: drums **Vocals:** Dolly Parton **Backing Vocals:** Rhonda Vincent, Darrin Vincent **Recorded:** Train Traxx (Nashville, TN), House of Prayer (Locust Ridge, TN), February 1998 **Technical Team:** Producers: Dolly Parton, Richie Owens / Sound Engineers: Richie Owens, J. Allen Williams Jr. / Mixing: Marshall Morgan / Mastering: Denny Purcell

The man she loves is gone—and, it is said, has rebuilt his life—but the narrator does not give up: She has not said goodbye, will never say it, and will always hope for his return.

This piece does not depart from the tradition of Dolly's ballads; this one is in three time, played by all the available string instruments (except the banjo) and the drums, which are very discreet. The bass drum's attack on the notes of the double bass and the snare drum's sweeps are distinctive.

The Camel's Heart

Dolly Parton / 3:15

Musicians: Richie Owens: acoustic guitar, mandolin / Bob Ocker: electric guitar / Gary Davis: banjo / Al Perkins: pedal steel / Mark Brooks: bass / Bob Grundner: drums, percussions **Vocals:** Dolly Parton **Backing Vocals:** Rhonda Vincent, Darrin Vincent **Recorded:** Train Traxx (Nashville, TN), House of Prayer (Locust Ridge, TN), February 1998 **Technical Team:** Producers: Dolly Parton, Richie Owens / Sound Engineers: Richie Owens, J. Allen Williams Jr. / Mixing: Marshall Morgan / Mastering: Denny Purcell

Tired of her lover's infidelities, the narrator decides to put an end to her grief and to this relationship. This song invites us to mount a horse, suggested by the pattern of the drums, and to ride until we are exhausted, as if to symbolize the new beginning sought by the neglected lover. The other instruments, as well as the chord grid (notably the sequence of the first two chords, at the very beginning of the song), are typical of Western music.

I Still Lost You

Dolly Parton / 3:36

Musicians: Richie Owens: acoustic guitar / Bob Ocker: electric guitar / Johnny Lauffer: piano / Al Perkins: pedal steel / Randy Leago: accordion / Mark Brooks: bass / Bob Grundner: drums **Vocals:** Dolly Parton **Backing Vocals:** Richard Dennison, Jennifer O'Brien, Joy Gardner **Recorded:** Train Traxx (Nashville, TN), House of Prayer (Locust Ridge, TN), February 1998 **Technical Team:** Producers: Dolly Parton, Richie Owens / Sound Engineers: Richie Owens, J. Allen Williams Jr. / Mixing: Marshall Morgan / Mastering: Denny Purcell

What is the point of wanting to stir up the embers of a lost love? The narrator has already given everything; she does not want to suffer any more.

This ballad is more of a pop song than "I'll Never Say Goodbye." The accordion brings the acoustic touch, but the electric bass and the metallic sound of the electric guitar are very perceptible. On this track, as on the whole album, the simplicity remains—while huge reverbs were applied in the 1980s (on the vocals and the snare drum, in particular), here we just find something that is applied to "loosen up" the sound.

Paradise Road

Dolly Parton / 3:11

Musicians: Richie Owens: acoustic guitar, pedal steel / Bob Ocker: electric guitar / Gary Mackey: mandolin / Johnny Lauffer: organ / Al Perkins: pedal steel / Mark Brooks: bass / Bob Grundner: drums **Vocals:** Dolly Parton **Backing Vocals:** Richard Dennison, Jennifer O'Brien, Joy Gardner, Rhonda Vincent, Darrin Vincent **Recorded:** Train Traxx (Nashville, TN), House of Prayer (Locust Ridge, TN), February 1998 **Technical Team:** Producers: Dolly Parton, Richie Owens / Sound Engineers: Richie Owens, J. Allen Williams Jr. / Mixing: Marshall Morgan / Mastering: Denny Purcell **Single:** Side A: Honky Tonk Songs / Side B: Paradise Road **Release:** Decca Records/Blue Eye Records, May 5, 1998 (ref.: DRNDS-72061) **Best US Chart Ranking:** 74 on Billboard Hot Country Songs

Through writing about childhood poverty that is almost autobiographical, the songwriter explores the inner world of her protagonist, supported by her dreams and her faith. The latter, which nothing can dent, opens up "the road to Paradise" for her.

From which instrument do the notes held under the guitar and pedal steel chords come? From an organ or a bass? As the intensity does not vary, one thinks at first of the organ; then, listening more carefully to the attacks of the notes, one guesses that this is the sound of the fingers on the strings close to the microphone, at 0:20 and at 0:44 in particular. The instruments are all playing fully only after 1:00. The melody of the song then changes, and the backing singers accompany Dolly Parton almost until the end. The organ, discreet upon its entry, plays increasingly loudly until closing the piece with its layers. The combination of instruments on the intro is similar to that of "I'll Never Say Goodbye," with Richie Owens's chords on folk guitar, with his theme on pedal steel, and with the mandolin added to Al Perkins's pedal steel. The guitar comes later, during the instrumental part of the ensemble. We notice a significant reverb on Dolly's voice, in particular at the beginning, a sensation accentuated by the few instruments that accompany her. It is on this number—and also "I Wanna Go Back There" and "Shine On"—that the star sings the highest.

A promotional photo of
Dolly Parton from 1998.

Shine On

Dolly Parton / 4:11

Musicians: Richie Owens: bouzouki, autoharp **Vocals:** Dolly Parton
Backing Vocals: Richard Dennison, Jennifer O'Brien, Joy Gardner,
Rhonda Vincent, Darrin Vincent, Louis Nunley, Jimmy Boling and the
House of Prayer Congregation **Recorded:** Train Traxx (Nashville, TN),
House of Prayer (Locust Ridge, TN), February 1998 **Technical Team:**
Producers: Dolly Parton, Richie Owens / Sound Engineers: Richie
Owens, J. Allen Williams Jr. / Mixing: Marshall Morgan / Mastering:
Denny Purcell

Dolly Parton gives all the energy she is capable of in this
concluding gospel song, and the listener, whether a believer
or not, feels regenerated.

While Dolly's earlier gospel songs were tinged with pop,
"Shine On"—despite the light chords of the Greek stringed
instrument the bouzouki—is closer to the traditional songs
heard in churches. The end of the song, with all-powerful
vocals, closes the album in an apotheosis.

ALBUM

Precious Memories

Precious Memories . Power in the Blood . In the Sweet Bye & Bye .
Church in the Wildwood . Keep on the Firing Line . Amazing Grace . Old Time Religion .
Softly and Tenderly . Farther Along . What a Friend We Have in Jesus .
In the Garden . When the Roll Is Called Up Yonder

RELEASE DATE
United States: April 17, 1999
Reference: Blue Eye Records, Nashville (TN)—
not intended for general sale
Best US Chart Ranking: Did Not Chart

All the proceeds from *Precious Memories* were donated to the Dollywood Foundation.

Rediscovering The Sacred Fire

Precious Memories is Dolly Parton's thirty-fifth solo album. Produced by Richie Owens, it was released by Blue Eye Records on April 17, 1999. This gospel opus, consisting of covers, is exceptional in the star's discography, because it was recorded and sold exclusively for the benefit of the Dollywood Foundation. You can listen online to the ten titles covered and sung by Dolly, but the album is not available for sale. It has therefore not been ranked in the charts, and no single has been released.

A Tireless Businesswoman

Dolly Parton is a tireless, determined, and insightful artist and businesswoman. Some might say that when it comes to marketing and promoting her image, she is as outrageous as she is in her choice of outfits, but they would be underestimating the star's intelligence. In her early fifties, Dolly was on her way to becoming an icon in America. To finance her numerous projects, in particular the Imagination Library and the Dollywood Foundation, she was pulling out all the stops: an amusement park, a production company, hotels, restaurants, cosmetics, lingerie…while questioning herself artistically after *Hungry Again*, she was committing herself intensively to setting up philanthropic projects, which included *Precious Memories*. This album, whose proceeds were entirely donated to her foundation, therefore did not reach the charts.

On April 1, 1999, on the occasion of the twentieth week of the hundred best hits on TNN, a special program was broadcast on the channel: *Dolly Parton's Precious Memories*. The star sings several songs from this gospel opus, accompanied by her brother Randy, her sister Rachel, and guests such as Alison Krauss. Family, faith, and music, the triptych that serves as a foundation for Dolly Parton, are in the spotlight.

Precious Memories

In this second gospel album, the singer pays tribute to texts and lyricists from a long tradition (from the eighteenth to the twentieth centuries) that, in a way, chronicle the hope of a better life, and the passion that inspires believers. In the liner notes of her previous album, *Hungry Again*, Dolly explained her need to take a break and reconnect with herself—we should remember that in 1998, she retreated to the heart of her native Tennessee for three months to practice meditation, prayer, and fasting. Beyond its philanthropic purpose, *Precious Memories* is perhaps also the result of a desire to consolidate the gains of this spiritual and creative retreat.

Album Cover

In this image by Wade Perry, a country chapel and an old wooden carriage stand out against wooded hills. In the foreground, a hymn book is opened at the score of "Precious Memories." On it, like an object from the abandoned past, a portrait of Dolly is reflected in a pocket mirror.

The Kingdom Heirs gospel choir on stage at the 47th Annual Gospel Music Association Dove Awards, presented at the Allen Arena in Nashville, 2016.

BACKING VOCALS

For *Precious Memories*, the Kinfolks ("family people") bring together Louis, Bill, John Henry, and Dorothy Jo Owens, from the maternal side of Dolly Parton's family. As for the quartet the Kingdom Heirs, this includes Steve French, Arthur Rice, David Sutton, and Eric Bennett.

Precious Memories

J. B. F. Wright / 3:15

Musicians: Mark Brooks: bass / Gary Davis: acoustic guitar / Bob Grundner: drums / Johnny Lauffer: piano / Al Perkins: pedal steel **Vocals:** Dolly Parton **Recorded:** Studio 19 and Studio 20 (Nashville, TN), 1998 **Technical Team:** Producer: Richie Owens / Sound Engineers: Danny Brown, Darrell Puett / Song Arrangements: Dolly Parton / Mixing: Dave Matthews / Additional Recordings (overdubs): Jim Pace

"Precious Memories" is a traditional gospel song that was written in 1925 by J. B. F. Wright, who was born, like Dolly Parton, in Tennessee. Among the many artists who have covered it are Aretha Franklin (1972), Johnny Cash (1975), Tammy Wynette and Emmylou Harris (1987), Bob

Dylan (1986), and Stella Parton, on her album *Appalachian Gospel* (2003).

"Precious Memories" celebrates childhood memories, angels, and sacred scenes. In this number, Johnny Lauffer's piano steals the show from the guitars. His delicately arpeggiated playing is the backbone upon which Al Perkins's aerial pedal steel, Gary Davis's acoustic guitar arpeggios, and a bass/drums section (played by Mark Brooks and Bob Grundner, respectively) are grafted with exemplary restraint. As always, Dolly refines her interpretation, balanced between strength and sweetness, in the image of her inextinguishable fervor and of all these precious memories.

Power In The Blood

Lewis E. Jones / 2:11

Musicians: Mark Brooks: bass / Gary Davis: acoustic guitar, banjo / Bob Grundner: drums / Johnny Lauffer: piano / Al Perkins: dobro
Vocals: Dolly Parton **Backing Vocals:** The Kinfolks, The Kingdom Heirs **Recorded:** Studio 19 and Studio 20 (Nashville, TN), 1998
Technical Team: Producer: Richie Owens / Song Arrangements: Dolly Parton / Sound Engineers: Danny Brown, Darrell Puett / Mixing: Dave Matthews / Additional Recordings (overdubs): Jim Pace

Illinois native Lewis Edgar Jones wrote more than two hundred hymns, many inspired by pastors' sermons. In this song praising Jesus, the work of the land, and the bonds of blood, Dolly, backed by a full chorus, gives her all. This time, it is Gary Davis's frailing banjo and the powerful voices of the Kinfolks that take the lead in this song made for a country-style dance. Al Perkins adds a touch of edginess with his heartfelt dobro licks, while the rhythm section flows forward seamlessly, like a single player, and the acoustic guitar strums relentlessly. Dolly and her musicians give a new lease on life to this gospel song, whose up-tempo orchestration invites you to clap your hands, stand up, and sing along to the glory of the Savior and the working-class heroes.

In The Sweet Bye & Bye

S. Fillmore Bennett, Joseph P. Webster / 3:37

Musicians: Mark Brooks: bass / Gary Mackey: fiddle / Gary Davis: acoustic guitar / Bob Grundner: drums / Johnny Lauffer: piano, strings / Al Perkins: pedal steel **Vocals:** Dolly Parton **Backing Vocals:** Rachel Dennison, Randy Parton **Recorded:** Studio 19 and Studio 20 (Nashville, TN), 1998 **Technical Team:** Producer: Richie Owens / Song Arrangements: Dolly Parton / Sound Engineers: Danny Brown, Darrell Puett / Mixing: Dave Matthews / Additional Recordings (overdubs): Jim Pace

Bennett said that Webster, a sensitive musician, was often melancholy, and that the best remedy for him was to play music. He wrote the words to this hymn—about the sweet and wonderful life that will come after earthly life—and Webster, enthused by this text, took it up, playing the violin and annotating the vocal parts on his score.

Gary Davis opens this ballad with a delicate acoustic guitar arpeggio that immediately sets the atmosphere for the listener. It seems that Johnny Lauffer, in addition to his piano part judiciously confined to the high register, also plays the double bass with his bow in a wide range that is rather unusual, even for a seasoned multi-instrumentalist. Gary Mackey's fiddle blends gracefully with Al Perkins's pedal steel, and Rachel Dennison and Randy Parton's vocal harmonies beautifully enhance Dolly's melody and voice. Mark Brooks on bass and Bob Grundner on drums play the bare essentials and know how to stop to make room for the voices, the narration, and the fine arrangements. The mark of great session men.

Church In The Wildwood

William S. Pitts / 2:39

Musicians: Mark Brooks: bass / Sam Bush, Gary Mackey: mandolin, fiddle / Gary Davis: acoustic guitar, electric guitar / Bob Grundner: drums / Johnny Lauffer: piano / Al Perkins: dobro **Vocals:** Dolly Parton **Backing Vocals:** Rachel Dennison, Steven Hill, Liana Manis, Randy Parton **Recorded:** Studio 19 and Studio 20 (Nashville, TN), 1998 **Technical Team:** Producer: Richie Owens / Song Arrangements: Dolly Parton / Sound Engineers: Danny Brown, Darrell Puett / Mixing: Dave Matthews / Additional Recordings (overdubs): Jim Pace

During a particular stage of a journey undertaken in 1857, William S. Pitts was moved by the beauty of a wooded valley, in which he imagined a "little brown church." For the narrator of his song, written on his return, no place was dearer to his childhood—an echo of Dolly and her grandfather's church. The orchestration is lively and bouncy. Johnny Lauffer's piano and Al Perkins's dobro twirl together. The drums in cross stick and bass drum on the crotchets and the staccato bass carry everyone along in their wake; the acoustic and electric guitars, as well as the fiddle and mandolin, are very far back in the mix. The backing vocals are always present, with Dolly and her musicians having the very clear intention of involving the audience in a sing-along (singing with the artist and the musicians, all together).

Keep On The Firing Line

Bessie F. Hatcher / 2:54

Musicians: Mark Brooks: bass / Gary Mackey: mandolin / Gary Davis: acoustic guitar, banjo / Bob Grundner: drums / Johnny Lauffer: piano / Al Perkins: dobro **Vocals:** Dolly Parton **Backing Vocals:** The Kinfolks, The Kingdom Heirs **Recorded:** Studio 19 and Studio 20 (Nashville, TN), 1998 **Technical Team:** Producer: Richie Owens / Song Arrangements: Dolly Parton / Sound Engineers: Danny Brown, Darrell Puett / Mixing: Dave Matthews / Additional Recordings (overdubs): Jim Pace

The brave who fight for good causes have God's support and will be rewarded whether they survive or perish. The lyrics of this song encourage the soldiers to stay in the line of fire, as this is God's will. From the very first bars, Gary Davis's frenetic banjo sets the tone: No one will be able sit still and silent for the short 2:54 of this song, halfway between gospel and patriotic anthem, intended to raise the morale of the troops at the front. The guitar and mandolin turnarounds and other dobro solos are everywhere, in bluegrass style. The rhythm section sets the pace with an unwavering spirit and metronomic evenness, the Kingdom Heirs choir lends a hand to the Kinfolks, and Dolly can then soar in search of that special tone of her voice, with her secret for producing a sound so energetic, stimulating, and full-throated, without holding anything back.

Amazing Grace

John Newton / 3:48

Musicians: Mark Brooks: bass / Gary Davis: acoustic guitar / Bob Grundner: drums / Johnny Lauffer: piano, organ / Al Perkins: pedal steel **Vocals:** Dolly Parton **Recorded:** Studio 19 and Studio 20 (Nashville, TN), 1998 **Technical Team:** Producer: Richie Owens / Song Arrangements: Dolly Parton / Sound Engineers: Danny Brown, Darrell Puett / Mixing: Dave Matthews / Additional Recordings (overdubs): Jim Pace

"Amazing Grace" is a Christian hymn originally written in 1772 by the Anglican clergyman and English poet—and repentant slave owner—John Newton, published in 1779, but associated with the "New Britain" tune only since 1835. This hymn, which evokes the power of faith, hope, forgiveness of sins, and salvation by divine grace, is extremely popular in the English-speaking world, especially in the United States, where it is sung at both religious ceremonies and secular celebrations. Judy Collins, Elvis, Johnny Cash, Aretha Franklin, Rod Stewart, Whitney Houston, Jessye Norman…the Library of Congress has a collection of some three thousand versions. The Queen of Country, who had been singing this standard regularly since she was a child, delivers here, with her band, a classic, well-judged interpretation. The progressive orchestration suits the spirit of the song well. From 1:56, the famous sound of a Hammond organ, passed through a Leslie cabinet—an archetypal sound of gospel—also reinforces the gospel color of the arrangement provided by Dolly Parton, while rubbing shoulders with the country instrument par excellence, the pedal steel. A version that is not short on scope, rather restrained, but effective.

Old Time Religion

Traditional / 1:36

Musicians: Mark Brooks: bass / Sam Bush: mandolin / Gary Davis: acoustic guitar / Bob Grundner: drums / Johnny Lauffer: piano / Al Perkins: dobro **Vocals:** Dolly Parton **Backing Vocals:** The Kingdom Heirs **Recorded:** Studio 19 and Studio 20 (Nashville, TN), 1998 **Technical Team:** Producer: Richie Owens / Song Arrangements: Dolly Parton / Sound Engineers: Danny Brown, Darrell Puett / Mixing: Dave Matthews / Additional Recordings (overdubs): Jim Pace

"Old Time Religion" is a traditional gospel tune from 1873, which has become a classic and has been included in many Protestant hymns. Dolly sings it in a country-gospel style, supported by the warm, deep voices of the Kingdom Heirs, reminiscent of African American spirituals. Here, each musician works to make us feel the swing of the ternary pulse; Johnny Lauffer allows himself a few turnarounds on the piano, and Al Perkins graces us from the intro with his melodic dobro flashes. The production is nicely done. The audience is invited to stand up and join in with the joy and happiness!

A model of the Kona lap guitar, made in Hawaii around 1927.

Farther Along

Traditional / 3:43

Musicians: Mark Brooks: bass / Sam Bush: mandolin, fiddle / Gary Davis: acoustic guitar / Bob Grundner: drums / Al Perkins: Kona lap guitar **Vocals:** Dolly Parton **Backing Vocals:** Rachel Dennison, Randy Parton **Recorded:** Studio 19 and Studio 20 (Nashville, TN), 1998
Technical Team: Producer: Richie Owens / Song Arrangements: Dolly Parton / Sound Engineers: Danny Brown, Darrell Puett / Mixing: Dave Matthews / Additional Recordings (overdubs): Jim Pace

A gospel song from the American South, "Farther Along" is a song whose authorship is disputed. Dolly recorded it with Linda Ronstadt and Emmylou Harris for the album *Trio*. The title evokes a Christian's dismay at the apparent prosperity of the wicked, contrasted with the suffering of the righteous. The repeated theme is related to the protagonist's hope that "farther along" (presumably in heaven) the truth will be revealed. The typically mountain music arrangement of this traditional song gently takes the listener by the hand and leads them onto the front porch of a southern Appalachian cabin: mandolin tremolos and fiddle counterpoints (both played by Sam Bush), acoustic guitar rhythm played in fingerpicking style by multi-instrumentalist Gary Davis, a few discreet notes of Kona lap guitar (the legendary Hawaiian guitar that is played on the lap, made in the workshops of the luthier Weissenborn from the 1920s) interpreted by Al Perkins. Rachel Dennison and Randy Parton on the backing vocals complete the hyper-realistic picture provided by Dolly Parton, who is a master in the art of reproducing this kind of picturesque sketch. Sometimes, three chords, a few words, and a clear melodic line are sufficient.

Softly And Tenderly

Will L. Thompson / 3:47

Musicians: Mark Brooks: bass / Gary Davis: acoustic guitar / Bob Grundner: drums / Johnny Lauffer: piano / Al Perkins: pedal steel
Vocals: Dolly Parton **Backing Vocals:** Rachel Dennison, Liana Manis
Recorded: Studio 19 and Studio 20 (Nashville, TN), 1998
Technical Team: Producer: Richie Owens / Song Arrangements: Dolly Parton / Sound Engineers: Danny Brown, Darrell Puett / Mixing: Dave Matthews / Additional Recordings (overdubs): Jim Pace

This Christian hymn was composed and written in 1880 by Will L. Thompson, who was a member of the Churches of Christ. Other hymns and gospel songs by him are still in use, but "Softly and Tenderly" is the best known of his compositions. It is the first country waltz ballad on the album. Still in a traditional vein, Dolly Parton's arrangement brings together all the musical ingredients that have rocked her since her early youth: pedal steel, the sound of the Hammond organ warmed by the rotary system of the Leslie cabinet, a gracefully breezing piano, and folk guitar arpeggios and strumming. The ensemble is supported by an ascetic rhythm section that maintains the tempo with the necessary touch and control to keep a slow waltz going, evoking the sweetness and tenderness of the Christian Word. The playing directions are, one might say, in the text itself: "Softly and tenderly, Jesus is calling…" Dolly and her musicians have always excelled in this kind of exercise.

A glamorous promotional photo of Dolly taken during the recording sessions for *Precious Memories*.

What A Friend We Have In Jesus

Joseph M. Scriven, Charles Crozat Converse / 3:47

Musicians: Mark Brooks: bass / Gary Davis: acoustic guitar / Bob Grundner: drums / Johnny Lauffer: piano / Al Perkins: pedal steel
Vocals: Dolly Parton **Backing Vocals:** Rachel Dennison, Liana Manis
Recorded: Studio 19 and Studio 20 (Nashville, TN), 1998
Technical Team: Producer: Richie Owens / Song Arrangements: Dolly Parton / Sound Engineers: Danny Brown, Darrell Puett / Mixing: Dave Matthews / Additional Recordings (overdubs): Jim Pace

In 1855, the preacher Joseph M. Scriven, who had emigrated to Canada, wrote this poem to comfort his mother, who had remained in Ireland. Published anonymously, this hymn—set to music by Converse in 1868—was attributed to Scriven in the 1880s. It is probably with closed eyes that Dolly and her musicians, comfortably installed in Nashville's Studio 19 and Studio 20, interpret this folk music standard in the purest country tradition. If the Nashville sound orthodoxy had to have an anthem, this could be it. Each instrument is in its rightful place and contributes fully to this creation.

In The Garden

C. Austin Miles / 2:54

Musicians: Mark Brooks: bass / Gary Davis: acoustic guitar / Bob Grundner: drums / Johnny Lauffer: piano / Al Perkins: pedal steel
Vocals: Dolly Parton **Backing Vocals:** Rachel Dennison, Liana Manis
Recorded: Studio 19 and Studio 20 (Nashville, TN), 1998
Technical Team: Producer: Richie Owens / Song Arrangements: Dolly Parton / Sound Engineers: Danny Brown, Darrell Puett / Mixing: Dave Matthews / Additional Recordings (overdubs): Jim Pace

This gospel song was written by American songwriter C. Austin Miles, a former pharmacist turned editor and director of Hall-Mack Publishing. According to his great-granddaughter, the song was born in a cold and dreary basement with no windows. It was published in 1912 and popularized by two members of Miles's staff, Homer Rodeheaver and Virginia Asher, during evangelistic campaigns in the early twentieth century. Gary Davis's acoustic guitar and Johnny Lauffer's piano blend their arpeggios to create this bed made of lace, so fragile and delicate, upon which Dolly at first barely dares to lay her voice. Then the rhythm section and the backing vocals make their entrance, calm and composed, soon joined by the aerial pedal steel of Al Perkins, like a walk in an English garden. Then, with the horizon just emerging, the arrangement of "In the Garden" ends as it began, leaving the listener with a few impressionistic touches of piano and guitar, as though in a waking dream.

When The Roll Is Called Up Yonder

James Milton Black / 2:03

Musicians: Mark Brooks: bass / Gary Mackey: mandolin / Gary Davis: acoustic guitar, banjo / Bob Grundner: drums / Johnny Lauffer: piano / Al Perkins: pedal steel **Vocals:** Dolly Parton **Backing Vocals:** The Kinfolks, The Kingdom Heirs **Recorded:** Studio 19 and Studio 20 (Nashville, TN), 1998 **Technical Team:** Producer: Richie Owens / Song Arrangements: Dolly Parton / Sound Engineers: Danny Brown, Darrell Puett / Mixing: Dave Matthews / Additional Recordings (overdubs): Jim Pace

This Christian hymn was written in 1893 by composer James Milton Black. One of his sources of inspiration was *The Book of Life*. The other was an event related to the Sunday school class he taught: Worried about the absence of a child who was ill, he went to the child's home and called a doctor; back home and finding nothing suitable in his repertoire of hymns, he decided to write this one. There are more than five hundred recorded versions, including those of Loretta Lynn, Johnny Cash, Jim Nabors, and Willie Nelson.

As is often the case, Dolly wanted to close her album on a joyful and unifying note. Everyone is called back on stage for a final number: Gary Davis, always impeccable on acoustic guitar and banjo; Gary Mackey and his fluid, agile mandolin; Al Perkins and his voluble pedal steel; Johnny Lauffer, with his breezy piano, invariably perfectly in rhythm; the rhythm section itself, that nothing seems to be able to disturb; the backing vocals of the Kinfolks and the Kingdom Heirs; and only two minutes suffice to wrap up the whole thing. On this track, Dolly's voice is as though veiled, on the verge of cracking, probably because of the number of enthusiastic takes, as she refused to take it easy—another proof of her legendary generosity. What better way to end a gospel album?

Dolly, Businesswoman and Philanthropist: An Entertainment Magnate with a Generous Heart

Dolly has often said that the best advice on how to manage her career was given to her by her father: that she should never let others take advantage of her. Wise advice that helped her to develop her business sense, combining her passion for music with singing, with professionalism. The artist founded her publishing company Owe-Par at the age of twenty to protect her copyrights. Then she created two labels, Dolly Records and Butterfly Records, and one successful project followed another. In the eyes of her fans and business partners, Dolly is an inspiring role model as a woman, artist, philanthropist, and entrepreneur.

In 2020, Dolly Parton's fortune was estimated at $800 million, and in the same year, her crisis management acumen became the focus of an academic presentation for entrepreneurs and managers.

Honor Your Roots

Dollywood in Pigeon Forge, Tennessee, is not just one of the most visited amusement parks in the United States. It is a celebration: a tribute to her native Sevier County, to her childhood spent in the heart of this splendid nature, to her parents, who faced so many hardships in poverty to raise their twelve children. For an artist, the story—family, marital, professional, etc.—that she offers to her public must be a message of emotion, of life, of singularity, sometimes of mystery, and always of a process of identification, in order to generate affinity, even empathy. Since her beginnings, the star has articulated her story around the same elements: her family, the material poverty in which she grew up, but also the richness of the heart—of which the song *Coat of Many Colors* is the symbol and the torch—the love of her parents, courage, faith, and the passion of music. Strong, authentic values, whose regular reaffirmation, like a mantra, a sort of spiritual backbone, confers upon Dolly Parton a clear, endearing, and solid image: that of a female artist you can count on. Her constancy is largely responsible for

this; since the beginning of her career, Dolly has always been present, always available.

An Ability to Sustain and Nurture Her Image

The Nielsen Institute confirms Dolly Parton's brand power in the US, with a "Q Score" (which measures public appeal and brand affinity) that places her in the top ten highest-ranked celebrities in all types of entertainment. She has an accurate sense of her own worth, which enables her to run the best promotional campaigns for her albums, movies, and TV shows, as well as her amusement park, the best example of what the star can achieve in pure business. Around her image as a glitzy, glamorous country queen, the artist has generated a whole range of merchandise: from mugs to socks, from T-shirts to canine accessories. In 2020, the star launched an idea that has gone viral on social networks: the #dollypartonchallenge, which challenges celebrities to post a mosaic of four different profile pictures for Facebook, Tinder, Instagram, and LinkedIn. Many celebrities have taken up the challenge, and even museums, such as the Musée d'Orsay in Paris, as well as the multinational auction house Sotheby's, have participated. A simple and smart challenge, and Dolly hits the nail on the head.

The Philanthropist

Dolly Parton redistributes (her wealth), supports (causes), and her popularity is exponential. As a philanthropist, she funds many projects, notably in medical research (development of the Moderna vaccine during the COVID-19 pandemic, for example), and also in the educational and cultural fields, through the Dollywood Foundation, which helps and supports young people in their studies and manages the Imagination Library, a program that gives books to underprivileged children up to the age of five.

In 2007, Dolly Parton received the Woodrow Wilson Award, presented by the Wilson Center (part of the

Dolly Parton poses with a guitar outside her offices in Nashville (2001).

Smithsonian Institution in Washington, DC) for outstanding work on behalf of local communities and the world at large.

An Example for Managers Everywhere

Dolly's ability to manage communication tools and respond to extraordinary events with financial and emotional support has earned her the respect of all. In January 2020, the business magazine *Forbes* published a presentation for members of the Public Relations Society of America, entrepreneurs and managers, based on the premise that every company should have a Dolly Parton. In it, Professor Lance Kinney deciphers how the star communicates during a crisis, using as an example the 2016 wildfires that ravaged part of Tennessee, leaving dozens of families destitute. Like any good crisis manager, Dolly began by studying the situation, then responded strategically and effectively to the magnitude of this disaster. She knew the area and its people, and even though her own businesses were not affected by the fires, she stepped in to assist those who had not been spared. Dolly mobilized

her media and musical entourage, attracted attention by posting a video on social networks, and had the intelligence to present a strong image of the future of the region by saluting the courage of the inhabitants, who were struggling to overcome this crisis. Then the star organized a telethon, which brought in several million dollars, part of which was donated monthly to the needy. A year later, in 2017, against all odds, tourists did not desert the region and local businesses recorded record revenues. Not only did the victims of this tragedy benefit from financial aid and moral support, but Dolly's strategy has enabled them to look to the future with greater peace of mind. In this region, which was hit hard during the Great Depression, no one wants to go through such a situation again. Fortunately, an angel is watching over Tennessee: In the difficult times, Dolly never forgets her family.

In November 2022, the online magazine *Outsider* reported that Dolly Parton, at the age of seventy-six, plans to create a museum in Nashville, and perhaps open a bar and grill or a restaurant. The adventure continues!

ALBUM

Trio II

Lover's Return . High Sierra . Do I Ever Cross Your Mind . After the Gold Rush . The Blue Train .
I Feel the Blues Movin' In . You'll Never Be the Sun . He Rode All the Way to Texas .
Feels Like Home . When We're Gone, Long Gone

RELEASE DATE
United States: February 9, 1999
Reference: Asylum Records, Los Angeles (CA)—62275-2
Best US Chart Ranking: 4

Three: A Very Lucky Number

Almost twelve years after *Trio*, their first collaboration, Dolly Parton, Linda Ronstadt, and Emmylou Harris did it again. Also produced by George Massenburg, *Trio II* was released on Asylum Records on February 9, 1999. It ranked sixty-two on the Billboard 200 and went gold.

Flashback

In 1998, Dolly parted very amicably with her manager, Sandy Gallin, who had helped her to achieve success in pop music with *Here You Come Again*. The first consequence was that the company Sandollar Productions, in which they were both involved, which produced or co-produced TV movies, TV shows, and films, should have been dissolved, but the projects in progress were maintained, such as *Buffy the Vampire Slayer.*

Dolly was performing less, and commercially she was no longer at the level at which she had been at the beginning of her partnership with Gallin. They remained on very good terms, and from time to time, in the spirit of their friendship, Sandy Gallin still gave Dolly advice. Dollywood celebrated its fourteenth season, while honors and awards rained down on the star—Dolly Parton was one of the five most popular singers of the twentieth century. In 1999, she was inducted into the prestigious Country Music Hall of Fame, becoming only the second living artist to be inducted (after Chet Atkins, in 1973).

Trio II, Twelve Years Later

Although beautifully sung by Emmylou Harris, Linda Ronstadt, and Dolly Parton, whose voices intertwine with power and sweetness at the same time, the covers of this second *Trio* initially generated less enthusiasm than the first. However, the critics praised the work of producer George Massenburg, agreeing that this was a good album. According to the writer Stephen Miller,[2] the recording conditions were sometimes tense between the three artists, because Dolly was busy with her other projects and not always available. Linda and Emmylou even considered inviting Dolly Parton to appear as a guest star—which she refused to do. For the same reason of incompatible schedules, no big tour was organized, only the bare essentials for promotion. The trio's performances were featured on *CBS This Morning*, *The Tonight Show with Jay Leno* (NBC), and *The Rosie O'Donnell Show* (NBC).

Album Cover

On a pinkish sepia background, the portraits of Emmylou, Linda, and Dolly as children are reminiscent of the past, as are the interior photos, which radiate the same nostalgic charm. The respective schedules of the three artists did not allow for a collective photo session.

Lover's Return

A. P. Carter, Maybelle Carter, Sara Carter / 4:00

Musicians: Mark Casstevens, Carl Jackson: acoustic guitar / David Grisman: mandolin / David Lindley: autoharp / Roy Huskey Jr.: double bass / Alison Krauss: fiddle, uncredited: bass **Vocals and Backing Vocals:** Dolly Parton, Emmylou Harris, Linda Ronstadt **Recorded:** The Site, Marin County (CA), 1994 **Technical Team:** Producer: George Massenburg / Co-producer: John Starling / Production Assistants: Gail Rosman, Janet Stark / Sound Engineers: Nathaniel Kunkel, Kevin Scott / Mixing: Linda Ronstadt / Mastering: Doug Sax

Written by members of the Carter Family, "Lover's Return" tells the story of the return of an old love, the story of a feeling that is still present but which has aged, like the protagonists. The narrator's heart having been wounded, the returned man will have only her friendship, because God does not give back the youth of the past. On this ballad, where the instruments are distributed on each side of the mix to leave the central space for the three voices, Linda Ronstadt provides the lead, while the voice of Emmylou Harris, which is higher, intervenes more infrequently. Throughout the album, the latter switches from one desk to the other with ease.

High Sierra

Harley Allen / 4:21

Musicians: Mark Casstevens, Carl Jackson: acoustic guitar / David Grisman: mandolin / Roy Huskey Jr.: double bass / Alison Krauss: fiddle / Al Perkins (?): pedal steel **Vocals and Backing Vocals:** Dolly Parton, Emmylou Harris, Linda Ronstadt **Recorded:** The Site, Marin County (CA), 1994 **Technical Team:** Producer: George Massenburg / Co-producer: John Starling / Production Assistants: Gail Rosman, Janet Stark / Sound Engineers: Nathaniel Kunkel, Kevin Scott / Mixing: Linda Ronstadt / Mastering: Doug Sax **Single:** High Sierra **Release:** Asylum Records, February 1999 (Ref.: apcd-1252)

The ups and downs of the feeling of love, from the peaks of passion to the abysses of disappointment, draw an exterior landscape of mountains and valleys in total correspondence with the contrasting interior landscape of the narrator. In comparison with *Trio*, and largely due to the mastering (the final stage of mixing, which consists of giving the album its overall color), the sound is airier, the voices are treated differently, less enclosed in the midrange

and more intelligible—the same is true for the instruments. The vocals are tighter in the mix; the lead is always in the center, and it is Emmylou Harris who gives us the opportunity to admire her vocal power. The harmonies work perfectly, always adapting to the three singers. The mandolin, familiar to Dolly Parton but particularly highlighted on this album, is present on almost all of it, in accompaniment or solo, as well as the violin. A rather discreet pedal steel, probably in the hands of Al Perkins—the star's historical musician, who also plays on the rest of the album—can be heard on the extreme left of the mix. Finally, the depth of the held notes of the double bass is very interesting: The sound, at the same time precise and round, contains a lot of harmonics, and, in the bottom of its range, the vibration of the strings is clearly perceptible.

Do I Ever Cross Your Mind

Dolly Parton / 3:16

Musicians: Mark Casstevens, Carl Jackson: acoustic guitar / David Grisman: mandolin / Roy Huskey Jr.: double bass / Larry Atamanuik: drums / Alison Krauss: fiddle **Vocals and Backing Vocals:** Dolly Parton, Emmylou Harris, Linda Ronstadt **Recorded:** The Site, Marin County (CA), 1994 **Technical Team:** Producer: George Massenburg / Co-producer: John Starling / Production Assistants: Gail Rosman, Janet Stark / Sound Engineers: Nathaniel Kunkel, Kevin Scott / Mixing: Linda Ronstadt / Mastering: Doug Sax **Single:** A Trio from the Trio—One Angelic Sound: After the Gold Rush / Feels Like Home / Do I Ever Cross Your Mind **Release:** Asylum Records, April 1999 (Ref.: apcd-1294)

Dolly, as the author of this song, first performed it in 1976 as a duet with Chet Atkins. She did not record the solo version until 1982, for the album *Heartbreak Express*. A woman wonders about the man she once loved: Does he still think about her, even if only from time to time?

Compared to the version released on *Heartbreak Express*, this version, which can be described as acoustic, is closer to the original, where two guitars and two voices could be distinguished. The rhythm, adapted to the orchestration of the album, reminds us of Chet Atkins's picking style, on a slower tempo. On this number we have fiddle, mandolin, bass, drums, and folk guitar.

The glass harmonica was invented by Benjamin Franklin in 1761. Musician Dennis James plays the instrument on the Neil Young cover "After the Gold Rush."

The glass harmonica (or armonica), made of glass bowls threaded on a metal axle and wetted, is played in a sitting position, like the pedal steel. The size of the bowls is calculated so that the instrument is tuned like a piano: The larger ones correspond to the bass, the smaller ones to the treble.

After The Gold Rush

Neil Young / 3:31

Musicians: Robby Buchanan: piano / Dennis James: glass harmonica / David Campbell, Linda Ronstadt: strings / Helen Voices: synthesizers **Vocals and Backing Vocals:** Dolly Parton, Emmylou Harris, Linda Ronstadt **Recorded:** The Site, Marin County (CA), 1994 **Technical Team:** Producer: George Massenburg / Co-Producer: John Starling / Production Assistants: Gail Rosman, Janet Stark / Sound Engineers: Nathaniel Kunkel, Kevin Scott / Mixing: Linda Ronstadt / Mastering: Doug Sax **Single:** A Trio from the Trio—One Angelic Sound: After the Gold Rush / Feels Like Home / Do I Ever Cross Your Mind **Release:** Asylum Records, April 1999 (Ref.: apcd-1294)

For the interpretation of this Neil Young song (1970), Dolly takes the lead vocals. As in "Lover's Return," Emmylou Harris explores the tessitura, but in the low register, leaving the very high notes to Linda Ronstadt, whom we had been more used to hearing in the bottom range. Synthesizers have replaced the album's orchestra, notably a glass harmonica, played by Dennis James. Because of the absence of the plucked strings, this version sounds a little more like the original version, which had the piano as the only instrument. The strings and synth layers, the reverberated high voices, and the glass harmonica give the music an airy, almost spacey dimension.

(L to R) Linda Ronstadt, Dolly Parton, and Emmylou Harris, pictured at CBS Studios, recorded two albums together: *Trio* and *Trio II*.

Roy Huskey Jr, bassist, and a frequent Dolly Parton collaborator.

The Blue Train

Jennifer Kimball, Tom Kimmel / 4:57

Musicians: Leland Sklar: bass / Dean Parks: electric guitar / Mark Casstevens: acoustic guitar / Jim Keltner: drums / Robby Buchanan: keyboards / Ben Keith: pedal steel **Vocals and Backing Vocals:** Dolly Parton, Emmylou Harris, Linda Ronstadt **Recorded:** The Site, Marin County (CA), 1994 **Technical Team:** Producer: George Massenburg / Co-producer: John Starling / Production Assistants: Gail Rosman, Janet Stark / Sound Engineers: Nathaniel Kunkel, Kevin Scott / Mixing: Linda Ronstadt / Mastering: Doug Sax

Everything is metaphorical in this song: The narrator, as in a dream, rides the blue train, the train of the blues and painful memories. These poetic lyrics evoke the ruin of a story, the weight of the past, where something has broken.

On this very pop-sounding song, Emmylou Harris sings almost alone, with Linda Ronstadt providing some of the backing vocals and Dolly Parton intervening only at the very end. Many effects are applied to the voices, as well as to the snare drum, enriched with a delay.

I Feel The Blues Movin' In

Del McCoury / 4:31

Musicians: Roy Huskey Jr.: bass / Carl Jackson, Mark Casstevens: acoustic guitar / Jim Keltner: drums / Alison Krauss: fiddle / David Grisman: mandolin **Vocals and Backing Vocals:** Dolly Parton, Emmylou Harris, Linda Ronstadt **Recorded:** The Site, Marin County (CA), 1994 **Technical Team:** Producer: George Massenburg / Co-producer: John Starling / Production Assistants: Gail Rosman, Janet Stark / Sound Engineers: Nathaniel Kunkel, Kevin Scott / Mixing: Linda Ronstadt / Mastering: Doug Sax

The lyrics of this song, also metaphorical, full of blues and spleen, express lost love and the loneliness of a broken heart. Musically, the country spirit is back, except for the delay on Dolly's voice—four repetitions fading in and out are in fact perceptible—a novelty in her discography.

You'll Never Be The Sun

Donagh Long / 4:43

Musicians: Mark Casstevens, Gary Davis: acoustic guitar / Edgar Meyer: acoustic bass / David Campbell: strings **Vocals and Backing Vocals:** Dolly Parton, Emmylou Harris, Linda Ronstadt **Recorded:** The Site, Marin County (CA), 1994 **Technical Team:** Producer: George Massenburg / Co-producer: John Starling / Production Assistants: Gail Rosman, Janet Stark / Sound Engineers: Nathaniel Kunkel, Kevin Scott / Mixing: Linda Ronstadt / Mastering: Doug Sax

Continuing the poetic theme of the album, the narrator of this song assures us that even though the other person is not the sun, the moon, or the stars, and cannot compete with them, they will always be, no matter what, a beacon, a light in life.

These lyrics by Irish singer-songwriter Donagh Long have been sung by, among others, Dolores Keane (*Solid Ground*, 1993) and John McDermott (*Love Is a Voyage*, 1995). All the versions respect the original, each artist bringing a little of their own world to it. In this case, it is the vocal harmonies that constitute the added value. The instrumentation is restrained and the guitars are complementary: One plays arpeggios with bass notes, while the other plays high melodies. The layers of the violins contribute a binding element.

He Rode All The Way To Texas

John Starling / 3:07

Musicians: Leland Sklar: bass / Dean Parks: acoustic guitar, electric guitar / Mark Casstevens: acoustic guitar / Jim Keltner: drums / Robby Buchanan: piano / David Grisman: mandolin **Vocals and Backing Vocals:** Dolly Parton, Emmylou Harris, Linda Ronstadt **Recorded:** The Site, Marin County (CA), 1994 **Technical Team:** Producer: George Massenburg / Co-producer: John Starling / Production Assistants: Gail Rosman, Janet Stark / Sound Engineers: Nathaniel Kunkel, Kevin Scott / Mixing: Linda Ronstadt / Mastering: Doug Sax

Aboard an old freight train, a man is heading for Texas and freedom, without looking back at the woman he leaves behind—he will not miss her—and is shedding no tears. This tension between love and choosing another life is a recurring theme in Dolly's work.

This very slow ballad marks the reappearance of amplified instruments such as bass and electric guitar. The effect is similar to a rock ballad. In the middle of some simple playing, notably that of the piano, the full percussion makes a remarkable return, with many breaks, giving the piece an individual color.

For Dolly Addicts

Trio II was nominated for a Grammy Award for Best Country Album, and the song "After the Gold Rush" won the award for Best Country Collaboration with Vocals.

SINGLE

Feels Like Home
Randy Newman / 4:47

Musicians: Leland Sklar: bass / David Grisman: mandolin / Mark Casstevens: acoustic guitar / Dean Parks: electric guitar, mandolin / Jim Keltner: drums / Robby Buchanan: piano, organ / David Campbell: strings **Vocals and Backing Vocals:** Dolly Parton, Emmylou Harris, Linda Ronstadt **Recorded:** The Site, Marin County (CA), 1994 **Technical Team:** Producer: George Massenburg / Co-producer: John Starling / Production Assistants: Gail Rosman, Janet Stark / Sound Engineers: Nathaniel Kunkel, Kevin Scott / Mixing: Linda Ronstadt / Mastering: Doug Sax **Single:** A Trio from the Trio—One Angelic Sound: After the Gold Rush / Feels Like Home / Do I Ever Cross Your Mind **Release:** Asylum Records, April 1999 (Ref.: apcd-1294)

Feeling "at home" in each other's arms, the heart pounding but safe, and finally catching a glimpse of the light, even in the dark, this is the beginning of a new life. Recorded in 1994 as part of the *Trio II* project and performed in 1995 by Bonnie Raitt in the musical *Randy Newman's Faust*, this song was dear to Linda's heart, and she modified it for the 1999 album.

After "He Rode All the Way to Texas," this is an "electric" ballad, a little more grandiloquent and solemn, with violins and an organ that considerably enrich the refrains. Two mandolins also intervene on the choruses, producing fast, repeated notes—a specific playing feature of this instrument. The voices are very reverberated, as on most of the tracks of the album. We almost fall back into the 1980s with an excess of effects. Fortunately, these had gained in quality and naturalness over time. It contrasts nevertheless with the small effect applied to the electric guitar, limited to a light overdrive. As for the piano, it takes things slightly easier, sometimes accompanying Emmylou Harris alone.

We note on this album a development since *Trio I*, where Dolly Parton was omnipresent. In this case, Dolly leaves much more space to her two friends, takes the lead much less often, and remains rather discreet in the backing vocals, with few interventions.

When We're Gone, Long Gone
Kieran Kane, James Paul O'Hara / 4:00

Musicians: Roy Huskey Jr.: double bass / Carl Jackson, John Starling: acoustic guitar / Jim Keltner: drums / David Grisman: mandolin / Alison Krauss: fiddle **Vocals and Backing Vocals:** Dolly Parton, Emmylou Harris, Linda Ronstadt **Recorded:** The Site, Marin County (CA), 1994 **Technical Team:** Producer: George Massenburg / Co-producer: John Starling / Production Assistants: Gail Rosman, Janet Stark / Sound Engineers: Nathaniel Kunkel, Kevin Scott / Mixing: Linda Ronstadt / Mastering: Doug Sax

This is the conclusion of an album that depicts love in (almost) all its facets.

On this other very acoustic ballad, which could have been performed identically without any electricity, Alison Krauss on the fiddle finally plays a solo; her beautiful melody at the end of the piece is perfectly accompanied, notably by the characteristic notes of the mandolin.

ALBUM

The Grass Is Blue

Travelin' Prayer . Cash on the Barrelhead . A Few Old Memories .
I'm Gonna Sleep with One Eye Open . Steady as the Rain . I Still Miss Someone .
Endless Stream of Tears . Silver Dagger . Train, Train . I Wonder Where You Are Tonight .
Will He Be Waiting for Me . The Grass Is Blue . I Am Ready

RELEASE DATE
United States: October 26, 1999
Reference: Sugar Hill Records / Blue Eye Records—SHCD 3900
Best US Chart Ranking: 24

Blue Blood in the Veins

The Grass Is Blue is the thirty-fifth solo album by Dolly Parton. Produced by Steve Buckingham, it was released by Sugar Hill Records / Blue Eye Records on October 26, 1999. The critics were very enthusiastic. The singles from the album were sent to country and folk radio stations but did not make it into the charts. The album itself peaked at number 198 on the Billboard 200.

The End of the Millennium

At the national level, even though President Bill Clinton was not impeached in the end following the Lewinsky affair, which had started the previous year, America did not have much respite, as it participated in Operation Allied Force, launched by NATO against the Serbs during the war in Kosovo, while antiglobalization activists demonstrated vigorously during the third ministerial conference of the World Trade Organization (WTO). Directed by the Wachowskis, the film *The Matrix* was released, opening a new cinematic era. The end of the century was approaching, bringing with it expectations but also the fear of the "Y2K bug" at the dawn of the new millennium.

After saying goodbye to her first mentor, Cas Walker, who died in 1998 at the age of ninety-six, Dolly continued to move forward on the road to her dreams. She teamed up with Sugar Hill Records and producer Steve Buckingham, who brought together the best bluegrass musicians of the day to produce *The Grass Is Blue*. Dolly had already enjoyed success with bluegrass: in her early days, with "Mule Skinner Blues (Blue Yodel No. 8)," a top ten cover of a Jimmie Rodgers song recorded in 1930, but also more recently, with some of the tracks on the album *Trio*. While Dolly grew up with this music, which runs in her veins, this was the first time she devoted an entire album to it.

Smoky Mountain DNA

According to Steve Buckingham, the recording of the album took only one month to organize.[2] The best bluegrass musicians immediately responded when asked to participate, as did backup singers including Patty Loveless, who owed the launch of her career to Dolly's support, and who would not have missed this artistic opportunity for anything in the world. They all wanted to be part of the adventure and agreed that Dolly Parton's voice was the most suitable for bluegrass. The album notes make it clear that all the musicians love Dolly—as does almost everyone else.

And so Dolly closed out the millennium with an album that was firmly rooted in her childhood, her native region, her genealogy. Bluegrass, between ballads and steady rhythms, is precisely what Dolly loves and masters, both in the writing of the songs and in the production.[2] Like so many previous albums, this opus—which includes covers chosen by either the artist or her producer—demonstrates Dolly Parton's talent and creativity.

Album Cover

Dennis Carney created a black-and-white portrait of Dolly for an understated cover, simply illuminated by the artist's smile, her chin resting on her guitar. Inside the CD booklet, we discover photos of her musicians, including Jerry Douglas, Steve Buckingham, Bryan Sutton, and Sam Bush, who express both their admiration and their pleasure to be playing with her.

1999

In "A Few Old Memories," Dolly Parton's protégé Patty Loveless shares the backing vocals with Rhonda Vincent.

Travelin' Prayer

Billy Joel / 4:16

Vocals: Dolly Parton **Musicians:** Barry Bales: bass / Jerry Douglas: dobro / Sam Bush: mandolin / Stuart Duncan: fiddle / Bryan Sutton: guitar / Jim Mills: banjo **Backing Vocals:** Alison Krauss, Dan Tyminski **Recorded:** Sound Kitchen, The Doghouse, Nashville, August 1999 **Technical Team:** Producer: Steve Buckingham / Production Assistant: Jennie Carey / Mixing: Gary Paczosa / Digital Editing: Toby Seay, Chuck Turner / Mastering: Doug Sax

By way of an overture, Dolly and her musicians transform this song, written and performed by Billy Joel (1973), into a dynamic bluegrass version that makes "Travelin' Prayer" sound like it comes from the mountains. The song's protagonist offers a fervent prayer to God to watch over her man who has gone on a journey.

Like a miraculously preserved daguerreotype, the sweet melody played on the fiddle by virtuoso Stuart Duncan sets the tone of this album as a tribute to Dolly Parton's musical roots. From 0:48 onward, the song suddenly breaks out of this generously reverberated atmosphere and goes headlong into a frenzied bluegrass. Jim Mills's breathless banjo frailing, Sam Bush's triple-gallop mandolin, Jerry Douglas's lightning dobro strokes, and Bryan Sutton's acoustic guitar sparks—with his strumming punctuated by ultraviolet flat-picking phrasing—are all driven by the well-oiled engine of this infernal music box: Barry Bales's double bass. In a heroic display, Dolly catches the wagon as it passes, like Buster Keaton in *The General* (1926), and performs this prayer with exceptional energy, backed by the unerring vocals of Alison Krauss and Dan Tyminski. Steve Buckingham's production is once again up to the challenge and goes straight to the point, dry and precise as it should be, to highlight the expressiveness and talent of the best bluegrass musicians of the day.

Cash On The Barrelhead

Charlie Louvin, Ira Louvin / 3:08

Vocals: Dolly Parton **Musicians:** Jerry Douglas: dobro / Sam Bush: mandolin / Stuart Duncan: fiddle / Jim Mills: banjo / Barry Bales: bass / Steve Buckingham: rhythm guitar **Backing Vocals:** Claire Lynch, Keith Little **Recorded:** Sound Kitchen, The Doghouse, Nashville, August 1999 **Technical Team:** Producer: Steve Buckingham / Production Assistant: Jennie Carey / Mixing: Gary Paczosa / Digital Editing: Toby Seay, Chuck Turner / Mastering: Doug Sax

"Cash on the Barrelhead," written by the famous Louvin Brothers, a country duo from Alabama, tells the story of a penniless drifter forced to choose between paying a fine and sleeping in jail. It was one of the favorite songs of Carl Dean,[2] Dolly's husband.

Steve Buckingham replaces Bryan Sutton on acoustic guitar. Surprisingly, the credits even state that this is a 1941 Gibson Super 400, an Archtop model used more often in jazz than in bluegrass or country music. Perhaps this is a way of highlighting Buckingham's judicious instrumental choice for playing this dry and very swinging rhythm section. Douglas, Bush, Duncan, Mills, and Bales play with a disconcerting ease. Dolly and her musicians are at home, and you can hear and feel it. Claire Lynch and Keith Little sing backing vocals impeccably, with their 1950s-style close harmonies, like a musical filter adding the final sepia touch.

A Few Old Memories

Hazel Dickens / 4:02

Vocals: Dolly Parton **Musicians:** Jerry Douglas: dobro / Sam Bush: mandolin / Stuart Duncan: fiddle / Bryan Sutton: guitar / Jim Mills: banjo / Barry Bales: bass **Backing Vocals:** Patty Loveless, Rhonda Vincent **Recorded:** Sound Kitchen, The Doghouse, Nashville, August 1999 **Technical Team:** Producer: Steve Buckingham / Production Assistant: Jennie Carey / Mixing: Gary Paczosa / Digital Editing: Toby Seay, Chuck Turner / Mastering: Doug Sax **Single:** A Few Old Memories / Train, Train **Release:** Sugar Hill Records / Blue Eye Records, October 25, 1999 (CD ref.: SUG-CD-3900)

In "A Few Old Memories," the first country waltz on this album, released as a promotional single but not offered for sale, a woman is surprised by the emotion she feels when she finds old memories, letters yellowed by time and a photo, which she pretends are insignificant, but which nevertheless make her shed a few tears...

The whole team is present. Their interpretation of this ballad (composed and recorded by Hazel Dickens in 1987) seems to come from another time. The gentle swaying of the 3/4 time, with a deliberately trundling charm, is reinforced by the clarity of Steve Buckingham's production. The bouncy interplay created by the articulations of each instrument, arpeggiated, picked, scraped, slid, or rubbed, has rarely sounded closer, or more distinct and authentic. The listener is thus projected into the midst of this pocket orchestra, on the porch of a cabin in the Great Smoky Mountains, on a summer evening. Patty Loveless, Dolly Parton's protégé, shares the backing vocals with Rhonda Vincent. The three singers harmonize with such ease that one might think they shared the same "old memories." The illusion, in any case, is perfect.

I'm Gonna Sleep With One Eye Open

Lester Flatt / 3:04

Vocals: Dolly Parton **Musicians:** Jerry Douglas: dobro / Sam Bush: mandolin / Stuart Duncan: fiddle / Bryan Sutton: guitar / Jim Mills: banjo / Barry Bales: bass / Steve Buckingham: rhythm guitar **Backing Vocals:** Stuart Duncan, Jerry Douglas, Sam Bush, Barry Bales **Recorded:** Sound Kitchen, The Doghouse, Nashville, August 1999 **Technical Team:** Producer: Steve Buckingham / Production Assistant: Jennie Carey / Mixing: Gary Paczosa / Digital Editing: Toby Seay, Chuck Turner / Mastering: Doug Sax

In this cover of a song by singer and guitarist Lester Flatt, the protagonist declares that from now on she will sleep with one eye open, because she knows where her man goes every night: the local honky-tonk bar. He thought he was smart, but she will be twice as smart as he is. This song could have been written by Dolly Parton, so familiar is this theme to the songwriter.

Another very swinging song, with a character accentuated by the respective playing of Bryan Sutton on acoustic guitar, flat-picking, and Steve Buckingham on rhythm guitar (probably the same 1941 Gibson Super 400 he used on "Cash on the Barrelhead"). The groove of "I'm Gonna Sleep with One Eye Open" makes you want to click your fingers and dance. Each musician has their own solo, with their own feeling, each in turn more alert and voluble than the others.

"I Still Miss Someone" was written by Johnny Cash and his nephew Roy Cash Jr., a former Navy officer.

Steady As The Rain

Dolly Parton / 3:05

Vocals: Dolly Parton **Musicians:** Jerry Douglas: dobro / Sam Bush: mandolin / Stuart Duncan: fiddle / Bryan Sutton: guitar / Jim Mills: banjo / Barry Bales: bass **Backing Vocals:** Claire Lynch, Keith Little
Recorded: Sound Kitchen, The Doghouse, Nashville, August 1999
Technical Team: Producer: Steve Buckingham / Production Assistant: Jennie Carey / Mixing: Gary Paczosa / Digital Editing: Toby Seay, Chuck Turner / Mastering: Doug Sax

The song "Steady as the Rain" was originally intended for Stella Parton, Dolly's sister, who made it a hit in 1979. The narrator, heartbroken and darkened by an unhappy love, draws a sad parallel between the falling raindrops and her flowing tears.

This is Dolly Parton's first of four compositions on this album. This up-tempo 4/4 flies like a butterfly just out of its chrysalis, meeting the world, ephemeral and eager for freedom. The questions and answers fly from all sides in this fluid and light orchestration, as if to counterbalance the tragic content of the text—a true trademark of Dolly's. The singer does not hesitate to stretch her vocal cords and seek friction, notably on the word *tears*, where her slightly saturated voice works wonders, recalling in passing the warm and breaking voice of her colleague Kim Carnes.

I Still Miss Someone

Johnny R. Cash, Roy Cash Jr. / 3:38

Vocals: Dolly Parton **Musicians:** Jerry Douglas: dobro / Sam Bush: mandolin / Stuart Duncan: fiddle / Bryan Sutton: guitar / Barry Bales: bass **Backing Vocals:** Alison Krauss, Dan Tyminski **Recorded:** Sound Kitchen, The Doghouse, Nashville, August 1999
Technical Team: Producer: Steve Buckingham / Production Assistant: Jennie Carey / Mixing: Gary Paczosa / Digital Editing: Toby Seay, Chuck Turner / Mastering: Doug Sax

"I Still Miss Someone," written by Johnny Cash and his nephew Roy Cash Jr., seems like a perfect match for Dolly, especially in this bluegrass version. The narrator of this slow ballad expresses her regrets and pain at having lost the man she loved, whom she misses terribly.

Stuart Duncan on the fiddle opens the dance on this country standard. This song sounds like the echo of a last dance in the middle of the Grand Ole Opry. The reminiscence of a love gone forever, of those arms in which one loved to sway, gently captures us. The fine team deploys the paraphernalia of the serenade band and enables Dolly to lay down her vocals without an ounce of affectation but with all the vigor of true feelings. Steve Buckingham's production hits the nail on the head once again, with restraint.

1999

Endless Stream Of Tears

Dolly Parton / 2:40

Vocals: Dolly Parton **Musicians:** Jerry Douglas: dobro / Sam Bush: mandolin / Stuart Duncan: fiddle / Bryan Sutton: guitar / Jim Mills: banjo / Barry Bales: bass **Backing Vocals:** Rhonda Vincent, Darrin Vincent **Recorded:** Sound Kitchen, The Doghouse, Nashville, August 1999 **Technical Team:** Producer: Steve Buckingham / Production Assistant: Jennie Carey / Mixing: Gary Paczosa / Digital Editing: Toby Seay, Chuck Turner / Mastering: Doug Sax

In "Endless Stream of Tears," Dolly Parton once again evokes the sorrow of love: This one is so painful that the tears flow like an inexhaustible torrent. Only the bluegrass rhythm is optimistic. Another good example of one of Dolly's specialties: the "sad ass song." This one, on a fast tempo, offers an additional opportunity for the musicians of this fantastic group, reunited for one album, to show off their virtuosity. Dolly, Rhonda Vincent, and Darrin Vincent do not disappoint; they give a vocal performance worthy of the greatest singers, reminding us that bluegrass is a living music that has never stopped evolving.

Silver Dagger

Traditional / 4:55

Vocals: Dolly Parton **Musicians:** Jerry Douglas: dobro / Sam Bush: mandolin / Stuart Duncan: fiddle / Bryan Sutton: guitar / Jim Mills: banjo / Barry Bales: bass **Recorded:** Sound Kitchen, The Doghouse, Nashville, August 1999 **Technical Team:** Producer: Steve Buckingham / Production Assistant: Jennie Carey / Mixing: Gary Paczosa / Digital Editing: Toby Seay, Chuck Turner / Mastering: Doug Sax **Single:** (one track only): Silver Dagger **Release:** Sugar Hill Records / Blue Eye Records, February 2000 (CD ref.: SUG-CD-3900)

"Silver Dagger" is a traditional folk song, with a hint of murder ballad, which Dolly interprets with a surprising sweetness. We find in it a theme that is dear to her: the harsh female condition. Here, a mother sleeps beside her daughter, a dagger in her hand, to protect her from the lust of men and the suffering caused by their chronic infidelity. The narrator's father is a heartbreaker, and the mother refuses to allow her daughter to endure the same misfortunes. Thus warned, she has convinced her: better to stay alone and single.

Jim Mills's banjo drives this up-tempo arrangement of light and shade. Dolly's voice seems to stretch endlessly on this musical reel, which each instrumentalist takes pleasure in unwinding with an unequaled brilliance, as if plunged into a delicious trance, in a state of grace. A gem of modern bluegrass.

> One of the most famous covers of "Silver Dagger" is the one by Joan Baez, released in 1960.

Train, Train

Shorty Medlocke / 2:50

Vocals and Instrumental: Dolly Parton **Musicians:** Jerry Douglas: dobro / Sam Bush: mandolin / Stuart Duncan: fiddle / Bryan Sutton: guitar / Jim Mills: banjo / Barry Bales: bass **Backing Vocals:** Alan O'Bryant, Keith Little **Recorded:** Sound Kitchen, The Doghouse, Nashville, August 1999 **Technical Team:** Producer: Steve Buckingham / Production Assistant: Jennie Carey / Mixing: Gary Paczosa / Additional Engineering: Toby Seay / Digital Editing: Toby Seay, Chuck Turner / Mastering: Doug Sax **Single:** A Few Old Memories / Train, Train **Release:** Sugar Hill Records / Blue Eye Records, October 25, 1999 (CD ref.: SUG-CD-3900) NB: This track was released as a promo single, so was not ranked on any chart.

On the theme of an almost joyous separation, the narrator decides to let the man she loves go by train to Memphis; good for her, she'll find another.

Dolly and her band let loose on this classic by blues and bluegrass musician and composer Shorty Medlocke. Stuart Duncan, on fiddle, is once again sent to the front of the line, quickly joined by his fellow virtuosos. Nothing and no one can stop this fast-paced bluegrass locomotive before its terminus: Memphis, Tennessee.

The song "In the Pines," also known as "Where Did You Sleep Last Night," "Black Girl," and "My Girl," was performed, among others, by Bill Monroe and Lead Belly. Much later, in 1993, the band Nirvana recorded it during its famous *MTV Unplugged in New York* gig.

American folk and blues musician Lead Belly, ca. 1945.

I Wonder Where You Are Tonight

Johnny Bond / 3:14

Vocals: Dolly Parton **Musicians:** Jerry Douglas: dobro / Sam Bush: mandolin / Stuart Duncan: fiddle / Bryan Sutton: guitar / Jim Mills: banjo / Barry Bales: bass **Backing Vocals:** Claire Lynch, Keith Little **Recorded:** Sound Kitchen, The Doghouse, Nashville, August 1999 **Technical Team:** Producer: Steve Buckingham / Production Assistant: Jennie Carey / Mixing: Gary Paczosa / Additional Engineering: Toby Seay / Digital Editing: Toby Seay, Chuck Turner / Mastering: Doug Sax

Here too, Dolly sings of separation with gentleness and emotion. Even though the man she loved was colder than the rain, the narrator suffers from his departure and wonders where he is.

The theme of this midtempo ballad with its old-fashioned charm is reminiscent of "In the Pines," a traditional song from the southern Appalachians. An image emerges: a small group of musicians posing proudly under the front porch of a Smokies cabin, like a 1940s postcard. The magic happens every time.

Will He Be Waiting For Me

Dolly Parton / 3:26

Vocals: Dolly Parton **Musicians:** Jerry Douglas: dobro / Sam Bush: mandolin / Stuart Duncan: fiddle / Bryan Sutton: guitar / Jim Mills: banjo / Barry Bales: bass **Backing Vocals:** Claire Lynch, Keith Little **Recorded:** Sound Kitchen, The Doghouse, Nashville, August 1999 **Technical Team:** Producer: Steve Buckingham / Production Assistant: Jennie Carey / Mixing: Gary Paczosa / Additional Engineering: Toby Seay / Digital Editing: Toby Seay, Chuck Turner / Mastering: Doug Sax

The poetic writing in "Will He Be Waiting for Me" (originally recorded and released as "Will He Be Waiting" in 1972 on the album *Touch Your Woman*) combines, as is often the case with Dolly, nature and sentiment. Here, a woman regrets having left the man she loved and, on the way back to him, wonders if he still loves her. The bluegrass version transforms this song, both in the way Dolly sings and in the instrumentation. It must be said that even if this unstoppable melody could accommodate many treatments, the liveliness of bluegrass suits it like a glove.

On "The Grass Is Blue," composer and musician Dan Tyminski sings backing vocals with Alison Krauss.

The Grass Is Blue

Dolly Parton / 3:45

Vocals: Dolly Parton **Musicians:** Jerry Douglas: dobro / Sam Bush: mandolin / Stuart Duncan: fiddle / Bryan Sutton: guitar / Jim Mills: banjo / Barry Bales: bass **Backing Vocals:** Alison Krauss, Dan Tyminski **Recorded:** Sound Kitchen, The Doghouse, Nashville, August 1999 **Technical Team:** Producer: Steve Buckingham / Production Assistant: Jennie Carey / Mixing: Gary Paczosa / Additional Engineering: Toby Seay / Digital Editing: Toby Seay, Chuck Turner / Mastering: Doug Sax

This is probably one of the songs on the theme of separation that is the most illustrative of Dolly Parton's talent as a songwriter. Here, she poetically rearranges nature: The sky turns green and the grass is blue, the rivers flow backward, and the valleys overshadow the mountains. And what is true for nature is also true for feelings; the narrator affirms that she is fine while she mourns the end of her love story.

Combined with the voice of the Queen of Country, the backing vocals of Alison Krauss and Dan Tyminski bring the choruses to a peak on the second country waltz of this album. This song is of a rare emotional intensity; one would like it never to stop and to be able to soak up its sweet perfume, these colors that one would swear are more vivid and harmonious than those of real life. While, quite specifically, it is as though Dolly whispers to us here: "Look, look, though, how beautiful life is!"

I Am Ready

Rachel Parton Dennison / 2:45

Vocals: Dolly Parton **Backing Vocals:** Rhonda Vincent, Darrin Vincent, Louis Nunley **Recorded:** Sound Kitchen, The Doghouse, Nashville, August 1999 **Technical Team:** Producer: Steve Buckingham / Production Assistant: Jennie Carey / Mixing: Gary Paczosa / Additional Engineering: Toby Seay / Digital Editing: Toby Seay, Chuck Turner / Mastering: Doug Sax

The Grass Is Blue ends with an a cappella gospel, with chills guaranteed. Rhonda Vincent, Darrin Vincent, Louis Nunley, and Dolly Parton are at the peak of their art in this song: The synchronism and the precision of the harmonies are amazing, the nuances of dynamics are breathtaking, and the extra soul is tangible. Dolly always finds a way to close her albums with brilliance, with an original, positive, and unifying touch.

In *Rhinestone*, Sylvester Stallone performs the songs.

Soundtracks:
When Dolly Writes Music for the Movies

Since her first film, *9 to 5*, in 1980, Dolly Parton has sometimes written all the songs for the films in which she appears, and sometimes only some. We will review here only the most notable and acclaimed. Faithful to all of her solo albums, and even collaborative albums, Dolly alternates covers of her old titles with new ones. Despite the success of some films or TV movies, such as *Christmas on the Square*, these soundtracks were not systematically released, but they are available for listening via streaming.

Throughout her career, Dolly has confided several times that writing a song for a movie is an exercise that seems quite simple to her, since a plot already exists. Similarly, when she co-wrote the novel *Run, Rose, Run*,[20] with James Patterson while simultaneously composing the music, the lyrics came easily. And when she plays the roles of a singer or an angel, one could not dream of a better role for her!

For Dolly Addicts

With *Rhinestone*, the star was nominated for the tenth time for a Grammy Award. Although the film was not a huge success, the album was rather well received: it reached number 135 on the Billboard 200 chart and was released digitally on December 4, 2015. Four singles were taken from the album; two did not chart at all, while "Tennessee Homesick Blues" reached number one on the Billboard Hot Country Songs and "God Won't Get You" reached number ten.

Rhinestone

Tennessee Homesick Blues (3:35)
Too Much Water (2:41)
The Day My Baby Died (2:55)
One Emotion After Another (3:36)
Goin' Back to Heaven (4:15)
What a Heartache (4:42)
Stay out of My Bedroom (3:40)
Woke Up in Love (3:23)
God Won't Get You (4:15)
Drinkin' Stein (3:55)
Sweet Lovin' Friends (3:29)
Waltz Me to Heaven (3:21)
Butterflies (3:20)
Be There (3:12)

Album Release Date
United States: January 18, 1984
References: RCA Victor—ABL1-5032
Best US Chart Ranking: 32
Singles: Tennessee Homesick Blues / God Won't Get You / Goin' Back to Heaven / What a Heartache

Vocals: Rusty Buchanan, Dolly Parton, Floyd Parton, Randy Parton, Stella Parton, Sylvester Stallone, Kim Vassy **Musicians:** Mike Baird, Willie Ornelas: drums / Dennis Belfield, Leland Sklar: bass / John Bidasio: steel guitar / John Goux, Steve Watson: guitar / David Lindley: fiddle / Tommy Morgan: harmonica / Larry Muhoberac: piano / Herb Pedersen: guitar, banjo / Pete Robinson, Ian Underwood: synthesizer **Backing Vocals:** Richard Dennison, Linda Dillard, Randy Parton, Herb Pedersen, Joey Scarbury **Recorded:** Smoketree Ranch, Chatsworth, California, between August 1983 and June 1984 **Technical Team:** Producers: Dolly Parton, Mike Post / Sound Engineers: Doug Parry, Ray Sheilbley

Genesis and Lyrics

Rhinestone is the soundtrack album of the eponymous film directed by Bob Clark in 1984, in which Dolly Parton stars

alongside Sylvester Stallone. The soundtrack, produced by Mike Post and Dolly Parton, was released by RCA Victor on June 18, 1984. The songwriter wrote thirteen of the fourteen songs ("The Day My Baby Died" is the work of Phil Alden Robinson and Mike Post). The script itself was inspired by a song released in 1975, "Rhinestone Cowboy," which was written by singer-composer Larry Weiss. The songwriter's major themes are found in the film: the opposition between town and country, nature and culture, the blues of her native land and, of course, heartbreak.

Rhinestone is a slightly old-fashioned comedy that can be watched with sweet nostalgia. This musical film follows the story of a singer stuck in a sleazy New York City nightclub called Rhinestone. One day, Jake (Dolly Parton) boasts that she can train any man to be a country singer. Freddie, her boss, takes up the challenge and sets the stakes: If Jake loses, she will have to stay under contract for another five years and give in to his advances. He chooses Nick Martelli, a cab driver (Sylvester Stallone), who is not only unable to sing but also hates this kind of music. Jake takes him to Tennessee to teach him how to act like a real country music star.

Production

Although the movie *Rhinestone* was not a great success, the musical portion of the film was undeniably sound. The songs were all recorded before the movie was shot, and then they were played on set as scenes were filmed. A lot of technical details were introduced to get as close as possible to the real conditions, but some omissions are to be noted: wires are connected to all the microphones, but there is nothing to pick up the drums, for example. Also, just before Nick's first performance in Tennessee, we may notice that his guitar is not plugged in...yet he is going to play with the band. Sylvester Stallone is not used to holding a microphone, unlike Dolly. On her side, the guitar playing is less natural; when she interprets "What a Heartache," she uses only one finger on the left hand—it also seems almost impossible to play with such long nails! On the other hand, the lip-synching is perfect.

Given the context of the film, the songs could not match the sound frenzy of the 1980s, so Dolly did traditional contemporary, with full drums, electric guitar, violin, pedal steel guitar, and so on. One notices the presence of some of her usual musicians, like Bill Owens, Leland Sklar, Richard Dennison, and her brother and sister, Randy and Stella Parton.

To see Stallone swaying like this, singing (it is indeed him), while we think of Rocky Balboa or John Rambo makes us smile. The actor demonstrates self-deprecation. A reference to Rocky: "For the fight, he is a real tiger," he says!

In *Dumplin'*, Willowdean, an overweight girl, decides to enter a Miss Teen Bluebonnet pageant contest to lead a "revolution in heels."

Straight Talk

Blue Grace (1:03)
Light of a Clear Blue Morning (4:11)
Dirty Job (4:51)
Blue Me (4:51)
Straight Talk (3:20)
Fish out of Water (5:02)
Burning (4:12)
Livin' a Lie (4:53)
Thought I Couldn't Dance (3:58)
Burning to Burned (3:09)
Light of a Clear Blue Morning (Reprise) (4:11)

Album Release Date
United States: March 31, 1992
Reference: Hollywood Records—HR-61303-2
Best US Chart Ranking: 22
Singles: Straight Talk / Light of a Clear Blue Morning

Vocals: Dolly Parton **Musicians:** Russ Kunkel: drums / Steve Farris, David Lindley, Steve Lukather: guitar / Howard Levy: harmonica / Luis Conte: percussions / George Hawkins: bass / Horny Horns: brass / Jeffery C. J. Vanston: piano / Scotty Paige: saxophone **Recorded:** (?), December 1991 **Technical Team:** Producers: Dolly Parton, Greg Ladanyi

Genesis and Lyrics

Directed by Barnet Kellman, *Straight Talk* follows Shirlee Kenyon (Dolly Parton), a dance teacher who leaves her small town and her lover (Michael Madsen) to move to Chicago. One day, after an acclaimed radio appearance where Shirlee gives listeners advice on their love lives, she becomes very popular. Her success attracts the attention of journalist Jack Russell (James Woods), who starts digging into her past and falls in love with her.

The lead single was not a hit, but the album, consisting of ten of Parton's original compositions, reached number twenty-two on the US country charts. Two singles were released from it: "Light of a Clear Blue Morning" a 1976 track (released on *New Harvest...First Gathering*) that the artist revisited, and "Straight Talk"; Dominic Orlando's video for the latter song was made at SIR Stage Studios in Hollywood. Guest musicians for the video were Russ Kunkel, Jeffery C. J. Vanston, Kenny Gradney, Steve Farris, and Greg Ladanyi.

Production

For a romantic comedy in the middle of Chicago, the music could not be pure country, so the film is accompanied by a light pop sound. We note, however, that Dolly's intonations in the dialogues (which she didn't necessarily have in *Rhinestone*) and the syllables that she lets drag, are very characteristic. We also notice the presence of Toto's guitarist Steve Lukather. We may also recall that Toto's pianist, David Paich, performed on Dolly's *Heartbreaker* album in 1978.

Dumplin'

Here I Am (4:32)
Holdin' On to You (3:27)
Girl in the Movies (4:34)
Red Shoes (2:58)
Why (2:29)
Dumb Blonde (2:34)
Here You Come Again (3:28)
Who (2:34)
Push and Pull (3:33)
If We Don't (2:29)
Two Doors Down (4:06)
Jolene (New String Version) (3:20)

Album Release Date
United States: November 30, 2018
Reference: RCA Records / Dolly Records—19075-89908-2
Best US Chart Ranking: 4 on the Billboard Americana/Folk Albums
Singles: Here I Am / Girl in the Movies / Jolene

Vocals: Dorothy, Macy Gray, Elle King, Miranda Lambert, Sia, Mavis Staples, Dolly Parton **Musicians:** Willa Amai: piano and vocals / David Goodstein: drums / Barry Green: trombone / Alison Krauss: fiddle / Billy Mohler: bass / Eli Pearl: electric and acoustic guitar, pedal steel guitar / Damon Fox: piano, B3 organ, electric and acoustic guitar / David Davidson, Katelyn Westergard, David Angell, Kristin Weber: violin / Betsy Lamb: viola / Kristin Wilkinson, Avery Bright: cello / Steve Patrick: trumpet / Rhonda Vincent: mandolin / Sam Levine: baritone saxophone / Austin Hoke, Emily Nelson: strings / strings arrangements: Austin Hoke **Backing Vocals:** Jennifer Aniston, Maiya Sykes, Briana Lee, Lisa Vitale, Luc Edgemon, Linda Perry **Technical Team:** Producer: Linda Perry / Executive Producer: Dolly Parton / Sound Engineers: Linda Perry, Luis Flores, John McBride

Genesis and Lyrics

While Dolly Parton never appears on-screen in *Dumplin'* (released on Netflix in 2018), she is nonetheless the central character: She is the protagonist who offers a respite in the upsetting daily life of an overweight young woman, breathes a set of values into her, proposes a place for everyone in society. By adapting the eponymous novel by Julie Murphy published in 2015, director Anne Fletcher created a sensitive film and a true tribute to Dolly Parton, who embodies a role model and support for the younger generation.

The script is written around a mother, Rosie (Jennifer Aniston), a former beauty queen obsessed with her appearance, and her daughter Willowdean (Danielle Macdonald), whom she nicknames "dumpling," or "dumplin'." In her last year of high school, the girl mourns the death of her aunt Lucy, a huge Dolly fan. This film, about friendship and love, highlights the difficulty of knowing who you are when you are different, or how to feel at peace with yourself—Dolly Parton's favorite themes. The script includes various quotes from the star and elements from her world: a small rural town in the South, self-image, drag queens, or the social and physical difference assumed, joy but also grief, mourning, and death.

In collaboration with producer Linda Perry, Dolly Parton wrote several new songs; she also revisited old ones, such as "Dumb Blonde," which opens the film, "Here You Come Again," and "Jolene." What is special about this soundtrack is that Dolly Parton conceived it like some of her solo albums, inviting the artists she loves: Miranda Lambert, Australian singer-songwriter Sia, Mavis Staples, Elle King, Alison Krauss, Rhonda Vincent, and Macy Gray, among others.

The single "Here I Am" from this album reached number thirty-seven on the Billboard Hot Country Songs chart.

Production

On this soundtrack the star does a pure Dolly Parton. Whether it is with the covers of old songs or the new ones, written with Linda Perry, we are in the realms of folk, country, and a little rock, too. Only "Jolene" has a very original arrangement: a small symphonic orchestra with only violins, cellos, and no double bass. The arrangements of the old songs are well crafted because, even though they include many new ideas, they retain their essence. Moreover, the choices of collaborations are very convincing, and the enjoyment experienced by each guest artist is palpable.

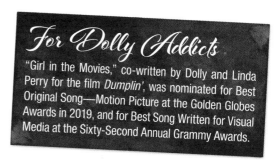

For Dolly Addicts

"Girl in the Movies," co-written by Dolly and Linda Perry for the film *Dumplin'*, was nominated for Best Original Song—Motion Picture at the Golden Globes Awards in 2019, and for Best Song Written for Visual Media at the Sixty-Second Annual Grammy Awards.

respectable citizen. However, the intervention of a senator forces Mona to close her establishment and some difficulties arise.

After *9 to 5*, this was the star's second role, and she was nominated for Best Actress in a Motion Picture—Musical or Comedy at the Golden Globe Awards.

Among the films or TV movies in which Dolly Parton acted, the star sometimes—partially—participated in the soundtracks. Dolly Parton has also written unpublished material or covered old hits for films whose soundtracks have never been released. In this book we will look at only those songs that have been well received.

The Best Little Whorehouse In Texas

I Will Always Love You (3:02)
Sneakin' Around (1:58)

Album Release Date
United States: July 12, 1982
References: MCA Records—MCA-6112,
Best US Chart Ranking: 5

Technical Team: Producer: Gregg Perry / Arrangements, Orchestration: Gregg Perry, Jack Hayes / Sound Engineers: Arnie Frager, Ernie Winfrey, Danny Wallin, Mickey Crofford, Mike Bradley

The Best Little Whorehouse in Texas is a film directed by Colin Higgins. The album was produced by Gregg Perry, although in 1982 he announced his departure from Dolly Parton's band. Most of the songs are by Carol Hall, but the soundtrack includes two Dolly Parton songs. The cover of her huge hit "I Will Always Love You" placed on the charts at number fifty-three on the Billboard Hot 100 chart and number seventeen on the Billboard Adult Contemporary chart, as well as hitting number one on the Hot 100. The second song was the unranked "Sneakin' Around" (available for listening on Spotify).

Adapted from the 1978 Broadway musical, *The Best Little Whorehouse in Texas* tells the story of Miss Mona (Dolly Parton), proprietress of the Chicken Ranch brothel outside Gilbert, Texas. Sheriff Ed Earl Dodd (Burt Reynolds) does not interfere with the Chicken Ranch and Mona, who is his lover. In the eyes of the people of Gilbert, this woman is a

In *The Best Little Whorehouse in Texas*, Burt Reynolds, with a towel around his hips, sings "Sneakin' Around" while Dolly Parton accompanies him in a sexy negligee, although she remains modest, as always. This is a light song about the taste for pretty, shiny things, the things that Ed and Mona love...like the pleasure of slipping into bed together.

Joyful Noise

Not Enough (4:30)
From Here to the Moon and Back (4:24)
He's Everything (4:37)

Album Release Date
United States: January 10, 2012
Reference: WaterTower Music—WTM-39273
Best US Chart Ranking: 1
Singles: From Here to the Moon and Back / He's Everything

Arranged and produced by Mervyn Warren, *Joyful Noise* is a 2012 American musical film about two particularly stubborn and charismatic women who are forced to cooperate when budget cuts threaten the existence of their small-town choir in Pacashau, Georgia. A conflict ensues between Vi Rose Hill (Queen Latifah) and G. G. Sparrow (Dolly Parton), the two leaders with opposing visions.

The *Joyful Noise* soundtrack features twelve tracks, drawing on gospel, country, pop, rock, and R&B, three of which are by Dolly Parton: "Not Enough," "He's Everything," and "From Here to the Moon and Back," which reached number two on the Billboard Christian Digital Song Sales chart—as well as interpretations of hits by Paul McCartney ("Maybe I'm Amazed," 1970) and Michael Jackson ("Man in the Mirror," 1987), among others.

A Smoky Mountain Christmas

Country Memories
Mountain Magic
Look on the Bright Side
(I'd Like to Spend) Christmas with Santa
Pretty Is as Pretty Does
A Smoky Mountain Christmas
Wrapped Up in You

A Smoky Mountain Christmas is an American musical film directed by Henry Winkler and starring Dolly Parton and Lee Majors (from the series *The Six Million Dollar Man*, 1973–1978), broadcast on ABC on December 14, 1986. The setting is a fantasy world where Lorna (Dolly Parton), leaving the city to spend Christmas in her native Tennessee, discovers seven runaway orphans in her house. All the songs are by Dolly Parton, except "(I'd Like to Spend) Christmas with Santa" written by Bill Owens, her uncle.

Blue Valley Songbird

Blue Valley Songbird
I Hope You're Never Happy
We Might Be in Love
Wildflowers
My Blue Tears
Runaway Feeling
Amazing Grace
Angel Band

Blue Valley Songbird is a 1999 American musical drama, directed by Richard A. Colla and starring Dolly Parton. Filmed in Nashville, it was first broadcast on the Lifetime channel on November 1, 1999. The film tells the story of a guitarist, Bobby (Billy Dean), who comes to the rescue of a country singer, Leanna Taylor (Dolly Parton). She is struggling with an abusive manager who also happens to be her partner. The soundtrack was not released in any version and includes old songs by the star ("Blue Valley Songbird," "I Hope You're Never Happy," "Wildflowers," "My Blue Tears," "Amazing Grace"), some of which are performed as a duet with the actor Billy Dean.

Christmas On The Square

Christmas Is
Christmas on the Square
Gotta Get Out
Maybe, Just Maybe
So Sorry
You
Queen of Mean
Keeper of Memories
Everybody Needs an Angel
Light Your Lamp
Wickedest Witch of the Middle
Try
Fairy Tale
Rearview Mirror
A Father's Prayer
When an Angel Knows Your Dreams
Happy Town
Just Dance
My Christmas Prayer
Forgive Me

In this 2020 TV movie, directed and choreographed by Debbie Allen, a cold-hearted wealthy woman returns to her hometown after her father's death and forces his tenants out of their home in order to secure a lucrative real estate deal with a shopping center developer. Eventually, after meeting an angel, played by Dolly Parton, she becomes warmer and more human, which leads to a form of redemption.

Despite its success and the two Emmy Awards that this TV movie won, the soundtrack, entirely written by Dolly Parton, was not released. On the other hand, the same year, the numbers "Christmas Is" and "Christmas on the Square" were released on the Christmas album *A Holly Dolly Christmas*. As for the song "Try," the original version was included on *Blue Smoke*, in 2014. On the artist's website, one can read of her surprise: "Who knew that when we were creating this movie, that it would be aired in the middle of the pandemic, and it would bring so much joy and so much hope to millions of people around the world?"

Little Sparrow

Little Sparrow . Shine . I Don't Believe You've Met My Baby . My Blue Tears .
Seven Bridges Road . Bluer Pastures . A Tender Lie . I Get a Kick out of You . Mountain
Angel . Marry Me . Down from Dover . The Beautiful Lie . In the Sweet Bye & Bye .
Little Sparrow (Reprise)

RELEASE DATE
United States: January 23, 2001
References: Sugar Hill Records / Blue Eye Records—SUG-CD-3927
Best US Chart Ranking:
3 on the Billboard Independent Albums

The star dedicated her new album to her father, Robert Lee Parton, who died in November 2000.

Mountain Music Blues

Little Sparrow is Dolly Parton's thirty-sixth solo album, produced by Steve Buckingham, and released on Sugar Hill Records / Blue Eye Records on January 23, 2001. It reached number ninety-seven on the Billboard 200, and number one on the OCC Country Artists Albums chart (UK), where it achieved a silver certification.

The Year 2000 Transition
The attacks of September 11, 2001, under the presidency of George W. Bush, marked the consciousness of the whole world forever.

As a counterpoint to this violence and its disastrous consequences, Peter Jackson's *The Lord of the Rings*, based on J. R. R. Tolkien's trilogy, re-enchanted the planet. Madonna began an international tour—even though her video for "What It Feels Like for a Girl" was censored—while Britney Spears caused a scandal with "I'm a Slave 4 U."

As for Dolly Parton, she continued her bluegrass trilogy, whose first opus, *The Grass Is Blue*, was a great success in 1999. Since she became associated with the Sugar Hill label, she was less constrained by commercial demands, which gave her more freedom to create longer songs.

The Disenchantment of Country and Folk Radio Stations
As the years went by, some country radio stations, surprisingly, still refused to play Dolly Parton's singles. Whatever the star did—pop, country, bluegrass, or gospel—and although she was acclaimed and rewarded by the most influential authorities in country music, these stations were reluctant to play her on the air. Without radio play, there is little or no chance of chart success. Fortunately for her fans, this did not prevent Dolly Parton from being more than ever appreciated by the critics who praised her new album. Beyond the nominations and awards in the United States, *Little Sparrow*, by reaching number one in the United Kingdom, confirmed the success of the Queen of Country in Europe, where she was invited to appear on several TV shows such as *Parkinson* and *So Graham Norton*. She was also on almost every US TV show—*Today* on NBC, *The Late Show with David Letterman* on CBS, to name but two, where Dolly, more beautiful than ever, created her own show and demonstrated her ability to handle the media.

With or without the promotional support of the radio, this mixture of bluegrass, Appalachian folk, country, and gospel, a music that was so Dolly, made *Little Sparrow* one of the star's major works.

Album Cover
The picture on the album cover reveals Dolly sitting on a wooden chair, in a dark room, with tones evoking the land and certainly her roots. Inside, in the same tones, are several photos of the star, guitar in hand or slung over her shoulder. Behind the lens is photographer Jim Herrington.

2001

Little Sparrow

Dolly Parton / 4:14

Vocals: Dolly Parton **Musicians:** Barry Bales: double bass / Jerry Douglas: resonator guitar / Stuart Duncan: fiddle / Bryan Sutton: guitar / Jim Mills: banjo / Chris Thile: mandolin **Backing Vocals:** Alison Krauss, Dan Tyminski **Recorded:** Ocean Way, The Doghouse, Nashville; Schnee Studio, Los Angeles, 2000 **Technical Team:** Producer: Steve Buckingham / Mixing: Gary Paczosa / Mastering: Robert Hadley, Doug Sax

The title track is a synthesis of dozens of the songwriter's songs exploring unhappy love affairs. The narrator speaks of love scorned, of men's lies and betrayal, and of her own heart being broken over and over again—"I am but the broken dream / Of a cold false-hearted lover."

She would like to be a bird to fly away freely, but she is only a fragile sparrow, easily crushed.

The title announces the style and color that the album will assume, namely very traditional, but not necessarily country. "Little Sparrow" is somewhat inspired by the music of the Appalachians, in a minor key that is quite rare for Dolly Parton. This general color can be found in the group the Dead South, which brings together the same family of instruments (guitar, mandolin, and fiddle). It is interesting to note that the title track of the album was not released as a single.

Shine

Ed Roland / 5:11

Vocals: Dolly Parton **Musicians:** Barry Bales: bass / Jerry Douglas: resonator guitar / Stuart Duncan: fiddle / Mark Kelly, Bryan Sutton: guitar / Jim Mills: banjo / Chris Tile: mandolin **Backing Vocals:** Keith Little, Claire Lynch **Recorded:** Ocean Way, The Doghouse, Nashville; Schnee Studio, Los Angeles, 2000 **Technical Team:** Producer: Steve Buckingham / Mixing: Gary Paczosa / Mastering: Robert Hadley, Doug Sax **Single:** Shine (Radio Edit) **Release:** Sanctuary Records, July 9, 2001 (special radio edition, ref.: SANPRO091) NB: This track was released as a promo single, so was not ranked on any chart.

In an audacious cover, Dolly Parton transforms a song by the alternative rock group Collective Soul into a country gospel. The song is about divine love, learning to love in order to be loved by God, and the chorus sounds like a prayer. Dolly takes all this material to transform this rock song into a real hymn. Thus, we leave the Appalachians for the South and the more traditional country music tinged with bluegrass. Since Dolly Parton's debut, the banjo had already been used on several albums, notably with Porter Wagoner, but with a very different playing style. At that time, the instrument was confined to a role of accompaniment with a few melodic incursions. Here, it is very much in the foreground, whether as an accompaniment, solo, or duet, with a fast-flowing play.

Many artists have appropriated rock songs and arranged them in country, bluegrass, or folk styles. Johnny Cash comes to mind, with his magnificent cover of "Hurt" by Nine Inch Nails, on his album *American IV: The Man Comes Around*, in 2002. We should also mention the group Steve 'n' Seagulls, who, more recently, made this style of covers in country or bluegrass its specialty, with, for example "Thunderstruck" by AC/DC in 2014 or "Self Esteem" by the Offspring in 2016. This requires considerable arranging to adhere to the target style, and especially a considerable amount of creativity to make the song your own without distorting it. Dolly Parton does this perfectly on "Shine."

I Don't Believe You've Met My Baby

Autry Inman / 3:02

Vocals: Dolly Parton **Musicians:** Barry Bales: double bass / Stuart Duncan: fiddle / Jerry Douglas: resonator guitar / Bryan Sutton: guitar / Jim Mills: banjo / Chris Thile: mandolin **Backing Vocals:** Keith Little, Claire Lynch **Recorded:** Ocean Way, The Doghouse, Nashville; Schnee Studio, Los Angeles, 2000 **Technical Team:** Producer: Steve Buckingham / Mixing: Gary Paczosa / Mastering: Robert Hadley, Doug Sax

Dolly had already performed this song in 1969, in *Always, Always*, in a duet with Porter Wagoner. The narrator goes to bed in tears and dreams that her lover is cheating on her, only to discover that he is not.

In this cover version, the key and tempo remain identical to the original version; only the duration of the piece is lengthened, due to the solos by violin, mandolin, and resonator guitar. The arrangement, adapted to the traditional style of the album, does not present any particular modification. It must be said that the original could almost have been included on the record, as it is so close to the color of the other tracks.

No "blue tears," but a blue dress for the dedication of *Little Sparrow* in Los Angeles, in 2001.

My Blue Tears

Dolly Parton / 3:03

Vocals: Dolly Parton **Musicians:** Byron House: double bass / Dermot Byrne: accordion / Jerry Douglas: resonator guitar / Stuart Duncan: fiddle / Mark Kelly: guitar **Backing Vocals:** Alison Krauss **Recorded:** Ocean Way, The Doghouse, Nashville; Schnee Studio, Los Angeles, 2000 **Technical Team:** Producer: Steve Buckingham / Mixing: Gary Paczosa / Mastering: Robert Hadley, Doug Sax

The first recording of "My Blue Tears" dates back to 1971, for the album *Coat of Many Colors*; the second one appears on the last disc of the compilation *The Complete Trio Collection*, released in 2016. In this song, the narrator refuses the benefits of the sun, such as flying like a free bird, anything that might make her feel good, because she is sad since her lover has left her.

This is a very acoustic ballad, with an accompaniment exclusively in arpeggios. The only notable chord (and even then, it is still played note by note) is the very last one of the piece. Unlike "I Don't Believe You Met My Baby," this cover has absolutely nothing to do with the one from 1971. On the other hand, it is closer to the version recorded in 1998 with Emmylou Harris and Linda Ronstadt.

Chris Thile, who played the mandolin on the *Little Sparrow* album, also plays the instrument for the Nickel Creek trio, which calls itself a "progressive acoustic" band.

Seven Bridges Road

Steve Young / 3:29

Vocals: Dolly Parton **Musicians:** Byron House: double bass / Jerry Douglas: resonator guitar / Stuart Duncan: fiddle / Bryan Sutton: guitar / Jim Mills: banjo / Chris Thile: mandolin **Backing Vocals:** Becky Isaacs Bowman, Sonya Isaacs, Carl Jackson **Recorded:** Ocean Way, The Doghouse, Nashville; Schnee Studio, Los Angeles, 2000 **Technical Team:** Producer: Steve Buckingham / Mixing: Gary Paczosa / Mastering: Robert Hadley, Doug Sax **Single:** Seven Bridges Road **Release:** Sugar Hill Records / Blue Eye Records, April 2, 2001 (CD ref.: ?) NB: This track was released as a promo single, so was not ranked on any chart.

Genesis and Lyrics

In this love song, the poetry of the landscape is associated with the narrator's feelings, and Dolly sings as if she were running, to escape or to reach something or someone.

This song is also a cover, arranged in a country-bluegrass style. It was composed in 1969 by the country guitarist, composer, and performer Steve Young. It has been covered by dozens of artists, including Joan Baez in 1970 on her album *One Day at a Time*, and the Eagles in 1980 for a live performance—whose version inspired many. It also appears on the 1990 album *Wildwood Flower*, by the Carter Family.

Production

This is a monster that Dolly Parton tackles, and she has the shoulders for it. The tempo she has chosen is one of the fastest of the existing versions. The rhythm is remarkable in its constancy and precision. The grid of three chords is not the most complicated one in existence, far from it. But it is very effective, and the arrangement is an asset. The bass marks each beat, while the mandolin marks the offbeats with muted chords. The guitar cements the two. It only remains for Stuart Duncan, Jerry Douglas, and Jim Mills to let their technique and their talent speak to us, providing hypnotic solos, which carry us into the wild. The sequence between the resonator guitar and the banjo works like a battle of speed between the two musicians, who finish together.

As for the vocals, the a cappella start is not at all indicative of the tempo that drives the song. The listener is taken by surprise with this crazy ride. The three voices remind us of the albums made with Emmylou Harris and Linda Ronstadt. From the middle of the song, the bass voice (the lowest of the backing vocals), Carl Jackson, perfectly integrated in the mix, brings a judicious diversity, which stands out from the double bass, although in the same range.

2001

Guitarist Steve Young's 1969 hit "Seven Bridges Road" has inspired many covers. He is pictured here at his home in Nashville.

The fiddle is a popular and traditional musical instrument, while the violin is more suited to classical music. Originally from Ireland, the fiddle is supported on the chest rather than between the shoulder and the chin. The strings are on less of a curve to enable several to be played simultaneously.

Bluer Pastures

Dolly Parton / 4:10

Vocals: Dolly Parton **Musicians:** Barry Bales: double bass / Jerry Douglas: resonator guitar / Stuart Duncan: fiddle / Bryan Sutton: guitar / Jim Mills: banjo / Chris Thile: mandolin **Backing Vocals:** Darrin Vincent, Rhonda Vincent **Recorded:** Ocean Way, The Doghouse, Nashville; Schnee Studio, Los Angeles, 2000 **Technical Team:** Producer: Steve Buckingham / Mixing: Gary Paczosa / Mastering: Robert Hadley, Doug Sax **Single:** Bluer Pastures **Release:** Sugar Hill Records / Blue Eye Records, April 2, 2001 (CD ref.: ?) NB: This track was released as a promo single, so was not ranked on any chart.

This song brings together several themes dear to the songwriter: leaving someone you love, someone who breaks your heart, leaving green pastures to go elsewhere and fulfill your dreams, getting older with each experience and understanding that you have lost the essential part of yourself. When time has taken its toll, when youth has faded and mistakes have been made, all that remains is to return home, where it all began, where love was.

This is the first track on the album where the mandolin is featured with melodies. It alternates with the banjo and the resonator guitar. Since the beginning of her career, Dolly Parton has been regularly accompanied by a fiddle. Throughout the song the banjo plays a melodic accompaniment (without chords), while the resonator guitar seems very free in its playing. It alternates between chords, accentuated or softer, and melodic lines, just like the mandolin. Chris Thile is also the mandolin player with the trio Nickel Creek.

A Tender Lie

Randy Sharp / 3:44

Vocals: Dolly Parton **Musicians:** Barry Bales, Byron House: double bass / Steve Buckingham: autoharp / Jerry Douglas: resonator guitar / Stuart Duncan: fiddle / Bryan Sutton: guitar / Jim Mills: banjo / Chris Thile: mandolin **Backing Vocals:** Alison Krauss, Dan Tyminski **Recorded:** Ocean Way, The Doghouse, Nashville; Schnee Studio, Los Angeles, 2000 **Technical Team:** Producer: Steve Buckingham / Mixing: Gary Paczosa / Mastering: Robert Hadley, Doug Sax **Single:** A Tender Lie **Release:** Sugar Hill Records / Blue Eye Records, April 2, 2001 (CD ref.: ?) NB: This track was released as a promo single, so was not ranked on any chart.

The narrator tries to convince herself that a "tender lie," the promise of a return, would be less difficult than admitting that she has lost the other forever.

This is a cover version of a song written by singer, songwriter, guitarist, and producer Randy Sharp for the band Restless Heart and their 1988 album *Big Dreams in a Small Town*. It is almost the same formation from the beginning of the album, with the exception of the autoharp chords that Steve Buckingham adds—difficult to identify at first listen, they become obvious later. A few chords in the intro, slightly to the left of the stereo mix, recur throughout the song. Finally, there is an instrumental reprise that seems to be a bonus (it is not really an outro: There is a general pause, and then an unexpected reprise).

I Get A Kick Out Of You

Cole Porter / 2:31

Vocals: Dolly Parton **Musicians:** Barry Bales: double bass / Jerry Douglas: resonator guitar / Stuart Duncan: fiddle / Bryan Sutton: guitar / Jim Mills: banjo / Chris Thile: mandolin **Backing Vocals:** Alison Krauss **Recorded:** Ocean Way, The Doghouse, Nashville; Schnee Studio, Los Angeles, 2000 **Technical Team:** Producer: Steve Buckingham / Mixing: Gary Paczosa / Mastering: Robert Hadley, Doug Sax

Everything seems to leave the protagonist indifferent—champagne, drugs—because nothing makes her feel better than her man. She is crazy about him, but the feeling is not mutual. Written by the songwriter Cole Porter for the musical *Anything Goes* in 1934, the song was first sung by the Broadway singer and actress Ethel Merman, and then covered dozens of times. The most famous version is probably that of Frank Sinatra in 1954. But there was also Ella Fitzgerald, and more recently, Tony Bennett with Lady Gaga.

The song starts with a sequence of solos by the mandolin, the resonator guitar, and the folk guitar. This is the first time in the album that it takes a melodic line. Each one has a very fast flow, reminiscent of gypsy jazz, a feeling accentuated by the rhythm established by the mandolin, with chords muffled by the left hand. These solos represent half the piece, and the singing the other half. This is a nice way for the singer to step aside and really let the orchestra take the lead.

Mountain Angel

Dolly Parton / 6:51

Vocals: Dolly Parton **Musicians:** Barry Bales: double bass / Steve Buckingham: dulcimer / Dermot Byrne: accordion / Jerry Douglas: resonator guitar / Stuart Duncan: fiddle / Bryan Sutton: guitar / Jim Mills: banjo / Chris Thile: mandolin / John Mock: whistle / Ciaran Tourish: bass whistle **Backing Vocals:** Rebecca Lynn Howard, Carl Jackson **Recorded:** Ocean Way, The Doghouse, Nashville; Schnee Studio, Los Angeles, 2000 **Technical Team:** Producer: Steve Buckingham / Mixing: Gary Paczosa / Mastering: Robert Hadley, Doug Sax

Dolly writes and sings a long song about the madness of love that leads to the despair of being abandoned. Tragic and beautiful, the story tells us that the protagonist was born as beautiful as an angel and then, when she became a woman, she fell in love and became pregnant by a man who left her without looking back. Left alone in the mountains, her child dead, as well as her parents, she sinks into madness and lies down on her baby's grave to die in turn. Since then, her spirit haunts the hills.

Having been absent on several albums, this marks the return of a choral piece. It is more precisely a musical narrative, because there are no references to musicals or operas. The length of the piece (6:51!) enabled the addition of unusual instruments, such as the dulcimer, traditional in the Appalachians. We also discover the whistle, a traditional Irish flute, in two different tessituras. We are more used to hearing the higher-pitched instrument, but it also exists in a lower register. The latter can be heard at 4:23, for example. The "normal" whistle, which is higher pitched, is hardly perceptible, and it seems to be drowned out by the violin and accordion. A few notes are nevertheless distinct around 5:19, before the resumption of the refrain.

Marry Me

Dolly Parton / 3:18

Vocals: Dolly Parton **Musicians:** Barry Bales: double bass / Jerry Douglas: resonator guitar / Stuart Duncan: fiddle / Bryan Sutton: guitar / Mike Snider: clawhammer banjo / Chris Thile: mandolin **Backing Vocals:** Becky Isaacs Bowman, Sonya Isaacs Tap Dancers: Bubba Richardson, Marcia Campbell **Recorded:** Ocean Way, The Doghouse, Nashville; Schnee Studio, Los Angeles, 2000 **Technical Team:** Producer: Steve Buckingham / Mixing: Gary Paczosa / Mastering: Robert Hadley, Doug Sax

This song is about a meeting, a kiss that goes further than just a kiss, the hopes of the narrator who intends to get married and to go far away with her man, far from her future mother-in-law. In this text, love is also synonymous with freedom, while the music is an invitation to party, directly inspired by the traditional Irish culture. One may recognize melodic lines from the Dubliners, such as "Lord of the Dance" (1975). The novelty is the banjo played in clawhammer style (the strings are more struck than plucked). One can also hear the tap dancers, as well as shouts of joy, as at a wedding.

Down From Dover

Dolly Parton / 5:09

Vocals: Dolly Parton, Mairéad Ní Mhaonaigh **Musicians:** Byron House: double bass / Dermot Byrne: accordion / Ciaran Curran: bouzouki / Jerry Douglas: resonator guitar / Stuart Duncan: fiddle / Mark Kelly, Dáithí Sproule: guitar / Pat McInnerney: percussion / John Mock: harmonium / Ciaran Tourish: bass whistle **Backing Vocals:** Maura O'Connell, Chip Davis, Monty Allen, Richard Dennison **Recorded:** Ocean Way, The Doghouse, Nashville; Schnee Studio, Los Angeles, 2000 **Technical Team:** Producer: Steve Buckingham / Mixing: Gary Paczosa / Mastering: Robert Hadley, Doug Sax

When Dolly Parton presented this song to Porter Wagoner in 1970, during their duet days, the showman told her that it was not suitable for radio because it was too long. A young girl finds herself pregnant by a man who left after seducing her, leaving her alone to face the family shame. "Down from Dover" is the story of many "girl mothers," as they were called in the 1960s. In this new version, as dark and poignant as ever, the songwriter's every word plunges us into this young woman's personal hell, making us hear her doubts and her hopes of seeing her lover come back.

On this track, the star is accompanied, in addition to her musicians, by the Irish band Altan. We find a bouzouki (a traditional Greek guitar), an accordion, a fiddle, and a guitar, but also the bass whistle (Irish bass flute), a harmonium, and percussion, including a shaker, throughout the song. The harmonium is from the organ family but uses accordion-like technology for the air supply and sound production. It can be heard here producing chord layers, especially at the end of the track.

All these musicians know each other and play for each other. We encounter the Irish singer and fiddler Mairéad Ní Mhaonaigh, or the guitarist Jerry Douglas, on projects with the Irish traditional musician Ciaran Tourish, for example.

In The Sweet By And By

S. Fillmore Bennett, Joseph Webster / 4:00

Vocals: Dolly Parton, Mairéad Ní Mhaonaigh **Musicians:** Byron House: bass / Dermot Byrne: accordion / Ciaran Curran: bouzouki / Jerry Douglas: resonator guitar / Dáithí Sproule: guitar / John Mock: harmonium / Ciaran Tourish: whistle **Backing Vocals:** Chip Davis, Monty Allen, Richard Dennison **Recorded:** Ocean Way, The Doghouse, Nashville; Schnee Studio, Los Angeles, 2000 **Technical Team:** Producer: Steve Buckingham / Mixing: Gary Paczosa / Mastering: Robert Hadley, Doug Sax

This song was previously recorded for the album *Precious Memories* in 1999, but this version is slower and softer. On this album, it was linked without a break to "The Beautiful Lie."

The 1999 version is rather pop sounding. Altan brings here the traditional Irish color of the whole album, with notably a verse in Gaelic. This language has different sounds from English and conveys a great sense of melancholy. We feel the weight of the history, and this is what makes it so beautiful, even more so in song.

The Beautiful Lie

David "Butch" McDade / 2:34

Vocals: Dolly Parton **Musicians:** Dermot Byrne: accordion / Stuart Duncan: fiddle **Recorded:** Ocean Way, The Doghouse, Nashville; Schnee Studio, Los Angeles, 2000 **Technical Team:** Producer: Steve Buckingham / Mixing: Gary Paczosa / Mastering: Robert Hadley, Doug Sax

This is another version of love and lying, when the relationship did not work out and you tell yourself a nice story to make yourself believe that love still exists.

David "Butch" McDade was the drummer for the country rock band Amazing Rhythm Aces. He wrote this track for the band's first album, *Stacked Deck* (1975). In this version we enjoy the purity of Dolly's voice accompanied only by an accordion and a fiddle. Note that the song begins on the same note as the previous one.

Little Sparrow

Dolly Parton / 1:37

Vocals: Dolly Parton **Musicians:** Jerry Douglas: resonator guitar / Stuart Duncan: fiddle / Bryan Sutton: guitar **Recorded:** Ocean Way, The Doghouse, Nashville; Schnee Studio, Los Angeles, 2000 **Technical Team:** Producer: Steve Buckingham / Mixing: Gary Paczosa / Mastering: Robert Hadley, Doug Sax

To close the album, the title song of the album is covered without words, but only vocalizations. The fiddle, the folk guitar, and the resonator guitar alternate melody and free accompaniment on the theme of the song. It acts as a kind of outro to the album. Some artists, especially in hip-hop, use this process: Throughout the record, they play interludes of a few seconds or tens of seconds, embroidering around the main theme. One thinks of the Fugees with *The Score* (1996), or the *Jazzmatazz* compilations by Guru.

ALBUM

Halos & Horns

Halos & Horns . Sugar Hill . Not for Me . Hello God . If . Shattered Image .
These Old Bones . What a Heartache . I'm Gone . Raven Dove .
Dagger Through the Heart . If Only . John Daniel . Stairway to Heaven

RELEASE DATE
United States: July 9, 2002
Reference: Sugar Hill Records / Blue Eye Records—SUG-CD-3946
Best US Chart Ranking: 4

Holding On with God's Help

Halos & Horns is Dolly Parton's thirty-seventh solo album, produced by the star herself. It was released by Sugar Hill Records / Blue Eye Records on July 9, 2002, and it reached number fifty-eight on the Billboard 200 and number one on the OCC Country Artists Albums chart in the United Kingdom, where it earned a silver certification.

The Impact of the Attacks

After the attacks of September 11, 2001, America was hurting and afraid. President George W. Bush decided to invade Afghanistan in March 2002 and went to war in Iraq in October. Steven Spielberg's *Minority Report*, which depicts a chilling world, was released in cinemas while writers James Patterson, Stephen King, Michael Crichton, Tom Clancy, and John Grisham made the *New York Times* bestseller list. The American mood was one of noir, spy, and horror novels, a cathartic way to deal with the anxieties of everyday life.

Between 2001 and 2002, although she cancelled several public events, Dolly continued to work. She was notably invited to collaborate on *Big Mon*, a tribute album to Bill Monroe, father of bluegrass, produced by Ricky Skaggs, on which she performed "Cry, Cry Darlin'." After *The Grass Is Blue* in 1999 and *Little Sparrow* in 2001, the star concluded her trilogy of bluegrass music with *Halos & Horns*. Twelve of the fourteen songs are her own.

On Tour Again

The reviews were good, the United Kingdom confirmed its enthusiasm, and Dolly prepared to tour again. In September, Governor Don Sundquist appointed her as the official ambassador of Tennessee to promote the state as an economic and creative player in Hollywood music and film production. During a press conference at Dollywood, the star announced the future release of her album as well as the tour. Of course, the events of September 11 were terrible, but Dolly confided to the *Knoxville News Sentinel* that she was doing everything to remain herself, preserving as much of her well-being as possible to help others while pursuing her projects.[2]

And in fact, all the musicians on *Halos & Horns*, even though they were impressed when she arrived in the studio, agreed that within minutes the atmosphere was relaxed. The star's answer to collective or personal trauma lies in her serenity and creativity. Throughout this trilogy, Dolly revisits the bluegrass genre while bringing back many of the great names in country music—the Carter Family and the Louvin Brothers, to name a few.

Album Cover

This simple and very glamorous cover was created by photographer Annie Leibovitz. The blond Dolly, in a simple denim shirt, is lying dreamily in the grass. Inside, one of the portraits of the star, dressed in a denim jacket embroidered with rhinestones, low-cut and fitted, shows her in the middle of the road, guitar in hand, and shouting out.

For Dolly Addicts

For the promotion of the album, the Sugar Hill Records label posted short music videos on its website—"I'm Gone," "Shattered Image," "John Daniel," "Not for Me," "If Only," and "Stairway to Heaven."

On this album there are many backing vocalists, but it's not clear who sang on which track. We therefore note the presence of: Eric Bennett, Richard Dennison, Terry Eldredge, Steve French, Robert Hale, Randy Kohrs, Jennifer O'Brien, Dolly Parton, April Stevens, Beth Stevens, David Sutton, and Darrell Webb.

In November 2002, Dolly Parton sets the Clyde Auditorium in Glasgow, Scotland, on fire during her *Halos & Horns* tour.

Halos & Horns
Dolly Parton / 3:33

Vocals: Dolly Parton **Musicians:** Gary "Biscuit" Davis: banjo, acoustic guitar / Terry Eldredge: bass, double bass / Randy Kohrs: dobro / Jimmy Mattingly: fiddle, mandolin / Brent Truitt: mandolin / Steve Turner: drums, snare drum, tambourine, washboard / Darrell Webb: mandolin / Kent Wells: acoustic, baritone, and electric guitars **Recorded:** Southern Sound Studios, Knoxville Tennessee, February 2002 **Technical Team:** Producer: Dolly Parton / Sound Engineers: Danny Brown, Phil van Peborgh, Scottie Hoaglan / Mixing: Danny Brown / Mastering: Seva

Through the sinner-saint dichotomy, Dolly explores the ups and downs of humanity. According to the Dollymania website, the idea came to her while preparing a pitch for Fox. This parable on human nature is the opportunity to start the album with a country waltz with bluegrass accents. The main ingredients are there: banjo, acoustic guitar, dobro, fiddle, mandolin, double bass (an instrument used sparingly by Dolly Parton) and devilishly precise vocal harmonies. Dolly is in top form: the mastery of her voice, the accuracy, the way she projects the sound forward while maintaining the dynamics, is impressive. We enter straight into the last album of her bluegrass trilogy, and this looks promising.

Sugar Hill
Dolly Parton / 2:50

Vocals: Dolly Parton **Musicians:** Gary "Biscuit" Davis: banjo, acoustic guitar / Terry Eldredge: bass, double bass / Robert Hale: acoustic guitar / Randy Kohrs: dobro / Jimmy Mattingly: fiddle, mandolin / David Sutton: harmonica / Steve Turner: drums, snare drum, tambourine, washboard / Darrell Webb: mandolin / Kent Wells: acoustic, baritone, and electric guitars **Recorded:** Southern Sound Studios, Knoxville Tennessee, February 2002 **Technical Team:** Producer: Dolly Parton / Sound Engineers: Danny Brown, Phil van Peborgh, Scottie Hoaglan / Mixing: Danny Brown / Mastering: Seva

When the song was first recorded in 2002, Dolly said she was initially inspired by the name of her production company, Sugar Hill. Then she turned to her personal life, meeting Carl, their long marriage, and combined the two ideas. The result is this story of an elderly couple returning to where their love story began. In 2019, an episode of the Netflix series *Heartstrings* was set around this song.

On this joyously nostalgic track, the acoustic guitar strumming and chord progression recall both standards by Buddy Holly and Bo Diddley's rhythmic staccato playing. This fifties rock 'n' roll base is gently counterbalanced by a purely acoustic and bluegrass arrangement, which gives this track, despite its formally hybrid aspect, an undeniable fluidity.

Not For Me
Dolly Parton / 3:20

Vocals: Dolly Parton **Musicians:** Gary "Biscuit" Davis: banjo, acoustic guitar / Terry Eldredge: bass, double bass / Robert Hale: acoustic guitar / Randy Kohrs: dobro / Jimmy Mattingly: fiddle, mandolin / Brent Truitt: mandolin / Kent Wells: acoustic, baritone, and electric guitars **Recorded:** Southern Sound Studios, Knoxville Tennessee, February 2002 **Technical Team:** Producer: Dolly Parton / Sound Engineers: Danny Brown, Phil van Peborgh, Scottie Hoaglan / Mixing: Danny Brown / Mastering: Seva

"Not for Me" is the sad tale of a woman for whom the sun no longer shines: She has not found love and even seems to believe that the love she longs for is not for her. Dolly, who wrote this song at least thirty years earlier, before she even arrived in Nashville in 1964, found it while searching for an old song for the Dollywood Museum. Terry Eldredge's double bass kicks off this lovely ballad. The delicacy of the instrumentalists' touch is striking, especially Randy Kohrs's playing and the expressiveness of his dobro, like a second voice echoing Dolly's. Arpeggios and the soft strumming of folk guitar, chords of banjo and resonator guitar (the dobro's equivalent), melodic counterpoints of mandolin and fiddle...the musicians use all their talent and sensitivity to illustrate Dolly's song and enable her to make her voice resonate.

Hello God

Dolly Parton / 2:59

Vocals: Dolly Parton **Musicians:** Gary "Biscuit" Davis: banjo, acoustic guitar / Terry Eldredge: bass, double bass / Randy Kohrs: dobro / Jimmy Mattingly: fiddle, mandolin / Brent Truitt: mandolin / Steve Turner: drums, snare drum, tambourine, washboard / Darrell Webb: mandolin / Kent Wells: acoustic, baritone, and electric guitars **Recorded:** Southern Sound Studios, Knoxville Tennessee, February 2002 **Technical Team:** Producer: Dolly Parton / Sound Engineers: Danny Brown, Phil van Peborgh, Scottie Hoaglan / Mixing: Danny Brown / Mastering: Seva **Single:** track 1: Hello God / track 2: Dolly Parton's Commentary on Hello God / track 3: Hello God Single with Commentary Introduction **Release:** Sugar Hill Records / Blue Eye Records, November 11, 2002 (CD ref.: SUG-CD-3946S4) **Best US Chart Ranking:** 60

This gospel number, this call to God to ask him why there is so much cruelty and death on earth, so much hatred in the world, was written just after the attacks of September 11. Dolly Parton captures the fragility of life, the loneliness of the believer who fears that God is no longer there to support him. On a ballad tempo, the orchestration provided here by Dolly, Gary Davis, and the team of musicians is significantly expanded: This is the first track on the album with drums and electric guitar. The latter, played by Kent Wells, doubles the melodic fiddle parts from 1:38 with a generously saturated sound bathed in a deep tremolo—epic effect guaranteed. The arrangement rises in power from the beginning to the end of the piece. The massive backing vocals contribute significantly to bring the orchestration to its climax, to reach its final amplitude and this larger-than-life sound.

If

David Gates / 3:19

Vocals: Dolly Parton **Musicians:** Gary "Biscuit" Davis: banjo, acoustic guitar / Terry Eldredge: bass, double bass / Randy Kohrs: dobro / Jimmy Mattingly: fiddle, mandolin / Brent Truitt: mandolin / Steve Turner: drums, snare drum, tambourine, washboard / Kent Wells: acoustic, baritone, and electric guitars **Recorded:** Southern Sound Studios, Knoxville Tennessee, February 2002 **Technical Team:** Producer: Dolly Parton / Sound Engineers: Danny Brown, Phil van Peborgh, Scottie Hoaglan / Mixing: Danny Brown / Mastering: Seva

"If" was written by the singer-songwriter David Gates in 1971 and made famous by the soft-rock band Bread. On Dollymania, we can read that Dolly liked this song for

a long time and that she wanted to record her own version, which is quite different from Bread's. The song was released as a single in the United Kingdom only.

The folk guitar picking and the electric guitar at the beginning, passed through a kind of fast vibrato effect (maybe from a Uni-Vibe pedal, or a Pulsar from Electro-Harmonix), might lead one to believe that after the arrangement a folk-rock ballad line would follow, very close to the original version. However, from 1:07, the arrangement starts on a country-folk rhythm with a fast tempo, supported by Steve Turner's brush playing on drums, Gary Davis's clawhammer banjo, and the strumming of the acoustic guitar, all in keeping with the color of the album. The dobro, the mandolin, and the fiddle take turns, gracing the listener with some melodic phrasing of which only they know the secret. This track brings a particular freshness to Dolly Parton's long discography; the public is unused to hearing her voice over this type of harmonic structure, far from the Partonian universe and yet seeming to flow from the first listening. One then realizes that the extent of Dolly's range has yet to reach its limits.

Shattered Image

Dolly Parton / 3:29

Vocals: Dolly Parton **Musicians:** Gary "Biscuit" Davis: banjo, acoustic guitar / Terry Eldredge: bass, double bass / Robert Hale: acoustic guitar / Randy Kohrs: dobro / Jimmy Mattingly: fiddle, mandolin / Brent Truitt: mandolin / Steve Turner: drums, snare drum, tambourine, washboard / Kent Wells: acoustic, baritone, and electric guitars **Recorded:** Southern Sound Studios, Knoxville Tennessee, February 2002 **Technical Team:** Producer: Dolly Parton / Sound Engineers: Danny Brown, Phil van Peborgh, Scottie Hoaglan / Mixing: Danny Brown / Mastering: Seva

This song had already appeared on the album *All I Can Do* (1976). Dolly decided to rerecord it as a response to all the vicious tabloid publications that trashed the image of those who made the front page. The songwriter had always defended, for everyone and for herself, the right to be different, the freedom to be whoever you want to be, whenever you want, and however you want. While Dolly's appearance no longer seemed to be an object of ridicule at the beginning of this millennium, this was not the case for all artists: Many of them were smeared and humiliated by the press, and this was a subject that mattered to the star.

The voluble dobro of Randy Kohrs opens this song with a touch of telluric country blues. The arrangement has a bayou feel to it: the pulse of the double bass stomp, the washboard rhythm, the haunting fiddle, the acidic dobro lines, and the meandering melody...all of this is reminiscent of Cajun music and the humidity of the Mississippi Delta.

2002

"If" was written by singer-songwriter David Gates in 1971 and made famous by the soft rock band Bread.

What A Heartache

Dolly Parton / 4:17

Vocals: Dolly Parton **Musicians:** Gary "Biscuit" Davis: banjo, acoustic guitar / Terry Eldredge: bass, double bass / Randy Kohrs: dobro / Jimmy Mattingly: fiddle, mandolin / Kent Wells: acoustic, baritone, and electric guitars **Recorded:** Southern Sound Studios, Knoxville Tennessee, February 2002 **Technical Team:** Producer: Dolly Parton / Sound Engineers: Danny Brown, Phil van Peborgh, Scottie Hoaglan / Mixing: Danny Brown / Mastering: Seva

This is the third time Dolly has covered this song. Probably because she loves this song and hopes that one day someone will take it and make it a huge hit, as with "I Will Always Love You."

This album was an opportunity to do an entirely acoustic version. The drone held on the accordion on the B at the beginning of the song, returning first discreetly from 1:20 to 2:00, then from 2:30 to the end, gives a special color to this arrangement, a surprising hypnotic quality for a ballad of this caliber. The recording, especially of the acoustic guitars and the double bass, is meticulous. Each instrument seems to retain its full spectrum and to be able to express itself fully, with plenty of dynamics, body, and depth. A production feat with a restrained and careful mix, probably its best version. For this reason alone, Dolly did well to pull this composition out of her hat once again, a classic in the hearts of fans.

These Old Bones

Dolly Parton / 5:37

Vocals: Dolly Parton **Musicians:** Bob Carlin: clawhammer banjo / Gary "Biscuit" Davis: banjo, acoustic guitar / Terry Eldredge: bass, double bass / Robert Hale: acoustic guitar / Randy Kohrs: dobro / Jimmy Mattingly: fiddle, mandolin / Steve Turner: drums, snare drum, tambourine, washboard / Darrell Webb: mandolin / Kent Wells: acoustic, baritone, and electric guitars **Recorded:** Southern Sound Studios, Knoxville Tennessee, February 2002 **Technical Team:** Producer: Dolly Parton / Sound Engineers: Danny Brown, Phil van Peborgh, Scottie Hoaglan / Mixing: Danny Brown / Mastering: Seva

The title came to Dolly Parton in a dream the night before she wrote this song, which tells the story of a clairvoyant mountain woman who never saw her daughter grow up. In 2019, Dolly revisited the story for an episode of the Netflix series *Heartstrings*.

This time it is Darrell Webb's turn to introduce the piece with a bouncy, light mandolin rhythm. Dolly seems to be having a wild time playing this elderly and probably toothless Southern Appalachian country girl. She is a specialist in this kind of antic, never missing an opportunity to do her act, and she is a born entertainer.

Dolly Parton at Irving Plaza in New York, July 2002.

I'm Gone

Dolly Parton / 5:07

Vocals: Dolly Parton **Musicians:** Gary "Biscuit" Davis: banjo, acoustic guitar / Terry Eldredge: bass, double bass / Robert Hale: acoustic guitar / Randy Kohrs: dobro / Jimmy Mattingly: fiddle, mandolin / David Sutton: harmonica / Brent Truitt: mandolin / Steve Turner: drums, snare drum, tambourine, washboard / Darrell Webb: mandolin / Kent Wells: acoustic, baritone, and electric guitars **Recorded:** Southern Sound Studios, Knoxville Tennessee, February 2002 **Technical Team:** Producer: Dolly Parton / Sound Engineers: Danny Brown, Phil van Peborgh, Scottie Hoaglan / Mixing: Danny Brown / Mastering: Seva NB: This track was released as a promo single, so was not ranked on any chart.

In this new song about the separation of a couple, the woman leaves because she can no longer stand living with such a pathetic and violent man. She throws her wedding ring out the train window and wants to take back her maiden name and find her freedom. There is energy in the writing, and one can well imagine the wife leaving her hell.

The dance opens with a lively, percussive clawhammer playing; in the background, Darrell Webb strums the backbeat in syncopated mandolin ghost notes, and David Sutton breathes extra groove into the harmonica. Then folk guitars and double bass make their entrance along with Dolly's voice, to broaden the sonic spectrum and clarify the harmony. At 0:46, everyone comes in on the chorus, the bluegrass party can begin, and we are off to four minutes of virtuoso mountain music. The orchestration plays on the nuances of intensity and thickness of the spectrum, with a clear intent to let the verses breathe and to create restarts before the choruses and the ad lib at the end. All of this works perfectly; the listener has no time to get bored, always challenged by a relevant musical event.

Raven Dove

Dolly Parton / 3:35

Vocals: Dolly Parton **Musicians:** Gary "Biscuit" Davis: banjo, acoustic guitar / Richard Dennison: piano / Terry Eldredge: bass, double bass / Randy Kohrs: dobro / Jimmy Mattingly: fiddle, mandolin / Brent Truitt: mandolin / Steve Turner: drums, snare drum, tambourine, washboard / Kent Wells: acoustic, baritone, and electric guitars **Recorded:** Southern Sound Studios, Knoxville Tennessee, February 2002 **Technical Team:** Producer: Dolly Parton / Sound Engineers: Danny Brown, Phil van Peborgh, Scottie Hoaglan / Mixing: Danny Brown / Mastering: Seva

This gospel song, a biblical-sounding text written in the middle of the night, is the result of a lightning inspiration that echoes the pain and stupor the songwriter felt after the September 11 attacks. Richard Dennison's piano lays down the first chords, supported by Brent Truitt's mandolin tremolos. Dolly sings a few discreet vocals, then sings the first verse with great restraint, her voice gradually increasing in intensity, until the first chorus. This time once more, the whole orchestra comes in to create a sound carpet to complement her vocals; the Queen of Country does not hesitate to push her chest voice to its limits. Jimmy Mattingly's fiddle and the backing vocals are the main assets of the chorus arrangements, while the verses are essentially based on the piano, bass, drums played in cross stick, and the ghostly tremolos of the mandolin. This play of light and shadow, symbolized in the lyrics by the allegory of the raven that turns into a dove ("When the raven of darkness turns into a white dove of peace"), enables this country gospel parable to reach the mystical quality promised from the first verse: a series of suspended chords, oscillating between *C* and *F*, until the change of key of the chorus, firmly anchored in *A* minor. A deep and sensitive piece of finely honed craftsmanship that recalls the best moments of Dolly's discography in the 1970s.

Dagger Through The Heart

Dolly Parton / 3:52

Vocals: Dolly Parton **Musicians:** Gary "Biscuit" Davis: banjo, acoustic guitar / Terry Eldredge: bass, double bass / Randy Kohrs: dobro / Jimmy Mattingly: fiddle, mandolin / Brent Truitt: mandolin / Steve Turner: drums, snare drum, tambourine, washboard / Kent Wells: acoustic,

Touring for her album *Halos & Horns*, the tireless Dolly performed at the Hammersmith Apollo in London.

baritone, and electric guitars **Recorded:** Southern Sound Studios, Knoxville Tennessee, July 8, 2002 **Technical Team:** Producer: Dolly Parton / Sound Engineers: Danny Brown, Phil van Peborgh, Scottie Hoaglan / Mixing: Danny Brown / Mastering: Seva **Single:** Dagger Through the Heart **Release:** Sugar Hill Records / Blue Eye Records, November 11, 2002 (CD ref.: SUG-CD-3946S11) NB: This track was released as a promo single, so was not ranked on any chart.

The protagonist narrates how she is regularly cheated on, mistreated, and humiliated by her lover, as if he were stabbing her in the heart. Yet she stays. A classic Dolly, the drama of the married woman who can't leave the man who makes her suffer. A video was shot in Nashville on June 14 and aired on *CMT Most Wanted Live* beginning July 20, 2002.

This ritornello of which Dolly knows the secret is in the category of "sad ass songs" but on a mid-tempo track conducive to dance—it becomes a song about not getting discouraged. The musicians knit an elegant fabric, and everything here is of a great fluidity, which is somewhat the trademark of this album. With such a team, how could it be otherwise?

If Only

Dolly Parton / 3:40

Vocals: Dolly Parton **Musicians:** Gary "Biscuit" Davis: banjo, acoustic guitar / Terry Eldredge: bass, double bass / Robert Hale: acoustic guitar / Randy Kohrs: dobro / Jimmy Mattingly: fiddle, mandolin / Brent Truitt: mandolin / Steve Turner: drums, snare drum, tambourine, washboard **Recorded:** Southern Sound Studios, Knoxville Tennessee, February 2002 **Technical Team:** Producer: Dolly Parton / Sound Engineers: Danny Brown, Phil van Peborgh, Scottie Hoaglan / Mixing: Danny Brown / Mastering: Seva

This was originally written for a film about Mae West, the famous actress, singer, and sex symbol of the 1920s through 1940s, but it was judged too sad for the soundtrack. "If Only" is a melancholic ballad of the kind that the songwriter and her fans like. The arrangement of this song, in the style of early '60s Nashville Dolly (the only thing missing is the pedal steel guitar), is a little out of place on the album, as it is in the purest country tradition. It must be said that the song itself does not allow for any other treatment. We are quite far from bluegrass if we put aside the instrumentation, which would suit the most roots kind of mountain music just as well as it would the modern acoustic Nashville sound.

John Daniel

Dolly Parton / 5:03

Vocals: Dolly Parton **Musicians:** Gary "Biscuit" Davis: banjo, acoustic guitar / Terry Eldredge: bass, double bass / Robert Hale: acoustic guitar / Randy Kohrs: dobro / Jimmy Mattingly: fiddle, mandolin / Brent Truitt: mandolin / Kent Wells: acoustic, baritone, and electric guitars **Recorded:** Southern Sound Studios, Knoxville Tennessee, February 2002 **Technical Team:** Producer: Dolly Parton / Sound Engineers: Danny Brown, Phil van Peborgh, Scottie Hoaglan / Mixing: Danny Brown / Mastering: Seva

This rather cheerful song, also written more than thirty years earlier and never before recorded, tells of the arrival in town of a young lumberjack who seduces the narrator because he seems different from the other men. As she tries to find out who this John Daniel is, she discovers that he is a charismatic preacher capable of moving crowds.

The bouncy groove, first infused by Randy Kohrs's syncopated dobro playing, then by finger-picking folk guitar and double bass, puts this song in the honky-tonk tradition. The objective, clearly stated here by Dolly and her musicians: to give the listener an irrepressible desire to tap their feet on the first beat and to clap their hands on the second. And it works: no need to be a hillbilly to be carried away and enter the dance. When John Daniel was preaching, he was able to transcend the crowds, Dolly tells us. We take her word for it.

Stairway To Heaven

Jimmy Page, Robert Plant / 6:31

Vocals: Dolly Parton **Musicians:** Gary "Biscuit" Davis: banjo, acoustic guitar / Terry Eldredge: bass, double bass / Randy Kohrs: dobro / Jimmy Mattingly: fiddle, mandolin / Brent Truitt: mandolin / Steve Turner: drums, snare drum, tambourine, washboard / Kent Wells: acoustic, baritone, and electric guitars **Recorded:** Southern Sound Studios, Knoxville Tennessee, February 2002 **Technical Team:** Producer: Dolly Parton / Sound Engineers: Danny Brown, Phil van Peborgh, Scottie Hoaglan / Mixing: Danny Brown / Mastering: Seva

According to the Dollymania website, by covering this rock classic composed and immortalized by the band Led Zeppelin, Dolly was aware that she was tackling a big piece. She wrote to Robert Plant, who found her bluegrass version very good. All that remained for the star was to convince the public, because the critics were already convinced.

Surprisingly, from the first notes of fiddle on the acoustic guitar arpeggios, we feel that this cover is going to flow. The idea was audacious, but the entirely acoustic arrangement carried by the banjo, mandolin, double bass, and the drums played with jumbo brushes (sticks made of thinner wooden sticks to absorb the impact and to produce a duller and less powerful sound than the standard sticks) suits this composition wonderfully well, revealing its resolutely folk aspect and enabling the listener to better perceive its ancestral essence. Dolly's voice, too, seems tailor-made for interpreting this timeless melody. The final climax can hold its head up high in comparison with Led Zeppelin's version: The backing vocals open up their voices, and seventh heaven is not far away.

Dolly hosts an Imagination Library press event at London's Savoy Hotel on December 4, 2007.

Spot Goes to School
Eric Hill

In 2020, Nick Geidner, a journalism professor and director of Land Grant Films, produced and directed a documentary titled *The Library That Dolly Built*, which is available on streaming.

The Book Lady's Imagination Library

Created in 1995 and sponsored by Dolly Parton, the Imagination Library is a charitable program that provides free books to children. Because her own father didn't know how to read, and due to her own love of storytelling, Dolly decided to offer books to kids all across the English-speaking world to help them imagine who they might become when they grow up.

Feeding the Imagination Through Reading

The seed of what would eventually become the Imagination Library was Dolly's belief that all children have dreams of what they might become when they're older—a pilot, a doctor, an astronaut, a decorator, a gardener—or perhaps an artist, as was the case with Dolly herself. She also believed that a child's hopes for the future require nourishment in order to take root and to grow, and a love of books is the perfect substance to feed a young person's belief in themselves and their own potential. Indeed, there is no more powerful lever for growth in a young child than the imagination, which can be nurtured and fed through a love of stories that are either read or shared. Each story contains a character, a situation, or a sentence that might lodge itself in the mind of a child and grow into a dream for the future. Thus, the concept that Dolly eventually named "The Imagination Library" took shape: children from birth to age five would be offered a free book each month, sent via the mail.

Far Beyond Tennessee

When it began, Imagination Library focused on helping the children in Dolly's native region of eastern Tennessee, where the performer's own love of words and stories began. Eventually, the program expanded beyond Sevier County and became available to the entire state of Tennessee. After that, as the program grew in popularity, it eventually expanded across the United States and into Canada, the United Kingdom, Ireland, and Australia. These programs were all co-funded by Dolly Parton and by local organizing committees. In 2018 the Library of Congress in Washington, D.C., hosted Dolly as she dedicated the hundred-millionth book in her library which, fittingly, was a copy of *Coat of Many Colors*, a children's adaptation of Dolly's popular song. As of 2023, the official website for Dolly Parton's Imagination Library lists more than 2.4 million children as beneficiaries of its programs, with more than 204 million copies donated.

ALBUM

For God and Country

The Lord Is My Shepherd . The Star-Spangled Banner . God Bless the USA .
Light of a Clear Blue Morning . When Johnny Comes Marching Home . Welcome Home .
Gee, Ma, I Wanna Go Home . Whispering Hope . There Will Be Peace in the Valley for Me .
Red, White and Bluegrass . My Country 'Tis . I'm Gonna Miss You . Go to Hell . Ballad of
the Green Beret . Brave Little Soldier . Tie a Yellow Ribbon . Color Me America .
The Glory Forever

RELEASE DATE
United States: November 11, 2003
References: Welk Music Group / Blue Eye Records—79756-2
**Best US Chart Ranking:
6 on the Billboard Independent Albums**

The Patriotic Album

For God and Country is Dolly Parton's thirty-eighth solo album. Produced by the singer Kent Wells and Tony Smith, it was released by Welk Music Group / Blue Eye Records on November 11, 2003. It reached number 167 on the Billboard 200 and number twenty-three on the Billboard Top Country Albums chart.

A Dark Year for America

In 2003, America was at war, still reeling from the attack on the World Trade Center; George W. Bush obtained an additional allocation of more than $80 billion to continue military operations in Iraq and Afghanistan, and American forces captured Saddam Hussein. The year was punctuated by disastrous events: the space shuttle *Columbia* disintegrated over Texas, killing seven astronauts; a few months later, a series of tornadoes hit the United States. The world of jazz was also in mourning, as the great singer Nina Simone died on April 21 at her home (in France). Dolly Parton reminded everyone just how patriotic she was, an American to the core. The country was doing badly, and Dolly's charts were not doing much better: Whether it was the compilation of her songs that was just released, *Ultimate Dolly Parton*, or her covers, honored by Norah Jones, Alison Krauss, and Emmylou Harris, among others, in *Just Because I'm a Woman: Songs of Dolly Parton*, sales were plummeting.

Patriotic and Country

The reception of *For God and Country* was also mixed, judging by the sales over two years—fewer than ninety thousand copies in the United States. However, it was not for lack of promotion, because Dolly was seen on almost every television set. In the press, the critic Brian Mansfield of the newspaper *USA Today* did not question the sincerity of the star, while the website AllMusic saw in it, beyond the patriotic aspect, the expression of her country roots. Some people found this album opportunistic, even clearly propagandistic. Whatever the case, no one doubts that the star felt the need to react, in her own way, to the shock of the 2001 attacks. Would her fans have understood if she had kept silent?

This album also has a spiritual dimension, with the hope that God will sustain America as the world teeters.

Album Cover

This very patriotic cover, by photographer Dennis Carney, is reminiscent of the posters that the United Service Organizations (USO) used to put up to brighten up the soldiers' daily lives during the Second World War. Facing the microphone, Dolly, pin-up style, blends into the American banner in the background.

For Dolly Addicts

In 2003, Dolly received the prestigious BMI Icon Award as an exceptional songwriter and for her influence upon young musicians and singers.

The Technical Team for This Album: The credits for each track on this album are not always complete. We note the presence of the following: Producers: Dolly Parton, Kent Wells, Tony Smith / Sound Engineers: Chuck Ainlay, Dave Sinco, Michael Davis, Patrick Murphy, Russ Long, Tony Smith / Mixing: Chuck Ainlay, John Guess / Mastering: Benny Quinn / Backing Vocals Supervisor: Hannah Dennison

The Lord Is My Shepherd

Traditional, arranged by Dolly Parton / 2:09

Vocals, Arrangements: Dolly Parton **Backing Vocals:** Monty Allen, Bob Bailey, Richard Dennison, Robert Hale, Steven Hill, Louis Nunley, David Slater, Darrell Webb, Kent Wells Backing Vocals Direction: Hannah Dennison **Recorded:** Two Monkeys Productions, Nashville, 2003

Dolly opens the album with a Christian hymn that praises the presence of God among men and women. Published in 1650, this traditional text, based on Psalm 23 of the Bible, is commonly attributed to Francis Rous, an English politician and Puritan theologian. Dolly is accompanied by an all-male choir a cappella. After singing with them at the beginning, she begins to recite a passage from the Bible, speaking softly into the microphone, achieving the whispering effect that crooners, in the original sense of the word, were looking for.

The Star-Spangled Banner

Francis Scott Key / 3:03

Vocals: Dolly Parton **Musicians:** (?): string ensemble / Michael Davis, Paul Hollowell: piano **Recorded:** Two Monkeys Productions, Nashville, 2003

Tenacity often pays off. It took a good dose of it for Maryland congressman John Charles Linthicum, who introduced a bill six times to have "The Star-Spangled Banner" recognized as the official national anthem before he got his wish. This tune was written by Francis Scott Key, a lawyer and poet in his spare time, during the War of 1812. It asks the question: Beyond the ravages and battles, will the banner of liberty still fly?

To emphasize the power of the United States, one could have imagined a wind band with brass and percussion. But this track has both an intimate and solemn character, provided by a string ensemble and a single piano. In the middle of the song, Dolly Parton interrupts herself to explain the reasons that drove her to record this titanic album, which is particularly long (eighteen titles, one hour and eleven minutes) compared to her previous albums.

God Bless The USA

Lee Greenwood / 3:34

Vocals: Dolly Parton **Musicians:** Charlie Anderson, Jay Weaver: bass / Michael Davis, Paul Hollowell: piano, Hammond B3 / Robert Hale, Bruce Watkins, Kent Wells: acoustic guitar / Jimmy Mattingly: fiddle, mandolin / Billy Thomas, Steve Turner: drums, percussion / Darrell Webb: mandolin / Kent Wells: electric guitar **Backing Vocals:** Monty Allen, Bob Bailey, Richard Dennison, Vicki Hampton, Steven Hill, Louis Nunley, Jennifer O'Brien, David Slater, Sheryl Thomas, Darrell Webb, Lynn Wright Backing Vocals Direction: Hannah Dennison **Recorded:** Two Monkeys Productions, Nashville, 2003

This song in praise of America, freedom, and those who died for the country, was released in 1984 on the album *You've Got a Good Love Comin'* by country singer and songwriter Lee Greenwood. This explains the eighties keyboard sound that almost haphazardly seemed to have slipped into the intro of this new version—as a nod to the unabashed era of the genesis of this ultrapatriotic song.

Light Of A Clear Blue Morning

Dolly Parton / 4:50

Vocals: Dolly Parton **Musicians:** Charlie Anderson, Jay Weaver: bass / Gary "Biscuit" Davis: banjo / Michael Davis, Paul Hollowell: piano, Hammond B3 / Robert Hale, Bruce Watkins, Kent Wells: acoustic guitar / Billy Thomas, Steve Turner: drums, percussion / Darrell Webb: mandolin / Kent Wells: electric guitar **Backing Vocals:** Monty Allen, Bob Bailey, Richard Dennison, Vicki Hampton, Steven Hill, Louis Nunley, Jennifer O'Brien, David Slater, Sheryl Thomas, Darrell Webb, Lynn Wright Backing Vocals Direction: Hannah Dennison **Recorded:** Two Monkeys Productions, Nashville, 2003

A Dolly cover of a song previously recorded for *New Harvest...First Gathering*. In the original version, she had a lot of emotion in the voice—at that time, she had just begun an important new chapter of her life by saying goodbye to Porter Wagoner and his show.

The 2003 arrangement is more enriched by the presence of the choirs in particular, but also by the greater emphasis given to the instrumental parts. Although the tempo is slightly faster and the tonality more bass oriented, the progression of the original song is respected: After a rather quiet start, with a piano intro, Dolly and her musicians accelerate to finish on a sustained rhythm.

2003

When Johnny Comes Marching Home

Louis Lambert / 4:19

Vocals: Dolly Parton **Musicians:** Charlie Anderson, Jay Weaver: bass / Michael Davis, Paul Hollowell: piano, Hammond B3 / Robert Hale, Bruce Watkins, Kent Wells: acoustic guitar / Jimmy Mattingly: fiddle, mandolin / Billy Thomas, Steve Turner: drums, percussion / Darrell Webb: mandolin / Kent Wells: electric guitar / (?): whistle **Backing Vocals:** Monty Allen, Bob Bailey, Richard Dennison, Vicki Hampton, Steven Hill, Louis Nunley, Jennifer O'Brien, David Slater, Sheryl Thomas, Darrell Webb, Lynn Wright Backing Vocals Direction: Hannah Dennison **Recorded:** Two Monkeys Productions, Nashville, 2003

If you have the impression when listening to the first notes of being suddenly immersed in a John Wayne film, that is quite understandable. Written by Irish songwriter Patrick Gilmore in 1863 and published under a pseudonym while he was serving in the Union Army, this popular song dates back to the Civil War. It is even said to be a cover of a nineteenth-century Irish antiwar song, "Johnny, I Hardly Knew Ya," and was later reinterpreted by many punk bands such as the Clash and the Dropkick Murphys. In spite of the opposition to the war clearly expressed by the text, the instrumentation is clearly military.

Welcome Home

Dolly Parton / 4:20

Vocals: Dolly Parton **Musicians:** Charlie Anderson, Jay Weaver: double bass / Gary "Biscuit" Davis: banjo / Robert Hale, Bruce Watkins, Kent Wells: acoustic guitar / Randy Kohrs: dobro / Jimmy Mattingly: fiddle, mandolin / Billy Thomas, Steve Turner: drums / Darrell Webb: mandolin / Kent Wells: electric guitar **Backing Vocals:** Monty Allen, Bob Bailey, Richard Dennison, Vicki Hampton, Steven Hill, Louis Nunley, Jennifer O'Brien, David Slater, Sheryl Thomas, Darrell Webb, Lynn Wright Backing Vocals Direction: Hannah Dennison **Recorded:** Two Monkeys Productions, Nashville, 2003

The songwriter positions herself here from the point of view of a father who awaits the return of his son, sees him arrive, and ends up falling into his arms, happy and emotional. The video, shot in January 2004 in Port Hueneme, California, features several hundred men and women from the US Navy.

This song marks a return to a more traditional style of country music, with its characteristic instruments, lacking only the piano and the pedal steel guitar. A male voice accompanies Dolly throughout almost the entire song. In front of the rhythm and the playing of the musicians, which plunges the listener into the midst of the seventies, the backing vocals, somewhat in the gospel style, feel slightly out of place.

Gee Ma, I Wanna Go Home

Traditional / 5:19

Vocals: Dolly Parton **Musicians:** Charlie Anderson, Jay Weaver: bass / Gary "Biscuit" Davis: banjo / Michael Davis, Paul Hollowell: piano / Robert Hale, Bruce Watkins, Kent Wells: acoustic guitar / Randy Kohrs: dobro / Jimmy Mattingly: fiddle, mandolin / Billy Thomas, Steve Turner: drums, percussion / Darrell Webb: mandolin / Kent Wells: electric guitar **Backing Vocals:** Monty Allen, Bob Bailey, Richard Dennison, Vicki Hampton, Steven Hill, Louis Nunley, Jennifer O'Brien, David Slater, Sheryl Thomas, Darrell Webb, Lynn Wright Backing Vocals Direction: Hannah Dennison **Recorded:** Two Monkeys Productions, Nashville, 2003

"Gee, Ma, I Want to Go Home" (or "I Don't Want No More of Army Life") is a traditional and humorous song, a kind of satire of life in the armed forces. Once again, the way Dolly sings it echoes some of the American war movies, with their valiant, tired, or embittered heroes. We can imagine that this arrangement with a country flavor was a natural choice, as the original already uses many of Dolly's style codes.

Whispering Hope

Jim Reeves / 2:30

Vocals: Dolly Parton **Backing Vocals:** Monty Allen, Bob Bailey, Richard Dennison, Vicki Hampton, Steven Hill, Louis Nunley, Jennifer O'Brien, David Slater, Sheryl Thomas, Darrell Webb, Lynn Wright Backing Vocals Direction: Hannah Dennison **Recorded:** Two Monkeys Productions, Nashville, 2003

This song of hope projects the listener into the middle of a church with a choir. Then Dolly's voice soars for a short moment before calling out to the listener. Once again, the general reverb seems almost too short for a church: It lacks a little space around the voices. As a result, when Dolly intervenes, the treatment of her singing is surprising, giving the impression of a kind of vocal collage.

Country, pop, glamour, and rock…Dolly at the Kodak Theater in Hollywood, during the 2003 Lifetime "Women Rock! Girls and Guitars" show.

trill of the pianist, give a jazzy color to the whole. The real strength of this arrangement lies in the depth and experience of the voices of the male choir: Their slow, warm vibrato evokes the Blind Boys of Alabama, a gospel group founded in 1939. For a final touch, a layer of slightly synthetic strings plays in the background. Dolly's speech at the end of the piece heralds the next one, a bluegrass number.

There Will Be Peace In The Valley For Me

Thomas A. Dorsey / 4:09

Vocals: Dolly Parton **Musicians:** Charlie Anderson, Jay Weaver: bass / Gary "Biscuit" Davis: banjo / Michael Davis, Paul Hollowell: piano, Hammond B3 / Robert Hale, Bruce Watkins, Kent Wells: acoustic guitar / Randy Kohrs: dobro / Jimmy Mattingly: fiddle, mandolin / Billy Thomas, Steve Turner: drums, percussion / Darrell Webb: mandolin / Kent Wells: electric guitar **Backing Vocals:** Monty Allen, Bob Bailey, Richard Dennison, Steven Hill, Louis Nunley, David Slater, Darrell Web Backing Vocals Direction: Hannah Dennison **Recorded:** Two Monkeys Productions, Nashville, 2003

This gospel song—one of the first to sell more than a million copies—was written in 1939 for the singer Mahalia Jackson. It was covered by Elvis Presley, who dedicated it to the Hungarian refugees fleeing the Russian invasion of their country in 1956. This ballad from the interwar period is updated here by Dolly and her musicians. The slow tempo supported by a drum on brushes, the harmony heightened by the richness of the chords of the rhythm guitar and the

Red, White And Bluegrass

Dolly Parton / 4:24

Vocals: Dolly Parton **Musicians:** Charlie Anderson, Jay Weaver: bass / Gary "Biscuit" Davis: banjo / Robert Hale, Bruce Watkins, Kent Wells: acoustic guitar / Randy Kohrs: dobro / Jimmy Mattingly: fiddle, mandolin / Billy Thomas, Steve Turner: drums, percussion / Darrell Webb: mandolin / Kent Wells: electric guitar **Backing Vocals:** Monty Allen, Bob Bailey, Richard Dennison, Vicki Hampton, Steven Hill, Louis Nunley, Jennifer O'Brien, David Slater, Sheryl Thomas, Darrell Webb, Lynn Wright Backing Vocals Direction: Hannah Dennison **Recorded:** Two Monkeys Productions, Nashville, 2003

This rather catchy song is a hymn to America, to what constitutes the essence of its inhabitants, in *red*, *white*, and *bluegrass*. It has all the instruments of a traditional bluegrass song, which are more or less the same as for country music (only the pedal steel guitar is missing). On the other hand, in this piece, the tempo is much faster and accelerates even more at the end, after a pause. This enables the musicians, especially the soloists on mandolin, banjo, and fiddle, to display the wonders of their technical skills to the listener.

My Country 'Tis

Samuel Francis Smith / 2:50

Vocals: Dolly Parton **Musicians:** Charlie Anderson, Jay Weaver: bass / Gary "Biscuit" Davis: banjo / Michael Davis, Paul Hollowell: piano, Hammond B3 / Robert Hale, Bruce Watkins, Kent Wells: acoustic guitar / Randy Kohrs: dobro / Jimmy Mattingly: fiddle, mandolin / Billy Thomas, Steve Turner: drums, percussion / Darrell Webb: mandolin / Kent Wells: electric guitar **Backing Vocals:** Monty Allen, Bob Bailey, Richard Dennison, Vicki Hampton, Steven Hill, Louis Nunley, Jennifer O'Brien, David Slater, Sheryl Thomas, Darrell Webb, Lynn Wright Backing Vocals Direction: Hannah Dennison **Recorded:** Two Monkeys Productions, Nashville, 2003

"America (My Country, 'Tis of Thee)" is an American patriotic song written by Samuel Francis Smith in the nineteenth century; in it, the melody of the British national anthem, "God Save the King," is recognizable. It was used as the national anthem in the United States before "The Star-Spangled Banner" was adopted as the official anthem in 1931. It has a singular arrangement, in particular the alternation of even bars for the intro and odd bars for the verse, before returning to even bars for the instrumental parts. Throughout the instrumental parts, the presence of a bell reminds us of Big Ben—no doubt a nod to the land of origin of this melody. On a high tempo, the banjo and the fiddle in particular have a significant flow. Two fiddles are played in overdub by the faithful Jimmy Mattingly. The process used, which is relatively common when there is only one musician, consists of recording the same part twice and inserting a take on each side of the mix.

I'm Gonna Miss You

Dolly Parton / 4:59

Vocals: Dolly Parton **Musicians:** Charlie Anderson, Jay Weaver: bass / Michael Davis, Paul Hollowell: piano, Hammond B3 / Robert Hale, Bruce Watkins, Kent Wells: acoustic guitar / Billy Thomas, Steve Turner: drums, percussion / Kent Wells: electric guitar **Backing Vocals:** Monty Allen, Bob Bailey, Richard Dennison, Vicki Hampton, Steven Hill, Louis Nunley, Jennifer O'Brien, David Slater, Sheryl Thomas, Darrell Webb, Lynn Wright Backing Vocals Direction: Hannah Dennison **Recorded:** Two Monkeys Productions, Nashville, 2003

The cry of love and despair of a woman who will never see her man again: This epic pop ballad has no particular point of interest, except that it is one of the only songs in this style in the album. However, always at ease in this type of register, Dolly delivers a vocal performance that could have propelled this track into the main theme of a blockbuster such as *Armageddon*, or any other feature film highlighting the patriotic heroism of a man.

Go To Hell

Dolly Parton / 6:49

Vocals: Dolly Parton **Musicians:** Charlie Anderson, Jay Weaver: bass / Gary "Biscuit" Davis: banjo / Michael Davis, Paul Hollowell: piano, Hammond B3 / Robert Hale, Bruce Watkins, Kent Wells: acoustic guitar / Billy Thomas, Steve Turner: drums, percussion / Darrell Webb: mandolin / Kent Wells: electric guitar **Backing Vocals:** Monty Allen, Bob Bailey, Richard Dennison, Vicki Hampton, Steven Hill, Louis Nunley, Jennifer O'Brien, David Slater, Sheryl Thomas, Darrell Webb, Lynn Wright Backing Vocals Direction: Hannah Dennison **Recorded:** Two Monkeys Productions, Nashville, 2003

Dolly discusses with Satan the destruction of what is good and beautiful in the world. After a long Hammond organ–voice intro in a gospel praise style, the beginning of the instrumental part of the second part of the song, from 1:43 to 1:47, is directly inspired by "I Wish" (1976) by Stevie Wonder. Then we start into a fast and energetic gospel. Next, from 3:45 to 4:45, Dolly comes back as a preacher for her faithful before resuming the chorus, which is rather explicit.

The Ballad Of The Green Beret

Barry A. Sadler, Robert L. Moore Jr. / 5:13

Vocals: Dolly Parton **Musicians:** Charlie Anderson, Jay Weaver: bass / Michael Davis, Paul Hollowell: piano / Robert Hale, Bruce Watkins, Kent Wells: acoustic guitar / Randy Kohrs: dobro / Jimmy Mattingly: fiddle / Billy Thomas, Steve Turner: drums, percussion / Kent Wells: electric guitar / (?) **Backing Vocals:** Monty Allen, Bob Bailey, Richard Dennison, Vicki Hampton, Steven Hill, Louis Nunley, Jennifer O'Brien, David Slater, Sheryl Thomas, Darrell Webb, Lynn Wright Backing Vocals Direction: Hannah Dennison **Recorded:** Two Monkeys Productions, Nashville, 2003

This popular song, written by a soldier during the Vietnam War in 1966, salutes those heroes who have fallen for their country. It has a strong symbolic dimension given the context of the time, when many singers of the hippie and folk movements, now immensely famous (such as Bob Dylan, Joan Baez, Peter, Paul and Mary), were opposed to this conflict. Note the contradiction with "When Johnny Comes Marching Home," which was inspired by a song for peace.

Brave Little Soldier

Dolly Parton / 4:25

Vocals: Dolly Parton **Musicians:** Charlie Anderson, Jay Weaver: bass / Michael Davis, Paul Hollowell: piano / Robert Hale, Bruce Watkins, Kent Wells: acoustic guitar / Billy Thomas, Steve Turner: drums, percussion / Jimmy Mattingly: fiddle / Darrell Webb: mandolin / Kent Wells: electric guitar **Backing Vocals:** Monty Allen, Bob Bailey, Richard Dennison, Vicki Hampton, Steven Hill, Louis Nunley, Jennifer O'Brien, Dolly Parton, David Slater, Sheryl Thomas, Darrell Webb, Lynn Wright Backing Vocals Direction: Hannah Dennison **Recorded:** Two Monkeys Productions, Nashville, 2003

Here Dolly praises the young soldier's courage in the face of danger by singing with a children's choir. While the snare drum dominates the instruments—reproducing the roll of military drums, its pattern even being taken up by the ensemble of singers in onomatopoeia—sounds of the metallophone, of the music box type, are contrasted with this warlike rhythm to evoke childhood. The lyrics, however, call for commitment. This piece full of paradoxes offers different levels of reading, notably in the context of a patriotic album. Dolly rerecorded it in 2017 for the album *I Believe in You*, which was dedicated to youth.

Tie A Yellow Ribbon

L. Russell Brown, Irwin Levine / 3:21

Vocals: Dolly Parton **Musicians:** Charlie Anderson, Jay Weaver: double bass / Gary "Biscuit" Davis: banjo / Robert Hale, Bruce Watkins, Kent Wells: acoustic guitar / Randy Kohrs: dobro / Jimmy Mattingly: fiddle, mandolin / Billy Thomas, Steve Turner: drums / Darrell Webb: mandolin / Kent Wells: electric guitar **Backing Vocals:** Monty Allen, Bob Bailey, Richard Dennison, Vicki Hampton, Steven Hill, Louis Nunley, Jennifer O'Brien, David Slater, Sheryl Thomas, Darrell Webb, Lynn Wright Backing Vocals Direction: Hannah Dennison **Recorded:** Two Monkeys Productions, Nashville, 2003

The protagonist wonders, after being away for three years as a prisoner of war, if his wife will still want him...If he is expected, then he will see a yellow ribbon around the tree in front of his house, according to tradition. The original version by Tony Orlando and Dawn, released in 1973, had a very sixties Motown feel. It was a great success. Dolly Parton covers it here in a country bluegrass style with guitar, banjo, mandolin, fiddle, dobro, double bass, and drums. The song is interspersed with solos by each instrument (except for the double bass and drums). The music, which is very cheerful, contrasts with the text, rather pessimistic about the return to the relationship of the demobilized soldier.

Color Me America

Dolly Parton / 3:54

Vocals: Dolly Parton **Musicians:** Charlie Anderson, Jay Weaver: bass / Michael Davis, Paul Hollowell: piano / Robert Hale, Bruce Watkins, Kent Wells: acoustic guitar / Jimmy Mattingly: fiddle, mandolin / Billy Thomas, Steve Turner: drums, percussion / Darrell Webb: mandolin / Kent Wells: electric guitar **Backing Vocals:** Monty Allen, Bob Bailey, Richard Dennison, Vicki Hampton, Steven Hill, Louis Nunley, Jennifer O'Brien, David Slater, Sheryl Thomas, Darrell Webb, Lynn Wright Backing Vocals Direction: Hannah Dennison **Recorded:** Two Monkeys Productions, Nashville, 2003

For this song, the songwriter uses a metaphor relating to the three colors of the American flag. It is the second epic ballad of the album, a little more rock sounding than "I'm Gonna Miss You," with saturated guitar parts. The mandolin playing, which adapts to all of Dolly's musical styles, fits perfectly here.

The Glory Forever

Traditional / 1:58

Vocals: Dolly Parton **Backing Vocals:** Monty Allen, Bob Bailey, Richard Dennison, Steven Hill, Louis Nunley, David Slater, Darrell Webb **Recorded:** Two Monkeys Productions, Nashville, 2003

Dolly Parton ends this album of eighteen songs—some of them quite military, others more spiritual, like this traditional gospel paean to the glory of God—with an a cappella number.

The album ends as it began, with a liturgical song in which Dolly is accompanied by a male choir—at the beginning and at the end only. Note that this song is in the same key as "The Lord Is My Shepherd"; these two psalms could have been linked together. Unlike "Whispering Hope," the length of the reverbs is quite consistent with the desired effect, simulating a church setting. The melody and the range of the backing vocals are reminiscent of the mysticism of Orthodox ritual chants. The harmonies, which are specific to the piece, are unusual for those unaccustomed to this type of music.

2003

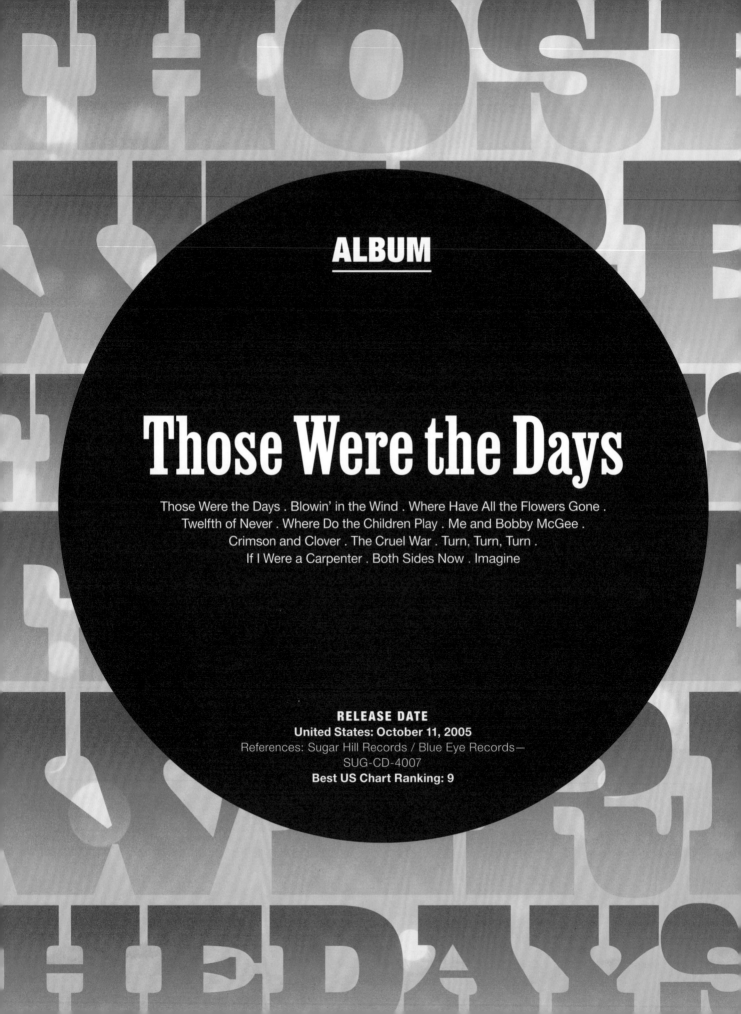

ALBUM

Those Were the Days

Those Were the Days . Blowin' in the Wind . Where Have All the Flowers Gone .
Twelfth of Never . Where Do the Children Play . Me and Bobby McGee .
Crimson and Clover . The Cruel War . Turn, Turn, Turn .
If I Were a Carpenter . Both Sides Now . Imagine

RELEASE DATE
United States: October 11, 2005
References: Sugar Hill Records / Blue Eye Records—
SUG-CD-4007
Best US Chart Ranking: 9

The Antiwar Album?

Those Were the Days is Dolly Parton's thirty-ninth solo album. Produced by the singer, it was released by Sugar Hill Records / Blue Eye Records on October 11, 2005. It reached number forty-eight on the Billboard 200 and number one on the OCC Country Artists Albums chart in the United Kingdom.

Nostalgia and Positioning

In 2005, Dolly Parton traveled throughout the country for her "Vintage Tour"; some dates were canceled due to the hurricanes that devastated Louisiana and destroyed parts of New Orleans and Texas. America was living through a period of contrasts, climatically and politically, between the second term of George W. Bush and the continuation of the Iraq War, as well as socially, with the abolition of the death penalty for those under eighteen by the Supreme Court and the recognition of same-sex marriage in California. When *Those Were the Days* was released, critics were divided: Some said it was one of Dolly Parton's best albums, some were less enthusiastic, while others wondered whether the songwriter was taking a stand against the war. It is sufficient to read the lyrics of these songs and to know the songwriter a little to conclude that she is indeed an activist for world peace.

Fruitful Years

Dolly does not skimp on resources or on guests (one to two per track)—we even find Porter Wagoner in the backing vocals, more than twenty years after their contract was ended. In total, twelve recording studios, forty musicians, and a technical team—almost as numerous—are involved. At that time, Wagoner was in great financial difficulty and Dolly, generous in friendship and not one to hold grudges, helped him out: Water had definitely flowed under the bridge between the former mentor and the star.[2]

Although music is of primary importance in the artist's life, it is not the only activity that keeps Dolly Parton busy. With 2.5 million visitors per season, Dollywood was expanding and the singer was investing in new attractions. On the eve of her sixtieth birthday, she was honored in many ways: She was one of five singers nominated for the CMA Best Female Vocalist of the Year Award. The prince of pop art, Andy Warhol, hung one of her portraits in his exhibition at the Bellagio Casino in Las Vegas. *Rolling Stone* magazine ranked her album *Coat of Many Colors* 299th in the top 500 albums of all time, and in 2004 she was honored by the US Library of Congress for her Imagination Library program against illiteracy.[2] The star turned superstar had the wind in her sails; she was now an icon, a voice, and a presence that could not be ignored.

Album Cover

Dennis Carney created this photograph in which, against a Flower Power–style background, Dolly is dressed as the perfect cowgirl (jeans, embroidered blouse, and long fringed bolero).

The Recording of This Album: A large number of musicians were involved in this opus, and individual track credits are not specified here: David Angell, Monisa Angell, David Davidson, Conni Ellisor, Jim Grosjean, Tom Howard, Jack Jezioro, Anthony Lamarchina, Carole Rabinowitz, Pam Sixfin, Alan Umstead, Catherine Umstead, Mary Kathryn Vanosdale: strings / Sam Bush, Danny Roberts, Chris Thile: mandolin / Richard Dennison: toy piano, Hammond B3, Wurlitzer / Stuart Duncan, Jimmy Mattingly: fiddle / Terry Eldredge, Yusuf Islam, Tony Rice, Brian Sutton, Kent Wells: acoustic guitar / David Foster, Paul Hollowell: piano / Dave Fowler, Terry Smith, Jay Weaver: bass / Andy Hall: dobro, harp / Jim Hoke: harmonica / Tommy James , Roger McGuinn, Kent Wells: electric guitar / Viktor Krauss: bowed double bass / Bob Mater: drums, percussion / Tony Smith: percussion / Joey Smith: accordion / David Talbot: banjo / Ilya Toshinsky: dulcimer, mandolaika, banjo / Dr. Ming Wang: erhu / Kent Wells: twelve-string guitar, six-string bass.

The sessions took place in 2004 and 2005 at: Two Monkeys Productions, the Tracking Room at Masterfonics, Ocean Way, Minutiae Studio, Nashville / Stir Studio, Cardiff, UK / Dollywood's Celebrity Theater, Pigeon Forge, Tennessee / Avatar Studios, Sound on Sound Recording, New York / Kensal Town Studio D, London / No Can Beat Studios, Hana, Hawaii / Taylor Made Studios, North Caldwell, New Jersey / Chartmaker Studios, Los Angeles.

In English-speaking countries, the most popular version of "Those Were the Days" is by Mary Hopkin (here in 1968), present on Dolly's version for some vocal harmonies.

The mandolaika is an instrument that is the result of a cross between the mandolin and the balalaika, which is very popular in Russia, and the erhu, a traditional Chinese musical instrument with bowed strings.

2005

Those Were The Days

Boris Fomin, Gene Raskin / 5:00

Vocals: Dolly Parton **Special Guests:** Mary Hopkin, The Moscow Circus **Backing Vocals:** Porter Wagoner and the Opry Gang **Technical Team:** Producer: Dolly Parton / Artistic Direction: Steve Buckingham / Sound Engineers: Matt Boynton, Steve Davis, Neil DeVor, Patrick Murphy, Gary Paczosa, Kelly Pribble, Alan Silverman, Glenn M. Taylor, Reed Taylor, J. Carter Tutwiler / Mixing: Benny Quinn

The return of Porter Wagoner, on backing vocals with the Opry Gang, the mainstay of the weekly *Grand Ole Opry* country radio show, is enough in itself to make this a distinctive song. The narrator observes with tenderness, and some regret, the time that has passed, her youth gone, giving way to a more mature and lonely woman. We also hear laughter and bar noises, and the Moscow Circus contributes a Slavic note between joy and nostalgia. Has anyone never hummed this melody? The music was composed by Boris Fomin, originally with the Russian words of the poet Konstantin Podrevsky, then with Gene Raskin's English lyrics, and this tune has been around the world a hundred times since. In English-speaking countries, the most popular version of this Russian classic is surely the one by singer Mary Hopkin, produced at the time by Paul McCartney himself, who is present here for some vocal harmonies. To complete the friendly atmosphere that reigns on this track, Dolly and Steve Buckingham do not hesitate to bring out the heavy artillery: mandolin, accordion, fiddle, banjo, dobro, string ensemble, and everything that clatters, vibrates, and brings warmth and joy.

Blowin' In The Wind

Bob Dylan / 3:21

Vocals: Dolly Parton **Special Guest:** Nickel Creek **Backing Vocals:** Richard Dennison, Terry Eldredge, Andy Hall, Vicki Hampton, Jamie Johnson, Jennifer O'Brien, Danny Roberts, David Talbot, Chuck Tilley, Kent Wells **Technical Team:** Producer: Dolly Parton / Artistic Direction: Steve Buckingham / Sound Engineers: Matt Boynton, Steve Davis, Neil DeVor, Patrick Murphy, Gary Paczosa, Kelly Pribble, Alan Silverman, Glenn M. Taylor, Reed Taylor, J. Carter Tutwiler / Mixing: Benny Quinn

The protest song par excellence, humanist and poetic, "Blowin' in the Wind" was written in 1962 in ten minutes by Bob Dylan, after a political discussion in a bar. Dolly is very comfortable with this song and joins the long list of artists who have covered it. (Dylan himself declined her invitation to participate in this cover.) Jim Hoke opens the proceedings on harmonica over acoustic guitar picking and some mandolin arpeggios delicately laid down by the young prodigy Chris Thile, member of Nickel Creek, the folk-bluegrass sensation of the time, here as a special guest. The presence of the band brings a breath of fresh air to this folk classic. Their voices blend wonderfully with Dolly's, the mandolin twirls, and Sara Watkins's fiddle gracefully flies over this eternal melody. An airy and optimistic version.

For the interpretation of "Where Have All the Flowers Gone," Dolly enlists the services of the singer and songwriter Lee Ann Womack.

Where Have All The Flowers Gone

Pete Seeger / 4:04

Vocals: Dolly Parton **Special Guests:** Norah Jones, Lee Ann Womack **Backing Vocals:** Richard Dennison, Terry Eldredge, Andy Hall, Vicki Hampton, Jamie Johnson, Jennifer O'Brien, Danny Roberts, David Talbot, Chuck Tilley, Kent Wells **Technical Team:** Producer: Dolly Parton / Artistic Direction: Steve Buckingham / Sound Engineers: Matt Boynton, Steve Davis, Neil DeVor, Patrick Murphy, Gary Paczosa, Kelly Pribble, Alan Silverman, Glenn M. Taylor, Reed Taylor, J. Carter Tutwiler / Mixing: Benny Quinn

Dolly sings this song with a kind of vulnerability in her voice. Flowers grow and are picked by girls who marry. Then their men go off to fight and die; it is time to lay flowers on the graves. The wheel of time spins relentlessly for the men who go to war and the women who become widows. To interpret this classic by Pete Seeger, the father of the American folk revival of the 1960s, Dolly enlists the services of singers and songwriters Norah Jones and Lee Ann Womack on vocal harmonies. The result is reminiscent of the prowess of the *Trio* group (Dolly Parton, Emmylou Harris, and Linda Ronstadt). After an introduction with an almost solemn depth to it, the orchestration and its very cinematographic strings arrangements provide a velvety setting for the three singers, Dolly, Norah, and Lee Ann, to unfold their seemingly effortless, sumptuous harmonies. A total success.

The Twelfth Of Never

Lisa Lee Reagan, Emily Bree Stevenson / 3:16

Vocals: Dolly Parton **Special Guest:** Keith Urban **Backing Vocals:** Richard Dennison, Terry Eldredge, Andy Hall, Vicki Hampton, Jamie Johnson, Jennifer O'Brien, Danny Roberts, David Talbot, Chuck Tilley, Kent Wells **Technical Team:** Producer: Dolly Parton / Artistic Direction: Steve Buckingham / Sound Engineers: Matt Boynton, Steve Davis, Neil DeVor, Patrick Murphy, Gary Paczosa, Kelly Pribble, Alan Silverman, Glenn M. Taylor, Reed Taylor, J. Carter Tutwiler / Mixing: Benny Quinn

A love song in duet with Australian country singer and guitarist Keith Urban. "Twelfth of Never" is first of all a popular expression that means that something will never happen. It evokes here the impossible disappearance of the narrator's love for someone else. The voices of Keith Urban and Dolly Parton are perfectly matched—one would swear that these two had spent their lives singing together. The band, made up of the most experienced country musicians of the day, rolls out the red carpet for them. This demonstration of restrained virtuosity enables the duo to vocalize freely on this country-bluegrass song that seemingly nothing could stop. At the end of the song, Keith Urban can be heard saying, "You give me chills, Dolly," and it's easy to see why. Dolly responds with her legendary childlike laughter, happy that the magic has worked once again.

Where Do The Children Play

Cat Stevens / 3:23

Vocals: Dolly Parton **Special Guest:** Yusuf Islam **Backing Vocals:** Richard Dennison, Terry Eldredge, Andy Hall, Vicki Hampton, Jamie Johnson, Jennifer O'Brien, Danny Roberts, David Talbot, Chuck Tilley, Kent Wells **Technical Team:** Producer: Dolly Parton / Artistic Direction: Steve Buckingham / Sound Engineers: Matt Boynton, Steve Davis, Neil DeVor, Patrick Murphy, Gary Paczosa, Kelly Pribble, Alan Silverman, Glenn M. Taylor, Reed Taylor, J. Carter Tutwiler / Mixing: Benny Quinn

Cat Stevens, who became Yusuf Islam upon his conversion to the Muslim faith, plays acoustic guitar for this song, which he wrote in 1970. By evoking the concrete playgrounds where children play, the lyrics denounce the long road of technological progress, paved by the destruction of our environment. This midtempo track features a rhythm section, as if to give the guest of honor a better opportunity to lay down his characteristic strumming, which is so direct and staccato. Dolly, who sings here in her lower register, seems to take a mischievous pleasure in imitating the fast and recognizable vibrato of Yusuf Islam's voice—their voices have at least two things in common, the energy and the tight vibrato. The dobro, fiddle, folk guitar, and backing vocals share the main theme, which is picked up in the high notes by the piano at the end of the song. At the beginning of the second verse, mandolin and acoustic guitar knit happily in the upper register. Then, from 1:34, the strings arrangements bring breadth and depth. To underline the point, a children's choir joins the party.

Me And Bobby McGee

Kris Kristofferson, Fred Foster / 3:49

Vocals: Dolly Parton **Special Guest:** Kris Kristofferson **Backing Vocals:** Richard Dennison, Terry Eldredge, Andy Hall, Vicki Hampton, Jamie Johnson, Jennifer O'Brien, Danny Roberts, David Talbot, Chuck Tilley, Kent Wells **Technical Team:** Producer: Dolly Parton / Artistic Direction: Steve Buckingham / Sound Engineers: Matt Boynton, Steve Davis, Neil DeVor, Patrick Murphy, Gary Paczosa, Kelly Pribble, Alan Silverman, Glenn M. Taylor, Reed Taylor, J. Carter Tutwiler / Mixing: Benny Quinn

The most famous version of this song, about freedom made in the USA, is probably the one that Janis Joplin recorded in 1971, the day before she died. Joplin sang it as if McGee were a man—unlike singer-songwriter and actor Kris Kristofferson, who sang it as a woman. Dolly Parton chose the male version, evoking the friend—or lover—with whom the narrator undertakes a road trip. Even though "Me and Bobby McGee" is undoubtedly the most country-folk song in her repertoire, Janis Joplin's style, much more rooted in blues and rock, is rather different from that of the Queen of Country. The arrangement she provides here with Steve Buckingham is logically closer to the original version than to Janis's. Moreover, with Kris Kristofferson as a guest singer on the chorus, this direction seemed to be obvious. However, Dolly allows herself some rugged and energetic vocals that we sense were inspired by the inimitable Janis's version, and it is convincing. From the intro, Jim Hoke's bluesy phrasing on harmonica propels the listener to the banks of the Mississippi, and the acoustic guitar sets off on a devilishly groovy strumming, impeccably supported by the rhythm section from 0:59 onward. The dobro strokes reinforce the blues aspect, the banjo brings a touch of mountain music, and the fiddle sprinkles the whole with a pinch of country-bluegrass. The quality of the sound recording and the dynamics of each instrument are beautifully preserved in the mix.

Crimson And Clover

Tommy James, Peter P. Lucia / 3:39

Vocals: Dolly Parton **Special Guest:** Tommy James **Backing Vocals:** Richard Dennison, Terry Eldredge, Andy Hall, Vicki Hampton, Jamie Johnson, Jennifer O'Brien, Danny Roberts, David Talbot, Chuck Tilley, Kent Wells **Technical Team:** Producer: Dolly Parton / Artistic Direction: Steve Buckingham / Sound Engineers: Matt Boynton, Steve Davis, Neil DeVor, Patrick Murphy, Gary Paczosa, Kelly Pribble, Alan Silverman, Glenn M. Taylor, Reed Taylor, J. Carter Tutwiler / Mixing: Benny Quinn

When a feeling in love could turn into a beautiful story... It is said that the title "Crimson and Clover" came first, before the song was even written. As Tommy James was waking up, he paired his favorite color, crimson red, with his favorite flower, the shamrock—"incarnate" shamrock trefoil, as it is known in Europe. This 1960s classic, originally recorded by Tommy James and the Shondells in 1968, was first revived by Joan Jett and the Blackhearts in 1981. Invited by Dolly to sing the harmonies, Tommy James surprises immediately with the clarity of his tone, identical in every way to what was his trademark during the Shondells' era: a pop tenor voice, clear and supple, capable of going from sensual ballads to rock or the most energetic rhythm 'n' blues. Despite this new arrangement—which gives pride of place to acoustic instruments—the main riff, so simple and identifiable, is respected until 1:21, where the song starts on a typically country tempo until 1:44, then time for a fiddle solo supported notably by a banjo rhythm in clawhammer mode. We then return to the original tempo until 2:30, when the musicians suddenly launch into a show of force, a real bluegrass explosion, until 3:11, ending gently with a final chorus in decrescendo. Dolly Parton, Steve Buckingham, and the whole team of virtuoso session men have clearly decided to show us all the colors...and it works very well!

The Cruel War

Traditional / 3:42

Vocals and Arrangement: Dolly Parton. **Special Guests:** Alison Krauss, Mindy Smith, Dan Tyminski **Backing Vocals:** Richard Dennison, Terry Eldredge, Andy Hall, Vicki Hampton, Jamie Johnson, Jennifer O'Brien, Danny Roberts, David Talbot, Chuck Tilley, Kent Wells **Technical Team:** Producer: Dolly Parton / Artistic Direction: Steve Buckingham / Sound Engineers: Matt Boynton, Steve Davis, Neil DeVor, Patrick Murphy, Gary Paczosa, Kelly Pribble, Alan Silverman, Glenn M. Taylor, Reed Taylor, J. Carter Tutwiler / Mixing: Benny Quinn

Dating from the Civil War and perhaps even earlier, this song is about a woman who refuses to lose her true love and offers to wear the military uniform to accompany him onto the battlefield. This is the most stripped-down arrangement on the album: arpeggiated acoustic guitar playing that borders on high art, two fiddles, sublime backing vocals by Alison Krauss, Mindy Smith, and Dan Tyminski as special guests, and a marching rhythm played on the snare drum that makes its entrance at 2:25 to illustrate the lyrics "So we marched into battle..." Close to perfection.

Turn, Turn, Turn

Pete Seeger / 3:17

Vocals: Dolly Parton **Special Guest:** Roger McGuinn **Backing Vocals:** Richard Dennison, Terry Eldredge, Andy Hall, Vicki Hampton, Jamie Johnson, Jennifer O'Brien, Danny Roberts, David Talbot, Chuck Tilley, Kent Wells **Technical Team:** Producer: Dolly Parton / Artistic Direction: Steve Buckingham / Sound Engineers: Matt Boynton, Steve Davis, Neil DeVor, Patrick Murphy, Gary Paczosa, Kelly Pribble, Alan Silverman, Glenn M. Taylor, Reed Taylor, J. Carter Tutwiler / Mixing: Benny Quinn

Ever since the book of Ecclesiastes was first written, this plea for peace and tolerance has known many interpreters. After having covered this great classic on her 1984 album *The Great Pretender*, in a version marked by the sound and production techniques of the 1980s, Dolly takes it up again with the American composer, singer, and guitarist Roger McGuinn. We return here to a version closer to that of the Byrds, and the presence of McGuinn on the backing vocals obliges. The arrangement, very folk-bluegrass at the beginning, soon assumes an almost theatrical dimension, which evokes the excesses of certain Broadway shows. Dolly's powerful voice and the choir, whose ranks swell until the end of the piece, are largely responsible for this. As a hat tip to Pete Seeger and Roger McGuinn, this big production pays tribute to this song, one of the standards of the sixties spirit.

If I Were A Carpenter

James Timothy Hardin / 2:54

Vocals: Dolly Parton **Special Guest:** Joe Nichols **Backing Vocals:** Richard Dennison, Terry Eldredge, Andy Hall, Vicki Hampton, Jamie Johnson, Jennifer O'Brien, Danny Roberts, David Talbot, Chuck Tilley, Kent Wells **Technical Team:** Producer: Dolly Parton / Artistic Direction: Steve Buckingham / Sound Engineers: Matt Boynton, Steve Davis, Neil DeVor, Patrick Murphy, Gary Paczosa, Kelly Pribble, Alan Silverman, Glenn M. Taylor, Reed Taylor, J. Carter Tutwiler / Mixing: Benny Quinn

A man asks a woman if she would still love him enough to marry him if he were just a carpenter. Folk musician and composer Tim Hardin performed this song (solo, guitar, and vocals), which was totally in tune with the times, during the legendary Woodstock festival in 1969, in a version that left a lasting impression. To sing with her this classic among classics, many times covered (by Bobby Darin in 1966, the Four Tops in 1967, Johnny Cash in 1970, Robert Plant in 1993, and so many others), there is no doubt that Dolly Parton would have called upon Hardin himself if he had still been around. Instead, she invites a rising but already confident star of modern country music: Joe Nichols. Between them, they deliver a country version solidly anchored in the Nashville sound of the 2000s.

Dolly Parton in concert at the Gwinnett Center in Duluth, Georgia, November 25, 2005.

Both Sides Now

Joni Mitchell / 3:33

Vocals: Dolly Parton **Special Guests:** Judy Collins, Rhonda Vincent **Backing Vocals:** Richard Dennison, Terry Eldredge, Andy Hall, Vicki Hampton, Jamie Johnson, Jennifer O'Brien, Danny Roberts, David Talbot, Chuck Tilley, Kent Wells **Technical Team:** Producer: Dolly Parton / Artistic Direction: Steve Buckingham / Sound Engineers: Matt Boynton, Steve Davis, Neil DeVor, Patrick Murphy, Gary Paczosa, Kelly Pribble, Alan Silverman, Glenn M. Taylor, Reed Taylor, J. Carter Tutwiler / Mixing: Benny Quinn

The inspiration came to Joni Mitchell during a plane trip, from the novel *Henderson the Rain King* by Saul Bellow. A strange play of mirrors: After reading a passage where the character in the book, also in a plane but on his way to Africa, gets lost in the clouds, Mitchell put down her book, looked at the sky, and wrote "Both Sides Now" in one go. This poetic song is perfect for Dolly Parton, because it describes two ways of looking at things: a romantic way and a realistic way, because everything, even love, has two sides. To give a new setting to this other emblematic song of the sixties, Dolly and Steve Buckingham start on an up-tempo bluegrass arrangement without compromise. No doubt, this very clear-cut choice was motivated by the idea of distinguishing themselves from the existing versions, already innumerable at the time. As special guests, Dolly welcomes the great folk musician Judy Collins—the first to record this classic in 1968, a year before Joni Mitchell decided to include it on her album *Clouds*—as well as fellow bluegrass musician Rhonda Vincent on vocal harmonies.

Imagine

John Lennon / 3:52

Vocals: Dolly Parton **Special Guest:** David Foster **Backing Vocals:** Richard Dennison, Terry Eldredge, Andy Hall, Vicki Hampton, Jamie Johnson, Jennifer O'Brien, Danny Roberts, David Talbot, Chuck Tilley, Kent Wells **Technical Team:** Producer: Dolly Parton / Artistic Direction: Steve Buckingham / Sound Engineers: Matt Boynton, Steve Davis, Neil DeVor, Patrick Murphy, Gary Paczosa, Kelly Pribble, Alan Silverman, Glenn M. Taylor, Reed Taylor, J. Carter Tutwiler / Mixing: Benny Quinn

In a duet with the Canadian singer, producer, and musician David Foster, the star covers John Lennon's huge hit, which was inspired by his wife, Yoko Ono, who has since been credited as co-writer. The song, whose lyrics are universal in their ideal vision of a human society without war, without borders, and without religion, was released as a preview on iTunes on September 27, 2005. Images of Lennon's house were included in the clip, shot in New York and broadcast on the CMT website and on *CMT Hot 20 Countdown*. After a very cinematic orchestral intro, the arrangement slowly builds up: first the piano, emblematic and inseparable from "Imagine," and the discreet acoustic guitar, then the mandolin and the fiddle. This is followed by the rhythm section and the choir, and then the song takes a step up with the arrival of the dobro and David Foster's voice at 1:53, until the return of the lush string ensemble. The piece ends on a climax in the form of a final bouquet. Dolly definitely likes to finish her albums in style.

For the 2005 film *Transamerica*, a road movie by director Duncan Tucker about a transgender woman, Dolly wrote and performed "Travelin' Thru," which was nominated four times for Best Song—Academy Awards, Grammy Awards, Golden Globes, and Broadcast Film Critics Association.

Dolly, Actress and Producer: Four Decades on the Small Screen and the Big Screen

At the end of the 1970s, the Queen of Country was simultaneously courting a pop audience and the Hollywood studios. It was with *9 to 5*, a comedy about the work world directed by Colin Higgins and co-starring Jane Fonda and Lily Tomlin, that Dolly made her debut on the big screen. The following panorama explores the main stages of more than forty years of her career as an actress and a producer. Dolly fascinates, and the cinema had no choice but to pick up on her iconic dimension.

Born to Embody Her Image

In 1980, when *9 to 5* was released, the critics were unanimous: Dolly Parton was a born actress. Yet she had never trained as an actress and had never been an extra. Her big dream? To be a world-famous singer and songwriter. Becoming an actress was just the icing on the cake, helping to increase her influence in showbiz and the entertainment industry. True to form, Dolly gave a thousand percent and took an interest in all aspects of film and television production. Over the course of four decades, she has acted, composed and written, and acted as a producer or coproducer... and sometimes even cooked for the crew. The roles she chooses are quite close to her public personality. When she is not playing a singer or a guardian angel, as in the musical *Christmas on the Square* (2020), which she coproduced for Netflix, the star appears on-screen as Dolly Parton. Beauty, love and faith, dreams, and a touch of magic, not to mention music, are the elements that visibly guide her choices in fiction. In 2022, the documentary *Still Working 9 to 5*, directed by Camille Hardman and Gary Lane, comes full circle by revisiting and questioning the impact of this film on society.

Between Drama and Comedy

Dolly Parton has acted mostly in musicals, both light and dramatic. In *9 to 5*, she was Doralee Rhodes, a voluptuous secretary determined to settle her account with her tyrannical boss; in *The Best Little Whorehouse in Texas* (1982), she played a brothel keeper and the lover of the sheriff. Produced by her company Sandollar, *Wild Texas Wind* (1991) tells the story of a singer struggling with her alcoholic manager. The human dimension is as important as the respect for all women, because the subtext of these comedies is the condition of women—as is also the case in *Steel Magnolias* (1989), which tells the story of several inhabitants of a small town in Louisiana through their meetings and conversations in a beauty salon. The TV movie *Blue Valley Songbird* (1999), which Dolly produced herself, is an opportunity to address the issue of domestic violence—a theme that recurs in her songs: The public discovers her as a singer abused by her lover and manager. In *Rhinestone*, another musical film, she is Jake, a talented country singer who boasts that she can make a star out of anyone. In this case, however, the audience did not buy into her so much, as *Rocky* fans probably found it difficult to see Sylvester Stallone as Nick Martinelli, a country singer coached by Jake-Dolly. In *Straight Talk* (1992), Dolly plays a dance teacher who, after various adventures, becomes a radio host—she wrote ten songs for the soundtrack. In 2012, she costarred with singer, rapper, and actress Queen Latifah in *Joyful Noise*, about the trials and tribulations of a choir competing to bring hope to their community. In all, Dolly has appeared in more than a dozen films and numerous dramas and sitcoms, including the Fox sitcom *Babes* (1991) and the *Simpsons* episode "Sunday, Cruddy Sunday." Passionate and inquisitive, she tries her hand at several genres but, on the whole, her roles are consistent and correspond to her... Can we imagine her playing a serial killer?

Dolly in Season 1 of *Dolly Parton's Heartstrings*, airing on Netflix in 2019.

Dolly and Netflix: The Art of Being Popular

The *Dolly Parton's Heartstrings* series (2019), for which Dolly is a coproducer, a host, an actress, and a singer, is perhaps one of the most emblematically illustrative projects of the way her creativity is organized. The songs become dramas that refer to the songs but also to her own story. As such, *Heartstrings* is a pure distillation of the star's multiple talents and interests—from coproducing to hosting, from writing to her presence as an actress and a singer. The documentary *Dolly Parton: Here I Am* (2019), directed by Francis Whately and also on Netflix, traces much of the iconic songwriter's life and career. In fact, simply looking at all of the productions, films, TV movies, and documentaries is sufficient to discover how Dolly Parton has a special talent for reusing her creations. As with the important themes of her songs, she picks up again and again on material already explored, always taking it further.

Symbol and Foil

There are several productions where, despite her absence, the star is nevertheless at the heart of the film. In *The Year Dolly Parton Was My Mom* (2011), directed by Tara Johns, she serves as the main thread in a young girl's search for herself upon learning that she is adopted. Released in 2020, *Dumplin'* tells the story of a teenage Dolly fan who mourns her aunt, falls in love, battles with her mother and, most important, her weight issues before entering a beauty pageant. This sensitive film deals with appearance and image, rejection and acceptance, subjects dear to the songwriter. On closer inspection, however, it must be said that Dolly Parton is not a great actress, and some of the films in which she has appeared have not always been well received. Nevertheless, in terms of popularity, as a role model and symbol, her imprint through drama is a measure of the breadth and depth of the impact the songwriter has had on several generations of filmmakers and audiences.

ALBUM

Backwoods Barbie

Better Get to Livin' . Made of Stone . Drives Me Crazy . Backwoods Barbie .
Jesus & Gravity . Only Dreamin' . The Tracks of My Tears . The Lonesomes . Cologne .
Shinola . I Will Forever Hate Roses . Somebody's Everything

RELEASE DATE
United States: February 26, 2008
Reference: Dolly Records, Nashville (TN)—DP925
Best US Chart Ranking: 2

Barbie Blues

Backwoods Barbie is Dolly Parton's fortieth solo album, produced by her and released on February 26, 2008, under her newly launched label, Dolly Records. The album reached number seventeen on the Billboard 200. Of the twelve songs included on the album, Dolly wrote seven, one of which was co-written with guitarist and producer Kent Wells. The other songs on the album are covers.

A Consecration and a World in Turmoil

After the release of her album *Those Were the Days* in 2005, the star celebrated her sixtieth birthday in 2006 and received a prestigious Kennedy Center Honor, which celebrates the best artists. Along with Dolly, four other major artists were honored: the British composer of the musical *Cats*, Andrew Lloyd Webber; the American director Steven Spielberg; the Indian conductor Zubin Mehta; and the American singer and composer Smokey Robinson. This was a key moment in Dolly's artistic life, as she never forgot that she came from the mountains of deep Tennessee. The award ceremony was held in the company of friends: Steve Buckingham; Alison Krauss, who performed "Jolene"; and Kenny Rogers, who sang "Islands in the Stream" as a duet with singer and actress Carrie Underwood. This evening was a real break in the midst of a whirlwind of concerts, business meetings, and TV and radio interviews that made up Dolly's daily life. In 2006 and 2007, Dolly went on tour with "An Evening with Dolly Parton," part of which took her to Europe (Great Britain, the Netherlands, Sweden), where her fans are numerous.

In 2008, the election of Barack Obama was a sign of change for the world, even as the American car industry was struggling and the Bernie Madoff fraud case was rocking the financial system, which was in crisis throughout the world.

A Fairy Story

In 2008, Dolly created her own label, Dolly Records, under which she released her new album, which included different bonus tracks depending on which store was selling the album: Best Buy, Target, Walmart, iTunes, or the Cracker Barrel, which sold a collector's edition. The *Backwoods Barbie* tour was scheduled: sixty-four concert dates, including seventeen in Europe, between March and November.

When the idea of the album first came to her, Dolly Parton had wanted to include "I Dreamed About Elvis," which she sang during her 2004 tour, the "Hello, I'm Dolly Tour." She also told the press her next album would be titled *Country Is as Country Does*, and that she had written the title track with her friend Mac Davis. Although her plans for the album changed, the song "Country Is as Country Does" was eventually released on the album *Better Day* in 2011.

Now in her sixties, Dolly was radiant and working on writing the musical adaptation of the 1980 film *9 to 5*. One thing is for sure—the star had never been busier, following the advice she often gave to others, and which she writes in the song that opened this album: "Better Get to Livin'"!

Album Cover

With its vivid yellow and pink tones, the immersion into the world of Barbie is obvious: Dolly, in a leopard-print negligee and pink taffeta housecoat, is wearing a dizzying wig. With legs that look abnormally long, she poses half recumbent on bales of hay in the back of a pickup truck. The message is clear: She may come from the countryside, may be undeniably outrageous, but we cannot reduce her to this image. While our pop culture superstar had suffered from the racy and misleading publications of the tabloids, she also knew how to play skillfully with her image. Inside the album, one shot shows a close-up of a tire flap on the Tennessee truck, where a silhouette appears of Dolly as a pinup figure with a hat on her head; another shows Dolly as a sophisticated farm girl, leaning against the door of her cabin; and another captures her smiling, at the wheel. These pictures are the work of photographer and contemporary artist Kii Arens.

For Dolly Addicts

On March 25, 2007, before her sold-out concert at Wembley, Dolly unveiled her handprints printed on a bronze plaque in Wembley Park's Square of Fame (UK).

All dressed in pink, Dolly Parton in concert at the National Indoor Arena in Birmingham, UK, July 2, 2008.

Better Get To Livin'

Dolly Parton, Kent Wells / 3:36

Musicians: Bryan Sutton, Kent Wells: acoustic guitar / Steve Mackey: bass / Lonnie Wilson: drums, percussion / Jerry McPherson, Kent Wells: electric guitar / Jimmy Mattingly: fiddle, mandolin / Dave Talbot: banjo / Paul Hollowell: piano / Paul Franklin: pedal steel guitar **Vocals:** Dolly Parton **Backing Vocals:** Rebecca Isaacs Bowman, Richard Dennison, Vicki Hampton, Sonya Isaacs, Jennifer O'Brien **Recorded:** Blackbird Studio A, Nashville (TN) **Technical Team:** Producers: Dolly Parton, Kent Wells / Sound Engineers: Ben "Snake" Schmitt, Brian Willis, Kyle Dickinson, Allen Ditto, Patrick Murphy / Mixing: Justin Niebank / Mastering: Jim DeMain, Alex McCullough **Single:** Better Get to Livin' **Release:** Dolly Records, August 28, 2007 (CD ref.:?) **Released:** iTunes, August 28, 2007 (ref:?) **Highest US Chart Ranking:** 48

Dolly gives us the key to a happy life: Love it; smile at it, even when it goes wrong; forgive it; and above all "live" against all odds. In the music video clip, shot in a carnival atmosphere (the star even dresses up as a horsewoman), Dolly tries to cheer up a friend.

The video for "Better Get to Livin'," directed by Steve Lippman, was shot on a farm near Pigeon Forge, TN, and posted on CMT and the CMT Top 20 Countdown. The one for "Backwoods Barbie," directed by Trey Fanjoy, shows Dolly, all dressed in pink, crossing Hollywood Boulevard. This was aired on CMT.

After her bluegrass trilogy and some rather folk albums, *Backwoods Barbie* signifies a change in direction, a return to pop. The star probably wants to mark the occasion of the launch of her label Dolly Records. With a very rock sound, the bass drum has a lot of attack and little bass. The snare drum slams, very compressed and probably triggered—that is, doubled by a sample in order to thicken the sound and enhance each impact. Mandolin, fiddle, and pedal steel guitar are the sure values of the piece. Yet, held by the legend that is Paul Franklin, the pedal steel parts full of overdrive blend perfectly into this modern arrangement and naturally find their place between the two other electric guitars and the two folk guitars. The distinctive sound of the steel bar sliding across the strings makes it easy to identify.

In this song designed to be widely broadcast on radio and television, all the codes of the hit are there: structure, duration, median tempo, catchy melody, catchy chorus.

Made Of Stone

Dolly Parton / 4:14

Musicians: Biff Watson: acoustic guitar / Mike Brignardello: bass / Steve Turner: drums, percussion / Tom Bukovac, Kent Wells: electric guitar / Jimmy Mattingly: fiddle, mandolin / Paul Hollowell: piano / Paul Franklin: pedal steel guitar **Vocals:** Dolly Parton **Backing Vocals:** Dolly Parton, Richard Dennison, Vicki Hampton, Jennifer O'Brien **Recorded:** Blackbird Studio A, Nashville (TN) **Technical Team:** Producers: Dolly Parton, Kent Wells / Sound Engineers: Ben "Snake" Schmitt, Brian Willis, Kyle Dickinson, Allen Ditto, Patrick Murphy / Mixing: Justin Niebank / Mastering: Jim DeMain, Alex McCullough

In this Dolly classic about men's infidelity, the wife, despite her humiliation and immense sorrow, does not manage to leave, because she obviously does not have a heart of stone. At the crossroads between pop rock and country, this ballad gathers all the instruments of the latter: folk and electric guitars, mandolin, fiddle, piano, but with saturated sounds for the guitars, very present, and a drumming rather characteristic of the former. In her performance, Dolly shows a range of emotions from vulnerability to compassion. The reverb effects applied to her voice and the snare drum come at the right time, giving a little air to the mix.

Drives Me Crazy

Roland Gift, David Steele / 4:14

Musicians: Bryan Sutton: acoustic guitar / Dave Talbot: banjo / Steve Mackey: bass / Lonnie Wilson: drums, percussion / Jerry McPherson, Kent Wells: electric guitar / Jimmy Mattingly: fiddle, mandolin / Paul Hollowell: piano / Paul Franklin: pedal steel guitar **Vocals:** Dolly Parton **Backing Vocals:** Alecia Nugent, Carl Jackson, Dolly Parton **Recorded:** Blackbird Studio A, Nashville (TN) **Technical Team:** Producers: Dolly Parton, Kent Wells / Sound Engineers: Ben "Snake" Schmitt, Brian Willis, Kyle Dickinson, Allen Ditto, Patrick Murphy / Mixing: Justin Niebank / Mastering: Jim DeMain, Alex McCullough **Single:** Drives Me Crazy **Release:** Dolly Records, January 12, 2009 (CD ref.:?)

This catchy cover of the hit by the English band Fine Young Cannibals released in 1989 on the album *The Raw and the Cooked* explains that desire and love drive you crazy. Dolly Parton does an efficient and creative job of creating this mix. On the guitar, there is no question of reproducing the British sound of the 1980s: Dolly and Kent Wells opt for an assertive FM rock sound. This more raw approach is particularly noticeable on the choruses with the use of power chords (chords with two tones: the tonic and fifth) from the electric guitar with a thick and compact saturation. The drum sounds are the same as in "Better Get to Livin'." The snare drum remains a little kitsch, with a resonance that carries a lot of harmonics struggling to blend in the tone of the arrangement. This is probably a conscious choice, but the rest is quite rock sounding. The fiddle and mandolin reproduce a stereo delay effect (very present on the voices) at the beginning of the song. The arrangement for the fiddles and mandolin allows them to take over the guitar and keyboard parts of the original. We can focus on the sound made by the banjo/fiddle mix at 0:10, where it is a kind of synthesizer party! Except for the funk guitar strumming on the verse, played here by Bryan Sutton on acoustic guitar, the only guitar sounds like a synthesizer. The last verse/chorus reverts to pure country with a change of rhythm and the highlighting of the banjo.

Backwoods Barbie

Dolly Parton / 3:21

Musicians: Biff Watson: acoustic guitar / Steve Mackey: bass / Steve Turner: drums, percussion / Brent Mason: electric guitar / Jimmy Mattingly: fiddle / Aubrey Haynie: mandolin / Hargus "Pig" Robbins: piano / Lloyd Green: pedal steel guitar **Vocals:** Dolly Parton **Backing Vocals:** Dolly Parton, Richard Dennison, Vicki Hampton, Jennifer O'Brien **Recorded:** Blackbird Studio A, Nashville (TN) **Technical Team:** Producers: Dolly Parton, Kent Wells / Sound Engineers: Ben "Snake" Schmitt, Brian Willis, Kyle Dickinson, Allen Ditto, Patrick Murphy / Mixing: Justin Niebank / Mastering: Jim DeMain, Alex McCullough **Single:** Backwoods Barbie **Release:** Dolly Records, March 9, 2009 (CD ref.:?)

Through an autobiographical story, Dolly traces the journey and desire of a girl who left her native countryside, leaving behind poverty and rags to go as high and far as she could. Now a beautiful and brilliant woman, she embraces the freedom of being herself with her unique blend of authenticity and superficiality, which can sometimes be construed as hillbilly extravagance. Moral of the fable: The Barbies of the fields are just as worthy as those of the cities, and clothes do not make the man, or woman!

Unlike "Made of Stone," this ballad is clearly country, with the characteristic swaying of the bass and drums. The

The fans will agree: Country Barbies are as good as city Barbies, and clothes don't make the man—or woman!

drums are played with brushes and the sound of the bass drum is more roots and less emphasized. We find the pedal steel guitar well forward, as well as the piano, which were both a little lost in the previous tracks. The fiddle and the folk guitar play their usual parts; the acoustic guitar delivers its strumming before taking a chorus and the fiddle twirls around the song. The mandolin, discreet but very present on the right of the mix, plays chords that are a little muffled, but its characteristic tone, high and woody, is perfectly recognizable.

This gospel song that Dolly borrows from songwriters Betsy Ulmer and Craig Wiseman is as epic as it is joyful. It expresses Dolly's faith beautifully, but also her joy of living through the ups and downs of life. The song starts out as a ballad and takes off on a very pop sound from the first chorus. The high concentration of instruments in the same range, between electric and folk guitars, fiddle, and keyboards, to which are added the backing vocals, which are very present, produces a somewhat overloaded finale. To be classified in the category of Christian pop songs that Dolly Parton has enjoyed performing since the end of the 1970s.

SINGLE

Jesus & Gravity

Betsy Ulmer, Craig Wiseman / 4:42

Musicians: Bryan Sutton, Kent Wells: acoustic guitar / Dave Talbot: banjo / Steve Mackey: bass / Lonnie Wilson: drums, percussion / Jerry McPherson, Kent Wells: electric guitar / Jimmy Mattingly: fiddle / Paul Hollowell: piano / Paul Franklin: pedal steel guitar **Vocals:** Dolly Parton **Backing Vocals:** Richard Dennison, Vicki Hampton, Jennifer O'Brien **Recorded:** Blackbird Studio A, Nashville (TN) **Technical Team:** Producers: Dolly Parton, Kent Wells / Sound Engineers: Ben "Snake" Schmitt, Brian Willis, Kyle Dickinson, Allen Ditto, Patrick Murphy / Mixing: Justin Niebank / Mastering: Jim DeMain, Alex McCullough **Single:** Jesus & Gravity **Release:** Dolly Records, February 12, 2008 (CD ref.:?)

Only Dreamin'

Dolly Parton / 5:37

Musicians: Kent Wells: acoustic guitar / Anthony Lamarchina, Carole Rabinowitz, Kirsten Cassel, Sarighani Reist: cello / Sam Bacco: percussion / John Mock: tin whistle, bodhran, harmonium / Chris Farrell, Gary Vanosdale, Jim Grosjean, Monisa Angell: viola / Alan Umstead, Carl Gorodetzky, Carolyn Bailey, Catherine Umstead, Conni Ellisor, David Angell, David Davidson, Janet Askey, Karen Winkelman, Mary Kathryn Vanosdale, Pamela Sixfin, Zeneba Bowers: violin / Craig Nelson: bass, violin / Kristin Wilkinson: strings arrangements **Vocals:** Dolly Parton **Backing Vocals:** Dolly Parton, Jamie Johnson, Terry Elredge, Richard Dennison, Vicki Hampton, Jennifer O'Brien **Recorded:** Kent Wells Production (strings ensemble), Sound Kitchen, Franklin (TN), 2006/2007 **Technical Team:** Producers: Dolly Parton, Kent Wells / Sound Engineers: Ben "Snake" Schmitt, Brian Willis, Kyle Dickinson, Allen Ditto, Patrick Murphy / Mixing: Justin Niebank / Mastering: Jim DeMain, Alex McCullough

In this melancholic and poignant song, a woman mourns the departure of her lover, but resists the external, social pressure that tells her that she is stupid to dream of his return. This hope for the return of lost love is a recurring theme in Dolly's songs.

To bring the necessary depth to this folk ballad that evokes the spirit of the early settlers, Dolly calls on the Nashville String Machine, already present on the 1989 album *White Limozeen*. For the Irish touch, she invites John Mock to play the whistle (Irish flute) and the bodhran (a handheld percussion instrument played with a stick, made of a wooden circle over which a goat skin is stretched).

The Tracks Of My Tears

Smokey Robinson, Warren Moore, Marvin Tarplin / 3:35

Musicians: Biff Watson: acoustic guitar / Steve Mackey: bass / Steve Turner: drums, percussion / Brent Mason: electric guitar / Aubrey Haynie: mandolin / Paul Hollowell, Hargus "Pig" Robbins: piano / Lloyd Green: pedal steel guitar **Vocals:** Dolly Parton **Backing Vocals:** Dolly Parton, Richard Dennison, Vicki Hampton, Jennifer O'Brien **Recorded:** Blackbird Studio A, Nashville (TN) **Technical Team:** Producers: Dolly Parton, Kent Wells / Sound Engineers: Ben "Snake" Schmitt, Brian Willis, Kyle Dickinson, Allen Ditto, Patrick Murphy / Mixing: Justin Niebank / Mastering: Jim DeMain, Alex McCullough

Another song about the sadness of a lost love, well-paced and poetic, where the narrator explains that you can follow the "tracks of her tears" on her face, the imprint of grief.

This Motown classic, written by Smokey Robinson in 1965 for his band the Miracles, has been covered many times, notably by Linda Ronstadt in 1975 on her album *Prisoner in Disguise*. Dolly does a country-pop cover, while respecting the essence of the original song.

The Lonesomes

Dolly Parton / 3:19

Musicians: Biff Watson: acoustic guitar / Steve Mackey: bass / Steve Turner: drums, percussion / Brent Mason: electric guitar / Aubrey Haynie: fiddle / Hargus "Pig" Robbins: piano / Lloyd Green: pedal steel guitar **Vocals:** Dolly Parton **Backing Vocals:** Richard Dennison, Vicki Hampton, Jennifer O'Brien **Recorded:** Blackbird Studio A, Nashville (TN) **Technical Team:** Producers: Dolly Parton, Kent Wells / Sound Engineers: Ben "Snake" Schmitt, Brian Willis, Kyle Dickinson, Allen Ditto, Patrick Murphy / Mixing: Justin Niebank / Mastering: Jim DeMain, Alex McCullough

For this umpteenth sad-ass song, the songwriter chooses to take the listener into the back room of a smoky jazz club. What better setting indeed to welcome the blues of the narrator who feels lonely as hell? When the intro ends, you want to sing "Got You on My Mind," a song written by Howard Biggs and Joe Thomas in the early 1950s and covered by many artists, such as Eric Clapton in 2001. In spite of the not very jazzy backing vocals, Dolly offers us a song of the kind one could hear in the jazz clubs of New York in the aftermath of Prohibition. It all goes to show that a band made up of the finest session men from Nashville, with fiddle and pedal steel guitar in front, can sound like classic jazz.

Cologne

Dolly Parton / 3:43

Musicians: Bryan Sutton, Kent Wells: acoustic guitar / Mike Brignardello: bass / Steve Turner: drums, percussion / Rob McNelley, Kent Wells: electric guitar / Jimmy Mattingly: mandolin / Paul Hollowell: piano / Terry Crisp: pedal steel guitar **Vocals:** Dolly Parton **Backing Vocals:** Richard Dennison, Vicki Hampton, Jennifer O'Brien **Recorded:** Blackbird Studio A, Nashville (TN) **Technical Team:** Producers: Dolly Parton, Kent Wells / Sound Engineers: Ben "Snake" Schmitt, Brian Willis, Kyle Dickinson, Allen Ditto, Patrick Murphy / Mixing: Justin Niebank / Mastering: Jim DeMain, Alex McCullough

In this new version of unhappy love, it is, for once, the point of view of the mistress that is portrayed: She cannot wear perfume, at the risk of tipping off her lover's wife.

From the beginning, we feel all the melancholy that the song wants to radiate—that we imagine would be perfect for a romantic film. The small notes of mandolin are the most important marker. The rest is very pop, like most of the ballads on this album, but the electric guitar stands out: lots of bass, tremolo, and a good dose of overdrive of the Nobels ODR-1 type, the secret weapon of Nashville session guitarists.

Shinola

Dolly Parton / 4:13

Musicians: Mike Brignardello: bass / Steve Turner: drums, percussion / Bryan Sutton: electric guitar / Jimmy Mattingly: mandolin / Paul Hollowell: piano / Terry Crisp: pedal steel guitar **Vocals:** Dolly Parton
Backing Vocals: Richard Dennison, Vicki Hampton, Jennifer O'Brien.
Recorded: Emerald Studio A, Nashville (TN) **Technical Team:**
Producers: Dolly Parton, Kent Wells / Sound Engineers: Ben "Snake" Schmitt, Brian Willis, Kyle Dickinson, Allen Ditto, Patrick Murphy / Mixing: Justin Niebank / Mastering: Jim DeMain, Alex McCullough **Single:** Shinola
Release: Dolly Records, July 21, 2008 (US radio edition, ref.: 33451) NB: This track was released as a promo single, so was not ranked on any chart.

This track is a rarity in Dolly's discography because it's a song in which Dolly expresses anger, sometimes with verbal insults, against men who mistreat women, heartbreakers, philanderers, liars, and other toxic people. With humor and energy, the star does not mince her words.

The song starts strongly with the tempo given from the beginning by the bass drum. The folk guitar sets the rhythm with the mandolin that plays mainly muffled chords. Then everyone comes in powerfully after the first verse. The piano hammers out the drone at the bottom of the spectrum with the left hand, while the guitars (electric and pedal steel) swing out devilish country-rock licks, and, to "keep it going," the bass drives in the nails on the bass drum, on the quarter note. On the last verse, at 2:57, a "beep" covers the expletive. To express her anger, Dolly Parton does rock!

I Will Forever Hate Roses

Dolly Parton / 3:28

Musicians: Biff Watson: acoustic guitar / Steve Mackey: bass / Steve Turner: drums, percussion / Brent Mason: electric guitar / Aubrey Haynie: fiddle / Hargus "Pig" Robbins: piano / Lloyd Green: pedal steel guitar **Vocals:** Dolly Parton **Backing Vocals:** Dolly Parton, Darrin Vincent, Rhonda Vincent, Richard Dennison, Vicki Hampton, Jennifer O'Brien **Recorded:** Blackbird Studio A, Nashville (TN)
Technical Team: Producers: Dolly Parton, Kent Wells / Sound Engineers: Ben "Snake" Schmitt, Brian Willis, Kyle Dickinson, Allen Ditto, Patrick Murphy / Mixing: Justin Niebank / Mastering: Jim DeMain, Alex McCullough

When the beauty of roses becomes a symbol of separation and despair, and of the end of a love that had been thought to be eternal. "I Will Forever Hate Roses" is a variation of "Yellow Roses" on *White Limozeen.*

In the United States, live broadcasting had been almost nonexistent since the Janet Jackson "wardrobe malfunction" during the 2004 Super Bowl halftime show. To avoid such unfortunate events, the transmission is delayed by a few seconds.

It has been a long time since we had the traditional country waltz! With amends made to this timeless ballad by Dolly Parton. We note the bass mixed very forward and the stereo effect created by the guitars on both sides of the mix. We can hear the rhythm in the center (bass/drums), the two folk guitars panned out to the extreme, and the space for the piano and the electric guitar answers, as well as the pedal steel guitar and fiddle counterpoints. One can thus imagine an arc of a circle, in the center of which are the soloists, the backing vocals, and the lead voice.

Somebody's Everything

Dolly Parton / 4:18

Musicians: Biff Watson: acoustic guitar / Mike Brignardello: bass / Steve Turner: drums, percussion / Derek Wells, Tom Bukovac: electric guitar / Jimmy Mattingly: mandolin, fiddle / Paul Hollowell: piano / Paul Franklin: pedal steel guitar **Vocals:** Dolly Parton **Backing Vocals:** Dolly Parton, Billy Davis, Christine Winslow, Marty Slayton **Recorded:** Blackbird Studio A, Nashville (TN) **Technical Team:** Producers: Dolly Parton, Kent Wells / Sound Engineers: Ben "Snake" Schmitt, Brian Willis, Kyle Dickinson, Allen Ditto, Patrick Murphy / Mixing: Justin Niebank / Mastering: Jim DeMain, Alex McCullough

To conclude this album of unhappy love stories on a joyful and optimistic note, the narrator of "Somebody's Everything" declares that she wants it all—all the love, all the attention, all the joy, all that is good and beautiful.

Dolly ends this opus with a rock ballad, where the listener is held in suspense until the end. The first verse, quiet at the outset, with layers of organ and guitar chords, gains in intensity under the impetus of Dolly's singing to arrive at what will be the general atmosphere of the song. The bridge in "reduced mode" at 3:10 serves to relaunch the machine; the rise toward the climax is then engaged by the guitars, joined by the bass and the breaks of rather heavy drums, the backing vocals and the orchestral bells, the whole thing repeated until the end in fade-out.

Also a tribute to Dolly's roots, the Dollywood amusement park is nestled in the Great Smoky Mountains, in Pigeon Forge, Tennessee.

Sha-Kon-O-Hey! Land of Blue Smoke: An Homage to the Mountains

Release Date
United States: February 11, 2009
Reference: Dolly Records, Nashville (TN)—(?)
Best US Chart Ranking: (?)
My Mountains, My Home (4:02)
Hey Howdy Hey (2:04)
Working on a Dream (1:56)
Time Flies (2:34)
Heart of the Smokies (2:30)
Good Time (2:17)
Sha-Kon-O-Hey! (3:19)
Forever Home (3:26)

Musicians: (?) Vocals and arrangements: Dolly Parton
Backing Vocals: Richard Dennison, Vicki Hampton, Jennifer O'Brien
Recorded: (?) **Technical Team:** Producers: Dolly Parton, Tony Smith / Sound Engineers: (?) / Mixing: Marv Treutel

Sha-Kon-O-Hey! Land of Blue Smoke is a solo album by Dolly Parton, released by her and producer Tony Smith on Dolly Records on February 11, 2009, as part of the seventy-fifth anniversary celebration of the Great Smoky Mountains National Park. All songs were written by the songwriter to be performed at Dollywood. Dolly traces the history of Tennessee, its roots, the Cherokee people, and the migrants who shaped the landscape as well as the cities. This event album is sold only in the amusement park and the profits are donated to the nonprofit organization Friends of the Smokies.

Celebrating Heritage

"Sha-Kon-O-Hey!" written phonetically is a transcription of the Cherokee term *shaconage*, which means "the land of blue smoke." This land, dear to Dolly's heart, is the land of bluegrass and of the music of the Europeans of the eighteenth and nineteenth centuries who settled in this remote region, mixing to some extent with the American Indian population. These mountains are Dolly's heart, her soil, and her soul, an inexhaustible material that

the songwriter never stops working and sharing with her audience.

The lyrics of the songs pay tribute to this heritage. In the musical show that Dolly took pleasure in writing, everything contributes to enchanting the fans: the sets, the stunts, the scenography, the dancers, the acrobats, and a six-piece orchestra. We discover Scottish and Irish settlers, railroaders, Cherokee warriors, and even smugglers. This journey immerses the audience in the 1930s, during the Great Depression and its terrible consequences.

It was not until the mid-1930s that Congress decided to grant the Smokies national park status, when nearly 80 percent of its forests had been decimated. It was the joint efforts of the states of Tennessee and North Carolina, as well as private donors—including Dolly Parton in her own way—that made their restoration and preservation possible.

When Smoky Rhymes with Philanthropy

Dolly is not only a shrewd businesswoman. She is, first and foremost, a woman of the South, born in the heart of these mountains and who, all her life, has campaigned for their preservation and for their development. Although the star travels the world to give concerts and run the Imagination Library program, she inexorably returns to these lands to draw strength and creativity from them. In 2009, she was even named ambassador of the Great Smoky Mountains National Park, which has developed considerably in the past seventy-five years: With more than six hundred miles of trails covering an area of more than 500,000 acres, and featuring exceptional flora and fauna, forests, rivers, and blue mists that float over the peaks every morning, this park represents a significant ecological and tourist asset.

Opened in 1986, Dollywood is today at the top of the list of American amusement park attractions (in 2010, the star received an Applause Award, which, every two years, rewards the most attractive theme park in the world). The mountains of the Smokies satisfy the visitors' need for wilderness, and Dollywood has something to satisfy all the expectations of the songwriter's fans.

MIDI (Musical Instrument Digital Interface) is a protocol for standardizing communications between hardware devices, music software, and electronic instruments such as synthesizers, as well as related audio equipment.

Production

From a production point of view, this album is much less polished than Dolly's other work. Except for the backing vocals, the arrangements of some tracks are almost in demo form. Most of the instruments are played with a master keyboard or programmed in MIDI, which gives the sounds a naive, almost childish quality. The absence of the organic element in the instrumental portions of the song is particularly striking, especially on the strings, brass, winds, and percussions. On the first song, "My Mountains, My Home," it seems that even the backbeat and the banjo picking are done in MIDI; the same is true for the acoustic guitar parts (mixed in the background), which is almost the last straw for an album celebrating life in the Smoky Mountains. But Dolly is not afraid of paradox!

This is all the more confusing because the album was made in 2009, but it sometimes leaves the impression of listening to the credits of a 1990s cartoon. If we put aside the purely economic motives, perhaps we should detect a particular intention in this treatment and this anodyne sound, for songs that were, after all, composed for a show mainly intended for a younger audience. However, despite the lack of dynamics or relief and the absence of a human factor in the vast majority of arrangements, the songs remain well put together and the mix very balanced, and they are not lacking in breadth. Ultimately, this approach confers upon the sound a pleasant roundness and very easy access. It must be said that the queen of country knows her audience, especially the one that comes, sometimes from far away, to be entertained at Dollywood. *Sha-Kon-O-Hey!* shows the kitsch aspect that Dolly Parton accepted.

Album Cover

Dolly, with her long hair tied up and her guitar slung over her shoulder, poses with a smile. In the background, we can see the blue mountains of the national park. The artist who created this cover is uncredited.

ALBUM

Better Day

In the Meantime . Just Leaving . Somebody's Missing You . Together You and I .
Country Is as Country Does . Holding Everything . The Sacrifice . I Just Might .
Better Day . Shine Like the Sun . Get Out and Stay Out . Let Love Grow

RELEASE DATE
United States: June 28, 2011
Reference: Dolly Records and Warner Music Nashville,
Nashville (TN)—528216-2
Best US Chart Ranking: 11

An Antidote to Gloom

Better Day was Dolly Parton's forty-first solo album. Produced by her and Kent Wells, it was issued by Dolly Records in association with Warner Music Nashville on June 28, 2011. It went to number fifty-one on the Billboard 200 and to number one on the British and Australian charts. This new album was met with a very positive critical reception.

Giving the World a Voice

In 2011, the world was still feeling the effects of the economic storm created by the 2008 financial crisis. The passing of Peter Falk, the magnificent actor whose name will forever be associated with that of Lieutenant Columbo, was mourned by Hollywood, just as that of Steve Jobs was by Silicon Valley. The tsunami that devastated Japan led people to think more urgently about the effects of climate change. Poverty was increasing. The explosion and oil spill from the Deepwater Horizon drilling rig that occurred in April 2010 off the coast of Louisiana was still fresh in people's minds. Anxiety was on the rise in the US as elsewhere, with economic and social crises causing unrest. Militant action against restrictions, deprivations of freedom, and the excesses of capitalism were multiplying; and movements such as such as Occupy Wall Street, which began in New York in September 2011, quickly spread to the whole continent. Seeing the sad state of the world, Dolly hoped that with her *Better Day*, she could bring her fans a little happiness and relief from their troubles. According to critic Steve Leggett of AllMusic, Dolly's new album had "enough musical sunshine to light up even the grayest day."

Caring and Contemporary

Dolly set out in *Better Day* with two firm intentions. The first was to initiate a change of direction in her work, because she wanted this album to be more modern than previous ones. The second was to offer some comfort in this dark period when the imminent end of the world was being announced daily. While Dolly was sensitive to the doom-laden atmosphere weighing on her contemporaries, she refused to let herself be sucked in by the apocalyptic mood sweeping the planet. As she says in the lyrics of "In the Meantime," the first track on this album, the end will come in its own time and no one can predict when that will be, so we might as well make the most of every moment.

The sixty-five-year-old Dolly refuses to worry about doomsday. She is buzzing with the energy, enthusiasm, and joie de vivre that infuses her music. We need not fear that the superstar she has become will rest on her laurels: She is out to conquer new generations.

Combining Business and Philanthropy

The *Better Day* world tour was Dolly's tenth concert tour in North America, Europe, and Australia, the last being a country she hadn't visited for thirty years. Financially successful, with almost 275,000 tickets sold for a total of $34 million, the tour represented a moment of intense excitement for Dolly's many European and Australian fans. The tour kicked off on July 17, 2011, in Knoxville, Tennessee, with an inaugural concert to benefit the Dollywood Foundation. All proceeds from the concert were dedicated to the ever-expanding Imagination Library program.

Album Cover

Photographer and producer Fran Strine has produced an image of Dolly, all blond hair and sequined dress, standing before an enormous microphone. The typographic design—a combination of blue lettering and a black signature—aims to give a modern feel. Dolly's famous butterfly, a kind of logo, also features, just as it does on the inside cover, where we see a sunny Dolly, now dressed in yellow.

Note on this album: Despite extensive research, the release date and references of the singles have not been found.

In The Meantime

Dolly Parton / 4:04

Musicians: Steve Turner: percussion, drums / Mike Brignardello, Steve Mackey: bass / Rob McNelley, Jerry McPherson, Brent Mason, Kent Wells: electric guitar / Lloyd Green, Steve Hinson: pedal steel guitar / Steve Hinson: slide guitar / Andie Hall, Randy Kohrs: dobro / Paul Hollowell: Hammond B3 organ, keyboards, piano / Michael Davis: Hammond B3 organ, synthesizer / Hargus "Pig" Robbins: piano / Bryan Sutton, Biff Watson, Kent Wells: acoustic guitar / Richie Owens: harmonica **Vocals:** Dolly Parton **Backing Vocals:** Jamie Dailey, Christian Davis, Richard Dennison, Vicki Hampton, Becky Isaacs, Sonya Isaacs, Jennifer O'Brien, Darrin Vincent **Recorded:** (?), 2010/2011 **Technical Team:** Producers: Dolly Parton, Kent Wells / Sound Engineers: Patrick Murphy, Tony Smith / Mixing: Patrick Murphy / Mastering: Stephen Marcussen

The lyrics say that Dolly's had enough of these often alarmist predictions of the end of the world and the many imminent catastrophes. In this rock 'n' rolling celebration of faith and life, she advises her listeners to enjoy the present and seize life with both hands, trusting in the help of God.

The instrumentation for "In the Meantime" is essentially electric. Very rich in the middle of the spectrum, the interweaving of electric and folk guitars, keyboards, backing vocals, and harmonica communicates sheer joy. The drumming style is more rock than in the two previous albums, with a drier and more natural-sounding snare drum. In spite of the wealth of instruments, the mix is finely balanced, allowing us to hear each of the different entries and lines when appropriate.

Just Leaving

Dolly Parton / 3:00

Musicians: Steve Turner: percussion, drums / Steve Mackey: double bass / Rob McNelley, Jerry McPherson, Brent Mason, Kent Wells: electric guitar / Lloyd Green, Steve Hinson: pedal steel guitar / Steve Hinson: slide guitar / Aubrey Haynie, Jimmy Mattingly: fiddle, mandolin / Andie Hall, Randy Kohrs: dobro / Bryan Sutton, Biff Watson, Kent Wells: acoustic guitar / David Talbot: banjo **Vocals:** Dolly Parton **Backing Vocals:** Jamie Dailey, Christian Davis, Richard Dennison, Vicki Hampton, Becky

Isaacs, Sonya Isaacs, Jennifer O'Brien, Darrin Vincent **Recorded:** (?), 2010/2011 **Technical Team:** Producers: Dolly Parton, Kent Wells / Sound Engineers: Patrick Murphy, Tony Smith / Mixing: Patrick Murphy / Mastering: Stephen Marcussen

The title says it all: The narrator is leaving and that's that. Her determination to end a difficult relationship is very clear… even if she finds setting out for the unknown intimidating.

This new composition by Dolly Parton is clearly influenced by the mountain music sound. The intro starts with banjo and dobro, but also—rather surprisingly, given the overall folk/bluegrass style—some descending scales on metal chimes. The woody sound of the double bass and the deep notes of the bass guitar stand out clearly. Jimmy Mattingly's brilliant fiddle plays an important role, as at 2:05 and 2:16, where he gives it his all. The different instrumental lines are well defined, and the fact that there is no keyboard, contributes to the clarity of the mix.

Somebody's Missing You

Dolly Parton / 3:43

Musicians: Steve Turner: percussion, drums / Steve Mackey: double bass / Steve Hinson: slide guitar, pedal steel guitar / Aubrey Haynie, Jimmy Mattingly: fiddle, mandolin / Andie Hall, Randy Kohrs: dobro / Paul Hollowell, Hargus "Pig" Robbins: piano / Bryan Sutton, Biff Watson, Kent Wells: acoustic guitar **Voice:** Dolly Parton **Backing Vocals:** Emmylou Harris, Alison Krauss **Recorded:** (?), 2010/2011 **Technical Team:** Producers: Dolly Parton, Kent Wells / Sound Engineers: Patrick Murphy, Tony Smith / Mixing: Patrick Murphy / Mastering: Stephen Marcussen

A classic Parton song where the protagonist describes her feelings when her lover is not with her. The text lists one by one the many different thoughts that come into her mind. Over a gentle melody, and supported by Emmylou Harris and Alison Krauss's backing vocals, Dolly sings of the pain of missing someone—a pain that everyone experiences sooner or later. The style is reminiscent of the *Trio* albums. Alison Krauss takes on the challenge of replacing the legendary Linda Ronstadt, who announced her retirement in 2011, the same year that *Better Day* was recorded; in 2013, she was to reveal that she was suffering from Parkinson's disease, later rediagnosed as PSP (progressive supranuclear palsy). The dobro plays the main theme in the intro and also in most of the responses to the verses. Mandolin and fiddle enter here and there with ornamentation that is both rich and restrained.

Dolly in concert at the Allphones Arena in Sydney, Australia, November 2011.

Together You And I

Dolly Parton / 3:36

Musicians: Steve Turner: percussion, drums / Mike Brignardello, Steve Mackey: bass / Rob McNelley, Jerry McPherson, Brent Mason, Kent Wells: electric guitar / Lloyd Green, Steve Hinson: pedal steel guitar / Steve Hinson: slide guitar / Aubrey Haynie, Jimmy Mattingly: fiddle / Michael Davis: Hammond B3 organ, synthesizer / Hargus "Pig" Robbins: piano / Bryan Sutton, Biff Watson, Kent Wells: acoustic guitar / David Talbot: banjo **Vocals:** Dolly Parton, Kent Wells **Backing Vocals:** Jamie Dailey, Christian Davis, Richard Dennison, Vicki Hampton, Becky Isaacs, Sonya Isaacs, Jennifer O'Brien, Darrin Vincent **Recorded:** (?), 2010/2011 **Technical Team:** Producers: Dolly Parton, Kent Wells / Sound Engineers: Patrick Murphy, Tony Smith / Mixing: Patrick Murphy / Mastering: Stephen Marcussen

In this rather eighties-sounding classic ballad, Dolly Parton, duetting with guitarist Kent Wells, her co-producer, describes the overwhelming power of love. The instrumentation is highly concentrated, especially in the tessitura of the voice, making the whole a little confused, but appropriate nevertheless for a text evoking passionate and complete love. The emotional state of someone experiencing this kind of love is perfectly captured.

The singer, looking radiant here, does not give the impression of having made any sacrifices to get to the top.

Country Is As Country Does

Dolly Parton, Mac Davis / 3:20

Musicians: Steve Turner: percussion, drums / Mike Brignardello, Steve Mackey: bass / Rob McNelley, Jerry McPherson, Brent Mason, Kent Wells: electric guitar / Lloyd Green, Steve Hinson: pedal steel guitar / Steve Hinson: slide guitar / Aubrey Haynie, Jimmy Mattingly: fiddle / Hargus "Pig" Robbins: piano / Bryan Sutton, Biff Watson, Kent Wells: acoustic guitar **Vocals:** Dolly Parton **Backing Vocals:** Jamie Dailey, Christian Davis, Richard Dennison, Vicki Hampton, Becky Isaacs, Sonya Isaacs, Jennifer O'Brien, Darrin Vincent **Recorded:** (?), 2010/2011 **Technical Team:** Producers: Dolly Parton, Kent Wells / Sound Engineers: Patrick Murphy, Tony Smith / Mixing: Patrick Murphy / Mastering: Stephen Marcussen

Written with her friend Mac Davis for an album a few years earlier, this song expresses the idea that people are defined by their place of origin. There are two recurring themes in Dolly's songs: the country versus the city, and the celebration of one's roots. That said, having grown up in the country does not prevent one from living in the city. The song's lyrics also reflect on the impact that success, money, the pleasures of life, and the city can have on someone who has grown up in poverty. Dolly is clear: She remains attached to the country and country music.

This up-tempo track is made for dancing and country festivals. Despite his rocking drumming, Steve Turner seems to have opted for drum rods because the attack seems less marked than if he had used drumsticks. Guitars and fiddle are very prominent, constantly popping up with solos: It's celebration time!

Holding Everything

Dolly Parton / 3:36

Musicians: Steve Turner: percussion, drums / Mike Brignardello, Steve Mackey: bass / Rob McNelley, Jerry McPherson, Brent Mason, Kent Wells: electric guitar / Lloyd Green, Steve Hinson: pedal steel guitar / Steve Hinson: slide guitar / Aubrey Haynie, Jimmy Mattingly: fiddle / Michael Davis: Hammond B3 organ, synthesizer / Hargus "Pig" Robbins: piano / Bryan Sutton, Biff Watson, Kent Wells: acoustic guitar / David Talbot: banjo **Vocals:** Dolly Parton, Kent Wells **Backing Vocals:** Jamie Dailey, Christian Davis, Richard Dennison, Vicki Hampton, Becky Isaacs, Sonya Isaacs, Jennifer O'Brien, Darrin Vincent **Recorded:** (?), 2010/2011 **Technical Team:** Producers: Dolly Parton, Kent Wells / Sound Engineers: Patrick Murphy, Tony Smith / Mixing: Patrick Murphy / Mastering: Stephen Marcussen

In this rather eighties-sounding classic ballad, Dolly Parton, duetting with guitarist Kent Wells, her co-producer, describes the overwhelming power of love. The instrumentation is highly concentrated, especially in the tessitura of the voice, making the whole a little confused, but appropriate nevertheless for a text evoking passionate and complete love. The emotional state of someone experiencing this kind of love is perfectly captured.

"The Sacrifice" gives us an opportunity to hear a different Dolly Parton than the one projected on stage at the 53rd Grammy Awards, here, in 2011.

The Sacrifice

Dolly Parton / 3:26

Musicians: Steve Turner: percussion, drums / Mike Brignardello, Steve Mackey: bass / Rob McNelley, Jerry McPherson, Brent Mason, Kent Wells: electric guitar / Lloyd Green, Steve Hinson: pedal steel guitar / Steve Hinson: slide guitar / Aubrey Haynie, Jimmy Mattingly: fiddle, mandolin / Andie Hall, Randy Kohrs: dobro / Paul Hollowell: Hammond B3 organ / Hargus "Pig" Robbins: piano / Bryan Sutton, Biff Watson, Kent Wells: acoustic guitar / David Talbot: banjo **Vocals:** Dolly Parton **Backing Vocals:** Jamie Dailey, Christian Davis, Richard Dennison, Vicki Hampton, Becky Isaacs, Sonya Isaacs, Jennifer O'Brien, Darrin Vincent **Recorded:** (?), 2010/2011 **Technical Team:** Producers: Dolly Parton, Kent Wells / Sound Engineers: Patrick Murphy, Tony Smith / Mixing: Patrick Murphy / Mastering: Stephen Marcussen

In this very personal song, Dolly sings of the sacrifices she has made on the way to fame. The moral? Everything has a price.

Musically, "The Sacrifice" is something of a hybrid: a traditional lineup playing with a pop rhythm. Fiddle, dobro, banjo, and guitars are all there. The mandolin is used

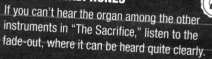

ON YOUR HEADPHONES
If you can't hear the organ among the other instruments in "The Sacrifice," listen to the fade-out, where it can be heard quite clearly.

sparingly, playing rhythmic parts on the choruses, especially on the last one, where you can hear its chords in the upper part of the spectrum. On the verses, the hi-hat supports the strumming of the acoustic guitar and its eighth-note triplets (two triplets in each 2/4 measure) creating a rhythmic pattern seldom found in country music. Also unusual is the duet between bass and dobro. This can be heard at the end of the first refrain, at 1:05, where the two musicians seem to be playing two totally unrelated but nevertheless harmonious parts. The same thing happens at the end of the second refrain, but this time with fiddle. As with the preceding track, the song ends with all the instruments—plus a few more—playing together. Added in to the already densely accompanied refrains, we hear layers of Hammond organ that bring a wonderful depth to the whole.

With the cast of the musical *9 to 5* and actress Allison Janney (to her right) at the 63rd Annual Tony Awards ceremony, in 2009 in New York City.

For Dolly Addicts

Four tracks on the album were written by Dolly for the Broadway musical *9 to 5*: "I Just Might," "Shine Like the Sun," "Get Out and Stay Out," and "Let Love Grow."

I Just Might

Dolly Parton / 3:57

Musicians: Steve Turner: percussion, drums / Mike Brignardello, Steve Mackey: bass / Rob McNelley, Jerry McPherson, Brent Mason, Kent Wells: electric guitar / Lloyd Green, Steve Hinson: pedal steel guitar / Steve Hinson: slide guitar / Aubrey Haynie, Jimmy Mattingly: mandolin / Paul Hollowell: Hammond B3 organ, keyboards, piano / Michael Davis: Hammond B3 organ, synthesizer / Hargus "Pig" Robbins: piano / Bryan Sutton, Biff Watson, Kent Wells: acoustic guitar **Vocals:** Dolly Parton **Backing Vocals:** Jamie Dailey, Christian Davis, Richard Dennison, Vicki Hampton, Becky Isaacs, Sonya Isaacs, Jennifer O'Brien, Darrin Vincent **Recorded:** (?), 2010/2011 **Technical Team:** Producers: Dolly Parton, Kent Wells / Sound Engineers: Patrick Murphy, Tony Smith / Mixing: Patrick Murphy / Mastering: Stephen Marcussen

There is not one Dolly Parton album that does not have a love song where the broken-hearted narrator wonders how she will be able to move on. Written for the musical *9 to 5*, "I Just Might" offers an answer to this sad situation: Trust in your inner strength and try your best. The ballad form is of course de rigueur for the text of this umpteenth "sad-ass song." In addition to the pianos and slightly maudlin guitar, the strings arrangements played on the synthesizer further contributes to what might seem a rather predictable piece. But Dolly's interpretation is deeply felt and makes all this perfectly credible.

Better Day

Dolly Parton / 3:22

Musicians: Steve Turner: percussion, drums / Steve Mackey: double bass / Rob McNelley, Jerry McPherson, Brent Mason, Kent Wells: electric guitar / Lloyd Green, Steve Hinson: pedal steel guitar / Steve Hinson: slide guitar / Aubrey Haynie, Jimmy Mattingly: fiddle / Andie Hall, Randy Kohrs: dobro / Hargus "Pig" Robbins: piano / Bryan Sutton, Biff Watson, Kent Wells: acoustic guitar **Vocals:** Dolly Parton **Backing Vocals:** Jamie Dailey, Christian Davis, Richard Dennison, Vicki Hampton, Becky Isaacs, Sonya Isaacs, Jennifer O'Brien, Darrin Vincent **Recorded:** (?), 2010/2011 **Technical Team:** Producers: Dolly Parton, Kent Wells / Sound Engineers: Patrick Murphy, Tony Smith / Mixing: Patrick Murphy / Mastering: Stephen Marcussen

Dolly opens the title track with a long spoken section before moving on to the blues, the perfect style to evoke the life's difficulties. There are better days, the lyrics say, and what a relief it is to hear it! The song has a very unplugged sound, despite the electric guitar. Piano on the principal line, dobro, drums with brushes, double bass, acoustic guitar, and fiddle; the slow tempo carries all the melancholy of the text, but also hope for a more joyful future.

Shine Like The Sun

Dolly Parton / 3:12

Musicians: Steve Turner: percussion, drums / Mike Brignardello, Steve Mackey: bass / Rob McNelley, Jerry McPherson, Brent Mason, Kent Wells: electric guitar / Lloyd Green: pedal steel guitar / Paul Hollowell: Hammond B3 organ, keyboards, piano / Michael Davis: Hammond B3 organ, synthesizer / Hargus "Pig" Robbins: piano / Bryan Sutton, Biff Watson, Kent Wells: acoustic guitar / David Talbot: banjo **Vocals:** Dolly Parton **Backing Vocals:** Jamie Dailey, Christian Davis, Richard Dennison, Vicki Hampton, Becky Isaacs, Sonya Isaacs, Jennifer O'Brien, Darrin Vincent **Recorded:** (?), 2010/2011 **Technical Team:** Producers: Dolly Parton, Kent Wells / Sound Engineers: Patrick Murphy, Tony Smith / Mixing: Patrick Murphy / Mastering: Stephen Marcussen

This strongly rhythmical song was another of those written for the musical *9 to 5*. Its message is that you should never give up on your dreams, on yourself, on love. When a love affair becomes toxic you must leave it, move on, and put yourself back together again; every one of us can shine. Track after track on this album pulsates with the same positive energy. This particular number is very characteristic of the pop music of the 1990s, particularly in the electric guitar theme at 2:00, recalling among other things the memorable theme tune from *Beverly Hills, 90210* (1990–2000). And despite the essentially modern sound, Dolly Parton brings about the almost impossible by always (or almost always) integrating a traditional country music instrument. Here it is the banjo with its characteristic clawhammer strumming.

Get Out And Stay Out

Dolly Parton / 3:05

Musicians: Steve Turner: percussion, drums / Mike Brignardello, Steve Mackey: bass / Rob McNelley, Jerry McPherson, Brent Mason, Kent Wells: electric guitar / Lloyd Green: pedal steel guitar / Aubrey Haynie, Jimmy Mattingly: fiddle / Paul Hollowell: Hammond B3 organ, keyboards, piano / Michael Davis: Hammond B3 organ, synthesizer / Bryan Sutton, Biff Watson, Kent Wells: acoustic guitar **Vocals:** Dolly Parton **Backing Vocals:** Jamie Dailey, Christian Davis, Richard Dennison, Vicki Hampton, Becky Isaacs, Sonya Isaacs, Jennifer O'Brien, Darrin Vincent **Recorded:** (?), 2010/2011 **Technical Team:** Producers: Dolly Parton, Kent Wells / Sound Engineers: Patrick Murphy, Tony Smith / Mixing: Patrick Murphy / Mastering: Stephen Marcussen

Tired of a lover who lies, cheats on her, and breaks her heart, the narrator claims her right to freedom and happiness. She tells her man to get out and stay out. Although this is a recurring theme in Dolly's songs, rarely has a protagonist expressed herself so strongly and decidedly.

As for the production, this track is not unlike "Shine Like the Sun," with a mainstream electronic pop sound and synthesized violins. Nevertheless, piano, fiddle, pedal steel guitar, and acoustic guitar all feature. It is as though these traditional instruments were helping Dolly to give of her best, especially in texture and interpretation.

Let Love Grow

Dolly Parton / 3:41

Musicians: Steve Turner: percussion, drums / Mike Brignardello, Steve Mackey: bass / Rob McNelley, Jerry McPherson, Brent Mason, Kent Wells: electric guitar / Lloyd Green: pedal steel guitar / Paul Hollowell: Hammond B3 organ, keyboards, piano / Michael Davis: Hammond B3 organ, synthesizer / Hargus "Pig" Robbins: piano / Bryan Sutton, Biff Watson, Kent Wells: acoustic guitar **Vocals:** Dolly Parton, Kent Wells **Backing Vocals:** Jamie Dailey, Christian Davis, Richard Dennison, Vicki Hampton, Becky Isaacs, Sonya Isaacs, Jennifer O'Brien, Darrin Vincent **Recorded:** (?), 2010/2011 **Technical Team:** Producers: Dolly Parton, Kent Wells / Sound Engineers: Patrick Murphy, Tony Smith / Mixing: Patrick Murphy / Mastering: Stephen Marcussen

Continuing with its main theme, the album closes with a dynamic song encouraging the listener never to give up. Love is everywhere, and it can appear where we least expect it. Dolly urges the listener to remain open to the beautiful experiences that life can bring.

After "Holding Everything," we have here a second song where Dolly duets with Kent Wells. And, strangely, these two songs are similar to one another in many ways, ranging from the orchestral lineup to the tempo, halfway between ballad and pop song. But "Let Love Grow" differs in the introduction of a gospel sound. From the second refrain, the backing vocals enter gradually until they are firmly established. A quasi–a cappella section introduces the famous modulation that we have almost begun to miss. The bass voices are well brought out, recalling some of the backing vocals in seventies Motown or sixties doo-wop numbers. The singer's lead line floats, gospel-style, over the backing.

ALBUM

Blue Smoke

Blue Smoke . Unlikely Angel . Don't Think Twice . You Can't Make Old Friends .
Home . Banks of the Ohio . Lay Your Hands on Me . Miss You, Miss Me . If I Had Wings .
Lover du Jour . From Here to the Moon and Back . Try

RELEASE DATE
United States: January 31, 2014
References: Dolly Records, Nashville (TN) and Sony Masterworks,
New York (NY)—88843 06568 2
Best US Chart Ranking: 2

Dolly Parton and Kenny Rogers's single, "You Can't Make Old Friends," peaked at number fifty-seven on the Billboard Country Airplay chart and marked the star's return to the Airplay chart for the first time since "Jesus & Gravity" in 2008.

An Optimistic Album

Blue Smoke was Dolly Parton's forty-second solo album. Produced by Kent Wells, it was released on January 31, 2014, on the Dolly Records label, in association with Sony Masterworks. It was listed at number six on Billboard 200 and number one in the Australian and British charts. The majority of music critics gave this new album enthusiastic reviews.

Flashback

With such a long career and so many important collaborations, Dolly was inevitably confronted with the death of several of her closest friends. February 2012 saw the passing of Whitney Houston, the singer forever associated in the mind of millions of listeners with her cover of "I Will Always Love You." When her version of this song was played at her funeral, Dolly was deeply moved. In May, the music scene mourned the death of Donna Summer, composer of "Starting Over Again," a hit for Dolly in 1980. During this same period, Robin Gibb, member of the Bee Gees and one of the authors of "Islands in the Stream," passed away. But the events of the tragedy-filled year 2012 did not affect only the musical world. On the night of July 19–20, a shooting in a movie theater in Aurora, Colorado, shocked the entire nation, bringing back memories of the 1999 shooting in Columbine, which is only about twenty miles from Aurora. Emotions ran so high that President Barack Obama and his opponent, Mitt Romney, temporarily suspended their campaigning for the forthcoming presidential elections—without, however, reopening the debate on firearms.

The year 2013 saw America agonizing over Edward Snowden's revelations after exposing the National Security Agency spying methods and unleashing a scandal that rocked the whole world. This difficult period in America's history may perhaps explain why Dolly Parton—always keen to record the life around her in her songs—wanted to spread a message of peace and love, hope and confidence, as if to offer an alternative to this almost permanent climate of violence. Seen in this light, *Blue Smoke* is an attempt to soothe the hearts of her fans and tip the balance from despair to hope.

Celebrating the Misty Mountains

As Dolly posted on her website at the time this album was released: "It was a song that brought me out of the Smoky Mountains and it will be a song that lays me back down in the ground in the Smoky Mountains." *Blue Smoke* offered Dolly's fans her characteristic mixture of bluegrass, gospel, country, and mountain music. The promotion, as always, was both effective and important, and the *Blue Smoke* world tour was notably wide-ranging. Dolly's fans were offered many opportunities to see their favorite star: No fewer than 47 concert dates were planned—11 in North America, 13 in Australia, and 23 in Europe. Dolly treated her different audiences to a bonus version of her album, which was made available at Walmart. This version contained four extra tracks including three unreleased songs—"Get Up, Get Out, Get On," "Olive Branch," and "Angels in the Midst"—and a boxed set for the UK edition, which, in addition to the CD

A banner saying "Dolly take me to your bosom" was carried by fans not lacking in humor at the UK's Glastonbury Festival in 2014.

of the album, also included a second CD with twenty of the songwriter's songs, standards, and biggest hits. Dolly also appeared on the video platform *QVC Session Live* with five tracks from the album *Live from London* and an interview, as well as on streaming platforms (audio and video) including Spotify and Yahoo Music. And that was not all! It is well known that Dolly is an expert at using every kind of communication tool available: She has five million followers on Twitter and four million on Instagram and Facebook, and it is estimated that her recently set up TikTok account will attract similar numbers. Dolly has indubitably taken advantage of all these new networks that unite her millions of fans around the world. That said, Dolly seems to prefer a more traditional medium: television.

Queen of the Festival

Held at Pilton (Somerset) in the UK, the Glastonbury Festival of Contemporary Performing Arts, or, more simply, the Glastonbury Festival, is one of the most important musical festivals in the world. The Rolling Stones performed there in 2013, and the following year Dolly Parton drew an astonishing crowd for an unforgettable concert in which she had 200,000 fans eating out of the palm of her hand. It was a huge success on every level—even the sun came out, which doesn't always happen in that part of the world. According to her biographer Stephen Miller,[2] Dolly prefers playing in smaller venues, but her Glastonbury performance shows that she is quite capable of managing an enormous audience. That same evening, she received an award from the Recording Industry Association of America in recognition of her lifetime achievement, and for selling over 100

million records worldwide. Wearing a dazzling white outfit with rhinestones and a piece of jewelry of her own making—a three-row pearl necklace attached to the bottom of her blouse—Dolly stood out in contrast to the members of her band, who were all dressed in dark outfits. Held outdoors, Glastonbury is notorious among festival-goers for its tendency to turn into a sea of mud when it rains—a not infrequent occurrence! In honor of the festival, Dolly composed a special song called "The Mud Song." The crowd was quick to join in with the chorus: "*Mud, mud, mud.*"

The next day, Dolly was on the front page of all the British newspapers and on television. She was dubbed the Queen of Glastonbury, as confirmed by the *BBC News* announcing that she had attracted the largest crowd ever seen at the festival. One slight reservation came from critic Rebecca Nicholson's five-star review in the online *Guardian*: Was Dolly completely ridiculous or completely sublime? Dolly had the deciding word: "It was corny, but it was fun."[2] The only real shadow cast was that by journalist Kay Burley of *Sky News*, who asserted that Dolly was miming. This was met with a general outcry from the web and networks and a scathing response from the singer speaking to *The Sun* newspaper: "*My boobs* are *fake, my hair's fake, but* what is *real* is *my voice* and *my heart.*" That silenced the doubters!

Album Cover

Dolly is depicted in the foreground of a painted representation of the misty blue mountains that are so dear to her heart. She wears a simple denim shirt and a radiant smile in typical Dolly fashion. The artist who created this cover is uncredited.

In 2014, Dolly embarked on her *Blue Smoke* world tour.

Blue Smoke

Dolly Parton / 3:33

Musicians: Kent Wells: acoustic guitar / Jimmy Mattingly: fiddle, mandolin / Danny Roberts: mandolin / Bob Mater: drums / Scott Vestal: banjo / Randy Kohrs: dobro **Vocals:** Dolly Parton **Backing Vocals:** Jamie Johnson, Christian Davis, Richard Dennison, Terry Eldredge
Recorded: Kent Wells Productions, Franklin (TN), 2013
Technical Team: Producer: Kent Wells / Sound Engineers: Patrick Murphy, Kent Wells / Mixing: Patrick Murphy, Kent Wells

Fans at the Glastonbury Festival (UK) were immediately hooked by this track dedicated to the story of a separation. Cheated on by an unfaithful, lying lover, the narrator is leaving the mountains on the "heartbreak train," a metaphor already used by Dolly in "Heartbreak Express." The train's name is *Blue Smoke*; it does not represent only regret—Dolly's energy brings back some joy in her heroine's heart. And the rhythm of the song makes us want to dance or click our fingers.

The arrangements for this dynamic track fall into three distinct phases: The first part, up to 1:49, establishes the basis of the song on a binary country folk rhythm where the drums, played by Bob Mater using brushes, evoke the sound of a locomotive traveling at full speed. Randy Kohrs gives a very bluesy, lively, and agile performance on the dobro. Then, from 1:49 to 2:25, after a pause for a stop in the Smoky Mountains, the tempo picks up for a fast-paced bluegrass section. Scott Vestal's clawhammer banjo playing energizes the rest of the musicians, handing over to Jimmy Mattingly on fiddle. Finally, from 2:25, Dolly and her backing singers launch into a section of gospel-style singing and clapping. The rest of the group quickly join in and the song returns to the tempo of the first section that unfolds until the a cappella ending with the words "Rolling down the track." At the very end, the instrumentalists finish with a drawn-out chord on fiddle, banjo, acoustic guitar, and dobro, evoking the trail of dust as the train arrives. Dolly's energetic and breathless vocal line sets the tone for the album; the Queen of Country is back and in great form. The production by Kent Wells is magnificent.

The single of "Blue Smoke," featuring "Home" on the B-side, was released as a limited edition on Dolly Records that was only available in the US and UK.

Unlikely Angel

Dolly Parton / 3:23

Musicians: Kent Wells: acoustic guitar, drum programming / Jimmy Mattingly: fiddle, mandolin / Jay Weaver: double bass / Randy Kohrs: dobro **Vocals:** Dolly Parton **Backing Vocals:** Richard Dennison, Vicki Hampton, Rebecca Isaacs, Sonya Isaacs, Jennifer O'Brien **Recorded:** Kent Wells Productions, Franklin (TN), 2013 **Technical Team:** Producer: Kent Wells / Sound Engineers: Patrick Murphy, Kent Wells / Mixing: Patrick Murphy, Kent Wells

Dolly wrote this song for a 1996 Michael Switzer TV movie, *Unlikely Angel,* aired on CBS and produced by Sandollar Productions. In this fantasy comedy, she plays Ruby Diamond, a singer who dies in a car accident and goes to heaven. There she meets Saint Peter, who tells her she can return to Earth if she agrees to reunite a family that's in trouble. The song tells the story of finding new love with a person sent "straight down to me from heaven."

Beautifully produced by Kent Wells, this ballad is free of excessive reverb and unnecessary orchestral effects. The brilliance brought by the ensemble of dobro, acoustic guitar playing arpeggios, mandolin, and fiddle gives an organic depth to the arrangement, as well as a feeling of intimacy and human warmth, reinforced by Jay Weaver on the double bass. These carefully and delicately woven notes by skilled musicians provide Dolly and her backing singers with the texture onto which they can superimpose their gentle, angelic voices. The discreet touches of percussion were programmed by Kent Wells himself; you could swear they were played by live musicians.

Don't Think Twice

Bob Dylan / 3:21

Musicians: Bob Mater: drums / Steve Turner: drums, percussion / Scott Vestal: banjo / Bryan Sutton: acoustic guitar / Randy Kohrs: dobro / Stuart Duncan: fiddle / Jay Weaver: double bass / Jim Hoke: harmonica **Vocals:** Dolly Parton **Backing Vocals:** Rebecca Isaacs, Sonya Isaacs **Recorded:** Kent Wells Productions, Franklin (TN), 2013 **Technical Team:** Producer: Kent Wells / Sound Engineers: Patrick Murphy, Kent Wells / Mixing: Patrick Murphy, Kent Wells

Not for the first time, here Dolly Parton has chosen to cover a song by Bob Dylan. "Don't Think Twice, It's All Right" was written in 1962. This classic American folk number suits Dolly so well that one wonders why she took so long to add it to her repertoire. The bluegrass sound from Randy

Kohrs on dobro, Scott Vestal on banjo, and Stuart Duncan on fiddle seems to come straight from its original roots, and the Isaacs sisters' backing vocals add a deliciously edgy note. Kent Wells's production, clear, precise, and natural as always, works its habitual magic. When the evidence is there, "don't think twice, it's all right."

You Can't Make Old Friends

Ryan Hanna King, Don Schlitz, Caitlyn Smith / 3:57

Musicians: Greg Morrow: drums / Jimmie Lee Sloas: bass / Ilya Toshinsky: acoustic guitar / J. T. Corenflos, Dann Huff: electric guitar / Charlie Judge: piano, strings, synthesizer / Paul Franklin: pedal steel guitar / Eric Darken: percussion **Vocals:** Dolly Parton, Kenny Rogers **Recorded:** Starstruck Studios, Nashville (TN), 2013, Starstruck Studios and Doppler Studios, Atlanta (GA), (?) **Technical Team:** Producer: Dann Huff / Sound Engineers: Steve Marcantonio, Russell Terrell / Mixing: Steve Marcantonio

This song features Dolly Parton duetting with Kenny Rogers, and it came out as a single in December 2013, following the release of Rogers's album of the same name. It was nominated at the 56th Grammy Awards in the category Best Country Duo. With Dann Huff at the helm, this ballad in the form of a tribute to friendship sounds very different from the first three tracks of the album. The production trademarks of the mainstream Nashville sound are all here. On all of the harmonic instruments and vocals, we find the delay/long reverb mix, pushed gradually as the song's intensity increases. The strings arrangements are coupled with the synthesizer layers and, in addition, we hear descending scales on the chimes, electric guitar arpeggios (played by Dann Huff himself), the muffled acoustic guitar rhythm played with fingers, the strings gently slapped on the neck at the same time as the snare backbeat, minimalist and straight drums played with brushes, a full bass sound kept below 150 Hz, a discreet but extremely dynamic and expressive piano, and the mellow and ethereal pedal steel guitar played by Paul Franklin. Kenny Rogers, Dolly Parton, Dan Huff, and Steve Marcantonio leave nothing to chance in the elegant production of this thought-provoking piece.

Home

Dolly Parton, Kent Wells / 3:22

Musicians: Kent Wells: acoustic and electric guitars, drum programming / Paul Hollowell: piano, Hammond B3 organ / Nick Buda: drums, percussion / Derek Wells, J. T. Corenflos: electric guitar / Jimmie Lee Sloas: bass / Aubrey Haynie: fiddle, mandolin **Vocals:** Dolly Parton **Backing Vocals:** Richard Dennison, Vicki Hampton, Jennifer O'Brien, Monty Allen **Recorded:** Kent Wells Productions, Franklin (TN), 2013 **Technical Team:** Producer: Kent Wells / Sound Engineer: Patrick Murphy / Mixing: Patrick Murphy, Kent Wells

Co-written by Dolly Parton and Kent Wells (who is wearing his producer's hat again), this very autographical song tells the story of a young woman who leaves her home to become a singer. Both in the composition and in the sound created by the musicians, this song seems to be another example of a number where Dolly and Kenny are aiming at producing an international hit: The banjo alongside the saturated electric guitars, the very pop-style drumming, slamming and compressed, all fit well with the programming. Aubrey Haynie's fiddle and mandolin fuse into the dense arrangement but stand out clearly at important moments. The backing vocals bring the ultimate touch of polish to this very radio-friendly track.

Banks Of The Ohio

Traditional song arranged by Dolly Parton / 3:48

Musicians: John Mock: harmonium / Bryan Sutton: acoustic guitar / Stuart Duncan: fiddle **Vocals:** Dolly Parton **Backing Vocals:** Carl Jackson, Val Storey **Recorded:** Kent Wells Productions, Franklin (TN), 2013 **Technical Team:** Producer: Kent Wells / Sound Engineer: Patrick Murphy / Mixing: Patrick Murphy

"Banks of the Ohio" is an anonymous murder ballad dating from the nineteenth century. It tells how Willie, taking a walk with his girl with the intention of proposing to her, is turned down. When they are alone on the banks of the river, the spurned lover kills her. Singing partly a cappella, Dolly makes this song into a beautiful ballad. The central part of the track, from 1:05 and 2:31, features John Mock on harmonium, Stuart Duncan on fiddle, and Bryan Sutton on acoustic guitar. Carl Jackson's remarkable voice is almost equal in precision to Dolly Parton's, and Val Storey brings in a third, higher harmony to reinforce the climaxes (both orchestrated and a cappella).

Lay Your Hands On Me

Jon Bon Jovi, Richie Sambora / 4:13

Musicians: Kent Wells: acoustic and electric guitars / Paul Hollowell: piano, Hammond B3 organ / Mike Brignardello: bass / Jimmy Mattingly: fiddle, mandolin / Randy Kohrs: dobro / Pat Buchanan: electric guitar / Steve Turner: drums, percussion / Steve Hinson: lap steel guitar / Scott Vestal: banjo **Vocals:** Dolly Parton **Backing Vocals:** Richard Dennison, Vicki Hampton, Jennifer O'Brien, Carl Jackson, Val Storey, Kyle Dickinson **Recorded:** Sound Kitchen Studio and Kent Wells Productions, Franklin (TN), 2013 **Technical Team:** Producer: Kent Wells / Sound Engineer: Patrick Murphy / Mixing: Patrick Murphy

"Lay Your Hands on Me" originally came out in August 1989 in the version by rock singer Jon Bon Jovi. In 2014, and with Bon Jovi's blessing, the song was given the gospel treatment. The narrator begs God, "lay your hands on me," to bring about a miracle. At the Glastonbury concert, Dolly Parton was accompanied both on voice and guitar by the co-writer of the original song, Richie Sambora. Like "Home," this arrangement features several electric instruments. The elaborate guitar riff (composed by Sambora) is here played in unison with Jimmy Mattingly's fiddle, sometimes supported by Randy Kohrs on dobro and Steve Hinson on lap steel. The mixture of genres—mainstream hard rock and modern country—works extraordinarily well. Dolly's penchant for this kind of fusion, which is ideally suited to her powerful voice and energetic temperament, is evident in her albums from the late 1970s onward.

Miss You, Miss Me

Dolly Parton / 4:00

Musicians: Thomas Rutledge: acoustic guitar / Michael Davis: keyboards / Jimmy Mattingly: mandolin / Richard Dennison: piano **Vocals:** Dolly Parton **Backing Vocals and Overdubs:** Patrick Murphy **Recorded:** Kent Wells Productions, Franklin (TN), 2013 **Technical Team:** Producer: Kent Wells / Sound Engineers: Michael Davis, Digital Audio Post, Nashville (TN) / Mixing: Patrick Murphy

The narrator in this song is a little girl who is asking her parents, and particularly her father, to resolve their differences. She is suffering from the situation and missing their love. The delicate arpeggios played on the acoustic guitar by Thomas Rutledge provide the backbone of this fine orchestration. Jimmy Mattingly's mandolin and tremolo playing, Richard Dennison's light touch on the piano, and Michael Davis's keyboards, which literally merge with the strings arrangements…all this allows Dolly to lay the vocals gently on top, giving a nuanced interpretation of this piece. One more little jewel in her collection.

Dolly and her guitarist in the middle of a show at the Lanxess Arena in Cologne, Germany, in 2014.

Lover du Jour

Dolly Parton / 4:11

Musicians: Kent Wells: acoustic guitar / Paul Hollowell: piano, Hammond B3 organ / Mike Brignardello: bass / Jimmy Mattingly: fiddle, mandolin / Randy Kohrs: dobro / Pat Buchanan: electric guitar, harmonica / Steve Turner: drums, percussion / Steve Hinson: lap steel guitar **Vocals:** Dolly Parton **Backing Vocals:** Richard Dennison, Vicki Hampton, Jennifer O'Brien, Patrick Murphy **Recorded:** Kent Wells Productions, Franklin (TN), 2013, and Blackbird Studios, Nashville (TN) **Technical Team:** Producer: Kent Wells / Sound Engineer: Patrick Murphy / Mixing: Patrick Murphy

If I Had Wings

Dolly Parton / 4:06

Musicians: Kent Wells: acoustic guitar, drum programming / Jimmy Mattingly: fiddle, mandolin / Jay Weaver: double bass / Randy Kohrs: dobro **Vocals:** Dolly Parton **Backing Vocals:** Richard Dennison, Vicki Hampton, Jennifer O'Brien **Recorded:** Kent Wells Productions, Franklin (TN), 2013 **Technical Team:** Producer: Kent Wells / Sound Engineers: Patrick Murphy, Kent Wells / Mixing: Patrick Murphy

Where would the narrator go if she had wings? Dolly returns her to her campaign to cheer people up: Since we can't change the past, let us make the present and future better. The melody is similar to that of the traditional song "The Wayfaring Stranger," popular with folk and gospel singers from the early nineteenth century. The similarity is all the greater given both the very traditional folk treatment and the theme of the song: exile, migration, journeying. The backing vocals by Richard Dennison, Vicki Hampton, and Jennifer O'Brien brighten the cloudy skies created by a sparse orchestration that, nevertheless, has a certain mystic quality, drawing as it does on traditions of the blues and the mountain music of the first settlers.

In this humorous song, the narrator explains to a Don Juan–type figure that, to use a culinary metaphor, she will never be his dish of the day. The mood is light and the music really swings. The song is introduced by Randy Kohrs's super-bluesy dobro playing, which sets the tone for this bayou-flavored arrangement. The syncopation of the guitars (acoustic, electric, lap steel, and dobro), coupled with the heady (but not heavy) stomp of the rhythm section, plunge the listener into an irresistible country funk groove that is particularly danceable for a midtempo number. You can hear that the drummer Steve Turner is in his element here with his cross stick playing on the edges of the snare drum, or in rim shot (not to mention the finesse of his hi-hat playing). Paul Hollowell's Hammond B3 electric organ also makes a fine contribution to the swamp sound, where Dolly sounds as if she's having a ball!

Dolly as a country priestess, glamorous in her iridescent fringe dress reminiscent of the colors of the LGBTQIA+ flag. Here at a show in aid of the Imagination Library, in 2015.

From Here To The Moon And Back

Dolly Parton / 4:02

Musicians: Jim "Moose" Brown: piano / Dennis Crouch: double bass / Bobby Terry: acoustic guitar / Mickey Raphael: harmonica / Bobby Wood: synthesizer / Tommy White: steel guitar / Chad Cromwell: drums / Steve Gibson: electric guitar / Willie Nelson: "Trigger" (acoustic guitar) / Nashville String Machine: strings **Vocals:** Dolly Parton, Willie Nelson **Recorded:** Georgetown Masters, Ben's Studio and Sound Emporium Recording Studios, Nashville (TN), 2013 **Technical Team:** Producer: Buddy Cannon / Sound Engineers: Drew Bollman, Butch Carr / Mixing: Butch Carr / Mastering: Andrew Mendelson

Dolly Parton previously recorded this number in 2012 with Jeremy Jordan and Kris Kristofferson for the movie *Joyful Noise*. Two years later she chose her friend Willie Nelson to sing with her in a slow dance tune with lyrics celebrating eternal, constant, and vital love. Nelson sings first in this slow country waltz, accompanying himself on his faithful "Trigger"—the name he gave to his acoustic guitar—giving us a short but tuneful solo between 2:26 and 2:40, before the reprise of the last refrain. In Willie Nelson's calloused hands, the sound produced by this nylon-string guitar with its patinated wood, bearing the marks of thousands of hours of playing, is unique. As for the production, the team is changed once again, this time with Buddy Cannon at the controls. The sound color, although purely country and without any obvious trace of bluegrass, fits quite well with tracks produced by Kent Wells. We find similar attention to detail in the whole, even if the sound here is slightly more spacious and with more reverb, thanks to strings arrangements provided by the Nashville String Machine that are a perfect match for this ballad "from here to the moon and back." Although we miss the perfect symbiosis of Dolly Parton and Kenny Rogers, her voice and that of Willie Nelson work wonderfully well together. The performance by two old friends, complementing one another with their different timbres, is a treat for the ears. Dolly even regales us with an overdubbed third harmony line on the refrains.

Try

Dolly Parton / 4:47

Musicians: Kent Wells: acoustic and electric guitars, arrangements, drum programming / Paul Hollowell: piano, Hammond B3 organ, keyboards / Steve Mackey: bass / Pat Buchanan: electric guitar / Nick Buda: drums, percussion / Jimmy Mattingly: fiddle, mandolin / Steve Hinson: lap steel guitar **Vocals:** Dolly Parton **Backing Vocals:** Richard Dennison, Vicki Hampton, Jennifer O'Brien **Recorded:** (?), 2010/2011 **Technical Team:** Producers: Dolly Parton, Kent Wells / Sound Engineers: Patrick Murphy, Tony Smith / Mixing: Mark Needham

This twelfth song returns to the theme of *Better Day*, offering hope to dreamers. Dolly's words say you should never give up on your dreams and you should always aim to go higher. Here we finish with the album's fourth big production number (if we include the rocking "Lay Your Hands on Me"), with Kent Wells back at the helm. This time, it is a midtempo ballad full of energy. In the first verse, the trick of a syncopated rhythmic acoustic guitar over drum programming, enhanced by a shaker marking the eighth notes, is a staple of mainstream pop from 2000 to 2010. The larger-than-life arrangement is gradually fleshed out as it reaches the ultimate climax. Piano, Hammond B3 organ, keyboards, incisive electric guitar lines, bass/drums, lap steel guitar, fiddle, mandolin, strings, and multiple takes of back vocals all combine to create a choral effect, and everything is carefully arranged. As usual, Dolly ends on an uplifting note.

Pure & Simple

Pure and Simple . Say Forever You'll Be Mine . Never Not Love You .
Kiss It (And Make It All Better) . Can't Be That Wrong . Outside Your Door .
Tomorrow Is Forever . I'm Sixteen . Head over High Heels . Forever Love

RELEASE DATE
United States: August 19, 2016
References: Dolly Records and RCA Nashville (TN)—
88985-35123-2
Best US Chart Ranking: 1

For Mother's Day 2016, Dolly offered, as a free download on her website, the song "Mama" (also released as a bonus track on the album version created for sale at Walmart). This song is a beautiful tribute to all mothers, but especially to her own.

The Colors of Love

Pure & Simple was Dolly Parton's forty-third solo album and one she produced herself. Released on August 19, 2016, via Dolly Records in association with the RCA Nashville label, this album hit number eleven on the Billboard 200; it went to number nine on the Australian charts, and to number one on the British charts. Celebrating fifty years of marriage to Carl Dean that same year, here Dolly offers ten songs about love that are both personal and universal. The album received a lot of critical attention in the US, Canada, and the UK, probably because it was the first time in twenty-five years that one of her albums had gone to number one on the Billboard Top Country Albums chart.

Dolly in Her Prime

While America still led the world, the country continued to grapple with climate change and political crises. Soon to hand over the presidency to Donald Trump, Barack Obama traveled to Cuba in the first visit by an American president since 1928. Attacks and shootings continued to plague the American people; meanwhile, Dolly Parton was celebrating her seventieth birthday and bringing out her new album, *Pure & Simple*.

Two important changes had occurred in the singer-songwriter's commercial strategy: the return to RCA, her label between 1967 and 1986, and a contract with Sony Music, which would from now on distribute her albums throughout the world. In August 2015, Dolly had given a number of small-scale concerts under the title *Dolly Parton: Pure and Simple* in the Ryman Auditorium in Nashville, and then at Dollywood. These events were to be the inspiration behind the album and the tour. The album coincided with the moment she and her husband renewed their marriage vows, and Dolly wanted it to represent all the colors of love. Her most devoted fans gave *Pure & Simple* a triumphant reception, and the public at large also enjoyed it. The album was listed in the top 10 of several charts in America and abroad.

The Art of Promotion

Her contract with Sony Music made it possible for Dolly to release new versions of her old songs and albums. She gave interview after interview, always smiling and enthusiastic. She gave concerts, played at the Ohio State Fair—one of the biggest in the US—where her show was sold out, took part in several TV programs, and her presence on social media attracted millions of followers and had an important impact on the promotion of her new album.

The indefatigable singer announced to the press that she was planning a tour with sixty-four concert dates. She also brought out a compilation album, *The Complete Trio Collection,* consisting of the two albums *Trio* and *Trio II* along with some previously unreleased recordings made with Emmylou Harris and Linda Ronstadt.

In June, Dolly held a press conference in Toronto to promote the *Pure & Simple* tour in Canada, and on August 19, several versions of the album were released simultaneously. One, which was intended for Walmart, contained the bonus track "Mama," from the Dollywood production of *My People* that was performed from 2013 to 2017. Another version, created for the British market, included two bonus songs and a live CD recording of Dolly's 2014 performance at Glastonbury. As part of a partnership with Cracker Barrel, *Pure & Simple* was also released in a deluxe version with a large booklet including many photos of Dolly, memorable stories about her life, and two live songs from the Glastonbury concert, as well as coupons for Parton attractions and a fridge magnet.

Album Cover

Seated by the riverside, Dolly is dressed all in white—"pure and simple"—a straw hat beside her and her guitar across her knee. This cover, designed by Fran Strine, varies somewhat among the versions of the album that were released. One version, for example, shows a close-up of a smiling Dolly holding a branch of flowers.

Dolly Parton shares the stage with pop icon Katy Perry at the Country Music Awards at the Grand Garden Arena in Las Vegas on April 3, 2016.

Dolly announced the UK release of the single "Pure and Simple" on Twitter. It was first heard on Ken Bruce's show on BBC Radio 2 on July 7. The next day, the track was available on all digital platforms.

Pure And Simple

Dolly Parton / 2:44

Musicians: Richard Dennison: electric piano / Paul Franklin: pedal steel guitar / Kevin Grantt: double bass / Tom Hoey: drums, percussion / Jimmy Mattingly: mandolin / Tom Rutledge: acoustic guitar **Vocals:** Dolly Parton **Backing Vocals:** Monty Lane Allen, Richard Dennison **Recorded:** Kent Wells Productions, Franklin (TN), 2015–2016 **Technical Team:** Producer: Dolly Parton / Mixing: Patrick Murphy

The color of this love is that of eternity, the sublime, the transcendent dream, the divine. This typically Dolly theme still seduces her fans. While means of communication may evolve, as far as music is concerned Dolly remains faithful to the good old recipes: This timeless ballad could have been composed in the 1970s. To illustrate this "pure and simple" love, Dolly opts for a typical Nashville sound lineup: drums played lightly with brushes, straightforward bass line moving with the bass drum, Wurlitzer-style electric piano—full with a slight saturation, especially in the attack. The folk guitar dominates the accompaniment, and the two solos—on mandolin and steel guitar—make an effective contribution. The only indications of modernity in this song are the gentle and sophisticated backing vocals and the clarity of the recording.

Say Forever You'll Be Mine

Dolly Parton / 2:49

Musicians: Tom Rutledge: acoustic guitar / Jimmy Mattingly: fiddle **Vocals:** Dolly Parton **Recorded:** Kent Wells Productions, Franklin (TN), 2015–2016 **Technical Team:** Producer: Dolly Parton / Mixing: Patrick Murphy, Nathan Smith

Duetting with Porter Wagoner, Dolly first sang "Say Forever You'll Be Mine" in 1975 on the album of the same name. The 2016 version is very different. Here she is alone at the mic, alternating the very soft sung parts with spoken words, as if the narrator were whispering her love into her lover's ear. The color of this second title is that of belonging: You are mine, I am yours, even though no one can promise that there will never be clouds in the sky of this love. The intimacy of the song is underlined by the acoustic guitar played in arpeggios by Tom Rutledge and the subtle fiddle counterpoints, played by the great Jimmy Mattingly. There are a few overdubs: The violin and the acoustic guitar lines are doubled and then two voices are arranged on the left and on the right of the mix during the spoken part. For the final modulation, Jimmy Mattingly piles up the overdubs, creating a veritable string ensemble instilling the song with a mood of shining and solemn hope.

Dolly Parton upon her arrival at the 51st Academy of Country Music Awards, April 3, 2016.

Never Not Love You

Dolly Parton / 3:36

Musicians: Tom Rutledge: acoustic guitar, banjo / Richard Dennison: piano / Steve Mackey: bass / Paul Franklin: pedal steel guitar / Tom Hoey: drums, percussion / Jimmy Mattingly: mandolin **Vocals:** Dolly Parton **Backing Vocals:** Richard Dennison, Vicki Hampton, Jennifer O'Brien **Recorded:** Kent Wells Productions, Franklin (TN), 2015–2016 **Technical Team:** Producer: Dolly Parton / Mixing: Patrick Murphy

The narrator, as a demonstration of her love, lists all the things she will never do, such as winning a Pulitzer Prize or climbing Mount Everest. One thing that will never happen is that she stops loving her lover.

The mixing of this track is interesting, the balance of a remarkable precision. The bass drum is very prominent, the attack powerful, and the sound quite dry. The bass is also well to the fore, while the banjo and mandolin are in the background but still clearly audible. The strummed twelve-string acoustic guitar has the first four pairs of strings tuned in octaves, while the last two pairs of strings are simply doubled. The result is a chorus-like effect, very rich at the top end and slightly metallic, like a dulcimer or a bouzouki.

Kiss It (And Make It All Better)

Dolly Parton / 3:48

Musicians: Tom Rutledge: acoustic guitar / Kent Wells: electric guitar / Paul Hollowell: piano / Michael Davis: programming of strings / Steve Mackey: bass / Paul Franklin: pedal steel guitar / Steve Turner: drums **Vocals:** Dolly Parton, Richard Dennison **Backing Vocals:** Richard Dennison, Vicki Hampton, Jennifer O'Brien **Recorded:** Kent Wells Productions, Franklin (TN), 2015–2016 **Technical Team:** Producer: Dolly Parton / Mixing: Patrick Murphy

Love is a balm, a tonic, able to make a broken heart beat again, bringing back a smile to the lips and a light in the eyes. If this little miracle of life has such restorative power, can a new love erase the pain of a love that is lost?

This archetypical mainstream pop ballad starts out very smoothly: piano, guitars, and vocals featuring on the first verse with the rest of the band entering at the refrain. This format can also be found in Aerosmith's "I Don't Want to Miss a Thing," with the faders rising on the chorus, or Ed Sheeran's "Visiting Hours" off his *Equals* album (2021). Kent Wells's touch on the electric guitar reminds us of Mark Knopfler, the famous front man of the English band Dire Straits, himself very influenced by the playing of the great Nashville session men.

Dolly posing with her Country Music Award at the Bridgestone Arena in Nashville, 2016.

Can't Be That Wrong

Dolly Parton / 3:56

Musicians: Tom Rutledge: acoustic guitar, electric guitar / Richard Dennison: piano / Tom Hoey: percussion / Steve Mackey: bass **Vocals:** Dolly Parton **Backing Vocals:** Richard Dennison, Vicki Hampton, Jennifer O'Brien **Recorded:** Kent Wells Productions, Franklin (TN), 2015–2016 **Technical Team:** Producer: Dolly Parton / Mixing: Patrick Murphy

"Can't Be That Wrong" echoes the theme of "God Won't Get You," released in 1984 for the film *Rhinestone*. The songwriter explores the contradictory feelings of adulterous love. Should one give in to temptation by taking a second lover, but suffer shame and guilt for betraying the first? Or not have an extramarital affair and feel the pain of passing up an opportunity to love and be loved? A classic theme in Dolly's repertoire, a biblical and universal dilemma.

Musically, this is an unusual song for Dolly Parton. For the first cycle of verses she sings accompanied only by Tom Rutledge with his acoustic guitar. She is then joined by the rest of the band, which makes a very smooth entrance. Here, Tom Hoey plays a percussion set with bongo, shaker, metal chimes, light bass drum, and a cymbal. The very aquatic sound of the electric guitar, an effect reminiscent of bubbles of water, is obtained by a clever combination of tremolo, chorus, and Uni-Vibe (sound modulation pedal).

Outside Your Door

Dolly Parton / 3:03

Musicians: Tom Rutledge: acoustic guitar / Kent Wells: electric guitar / Paul Hollowell: piano, organ / Paul Franklin: pedal steel guitar / Steve Mackey: bass / Steve Turner: drums **Vocals:** Dolly Parton **Backing Vocals:** Richard Dennison, Vicki Hampton, Jennifer O'Brien **Recorded:** Kent Wells Productions, Franklin (TN), 2015–2016 **Technical Team:** Producer: Dolly Parton / Mixing: Patrick Murphy

Like a blazing sun, the narrator joyfully prepares to meet her lover, with two bottles of wine to celebrate their reunion: "Only a door separates us from love." The simple video shows a woman's hands writing the text in a notebook, perhaps suggesting a diary.

Here we are back with a country-style pop song, the use of drums being much more natural-sounding than in the previous albums, where the aim was a rock sound. An electric piano and an organ are employed, forming a balanced duo on the left and right of the mix. Their respective lines are easily distinguished but do not mask the other instruments, a tribute as much to the quality of the mixing as to the quality of the arrangements. As for Dolly, she does not push her voice, keeping it instead within a comfortable range—this is not the moment for extremes of lyricism. In keeping with the whole of this album, this song is intimate and inward-looking.

Tomorrow Is Forever

Dolly Parton / 3:10

Musicians: Tom Rutledge: acoustic and electric guitars / Paul Franklin: pedal steel guitar / Kevin Grantt: double bass / Tom Hoey: drums, percussion / Jimmy Mattingly: mandolin **Vocals:** Dolly Parton **Backing Vocals:** Richard Dennison, Monty Lane Allen **Recorded:** Kent Wells Productions, Franklin (TN), 2015–2016 **Technical Team:** Producer: Dolly Parton / Mixing: Patrick Murphy

Central to these lyrics is the relationship between the past (the color of sorrow) and the future of love (the color of joy). The narrator affirms that tomorrow everything is possible, even eternal love. On the musical side, we return to the 3/4 time of a slow country waltz, the arrangement based exclusively on plucked strings and drums. The mandolin plays a more important role than on the rest of this album, as does the pedal steel guitar. Until now, these two instruments—so important in Dolly's compositions—have remained rather in the background.

I'm Sixteen

Dolly Parton / 3:34

Musicians: Tom Rutledge: acoustic guitar / Kent Wells: electric guitar / Paul Hollowell: piano, organ / Steve Turner: drums / Steve Mackey: bass **Vocals:** Dolly Parton **Backing Vocals:** Richard Dennison, Vicki Hampton, Jennifer O'Brien, Jeff Pearles **Recorded:** Kent Wells Productions, Franklin (TN), 2015–2016 **Technical Team:** Producer: Dolly Parton / Mixing: Patrick Murphy

In this nostalgic song, the narrator feels like she felt when she was sixteen, experiencing the same crazy passion. The nostalgia is all the more marked as the melody of the chorus resembles the riff of "Do I Ever Cross Your Mind," interpreted by the king of picking, Chet Atkins. It is, however, infinitely more modern with its riffs and licks of electric guitar—very blues rock. Jeff Pearles's bass voice is wonderfully effective as always.

Head Over High Heels

Dolly Parton / 2:50

Musicians: Tom Rutledge: acoustic guitar, banjo / Kent Wells: electric guitar / Paul Hollowell: organ / Steve Turner: drums / Steve Mackey: bass / Paul Franklin: pedal steel guitar **Vocals:** Dolly Parton **Backing Vocals:** Richard Dennison, Vicki Hampton, Jennifer O'Brien **Recorded:** Kent Wells Productions, Franklin (TN), 2015–2016 **Technical Team:** Producer: Dolly Parton / Mixing: Patrick Murphy

Dolly sings here about passionate love. She describes the ritual of a woman's preparation for her date. She makes herself beautiful and desirable, putting on her high heels and her makeup, doing what almost every woman in the world does when she wants to seduce her lover.

The banjo takes an active part in the accompaniment. It comes in from the beginning of the piece although it can be confused at first with the palm-muted electric guitar. The organ has a similarly discreet role, with layers and small notes. This addition of rhythmic elements enormously enriches a song that is probably the most electric of the entire album. The electric guitar, with distortion, brings the rock touch. At the end, it goes down in pitch in one phrase, as if the song were collapsing—perhaps to evoke the moment when the protagonist can finally take off her stilettos?

Forever Love

Dolly Parton / 3:30

Musicians: Tom Rutledge: acoustic guitar / David Davidson, David Angell: violin / Kristin Wilkinson: alto / Anthony Lamarchina: cello / David Davidson: strings arrangements **Vocals:** Dolly Parton **Recorded:** Kent Wells Productions, Franklin (TN), 2015–2016 **Technical Team:** Producer: Dolly Parton / Mixing: Patrick Murphy

In this finale, all the colors of love are gathered together. Dolly, who dedicated "Forever Love" to her husband, also sang it during their vow renewal ceremony. There is a full chamber orchestra. The classical guitar, with its nylon strings, brings an original sound to the ensemble, making it a little more modern than the chamber orchestra alone. Dolly sings and croons very close to the mic, the breathiness of her voice sounding like a caress. Unusually for a Dolly song, the conclusion is intimate and essentially private.

I Believe in You: The Young Persons' Album

I Believe in You (Dolly Parton / 2:00)
Coat of Many Colors (Dolly Parton / 2:56)
Together Forever (Dolly Parton / 2:26)
I Am a Rainbow (Dolly Parton / 1:58)
I'm Here (Dolly Parton / 2:27)
A Friend Like You (Dolly Parton / 1:52)
Imagination (Dolly Parton / 2:23)
You Can Do It (Dolly Parton / 1:53)
Responsibility (Dolly Parton / 1:54)
You Gotta Be (Dolly Parton / 1:54)
Makin' Fun Ain't Funny (Dolly Parton / 2:19)
Chemo Hero (Dolly Parton / 2:09)
Brave Little Soldier (Dolly Parton / 2:34)
A Reading of "Coat of Many Colors" (bonus track / Dolly Parton / 2:45)

Album Release Date
United States: September 29, 2017
References: Dolly Records and RCA Nashville, Nashville (TN)—88985-48348-2
Best US Chart Ranking: 3

Musicians: Paul Brannon: guitars / Richard Dennison, Tim Hayden: claviers / Tom Hoey: drums, percussion / Steve Mackey, Danny O'Lannerghty: bass / Tom Rutledge: acoustic guitar, bass, MIDI guitars / Tom Reeves: drums / Kent Wells: electric guitar **Vocals:** Dolly Parton
Backing Vocals: Richard Dennison, Jennifer O'Brien, Vicki Hampton, The Inner Child Chorus, Shelley Jennings, Melodie Kirkpatrick, Shane McConnell **Recorded:** Westpark Sound, Franklin (TN) (?)
Technical Team: Producers: Tom McBryde, Richard Dennison, Tom Rutledge / Executive Producers: Paul T. Couch, Dolly Parton / Sound Engineers: Tom Rutledge, Tom Reeves, Chris Latham, Nathan Smith / Mixing: Tom Reeves / Mastering: John Mayfield

I Believe in You is Dolly Parton's forty-fourth solo album and her first young persons' album. Produced by Tom McBryde, Richard Dennison, and Tom Rutledge, and co-produced by Dolly Parton and Paul T. Couch, it was released on September 29, 2017, on Dolly Records, in association with RCA Nashville. With the Dollywood Foundation, which supports students, and the Imagination Library program, which fights illiteracy, Dolly is committed to young people: She "believes in them," as the album title indicates. The album reached number 173 on the Billboard 200 and number 20 on the Top Country Albums chart. A video clip in the form of a cartoon was produced for each song.

Supporting New Generations
As Donald Trump, the newly elected president, was moving into the White House, a climate of opposition was intensifying, and many anti-Trump Americans were demonstrating or even leaving the country. The year 2017 was also focused on the defense of women's rights (with the Women's March on Washington), the LGBTQIA+ community, and the fight against racial inequality. In the midst of all this sociopolitical upheaval, while the far right mobilized in Charlottesville, Virginia, a total eclipse crossed the United States.

I Believe in You is done in the same spirit as "Coat of Many Colors," which the album reproduces and of which it delivers a reading by Dolly Parton. As a child, the star drew strength, courage, and inspiration from dreams, stories, and songs of her family, whose only book was the Bible. When the album was released, the critics were divided—some found it moralizing—while children all over the United States were using it as a tool for reflection and reproducing the multicolored paper coat.

With the Dollywood Foundation, which supports students, and the Imagination Library program, which combats illiteracy, Dolly has shown a constant commitment to young people.

A Coat of Advocacy

From her own traumatizing experience of poverty, Dolly has crafted a song, a children's show, and two illustrated books. The second book, published in 2016, offered a free download of "Makin' Fun Ain't Funny." The Queen of Country's story also inspired a comedy drama, *Dolly Parton's Coat of Many Colors*, directed by Stephen Herek, in which the star provides the voiceover. Broadcast on NBC on December 10, 2015, it earned her the Tex Ritter Award (which recognizes a film using country music) at the Academy of Country Music ceremony. The sequel, *Dolly Parton's Christmas of Many Colors: Circle of Love*, in which the star makes an appearance, aired on NBC on November 30, 2016. But Dolly did not stop there. At Dollywood she created a show called the *Imagination Playhouse*, in which artists transform her songs into a twenty-minute musical. "I Believe in You"—the artist's credo—was written for one of these shows, with proceeds benefiting the Dollywood Foundation.

Genesis and Lyrics

There is hardly an album in Dolly's catalog that doesn't evoke the rainbow of life: no sun without rain, no laughter without tears. In "I Am a Rainbow," she emphasizes the uniqueness of each child and the strength they carry within. It is up to each child to color the world in their own way. Dolly puts imagination back at the heart of everyday life. Whatever happens to you, she says in "Imagination," you can always find refuge in your imagination: flying, traveling, dreaming, becoming a hero or anything you like. Interviewed by Lisa Butterworth for *Bust* magazine in 2014, Dolly explains, "If you're gonna make a dream come true, you gotta work it. You can't just sit around. That's a wish. That's not a dream."[1] Indeed, Dolly has spoken extensively about her propensity for imagining the unfolding of her projects, and about her lifelong faith. She conveys her culture of the American dream that has seduced the world. "You Can Do It" works like a mantra, whether you are big or small.

I Believe in You is Dolly's first album written and recorded for children. Here, at her press conference in front of media representatives and their children in 2017.

Be strong like a bear, know how to anticipate the times ahead like a squirrel putting aside nuts for winter, fly like an eagle...these are among the recommendations listed in "You Gotta Be." But it is probably the text of "Responsibility" that some critics must have found moralistic in terms of its views of work: Everyone, big or small, has a job to do every day (working, doing their homework...), and the world works better when everyone does their part.

Finally, "Chemo Hero" pays tribute to all the children who face the ordeal of chemotherapy (the disease of cancer, the pain, the hair loss), as well as to their parents. Perhaps this is what the songwriter intends to symbolize in "Brave Little Soldier," a cover of a track from the 1994 album *Heartsongs: Live from Home*?

Production

As with *Sha-Kon-O-Hey! Land of Blue Smoke* (recorded eight years earlier to provide music for the Dollywood show of the same name), *I Believe in You* relies heavily on programming and sounds played on a MIDI controller, whether a master keyboard, a MIDI guitar, a wind controller or an electronic pad. Indeed, for these fourteen titles intended for young people, Dolly Parton and Tom McBryde, the producer, do not hesitate to use the naive and familiar sounds that have illustrated children's television programs since the end of the 1980s. The brass sounds especially—trumpet, saxophone, or brass ensemble, found throughout this album—are probably the most identifiable and typical of cartoon music.

The less experienced ear can easily identify the synthetic aspect and the lack of expressiveness of most of the sounds. The strings and the percussive elements remain, however, the most impressive, even though one does not feel on this album the desire to humanize the sound and to make it as organic as possible (at the cost of tedious manipulations). The option of the MIDI, chosen both for practical reasons and for the bright and joyful side of the sounds, produces an environment that is certainly clear, readable, and reassuring for the children, but very sanitized.

In such a context, Dolly's antics work wonders, as the Queen of Country never misses an opportunity to connect with her inner child. Her spiritedness, as always, is perfectly authentic. And the children are not mistaken.

Album Cover

Trey Fanjoy's images show Dolly on the front cover wearing a blue dress like a fairy with butterfly wings, while on the back she is reading children's books in a tailored suit with a pair of tiny glasses. Inside, a Dennis Carney photograph immortalizes the artist with two little girls who are kissing her on the cheeks.

Dollymania

From the beginning of her career, Dolly Parton has been dedicated to her fans. She always remembered her years on *The Porter Wagoner Show* and the attitude Porter took toward his fans, and she remained inspired by it. Since the advent of networking, fans have been making or breaking the lives of their idols. What is this strange relationship between the fan and the star?

Characteristics of Dollymania

At the beginning of December 2022, a big splash was made in the community of Dolly's fans, who are counted in the millions and come from all walks of life and every socio-economic group: Dolly arrived on TikTok! The impressive professional longevity of the star, her constant presence, and the values she stands for probably help to explain her countless admirers.

Everyone loves Dolly…but what are the traits and values that electrify her fans? Perceived as an endearing and generous personality and an independent female artist, the star represents the freedom to be yourself, an acceptance of differences, the joy of living with humor and faith, and an exceptional work ethic. She embodies the American dream, and she's a source of energy and hope for her fans. She is beautiful and extravagant, with a confident blend of sophistication and simplicity, authenticity, and superficiality. Above all, with her touching stories, and her music that fuses country, pop, and gospel, Dolly represents love, and the poetry of words. It is no surprise that she embodies such vitality and grace.

When a Star Endorses Her Fans

Dolly's fans are seemingly always ready for anything! They relay information; manage fan clubs and a colossal mass of photos, videos, and archives; and also spend time and money without counting the cost. On the Internet, sites and forums abound and, among them, the famous Dollymania.net stands out. It is managed by Duane Gordon, one of her greatest admirers, to whom academics, biographers, and journalists owe a great deal. On this well-documented site, which he has maintained with impeccable consistency by devoting his days to the star since the late 1990s, Gordon transcribes, relays, and comments with admiration on Dolly Parton's career. The star herself has thanked him for his professional, passionate, and respectful approach.

But Dollymania does not stop there: In New York City every year, Dollypalooza takes place. This is a collective artistic performance that celebrates the singer in a rather singular way: At this gigantic party, men and women dress up as Dolly and perform her songs in front of a crowd of fans. This event features the extravagance ("palooza") of Dolly's outfits, wigs, rhinestones, and makeup, along with quizzes, costume contests, and burlesque shows. There are also prizes to be won at auctions—a host of items in the star's image, from T-shirts to greeting cards, beauty masks, kitchen aprons, pairs of socks, bags, wigs, posters, and even a pinball machine.

In 2019, Dolly signed a contract with IMG, which specializes in marketing, events, sports, and fashion. This was an opportunity for her to expand her brand and to launch herself in fashion, perfumes, and accessories. The latest relates to the canine world: On her website she dedicates several articles to it and offers for sale various objects for dogs, all bearing the Dolly name. After all, her first success was "Puppy Love."

Once a Fan, Always a Fan?

Despair, distress, and sadness were just some of the emotions expressed by devastated fans when Dolly announced, in March 2022, that she was ending her tours. These were not just words shared on social networks; they are a psychological, emotional, and affective reality expressed by the star's fans. This change also reflects a new economic reality, which is evidenced by a recent study that found that 40 percent of American fans are responsible for 75 percent of music spending, which amounts to between $20 billion and $26 billion each year. There is a bridge called the Dolly Parton Bridge in Memphis, Tennessee, a statue in Sevierville, Tennessee, and even an official Dolly doll. A petition has even been launched in Tennessee to replace Confederate monuments with statues of the star! Dolly and her fans have created a love story that has lasted for six decades. As further proof of this boundless love, the star has in her home a multitude of gifts sent by her fans—probably enough for a "Dolly Parton Fans" retrospective!

ALBUM

A Holly Dolly Christmas

Holly Jolly Christmas . Christmas Is . Cuddle Up, Cozy Down Christmas .
Christmas on the Square . Circle of Love . All I Want for Christmas Is You .
Comin' Home for Christmas . Christmas Where We Are . Pretty Paper .
I Saw Mommy Kissing Santa Claus . You Are My Christmas .
Mary, Did You Know?

RELEASE DATE
United States: October 2, 2020
References: Butterfly Records, Los Angeles (CA) and
12-Tone Music Group, New York (NY)—190296823015
Best US Chart Ranking: 1

A Christmas Unlike Any Other

A Holly Dolly Christmas is Dolly Parton's third Christmas album. Produced by Kent Wells, it was released on October 2, 2020, on Dolly's own label, Butterfly Records, in association with 12-Tone Music Group. It reached number sixteen on the Billboard 200 and number one on the US Top Country Albums chart.

The World in a State of Shock

In 2020, the COVID-19 pandemic affected the entire planet, and the massive containment of populations, managed differently in different countries, was experienced as a challenge and a trauma. The United States, under the presidency of Donald Trump, over whom the threat of impeachment hung, was also experiencing severe economic turmoil. The country was divided on how to respond to the outbreak. The year ended with the election of Joe Biden as president, in a time also marked by social unrest and climate disruption.

In September, Dolly Parton lost another dear friend, singer-songwriter Mac Davis. Knowing that COVID-19 was not to be taken lightly, Dolly became involved in convincing her fellow citizens to get vaccinated. On the one hand, she donated one million dollars to Vanderbilt University to support research; and on the other hand, on March 3, 2021, she was filmed while receiving the vaccine, singing "Vaccine, vaccine, vaccine, vacciiiine / I'm begging you please don't hesitate" to the tune of "Jolene," and then she disseminated the video on social media in order to encourage the population to do the same. Finally, she released this Christmas album, undoubtedly with a view to boosting morale, seeking to instill a little warmth and tenderness, as well as some joyful rhythm with which to see out a year that had been so terrible for so many. In so doing, she returns to her most essential values.

Being Together

Even though Dolly Parton takes action, writes, and brings people together, since the beginning of her career she has refused to be associated with any specific political movement. This is the reason for her refusal to accept certain awards, such as the Medal of Freedom—one of the most prestigious civilian decorations in the United States—that both Donald Trump and Joe Biden wanted to give her.

At the end of a year in which everyone, from one end of the planet to the other, had been subjected to the wearing of masks, protective measures, social distancing, confinement, illness, and in some cases the loss of loved ones, being together had never seemed so important. With this album, Dolly decided to honor the holiday season and celebrate the spirit of Christmas with warmth and humanity, through music, and in collaboration with her artist friends.

Album Cover

The star, dressed all in red and smiling, wears a few holly leaves (on her neck, wrist, and hip). Inside, we see her dressed as Mrs. Claus, wearing a red hat with a white pompom, and also taking a batch of cookies out of the oven. These photographs were taken by Stacie Huckeba.

Album Recording and Production: Recording sessions took place at several studios: Sound Stage Studios, Adventure Studios, Velvet Apple Music Studio, Little Big Sound, Quad Studios (Nashville, TN) / Kent Wells Productions, Dark Horse Recording, Paragon Studios (Franklin, TN) / The Jazz/Pop Sweatshop, Vancouver (BC, Canada) / Monk Music Studios, East Hampton (NY) / Pedernales Recording Studio, Spicewood (TX): 2009, 2016–2020.

Technical Team: Producers: Kent Wells, Richard Dennison, Tom Rutledge / Executive Producer: Dolly Parton / Sound Engineers: Steve Chadie, Joey Crawford, Cynthia Daniels, Ryan Enockson, Patrick Murphy, Tom Rutledge, Cody Simpson, Paul David Hager, Kevin Willis

Holly Jolly Christmas

Johnny Marks / 3:21

Musicians: Dennis Crouch: double bass / Michael Davis: keyboards, Hammond B3 organ / Lloyd Green: pedal steel guitar / Steve Turner: drums, percussion / Paul Hollowell: piano / Jimmy Mattingly: fiddle / Tom Rutledge: acoustic guitar / Kent Wells: electric guitar **Vocals:** Dolly Parton **Backing Vocals:** Richard Dennison, Vicki Hampton, Jennifer O'Brien

How to get out of COVID-19 and gloom? With one of the most covered holiday songs, originally performed in 1964 by American singer and actor Burl Ives. The star puts all her heart into making this song lively and joyful, in a mixture of swing and Christmas singing. We note the double bass playing and its very deep notes. Almost all the orchestra is brought in for the swing part, while the backing vocals along with the percussion and their bells provide the magical touch.

Christmas Is

Dolly Parton / 3:17

Musicians: Michael Davis: keyboards / Lloyd Green: pedal steel guitar / Richard Dennison: piano / Tom Hoey: drums, percussion / Paul Hollowell: piano / Gary Lunn: bass / Jimmy Mattingly: fiddle, mandolin / Tom Rutledge: acoustic guitar / Kent Wells: electric guitar, classical guitar Orchestration: Michael Davis **Vocals:** Dolly Parton, Miley Cyrus **Backing Vocals:** Richard Dennison, Vicki Hampton, Jennifer O'Brien

Together with her goddaughter, the famous actress and singer Miley Cyrus, Dolly performs this song she wrote for the TV movie *Christmas on the Square*, which conveys messages of love and compassion to end the year better than it began. Among other instruments, the piece involves several keyboards (synthesizer, piano) and guitars (electric, folk, classical), the fiddle, and the mandolin. The mix emphasizes the two main vocals—at the expense, perhaps, of the backing vocals, which are drowned out by the orchestra. The grain of Miley Cyrus's voice, with a lot of midrange and lots of breathiness, is recognizable among the rest. In spite of the sounds of electronic layers that line the piece, one notices the glockenspiel (a small metallophone resembling an instrument for a child) and the bells, which open and close the song.

Cuddle Up, Cozy Down Christmas

Dolly Parton / 3:39

Musicians: Roy Agee: trombone / David Angell, Wei Tsun Chang, Janet Darnell, David Davidson, Stefan Petrescu, Karen Winkelman, Mary Kathryn Vanosdale: violin / Monisa Angell, Chris Farrell: viola / Steve Turner: drums, percussion / Paul Hollowell: piano / Sam Levine: saxophone, flute, clarinet / Dennis Crouch: double bass / Paul Nelson, Sarighani Reist: cello / Kent Wells: acoustic guitar, electric guitar, percussion Orchestration: Roy Agee, David Davidson, Michael Davis, Sam Levine **Vocals:** Dolly Parton, Michael Bublé

This duet with Canadian singer Michael Bublé is dedicated to lovers who dream of only one thing at Christmas: staying cuddled up to each other while watching the snow fall.

While the first track of the album, "Holly Jolly Christmas," is very swinging, "Cuddle Up, Cozy Down Christmas" has a rather jazzy tone. The playing of the big band, the sleigh bells, the sounds of bells, and the very bouncy interventions of the flutes produce a very successful mix of genres. The intro, in the form of a snare drum call, is identical to the first track of the album. The drums pattern is also reminiscent of "Holly Jolly Christmas," but on a slower tempo. The bass drum plays on all the beats, the snare drum plays the strong beats two and four of the measure with some liberties taken that help to fuel the groove of the song. Bells or a tambourine replace the hi-hat, which is played on the pedal on all the beats. Some of the musicians play the part of several instruments, which entails a large number of takes, especially overdubs (note the flute lines at around the 0:30 mark).

Christmas On The Square

Dolly Parton / 3:15

Musicians: Dennis Crouch: double bass / Michael Davis: keyboards / Lloyd Green: pedal steel guitar / Steve Turner: drums, percussion / Paul Hollowell: piano / Jimmy Mattingly: fiddle / Rhonda Vincent: mandolin / Tom Rutledge: acoustic guitar / Kent Wells: electric guitar, banjo **Vocals:** Dolly Parton **Backing Vocals:** Richard Dennison, Vicki Hampton, Darrin Vincent, Jennifer O'Brien, Rhonda Vincent

Dolly poses for the traditional portrait in front of the Christmas tree in Nashville.

Christmas on the Square is a 2020 American Christmas musical film directed and choreographed by Debbie Allen. Released on Netflix, it won the award for Best TV Movie at the 73rd Primetime Emmy Awards. In it, Dolly Parton plays an angel supporting the residents of a town in their struggle against the wealthy Regina Fuller, who is determined to spoil Christmas for them by evicting them to sell their land to a shopping center developer. The song is a complete panorama of what goes on in the streets illuminated for the festive holidays, of what is eaten and drunk, of the snowball games, of the coats that are worn, and the presents that are given.

This is the first real country song on the album. The banjo contributes its very recognizable tone and playing. When it stops playing on the second verse, the sound of the song changes dramatically. The fiddle is well surrounded in the mix, framed on the right by the banjo, and on the left by the mandolin. The backing vocals are a little overplayed, but this fits well with a Christmas soundtrack.

Circle Of Love
Dolly Parton / 3:42

Musicians: Michael Davis: keyboards, Hammond B3 organ, percussion / Richard Dennison: piano / Tom Hoey: drums, percussion / Steve Mackey: bass / Tom Rutledge: acoustic guitar / David Angell, Wei Tsun Chang, Janet Darnell, David Davidson, Stefan Petrescu, Karen Winkelman, Mary Kathryn Vanosdale: violin / Monisa Angell, Chris Farrell: viola / Carole Rabinowitz: cello Orchestration: David Davidson
Vocals: Dolly Parton **Backing Vocals:** Richard Dennison, Vicki Hampton, Jennifer O'Brien

This song, written by Dolly Parton, was performed by country singer Jennifer Nettles for the TV movie *Dolly Parton's Christmas of Many Colors: Circle of Love*, made for NBC and broadcast on November 30, 2016. In this gospel song we find the three-beat ballad to which the string ensemble adds grandiloquence, in contrast to the usually less solemn style.

All I Want For Christmas Is You

Mariah Carey, Walter Afanasieff / 4:04

Musicians: Michael Davis: keyboards / Lloyd Green: pedal steel guitar / Steve Turner: drums, percussion / Kent Wells: banjo / Michael Davis: keyboards / Paul Hollowell: piano / Gary Lunn: bass / Jimmy Mattingly: fiddle / Tom Rutledge: acoustic guitar **Vocals:** Dolly Parton, Jimmy Fallon **Backing Vocals:** Richard Dennison, Vicki Hampton, Jennifer O'Brien

Written and sung by Mariah Carey in 1994, "All I Want for Christmas Is You" is about the romance of Christmas. Dolly Parton and comedian, actor, and host Jimmy Fallon start by talking about Christmas and then sing about how they do not want anything, because they are each other's greatest gift. The banjo provides the "country guarantee" for the song in its play, with plenty of flow. It stops playing during the solo verse by Jimmy Fallon to emphasize his singing, which is pretty good for someone whose day job is not singing.

Comin' Home For Christmas

Dolly Parton, Kent Wells / 4:28

Musicians: Michael Davis: keyboards, Hammond B3 organ / Steve Turner: drums, percussion / Paul Hollowell: piano / Steve Mackey: bass / Jimmy Mattingly: fiddle / Kent Wells: electric guitar, acoustic guitar **Vocals:** Dolly Parton **Backing Vocals:** Richard Dennison, Vicki Hampton, Jennifer O'Brien

This gentle song reminds us of the importance of being with family at this time of the year, gathered around the tree or a beautiful well-stocked table, enveloped in comforting warmth. A touch of Tennessee and nostalgia shines through, especially with the rather slow tempo featuring many minor chords. The profusion of instruments playing in the same range announces, with great solemnity, the long-awaited return of the narrator.

Christmas Where We Are

Jada Roberts, Barry Jobe / 3:10

Musicians: Michael Davis: keyboards / Lloyd Green: pedal steel guitar / Richard Dennison: piano / Steve Turner: drums, percussion / Paul

Hollowell: piano, Hammond B3 organ / Gary Lunn: bass / Jimmy Mattingly: fiddle, mandolin / Tom Rutledge: acoustic guitar / Kent Wells: electric guitar, programming Orchestration: Roy Agee, David Davidson, Michael Davis, Sam Levine **Vocals:** Dolly Parton, Billy Ray Cyrus **Backing Vocals:** Richard Dennison, Vicki Hampton, Aaron McCune, Jennifer O'Brien **Vocal Harmonies:** Heidi Parton Backing Vocals Arrangements: Lakieta Bagwell-Garves

This text, sung as a duet with singer Billy Ray Cyrus, references "All I Want for Christmas Is You." The important thing, in the narrator's eyes, is to spend Christmas with her lover, no matter where they end up.

The song was written and composed by Dolly's niece, Jada Roberts (aka Jada Star), and her songwriting partner Barry Jobe (aka BarryJ) for the 2019 Dollywood Christmas show, *A Songbook Christmas*. This song fits in well with the contemporary pop landscape, featuring electric guitar solos, mandolin, multiple drum breaks, and doubling with a drum machine at times. The music was rearranged for the Dolly and Billy Ray Cyrus version: A fiddle was added and, above all, the general sound of the mix is very different. While it is bright, almost aggressive with Jada Star and BarryJ, here there is much more low and midrange roundness. In a rare combination, the fiddle and mandolin play a melody in unison, creating a distinctive timbre. Even though the weight of the years is felt in the voice of Miley Cyrus's father, the precision is still there.

Pretty Paper

Willie Nelson / 3:33

Musicians: Michael Davis: organ / Lloyd Green: pedal steel guitar / Steve Turner: drums, percussion / Paul Hollowell: piano / Gary Lunn: double bass / Jimmy Mattingly: fiddle / Paul Nelson, Carole Rabinowitz, Sarighani Reist: cello / David Angell, Wei Tsun Chang, Janet Darnell, David Davidson, Stefan Petrescu, Karen Winkelman, Mary Kathryn Vanosdale: violin / Tom Rutledge: acoustic guitar / Willie Nelson: folk guitar / Kent Wells: electric guitar Orchestration: David Davidson, Michael Davis **Vocals:** Dolly Parton, Willie Nelson **Backing Vocals:** Richard Dennison, Vicki Hampton, Jennifer O'Brien

Inspired by a disabled street vendor who sold "pretty paper, pretty ribbons" while crawling along a downtown sidewalk in Fort Worth, Texas, "Pretty Paper" was recorded by Willie Nelson in November 1964. Forty years of mystery surrounded the song until, in 2013, its protagonist was formally identified by the *Fort Worth Star-Telegram*: It was a man named Frankie Brierton, from Santo, Texas, who lost the use of his legs to a case of childhood meningitis.

The duo of Dolly Parton and Willie Nelson offer a very beautiful version of this song. Nelson's voice is instantly recognizable, just like his folk guitar with its overdrive effect. In particular we hear the resonance of the drum in this song. The very first notes of the intro, with the backing vocals, do not really suggest a ballad at this slow pace, but the descent of violins breathes the right tempo into the orchestra. The pedal steel guitar, fiddle, piano, and string ensemble seem to enjoy great freedom while remaining attuned to the other musicians.

I Saw Mommy Kissing Santa Claus

Tommy Connor / 2:44

Musicians: Dennis Crouch: double bass / Michael Davis: keyboards, percussion / Lloyd Green: pedal steel guitar / Steve Turner: drums, percussion / Paul Hollowell: piano / Jimmy Mattingly: fiddle / Tom Rutledge: acoustic guitar / Kent Wells: electric guitar **Vocals:** Dolly Parton **Backing Vocals:** Richard Dennison, Vicki Hampton, Jennifer O'Brien

Written and composed by the British author Tommy Connor, "I Saw Mommy Kissing Santa Claus" was recorded for the first time by a young boy aged thirteen, the American singer Jimmy Boyd in 1952. The Ronettes took over in 1963, then the Jackson 5 in 1970. The song tells the story of a child who, the day before Christmas, surprises his mother in the arms of Santa Claus, kissing him. He wonders, how will his father react when he hears the news? The song created a rather unexpected controversy when it was first released: The influential Roman Catholic Archdiocese of Boston condemned Jimmy Boyd for having apparently portrayed an adulterous link between kissing and Christmas, but relented after Boyd declared publicly that the dad and Santa Claus were of course the same person.

We find here the swinging spirit of "Holly Jolly Christmas," but the Christmas effects are much more marked, with omnipresent sleigh bells, and the feeling that the backing singers are gathered around the fire. The intro features the well-known "Jingle Bells" tune, which also returns at the very end. A keyboard replicating the sound of the violin plays with the piano during Dolly's narrative. The sound is much brighter here than on the album (using real violins), and the key stroke attacks are clearly audible.

You Are My Christmas

Dolly Parton / 4:14

Musicians: Michael Davis: keyboards / Lloyd Green: pedal steel guitar / Richard Dennison: piano / Steve Turner: drums, percussion / Paul Hollowell: piano / Gary Lunn: bass / Jimmy Mattingly: fiddle / Tom Rutledge: acoustic guitar / Kent Wells: electric guitar **Vocals:** Dolly Parton, Randy Parton **Backing Vocals:** Richard Dennison, Vicki Hampton, Aaron McCune, Jennifer O'Brien, Heidi Parton Backing Vocals Arrangement: Lakieta Bagwell-Garves

In this duet, Dolly and her brother Randy celebrate a love that has become a perpetual Christmas present. Heidi Parton, Dolly's niece and Randy's daughter, was also invited to join the fun and she appears in the backing vocals. This pop song about Christmas is a real family affair: The sleigh bells, and the common thread of the album, are obviously present. The keyboard intro oscillates between the sound of the harmonica and the accordion.

Mary, Did You Know?

Mark Lowry, Buddy Greene / 4:26

Musicians: David Angell, Wei Tsun Chang, Janet Darnell, David Davidson, Stefan Petrescu: violin / Monisa Angell, David Davidson, Chris Farrell: viola / Michael Davis: keyboards / Steve Turner: drums, percussion / Paul Hollowell: piano / Gary Lunn: bass / Paul Nelson, Sarighani Reist: cello / Kent Wells: classical guitar, electric guitar Orchestration: David Davidson **Vocals:** Dolly Parton **Backing Vocals:** Richard Dennison, Vicki Hampton, Jennifer O'Brien

"Mary, Did You Know?" is addressed to Mary, mother of Jesus, inviting the listener to admire her relationship with her son. It should be noted that songs about the Blessed Virgin are rare in Dolly Parton's work. This song falls into the category of a choral song or musical—a story with a beginning and an end. The playing of drums, bass, and guitars is radically different from pop songs.

It is noticeable that the star's voice is slightly altered, especially when she speaks at length or sings softly near the microphone. On the other hand, when she delivers more power, the breathiness disappears and her confidence seems to return. A beautiful ending to the album.

Dolly as a Writer, Songwriter, and Storyteller

Dolly Parton has said (and written) it many times: If her audience could remember only one thing about her, she would want to be remembered as a talented songwriter. This caught the attention of music professor Lydia R. Hamessley, who, in her book *Unlikely Angel: The Songs of Dolly Parton*, details the star's career by exploring her songwriting. Of course Dolly is world famous as a singer, but she is inherently a writer—everything that happens in her life, both in and around her, eventually gets turned into words.

A Breath and a Signature

Dolly Parton has written more than three thousand songs and published several books, including an autobiography, children's stories, a cookbook, poems, and, in 2022, a novel written with James Patterson called *Run, Rose, Run*[20] (Little, Brown). Dolly was not yet forty years old when she wrote about herself for the first time outside of her songs, which were not always autobiographical. In *Dolly: My Life and Other Unfinished Business*,[1] published in 1994, she expresses herself in a simple and direct way, often with humor, addressing her reader as if they were at her side during the writing process. Dolly Parton writes as she breathes, as she speaks, as she composes, and her songs are little stories that her fans can relate to. Her remarkable command of language makes her a poet, a storyteller, and a songwriter all in one. She knows how to associate one word with another to give it a resonance, a very specific emotional charge, just as she uses particular figures of speech to evoke a boat.

For a celebrity, the exercise of autobiographical writing is never simple: There is a balance that has to be struck between emotion and memory, and sometimes a delicate choice has to be made between what belongs in the public domain and what will remain secret.

Dolly's entire discography evokes a link between her present life and work, and the music she heard as a child, growing up among the Great Smoky Mountains and the music of Appalachia. From this alchemy between past and present, she derives short stories in which her audience can see, hear, and feel what she herself saw, heard, and felt growing up. Her songs are a distillation of her heritage and the heritage of her ancestors passed down through her family, such as the murder ballads, Bible stories, and church songs like the popular Christian hymn "Amazing Grace," that constantly appear in Dolly's work.

The Dolly Library

For fans who would like to build a "Dolly library," there are many places to start. Food lovers will turn to *Dolly's Dixie Fixin's*, her book of recipes gleaned from her family and Dollywood, where Tennessee cuisine is part of the park's many attractions. Dolly Parton has never hidden the fact that she loves to cook and eat. Here too, the star brings together a subject that comes from her childhood as well as from her adult life. How could she not know that cooking for others is a labor of love?

Love and dreams are the other pillars that guide her writing and her life, and never has this been more clearly laid out than in a commencement speech she gave in 2009 at the University of Tennessee in Knoxville. When the speech became popular and widely shared, in true Dolly form the singer transformed her speech into a book, *Dream More: Celebrate the Dreamer in You*, which helped support the Imagination Library program.

Dolly explores her relationship with her songs and how they were written in the beautiful book *Songteller: My Life in Lyrics*, published in 2020. She also seemingly loves the idea of sharing her desire to dream big with all of her fans. So, it was a natural progression for the songwriter to take up her pen to tell stories to younger people. Her latest book, *Billy the Kid Makes It Big*, was released in April 2023. The book, aimed at children ages four to seven, tells the story of a dog who loves to bark when he hears country music. He decides to become a star and goes to Nashville, where he overcomes many obstacles with the help of his new friends. We find these themes once more developed on her children's album *I Believe in You*, which was released in 2017 and preaches the value of friendship and not giving up on yourself or your dreams.

In her life as a star, Dolly has invested a lot of time and money in the support of literature, including, among others, with her Imagination Library program; and also with *I Am a Rainbow*, another children's book; and *Just the Way I Am*, a collection of poems based on many of her best songs. *Coat of Many Colors* was published twice, with two different illustrators.

If you are interested in reading everything related to Dolly Parton, then look for authorized biographies, such as *Dolly*[3] by Alanna Nash, as well as unauthorized ones, such as *Smart Blonde: The Life of Dolly Parton*[2] by Stephen Miller, which is very comprehensive. Finally, read and reread the great Dolly interviews by adding *Not Dumb, Not Blonde: Dolly in Conversation*[5] to your collection. It's a great compilation of interviews from 1967 to 2014. All of these books evoke Dolly Parton at every stage of her long and successful career.

A (Non-Exhaustive) List of Works Written by Dolly Parton

Billy the Kid Makes It Big, illustrated by MacKenzie Haley, Penguin Young Readers, 2023

Songteller: My Life in Lyrics, Chronicle Books, 2020

Coat of Many Colors, illustrated by Brooke Boynton-Hughes, Penguin Young Readers, 2016

Dream More: Celebrate the Dreamer in You, Putnam, 2012

I Am a Rainbow, illustrated by Heather Sheffield, Putnam, 2009

Dolly's Dixie Fixin's, Viking Studio, 2006

Coat of Many Colors, illustrated by Judith Sutton, HarperCollins, 1994

Dolly: My Life and Other Unfinished Business, HarperCollins, 1994

Just the Way I Am, Blue Mountain Press, 1979

ALBUM

Run, Rose, Run

Run . Big Dreams and Faded Jeans . Demons . Driven . Snakes in the Grass .
Blue Bonnet Breeze . Woman Up (And Take It Like a Man) . Firecracker .
Secrets . Lost and Found . Dark Night, Bright Future . Love or Lust

RELEASE DATE
March 4, 2022
Reference: Butterfly Records, Los Angeles (CA)—RRR001LPB
Best US Chart Ranking: 1

Full Circle

Dolly Parton had not released a solo album since *I Believe in You* in 2017. Accompanied by the eponymous novel co-written with James Patterson, *Run, Rose, Run* is the artist's forty-fifth solo album. Produced by Butterfly Records, the star's own label, it was released on March 4, 2022. It reached number thirty-four on the Billboard 200 and was a hit on the American, European, and Australian charts.

Songwriter and Novelist

At seventy-six years old, while at the height of her fame, and while involved in many side projects, including her foundation, Dollywood; the launch of her perfume, Scent from Above; attending various award ceremonies; and her support for scientific research during the COVID-19 pandemic, Dolly continued to push herself into trying new things. *Run, Rose, Run*[20] was her first novel-writing experience, and it inspired twelve songs. Dolly became the source of inspiration for this novel, which sent her back, through the powers of fiction, to her arrival in Nashville in 1964, just like AnnieLee, the heroine of *Run, Rose, Run*.

Both in terms of production and superstar associations—and as a cultural object for the entertainment industry—*Run, Rose, Run* was an unprecedented and eventful project. Like a soundtrack for a movie, this album became the first original soundtrack ever created for a book. This was an opportunity for Dolly to sing not just as herself, but as three distinct people, since each song on the album refers to different characters in the novel and the situations they experience. *Run, Rose, Run* is a multimedia project of sorts—a novel, twelve songs, various album formats (vinyl, CD, and MP3) carried by various retailers and streaming platforms, plus a virtual tour on YouTube with her co-author, James Patterson. A podcast and an audiobook with young country pop singer Kelsea Ballerini were created; and a film is also in preparation, produced by Sony Pictures and Reese Witherspoon's Hello Sunshine company.

Run, Rose, Run was written in collaboration with best-selling author James Patterson, the writer behind numerous *New York Times* bestsellers, and the author of the book *Along Came a Spider,* upon which Lee Tamahori's 2001 film adaptation *Along Came a Spider*[22] was based. This was not James Patterson's first collaborative novel, nor was it his first book to feature a main character who is a singer. In 1996 *Hide and Seek*[23] was published, the story of Maggie Bradford, a singer-songwriter who, despite her talent and public acclaim, still faced perils and demons. Patterson loves music—and although he says he prefers rock, he is not impervious to country—and Parton loves to write with passion. *Run, Rose, Run* is a drama about how the heroine, AnnieLee Keyes, slams the door on her past and runs away to Nashville armed with nothing more than a big dream and faded jeans, which is what "Big Dreams and Faded Jeans," the album's lead single, refers to. We will not reveal any more about the plot.

The Album

The collaboration between the writer and the artist was, according to them both, fluid and exciting, almost a foregone conclusion. James Patterson even confided that he was surprised by the speed with which Dolly wrote the songs—seven songs in a just a few days. Yet behind the simple language and themes, which everyone can relate to, lies a real depth. Each track functions as a chapter in the book—so you can both hear and read the scene Dolly is singing about. As we read through the novel, we discover that anything goes in Nashville, even ripping off other artists. This is also echoed in *Run, Rose, Run*, which talks about the relationship between the dark side of the music industry and the dreams of artists. If we listen carefully to the lyrics, how can we not think of the young Dolly Rebecca Parton, who, as soon as she graduated from high school, left her family, friends, and hometown to go to Nashville by bus at the age of eighteen? Last but not least, *Run, Rose, Run* tells of female freedom, love, and the importance of fulfillment. As soon as this opus was released, the critics reacted positively to this mix of country and bluegrass, spiced up with a touch of rock energy and emotions from the ballad tradition.

Album Cover

In the background, we see a landscape drowned in the dark blue of night. In the foreground, which is tinted with darkness, we see a ground strewn with roses and Dolly Parton. Standing, luminous, in faded jeans and a red shirt tied at the midriff, her guitar rests on her leg, she has a hat screwed on top of her legendary blondness, and she is smiling. The strength of serenity seems to emanate from her, that of the goal achieved. This photograph was part of a set of images taken by Stacie Huckeba.

2022

Album Recording: Adventure Studios, Dailey & Vincent, KWP Productions, Velvet Apple Music Studio, Nashville (TN) / Ben's Den Recording Studio, Hendersonville (TN) / The Freeway, Franklin (TN) / The Soundhouse, Redding (CA), 2021

Technical Team: Producers: Tom Rutledge, Richard Dennison, Dolly Parton / Arrangements: Richard Dennison / Sound Engineers: Tom Rutledge, Ben Isaacs, Joe Corey, Lonnie Wilson, Kent Wells, Joey Crawford, Chris Latham, Darrin Vincent / Mixing: Mark Capps, Mark Needham

With James Patterson, promoting their book, *Run, Rose, Run*, and the accompanying album, in March 2022.

Jamie Dailey and Darrin Vincent have a well-established bluegrass group, Dailey & Vincent, that features a total of nine musicians.

Run

Dolly Parton / 2:45

Musicians: Lonnie Wilson: drums / Steve Mackey: bass / Kent Wells: acoustic and electric guitars / Richard Dennison: piano / Tom Rutledge: banjo / Jimmy Mattingly: fiddle **Vocals:** Dolly Parton **Backing Vocals:** Darrin Vincent, Jamie Dailey, Aaron McCune

"Run" opens the album with a catchy, foot-stomping tune, and Dolly Parton's passion shines through in the chorus. The message is clear: To achieve your dreams, you have to take risks, and sometimes run straight ahead without looking back. Break down walls, if you have to.

Dolly decided to treat her song in a country bluegrass style that a new generation of virtuoso and creative musicians has embraced. With bands like the Grascals, Old Crow Medicine Show, and songwriter Daryl Mosley, Nashville's bluegrass scene was enjoying a renaissance. She recorded in Dailey & Vincent's studios. Steve Mackey, Dolly's regular bassist, had no problem leaving the electric bass behind and switching to the indispensable double bass. Drummer Lonnie Wilson manages to remain discreet and efficient. Fiddler Jimmy Mattingly works in his favorite musical territory. Kent Wells recorded the strummed acoustic guitar part and the electric guitar overdubs. Producers Tom Rutledge and Richard Dennison, in true Nashvillian fashion, do not hesitate to step out of the booth to take over the banjo and piano, respectively.

The basic tracks that form the structure of "Run" are recorded with the musicians facing each other and eye-to-eye contact established, with Dolly recording a voice part that shines through. For the final vocal take, she sings accompanied by the backing vocals of Jamie Dailey, Darrin Vincent, and Aaron McCune.

Big Dreams And Faded Jeans

Dolly Parton / 4:07

Musicians: Lonnie Wilson: drums / Steve Mackey: bass / Kent Wells: acoustic and electric guitars / Richard Dennison: Hammond B3 organ / Pat Bergeson: harmonica **Vocals:** Dolly Parton **Backing Vocals:** Richard Dennison, Jennifer O'Brien, Vicki Hampton **Single:** Big Dreams and Faded Jeans **Release:** Ingrooves, UMG, January 14, 2022 (CD ref.: ?) NB: This track was released as a promo single, so was not ranked on any chart.

This track was released as a single before the album was released. It asks: Where do you go to make your dream come true? The answer is quickly found: Nashville, the city where one goes to build a future, whatever it is. How do you get there? In faded jeans, with your old guitar and dreams, with "a bag of songs" slung over your shoulder, as Dolly Parton says. The graphic choice of the video, like that of "Woman Up! (And Take It Like a Man)," immerses us in the imagination of the early 1960s. In this song, Dolly describes the life of the city's songwriters, a particular category of Nashvillian that has become legendary. What they all have in common is that they left home one day to try their luck in Music City (Nashville's nickname), which presupposes an unshakable faith in their destiny. These are the "Big Dreams" of the title. As for the "Faded Jeans," they are obviously the favorite accessory of these artists, along with some cowboy boots.

Dolly brings her band together again, also inviting harmonica player Pat Bergeson. The bass/drums rhythm section, the doubled acoustic/electric guitars, and Dolly on vocals: This is the core of a very experienced country band, joined by the Hammond B3 organ and the backing vocals.

2022

Demons

Dolly Parton / 3:24

Musicians: Lonnie Wilson: drums / Steve Mackey: bass / Kent Wells: electric guitar / Tom Rutledge: acoustic guitar / Richard Dennison: piano, keyboards / Charlie McCoy: harmonica **Vocals:** Dolly Parton, Ben Haggard **Vocal Harmonies:** Dolly Parton **Backing Vocals:** Richard Dennison, Jennifer O'Brien, Vicki Hampton

Merle Haggard was incarcerated at San Quentin State Prison between 1958 and 1960, where Johnny Cash recorded his famous concert "At San Quentin" in 1969, a year after his legendary live album *At Folsom Prison.*

"Demons" continues the story of the songwriter AnnieLee's saga: After the initial success comes the test of demons, which may come from all kinds of excesses as well as from the tie-wearing executives of Nashvillian show business, always ready to replace artistic inspiration with production methods similar to those of a car assembly line. It is not surprising that the offices of the record labels are located on Demonbreun Street! Dolly Parton, who managed to escape these evil geniuses, talks about them with Ben Haggard, the youngest son of the famous country outlaw Merle Haggard. The elder Haggard went through it all: prison, whiskey addiction, and the aimless wandering life of the musician blinded by a disjointed lifestyle. Unusually on one of her solo albums, Dolly lets Ben Haggard sing the first verse, only harmonizing with him on the second cycle. Legendary harmonica player Charlie McCoy lights up the whole thing in his inimitable style, discreet and always appropriate.

In the backing vocals of "Driven," we note the presence of Sonya Isaacs and Becky Isaacs Bowman, both from the bluegrass gospel group the Isaacs, which was founded in 1971 by the Isaacs family, survivors of the Holocaust.

The bluebonnet, a delicate blue flower covering entire fields of Texas, is one of the state's symbols.

Driven

Dolly Parton / 2:40

Musicians: Lonnie Wilson: drums / Steve Mackey: bass / Kent Wells: acoustic and electric guitars / Richard Dennison: piano / Tom Rutledge: banjo **Vocals:** Dolly Parton **Backing Vocals:** Sonya Isaacs, Becky Isaacs Bowman

If ever there was a song of motivation, it has to be "Driven"! Because the heroine is undoubtedly motivated—in spite of the ties holding her to Nashville. We find here a theme dear to the American culture: the freedom of the open road, and the promise of a better life.

Dolly's band reunites in its simplest version. Kent Wells doubles on electric and acoustic guitars. Co-producers Richard Dennison and Tom Rutledge play piano and banjo, respectively. But this bluegrass gospel is mostly about a fabulous trio with the two Isaacs sisters on backing vocals and Dolly Parton on lead vocals. It is obvious that she takes great pleasure in this very particular style, which reminds us of classics such as "New River Train" (a traditional song from the end of the nineteenth century). The only difference: From Dolly's pen, the traditional train is transformed into a car!

Snakes In The Grass

Dolly Parton / 2:41

Musicians: Lonnie Wilson: drums / Steve Mackey: bass / Kent Wells: electric guitar / Tom Rutledge: acoustic guitar / Richie Owens: Weissenborn resonator / Paul Hollowell: Hammond B3 organ **Vocals:** Dolly Parton **Backing Vocals:** Richard Dennison, Jennifer O'Brien, Vicki Hampton

One imagines that Dolly Parton must have brought her experience of the record industry to bear on the novel. One can also imagine that snakes are used as a metaphor, even if there are real ones, which one should avoid stepping on. One can also imagine that the venom of the reptile is as painful as that of some humans.

This country blues number owes much to the inspired playing of Richie Owens (related to Dolly's beloved uncle Bill Owens, guitarist and songwriter) on the Weissenborn resonator. Originally shaped like a Hawaiian guitar, the Weissenborn is made from the rare and protected koi wood. Popularized by Ben Harper among others, it is held flat on the knees, like a lap steel. Here, Owens chose a model with a metal resonator, like a dobro. The Hammond B3 organ, the acoustic guitar, and the electric guitar weave a harmonic backdrop.

Blue Bonnet Breeze
Dolly Parton / 5:19

Musicians: Tom Rutledge: acoustic guitar / Jimmy Mattingly: mandolin / David Davidson: first violin / David Angell: second violin / Monisa Angel: viola / Carole Rabinowitz: cello / David Davidson: strings arrangements **Vocals and Vocal Harmonies:** Dolly Parton **Single:** Blue Bonnet Breeze **Release:** Ingrooves, UMG, February 11, 2022 (CD ref.: ?)

The second single to be released before the album, this track takes the name of the bluebonnet, the field flower that has become one of the symbols of Texas. Here we are in the heart of Romeo and Juliet's drama, revisited in country style: They love each other, but because they do not come from the same background, their parents are opposed to their marriage. This thwarted destiny will push the young lovers to kill themselves. One cannot help but think of "The Bridge" when listening to "Blue Bonnet Breeze." The emotion is there, and Dolly Parton's voice vibrates with the tragic dimension of life and love. We have the feeling that she is whispering in our ear, which reinforces the intimate character of the composition.

For this country waltz dedicated to love, Dolly and her team opted for a string quartet with two violins, viola, and cello. A sophisticated sound…but hillbilly all the same, with the presence of mandolinist Jimmy Mattingly and co-producer Tom Rutledge on acoustic guitar. This very beautiful ballad in the Appalachian style was probably composed by Dolly on one of her acoustic guitars with a smaller, higher range. At 5:19, this track is also the longest on the album.

Woman Up (And Take It Like A Man)
Dolly Parton / 2:27

Musicians: Lonnie Wilson: drums / Steve Mackey: bass / Kent Wells: electric guitar / Tom Rutledge: acoustic guitar / Richard Dennison: Hammond B3 organ / Pat Bergeson: harmonica **Vocals:** Dolly Parton **Backing Vocals:** Richard Dennison, Jennifer O'Brien, Vicki Hampton **Single:** Woman Up (And Take It Like a Man) **Release:** Ingrooves, UMG, March 4, 2022 (CD ref.: ?)

This track was released as a single, on the same day as the album. As Dolly Parton says on her website, this song is rather like "9 to 5": We find the same ardor and the same determination to be a source of inspiration for the listener. The text reaffirms the importance of never giving up, and finding your place, even when others doubt you. In perfect harmony with the female characters in the novel, Dolly tells us that it is necessary to be a woman, but to think like a man—and especially in the music industry. She does not need to go back very far in her career and personal experience to find the inspiration for this hymn to women's inner resilience: She attributes to her heroine, AnnieLee, the indisputable communicative pugnacity she has possessed since her own beginnings.

It is obvious that this song for her sisters is very close to her heart. For this reason, she retains the core of her band. Harmonica player Pat Bergeson was hired to replace Charlie McCoy, who was probably busy elsewhere. This ideal configuration enables her to sculpt her vocals, accompanied by a vocal ensemble doped with gospel praise. The saturated electric guitars and the slamming sound of the drums, strongly compressed in parallel, give this modern country blues a rock energy that Elvis Presley himself would not have disowned.

Firecracker
Dolly Parton / 3:13

Musicians: Lonnie Wilson: drums / Steve Mackey: bass / Kent Wells: electric and acoustic guitars / Richard Dennison: piano / Scott Vestal: banjo / Jimmy Mattingly: fiddle **Vocals and Vocal Harmonies:** Dolly Parton / **Backing Vocals:** Rhonda Vincent, Val Storey

Here we learn a little more about AnnieLee, the heroine of the novel *Run, Rose, Run*, whose nickname is Firecracker—in other words, a woman as explosive as a stick of dynamite! In "Firecracker," which is a very catchy song, we find the same determination and the same will to succeed that we find in "Run."

The song is a pure bluegrass song conceived by Dolly on her short-scale guitar (three-quarter guitar). For added effect, this track features not one, but two superstar bombshells: Dolly herself and, in the backing vocals, her longtime friend Rhonda Vincent. Although the two singers are not of the same generation, they have a lot in common: Both are mountain natives, and both started singing at a very young age—six for Dolly, five for Rhonda. Accompanied by two bluegrass specialists, Jimmy Mattingly on fiddle and Scott Vestal on banjo, they explode on this aptly named track, recorded at the Dailey & Vincent studio in Nashville.

Secrets

Dolly Parton / 2:52

Musicians: Lonnie Wilson: drums / Steve Mackey: bass / Kent Wells: electric guitar / Tom Rutledge: acoustic guitar / Jimmy Mattingly: mandolin / Richard Dennison: keyboards **Vocals:** Dolly Parton
Backing Vocals: Richard Dennison, Jennifer O'Brien, Vicki Hampton

More languid than "Firecracker," "Secrets" makes you want to curl up in a warm embrace with someone with whom you feel safe. The major theme of this song is the dilemma that the heroine lives: how to open up to others when you carry a heavy secret and have lost all trust?

This nostalgic ballad is perhaps the most eloquent of Dolly Parton's compositions: Everyone wears a mask; only the soul is authentic. Here again, Dolly works in a tight configuration, just her and her band, which leaves her full scope to harmonize with her backing singers. The image of a discreet inner beauty. The chorus, the delay, the reverb of the electric guitar, and the keyboards (Yamaha CP-80 and DX7 types) give this production a flavor that is straight out of the 1980s. Only the mandolin part evokes the Appalachian tradition.

Lost And Found

Dolly Parton / 3:18

Musicians: Lonnie Wilson: drums / Steve Mackey: bass / Kent Wells: electric guitar / Tom Rutledge: acoustic guitar / Steve Hinson: pedal steel guitar / Dirk Johnson: keyboards **Vocals:** Dolly Parton, Joe Nichols
Backing Vocals: Richard Dennison, Jennifer O'Brien, Vicki Hampton

The second duet of the album, "Lost and Found" brings together Dolly Parton and Joe Nichols for a bittersweet ballad. The song speaks to us of time wasted brooding over regrets, of long-lost loves that haunt the night and prevent sleep, and of a new world that is just waiting for a sign from us for it to happen. It is also an invitation to leave solitude for a new love.

The office of lost and found objects and memories is evoked here by Dolly Parton in this nostalgic but never disillusioned ballad: nostalgic as the sound of Steve Hinson's pedal steel guitar, whose glissandi would make the most irascible of saloon cowboys cry into his beer; never disillusioned, because Dolly and her alter ego, AnnieLee, have a deep sense of destiny despite life's hard knocks. Dolly's partner here is country singer Joe Nichols, who, although he has calmed down considerably since his 2007 marriage to Heather Singleton, can almost be heard thinking: "Oo-wee! Potential new girlfriend!" In any case, he and Dolly harmonize perfectly on the verses, well supported by the backing vocals and the pedal steel guitar.

Dark Night, Bright Future

Dolly Parton / 2:37

Musicians: Lonnie Wilson: drums / Steve Mackey: bass / Kent Wells: electric and acoustic guitar / Tom Rutledge: banjo / Jimmy Mattingly: fiddle / Richard Dennison: piano **Vocals:** Dolly Parton
Backing Vocals: Appalachian Road Show, with Darrell Webb, Barry Abernathy, and Jim Van Cleve

After the rain comes the good weather, Dolly seems to be telling us. She reminds us that we have all laughed, bled, and cried, and that we can rise from our ashes, like the phoenix, to reach the sky: a true profession of faith, in the form of a philosophy of hope. To emphasize that the darker the night, the brighter the future, Dolly chose to invite Darrell Webb, Barry Abernathy, and Jim Van Cleve of the Appalachian Road Show, with whom she toured with Rhonda Vincent, to sing backing vocals. These gentlemen very effectively support the vocals of the Queen of Country with banjo and fiddle.

Love Or Lust

Dolly Parton / 3:20

Musicians: Richard Dennison: piano / Jimmy Mattingly: mandolin / David Davidson: first violin / David Angell: second violin / Kristin Wilkinson: viola / Sarighani Reist: cello / David Davidson: strings arrangements **Vocals:** Dolly Parton, Richard Dennison

To close this unique album, which straddles fiction and reality, this last song is sung as a duet with Richard Dennison, another fellow traveler in Dolly Parton's world. Whether it is about love or lust, the protagonists will go all the way—a finale as a hymn to the power of strong feelings.

In spite of Jimmy Mattingly's mandolin, the spirit of this waltz-like ballad is closer to Broadway than to traditional country music. Richard Dennison, with his expressive vibrato and emphatic yet articulate piano playing, gets it right. Two violins (no more fiddles here, no question of hitting the heel of the boots with the bow), a viola, and a cello. No backing singers, only Dolly's voice, full of changing emotions, to draw out the lesson learned from a more than fulfilled and accomplished life.

2022

Dolly Parton in
mid-performance
at the Hollywood
Bowl, 2011.

Live Albums—US

A Real Live Dolly
Release date: June 29, 1970 / Ref.: RCA Victor—LSP-4387 / Format: LP

Heartsongs (Live from Home)
Release date: September 27, 1994 / Ref.: Blue Eye Records, Columbia—CK 66123 / Format: LP

Live and Well
Release date: September 14, 2004 / Ref.: Blue Eye Records, Sugar Hill Records—SUG-DVD 3998 / Format: DVD, 2xCD

Live from London
Release date: November 10, 2009 / Ref.: Dolly Records—925-Butterfly 2AV / Format: CD, DVD, DVD-video

An Evening with Dolly (Live in the U.K.)
Release date: 2012 / Ref.: Music Catalogue Cracker Barrel Old Country Store—925-Butterfly 2AV / Format: CD, DVD, DVD-video

Compilations and Best Of—US

1960s–1970s

Hits Made Famous by Country Queens
Release date: April 13, 1963 / Ref.: Stereo-Fidelity—SF-19700, Somerset—S197 / Format: LP (Side A: Faye Tucker / Side B: Dolly Parton)

Dolly Parton Sings Country Oldies
Release date: April 13, 1968 / Ref.: Stereo-Fidelity—SF-29400 / Format: LP (Side A: Dolly Parton / Side B: Faye Tucker)

Dolly Parton and George Jones
Release date: 1969 / Ref.: Starday Records—SLP 429 / Format: LP (Side A: Dolly Parton / Side B: George Jones)

As Long as I Love
Release date: June 8, 1970 / Ref.: Monument—SLP 18136 / Format: LP

The Best of Dolly Parton
Release date: November 9, 1970 / Ref.: RCA Camden—LSP 4449 / Format: LP

Just the Way I Am
Release date: September 1972 / Ref.: RCA Camden—CAS-2583 / Format: LP

The World of Dolly Parton
Release date: 1972 / Ref.: Monument—KZG 31913 / Format: LP

Mine
Release date: September 1973 / Ref.: RCA Camden—ACL1-0307 / Format: LP

Best of Dolly Parton
Release date: July 14, 1975 / Ref.: RCA Camden—APL1-1117 / Format: LP

Best of Dolly Parton, Vol. 2
Release date: 1975 / Ref.: RCA—5706-2-RRE / Format: CD / RCA—5706-1-R / Format: LP

I Wish I Felt This Way at Home
Release date: 1975 / Ref.: Pickwick—ACL-7002 / Format: LP

Just Because I'm a Woman
Release date: 1976 / Ref.: Pickwick—ACL-7017 / Format: LP

This Is Dolly Parton
Release date: 1976 / Ref.: RCA—DHYK 0007 / Format: Cassette

In the Beginning
Release date: 1978 / Ref.: Monument—MG 762 / Format: LP

1980s

Dolly Parton & Kitty Wells
Release date: 1980 / Ref.: Exact Productions—EX-239 / Format: LP

Golden Favorites
Release date: 1981 / Ref.: RCA Victor – SVL1-0520 / Format: LP / RCA Special Products – SVL1-0520 / Format: Cassette / RCA Special Products—DPC1-0956 / Format: CD

Just the Way I Am
Release date: 1982 / Ref.: Pair, RCA Special Products—CAS-2583 / Format: LP

Greatest Hits
Release date: September 13, 1982 / Ref.: RCA—AHL1-4422 / Format: LP

The Winning Hand (with Kris Kristofferson, Willie Nelson, and Brenda Lee)
Release date: November 1, 1982 / Ref.: Monument—JWG2784-38389-1 / Format: 2xLP

Dolly in London
Release date: 1984 / Ref.: Pioneer Artists—PA-84-068 / Format: CD

Her Greatest Hits and Finest Performances
Release date: 1984 / Ref.: RCA—R1RS-5921-5934 / Format: 7xLP

Portrait
Release date: 1985 / Ref.: Pair—PDL2-1116 / Format: LP, Cassette

Collector's Series
Release date: June 3, 1985 / Ref.: RCA—6338-2-RRE / Format: CD / RCA—AHL1-5471 / Format: LP / RCA—AHK1-5471 / Format: Cassette

Think About Love
Release date: April 15, 1986 / Ref.: RCA—AHL1-9508 / Format: LP

Best of Dolly Parton, Vol. 3
Release date: September 22, 1987 / Ref.: RCA—5706-2-RRE / Format: CD / RCA—5706-1-R / Format: LP

The Best There Is
Release date: July 1987 / Ref.: RCA Victor—6497-1-R / Format: LP, Cassette

1990s

The RCA Years 1967–1986
Release date: 1993 / Ref.: RCA Victor—66127-2 / Format: 2xCD

I Will Always Love You: 36 All-Time Greatest Hits
Release date: 1993 / Ref.: GSC Music—#15071, BMG Direct Marketing—DMC31086 / Format: 3xCD

I Will Always Love You / The Essential Dolly Parton One
Release date: March 28, 1995 / Ref.: RCA—07863-66533-2 / Format: CD

**I Will Always Love You
(and Other Greatest Hits)**
Release date: 1996 / **Ref.**: Columbia—CK 67582 / **Format**: CD

Super Hits
Release date: 1996 / **Ref.**: RCA—07863-68852-4 / **Format**: CD

Legendary Country Singers
Release date: 1996 / **Ref.**: Time Life Music—TCD-650 R990-13 / **Format**: CD

I Believe: The Encore Collection
Release date: September 16, 1997 / **Ref.**: BMG Special Products—44617-2 / **Format**: CD

Greatest Hits
Release date: 1998 / **Ref.**: Columbia River Entertainment Group—CRG 210000 / **Format**: 2xCD

Super Hits
Release date: 1999 / **Ref.**: Columbia—CK 69086 / **Format**: CD

2000s

RCA Country Legends
Release date: 2002 / **Ref.**: BMG Heritage, RCA—07863 65101 2 / **Format**: CD

Country Legends
Release date: March 15, 2002 / **Ref.**: Green Hill—GHD5276, Spring Hill Music Group, Inc.—DRC13176 / **Format**: CD

Super Hits
Release date: 2002 / **Ref.**: Federal, Gusto Records—FED-CD-0500, BMG Special Products—DRC 13060 / **Format**: CD

Ultimate Dolly Parton
Release date: June 3, 2002 / **Ref.**: RCA Nashville, BMG Heritage—82876 52008 2 / **Format**: CD

All American Country
Release date: 2003 / **Ref.**: BMG Special Products—75517445212 / **Format**: CD

**All American Country
(with Porter Wagoner)**
Release date: 2003 / **Ref.**: BMG Special Products—75517478072 / **Format**: CD

Platinum & Gold Collection
Release date: May 4, 2004 / **Ref.**: RCA Nashville—82876 57229 2 / **Format**: CD

The Essential Dolly Parton
Release date: 2005 / **Ref.**: Legacy, RCA—82876 69240 2 / **Format**: 2xCD

American Music Legends
Release date: 2005 / **Ref.**: Music Catalog Cracker Barrel Old Country Store—CR02582, BMG—DRC13681 / **Format**: CD

Covered by Dolly
Release date: 2005 / **Ref.**: Sterling—35272 / **Format**: CD

Dolly Parton
Release date, US & Canada: 2006 / **Ref.**: Direct Source Special Products Inc.—ITEM#AD 70542 / **Format**: CD

Love Songs
Release date: 2006 / **Ref.**: RCA Nashville—82876 76176 2 / **Format**: CD

The Acoustic Collection 1999–2002
Release date: October 10, 2006 / **Ref.**: Sugar Hill Records, Blue Eye Records—SUG-CD-4008, SHCD 3900, SUG-CD-3927, SUG-CD-3946, SUG-DVD-4008 / **Format**: 3xCD, DVD

**Triple Feature: Eagle When She Flies/
White Limozeen/Slow Dancing
with the Moon**
Release date: 2007 / **Ref.**: Sony Music Custom Marketing Group—88697371532 / **Format**: 3xCD

Always, Always / Two of a Kind
Release date: 2007 / **Ref.**: American Beat Records—24792 / **Format**: CD

16 Biggest Hits
Release date: August 7, 2007 / **Ref.**: RCA Nashville, Legacy, Sony BMG—88697 13481 2 / **Format**: CD

Playlist: The Very Best of Dolly Parton
Release date: April 29, 2008 / **Ref.**: RCA Nashville, Legacy—88697104322 / **Format**: CD

Love Songs
Release date: 2008 / **Ref.**: Sony BMG Music Entertainment Custom Marketing Group—A722376 / **Format**: CD

16 Biggest Hits
Release date: 2009 / **Ref.**: RCA Nashville, Legacy—88697 41334-2 / **Format**: CD

From the Heart
Release date: January 20, 2009 / **Ref.**: RCA, Legacy—88697 41281 2 / **Format**: CD

Dolly
Release date: October 27, 2009 / **Ref.**: RCA Nashville, Legacy—88697 48086 2 / **Format**: 4xCD, remastered

2010s–2020s

**Letter to Heaven: Songs of Faith
and Inspiration**
Release date: May 4, 2010 / **Ref.**: RCA Nashville, Sony Legacy—88697 67482 2 / **Format**: CD

**The Fairest of Them All / My Favorite
Songwriter: Porter Wagoner**
Release date: June 14, 2010 / **Ref.**: The Omni Recording Corporation—OMNI-138 / **Format**: CD

**Playlist: The Very Best Gospel of Dolly
Parton**
Release date: October 12, 2010 / **Ref.**: RCA Nashville, Legacy — 88697 76943 2 / **Format**: CD

**Triple Feature: Coat of Many Colors /
My Tennessee Mountain Home / Jolene**
Release date, US & Canada: November 9, 2010 / **Ref.**: Sony Music—A774693 / **Format**: 3xCD, remastered reissue

Super Hits / Heartbreaker
Release date: November 9, 2010 / **Ref.**: Allegro Media Group, Sony Music Commercial Music Group—ALE 220003 / **Format**: 2xCD

The Box Set Series
Release date: January 28, 2014 / **Ref.**: RCA, Legacy —88843019462 / **Format**: 4xCD

**The Complete Trio Collection (with Linda
Ronstadt and Emmylou Harris)**
Release date: September 9, 2016 / **Ref.**: Warner Bros. Records, Asylum Records, Rhino Records—R2 550159 / **Format**: CD remastered reissue

The Chronological Classics 1959–1966
Release date: December 4, 2020 / **Ref.**: Kipepeo Publishing—ref.: none / **Format**: CDr

The Ultimate Collection
Release date: 2020 / **Ref.**: Time Life—34019-X, 34020-Z, 33988-X, 33997-X, 34007-X, 34014-X / **Format**: 19xDVD-Video

The Very Best of Dolly Parton
Release date: 2020 / **Ref.**: RCA, Legacy—19439751631 / **Format**: 2xLP

Early Dolly
Release date: July 23, 2021 / **Ref.**: Stardust Records—CL02341 / **Format**: LP

**Diamonds & Rhinestones:
The Greatest Hits Collection**
Release date: November 18, 2022 / **Ref.**: Sony, Legacy—19439977991 / **Format**: 2x LP

Albums Live, Best of, and Compilations—International

1974–2009

Dolly Parton
Release date, UK: 1974 / **Ref.:** RCA Camden—CDS 1164 / **Format:** LP

Both Sides of Dolly Parton
Release date, UK: March 20, 1978 / **Ref.:** RCA Victor—RCA 42765 / **Format:** LP

The Great Dolly Parton, Vol. 1 (D-I-V-O-R-C-E)
Release date, UK: 1979 / **Ref.:** RCA Camden—CDS 1171 / **Format:** LP / RCA Camden—CAM 482 / **Format:** Cassette

The Great Dolly Parton, Vol. 2
Release date, UK: 1975: **Ref.:** RCA Camden—CDS 1184 / **Format:** LP

Dolly Parton & Chris LeDoux
Release date, Denmark: 1979 / **Ref.:** Queen—1200479 / **Format:** LP, Cassette (Side A: Dolly Parton / Side B: Chris LeDoux)

The Best of Jim Reeves and Dolly Parton
Release date, South Africa: 1976 / **Ref.:** RCA Victor—38-569 / **Format:** LP (Side A: Jim Reeves / Side B: Dolly Parton)

The Hits of Dolly Parton
Release date, Germany: 1976 / **Ref.:** RCA Victor—PPL 1-8088 / **Format:** LP

18 Greatest Hits
Release date, Australia, Australasia: 1977 / **Ref.:** RCA—SP-186 / **Format:** LP, cassette

The Dolly Parton Story
Release date, UK: 1977 / **Ref.:** CBS—S CBS 31582, Embassy 31582 / **Format:** LP

The Dolly Parton Story
Release date, Canada: 1977 / **Ref.:** CBS—WP 90621 / **Format:** LP

Golden Highlights
Release date, Netherlands: 1978 / **Ref.:** Monument—MNT 54713 / **Format:** LP

Country Friends (with Johnny Cash)
Release date, Denmark: 1979 / **Ref.:** Queen—1420779 / **Format:** Cassette

The Dolly Parton Collection
Release date, UK: 1979 / **Ref.:** RCA Camden—PDA 053 / **Format:** 2xLP

Recital: Greatest Hits
Release date, France: 1979 / **Ref.:** K-Tel—BLP 7900 / **Format:** LP

Love Is Like a Butterfly
Release date, UK: 1980 / **Ref.:** Camden—CDS 1202 / **Format:** LP; CAMV 1202 / **Format:** Cassette

A Real Country...Dolly
Release date, Australia, New Zealand: 1981 / **Ref.:** RCA International—VAL1 0301 / **Format:** LP

The Very Best
Release date, South Africa: 1981 / **Ref.:** RCA Victor—38-747 / **Format:** LP, Cassette

The Very Best Of
Release date, UK: 1981 / **Ref.:** RCA Victor—RCA LP 5052 / **Format:** LP

The Very Best Of
Release date, Germany: 1981 / **Ref.:** RCA Victor—RCA PL 89007 / **Format:** LP

The Very Best Of
Release date, Israel: 1981 / **Ref.:** RCA Victor—RCA PL 43675 / **Format:** LP

Dolly
Release date, Netherlands: 1981 / **Ref.:** RCA International—NL-43743 / **Format:** LP

More of the Best of Dolly Parton
Release date, South Africa: 1982 / **Ref.:** RCA—TRC 3176 / **Format:** LP

I Love You
Release date, Benelux: 1982 / **Ref.:** RCA International—VLP-4525 / **Format:** LP

Dolly Parton
Release date, UK: 1982 / **Ref.:** RCA Camden—CDS 1208 / **Format:** LP

The Very Best Of
Release date, UK & Europe: 1983 / **Ref.:** RCA Victor—PL 89007 / **Format:** LP, Cassette

Queens of Country (with Donna Fargo)
Release date, UK: 1983 / **Ref.:** Sundown—SDLP1001 / **Format:** LP

The Love Album
Release date, Europe: 1983 / **Ref.:** RCA—PL 89245 / **Format:** LP

The Best of Dolly Parton
Release date, UK: 1984 / **Ref.:** Reader's Digest—GDOL-A-070 / **Format:** 4xLP

King & Queen of Country (with Kenny Rogers)
Release date, New Zealand: 1984 / **Ref.:** Lucky—LUC-049 / **Format:** LP

Two of a Kind (with Donna Fargo)
Release date, Portugal: 1984 / **Ref.:** Movie Play Portuguesa, Breakaway Tapes—20021 / **Format:** Cassette

With Love from Dolly Parton
Release date, Germany: 1985 / **Ref.:** RCA Camden—CL89520 / **Format:** LP

With Love from Dolly Parton
Release date, Europe: 1985 / **Ref.:** RCA Camden—CK 89520, Cassette

Lynn Anderson & Dolly Parton
Release date, Netherlands: 1985 / **Ref.**: Success—204210 / **Format**: LP

Lynn Anderson & Dolly Parton
Release date, Europe: 1985 / **Ref.**: Success—2042CD / **Format**: CD

Dolly Parton & Friends: Letter to Heaven
Release date: 1985 / **Ref.**: Success—LP 205110 / **Format**: LP

The Love Album 2
Release date, Europe: 1985 / **Ref.** RCA—PL89514 / **Format**: LP, CD

The Love Album 2
Release date, Netherlands: 1985 / **Ref.** RCA—PD89514 / **Format**: LP, CD

The Love Album 2
Release date, Indonesia: 1985 / **Ref.** BMG—BMG5163 / **Format**: Cassette

Magic Moments with Dolly Parton
Release date, UK & Europe: 1985 / **Ref.**: RCA—NK 89620 / **Format**: Cassette

16 Greatest Love Songs
Release date, South Africa: 1985 / **Ref.**: RCA Victor — MMTL 1315 / **Format**: LP

Dolly Parton's 16 Biggest Hits
Release date, Australia: 1986 / **Ref.**: J&B records — JB277C / **Format**: Cassette

Dolly Parton's 16 Biggest Hits
Release date, New Zealand: 1986 / **Ref.**: RCA — VPL1 0640 / **Format**: LP

Autograph
Release date, Yugoslavia: 1986 / **Ref.**: Jugodisk—LPS-1104 / **Format**: LP

The Very Best of Willie & Dolly
Release date, Australia 1987 / **Ref.**: Reader's Digest—RD4-420 / **Format**: 8xLP

The Very Best of Kenny Rogers & Dolly Parton
Release date, Benelux, Netherlands: 1987 / **Ref.**: EVA Imperial—PL/PK/PD 71317 / **Format**: 2xLP, Cassette, CD

Her Greatest Hits
Release date, Netherlands: 1987 / **Ref.**: RCA BV Holland—SPLP 010487 / **Format**: 2xLP

16 Top Tracks from Dolly Parton Diamond Series
Release date, Australia: 1988 / **Ref.**: RCA—BPCD5014 / **Format**: CD

Everything's Beautiful
Release date, Europe: 1988 / **Ref.**: Success—2186CD / **Format**: CD

14 of Her Greatest Hits
Release date, Canada: 1988 / **Ref.**: RCA—ADM 4012 / **Format**: Cassette

The Very Best of Dolly Parton
Release date, Canada: 1988 / **Ref.** RCA Special Products—ADM R-1004 / **Format**: 2xCD

Greatest Hits
Release date, UK & Europe: 1989 / **Ref.**: RCA—PL 90407 / **Format**: LP

Country Heroes: Dolly Parton
Release date, Europe: 1989 / **Ref.**: Ariola Express—295 050, 495 050 / **Format**: CD, Cassette

Country Heroes: Dolly Parton
Release date, Poland: 1989 / **Ref.**: As—A 9148 / **Format**: Cassette

Anthology
Release date, UK: 1991 / **Ref.**: Connoisseur Collection—VSOP CD 165 / **Format**: CD

Country Girl
Release date, UK: 1991 / **Ref.**: EMI Records Ltd.—CDB 7 96216 2, CD

As Long as I Love
Release date, Europe: 1992 / **Ref.**: Zillion Records—2610712 / **Format**: CD

Jolene
Release date, Europe: 1992 / **Ref.**: RCA—74321 120702 / **Format**: CD

Country Classics
Release date, Europe: 1993 / **Ref.**: Reader's Digest—RDCD 441-443 / **Format**: 3xCD

The Little Things (18 Great Country Songs)
Release date, Belgium: 1993 / **Ref.**: Country Stars—CTS 55419 / **Format**: CD

The River Unbroken
Release date, France: 1993 / **Ref.**: Versailles VER 473918 2, Sony Music Special Marketing 473918 2 / **Format**: CD

The New Best of Dolly Parton
Release date, Japan: 1993 / **Ref.**: RCA—BVCP-2101 / **Format**: CD

The Collection
Release date, Germany: 1993 / **Ref.**: RCA, BMG—74321 13987 2 / **Format**: CD

Dolly Parton & Friends
Release date, Europe: 1993 / **Ref.**: Gold—GOLD 094 / **Format**: CD

The Greatest Hits
Release date, UK: 1994 / **Ref.**: Telstar—TCD 2739 / **Format**: CD

Here I Come Again
Release date, Australasia: 1994 / **Ref.**: Castle Communications (Australasia) Limited—PCD 10006 / **Format**: CD

Best Selection
Release date, Japan: July 6, 1994 / **Ref.**: RCA—BVCP- 2630 / **Format**: CD

Heartsongs (Live from Home)
Release date, Europe: 1994 / **Ref.**: Blue Eye Records, Colombia—477276 2 / **Format**: CD

Heartsongs (Live from Home)
Release date, South Africa: 1994 / **Ref.**: Gallo Record Company, Colombia—CDCOL 3919 K / **Format**: CD

Heartsongs (Live from Home)
Release date, Indonesia: 1994 / Ref.: Blue Eye Records—472 276 4, Colombia—C-7961094 / Format: CD

Heartsongs (Live from Home)
Release date, Poland: 1994 / Ref.: MJM Music PL—345 M, Colombia—47-477276-40 / Format: CD

Heartsongs (Live from Home)
Release date, France: 1994 / Ref.: Colombia—427276 4 / Format: CD

Heartsongs (Live from Home)
Release date, Australia: 1994 / Ref.: Colombia—477276 2 / Format: CD

The Great Dolly Parton
Release date, Portugal, Spain: 1995 / Ref.: Goldies—GLD 63184 / Format: CD

2 Gether on 1
Release date, Europe: September 4, 1995 / Ref.: RCA—74321 29456 2 / Format: CD

24 Karat Gold
Release date, Netherlands: 1996 / Ref.: BMG—74321 390052 / Format: 2xCD

The Essential Dolly Parton Volume Two
Release date, Europe: 1997 / Ref.: RCA, BMG—07863 66933 2 / Format: CD

The Best of Dolly Parton
Release date, Europe: 1997 / Ref.: Camden, BMG—74321 476802 / Format: CD

A Life in Music: The Ultimate Collection
Release date, UK & Ireland: October 27, 1997 / Ref.: RCA—74321 44363 2 / Format: CD

Wildest Dreams
Release date, Austria: 1998 / Ref.: Sony Music Entertainment (Germany) GmbH—07-985646-10 / Format: CD

The Ultimate Collection
Release date, Australia: 1998 / Ref.: RCA, BMG—74321562892 / Format: 2xCD

Love Songs
Release date, Europe: 1999 / Ref.: Camden, BMG—74321 674402 / Format: CD

Dolly Parton and Friends
Release date, Germany: 2003 / Ref.: Planet Song—8511 / Format: DVD, DVD-video, PAL

Legendary Dolly Parton
Release date, Australia: 2000 / Ref.: RCA, BMG—74321 75310 2 / Format: 3xCD

Favoritter
Release date, Norway: 2000 / Ref.: BMG Norway AS—74321 317432 / Format: CD

Midnight Country: Dolly Parton (Volume 2)
Release date, UK: 2001 / Ref.: Dressed to Kill, Metrodome—METRO815 / Format: CD

Legendary Dolly Parton
Release date, UK: 2001 / Ref.: BMG—74321 892502 / Format: 3xCD

Gold Greatest Hits
Release date, Europe: February 19, 2001 / Ref.: BMG, RCA, C2M—74321 840202 / Format: CD

Mission Chapel Memories, 1971–1975
Release date, Australia: October 9, 2001 / Ref.: Raven Records—RVCD-121 / Format: CD

Queen of Country
Release date, Denmark: 2001 / Ref.: BMG Heritage—74321843592 / Format: 2xCD

Jolene & My Tennessee Mountain Home
Release date, UK & Ireland: 2001 / Ref. Camden Deluxe, BMG—74321 822362 / Format: CD, reissue

Dolly Parton & Friends (with Sandy Posey and Donna Fargo)
Release date, Europe: 2001 / Ref.: Forever Gold—FG036 / Format: CD

Here You Come Again
Release date, Sweden: 2001 / Ref.: BMG Sweden, RCA—74321 84526 2 / Format: CD

Joshua & Coat of Many Colors
Release date, Europe: 2001 / Ref.: Camden Deluxe—74321 869642 / Format: CD

Greatest Hits
Release date, UK & Europe: 2002 / Ref.: Camden—74321 985262 / Format: CD

The Ultimate Collection
Release date, Belgium: 2002 / Ref.: BMG Belgium—74321 928292 / Format: CD

The Collection
Release date, UK: 2002 / Ref.: Marks & Spencer—MS4802Y / Format: CD

Love Songs
Release date, Europe: January 6, 2003 / Ref.: RCA, BMG—74321 96239 2 / Format: CD

Ultimate Dolly Parton
Release date: June 3, 2002 / Ref.: RCA Nashville, BMG Heritage—82876 52008 2 / Format: CD

The Bluegrass Collection
Release date, UK: October 27, 2003 / Ref.: BMG UK & Ireland—82876 567282 / Format: CD

The Best Of
Release date, Europe: 2004 / Ref.: Sony Music—519087 2 / Format: CD

Artist Collection
Release date, Europe: 2004 / Ref.: RCA, BMG—82876636262 / Format: CD

The Collection
Release date, UK: 2004 / Ref.: Spectrum Music, Universal—982 014-3 / Format: CD

The Only Dolly Parton Album You'll Ever Need
Release date, UK & Ireland: June 7, 2004 / Ref.: BMG—82876626282 / Format: CD

The Great Dolly Parton
Release date: 2004 / Ref.: Rajon Music Group—CDR0296 / Format: 3xCD

Live and Well
Release date, Europe: 2004 / Ref.: Blue Eye Records, Sugar Hill Records—SUG-CD 3998 / Format: 2xCD

Live and Well
Release date, Australia: 2004 / Ref.: Sugar Hill Records—SHCD3998 / Format: 2xCD

Dolly Parton and Friends
Release date, Europe: 2005 / **Ref.:** Planet Song—8511 / **Format:** DVD, DVD-video, PAL

The Essential Dolly Parton
Release date, Europe, Australia: 2005 / **Ref.:** Sony BMG Music Entertainment, RCA, Legacy—82876 69240 2 / **Format:** 2xCD

The Essential Dolly Parton
Release date, Japan: 2005 / **Ref.:** RCA, BMG—BVCM-37660/61 / **Format:** 2xCD

The Essential Dolly Parton
Release date, South Africa: 2005 / **Ref.:** Sony Music—CDRCA7168 / **Format:** 2xCD

Legends
Release date, Europe: 2005 / **Ref.:** Sony BMG Music Entertainment—82876673662 / **Format:** 3xCD, reissue

Country Legends
Release date, Portugal: 2005 / **Ref.:** IMC Music Ltd.—CL76663 / **Format:** CD

Singer Songwriter & Legendary Performer
Release date, UK: February 25, 2007 / **Ref.:** The Mail on Sunday, Upfront, Live Nation—UPDP01 / **Format:** CD

Burlap & Satin and Real Love
Release date, UK & Europe: March 5, 2007 / **Ref.:** RCA, Sony BMG Music Entertainment: 88697061132 / **Format:** CD

Great Balls of Fire and Dolly, Dolly, Dolly
Release date, UK & Europe: March 5, 2007 / **Ref.:** RCA, Sony BMG: 88697061162 / **Format:** CD

**All I Can Do and New Harvest…
First Gathering**
Release date, Europe: March 5, 2007: **Ref.:** RCA, Sony BMG Music Entertainment—88697061082 / **Format:** CD

The Very Best of Dolly Parton
Release date, Europe, Australia, Canada: March 25, 2007 / **Ref.:** Sony BMG Music Entertainment—88697060742 / **Format:** CD

The Very Best of Dolly Parton, Volume 2
Release date, Europe: August 20, 2007 / **Ref.:** Sony BMG Music Entertainment—88697119562 / **Format:** CD

Official Masters Greatest Hits
Release date, Canada: 2008 / **Ref.:** Sony BMG—88697370472 / **Format:** 2xCD

Collector's Edition
Release date, Canada: June 24, 2008 / **Ref.:** Madacy Entertainment—TC2 53612, Sony BMG Music Entertainment Custom Marketing Group—TCE2 53613 / **Format:** 3xCD

Original Album Classics
Release date, Europe: 2008 / **Ref.:** RCA, Legacy, Sony BMG Music Entertainment—88697271112 / **Format:** 5xCD, reissue

Live from London
Release date, Australia: 2009 / **Ref.:** Dolly Records—925-Butterfly 2AV, 274463 / **Format:** CD, DVD, DVD-video

Dolly
Release date, Europe: 2009 / **Ref.:** Sony Music, RCA Nashville, Legacy—88875006172 / **Format:** 4xCD, remastered reissue

Greatest Hits
Release date, Europe: 2009 / **Ref.:** Sony Music—88697458602 / **Format:** CD

2010s–2020s

3 Original Album Classics
Release date, Europe: February 8, 2010 / **Ref.:** Sony Music, Legacy, Columbia—88697645782 / **Format:** 3xCD, reissue

The Gospel Collection
Release date, UK: November 2, 2010 / **Ref.:** Camden—88697794862 / **Format:** CD

Original Artists (with Don Williams)
Release date, South Africa: 2011 / **Ref.:** PT Music—SSDB 655 / **Format:** 2xCD

Original Album Classics
Release date, Germany: 2011 / **Ref.:** Sony Music, Legacy, Columbia—88697928832 / **Format:** 5xCD, reissue

14 Great Hits
Release date, South Africa: 2011 / **Ref.:** Sony Music Entertainment Africa (Pty) Ltd. –CDSM516 / **Format:** CD

The Very Best of Dolly Parton
Release date, New Zealand: December 20, 2013 / **Ref.:** Sony Music—88843030422 / **Format:** 2xCD

The Real…Dolly Parton
Release date, Europe: October 8, 2013 / **Ref.:** Sony Music—88883782442 / **Format:** 3xCD, remastered

The Box Set Series
Release date, Europe, Australia: 2014 / **Ref.:** RCA, Legacy, Sony Music—88843059732 / **Format:** 4xCD

Nashville Stories
Release date, Germany: July 24, 2015 / **Ref.:** Feel Good Music—1823 / **Format:** CD

The Complete Trio Collection
Release date, Europe: 2016 / **Ref.:** Warner Bros. Records, Asylum Records, Rhino Records—081227954086 / **Format:** CD reissue

The Complete Trio Collection
Release date, Australasia: 2016 / **Ref.:** Rhino Records—081227954086 / **Format:** CD reissue

**Diamonds & Rhinestones:
The Greatest Hits Collection**
Release date, Europe: 2022 / **Ref.:** RCA, Legacy, Sony Music—19439977991 / **Format:** 2x LP

**Diamonds & Rhinestones:
The Greatest Hits Collection**
Release date, Australia: 2022 / **Ref.:** RCA, Legacy, Dolly Records, Sony Music—19439978022 / **Format:** CD

Other Singles

Independently of the duets born from her alliance with Porter Wagoner, which we have not listed here, Dolly released the singles below with other artists. Some numbers used for the soundtracks of films where Dolly Parton more or less contributed were released as records. We have listed here the singles released outside the albums analyzed in this book.

We note, in 1982, an unexpected duet with Boy George of Culture Club for "Your Kisses Are Charity," the Queen of Country having been invited by the British group to record a song. This is also an opportunity to hear her in the reggae style of the huge hit "Do You Really Want to Hurt Me." As for *The Winning Hand*, an album mixing pop and country released the same year, this brings together three major Monument Records artists (Dolly Parton, Willie Nelson, and Brenda Lee) and the singer and songwriter Kris Kristofferson. This opus, composed of unreleased songs, rearranged or written for the occasion, constituted a great promotional operation for the label.

Collaborative Singles

Side A: It's Sure Gonna Hurt Side B: The Love You Gave **Release:** Mercury, 1962 (45 rpm ref.: 71982)

Side A: What Do You Think About Lovin' Side B: I Wasted My Tears **Release:** Monument Records, November 1964 (45 rpm ref.: 45-869)

Side A: Happy, Happy Birthday Baby Side B: Old Enough to Know Better (Too Young to Resist) **Release:** Monument Records, July 1965 (45 rpm ref.: 45-897)

Side A: Busy Signal Side B: I Took Him for Granted **Release:** Monument Records, January 1966 (45 rpm ref.: 45-913)

Side A: Don't Drop Out Side B: Control Yourself **Release:** Monument Records, February 1966 (45 rpm ref.: 45-922)

Side A: I'm Not Worth the Tears Side B: Ping Pong **Release:** Monument Records, January 1968 (45 rpm ref.: 45-1047)

Side A: Comin' for to Carry Me Home Side B: Golden Streets of Glory **Release:** RCA Victor, March 1971 (45 rpm ref.: 47-9971) **Best ranking:** 23 on Billboard Hot Country Songs

Side A: Washday Blues Side B: Just as Good as Gone **Release:** RCA Victor, June 1972 (45 rpm ref.: 74-0757)

Side A: The Seeker Side B: Love with Feeling **Release:** RCA Victor, May 1975 (45 rpm ref.: PB-10310)

Side A: Everything's Beautiful (In Its Own Way) (with Willie Nelson) Side B: Put It Off Until Tomorrow (with Kris Kristofferson), taken from the album *The Winning Hand* (November 1982) **Release:** Monument Records, November 1982 (45 rpm ref.: WS4-03408) **Best ranking:** 7 on Billboard Hot Country Songs

Side B: What Do You Think About Lovin' (with Brenda Lee), taken from the album *The Winning Hand* (November 1982) **Release:** Monument Records, March 1983 (45 rpm ref.: WS4-03781)

Side A: Islands in the Stream (with Kenny Rogers), written by the Bee Gees **Release:** RCA Victor, August 1983 (45 rpm ref.: PB-13615) **Best ranking:** 1 on Billboard Hot 100; gold disc, October 18, 1983; platinum disc, December 7, 1983

Singles Taken from Soundtracks

Side A: Tennessee Homesick Blues / Side B: Butterflies, taken from the film *Rhinestone* (1984) **Release:** RCA Victor, May 1984 (45 rpm ref.: PB-13819) **Best ranking:** 1 on Billboard Hot Country Songs

Side A: God Won't Get You / Side B: Sweet Lovin' Friends (with Sylvester Stallone), taken from the film *Rhinestone* (1984) **Release:** RCA Victor, August 1984 (45 rpm ref.: PB-13883) **Best ranking:** 10 on Billboard Hot Country Songs

Straight Talk, taken from the film *Straight Talk* (1992) **Release:** Hollywood Records, 1992 (CD ref.: PRCD-10129-2) **Best ranking:** 64 on Billboard Hot Country Songs

Light of a Clear Blue Morning, taken from the film *Straight Talk* (1992) **Release:** Hollywood Records, 1992 (CD ref.: PRCD-8564-2)

Burning (with Les Taylor), taken from the film *Straight Talk* **Release:** Hollywood Records, 1992 (CD ref.: PRCD-10203-2)

Glossary

Anacrusis: an initial short motif preceding the first beat.

Arpeggio: a chord played out note by note.

Backbeat: played on a 4/4 rhythm, this is the second beat marked by the snare drum. It is often used in up-tempo songs, when this beat is reinforced by a slamming guitar chord, usually played high on the neck.

Backing band: a group of musicians accompanying an artist on stage or in the studio.

Backing track: an instrumental or vocal track, sometimes only rhythmic, recorded to accompany a singer or band.

Ballad: in twentieth-century popular music, a slow song, usually slower than 95 bpm (beats per minute), suitable for a reflective mood or slow dancing. Its structure most commonly consists of verses interspersed with a refrain.

Bar chimes: a percussion instrument used mainly for musical color, as it is generally non-harmonic. It typically consists of solid aluminum cylinders or hollow copper tubes attached to a horizontal bar in order of length and pitch. It is played by sweeping the tubes horizontally with the fingers or with a stick.

Bottleneck: a glass or metal tube that the guitarist places over a finger and slides over the strings to obtain a metallic sound. Bluesmen developed this way of playing by using the neck of a bottle.

Brass band: a brass ensemble.

Bridge: transition between two passages of a song; usually refers to the sequence between the verse and the chorus. Also called a passage.

Cajun two-step: a traditional dance par excellence, danced in Louisiana by people of all ages, despite its fast rhythm.

Capo: short for *capotastro*, a device that can be attached to the neck of a guitar to change the pitch by pressing on the strings.

Charley: *see* **Hi-hat**.

Chicken picking: percussive, lively, and melodic fingerpicking on electric guitar, usually used in country music.

Chop: a guitar technique involving note-by-note play, whether of the "open" [without palm-muting], "closed" [with palm-muting], or "skank" [especially, off-beat Reggae] type—used above all in funk music.

Chorus: an effect obtained by adding an audio signal identical to the original signal, but with a very slight delay—about 20 milliseconds—and an imperceptibly different pitch. The result is a thickening of the sound, comparable to the insertion of choirs; hence the name *chorus*.

Clawhammer: playing with the thumb and forefinger attacking the strings from top to bottom. This technique takes its name from the fact that the hand that strikes the strings, stiffened from farm work, takes the form of an eagle's claw or a hammer with a nail-pulling end.

Close harmony: an arrangement using notes of a chord with a small interval between the parts. Vocal close harmony, in particular, was a genre that became very popular in the late 1930s, driven by the barbershop quartet fashion, then by the Louvin Brothers in the 1940s, the Andrews Sisters in the 1950s, and Simon & Garfunkel and the Beach Boys in the 1960s.

Coda: word of Italian origin meaning the concluding section of a piece of music.

Cross stick[ing]: a snare drum hit on the hoop of the drum, while the lower part—usually the tip—of the stick remains pressed to the skin.

Delay: an audio effect reproducing the acoustic phenomenon of an echo. Incorporated in a pedal-activated effect or on a mixing console, it can be applied to a voice or instrument to repeat a sound regularly by delaying its signal over time. A *slapback delay* is a short delay that creates the sensation of note bounce or thickening of the sound.

Distortion: a sound effect created by degrading the quality of an audio signal by saturating the channel of an amplifier. This is achieved through the "distortion" output of the amplifier or through the use of a distortion pedal.

Dobro: a make of guitar whose sound is amplified using a metallic resonator. The word *dobro* comes from a contraction of the name of its creators, Americans of Slovak origin: the *Dopyera Brothers*.

Doo-wop: a vocal style that consists of singing a melodious combination of onomatopoeia, often in close harmony. A typical group consists of a tenor surrounded by a trio or quartet.

Dulcimer: a narrow, elongated plucked or bowed string instrument in the shape of a figure eight, or in the shape of a teardrop, or in a variety of more or less rounded elongated shapes, played in traditional American music. Of Appalachian origin, it is descended from Northern European instruments—such as the German scheitholt or the Flemish hummel—brought over by settlers.

Fade-out: fading out of the music at the end of a piece.

Fiddle: name used to designate the violin in country music, mountain music, bluegrass, and Anglo-Saxon folk music.

Fingerpicking: fast arpeggiated guitar playing using the fingers, also known as fingerstyle or pattern picking.

Flanging: a sound effect obtained by adding the same signal to the original signal, but slightly delayed. This fixed delay is modulated by an LFO (low-frequency oscillation) synthesizer.

Flat picking: melodic and fast acoustic guitar playing with a pick/plectrum, typical of bluegrass.

Frets: raised metal bars built into the neck of some stringed instruments, especially guitars, at regular intervals. They allow the pitch of a note to be varied by controlling the vibrating length of the string between the resting point and the bridge, while ensuring harmonic accuracy.

Gate: processing that eliminates the resonance of a sound below a certain threshold, such as the resonance of a drum kit after impact.

Glissando: a slide between two notes.

Glockenspiel: an instrument with metal strips played with mallets, generally in a high register reminiscent of a music-box sound. A smaller sibling of the vibraphone.

Guitar hero: unofficial title given to a virtuosic and creatively brilliant guitarist. Frequently used to define electric six-stringers in the hard FM or metal styles of the 1980s, the term celebrates the greatest guitarists of the genre.

Harmonics: notes for which the left hand touches the string above the 5th, 7th, or 12th fret, so called because their frequencies are multiples of the open string frequency.

Hi-hat: a double cymbal opened and closed with a foot pedal control, used to mark the tempo. Also called a Charley or high hat.

Hillbilly: a term for a person lacking sophistication (colloquial, derogatory term connoting a "country person" from the hills), originally associated with the Appalachian region.

Hoedown: a country dance. *See also* **Square dance**.

Honky-tonk: a style of country music popularized by musicians such as Jimmie Rodgers and Hank Williams Sr. and played in bars of the same name, mainly in the southern United States.

Humming: singing with the mouth closed.

Lap steel: a type of electric guitar, similar to the pedal steel but more rudimentary, played on the knees (hence the name *lap*) with the help of a bottleneck or a steel bar sliding on the strings.

Layers: sustained notes.

Leslie cabinet/speaker: named after its inventor, Donald Leslie, an amplification cabinet equipped with a rotating speaker that creates a vibrato effect.

Licks: musical motifs.

Mastering: the next step after mixing in the production of a song or album, designed to give the recording an even quality and optimized sound volume (regardless of the listening medium), and to homogenize the tracks between them.

Midtempo: a song played at a moderate tempo.

Overdrive: usually in the form of an electric guitar pedal (mostly analogue, but also digital), an audio effect whose purpose is to re-create the saturation of an amplifier pushed to its gain limits. It usually has less gain than distortion.

Overdubs: a set of new recorded sounds (vocals and/or instruments) added to an existing recording.

Palm muting: a guitar and bass technique that consists of muffling the notes by placing the palm of the hand (right hand for right-handed players, left hand for left-handed players) on the strings near the bridge. The aim is to muffle the notes played with the pick.

Pattern: a rhythmic or melodic sequence that is repeated in a piece.

Pick: *see* **Plectrum**.

Picking: a playing technique using the thumb on the low strings, and the other fingers playing the melody on the higher strings.

Pizzicato: a playing technique used on bowed string instruments consisting of plucking the strings rather than using the bow.

Plectrum: the original name of the pick. It is possible to wear a kind of adapted ring on the finger (fingerpick), which allows a musician to play with the finger as well.

Praise: "prayer" song in gospel music.

Pump organ: a type of organ with an air chamber consisting of one or more manual keyboards and two pedals to operate the air bellows.

Resolution: the most common resolution, as it is usually the most recognizable to the listener, is often played on the *tonic* or *keynote,* the first tone of a scale.

Reverb: a natural or artificial echo effect applied to an instrument or voice during the recording or mixing of a song.

Reverse: intentional playing of a sound backward on an audio track.

Riff: a short fragment of a few notes that recurs regularly in a song and accompanies the melody. The origin of the word *riff* may be derived from an abbreviation of the English expression *rhythmic figure.*

Rimshot: hitting the skin of the snare drum at the same time as its rim, resulting in a loud, slamming sound.

Session man: a session musician.

Shuffle: a rhythmic figure that can be found especially in blues; it replaces a binary rhythm with a ternary rhythm. It offers more flexibility, and more life to the rhythm section, and opens up the field to its creativity.

Slap: a technique of playing the electric bass, practiced mainly in funk and disco music, in which the strings are struck by the thumb and pulled by the other fingers of the right hand.

Slapstick: a style of comedy whose humor is based on awkward actions and embarrassing events. The cinema of Charlie Chaplin, Buster Keaton, and Harold Lloyd exemplifies slapstick humor.

Songwriter: the author of a song.

Square dance: a type of country dance that starts with four couples facing each other in a square and whose steps and movements are announced by a leader. *See also* **Hoedown**.

Stab: isolated staccato punctuation, often played by the brass section or its keyboard equivalent, sampled or emulated by a synthesizer.

Strumming: a guitar technique that consists of sweeping up and down all the strings of the instrument with the right hand for right-handed players, and with the left hand for left-handed players.

Swamp blues: a style derived from Louisiana blues (associated with the bayou), with a funky and cheerful rhythm. It is influenced by traditional Acadian music and the zydeco of Louisiana Creoles living in the Baton Rouge area.

Swell effect: a "wave" effect obtained by using a volume pedal to control the attack of an electric guitar, a bass, or a steel guitar, and its continuous rise in volume. This technique is also called *violining*, in reference to the violin and other bowed instruments whose attack can be very progressive.

Syncopation: in the music theory of rhythm, a note or chord that is attacked on an offbeat and extended onto the next beat (which is always a strong beat). Syncopated patterns have an effect on the instinct to dance and are very common in funk and jazz music.

Tag: a short musical intervention by an instrument.

Tom: a drum used mainly for breaks. There are usually three: the alto and the medium tom (rack toms) attached to the bass drum, and the bass tom (floor tom) placed opposite the hi-hat.

Tonic (of the chord): the tonic is the first note of a key, and therefore of the major and minor scales. The tonic gives its name to the key associated with it. For example, the note C is the tonic of the "key of C," that is, the main note of a key, followed by the dominant and the subdominant.

Traditional: music that has come into the public domain.

Transients: the initial information in a soundwave.

Trill: fast and uninterrupted alternation between two adjacent notes.

Turnaround: a short phrasing leading, like a bridge, from one section to another that enhances the harmony with melodic counterpoints.

Twangy: derived from the word *twang*, meaning an accent, vibration, or nasal tone. On the electric guitar, a twangy sound (clear, brief, vibrant, and sharp) is achieved through special playing using a felt pad on the bridge or note-to-note playing muffled by the palm of the hand holding the pick.

Twelve-bar blues: twelve-bar is the most emblematic chord grid of the blues, which has become an essential basis of Anglo-Saxon popular music due to its popularity.

Up-tempo: a rapid tempo.

Vibe(s): a vocal technique consisting of singing a syllable over several notes. May also refer to a vibraphone (*see* **vibraphone**).

Vibraphone: a musical instrument in the percussion family, and more specifically in the keyboard category. Easily confused with the xylophone, it is made of metal bars instead of wood; it is often accompanied by a vibrato system with adjustable speed activated by a motor.

Wah-wah: an audio effect achieved by the oscillation of sound between low and high frequencies that produces a sound reminiscent of a human voice repeating the onomatopoeic "wah" sound. This effect, used mainly for electric guitars, is created using the pedal of the same name.

Yodeling: a singing technique that consists of rapidly and virtuosically switching from the chest (or "body") voice to the head (or "falsetto") voice. Among farms of the Midwest, the Amish from Switzerland and Alsace have perpetuated the art of yodeling. Its inspiration can be found in American country music.

Index

The singles, albums, and Portraits are in bold.

9 to 5 [Musical] 12, 526, 529, 544–545
9 to 5 [Movie] 12, 41, 51, 106, 269, 279–282, 285, 293–296, 486, 490, 526–527
9 to 5 [Single] 91, 278–280, **282**, 285–286, 293, 315, 350, 572, 579
9 to 5 and Odd Jobs 13, **278–289**, 293
12–Tone Music Group 566–567

ABBA 187
Abernathy, Barry 580
A Better Place to Live 126, 134–135
AC/DC 150
A Christmas to Remember 326, 330, 333
A Cowboy's Ways 304, 312–313
Act Like a Fool [Single] 292, 298, **302–303**
Acuff, Roy 18, 76, 177, 221, 227
Adams, Lucy 322
Adler, Rich 220–222, 224–227
Aerosmith 404, 559
Afanasieff, Walter 570
A Father's Prayer 491
A Few Old Memories [Single] 478, **481**, 483
Afraid to Live and Afraid of Dying 162, 166–167
A Friend Like You 562
After the Goldrush 438, 446
After the Goldrush [Single] 470, 472–**473**, 476
A Gamble Either Way 304, 309
Agee, Roy 568, 570
A Habit I Can't Break 96, 100
A Holly Dolly Christmas **566–573**
Alabama Sundown 162, 165–166, 190, 286
Alger, Pat 345
A Little At a Time 138, 144
Allen, Debbie 491, 569
Allen, Harley 472
Allen, Monty 498–499, 512–516, 552, 558, 561
All I Can Do **210–215**, 504
All I Can Do [Single] **212**, 214
All I Want for Christmas Is You 566, 570
All–Star Reveliers 14
Almost in Love 256, 264
A Lot of You Left in Me 138, 143
Altan 499
Alternative Country 22

Altman, Robert 513
Altshuler, Jean 81–83, 85
Always, Always 53, **78–87**, 170, 174
Always, Always [Single] 53, 78, **84**, 170
Always the First Time 52, 62
Amai, Willa 489
Amazing Grace 460, 464, 491, 572
Andersen, Mark 285
Anderson, Charlie 512–516
Anderson, Eddy 298–303, 306–310, 312–313
Anderson, Leroy 328
Anderson, Pamela 254
André of the Valley 350
Andrews Sisters (The) 434
Angel Band 491
Angell, David 489, 520, 532, 561, 568–571, 579–580
Angell, Monisa 520, 532, 568–569, 571, 579
Anglin, Jack 194
Animals (The) 206, 283
Aniston, Jennifer 489
Another Woman's Man 177
Anything's Better Than Nothing 78, 87
Appalachian Memories 304, 309
Applejack [Single] 120–121, 216, **221**–222, 225, 246, 299
A Reading of Coat of Many Colors 562
Arens, Kii 529
Armstrong, Louis 65, 109
Armstrong, Neil 53
Arnold, Eddy 46
Arrias, John 270, 272–276
Asher, Virginia 466
Askey, Janet 532
Asleep at the Wheel 22
As Long As I Love 38, **96–107**, 112
As Long As I Love 96, 100
A Smoky Mountain Christmas 491
A Smoky Mountain Christmas [Television Movie] 365, 491
As Much As Always 292, 300
As Soon As I Touched Him 230, 237
Astaire, Fred 365
Atamanuik, Larry 472
A Tender Lie [Single] 492, **497**
Atkins, Chet 18, 22, 32, 37–40, 177, 221, 227, 250, 301, 416, 471–472, 561
Aufray, Hugues 13
Avedon, Richard 315

Babcock, Joe 56–58, 60–63, 68–70, 72–75, 91–95, 144–145, 159–160
Babes [Television Movie] 526
Baby, Come Out Tonight 230, 233
Baby I'm Burnin' [Single] 240–241, 244, **248**
Baby Sister 37, 47
Bacco, Sam 398–400, 402–404, 406, 532
Back Home 154, 160
Backwoods Barbie **528–537**
Backwoods Barbie [Single] 528, 530–**532**
Badham, John 241
Badham, Mary 120–121
Baez, Joan 40, 68, 284, 359, 483, 496, 515
Bagwell-Garves, Lakieta 570–571
Bailey, Bob 390, 430, 432–435, 440, 512–516
Bailey, Carolyn 532
Bailey, Jerry 187, 199
Baird, Mike 486
Baker, Lois 454
Bakersfield Sound 22
Bales, Barry 480–485, 494, 497–498
Ball, Anita 221, 227, 244–248, 250–251, 258, 260–262, 264–265, 270, 272–276, 282–286, 288–289, 298, 300, 302–303, 306–310, 312–313, 367–368, 370–373
Ballade Country 30–31, 34, 46, 60–61, 73, 93, 98, 101, 104, 132, 144–145, 158, 202, 308, 312, 390, 393, 398, 417, 465
Ballerini, Kelsea 575
Band (The) 134–135
Banks of the Ohio 552
Barbara on Your Mind [Single] 177, 292, 299, **302**
Bardot, Brigitte 25, 139
Bare, Bobby 32, 46, 286
Barnes, Howard 310
Barnes, Matt 451
Barron, Steve 310
Bashful Brother Oswald 221, 227
Basie, Count 315
Basore, Stu 180–185, 189–193, 220–222, 224–227
Batteau, David 366
Baxter, Glenn 81, 86, 104–105
Baxter, Jeff 244–248, 250–251, 270, 272–276, 282, 298–303

Bayer Sager, Carole 251, 260
Bayers, Eddie 282–286, 288–289, 376–378, 380, 382–384, 432–435, 440, 442–444, 446–449
Beach Boys (The) 226
Bear Family Records 172, 557
Beasler, Norma Jean 25, 34, 47, 76, 79, 102, 113, 169–170, 174
Beatles (The) 25, 30, 60, 109, 120, 206, 226, 261, 280, 393
Because I Love You 204–205, 209
Becker, Walter 265
Beckett, Barry 376–378, 380, 382–384
Bee Gees (The) 228, 305, 336–337, 547
Before the Next Teardrop Falls 438, 444
Before You Make Up Your Mind 88, 92–93
Behind Closed Doors 438, 447
Belafonte, Harry 337, 390
Belfield, Dennis 328–330, 332–334, 486
Bellow, Saul 525
Belly, Lead 136, 484
Benay, Ben 232–237
Bennett, Eric 462, 502
Bennett, S. Fillmore 463, 499
Bennett, Tony 498
Benson, Ray 22
Berg, Matraca 440, 444
Bergeson, Pat 576, 579
Berinati, Lea Jane 221, 306–310, 312–313, 398–399, 402, 404, 406
Berlin, Irving 334
Bernard, Crystal 440
Bernard, Felix 328
Berry, Chuck 74–75
Blackberry tree 513
Best Woman Wins [Single] 396, 400, **403–404**
Be There 486
Better Day 529, **538–545**, 554
Better Day 538, 544
Better Get to Livin' [Single] **528–531**
Better Move It on Home [Single] 102, **106**
Beyoncé 199
Bidasio, John 486
Biden, Joe 567
Blyth, Ann 196
Big Dreams and Faded Jeans [Single] 574–**576**
Biggs, Howard 534
Big Wind 64, 70
Billy the Kid 22

Birkin, Jane 139
Black, Damon 62
Black, James Milton 466
Black, Michael 306–310, 312–313
Blackie, Kentucky 186, 190, 192
Blackwell, Otis 262, 320
Blaine, Hal 321
Blair, Hal 420
Blakeman, Robert 350, 375
Blalock, Arthur 50
Blalock, Mitchell 50
Blind Boys of Alabama (The) 514
Bloom, Steve 360
Blowin' in the Wind 518, 520
Blue Bonnet Breeze [Single] 574, **579**
Blue Eye Records 339, 342–343, 428–429, 438–440, 443, 449–454, 458, 460–461, 478–479, 481, 483, 492–494, 496–497, 500–501, 504, 507, 510–511, 518–519
Blue Grace 488
Bluegrass [Music] 13, 16–18, 21, 31, 42, 73, 94, 105, 107, 124, 130, 167, 214, 261, 372, 376, 390, 439, 464, 479–484, 493–494, 496, 501–502, 506, 508, 514, 516, 520, 522–525, 530, 536, 540, 547, 550–551, 554, 575–576, 578–579
Blue Grass Boys (The) 21
Blue Me 488
Bluer Pastures [Single] 492, **497**
Blue Ridge Boys (The) 76
Blues [Music] 17, 19, 21, 31, 61, 65, 74–75, 104, 113, 136, 150, 184–185, 191–192, 200, 213, 226, 250, 260, 264, 356, 360, 410, 412, 442, 474, 523, 534, 544, 550, 553, 561
Blue Smoke 546–555
Blue Smoke 546, 550
Bluestone, Harry 232–234, 236–237
Blues Traveler 442
Blue Valley Songbird 450, 456, 491
Blue Valley Songbird [Television Movie] 456, 491
Boberg, Carl 114

Birkin, Jane 139
Bob Wills & His Texas Playboys 21
Bogan, Joe 398
Bohanon, George 270, 272–276, 298–303
Boileau, Nicolas 132
Bolas, Niko 316–321
Bollman, Drew 554
Bond, Johnny 484
Bon Jovi, Jon 552
Bonnie & Clyde 117, 122
Boogie–woogie 21, 298
Book of Life 108–109, 114, 166
Boorman, John 21
Bordonali, Pete 306–310, 312–313
Bosworth, Richard 316–321, 366
Both Sides Now 518, 525
Boulder to Birmingham 210, 214
Bourke, Rory 245
Bowers, Zeneba 532
Bowie, David 12
Box Tops 145
Boyd, Jimmy 571
Boy George 471
Boynton, Matt 520, 522–525
Braddock, Bobby 63
Bradley, Mike 490
Bradley Kincaid, 194
Brannan, Richard Spady 340, 344
Brannon, Paul 562
Brave Little Soldier 510, 562, 564
Bread 504
Brémond, Jacques 20
Brewster, Paul 457
Bridges, Alicia 422
Bridges, James 337
Briggs, David 26, 40–42, 44–47, 81–87, 129–130, 132–134, 180–185
Bright, Avery 489
Brignardello, Mike 376–378, 380, 382–384, 531, 534–535, 540–545, 552–553
Britz, Chuck 282–286, 288–289, 298–303
Brooks, Clyde 221
Brooks, Garth 422
Brooks, Mark 454, 456–458, 462–466
Brooks, Phillips 393
Brown, Alexandra 270, 272–276
Brown, Danny 462–466, 502, 504–508
Brown, Darrell 366
Brown, Hylo 16
Brown, James 398
Brown, Jerry 361
Brown, Jim "Moose" 554
Brown, Milton 21
Brown, Russell 228, 516
Browne, Jackson 214, 360

Browning, Walter 60
Bruce, Bobby 366–368, 370–373
Bruce, Ken 558
Bryant, Boudleaux 359
Bryant, Felice 359
Bryner, Mark 346
Bubbling Over 162–175
Bubbling Over 162–163, 165
Bublé, Michael 568
Buchanan, Pat 552–554
Buchanan, Robby 306–310, 312–313, 473–476
Buchanan, Rusty 486
Buckingham, Steve 13, 339, 397–400, 402–404, 406, 409–410, 412–414, 416–418, 420, 422, 429–430, 432–435, 439–440, 442–444, 446–449, 479–485, 493–499, 520, 522–525, 529
Buda, Nick 552, 554
Buena Vista Social Club 351
Bukovac, Tom 531, 535
Bulling, Erich 328–330, 332–334
Bumgarner, Samantha 136
Bunch, Ray 398
Burke, Willi 316
Burlap & Satin 304–313
Burley, Kay 548
Burnett, Carol 260–261
Burnett, Jodi 356
Burning 488
Burning to Burned 488
Burns, Ken 359
Burton, Tim 387
Bush, George W. 361, 493, 501, 511, 519
Bush, George H. W. 375, 387, 397
Bush, Sam 463–465, 479–485, 520
Butler, Jerry 319
Butler, Rosemary 319
Butterflies 486
Butterflies [Movie] 189
Butterfly Records 566–567, 574–575
Butterworth, Lisa 563
Buttrey, Kenny 55–58, 60–63
But You Know I Love You [Single] 278, **288**–289
But You Loved Me Then 88, 93–94, 140, 200
Byrds (The) 33, 142, 317–318, 524
Byrne, Dermot 495, 498–499

Cajun [Music] 14, 16–17, 19, 105, 150, 377–378, 504
Cale, J.J. 45, 200
Callas, Maria 361

Calm on the Water 304, 313
Campbell, David 355–356, 366–368, 370–373, 473, 475–476
Campbell, Marcia 498
Campbell, Tom 340
Cannon, Buddy 554
Cannon, Chuck 410, 412, 414, 416–418
Can't Be That Wrong 556, 560
Caponetta, Debbie 328–330, 332–334
Capote, Truman 315
Capps, Jimmy 157–161
Capps, Mark 576
Caraeff, Ed 231, 242, 257, 305
Carey, Jennie 440, 442–444, 446–449, 480–485
Carey, Mariah 570
Cargill, Henson 26
Carlile, Brandi 12
Carlisle, Bob 378
Carlton, Larry 282–286, 288–289, 298–303
Carmichael Parks, Carol 260, 262, 264
Carnes, Kim 327, 342, 440, 444, 482
Carney, Dennis 205, 479, 511, 519, 564
Carr, Butch 554
Carrey, Jim 361
Carrigan, Jerry Kirby 40–42, 44–47, 56–58, 60–63, 68–70, 72–75, 81–87, 91–95, 129–130, 132–134, 148–152, 157–161, 180–185
Carson, Carl 392
Carson, Johnny 241
Carter, Anita 13, 40, 42–47, 81–87, 91, 105
Carter, A. P. 472
Carter, Brenda 81
Carter, Calvin 319
Carter, Jimmy 231, 269, 280
Carter, June 40, 250
Carter, Maybelle 136, 472
Carter, Sara 472
Carter Jr., Fred 68–70, 72–75
Carter Family (The) 136, 436, 472, 496, 501
Cash, Johnny 21, 26, 28, 40, 68, 197, 250, 294, 315, 317, 360, 393, 462, 464, 466, 482, 494, 524, 577
Cash, Rosanne 310
Cash, Tommy 26
Cashdollar, Cindy 22
Cash Jr., Roy 482
Cash on the Barrelhead 478, 481
Cassel, Kirsten 532

Casstevens, Mark 220–222, 224–227, 376–378, 380, 382–384, 398–400, 402–404, 406, 440, 443, 472, 474–476
Castro, Lenny 258, 260–261, 264, 270, 272–276, 282, 298–303, 340–342, 344–345
Cas Walker Show 9
Cates, Margie 430, 432–435
Cave, Nick 137
CBS Records 29
Chadbourne, Eugène 25
Chadie, Steve 568
Chambers, Kasey 46
Chanel, Coco 109
Chang, Wei Tsun 568–571
Change 428, 432
Chapel Hart (The) 180
Chapin Carpenter, Mary 410, 422
Chapman, Mike 367–368, 370–373
Chappelear, Charlie 220–222, 224–227
Charles, Robert 398
Chas [Single] 88, 91–**92**
Chater, Kerry 274
Chavis, Boozoo 14
Chemay, Joe 328–330, 332–334
Chemo Hero 562, 564
Cher 400
Chesnut, Jerry 102, 106
Chicken Every Sunday 116, 124
Childs, Ralph 220–222, 224–227
Christ Church, 375
Christ Church Choir (The) 414, 418
Christ Church Pentecostal Choir (The) 394
Christian, Terry 328
Christmas Is 491, 566, 568
Christmas on the Square 491, 566, 568–569
Christmas on the Square [Musical] 486, 491, 526, 569
Christmas Where We Are 566, 570
Christmas Without You [Single] 326, 328–**329**
(*I'd Like to Spend*) *Christmas with Santa* 491
Church in the Wildwood 460, 463
Ciccone, Christopher 439
Clancy, Tom 501
Clapton, Eric 135, 251, 534
Clark, Bob 315, 486
Clark, Gene 33, 142
Clark, Michael 142
Clark, Petula 318–319
Clark, Roy 107

Clash (The) 513
Clement, Jack 102, 104
Cliff, Jimmy 226
Cline, Gerald 196
Cline, Patsy 20, 22, 40, 147, **194–197**, 421, 424
Clinton, Bill 409, 451, 479
Coat of Many Colors 109, **126–137**, 147, 165, 177, 182, 200, 519
Coat of Many Colors [Single] 9, 46, 51, 91, 126–**129**–130, 134, 365, 509, 519, 562, 572–573
Cobb, Don 440, 442–444, 446–449
Cochran, Eddie 17, 70
Cochran, Hank 26
Coen brothers 57, 352
Cogbill, Tommy 306–310, 312–313
Cohen, Ethan 337
Cohen, Joel 337
Cohen, Paul 194
Cohn, Nudie 76, 245
Colella, Jeff 316–321
Coleman, Dabney 279
Colla, Richard A. 491
Collins, Judy 284, 464, 525
Collins Kids (The) 16–17
Cologne 528, 534
Color Me America 510, 516
Columbia Records 364–367, 370–378, 380–384, 386–387, 396–397, 399–400, 402–404, 406, 408–410, 412–413, 416, 418, 420, 428–429, 432, 434, 439
Colvard, Jimmy 157–161, 180–185, 189–193, 220–222, 224–227
Come Back to Me [Single] 338, 340, **345**
Comes and Goes 146, 149, 151
Comin' For to Carry Me Home! [Single] 113
Comin' Home for Christmas 566, 570
Connor, Tommy 571
Converse, Charles C. 466
Cooder, Ry 351
Cook, Betsy 355
Cooley, Eddie 320
Coolidge, Rita 226
Coon Creek Girls (The) 136
Cooper, Anderson 361
Cooper, Stoney 221
Cooper, Wilma Lee 221
Coots, J. Fred 388
Corbin, Everett 26, 79, 241
Corcoran, Paddy, 398, 410, 412
Corenflos, J. T. 551–552
Corey, Joe 576
Costello, Elvis 361

Couch, Paul T. 562
Could I Have Your Autograph [Single] 364, 367, **372**
Country Blues 94, 134, 184, 235, 397, 448, 504, 578–579
Country Folk 29, 133, 203, 504, 523, 550
Country Funk 93, 130, 200
Country Gospel 104, 215, 349, 464
Country Hillbilly 20
Country Hoedown 72, 130, 182, 201, 214, 289
Country Is as Country Does 529, 538, 541
Country Memories 491
Country [Music] 9–10, 12, **19–22**, **48–51**, **194–197**, 511
Country Music Association (CMA) 60, 80, 107, 129, 187, 199, 206, 250, 322, 375, 422
Country Music Hall of Fame and Museum (The) 40, 130–131, 164, 195–196, 315, 336, 359, 424, **436–437**, 471
Countrypolitan Sound 22, 130
Country Pop 22, 42, 165, 279, 282, 312, 373, 457
Country Road [Single] 396, **400**, 403
Country Rock 33, 42, 56, 128, 142, 212, 286, 375, 535
Country Shuffle 32, 34, 42, 73–74, 83, 86, 92, 98, 101, 104, 106, 132, 143–144, 158–160, 182, 184, 202, 213–215, 236, 312, 388, 390
Country Style 322–323
Country Waltz 73, 86–87, 92, 105, 202–203, 448, 465, 481, 485, 502, 535, 554, 561, 579
Country Western 21
Cowboy Copas 197
Cowgirl & the Dandy 230, 236
Cox, Jimmy 328–330, 332–334
Cox, Suzanne 430, 432–435
Cracker Jack 177
Craig, Betty 124
Craig, Charlie 124
Crawford, Jimmy 220–222, 224–227
Crawford, Joey 568, 576
Creedence Clearwater Revival 212
Creek, Nickel 520
Crichton, Michael 501
Crimson and Clover 518, 523

Crippled Bird 428, 430, 432, 452
Crisp, Terry 376–377, 380, 384, 534–535
Crofford, Mickey 490
Cromwell, Chad 554
Cronin, Kevin 376
Cropper, Steve 270, 272–276, 298–303
Crosby, David 33
Cross My Heart 408, 417
Crouch, Dennis 554, 568, 571
Crow, Sheryl 310
Crowell, Rodney 359, 410, 412, 414, 416–418
Crozat 466
Cry, Cry Darlin' 501
Cuesta, Stan 359
Cuevas, Manuel 76, 350
Cuddle Up, Cozy Down Christmas 566, 568
Cuomo, Bill 320–321, 366–368, 370–373
Cunningham, Austin 414
Curran, Ciarán 498–499
Curtiz, Michael 196
Cyrus, Billy Ray 409–410, 570
Cyrus, Miley 12, 220, 409–410, 568, 570

Da Costa, Paulinho 244–247
Daddy [Single] 53, 56, 64, 66, **73**, 104
Daddy Come and Get Me [Single] 53, 88, 90–**91**, 92
Daddy's Moonshine Still 116, 124–125
Daddy's Working Boots 154, 158, 285
Daddy Was an Old Time Preacher Man [Single] 102, **104**, 174
Daddy Won't Be Home Anymore 96, 100
Dagger Through the Heart [Single] 500, 507
Dailey, Jamie 540–545, 576
Dailey & Vincent 576
Dale, Dick 32
Dalhart, Vernon 73
Dalida 241
D'Amore, Richard 339
Daniels, Cynthia 568
Danoff, Bill 214
Darin, Bobby 93, 524
Dark As a Dungeon 278, 288
Darken, Eric 551
Dark Night, Bright Future 574, 580
Darnell, Janet 568–571
Davidson, David 489, 520, 532, 561, 568–571, 579–580
Davis, Betty Jack 32

Davis, Billy 535
Davis, Chip 498–499
Davis, Christian 540–545, 550
Davis, Danny 104–105
Davis, Eva 136
Davis, Gary 452, 456–458, 462–466, 475, 502, 504–508, 512–516
Davis, Jimmie 57
Davis, Katherine Kennicott 391
Davis, Mac 10, 68, 93, 178, 241, 375, 378, 382–383, 397, 406, 409–410, 418, 444, 529, 542, 567
Davis, Michael 388–394, 410, 412–414, 416–418, 512–516, 540–545, 552, 559, 568–571
Davis, Miles 85
Davis, Steve 520, 522–525
Davis Sisters (The) 32
Dawidoff, Nicholas 195
Dean, Billy 412, 491
Dean, Carl Thomas 9–10, 12, 46, 50–51, 66, 115, 147, 177, 269, 305, 481, 502, 557
Dean, Eddie 420
Dean, Ginny 115
Deason Sisters (The) 194
DeCaro, Denise 270, 272–276, 298, 300, 302–303
DeCaro, Nick 232–237, 244–248, 250–251
Decca 194–195, 197, 450–454, 458
Deck the Halls 387
DeFeo, Ronald Jr. 199
Delmore Brothers (The) 21
DeMain, Jim 530–532, 534–535
Deming, Mark 37–38, 211, 257
Demons 574, 577
DeMorris, Jeff 440, 442–444, 446–449
De Niro, Robert 231
Dennis, Quitman 258, 260–262, 264–265
Dennison, Hannah 512–516
Dennison (Parton), Rachel 177, 279, 409, 417, 454, 463, 465–466, 485
Dennison, Richard 13, 51, 177, 221, 244–248, 250–251, 258, 261, 264, 270, 272–276, 282–286, 288–289, 298, 300–303, 307–310, 312–313, 366–373, 376–377, 380–384, 388–391, 394, 398–399, 402, 404, 406, 409–410, 412, 414, 416–418, 430, 432–435, 446, 449, 453–454, 457–459, 486–487, 498–499, 502, 507, 512–516, 520, 522–525, 530–532, 534–536, 540–545, 550–554, 558–562, 568–571, 576–580

Densmore, Denny 316–321
De Palma, Brian 305
Deportee (Plane Wreck at Los Gatos) 278, 284
Derek and the Dominos 251
DeShannon, Jackie 414
Detroit City [Single] 278, **286**.
DeVor, Neil 520, 522–525
Dew, Joan 426
Diana Ross & the Supremes 30
DiCaprio, Leonardo 177
Dick, Charlie 196
Dickens, Hazel 481
Dickinson, Kyle 530–532, 534–535, 552
Diddley, Bo 135, 502
Dill, Danny 286
Dillard, Linda 486
Dillon, Lola Jean 26, 34
Dire Straits 359, 413, 559
Dirty Job 488
Disco 150, 199, 217, 231, 236, 241, 244, 248, 257–258, 271, 273, 283, 318
Disney, Walt 90
Ditto, Allen 530–532, 534–535
D–I–V–O–R–C–E 52, 63
Dixie Chicks (The) 137
Dobbe, Paul 282–286, 288–289, 298–303
Dobbins, Gene 245
Do I Ever Cross Your Mind [Single] 292, **301**, 471–**472**, 473, 476, 561
Doobie Brothers (The) 244
Dolly (Show) 163, 189, 205, 211, 228–229, 237, 336, 362–363
Dolly Doll 177
Dolly, Dolly, Dolly 268–277, 279
Dollymania 502, 504, 508, **565**
Dolly Parton's Christmas of Many Colors: Circle of Love [Movie] 51, 563, 569
Dolly Parton's Christmas on the Square [Television Movie] 568
Dolly Parton's Coat of Many Colors [Movie] 51, 563
Dolly Parton's Commentary on Hello God [Single] 504
Dolly Parton Day (The) 97
Dolly Parton & Friends [Series] 229
Dolly Parton Sings: My Favorite Songwriter, Porter Wagoner 146–153, 166, 171, 185
Dolly Records 12, 528–532, 535–536, 538–539, 546–547, 550, 556–557, 562
Dolly: The Seeker/We Used To 204–209
Dollywood 10–12, 50–51, 127–128, 156, 158, 177, 188, 322, 339, **346–347**, 365, 375, 420, 439, 461, 468,

471, 501–502, 519–520, 536–537, 557, 563–564, 570, 572, 575
Dollywood Foundation 420, 461, 468, 539, 562–563
Don't Call It Love [Single] 338, 341–**342**
Don't Let It Trouble Your Mind 52, 54, 56
Don't Let Me Cross Over 438, 448
Don't Make Me Have to Come Down There [Single] 10
Don't Think Twice 546, 551
Dorff, Steve 368, 440, 447, 449
Dorsey, Thomas A. 514
Douglas, Jerry 479–485, 494–499
Down [Single] 256, **260**
Down from Dover 88, 90, 95, 140, 492, 498–499
Down from Dover [Series] 90
Down on Music Row 154, 161
Downtown [Single] 314, **318**–319, 321
Doyle, Bobby 336
Do You Hear the Robins Sing 146, 148–149, 151, 166
Do You Think That Time Stands Still 256, 261, 264
Dozier, Lamont 320
Drake, Ervin 112
Drake, Pete 68–70, 72–75, 107, 129–130, 132–135, 148–152, 157–161, 180–185
Dreadnoughts (The) 513
Dreams Do Come True 396, 406
Dresser, Lee 320–321
Drinkin' Stein 486
Driven 574, 578
Drives Me Crazy [Single] 528, 531
Dropkicks Murphys (The) 513
Dr. Robert F. Thomas 154, 159
Dubliners (The) 498
Duffy 246
Dugmore, Dan 448
Dukes, Kevin 366–368, 370–373
Dumb Blonde [Single] 10, 24, **28–29**, 30, 32, 42, 54, 169, 258, 489
Dumler, Earl 258, 260–262, 264–265, 270, 272–276
Dumplin' [Movie] 28, 232, 488–489, 527, 567
Dump the Dude 364, 368
Duncan, Glen 398–400, 402, 404, 406
Duncan, Stuart 376–377, 380–381, 383, 390, 393, 430, 432–435, 480–485, 494–499, 520, 551–552
Dycus, Frank 417
Dylan, Bob 13, 26, 40, 55–56, 58, 62, 68–70, 92, 135, 148, 228,

273, 284, 359–360, 462, 515, 520, 551
Dyson, Bobby 13, 81–87, 129–130, 132–134,142, 144, 148–152, 157–161, 180–185, 189–193, 220–222, 224–227

Eagle When She Flies 13, 51, **396–407**, 409, 422
Eagle When She Flies [Single] 396, **402**, 406
Eagles (The) 360, 496
Early Morning Breeze 126, 133, 176, 182
Earth Wind & Fire 150
East, Javeline 398
East, Nathan 270, 272–276, 298–303
Easton, Sheena 336
Edgemon, Luc 489
Edgin, Dolores 40, 42, 44–47, 56–58, 60–63, 68–70, 72–75, 81–87, 91–95, 105, 159–160
Edwards, Kenny 351, 354–357, 360
Eggers, Bob 122
Eggers, Janice 122
Elbert, Donnie 320
Eldrige, Sheridan 270, 272–276
Eldredge, Terry 502, 504–508, 520, 522–525, 550
Electro/Dance [Music] 370, 409
Elizabeth I 90, 136
Elizabeth II 218
Ellington, Duke 177, 393
Ellisor, Conni 520, 532
Elliott, Ron 316–321
Elusive Butterfly [Single] 314, 316, **321**
Emmanuel, Tommy 301
Endless Stream of Tears 478, 483
English, Michael 410, 412, 414, 416–418
Enockson, Ryan 568
Epstein, Rob 361
Estel, Floyd 250
Etheridge, Melissa 46
Even a Fool Would Let Go 268, 274
Evening Shade 64–65, 72, 426
Everett, Les 103, 110, 128, 140, 147, 164, 174
Everly Brothers (The) 21
Everybody Needs an Angel 491
Everyday Hero 364, 370

Fagen, Donald 265
Falk, Peter 539
Fallen Angels (The) 359
Falling Out of Love with Me [Single] 210–212, **214**
Fallon, Jimmy 570
False Eyelashes 36, 40–41
Family 396, 406
Fanjoy, Trey 530, 541, 564
Farina, Sandy 276
Farrakhan, Louis 429
Farrell, Chris 532, 568–569, 571
Farris, Steve 488

Farther Along [Single] 348, 351, **358**, 461, 465
Fairy Tale 491
Feels Like Home [Single] 470, 472–473, **476**
Feiten, Buzzy 270
Fekaris, Dino 373
Feldman, Victor 328–330, 332–334
Feliciano, José 402
Fender, Freddy 14, 301, 404
Ferguson, Bob 12, 40–42, 44–47, 53, 55–58, 60–63, 68–70, 72–75, 79, 81–87, 91–95, 102, 104–107, 109, 112–115, 117, 120, 122–125, 129–130, 132–134, 139, 142–145, 147–152, 155, 157–161, 163, 165–168, 174–175, 177, 180–185, 187, 189–193, 199, 221, 420
Fergusson, Larry 328
Ferrer, Ibrahim 351
Ferrer, Nino 113
Fielder, Mary 221
Fikes, Lee 81
Findley, Chuck 258, 260–262, 264–265, 270, 272–276, 298–303, 318
Fine Young Cannibals 531
Firecracker 574, 579–580
First Noel 386, 388, 394
Fishell, Steve 351–352, 355–356
Fish out of Water 488
Fitzgerald, Ella 360, 393, 498
Flatt, Lester 21, 481
Fleck, Béla 376–378, 380, 383
Fletcher, Anne 28, 232, 489
Flippo, Chet 241–242
Flores, Luis
Flower Power 25, 79, 89, 139–140, 199, 519
Fogerty, John 489
Folk [Music] 33–34, 55, 98, 134–136, 142, 148–149, 180, 194, 200, 203, 235, 317, 321, 336, 349, 352, 355, 359–360, 443, 452, 466, 479, 483, 489, 493–494, 504, 515, 520, 522–525, 530, 534, 540, 550–551, 553
Follmar, Chrissy 388–394, 398
Fomin, Boris 520
Fonda, Jane 106, 269, 279–281, 526–527
Fool for Your Love 268, 274
Ford, Gerald 177, 187
Ford, Harrison 293
Ford, John 20
Forever Home 536
Forever Love 556, 561
Forgive Me 491
For God and Country 510–517
Forman, Milos 89
Fort, Hank 137
For the Good Times [Single] 438, 443, **449**

Foster, David 13, 232–237, 244–248, 250–251, 258, 264, 327–330, 332–334, 520, 525
Foster, Fred 12, 25–35, 37, 97–101, 103, 294, 339, 357, 523
Foster, Stephen 282
Fouce, Tom 328
Four Seasons (The) 247
Four Tops (The) 30, 248, 320, 524
Fowler, Dave 520
Fox, Damon 489
Frager, Arnie 490
Francisco, Don 384
Franco 109
François, Claude 247
Franklin, Aretha 69, 134, 152–153, 303, 462, 464
Franklin, Paul 376–377, 380, 382, 384, 398–400, 402, 404, 406, 410, 412–414, 416–418, 432–435, 448, 530–532, 535, 551, 558–561
French, Jeanne 264–265
French, Steve 462, 502
Fresh Out of Forgiveness 52, 55, 61, 134
Fricke, Janie 221
Friedkin, William 163
Friedman, Jeffrey 361
Friend, Cliff 420
Fritts, Donnie 318
Froman, Jane 112
From Here to the Moon and Back [Single] 310, **490**, 546, 554
Fuel to the Flame 24, 26, 32
Fugees (The) 499
Full Circle [Single] 408, **410**, 412
Funk [Music] 82, 93, 150, 192, 209, 226, 246, 251, 275, 553
Funk Brothers (The) 73, 133, 226
Furusho, Stuart 328

Gable, Clark 424
Gahr, David 218
Gainsbourg, Serge 25, 133, 139
Gallin, Sandy 12, 178, 205, 231, 257, 264–265, 294, 397, 439, 471
Galloway, Roy 258, 260, 270, 272–276, 298, 300–303
Games People Play 64, 69
Gannon, Kim 389
Garay, Val 13, 315–321
Garbo, Greta 387
Gardner, Ava 387
Gardner, Joy 453–454, 457–459
Garnett, Gale 320
Garney, Dennis 387
Garrish, Sonny 410, 412–414, 416–418
Gassman, Jan 232–237
Gates, Bill 451
Gates, David 504
Gatica, Humberto 328
Gay, Connie B. 196
Gaye, Marvin 30, 315

Gee Ma, I Wanna Go Home 510, 513
Geidner, Nick 509
Gentle Reign (The) 320
Gentry, Bobbie 29
George Baker Selection 165
Get Out and Stay Out 538, 544–545
Gettin' Happy 186, 191–192
Getting in My Way 216, 226
Gibb, Barry 337, 336
Gibb, Maurice 305
Gibb, Robin 305, 547
Gibson, Steven A. 376–378, 380, 382–384, 398–400, 402, 404, 406
Giedt, Jeff 376
Gift, Roland 531
Gilbert and Sullivan 361
Gill, Gene 61
Gill, Vince 376–377, 380, 382–384, 400, 410, 412, 414, 416–418, 432
Gillespie, Haven 388
Gilmore, Patrick 513
Gilstrap, Jim 244–248, 250–251
Gimble, Johnny 129–130, 132–134, 148–152, 157–161, 180–185
Girl in the Movies [Single] **489**, 567
Girl Left Alone [Single] 16–**17**, 345
Glascock, Brian 316–321
Glass, Philip 361
Glaub, Bob 340–342, 344–345, 366–368, 370–373
Glosson, Lonnie 84
God Bless the USA 510, 512
Goddard, Paulette 387
God's Coloring Book 230, **236**
God Won't Get You [Single] **486**–487, 560
Goin' Back to Heaven [Single] **486**
Goldband Records 9, 14, 16–17
Goldberg, Jan 293
Goldberg, Neil 293
Goldberg, Paul 316–321
Golden, Gene 435
Golden Streets of Glory **108**–**115**, 117, 166, 421
Golden Streets of Glory [Single] 108, **113**–114
Goldsboro, Bobby 236
Goldstein, Steve Golde 13, 316–321, 327, 329, 340–342, 344–345, 365–373
Good, Rodney 376
Good As Gold 78, 86–87
Good Time 536
Gordon, Jim 251
Gordon, T. Duane 48, 565
Gordy, Berry 30
Gore, Lesley 29, 92
Gorodetzky, Carl 532
Gospel [Music] 19–20, 46, 49, 90, 104, 109–110, 112–114, 122, 127,

134–135, 149, 151–152, 193–194, 200, 205, 208, 212, 215, 217, 220, 227, 231, 313, 321, 333, 349, 358, 375, 384, 387, 390, 397, 418, 435, 457, 459, 461–466, 485, 490, 493–494, 504, 507, 513–516, 532, 545, 547, 550, 552–553, 565, 569, 578–579
Go Tell It on the Mountain 386, 390
Go to Hell 510, 515
Gouldman, Graham 145
Goux, John 283, 328–330, 332–334, 486
Grace and Frankie Series 527
Graham, Bill 205, 211, 228
Graham, Irvin 112
Grammer, Billy 26, 113, 286
Grant, Gary 270, 272–276, 298–303, 318
Grantt, Kevin 558, 561
Grappelli, Stéphane 434
Grascals (The) 576
Gray, William B. 194
Graydon, Jay 232–237, 270, 272–276
Great Balls of Fire 13, **256–267**
Great Balls of Fire [Single] 256, **262**
Green, Ed 328–330, 332–334
Green, Lloyd 13, 40–42, 44–47, 56–58, 60–63, 68–70, 72–75, 81–87, 91–95, 376–377, 380, 384, 531, 534–535, 540–545, 568, 570–571
Greene, Buddy 571
Greene, William Bill 270, 272–276
Greene, Willie Jr. 298, 300–303
Green–Eyed Boy 428, 433
Greenwood, Lee 512
Grier, Carlos 398
Griff, Ray 102, 106
Grisman, David 258, 260–262, 264–265, 434, 472, 474–476
Grisham, John 501
Grobel, Lawrence 177, 242, 254–255, 375
Grosjean, Jim 520, 532
Gruber, Franz 332
Grundmann, Bernie 258, 260–262, 264–265
Grundner, Bob 453–454, 456–458, 462–466
Guerrero, Gene 80, 171
Guns N' Roses 273
Guru 499
Guthrie, Woody 284, 359
Gypsy 74
Gypsy Fever (The) 177–178, 217–218, 305
Gypsy, Joe and Me 64, 74, 234

Hager, Paul David 568
Haggard, Ben 577

Haggard, Merle 28–29, 34, 107, 199, 201, 203, 208, 215, 250, 442, 577
Hale, Owen 432–435
Hale, Robert 502, 504–506, 508, 512–516
Haley, Bill 20, 22
Hall, Andy 520, 522–525, 540, 543–544
Hall, Bobby 340–342, 344–345
Hall, Carol 490
Hall, Tom T. 58
Hallyday, Johnny 22, 110
Halos & Horns 13, 214, **500–509**
Halos & Horns [Song] 500, 502
Hamessley, Lydia R. 9, 572
Hammer, Jack 262
Hammond, Laurens 113
Hampton, Vicki 376–377, 380–384, 398–399, 402, 404, 406, 430, 432–435, 446, 449, 512–516, 520, 522–525, 530–532, 534–535, 536, 540–545, 551–554, 559–562, 568–571, 576–580
Happy Town 491
Hardin, James Timothy 524
Harding, Tom 376
Hardley, Robert 494–499
Hardman, Camille 526
Hard rock [Music] 552
Harper, Idy 136
Harper, Tex 75
Harper Lee, Katherine 120
Harper Valley PTA 52, 55, 58
Harrington, Jim 493
Harris, Emmylou 10, 13, 35, 46, 130, 194, 214, 228, 238–239, 245, 301, 349–352, 354–**359**, 360, 375, 400, 410, 412–414, 416–418, 422, 462, 465, 471–476, 495–496, 511, 522, 540, 557
Harrison, George 68
Harrison, Mike 217–218
Hatch, Tony 318
Hatcher, Bessie F. 464
Hawkins, George 488
Hawkins, Hawkshaw 197
Hawkins, Ronnie 26, 135
Hayden, Tim 562
Hayes, Jack 490
Haynie, Aubrey 531, 534–535, 540–545, 552
Hayworth, Rita 365
Hazard, Robert 272
Hazlewood, Lee 42, 95
Head over High Heels 556, 561
Heartbreaker 51, **240–255**, 260, 273, 275, 322, 488
Heartbreaker [Single] 240, 246, **251**
Heartbreak Express 73, **292–303**, 357, 472
Heartbreak Express [Single] 292–293, **298**, 302–303, 550
Heart of the Smokies 536

Heartsongs, Live from Home 564
Heartstrings [Series] 95, 122–123, 236, 346, 502, 527
Heaven's Just a Prayer Away 108, 113
Hekman, James 112
He Left Me Love 146, 152
Hello God [Single] 500, **504**
Hello God Single with Commentary introduction [Single] 504
Hello, I'm Dolly 12, **24–35**, 37, 47, 55, 65, 140, 169, 189, 218, 231, 246, 345, 421
Helmer, Jim 272
Helms, Norma 237
Help! 256, 261–262
Henderson, Don 232–237, 244–245, 246–248, 250–251, 270, 272–276
Henderson, Milton 68–70, 72–75, 91–95
Hendricks, Scott 316–321, 376
Hensley, Hilda 196
Herbig, Gary 258, 260–262, 264–265, 270, 272–276, 298–303
Here I Am [Documentary] 527
Here I Am [Single] 126, 129, **134**–135, 169, 200, 489
Here You Come Again 13, **230–239**, 241, 254, 258, 279, 284
Here You Come Again [Single] 178, 230–231, **232**, 234, 365, 471, 489
He Rode All the Way to Texas 470, 475–476
Herrington, Jim 451
Herzhaft, Gérard 20
He's a Go–Getter [Single] 52–**56**, 62, 73
He's Alive [Single] 374–375, 381, **384**
He's Everything [Single] 490
He Would Know 198, 203
Hey, Jerry 244–248, 250–251, 282
Hey Howdy Hey 536
Hey, Lucky Lady 207, 210, **215**
Hidalgo, David 444
Higgins, Colin 490, 526
Higgins, Sharon 62
(Your Love Has Lifted Me) Higher and Higher 216, 226
High and Mighty [Single] 408, 410, **418**
Highlight of My Life 176, 182
High Sierra [Single] 470, **472**
Highway Headin' South 186, 192
Hill, Lauryn 150
Hill, Steven 463, 512–516

Hillbilly Boogie [Music] 20–**21**
Hillbilly [Music] **20**, 31, 73–75, 99, 120, 132, 144, 201, 345, 508, 579
Hillbilly Willy 96, 99
Hine, Stuart K. 114
Hinson, Steve 540–544, 552–554, 580
Hip-Hop [Music] 150, 499
Hirsch, Ken 237
Hirshey, Gerri 257, 269
Hoaglan, Scottie 502, 504–508
Hobbs, John 328–330, 332–334
Hobo's Meditation [Single] 348, **352**, 354
Hodges, Yvonne 376–377, 380–384, 430, 432–435
Hoephinger, Mary 157–161
Hoey, Tom 558–562, 568–569
Hoffmann, Martin 284
Hoke, Austin 489
Hoke, Jim 520, 523, 551
Holding Everything 538, 542, 545
Holding on to Nothin' [Single] 37, 102, **106**, 174
Holdin' on to You 216, 222, 489
Hold Me 204, 209
Holiday, Jimmy 414
Holland, Brian 320
Holland, Eddie 320
Hollowell, Paul 410, 412–414, 416–418, 430, 432, 434–435, 512–516, 520, 530–532, 534–535, 540–541, 543–545, 552–554, 559–561, 568, 570–571, 578
Holly, Buddy 26, 360, 502
Holly Jolly Christmas 566, 568, 571
Hollywood Potters 292, 303
Hollywood Records 488
Holmes, Rupert 276
Home 546, 550, 552
Home for Christmas **386–395**
Home for Christmas with Dolly Parton: The Radio Special 387
Home for Pete's Sake 64, 66, 75
Honey Creek 51
Honky Tonk (Music)16, **20–21**, 26, 38, 40–41, 60, 70, 72, 86, 93, 109, 113, 143, 190, 194, 200–201, 262, 344, 454
Honky Tonk Angels 409, 454
Honky Tonk Songs [Single] **420–422**, 424, 426, 450, **454**, 456, 458
Honky Tonk Women (The) 454
Hoog, Karen 137
Hope (Owens), Dorothy Jo 17, 91, 102, 104, 112, 114, 122–123, 125, 174, 462
Hopkin, Mary 520

Hopkins Jr., John Henry 392
Horn, Jim 258, 260–262, 264–265, 270, 272–276, 298–303
Horton, Johnny 17
House, Byron 495–499
House [Music] 409
Houston, Whitney 183, 420, 432, 464, 547
Howard, Harlan 40–41, 82
Howard, Jan 40–41, 74
Howard, Rebecca Lyn 498
Howard, Tom 520
How Does It Feel 216, 224
How Great Thou Art 108, 114–115
Hubert Gregory & the Fruit Jar Drinkers 221
Huckeba, Stacie 567, 575
Huff, Dann 367–368, 370–373, 551
Hughes, Randy 196–197
Hughes, Teresa 454
Hughey, John 376–377, 380, 384
Hull, Craig 316–321
Humperdinck, Engelbert 16
Humphries, Mitch 306–310, 312–313, 410, 412–414, 416–418
Hungate, David 232–237, 244–248, 250–251, 432–435, 440, 448–449
Hungry Again **450–459**, 461
Hungry Again [Single] 450, **452**–453, 456
Huntsinger, David 376–378, 380–384
Hurst, Jack 79
Hush–a–Bye Hard Times 278, 282, 284
Huskey, Roy Jr 13, 40–42, 44–47, 56–58, 60–63, 68–70, 72–75, 81–87, 91–95, 398, 402, 472, 474, 476
Husky, Ferlin 17, 114–115
Hussein, Saddam 511
Hutchcroft, Kim 244–247, 282
Hutchinson, Pat 376
Hyde, Dick 270, 272–276
Hyde, Slide 298–303, 318

I Am a Rainbow 562–563
I Am Ready 478, 485
I Believe 108, 112–113
I Believe in Santa Claus [Single] 326, **328**–329, 333
I Believe in You 516, **562–564**, 575
I Believe in You 563
I Can't Be True [Single] 338, **344**–345
I Can't Help Myself (Sugar Pie, Honey Bunch) 315, 320
I Couldn't Wait Forever [Single] 96–98, **101**
I Don't Believe You've Met My Baby 78, 83, 492, 494–495
I Don't Trust Me Around You 96, 101

I Don't Want to Throw Rice 26, 30

I Don't Want You Around Me Anymore 96, 98

I Dreamed of a Hillbilly Heaven 420–421

If 500, 504

I Feel the Blues Movin' In 470, 474

If I Cross Your Mind 186, 190

If I Lose My Mind 126, 132

If I Were a Carpenter 518, 524

If Only 500–501, 508

I Forgot More Than You'll Ever Know 420

If I Had Wings 546, 553

If You Need Me 396, 398, 403

If We Don't 489

I Get a Kick Out of You 492, 498

I Hope You're Never Happy [Single] 338, 341, **345**, 491

I Just Might 538, 544

I Knew You When [Single] 268, 273, **276**

I Know You by Heart [Single] 364, **367**, 371–372

I'll Be Home for Christmas 386, 389

I'll Keep Climbing 108, 114

I'll Make Your Bed [Single] 408, 413, **416**

I'll Never Forget [Single] 198, 200, **203**

I'll Never Say Goodbye 450, 457–458

I'll Oilwells Love You 36, 41

I'll Remember You as Mine 204, 209

I'm a Drifter 210, 213

Imagination 562–563

Imagination Library 10, 461, 468, **500**, **509**, 519, 536, 539, 562, 572–573

Imagination Playhouse [Show] 563

Imagine 518, 525

I'm Doing This for Your Sake [Single] 88, **93**, 120

I'm Fed Up with You 64, 72

I'm Gone [Single] 500–501, **506**

I'm Gonna Miss You 510, 515–516

I'm Gonna Sleep with One Eye Open 478, 481

I'm Here 562

I'm in No Condition 24, 32–33

I'm Not Worth the Tears [Single] 38, 96–97, **101**

I'm Running Out of Love 36, 45

I'm Sixteen 556, 561

Ingram, James 421

Inman, Autry 83, 494

Inner Child Chorus (The) 562

In the Ghetto [Single] 44, 53, 64–65, **68**, 73, 178, 409

In the Good Old Days (When Times Were Bad) 19, **52–63**, 65, 134, 155, 377

In the Good Old Days (When Times Were Bad) [Single] 38, 47, 52, **56–57**, 142, 154, 159, 246

In the Meantime 538–541

In the Old Good Days (Where Times Were Bad) 8

In the Sweet Bye & Bye 493, 499

In the Sweet Bye & Bye 461, 463

I Really Don't Want to Know 304, 310–311

I Really Got the Feeling [Single] 240, **244**, 246, 248

I Remember [Single] 154, **157**, 160, 165

Isaacs, Ben 576

Isaacs, Sonya 496, 498, 530, 540–545, 551, 578

Isaacs (The) 578

Isaacs Bowman, Becky 496, 498, 530, 540–545, 551, 578

I Saw Mommy Kissing Santa Claus 566, 571

Isbell, James 68–70, 72–75

Islam, Yusuf 520, 523

Island Records 29

Islands in the Stream 228, 305, 336, 344, 529, 547

I Still Lost You 450, 458

I Still Miss Someone 478, 482

It Ain't Fair That It Ain't Right 116, 122

It Must Be You 176, 185

It's All Wrong, But It's All Right [Single] 230, **234**, 236

It's My Time 52, 55, 57

It's Not My Affair Anymore 256, 264–265

It's Such a Heartache 338, 342

It's Too Late to Love Me Now 240, 245

It Wasn't God Who Made Honky Tonk Angels 16, 194, 420–421

I've Had Enough 348, 356

I've Lived My Life [Single] 24, 31, **34–35**

Ives, Burl 568

I Walk the Line 21, 314, 317

I Wanna Fall in Love 240, 251

I Wanna Go Back There 450, 457–458

I Want to Be What You Need 198, 202

I Wasted My Tears [Single] 24, **31**

I Will Always Love You [Single] 10, 12, 156, 168, 171–172, 176–179, 181, **183**, 184–185, 187, 190, 199, 228, 251, 301, 315, 346, 421, 428, **432**, 434, 490, 547

I Will Forever Hate Roses 528, 535

I Wish I Felt This Way at Home [Single] 36, **40**–41, 46

I Wonder Where You Are Tonight 478, 484

I Wound Easy 96, 98

Jackson, Carl 388–394, 398, 410, 412, 414, 416–418, 430, 432–435, 472, 474, 476, 496, 498, 531, 552

Jackson, Gary 226

Jackson, Janet 535

Jackson, Mahalia 514

Jackson, Michael 30, 58, 293, 305, 310, 337, 365, 410, 490

Jackson, Mick 183

Jackson, Peter 493

Jackson, Wanda 29, 40

Jackson 5 (The) 571

Jagger, Mick 217, 360

Jamerson, James 73

James, Dennis 473

James, Sonny 26

James, Tommy 520, 523

James Brown and the JB's 398

Jamtaas, Phil 306–310, 312–313

Jarrh, Cliff 315

Jarvis, John 333, 376–377, 380, 382–384, 410, 412–414, 416–418

Jay, Penny 448

Jazz [Music] 21, 85, 113, 167, 177, 199, 207, 229, 302, 315, 336, 360, 389, 398, 434, 449, 481, 498–499, 511, 514, 534, 568

Jealous Heart 304, 308

Jeannie's Afraid of the Dark [Single] 37, 102, **105**, 107, 174

Jeffries, Larry 398

Jennings, Shelley 562

Jennings, Waylon 68

Jesus & Gravity [Single] 528, **532**, 547

Jezioro, Jack 520

Jimmy Boling and the House of Prayer Congregation 459

Jimmy Heap & the Melody Masters 16

Jingle Bells 386, 393

J.J. Sneed 116–117, 122–125

Joan Jett and the Blackhearts 523

Jobe, Barry 570

Jobs, Steve 539

Joe & Rose Lee Maphis 221

John Daniel 500–501, 508

Johnnie Wright and the Harmony Girls 194

Johnny Clegg & Savuka 341

Johns, Tara 205, 527

Johnson, Augie 244–248, 250–251

Johnson, Dirk 580

Johnson, Doug 376

Johnson, Jamie 520, 522–525, 532, 550

Johnson, Michael 389

Johnson, Robert 31

Jolene 133, 148, **176–185**, 200, 251, 432

Jolene [Single] 11, 33, 132, 156, 163, 176–178, **180**–181, 183, 187, 200, 215, 293, 302, 315, 403, 410, 424, 428, 435, **489**, 529, 567

Jones, Brad 376, 388–394, 398

Jones, George 28, 81, 104, 197, 397, 426, 454

Jones, Keziah 380

Jones, Lewis E. 463

Jones, Mel 440, 442–444, 446–449

Jones, Norah 46, 511, 522

Jones, Quincy 29

Jones, Rickie Lee 233

Jones, Tom 286

Jones Wall, Alisha 392–393, 404, 410, 417

Joplin, Janis 523

Jordan, Jeremy 554

Jordanaires (The) 316

Joshua 116–125

Joshua [Single] 92, 97, 109, 116–117, **120**, 122, 124, 177

Joy to the World 386, 394

Joyful Noise [Movie] 490, 526, 554

Judd, Wynonna 62

Judge, Charlie 551

Judge, Mike 409

Just as Good as Gone [Single] 150

Just Because I'm a Woman 36–51, 140

Just Because I'm a Woman [Single] 36, 38, 40, **46**, 122, 140, 192

Just Between You and Me 80, 169, 172, **174**

Just Between You and Me [Single] 106, 174

Just Between You and Me: The Complete Recordings 557

Just Dance 491

Justis, Bill 45

Just Leaving 538, 540

Justman, Paul 226

Just Someone I Used to Know [Single] 53, 102, **104**–105, 174

Just the Two of Us 37, 169, **174**

Just the Way I Am 79, 88, 93

Just When I Needed You Most [Single] 438, **443**, 449

Kane, Kieran 476

Kanter, Hillary 342

Karmazyn, Dennis 356

Katrina and the Waves 446

Kaye, Carole 321

Kaz, Eric 370

Keane, Dolores 475

Keaton, Buster 41, 480

Keeper of Memories 491

Keep on the Firing Line 460, 464

Keister, Shane 220–222, 224–227

Keith, Ben 474

Keith, Vivian 444

Kellman, Barnet 488

Kelly, Gene 65

Kelly, Mark 494–495, 498–499

Kelly Kirkland Strings (The) 221

Keltner, Jim 232–237, 244–248, 250–251, 258, 260–262, 264–265, 366–368, 370–373, 474–476

Kennedy, Jerry 42

Kennedy, John F. 9

Kent, Walter 389

Kentucky Gambler 198, 201

Kesey, Ken 89

Key, Francis Scott 512

Khomeyni, Rouhollah 269

Kid Connection (The) 406

Kimball, Jennifer 340–342, 344–345, 474

Kimmel, Bobby 360

Kimmel, Tom 474

Kincaid, Bradley 194

Kinfolks (The) 462–464, 466

King, Carole 303

King, Elle 489

King, Martin Luther 68, 305

King, Ryan Hanna 551

King, Stephen 231, 429, 501

Kingdom Heirs (The) 462–464, 466

Kinney, Lance 469

Kipner, Steve 310

Kiracofe, Mark 388–394

Kirby, Dave 13, 129–130, 132–134, 148–152, 157–161, 165, 180–185, 189–193, 220–222, 224–227

Kirkpatrick, Melodie 562

Kissinger, Henry 199

Kiss It (And Make It All Better) 556, 559

Klein, Gary 13, 231–237, 244–248, 250–251, 270, 272–276

Kling, Randy F. 200–203

Knechtel, Larry 282

Knopfler, Mark 359, 413, 559

Kohrs, Randy 502, 504–508, 513–516, 540, 543–544, 550–553

Kool and the Gang 251, 274

Koppelman, Charles 258, 260–262, 264–265, 270, 272–276

Koresh, David 409

Kortchmar, Danny 366–368, 370–373

Krampf, Craig 366–368, 370–373

Krauss, Alison 21, 46, 237, 398, 410, 412–414, 416–418, 430, 432–435, 443, 446, 461, 472, 474, 476, 480, 482, 485, 489, 494–495, 497–498, 511, 524, 529, 540

Krauss, Viktor 446, 520

Kristofferson, Kris 22, 26, 45, 72, 294, 310, 349, 449, 523, 554

Kroon, Jerry 220–222, 224–227

Krystall, Marty 356

Kunkel, Nathaniel 472–476

Kunkel, Russ 317–318, 351–356, 488

Kunz, John 388–394, 398

Laboriel, Abraham 258, 260–262, 264–265, 270, 272–276, 282, 298–303, 366–368, 370–373

LaChapelle, David 439

Ladanyi, Greg 488

Lady Gaga 498

Ladysmith Black Mambazo 440

Lamarchina, Anthony 520, 532, 561

Lamb, Betsy 489

Lambert, Louis 513

Lambert, Miranda 28, 489

Landau, Michael 328–330, 332–334, 367–368, 370–373

Landreth, Sonny 435

Lane, Gary 279, 526

Lane, Larry 279

Langdon, Harry 98–99, 254

Last Night's Lovin' 177

Latham, Chris 562, 576

Latifah, Queen 490, 526

Lauffer, Johnny 453–454, 457–458, 462–466

Lauper, Cyndi 272, 365, 370

Lawrence, D. H. 139

Lay Your Hands on Me 546, 552, 554

Leago, Randy 458

Lea Jane Singers (The) 189–193, 200–203, 206–209, 212–215

Led Zeppelin 136, 206, 246, 508

Lee, Albert 72, 270, 272–276, 298–303, 351, 354–358, 376–378, 380, 382–384

Lee, Brenda 69, 232, 236, 294, 310

Lee, Briana 489

Lee, Peggy 320

Leggett, Steve 539

Lehman, Acy 218

Leibovitz, Annie 365, 501

Leim, Paul 328–330, 332–334, 340–342, 344–345

Lennon, John 233, 261, 280, 305, 525

Leonard, David 316–321, 328

Leroy, Gregg 272

Let Her Fly 420–422

Let Love Grow 538, 544–545

Letter to Heaven 16, 116–117, 125

Leventhal, Herb 137

Levine, Gene 345

Levine, Irwin 228, 516
Levine, Sam 489, 568, 570
Lewis, Jerry Lee 28, 40, 69, 85, 262
Lewis, Margaret 85
Life's Like Poetry 210, 215
Lightfoot, Gordon 133
Light in the Attics Records 93
Light of a Blue Morning [Single] **488**
Light of a Clear Blue Morning [Single] 216, **220**, 224, 227, 488, 510, 512
Light Your Lamp 491
Lind, Bob 321
Lindley, David 232–237, 351, 354–357, 472, 486, 488
Lippman, Steve 530
Literature 11, **572–573**
Little Bird 52, 55, 60
Little Bit Slow to Catch On 36, 42
Little, Keith 481–484, 494
Little Pigeon Records 92
Little Sparrow 13, 95, 130, **492–499**, 501
Little Sparrow 492, 494, 499
Little Swiss Miss 22
Little Tiny Tasseltop 14
Little Willie John 320
Livin' a Lie 488
Living on Memories of You 176, 184–185, 200
Livingston, Laura 328
Locklin, Hank 307
Loeb, David 373
Loftus, Bob 366
Londin, Larrie 180–185, 189–193, 220–222, 224–227
Loneliness Found Me 138, 145
Lonely Comin' Down [Single] 146, 148, 151, 176, 183, **185**
Long, Donagh 475
Look on the Bright Side 491
Lord, Hold My Hand [Single] 108, 115, 151
Loretta and the Trailblazers 424
Los Super Seven 444
Lost and Found 574, 580
Loudermilk, John D. 57
Louvin, Charlie 481
Louvin, Ira 481
Louvin Brothers (The) 481, 501
Love and Learn 36, 45
Love and Music 163, 175
Love Is Like a Butterfly 147, **186–197**
Love Is Like a Butterfly [Single] 186, **189**, 190, 192–193, 199, 203, 228
Love Isn't Free 138, 144
Love Is Only As Strong (As Your Weakest Moment) 138, 144
Loveless, Patty 90, 400, 479, 481
Love or Lust 574, 580
Lover du Jour 546, 553
Lovesick Blues 420–422

Love's Return 470, 472
Love to Remember 198, 202
Love with Me 162, 166–167
Love, You're So Beautiful Tonight [Single] 156, 162–163, **168**, 180
Lovin' Spoonful (The) 235, 443
Lovin' You 230, 235
Lowry, Mark 571
Lubbock, Jeremy 328–330, 332–334
Lucas, George 231, 361
Lucia, Peter P. 523
Lukather, Steve 488
Lunn, Gary 568, 570–571
Lynch, Claire 481–482, 484, 494
Lynn, Loretta 34, 40, 62–63, 72, 74, 147, 194, 196, 307, 310, 409, 420–421, **424**–426, 447–448, 454, 466
Lynn, Oliver Vanetta 424
Lynne, Shelby 46
Lynyrd Skynyrd 213
──────────
Mabee, Patricia 366–368, 370–373
Macdonald, Danielle 489
Mackey, Gary 452, 456–458, 463–464, 466
Mackey, Steve 554, 559–562, 569–570, 576–580
Macy Gray, Dorothy 489
Madaio, Steve 244–248, 250–251
Maddox, Rose 147
Made of Stone 528, 531
Madonna 365, 375, 439, 493
Madsen, Michael 488
Magaha, Mack 13, 40–42, 44–47, 56, 60, 62, 68–70, 72–76, 81–87, 91–95, 102, 106–107, 129–130, 132–134, 148–152, 157–161, 180–185
Maher, Brent 220–222, 224–227
Majors, Lee 491
Make Love Work [Single] 364, **370**–371
Makin' Fun Ain't Funny 562–563
Making Plans 348, 351
Malena [Single] 53, 78, 82–**83**, 112
Mallah, Linda 273
Malloy, David 13, 339–342, 344–345
Malloy, Jim 104–107
Malo, Raul 448
Malone, Kenny 180–185
Mama, Say a Prayer 52, 62
Mammie 88, 94
Mandrell Sisters (The) 264, 266–267
Manis, Liana 444, 447–449, 463, 465–466
Mann, Barry 13, 232
Manoogian, Michael 231
Mansfield, Brian 511
Maphis, Joe 17, 221
Maphis, Rose Lee 331

Marcantonio, Steve 551
Marcussen, Stephen 540–545
Marks, Johnny 390, 568
Marley, Bob 199
Marotta, Rick 306–310, 312–313
Marry Me 492, 498
Martha & the Vandellas 30
Martin, Brice 356
Martin, Dean 307
Martin, Grady 26
Martin, Paul 86
Marvin, Hank 32
Marx, Richard 340–342, 344–345
Mary, Did You Know? 566, 571
Mason, Bob 377, 381
Mason, Brent 430, 432–435, 531, 534–535, 540–545
Massenburg, George 13, 349, 351–352, 354–358, 376, 471–476
Mater, Bob 520, 550–551
Mattea, Kathy 410
Matthews, Dave 462–466
Matthews, Myrna 232–237, 244–248, 250–251
Mattingly, Jimmy 388, 390, 392–393, 410, 412–414, 416–418, 430, 432–435, 502, 504–508, 512–516, 520, 530–532, 534–535, 540–545, 550–554, 558–559, 561, 568, 570–571, 576, 579–580
Mavericks (The) 448
May, Robert L. 390
Maybe, Just Maybe 491
Mayfield, Curtis 319
Mayfield, John 562
Maynard, Ken 21
Maynelli, Denise 282, 298, 300, 302–303
McAnally, Mac 376–377, 380, 382–384
McBride, John 489
McBryde, Tom 562, 564
McCall, Marti 232–237
McCartney, Paul 261, 490, 520
McConnell, Shane 562
McCord, Joyce 62, 84
McCord, Kathy 233
McCormick, George 40–42, 44–47, 56–58, 60–63, 68–70, 72–75, 81–87, 91–95, 105, 129–134
McCormick, Randy 340–342, 344–345, 435
McCoury, Del 474
McCoy, Charlie 26, 157–161, 577, 579
McCoy, Joltin' Jim 196
McCracken, Hugh 306–310, 312–313
McCuller, Arnold 319
McCullough, Alex 530–532, 534–535
McCune, Aaron 570–571, 576
McDade, David Butch 499
McDermott, John 475
McElhiney, Bill 81, 86

McElroy, Donna 306–310, 312–313
McEntire, Reba 46
McGarrigle, Kate 356
McGee, Kirk 221
McGhee, Stick 74
McGuffee, Joe 220–222, 224–227, 244–248, 250–251, 258, 260–262, 264–265, 282–286, 288–289, 298–303, 306–310, 312–313
McGuinn, Roger 33, 520, 524
McInerney, Pat 446, 498
McLoone, Annie 306
McMakin, Pat 282–286, 288–289, 298–303
McMillan, Terry 410, 412, 414, 416, 418, 430
McNelley, Rob 534, 540–545
McPherson, Jerry 530–532, 540–545
McQueen, Steve 280
Me and Bobby McGee 518, 523
Me and Little Andy [Single] 230, 232, **234**
Meaux, Huey 14
Medley: Winter Wonderland/ Sleigh Ride [Single] 326, **328**, 330
Medlock, Shorty 483
Mehta, Zubin 529
Mendelson, Andrew
Mendy Never Sleeps [Single] 53, 104
Menza, Don 318
Mercury, Freddie 229, 321
Merman, Ethel 498
Merrill, George 367
Metzger, John 128
Meyer, Edgar 475
MGM Records 58
Michael, George 365
Mighty Fine Band (The) 388–394, 398–400, 402–404, 406
Miles, C. Austin 466
Milete, Shirl 47
Miller, Eddie 302
Miller, J. D. 194, 420
Miller, Stephen 6, 49, 257, 269, 471, 548, 573
Mills, Irving 420
Mils, Jim 480–485, 494–496, 498
Milwaukee, Here I Come Mine 78–79, 81, 192
Mine 163
Mine 52, 60
Minnelli, Liza 231
Minogue, Kylie 137
Miracles (The) 534
Miranda, Billy 316–321
Miskulin, Joey 404, 406, 410, 412–413, 416
Mission Chapel Memories [Single] 138, 143, **145**
Miss You, Miss Me 546, 552
Mitchell, Eddy 22
Mitchell, Joni 135, 525
Mock, John 498–499, 532, 534, 552
Moffatt, Hugh 273

Mohler, Billy 489
Mohr, Joseph 332
Monday, Jerry 74
Monet, Darci 440, 444
Monroe, Bill 18, 21, 484, 501
Monroe, Marilyn 139, 254, 372
Montana, Pasty 20, 22, 137, 147, 194
Monument Records 12, 24–28, 30–35, 37, 96–101, 103, 294, 339
Moody, Clyde 16
Moore, Bob 26
Moore, Michael 361
Moore, Warren 534
Moore Jr., Robert L. 515
Moorer, Allison 46
More Than I Can Say [Single] 364, 366, **373**
More Than Their Share 88, 94
More Where That Came From [Single] 408–409, **413**, 416
Morford, Gene 232–237, 270, 272–276, 298, 300–303, 340–342, 344–345
Morgan, Helen 196
Morgan, Lorrie 403
Morgan, Marshall 282–286, 288–289, 298–303, 440, 442–444, 446–449, 452–454, 456–459
Morgan, Tommy 486
Moriarty 352
Morricone, Ennio 200
Morris, Farrell 220–222, 224–227, 376–378, 380, 383–384, 443–444, 447, 448–449
Morrison, Danny 165–166
Morrison, Jim 109
Morrison, Kim 377, 380–384
Morrison, Van 135, 433
Morrison, Voni 351
Morrow, Greg 551
Moscow Circus (The) 520
Mosley, Daryl 576
Moss, Wayne 40–42, 44–47, 56–58, 60–63, 68–70, 72–75, 81–87, 91–95
Most of All, Why? [Single] 204, 207
Motown 30, 63, 73, 133, 148, 222, 226, 248, 320, 345, 516, 534, 545
Mountain Angel 492, 498
Mountain Magic 491
Mountain music 17, 40, 42–43, 70, 75, 86–87, 130, 200, 390, 465, 501, 506, 508, 523, 540, 547
Moynihan, Maura 339
Muhoberac, Larry 486
Mulligan, Robert 120
Mundhenk, Danny 316–321
Murder Ballad 30, 109, **136–137**, 483, 552, 572
Murphy, Julie 489
Murphy, Patrick 520, 522–525, 531–532, 534–

535, 540–545, 550–554, 558–561, 568
My Blue Ridge Mountain Boy 53, **64–77**, 178, 234, 409
My Blue Ridge Mountain Home [Single] 53, 64, 66, 69, **73**, 140, 142, 292, 300, 433
My Blue Tears [Single] 51, 126, **130**, 132, 491–492, 495
My Christmas Prayer 491
My Country 'Tis 510, 515
My Dear Companion [Single] 348, **355**–356
Myers, Bill 118
Myers, Randy 414
My Eyes Can Only See You 186, 190
My Girl (My Love) 216, 222
My Hands Are Tied [Single] 53, 78, **86**, 104
My Heart Started Breaking [Single] 204, 206–**207**, 208
My Kind of Man 162, 167
My Mountains, My Home 536
My Tennessee Mountain Home 56, **154–161**, 163, 177, 228, 237, 285
My Tennessee Mountain Home [Single] 154, 156, **159**–160
──────────
Nabors, Jim 466
Nash, Alanna 6, 38, 48, 55, 66, 76, 102–103, 147, 218, 220–221, 229, 573
Nashville A–Team 26, 40, 69, 73–74, 91, 93, 133–134, 143, 158, 160, 201, 203, 213, 215
Nashville Edition (The) 129–130, 132–134, 148–152, 157–161, 180–185
Nashville Horns (The) 220–222, 224–227
Nashville sound 13, 19–20, **22**, 28, 32, 72, 75, 109, 133, 212, 283, 286, 372, 390, 422, 440, 466, 524, 551, 558
Nashville String Machine (The) 306–310, 312–313, 377, 384, 534, 554
Nathan, Steve 430, 432, 434–435
Ndegeocello, Meshell 46
Needham, Mark 554, 576
Negro Spiritual 49, 90, 109–110, 390, 464
Nelson, Craig 376–377, 380, 382–384, 532
Nelson, Emily 489
Nelson, Paul 568, 570–571
Nelson, Willie 10, 22, 26, 29, 40, 46, 95, 197, 294, 310–311, 315, 349, 397, 466, 554, 570–571
Nettles, Jennifer 569
Never Not Love You 556, 559
Newbury, Mickey 46
New Christy Minstrels 336

New Country 22
New Harvest…First Gathering 13, 164, **216–229**, 231–232, 245–246, 248, 299, 488, 512
Newman, Paul 196
Newman, Randy 476
New Salem Methodist Church Congregation (The) 388, 394
Newton, John 464
Newton–Jones, Olivia 180
Nichol, Jamie 220–222, 224–227
Nichols, Joe 524, 580
Nicholson, Jack 91
Nicholson, Rebecca 548
Nickel Creek 497, 520
Nickels and Dimes 51, 240, 250
Niebank, Justin 530–532, 534–535
Nilsson, Harry 233
Ní Mhaonaigh, Mairéad 498–499
Nine Inch Nails 494
Nirvana 484
Nitzsche, Jack 321
Nixon, Richard 68, 89, 135, 155, 177, 187
No Good Way of Saying Good–Bye 428, 435
No Reason to Hurry Home [Single] 53, 78, 81, 84, **86**
Norman, Jessye 464
Not Enough Love 490
Not for Me 500–502
Novog, Ilene Novi 356
Nugent, Alecia 531
Null, Cecil 420
Nunley, Louis 398–399, 402, 404, 406, 430, 432–435, 440, 446–449, 459, 485, 512–516

Oates, Ron 159–161, 270, 272–276, 282–286, 288–289, 298–303, 306–310, 312–313
Obama, Barack 529, 547, 557
O'Brien, Jennifer 388–391, 394, 398–399, 402, 404, 406, 410, 412–414, 416–418, 446, 449, 453–454, 457–459, 502, 512–516, 520, 522–525, 530–532, 534–536, 540–545, 551–554, 559–561, 568–571, 576–580
O'Bryant, Alan 356, 483
Ocker, Bob 453–454, 547–458
O'Connell, Maura 410, 412–414, 416–418, 498
O'Connor, Mark 351, 354–357, 404
O'Connor, Sinéad 46
O'Dell, Kenny 447
O'Donnell, Margo 479
O'Donughue, Michael 299
Oehler, Dale 430, 432–433, 435
Offspring (The) 494

Ogle, Judy 51, 166, 177–178, 218, 293, 306–310, 312–313, 454
O'Hara, James Paul 476
O'Hearn, Robert 366–368, 370–373
Oh, He's Everywhere 146, 152
O'Lannerghty, Danny 562
Old Black Kettle 154–155, 157, 228
Old Crow Medicine Show 576
Old Flames Can't Hold a Candle to You [Single] 268–269, **273**, 276
Old–Time Music 19–20
Old Time Religion 460, 464
O Little Town of Bethlehem 386, 393
Omartian, Michael 244–248, 250–251, 260–261, 264–265, 274
Once in a Very Blue Moon 338, 345
Once More 97, 170, **174**
Once Upon a Christmas 326–337
Once Upon a Christmas 326, 334
Once Upon a Memory 186, 192
One Emotion After Another 486
One of Those Days [Single] 304, 310, **312**
Only Dreamin' 528, 532
Only the Memory Remains 204, 209
On My Mind Again 198, 202
Ono, Yoko 525
Onorati, Henry 391
Ooo—Eee 304, 306
Orbison, Roy 26, 31, 42, 47, 359–360
Orlando, Dominic 488
Orlando, Tony 319
Ornelas, Willie 486
Osbon, Bruce 189–193
Osborne, Bobby 282
Osborne, Joan 46
Osborne, Sonny 282–286, 288–289
OSM Audio 97
Our Kids 390, 393
Outlaw Country 22
Outside Your Door 556, 560
Overall, Fran 306–310, 312–313
Owens (Parton), Avie Lee 8, 48, 50, 127, 129, 157, 221, 322, 357
Owens, Bill 9–10, 12, 14, 16–17, 25–26, 30–32, 34–35, 41, 45, 49–50, 61, 72, 76, 80, 91–92, 97–98, 100–101, 144, 167, 177, 357, 397, 406, 421, 487, 491, 578
Owens, Bonnie 34, 442
Owens, Buck 34
Owens, Jake 8, 50, 90, 104, 109–110, 114, 174, 195
Owens, Louis 92, 156
Owens, Rena 16

Owens, Richie 13, 451–454, 456–459, 461–466, 540, 578
Owe–Par Publishing Company 12, 76, 80, 468

Pace, Jim 462–466
Pachucki, Al 12, 40–42, 44–47, 56–58, 60–63, 68–70, 72–75, 81–87, 91–95, 104–107, 112–115, 120, 122–125, 129–130, 132–134, 142–145, 148–152, 157–161, 165–168, 180–185
Pacino, Al 14, 305
Packin' It Up 268, 276
Paczosa, Gary 388–394, 398, 440, 442–444, 446–449, 480–485, 494–499, 520, 522–525
Page, Jimmy 508
Page, June 56–58, 60–63, 68–70, 72–75, 81–87, 91–95
Page, Ricki 159–160
Paich, David 244–248, 250–251, 488
Paradise Road [Single] 450, 454, **458**
Parish, Mitchell 328
Parker, Ira 454
Parker, John David 398
Parker, John Lewis 310
Parker, Colonel Tom 12
Parks, Dean 13, 232–237, 248, 250–251, 257–258, 260–262, 264–265, 340–342, 344–345, 440, 443–444, 446, 448–449, 474–476
Parry, Doug 282–286, 288–289, 298–303, 486
Parsons, Gram 33, 214, 359
Parton, Bobby 48, 50
Parton, Cassie 51
Parton, David 50
Parton, Denver 50
Parton, Doris 48
Parton, Floyd 51
Parton, Freida 50–51, 285
Parton, Heidi 570–571
Parton, Larry 51
Parton, Lee 221, 493
Parton, Randy 51, 188, 221, 409, 417, 461, 463, 465, 486–487, 571
Parton, Robert Lee 8, 50, 73, 468, 493, 509
Parton, Stella 46, 49–51, 417, 462, 482, 486–487
Parton, Willadeene 48–51
Parton, William Walter 50
Patrick, Steve 489
Patterson, James 157, 486, 501, 572, 575
Patton, Robbie 273
Patton, Wayland 384
Pavarotti, Luciano 393
Paxton, Tom 102, 105
Payne, Bill 260–262, 265, 355–356, 358

Owens, Richie 13, 451–454, 456–459, 461–466, 540, 578
Peace Train/Isitimela Sokuthula [Single] 438–**440**
Pearl, Eli 489
Pearl, Johnny 221
Pearl, Minnie 103, 177, 221
Pearles, Jeff 561
Peborgh, Phil van 502, 504–508
Peck, Gregory 120–121
Peck, Orville 12
Peckinpah, Sam 337
Pedersen, Herb 261, 352, 355, 486
Peer, Bill 196
Pell, John 220–222, 224–227
Pendragon, Jana 451
Penn, Arthur 21
Pentatonix 180
Perkins, Al 232–237, 248, 250–251, 366–368, 370–373, 458, 462–466, 472
Perkins, Carl 21, 400, 406
Perkins, Gregg 400
Perkins, Stan 400
Perry, Gregg 13, 217, 220–222, 224–227, 244–248, 250–251, 257–258, 260–262, 264–265, 270, 272–276, 279, 282–286, 288–289, 293, 298–303, 305–310, 312–313, 315, 490
Perry, Linda 489, 567
Perry, Wade 461
Peter, Paul and Mary 148–149
Peters, Ben 444
Petersen, Wolfgang 397
Peterson, Oscar 434
Petrescu, Stefan 568–571
Petrie, Daniel 337
Peyton, Bernard 376–377, 380–384
Phillips, Bill 26, 28, 31
Phillips, Phil 14
Phillips, Sam 21
Pick, Tom 12, 142–145, 148–152, 200–203, 206–209, 212–215
Pickering, Bob 328
Pierpont, James Lord 393
Pigg, Dewayne 306–310, 312–313
Ping Pong [Single] 38, 101
Pink Floyd (The) 189
Pinmonkey 211
Pirro, Jason 451
Pitchford, Dean 342, 367
Pitts, William S. 463
Pixies (The) 444
Plant, Robert 508, 524
Platshon, David 316–321
Platters (The) 321
Playboy 139, 241–242, **254–255**, 257–258, 375
Pleasant As May 162, 167
Please Help Me I'm Falling (In Love with You) 420
Podrevsky, Konstantin 520
Police (The) 410
Pomus, Doc 316
Pool, Mike 376

Poor Folks Town [Single] 278, 288–**289**
Pop, Iggy 165
Pop [Music] 13, 22, 28–29, 33, 127, 133, 144–148, 147–148, 152, 187, 196,199, 205, 209, 211, 217, 220, 231–232, 237, 241, 244–245, 254, 257–258, 260, 270, 272, 274, 279, 299–300, 305, 310, 328, 330, 333, 336, 339, 345, 349, 352, 355, 365, 367, 372, 375, 397, 399, 406, 410, 412, 420, 433, 440, 458–459, 471, 474, 488, 490, 493, 499, 515–516, 523, 526, 529–532, 534, 541, 543, 545, 552, 554, 559, 565, 570–571
Popper, John 442
Porter, Cole 498
Porter & Dolly 79–80, 102, 104, 172, **175**, 269, 351
Porter 'n' Dolly 174–175, 205, 541
Porter Wagoner Show (The) 10, 25, 34, 37, 47, 54–55, 70, **76–77**, 79–82, 90, 97, 102–103, 105, 147, 163, 169–170, 172, 174, 177, 188, 205, 211, 217, 228, 339, 565
Porter Wagoner & the Opry Gang 520
Porter Wayne & Dolly Rebecca 170, **174**
Portnoy, Gary 274
Portuondo, Omara 351
Post, Mike 13, 279, 282–286, 288–289, 293, 486
Potter, Don 430, 432–435, 443–444
Powell, Hope 178, 188, 199, 211
Power in the Blood 460, 463
Preacher Tom 210, 215
Precious Memories 460–469, 499
Precious Memories 460–462
Presley, Elvis 12, 21, 25, 28, 32, 40, 45, 55, 68–69, 73, 133, 139, 143, 183, 248, 344, 372, 409, 514, 579
Presley, Priscilla 25
Prestidge, Eric 258, 260–262, 264–265
Preston, Rudy 75
Pretty Is As Pretty Does 491
Pretty Paper 566, 570–571
Pribble, Kelly 520, 522–525
Price, Ray 26
Pride, Charley 74
Prime of Our Love 292, 303
Prince 199, 368
Puccini, Giacomo 361
Puckett, Debbie Joe 221
Puckett, Dwight 221

Puett, Billy 220–222, 224–227
Puett, Darrell 462–466
Punk rock [Music] 22, 51, 513
Puppy Love [Single]9, 14–**16**, 17, 345, 565
Purcell, Denny 376, 388–394, 398, 440, 442–444, 446–449, 452–454, 456–459
Pure & Simple 556–565
Pure and Simple 556, 558
Push and Pull 489
Put a Little Love in Your Heart 408, 414
Put It Off Until Tomorrow [Single] 24, **30**–31, 34–35, 80, 420–421
Putman, Curly 10, 26, 28–29, 42, 63

Quant, Mary 139
Queen 387
Queen of Mean 491
Quinn, Benny 520, 522–525
Quinn, Mary Ellen 319

Rabinowitz, Carole 520, 532, 569–570
Rabourn, J. R. 451
Rae, Diana 384
Ragin, Melvin Wah Wah Watson 226
Ragtime 20–21, 191
Rainbow 364–373, 375
Raitt, Bonnie 476
Ram, Buck 321
Randy 176, 184
Raney, Wayne 84
Raphael, Mickey 554
Raskin, Gene 520
Ratner, Lisa 276
Raven Dove 500, 507
Raye, Collin 417
Rayfield, Bessie Elizabeth 50
R&B 14, 222, 226, 367, 490
RCA 12, 36–38, 40–42, 44–47, 52, 56, 64–65, 68–69, 73, 76, 78–79, 82–84, 88, 91–93, 102, 104–109, 113, 116, 120, 126, 129–130, 132–134, 138–139, 143, 145–147, 150–151, 154, 156–157, 159–165, 169, 174–177, 180–187, 189, 192–194, 198–200, 203–218, 220–222, 226–227, 230–231, 234, 236, 240–242, 244, 246, 248, 251, 256–257, 260, 262, 268–270, 273, 275–276, 278–279, 282–283, 285–286, 288–289, 292–293, 298–310, 312–321, 326–330, 333–334, 338–342, 344–345, 365, 436, 486, 489, 556–557, 562
Reagan, Lisa Lee 522
Reagan, Ronald 280, 305, 315, 318, 375
Real Love 338–347, 349

Real Love [Single] 338–339, **344**
Rearview Mirror 491
Rebennack, Mac 244–248, 250–251
Redding, Otis 222
Red Dirt 22
Redner, Lewis 393
Red Hot + Country 397
Red Hot Screaming Love 364, 368
Red Shoes 489
Red, White and Bluegrass 510, 514
Reed, Jerry 55–58, 60–63
Reed, Lou 316
Reese, Leona 74, 84
Reese, Mike 270, 272–276, 282–286, 288–289, 298–303
Reeves, Jim 513
Reeves, Tom 562
Rehrig, Bill 177
Reichenbach, Bill 244–248, 250–251, 282, 318
Reid, John 341
Reinhardt, Django 434
Reist, Sarighani 532, 568, 570–571, 580
Release Me 16, 195, 292, 302
Reno, Janet 409
REO Speedwagon 376
Remsen, Dorothy 258, 260–262, 264–265
Reneau, Bud 262
Reneau, George 16
Resnick, Patricia 279
Responsibility 562, 564
Restless Heart 497
Rew, Kimberley 446
Reynolds, Burt 193, 293, 296–297, 312–313, 426, 490
Reynolds, Dick 420
Rhinestone 486–487
Rhinestone [Movie] 315–316, 322–323, 332, 486, 488, 526, 560
Rhodes, Jack 420
Rhodes, Michael 306–310, 312–313
Rhodes, Speck 76, 79, 97
Rhythm and blues [Music] 20, 30, 61, 345, 523
Rice, Arthur 462
Rice, Sharon 351–352, 354–358
Rice, Tony 520
Rich, Allan 368
Rich, Charlie 68, 447
Richard, Cliff 32
Richards, John 328
Richardson, Bubba 498
Richey, George 426
Richie, Lionel 336–337, 410
Riddle, Jimmy 157, 220–222, 224–227
Riddle, Nelson 361
Riley, Jeannie C. 58–59
Rising Tide/Blue Eye Records 438–440, 443, 449
Ritchie, Jean 355, 357
River of Happiness 176, 181
Rivers, Dick 22

Rivers, Joan 205
Robbins, Hargus "Pig" 13, 40–42, 44–47, 56–58, 60–63, 68–70, 72–75, 81–87, 91–95, 129–130, 132–134, 148–152, 157–161, 180–185, 447–448, 531, 534–535, 540, 542–545
Robbins, Marty 357
Robert 88, 95
Roberts, Bruce 260
Roberts, Danny 520, 522–525, 550
Roberts, Jada 570
Robertson, Don 310, 420
Robinson, John 328–330, 332–334
Robinson, Pete 486
Robinson, Phil Alden 486
Robinson, Smokey 367, 371, 529, 534
Robinson, William 222
Robison, Carson 73
Rock'n'roll [Music] 14, 19–20, 22, 31, 69, 82, 89, 109, 113, 127, 134–135, 147–148, 165–166, 181, 184, 192, 199–200, 206, 209, 213–214, 220, 231, 241, 244, 246, 248, 262, 265, 273, 276, 285, 318, 336, 344–345, 349, 359–360, 376, 382–383, 399, 410, 422, 424, 444, 446, 453–454, 489–490, 494, 502, 504, 508, 516, 523, 530–531, 535, 540–542, 552, 554, 560–561, 575, 579
Rockabilly [Music] 16–17, 20–**21**, 22, 75, 80, 83
Rockin' Sidney 14
Rockin' Years [Single] 51, 396–397, **399**, 404
Rocksteady 213
Rodeheaver, Homer 466
Rodgers, Jimmie 19–20, 22, 70, 352, 436, 479
Rodgers, Nile 329
Rodman, Judy 306–310, 312–313
Rodriguez, Chris 430, 432–435, 440, 444
Rogers, Kenny 10, 12, 228, 237, 288–289, 305, 327–330, 332–334, **336–337**, 339, 344, 349, 356, 436, 529, 547, 551, 554
Rogut, Rail 366
Roland, Ed 494
Rollings, Matt 430, 432, 434–435, 440, 442–444, 446–447, 449
Rolling Stones (The) 20, 97, 226, 454, 548
Romano, Rick 282–286, 288–289, 298–303
Romantic Roy Huskey 398, 402
Romeo [Single] 408–**410**, 412, 418
Romney, Mitt 547
Ronettes (The) 571
Ronstadt, Linda 10, 13, 35, 130, 228, 238–239,

301, 349–352, 354–359, **360–361**, 375, 400, 410, 422, 446, 465, 471–476, 495–496, 522, 534, 540, 557
Rose, David 244
Rose, Fred 436
Rosenberg, Stuart 199
Rosewood Casket [Single] 348, 355, **357**
Rosman, Gail 472–476
Ross, Diana 63, 251, 327
Ross, Ken 440, 442–444, 446–449
Roth, Don 220–222, 224–227
Rous, Francis 512
Rouse, Ervin T. 21
Rowan, Brent 430, 432–435
Rubicam, Shannon 367
Ruboca Records 195
Rudolph the Red–Nosed Reindeer 386, 390, 393
Run 574, 576
Runaway Feelin' [Single] 396, 400, 402–**404**
Run, Rose, Run 574–583
Run That by Me One More Time 102, 106
Rupert, Eric 453
Russell, Johnny 351, 357
Russell, Leon 233, 321
Rutledge, Tom 13, 306–310, 312–313, 552, 558–562, 568–571, 576–580
Ryles, John Wesley 398–399, 402, 404, 406, 444, 447–448

Sacred Memories [Single] 186, 189, **193**
Sadler, Barry A. 515
Saint Phalle, Niki de 139
Salestrom, Jim 270, 272–276, 298, 300–303
Sambora, Richie 552
Same Old Fool 268, 272
Sandy's Song 256, 264–265
Sanford, Bill 129–130, 132–134, 148–152
Sangiamo, Nick 218
Santa Claus Is Coming to Town 386, 388
Satin Sheets 438, 448
Save the Last Dance for Me [Single] 314, **316**, 321
Saviano, Tom 270, 272–276, 282, 288, 298–303
Savin' It for You [Single] 364, **373**
Sax, Doug 351–352, 354–358, 472–476, 480–485, 494–499
Say Forever You'll Be Mine 556, 558
Sayer, Leo 274
Say Goodnight 268, 274
Scarbury, Joey, 282, 284–286, 288–289, 486
Scheuble, Brian 366
Schlitz, Don 551
Schmitt, Ben Snake 530–532, 534–535
Schmitt, Stephen 328

Schulman, Alan 440, 442–444, 446–449
Schwarzenegger, Arnold 257
Scorpions (The) 273
Scorsese, Martin 135, 214, 231
Scott, Kevin 472–476
Scott, Jim 306–310, 312–313
Scott, Ridley 293
Scott, Tom 270, 272–276, 298–303, 318, 340–342, 344–345, 366–368, 370–373
Scriven, Joseph M. 466
Scrivenor, Gove 412, 416–417
Scruggs, Earl 21
Scruggs, Gary 400
Seals, Troy 318
Seay, Ed 376
Seay, Toby 440, 442–444, 446–449, 452–454, 456–459, 480–485
Sebastian, John Benson 235, 443
Sebert, Pebe 273
Second Best 138, 143, 152
Secrets 574, 580
Seeger, Pete 317–318, 522, 524
Segundo, Compay 351
Seitz, Chuck 104–107
Sellers, Dale 106
Send Me the Pillow You Dream On 304, 307
Sethi, Anita 10
Settle, Mike 288
Seva 502, 504–508
Severs, Mike 298–303, 306–310, 312–313
Shabalala, Joseph 440
Shadows (The) 32
Sha–Kon–O–Hey! Land of Blue Smoke 536–537, 564
Sha–Kon–O–Hey! 536
Shamblin, Allen 414
Sharp, Randy 497
Sharp, Sid 282–286, 288–289
Shattered Image 10, 210, 214, 500–501, 504
She Don't Love You (Like I Love You) 314, 319
Sheeran, Ed 559
Sheffield, Buddy 420
Shelbley, Ray 486
Shelly, Michelle 440, 442–444, 446–449
Shelton, Stephen 328
Shendan, Sue 274
She Never Met a Man (She Didn't Like) 126, 132
Sheridan, Sue 275
Sherrill, Billy 426
Shine [Single] 492–**494**
Shine Like the Sun 538, 544–545
Shine On 450, 458–459
Shiner, Mervin 74
Shinola [Single] 528, **535**
Shirl, Jimmy 112
Shlosser, Rick 282, 285–286, 288–289
Shockley, Roy 68–70, 72–75, 81–87, 91–95, 104–107, 112–115,

120, 122–125, 129–130, 132–134, 142–145, 148–152, 157–161, 165–168, 180–185, 200–203, 206–209, 212–215
Shockley, Mike 142–145, 165–168, 180–185
Shook, Jerry 129–130, 132–134
Shuler, Eddie 14, 16
Shuler, Elsie 14
Shuler, Johnny 16
Shuman, Mort 316
Sia 489
Silbar, Jeff 341
Silent Night 326, 330, 332, 387, 451
Silver, Lisa 306–310, 312–313, 376–377, 380–384, 398–399, 402, 404, 406
Silver and Gold [Single] 396, **400**, 404
Silver Dagger [Single] 136, 478, **483**
Silverman, Alan 520, 522–525
Silver Threads and Golden Needles 420–422
Simeone, Harry 391
Simon, Paul 233, 310, 340–341, 434, 440
Simon & Garfunkel 68, 97
Simone, Nina 511
Simonton, Ed 440, 442–444, 446–449
Simply Red 375
Simpson, Cody 568
Simpson, O. J. 429
Simpsons (The) Series 526
Sinatra, Frank 47, 498
Sinatra, Nancy 42, 45, 95, 400
Sing for the Common Man [Single] 278, 282, **285–286**
Singleton, Shelby 58
Single Women [Single] 292, **299**, 302
Sittin' on the Front Porch Swing 420
Sixfin, Pam 520, 532
Skaggs, Ricky 13, 72, 261, 375–378, 380–384, 410, 412, 414, 416–418, 501
Skeeter Davis 26, 32, 69
Sklar, Leland 270, 272–276, 282, 284–286, 288–289, 298–303, 306–310, 312–313, 316–321, 352, 366–368, 370–373, 474–476, 486–487
Slater, David 512–516
Slayton, Marty 535
Slenzak, Ron 280
Sloas, Jimmie Lee 551–552
Slocum, Tom 359
Slow Dancing with the Moon 408–427
Slow Dancing with the Moon 408, 418
Slow Healing Heart [Single] 374, **380**, 382–383

Sly and the Family Stone 398
Smarr, Rod 220–222, 224–227
Smith, Caitlyn 551
Smith, Carl 226
Smith, Dick 328
Smith, Gary 13, 387–394, 397–400, 402–404, 406
Smith, Howard 388–391, 394, 398–399, 402, 404, 406
Smith, Jack 389–390, 392
Smith, Jerry 189–193
Smith, Joey 520
Smith, Mindy 46, 524
Smith, Myra 85
Smith, Nathan 558, 562
Smith, Samuel Francis 515
Smith, Steuart 430, 432–435
Smith, Terry 520
Smith, Tony 511, 520, 536, 540–545, 554
Smith, Tori 128
Snakes in the Grass 574, 578
Sneakin' Around 490
Snider, Mike 498
Snow, Tom 274, 342
Snowden, Edward 547
Softly and Tenderly 460, 465
Solee, Denis 306–310, 312–313
Somebody's Everything 528, 535
Somebody's Missing You 538, 540
Something Fishy [Single] 24, **31**, 34, 169
Something's Burning 438, 444
Something Special 208, **428–437**, 452
Something Special 428, 430
Sometimes an Old Memory Gets in My Eye 162, 167
Sonnier, Jo–El 14, 377–378
Sony Corporation 29
Sony Masterworks 546–547
Sony Music 177
So Sorry 491
Soul [Music] 30, 93, 113, 134, 148, 152
Sound Kitchen 532, 552
South, Joe 69
Southern, Hal 420
Sparks, Richard 218
Speakin' of the Devil [Single] 428, 432, **434**
Spears, Billie Jo 34
Spears, Britney 493
Spector, Phil 87, 351
Spicher, Buddy 129–130, 132–134, 220–222, 224–227, 270, 272–276, 298–303
Spielberg, Steven 231, 409, 501, 529
Spivey, Joe 448
Spotnicks (The) 21
Springsteen, Bruce 217, 284, 359, 366, 368
Sproule, Dáithí 498–499

Spruill, Stephanie 244–248, 250–251, 258, 260, 270, 272–276, 282–283, 286, 288, 298, 300, 302–303

Stadiem, William 387, 397

Stairway to Heaven 206, 500–501, 508

Staley, Karen 383

Stallone, Sylvester 315–316, 322–325, 486–487, 526

Stanwyck, Barbara 387

Staples, Mavis 489

Stapp, Jack 28

Stark, Janet 472–476

Starling, Duawne 430, 432–435, 440

Starling, John 352, 356, 358, 472–476

Star of the Show 256–259

Starr, Ringo 68

Starting Over Again [Single] 268, **270**, 272, 274–275, 547

Stay out of My Bedroom 486

Steady as the Rain 478, 482

Steel Magnolia [Movie] 526

Steele, David 531

Steely Dan 244, 265, 275

Steffey, Adam 448

Steinbeck, John 20

Steiner, Armin 220–222, 224–227, 232–237, 244–248, 250–251

Stembridge, Jerry 56–58, 60–63, 68–70, 72–75, 81–87, 91–95, 129–130, 132–134, 148–152

Stevens, April 502

Stevens, Beth 502

Stevens, Cat 97, 439–440, 523

Stevens, Even 342

Stevenson, Emily Bree 522

Sticka, Michael 322

Stillman, Al 112

Still on Your Mind 146, 152

Still Working 9 to 5 [Documentary] 526

St. Nicholas, Randee 397

Stone, Joss 246

Stone Poneys (The) 360

Storey, Val 552, 579

Straight Talk 488

Straight Talk [Movie] 409, 526

Straight Talk [Single] 409, **488**

Stravinski, Igor 199

Streisand, Barbra 65

Strine, Fran 539, 557

Strong, Tommy 28–35, 98–101

Stubenhaus, Neil 328–330, 332–334

Sudano, Bruce 270

Sugar Hill Records 478–479, 481, 500–501

Summer, Donna 270–271, 547

Sundquist, Don 501

Sure Thing [Single] 240, **246**, 251

Sutton, Bryan 479–485, 494, 496–499, 520,

530–532, 534–535, 540–545, 551–552

Sutton, David 462, 502, 506

Sutton, Greg 272

Swain, Brett 366

Swamp Blues 200, 214

Swamp Pop 14

Swan, Billy 46

Sweet Agony [Single] 268, 270, **275**

Sweet Lovin' Friends 486

Sweet Music Man 230, 237

Sweet Summer Lovin' [Single] 256, **262**

Swift, Taylor 12

Swindley, Ted 197

Switzer, Michael 551

Sykes, Maiya 489

Tackett, Fred 270, 272–276, 298–303, 328–330, 332–334

Take Me Back 186, 190

Take Me Back to the Country [Single] 374, 380, **383**

Talbot, David 520, 522–525, 530–532, 540–543, 545

Tamahori, Lee 575

Tapp, Demetris 40–41

Tarantino, Quentin 150, 400

Tarplin, Marvin 534

Taylor, Bobby 377, 381

Taylor, Glenn M. 520, 522–525

Taylor, Holly 90

Taylor, Reed 520, 522–525

Taylor–Good, Karen 306–310, 312–313

Teach Me to Trust 428, 435, 452

Techno [Music] 365, 409

Telephone 276

Telling Me Lies [Single] 348, **355**, 357

Tennessee Hillbillies 194

Tennessee Homesick Blues [Single] 486–487

Termen, Léon 144

Terrell, Russell 551

Terry, Bobby 554

That's the Way It Could Have Been 420

The Ballad of the Green Beret 510, 515

The Bargain Store 198–203

The Bargain Store [Single] 198–**200**, 203

The Beautiful Lie 492, 499

The Beginning 162, 165, 168

The Best Little Whorehouse in Texas 490

The Best Little Whorehouse in Texas [Movie] 41, 193, 293–294, 309, 312–313, 490, 526

The Best of Porter Wagoner & Dolly Parton 79, **102–103**, 147, 174

The Better Part of Life [Single] 154, 159–**160**

The Beverly Hillbillies [Movie] 421

The Bird That Never Flew 146, 148–149

The Blue Train 470, 474

The Bridge [Single] 36, 38, **44**, 53, 68, 74, 137, 140, 579

The Camel's Heart

The Carroll County Accident 54–55, 60

The Christmas Song [Single] 326, 328, **330**

The Company You Keep 24, 34, 47, 80

The Complete Trio Collection 557

The Cruel War 518, 524

The Day My Baby Died 486

The Fairest of Them All 88–**95**, 117, 200

The Fire's Still Burning 116, 125

The Fire That Keeps You Warm 210, 213

The Giving and the Taking [Single] 24, 28, **32**

The Glory Forever 510, 516

The Golden Streets of Glory 108–**115**, 117

The Grass Is Blue 13, **478–491**, 493, 501

The Grass Is Blue 478, 485

The Greatest Days of All 138, 142

The Greatest Gift of All [Single] 326, 330, **333–334**

The Great Pretender **314–325**, 524

The Great Pretender [Single] 314, 318, **321**

The House of the Rising Sun [Single] 206, 278, **283**, 286

The House Where Love Lives 78, 84

The Last One to Touch Me 116, 118, 122

The Last Thing on My Mind [Single] 102, **105**, 174

The Letter 145, 154–155, 157, 237

The Little Drummer Boy 386, 391

The Little Things [Single] 24, 30, **35**

The Lonesomes 528, 534

The Lord Is My Shepherd 510, 512

The Love I Used to Call Mine 204, 207

The Man 240, 250

The Master's Hand 108, 113, 166

The Monkey's Tale 64, 74–75

The Moon, the Stars and Me [Single] 374, 376, 382, **384**

The Mystery of the Mystery [Single] 126, 130, **132**

The Only Hand You'll Need to Hold 198, 202

The Only Way Out (Is to Walk over Me) 36, 42

The Pain of Loving You 102, 105, 348, 351

There [Single] 216, 220, **227**

There Never Was a Time 58, 78, 85

There Will Be Peace in the Valley for Me 510, 514

The Right Combination – Burning the Midnight Oil 175

The River Unbroken [Single] 364, **366**, 373

The Sacrifice [Single] 538, **543**

The Salt in My Tears [Single] 450, 452–**453**

The Seeker [Single] 204, **208**, 428, 435

These Old Bones 500, 505

The Star–Spangled Banner 510, 512, 515

The Tracks of My Tears 518, 522

The Twelfth of Never 518, 522

The Way I See You 126, 133

The Wrong Direction Home 154, 160

The Year Dolly Parton Was My Mom [Movie] 527

Thiele, Doug 264

Thile, Chris 494, 496–498, 520

Think About Love 318

Think About Love [Single] 338, **340**, 345

This Boy Has Been Hurt 96, 100

Thomas, Billy 512–516

Thomas, Joe 534

Thomas, Randy 378

Thomas, Robert F. (Dr.) 158–159

Thomas, Sheryl 512–516

Thomasson, Mort 28–35

Thompson, Bobby 148–152, 157–161, 180–185, 189–193, 220–222, 224–227

Thompson, Hank 16, 194–195, 357

Thompson, Linda 355

Thompson, Will L. 465

Those Memories of You [Single] 348, 355–**356**

Those Were the Days 518–527

Those Were the Days 518, 520

Thought I Couldn't Dance 488

Tie a Yellow Ribbon 510, 516

Tie Our Love (in a Double Knot) [Single] 338, 340–**341**, 345

'Til Death Do Us Part [Single] 53, 64, **69**, 73

Tilley, Chuck 520, 522–525

Tillis, Mel 286

Tillis, Pam 410, 430, 432–435

Tillotson, Johnny 307

Time and Tears 450, 457

Time Flies 536

Time for Me to Fly [Single] 374, **376**

Today I Started Loving You Again 438, 442

Together Always 175, 323

Together Forever 562

Together You and I [Single] 538, **541**

Tolkien, J. R. R. 493

To Know Him Is to Love Him [Single] 348, **351**, 358

Tomlin, Lily 279–280, 526–527

Tomlinson, Tommy 113

Tommy James and the Shondells 523

Tomorrow Is Forever [Single] 53, 102, **104–105**, 556, 561

Tony Orlando and Dawn 319, 516

Too Lonely Too Long 96, 101

Too Much Water 486

Tormé, Mel 330

Torry, Clare 189

Toshinsky, Ilya 520, 551

Tosti, Blaise 185, 245, 262, 367–368, 370, 372–373

Toto 244, 246, 488

Touch Your Woman **138–145**, 147, 152, 160, 199, 484

Touch Your Woman [Single] 138, 140, **143**, 145, 195

Tourish, Ciaran 498–499

Train, Train [Single] 478, 481, **483**

Traugott, Wally 328

Travelin' Family Band (The) 177, 188, 218

Traveling Man [Single] 126, 130, 157, 162, **165–**166

Travelin' Prayer 478, 480

Travelin' Thru 526

Travis, Merle 63, 288

Treasures 438–449

Tree Publishing 28–29

Trent, Buck 13, 56–58, 60, 62–63, 68–70, 72–76, 84, 91–95, 129–130, 132–134, 148–152, 157–161, 180–185, 366–368, 370–373

Trent, Charles 40–42, 44–47

Treutel, Marv 536

Trindl, Gene 327

Trio 13, 35, 167, 228, 238–239, **348–363**, 375, 400, 410, 420–422, 465, 471–472, 479, 522, 540, 557

Trio II 356, 422, 446, **470–477**, 522, 540, 557

Truitt, Brent 502, 504, 506–508

Trump, Donald 361, 557, 562, 567

Try 491, 546, 554

Try Being Lonely [Single] 36, 38, **47**, 56

Tubb, Ernest 221

Tubert, Bob 40

Tucker, Duncan 526

Tucker, Tanya 46, 410

Turnbough, Zedrick 232–237

Turner, Chuck 480–485

Turner, Ike & Tina 212

Turner, Steve 388–391, 393–394, 410, 412–414, 416–418, 432–435, 502, 504–508, 512–516, 531, 534–535, 540–545, 551–553, 559–561, 568, 570–571

Turner, Tina 361

Turn, Turn, Turn 518, 524

Turn, Turn, Turn (To Everything There Is a Season) 314, 317

Tutwiler, J. Carter 520, 522–525

Twain, Mark 74

Twain, Shania 12, 45–46, 422

Twillie, Carmen 367–368, 370–373

Twitty, Conway 34, 63

Two Doors Down [Single] 230, 234, **236**, 315, 489

Two Lovers [Single] 364, 370–**371**

Two of a Kind 175, 351

Two of a Kind [Single] 106

Tyler, Linda 232–237, 244–248, 250–251, 258, 260–262, 264–265

Tyminski, Dan 443, 480, 482, 485, 494, 497, 524

Tyson, Mike 429

Uhlmann, Tai 293

Uhrig, Paul 388–392, 394, 410, 412–414, 416–418, 432–435

Ulmer, Betsy 532

Ultimate Dolly Parton

Umstead, Alan 520, 532

Umstead, Catherine 520, 532

Underwood, Carrie 529

Underwood, Ian 282–286, 288–289, 486

Universal 197, 439

Unlikely Angel 546, 551

Unlikely Angel [Television Movie] 551

Urban, Keith 522

USA for Africa 337

Vadim, Roger 139

Valentine, Rena Kansas 50

Van Cleve, Jim 580

Van Halen 318

Vanosdale, Gary 532

Vanosdale, Mary Kathryn 520, 532, 568–570

Van Shelton, Ricky 399

Vanston, C. J. 488

Van Warmer, Randy 443

Van Zandt, Townes 359

Vartan, Sylvie 22

Vassy, Kin 328–330, 332–334, 486

Vaughan, George 70

Veal, Charles 355

Vecsey, George 424

Vera, Billy 244

Vestal, Scott 550–552, 579

Vicari, Tommy 328

Vigran, John 366–368, 370–373

Villon, François 136

Vincent, Darrin 410, 412, 414, 416–418, 452–453, 456–459, 483, 485, 497, 535, 540–545, 568, 576

Vincent, Rhonda 21, 410, 412–414, 416–418, 452–454, 456–459, 481, 483, 485, 489, 497, 525, 535, 568, 579–580

Vitale, Lisa 489

Vito, Rick 367–368, 370–373

Voices, Helen 473

Volinkaty, John E. 448

Wachtel, Waddy 317–318, 320–321, 366–368, 370–373

Wachowski, Lana 479

Wachowski, Lilly 479

Wagoner, Porter 10, 12–13, 25–26, 34, 37, 47, 53, 60, 62, 65, 70, 74, 76–77, 79–87, 91–92, 94–95, 97, 102–107, 109–110, 114, 117, 127–128, 132–133, 143, 145, 147–152, 155, 163, 166–175, 177–179, 182, 185, 187, 190, 192, 199, 202–203, 205, 211, 220, 229, 232, 245, 257–258, 269, 279, 310, 339, 349, 351, 432, 494, 499, 512, 519–520, 541, 557–558

Wagonmasters 76–77, 79–80, 97

Wait Till I Get You Home [Single] 374, 377–378, 383

Waldman, Randy 328–330, 332–334

Waldschlager, Brian 453

Walker, Cas 14, 16, **18**, **97**, 439, 479

Walker, Ray 221, 306–310, 312–313

Walker, Wayne P. 70

Walker Jr., Billy Joe 328–330, 332–334, 340–342, 344–345

Walking on Sunshine 438–439, 446

Wallin, Danny 490

Walls of My Mind 116, 122

Walsh, Marty 282, 306–310, 312–313

Walters, Barbara 257

Waltz Me to Heaven 486

Wang, Dr. Ming 520

Warden, Ann 177

Warden, Don 157–161, 177, 205

Warhol, Andy 25, 217–218, 339, 387, 519

Warner Bros Records 348–349, 351–352, 354–358

Warner Music Nashville 538–539

Warren, Mervyn 490

Warwick, Dee Dee 360

Warwick, Dionne 422

Washday Blues [Single] 146–148, **150**

Waters, Julia 258, 260, 321, 366–368, 370–373

Waters, Luther 320–321

Waters, Maxine 258, 260, 321, 366–368, 370–373

Waters, Muddy 135

Waters, Oren 320–321

Waters Family (The) 321

Watson, Biff 531, 534–535, 540–545

Watson, Steve 486

Watkins, Bruce 410, 412–414, 416–418, 512–516

Watkins, Sara 520

Watts, Isaac 394

Wayne, John 513

Weaver, Jay 512–516, 520, 551, 553

Webb, Darrell 502, 504–506, 512–516, 580

Webb, Jay Lee 424

Webb, Loretta 424

Webber, Andrew Lloyd 529

Weber, Kristin 489

Webster, Joseph 463, 499

We Found It 163, 175

We Got Too Much [Single] 338, **341**, 342

We Had All the Good Things Going 64, 74

We Had It All 314, 318

Weil, Cynthia 13, 232

Weiss, Larry 412, 486

Weissenborn 465

Weissmuller, Johnny 315

Welcome Home 510, 513

Welk Music Group 510–511

Welles, Orson 424

We'll Get Ahead Someday [Single] 37, 102, 105, **107**, 174

Wells, Derek 535, 552

Wells, Kent 13, 388–390, 392, 394, 410, 412–414, 416–418, 502, 504–508, 511–516, 520, 522–525, 529–532, 534–535, 539–545, 547, 550–554, 558–562, 567–568, 570–571, 576–580

Wells, Kitty 16, 20, 31, 147, **194**–196, 200, 221, 421

Wells, Mary 63

Wells, Robert 330

We'll Sing in the Sunshine 314, 320

Wells–Wright, Carol Sue 195

Wells–Wright, Robert 195

Wells–Wright, Ruby 195

We Might Be in Love 491

Wendell, Bud 97

Wesley Work Jr., John 390

West, Dottie 196, 336

West, Mae 508

West, Speedy 21

We're Through Forever ('Til Tomorrow) 240, 245

Westergard, Katelyn 489

We Three Kings 386, 392

We Used To [Single] **206**–208

What a Friend We Have in Jesus 460, 466

What a Heartache [Single] 293, 396, 399, **404**, 406, **486**–487, 500, 505

What Ain't to Be, Just Might Happen 146, 148

What Do You Think About Lovin' [Single] 31

Whately, Francis 169, 527

What Is It My Love [Single] 375, **381**, 384

What Will Baby Be [Single] 408, 410, **412**

Wheeler, Onie 180–185

Whenever Forever Comes 408, 417

When I'm Gone 198, 201

When I Sing for Him [Single] 146, **151**

When Jesus Comes Calling for Me 450, 457

When Johnny Comes Marching Home 510, 513, 515

When Possession Gets Too Strong 88, 92

When Someone Wants to Leave 176, 181

When the Roll Is Called Up Yonder 460, 466

When the Sun Goes Down Tomorrow 210, 213

When We're Gone, Long Gone 471, 476

Where Beauty Lives in Memory 216, 225

Where Do the Children Play 518, 523

Where Have All the Flowers Gone 518, 522

Wickedest Witch of the Middle 491

Whispering Hope 510, 513, 516

White, Bergen 377, 381, 384

White, Bukka 31

White, Clarence 33

White, Jack 424

White, Lari 410, 412–414, 416–418

White, Ronald 222

White, Tommy 554

White, Tony Joe 26, 45, 93, 200

White Christmas [Movie] 334–335

White Christmas [Single] 326, 333–334

White Limozeen 13, 178, **374–385**, 398, 534–535

White Limozeen [Single] 374, **382**,

White Stripes (The) 180, 424

Who (The) 275, 285

Why 489

Why Can't We 408, 414, 417

Why Don't You Haul Off & Love Me 78, 84

Why'd You Come in Here Lookin' Like That [Single] 374, **378**, 383

Why, Why, Why [Single] 96–**98**, 99, 101

Wiginton, Hurshel 81–87, 159–160

Wildest Dreams [Single] 396, 402, **406**

Wildflowers [Single] 348, 352, **354**–355, 491

Wild Texas Wind [Movie] 405, 526

Wilkinson, Kristin 489, 532, 561, 580

Will He Be Waiting? 138, 142

Will He Be Waiting for Me 484

Williams, Dub 302

Williams, Hank 16, 20, 32–33, 91, 436

Williams, Larry 244–248, 250–251

Williams, Robert 390, 393

Williams, Terry 340–345

Williams, Tex 21

Williams Jr., Hank 26, 32–33, 69

Williams Jr., J. Allen 452–454, 456–459

Willis, Brian 530–532, 534–535

Willis, Kevin 568

Willis Brothers (The) 221

Wilma Lee & Stoney Cooper 221

Wilson, Dennis 398–399, 402, 404, 406

Wilson, Jackie 226

Wilson, Jay 245

Wilson, Lonnie 530–532, 576–580

Wilson, Marie 87

Winbush, Angela 244–248, 250–251

Winfrey, Ernie 306–310, 312–313, 490

Wings of a Dove 108, 114–115, 420–421

Winkelman, Karen 532, 568–570

Winkler, Henry 365, 491

Winslow, Christine 535

Wiseman, Craig 532

With Bells On 326, 332

Witherspoon, Reese 575

With You Gone 240, 247

WNYC Studios 97

Wogan, Terry 339

Woke Up in Love 486

Wolfe, Bruce 422

Wolfert, Dave 232–237, 244–248, 250–251, 275

Womack, Lee Ann 522

Woman Up (And Take It Like a Man) [Single] 574, 576, **579**

Wonder, Stevie 30, 163, 192, 248, 273, 275, 301, 328–329

Wood, Bobby 554

Woods, James 488

Woodstock 53, 65, 132, 199, 214, 235

Worden, Casey 221

Worden, Kelly 221

Worden, Mickie 221

Working Girl [Single] 278, 283, **286**

Working on a Dream 536

Wouldn't It Be Great 420

Wrapped Up in You 491

Wright, Johnnie 31, 194–195, 221

Wright, J. B. F. 462

Wright, Lynn 512–516

Wynette, Tammy 22, 63, 68, 178, 194, 197, 312, 397, 409, 420–422, 424, **426–427**, 448, 454, 462

Yellow Roses [Single] 374, **377**, 535

Yep Roc Records 16

Yes, I See God 108, 112

Yodel 19, **22**, 120, 246, 413

You 491

You Are [Single] 216, 221–**222**

You Are My Christmas 566, 571

You Can Do It 562–563

You Can't Make Old Friends 546–547, 551

You Can't Reach Me Anymore 123

You Gotta Be 562, 564

(You Got Me Over) a Heartache Tonight 408, 412

You'll Always Be Special to Me 198, 203

You'll Never Be the Sun 470, 475

Young, Chip 40–42, 44–47, 68, 148–152, 157–161, 180–185

Young, Curtis 376–378, 380–384, 398–399, 402, 404, 406

Young, Liana 376–377, 380–384

Young, Loretta 424

Young, Neil 40, 135, 233, 359, 446, 473

Young, Red 270, 272–276

Young, Reggie 282–286, 288–289, 298–303, 376, 380, 383–384, 430, 432–435, 440, 442–444, 446–449

Young, Steve 496

Yount, Robert 302

You're Gonna Be Sorry 36, 40

You're the One That Taught Me How to Swing 186, 192

You're the Only One [Single] 256, **260**

You're the Only One I Ever Needed 268, 273–274

Your Ole Handy Man 24, 26, 30–31

Yours Love [Single] 53, 78, **82–83**

Zanetis, Alex 70

Zimmerman, David 349

Zydeco 17

Bibliography

0—Lydia Hamessley, *Unlikely Angel: The Songs of Dolly Parton*, Urbana: University of Illinois Press, 2020.

1—Dolly Parton, *My Life and Other Unfinished Business*, New York: HarperCollins,1995.

2—Stephen Miller, *Smart Blonde: Dolly Parton*, London: Omnibus Press, 2015.

3—Alanna Nash, *Dolly*, Los Angeles: Reed Books, 1978.

4—Leonore Fleischer, *Dolly: Here I Come Again*, Toronto: PaperJacks, 1987.

5—Randy Schmidt, ed., *Not Dumb, Not Blonde: Dolly in Conservation*, London: Omnibus Press, 2017.

6—*Dolly Parton's Heartstrings*, Netflix, 2019.

7—*Dolly Parton: Here I Am*, directed by Francis Whately, documentary, Man Alive Productions, 2019.

8—"Dolly Rebecca Parton," Smoky Mountain Ancestral Quest, https://smokykin.com/tng/pedigree.php?personID=I48409.

9—*The Last Hillbilly*, directed by Diane Sara Bouzgarrou and Thomas Jenkoe, documentary, Films de Force Majeure, 2020.

10—Tony Byworth, *Giants of Country Music*, London: Hamlyn, 1984.

11—Steve Eng, *A Satisfied Mind: The Country Music Life of Porter Wagoner*, Nashville: Rutledge Hill Press, 1992.

12—Gérard Herzhaft and Jacques Brémond, *Le guide de la country music et du folk* (Guide to Country Music and Folk), Paris: Fayard, 1999.

13—David Evans, *Big Road Blues*, Berkeley: University of California Press, 1982.

14—Paul Hemphill, *The Nashville Sound: Bright Lights and Country Music*, New York: Simon & Schuster, 1970.

15—John Humphries and Michael Preston, *Music Master: The World's Greatest Record Catalogue, 1984*, Hastings, UK: John Humphries, 1984.

16—Ken Kesey, *One Flew over the Cuckoo's Nest*, New York: Signet, 1962.

17—*The Dolly Parton Scrapbook*, Meridianville, AL: Dolly Parton Fan Club, ca. 1976. A PDF version is available on the Internet Archive website at https://archive.org/details/the-dolly-parton-scrapbook/mode/2up.

18—Christopher S. Wren, *Johnny Cash—Winners Got Scars Too: The Life of Johnny Cash*, London: W.H. Allen & Co., 1973.

19—Dolly Parton and Robert K. Oermann, *Dolly Parton, Songteller: My Life in Lyrics*, San Francisco: Chronicle Books, 2020.

20—Dolly Parton and James Patterson, *Run, Rose Run*, Boston: Little, Brown and Company, 2022.

21—Willadeene Parton, *Smoky Mountain Memories: Stories from the Hearts of the Parton Family*, Nashville: Rutledge Hill Press, 1996.

22—James Patterson, *Along Came a Spider*, Boston: Little, Brown and Company, 1993 / *Le Masque de l'araignée*, JC Lattès, 1993.

23—James Patterson, *Hide and Seek*, Boston: Little, Brown and Company, 1996 / *La Diabolique*, JC Lattès, 1998.

24—Michel Rose, *Encyclopédie de la country et du rockabilly (Encyclopedia of Country and Rockabilly)*, edited by Jacques Grancher, Paris: J. Grancher, 1986.

25—Stella Parton, *Tell It Sister, Tell It: Memories, Music and Miracles*, self-pub., Attic Entertainment, 2011.

26—*To Kill a Mockingbird*, produced by Robert Mulligan, Brentwood Productions, 1962.

27—Harper Lee, *To Kill a Mockingbird*, New York: J. B. Lippincott & Co., 1960 / *Ne tirez pas sur l'oiseau moqueur*, Le Livre contemporain, 1961.

28—Nicholas Dawidoff, *In the Country of Country*, London: Faber and Faber, 1997.

Web Sources

- allmusic.com
- chapelhart.com
- countrymusichalloffame.org
- countryuniverse.net
- dla.acaweb.org (Digital Library of Appalachia)
- dollymania.net
- dollyparton.com
- dollypartonchallenge.com
- highwayqueens.com
- imaginationlibrary.com
- loc.gov (Library of Congress)
- robertchristgau.com
- ronstadt-linda.com
- stellaparton.com
- tennesseeencyclopedia.net
- urbania.ca

Other Sources

- *NZ in Lockdown: 10 Essential Things You Need to Know about Covid-19*, nowtolove.co.nz.
- Complainte sur les vampires de Bourganeuf (Lament of the Vampires of Bourganeuf), 1914, criminocorpus.org.
- *The History of Murder Ballads and the Women Who Flipped the Script*, sheshreds.com.

ACKNOWLEDGMENTS

The publisher would like to warmly thank Lalie Walker, Damien Somville, Simon Benoît, and the whole team for their professionalism and patience throughout the production of this book. Thanks also to Marie-Hélène Sauvage and Valérie Nidgélian for their support. In particular, thanks to: Gilbert Rouit, president and founder of the Country Music Memorial Association, as well as Romain Decoret, Gilles Vignal, and Marcel Rapp for their contributions.

PHOTO CREDITS

About the Authors

Simon Benoît is a guitarist who has explored many styles: from classical to Brassens, from jazz to punk, from bossa to blues. He has worked as a sound engineer for fifteen years, and he is a curious professional, driven by the desire to learn and share.

Damien Somville started his career working at record companies like Atmosphériques and Warner while developing his skills as an author/composer and stage musician. In 2015, he opened his own production studio in Paris, Plastic Folk Invention.

Lalie Walker is a writer, scriptwriter, and essayist who has always been passionate about languages, literature, the arts, science, and human nature.